# LONDON
# THE ILLUSTRATED HISTORY

# LONDON
## THE ILLUSTRATED HISTORY

Cathy Ross & John Clark

PENGUIN BOOKS

PENGUIN BOOKS

Published by the Penguin Group
Penguin Books Ltd, 80 Strand, London WC2R 0RL, England
Penguin Group (USA) Inc., 375 Hudson Street, New York, New York 10014, USA
Penguin Group (Canada), 90 Eglinton Avenue East, Suite 700, Toronto, Ontario,
    Canada M4P 2Y3 (a division of Pearson Penguin Canada Inc.)
Penguin Ireland, 25 St Stephen's Green, Dublin 2, Ireland
    (a division of Penguin Books Ltd)
Penguin Group (Australia), 707 Collins Street, Melbourne, Victoria 3008,
    Australia (a division of Pearson Australia Group Pty Ltd)
Penguin Books India Pvt Ltd, 11 Community Centre, Panchsheel Park,
    New Delhi – 110 017, India
Penguin Group (NZ), 67 Apollo Drive, Rosedale, Auckland 0632, New Zealand
    (a division of Pearson New Zealand Ltd)
Penguin Books (South Africa) (Pty) Ltd, Block D, Rosebank Office Park,
    181 Jan Smuts Avenue, Parktown North, Gauteng 2193, South Africa

Penguin Books Ltd, Registered Offices: 80 Strand, London WC2R 0RL, England

www.penguin.com

First published by Allen Lane 2008
Published in Penguin Books 2011
6

Text and illustrations copyright © Museum of London, 2008
Design, new maps and new artwork © Penguin Books Ltd., 2008

The moral right of the author has been asserted

Set in Bliss and ITC Giovanni
Typeset by Darren Bennett and Simon Hall
Printed in India by Replika Press Pvt. Ltd.

A CIP catalogue record for this book is available from the British Library

ISBN: 978–0–141–01159–2

**Produced for Penguin Books by Simon Hall**
Designed by Darren Bennett
Edited by Fiona Plowman and Antonia Cunningham
Proofreading by Ronnie Hanna
Additional picture research by Veneta Bullen and Prerona Prasad
Cartography by Richard Watts (Total Media Services)
Additional cartographic editing by John Haywood
Illustrations by Roger Hutchins
Index by Gerard M.-F. Hill

# CONTENTS

# PREFACE

I am delighted to introduce a book that gives all of us a great deal of pride.

At the Museum, our task is to reflect London back to Londoners. We have a collection of over 3 million artefacts, images and recordings – large enough in itself, but small when you consider that these are supposed to represent the experiences of the many millions of people who have shaped and been shaped by London over the centuries. Our task is impossible, but compelling.

This book has presented a similar challenge. Distilling the story of our city down to 350 pages, balancing detail and overview, doing justice to new stories as well as old, has not been easy – but it has been highly enjoyable. Our hope is that this book will stimulate all its readers, encouraging them to explore for themselves the fascinating web of stories that London offers. Our choice has been to tell the story of London thematically so that, as well as following the capital's history chronologically down to the present day, the reader can explore the developing stories of London art, trade, crime, immigration and books – and many other distinct strands – through the centuries. Illustrating these interwoven stories are the unique pictures, objects and reconstructions from our collection, as well as many new maps specially created for this project.

This collaboration with Penguin comes at an exciting time for the Museum of London. The Museum opened in 1976 and, like many maturing cultural institutions, we have recently felt the need to freshen ourselves up. We have been looking critically at the story of London we tell, and how we can best fit ourselves to the 21st century. This book is part of this process, as are our growing presence on the web (www.museumoflondon.org.uk), our second site in East London (Museum of London, Docklands) and the current redevelopment of our original London Wall site.

The last of these, the biggest alteration to the museum since 1976, will be completed in 2010, when visitors will find an entirely new suite of galleries exploring London from the Great Fire to the present day. It is a very exciting project for us, and I hope that this book will whet the appetites of readers and encourage them to come and see it for themselves.

Many people helped bring this project to fruition. Among those external to the Museum, special thanks are due to Simon Hall for project management. At Penguin, Georgina Laycock (and before her Nigel Wilcockson) has been constantly supportive.

From the Museum of London staff, the biggest thanks are due to the team of writers in our two curatorial departments, run by Cathy Ross and John Clark. Many members of staff 'did Penguin duty' over the course of the project, compiling material and writing about their own areas of expertise – including some who have since left the Museum: the initials at the bottom of each main spread identify the author or authors. Caroline Juby and Danielle Schreve of Royal Holloway, University of London, also contributed to the chapter on Prehistory.

Special thanks go to two people whose contribution was absolutely central: for chapters 7 to 15, Anna Sparham was invaluable in managing the photography and identifying and providing images; Sean Waterman was key in the provision of images for the earlier chapters. Images and objects have a particular eloquence, and the Museum of London is particularly conscious of the value they add to an understanding of the past.

I hope you enjoy the book.

**Professor Jack Lohman**
Director, Museum of London
June 2008

# CONTRIBUTORS

| | | | |
|---|---|---|---|
| AD | Annette Day | JC | John Clark |
| AG | Adrian Green | JFC | Jonathan Cotton |
| AL | Anna Lobbenberg | JH | Julia Hoffbrand |
| AS | Anna Sparham | JMNH | Jenny Hall |
| AW | Alex Werner | JK | Jackie Keily |
| BC | Beverley Cook | JL | Jenny Lister |
| CJ | Caroline Juby *Royal Holloway College* | JS | John Schofield |
| CR | Cathy Ross | KF | Karen Fielder |
| DS | Danielle Schreve *Royal Holloway College* | MB | Mark Bills |
| EE | Edwina Ehrman | MJ | Meriel Jeater |
| ES | Emma Shepley | MoL | Museum of London (multiple authors) |
| FG | Francis Grew | OC | Oriole Cullen |
| FM | Francis Marshall | SG | Sarah Gudgin |
| HF | Hazel Forsyth | TW | Tom Wareham |
| HS | Hedley Swain | | |

All contributors are current or former Museum of London staff members unless otherwise noted.

## PROJECT EDITOR'S NOTE

When Nigel Wilcockson of Penguin asked me to produce a new illustrated atlas of London history, I felt a certain trepidation. I was afraid it would prove all but impossible to do justice in a single book to the endlessly fascinating story of the rich, complex, diverse world city in which I have lived for most of my adult life.

What I hadn't taken into account was the knowledge, patience and enthusiasm of our partners in the project, the staff of the Museum of London. Cathy Ross and John Clark (and John's predecessor, Hedley Swain) found time to organize and motivate their colleagues, to grapple with detail and overview – and to pull together the resources of the Museum into a coherent story.

On our side, Darren Bennett produced an elegant, flexible book design and the meticulous DTP management that is his trademark. Richard Watts created beautiful maps, and Roger Hutchins a new series of his superb artworks. Fiona Plowman and Antonia Cunningham dealt calmly with the editorial crises that a complex project throws up, Ronnie Hanna supported us with a fast and intelligent proofread, and Gerard Hill supplied an exceptional index. Veneta Bullen and Prerona Prasad added a professional picture-research edge to the work of Anna and Sean at the Museum. John Haywood gave the map commissioning work a shot in the arm at a crucial stage, and our publisher Georgina Laycock has been unstinting in her support.

The result is a multi-faceted book in which a true history of the city emerges from a multiplicity of voices, themes, images, maps and ideas for further exploration – a history of the everyday lives of Londoners that fully lives up to the remit of the Museum.

**Simon Hall**
June 2008

*London from Southwark,*
*c. 1630 (detail)*
One of only four paintings of
London before the Great Fire,

# PRELUDE: LONDON'S PAST REDISCOVERED

Londoners have always had a sense of their city's history, but systematic investigation began only in the 17th century – and true archaeology only in the mid-20th.

**Stukeley's map of Roman London, 1724**
*The antiquarian William Stukeley's map was based on traditional literary sources and included a good deal of conjecture. Nonetheless, it was the first serious attempt to map the city's Roman past.*

In the 5th century AD Roman Londinium lay in ruins and a new people, the Anglo-Saxons, farmed the countryside around. They had no use for towns; they did not build in stone. What did they make of the ruins that littered the landscape? Later poets were to romanticize them as 'the work of giants', but as a new Saxon town Lundenwic grew up to the west of the Roman city, as links were established with Christian Europe and the remains of the Roman empire there, many people were aware of the history behind the romance. A 9th-century Anglo-Saxon bishop described London: it was, he wrote, 'built by the skill of the ancient Romans'. In 886 Saxon Lundenwic was abandoned in its turn, and Londoners moved back inside the still impressive stone walls of Londinium. There they came into daily contact with the relics of a lost civilisation. Every time they dug a pit they came across building foundations, an old road surface or mysterious artefacts. When they built new stone churches, they built them of stone and tiles taken from Roman buildings.

Yet the Roman past disappeared into a mist of legends. In about 1136 a book claiming to be an authentic account of the history of Britain before the coming of the Anglo-Saxons burst upon a startled world. Geoffrey of Monmouth's *History of the Kings of Britain* was largely fictional, but was accepted by historians as true for over 400 years. Geoffrey told how a party of Trojan refugees first settled Britain, and named it after their leader Brutus. Brutus founded a capital city on the Thames, and called it *Troia Nova* or New Troy. Later, rebuilt by (an equally legendary) King Lud, it was renamed *Kaer Lud* and eventually London.

So medieval Londoners saw their city as New Troy. It was said that Brutus had built the Tower of London 2000 years before the time of William the Conqueror. St Peter's church on Cornhill

**A Roman house and bath house**
*The remains of a Roman house and bath house were excavated during building works in Lower Thames Street in 1848. The finds aroused significant public interest.*

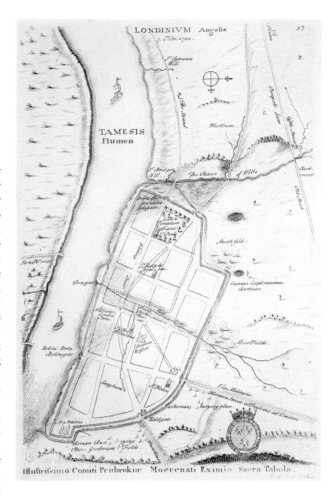

GENERAL VIEW OF THE REMAINS OF THE ROMAN VILLA, ON THE SITE OF THE NEW COAL EXCHANGE.

claimed to be the oldest church in the city on the grounds that it was on the site of a cathedral built by another legendary king, Lucius, in AD 179 – the parishioners may well have been aware of the massive foundations of the cathedral-like Roman basilica that underlay the area.

## FROM ANTIQUARIANISM TO ARCHAEOLOGY

By the end of the 16th century, historians like John Stow and William Camden were questioning the veracity of Geoffrey's 'British history'. They turned to classical authors for their knowledge of Roman Britain, and did not at first consider what we would call archaeological evidence. William Camden suggested (on very shaky grounds) that St Paul's cathedral stood on the site of a Roman temple dedicated to the goddess Diana, and others repeated his suggestion during the 17th century.

In 1666 came the Great Fire, which destroyed St Paul's along with a large part of the old City. During the rebuilding works, particularly around the cathedral site, strange objects and structures came to light. A new breed of antiquarians recorded and collected these finds, and just as medieval Londoners had interpreted the past in terms of New Troy, these classically-educated gentlemen saw their discoveries in the light of what they knew of the Roman world and the uncivilized 'Ancient Britons' that Julius Caesar had described. John Conyers, an apothecary since described as 'London's first archaeologist', sketched a Roman pottery kiln and the pottery found with it on the site of the cathedral. He also

**Roman river god, 2nd century AD**
*This sculpture fragment was found by workmen in Walbrook in 1899. It probably came fom the temple of Mithras, which was not discovered until much later, in 1954, by W. F. Grimes of the London Museum.*

found what we recognize as a Palaeolithic flint hand-axe at Battle Bridge (King's Cross); since it was found near the bones of an elephant (probably an extinct straight-tusked elephant) he interpreted it as a weapon used by a Celtic warrior against the elephants that accompanied Claudius's army in the Roman invasion in AD 43. In the absence of any knowledge of the extinct prehistoric fauna of Britain, Claudius's elephants seemed to be the only ones historically recorded that could account for the presence of this exotic animal in the London area.

In 1724 the well-known antiquary William Stukeley published what seems to have been the first attempt to reconstruct a plan of Roman London (see opposite). Although it marks sites to the north and east of the city where Roman burials had been found, it is largely conjectural. Prominent is the Templum Dianae, William Camden's Temple of Diana.

The later 18th century added little to our knowledge of London's past, but the large-scale building programmes of the 19th century, with new public works and offices, warehouses and public buildings with deep foundations, led to the discovery (and destruction) of many Roman remains, while medieval buildings were demolished without record. Antiquaries such as Charles Roach Smith recorded what they could and built up collections of finds – complaining about the destruction that they saw. Archaeological societies were founded to publish reports and encourage public interest, and in 1874 the Guildhall Museum opened in a new building in Basinghall Street. On show were finds made during building works, such as a fine Roman mosaic from Bucklersbury still to be seen in the Museum of London. The Guildhall Museum's curator occasionally visited building sites to record discoveries, and its later rival, the London Museum, employed an agent to acquire archaeological finds direct from the workmen to add to its collection.

**The Bucklersbury Mosaic**
*This fine mosaic floor from a 3rd-century Roman house was discovered in 1869 near the Mansion House during the construction of Queen Victoria Street. It measures 6 metres by 3.6 metres (about 20 ft by 10 ft). The building works of the 19th century unearthed large numbers of artefacts from Roman and medieval London.*

Only in 1928 was a professional archaeologist appointed, by the Society of Antiquaries, to observe and record finds made during city building works; only in 1946, after the huge destruction of World War II, was the first scientific excavation undertaken by the newly established Roman and Mediaeval London Excavation Council. The 1970s saw the creation of full-time archaeological units at the Guildhall Museum, in Southwark and elsewhere, and the now-familiar procedure by which archaeological investigation precedes building work on every important site began to take shape. Yet it was not until 1985 that archaeologists rediscovered Lundenwic, the Saxon town on the Strand whose inhabitants had long ago wondered at the ruins of Roman Londinium.          **JC**

# PREHISTORY

We are used to thinking of London as one of the world's great cities, but it was actually founded less than 2000 years ago. Yet for at least half a million years before this the Thames valley was home to groups of nomadic hunters and gatherers, and later to more settled communities of herders and farmers.

Direct traces of the earliest humans are few, and it is likely that they were only occasionally present in the area in small numbers. However, their flint tools and the bones of animals they hunted have been found across the capital.

The appearance of anatomically modern humans around 40,000 years ago coincided with a renewed phase of climate change.

New tools hint at new ways of hunting and, following a complete desertion of these islands either side of the last Ice Age around 20,000 years ago, the London area was gradually re-colonized.

After the final retreat of the glaciers some 10,000 years ago, a warming climate encouraged the growth of thick forests, and people adopted a more settled lifestyle. They created clearings in the woods along the Thames – initially for hunting, then for growing plants and rearing domesticated animals, especially cattle. Some clearings were

Early in the second millennium BC rising water levels drowned much of the valley floor. Wooden trackways were thrown across marshy areas to maintain access to traditional grazing grounds. Further back from the river, farmsteads of sturdy houses were set in hedged fields. The best land was much prized and may have been owned by powerful individuals who grew rich on agricultural surpluses and trade in metals.

By the early 1st millennium BC, however, long-established trade contacts broke down and formerly important enclosures were abandoned. Increasingly, people lived in open hamlets of roundhouses. Some specialized in metalworking, others in the production of cloth. In the century or so before the Romans arrived new enclosures protected market centres, farmsteads and religious sites. Fancy imports from Europe largely bypassed the London area and ended up in aristocratic graves in Essex and Hertfordshire.

The impact of the Roman conquest on the people of the London area is still difficult to assess. For some it may simply have meant exchanging a tribal landlord for a Roman tax official. It is undeniable, however, that once it was founded, the new Londinium exerted a profound influence on the region – an influence that has been felt ever since.

**Central London in the 2nd millennium BC, looking south west**
The Thames was much wider and shallower than it is today, and bordered by extensive mudflats. It was probably tidal as far upstream as Vauxhall. The areas of modern Bermondsey and north Southwark (centre) and Westminster (centre right) were gravel islands, while a number of now-lost tributary streams such as the Fleet (bottom right) are clearly visible. Much of the landscape at this time would have been divided up into field systems, generating an agricultural surplus for the local communities.

# THE THAMES VALLEY

The origin of the Thames lies deep in the past. Once it was diverted into its modern valley nearly half a million years ago, animals and early humans came and went as climate and sea levels fluctuated.

During the Early Pleistocene period (1.8 million–780,000 years ago), the climate in Britain was sub-tropical and generally stable. At this time, the rivers mainly transported fine sands and silts and occupied small channels. Some parts of modern Norfolk, Suffolk and Essex were under a shallow sea (see Map 1), as revealed by sediments typical of marine conditions, together with marine shells and bones of seals, whales and fish. Britain was connected to Europe by a land bridge that allowed many species of animal to cross over from the continent, including mastodons, tapirs, red panda, extinct horses and an early form of mammoth.

## EARLY RIVERS

As the Pleistocene progressed, periods of cold became more common and the rivers gained power, eroding and transporting sands and gravels over much greater distances. The former headwaters of the Thames, for example, which then flowed further north than its present day course, extended into north Wales and carried the local igneous and metamorphic rocks to the North Sea. At this time, however, the Thames was merely a tributary of the now-gone Bytham River, the largest in Britain's history, which flowed from the Midlands through northern Norfolk out into the North Sea basin.

From about 800,000 to 480,000 years ago, the increased activity of northern European rivers continued with many developing larger channels (see Map 2). The climate began to fluctuate dramatically between cold glacial periods (sometimes with large ice sheets covering much of Britain) and warmer interglacials. Britain remained connected to the Continent but during times of glaciation sea level fell by as much as 100 metres (328 ft). At this time, the 'Channel River' flowed out into the Atlantic Ocean, fed by the major European rivers, such as the Rhine, Thames and Meuse.

It was approximately 800km (497 miles) long and more than three times longer than the present-day Thames.

Around this time, early humans (probably of the species *Homo heidelbergensis*) began to enter Britain across the land bridge to the Continent. Stone tools discovered on the coast of East Anglia date back as far as 700,000 years ago and were found with animal bones and insect remains indicative of Mediterranean-style warmth.

## THE GREAT GLACIATION

The Anglian glaciation, which began 480,000 years ago, was the most extensive known in Britain's prehistory, with ice extending as far south as Finchley in modern north London. Rivers flowing into what is now the North Sea basin were blocked by the glacier, creating an enormous ice-dammed lake (see Map 3). The ice sheet also blocked the original course of the Thames through the Vale of St Albans and modern Colchester, and diverted it south into its present-day valley, as well as destroying the Bytham River and carving out the low-lying Fens of East Anglia. Eventually, catastrophic overspill of the ice-dammed lake breached the land bridge joining Britain to the Continent, thereby creating the Straits of Dover and isolating Britain from the rest of Europe for the first time.

## CLIMATIC FLUCTUATIONS

The period from the Anglian glaciation to about 130,000 years ago was characterized by fluctuating climates of cold glacial and warm interglacial conditions. There were further glaciations in which the landscape was again remodelled by the advancing ice (see Map 4), but not on the scale of the Anglian. During these ice ages, the sea level was low enough to reconnect Britain to the Continent, thereby allowing early Neanderthals (the descendants of *Homo heidelbergensis*) and animals to cross once more. In addition to early humans, the warm interglacials saw Britain inhabited by lions, straight-tusked elephants and several species of extinct rhinoceros, giant deer and aurochs (ancient wild ox). During the glaciations, these were replaced by herds of cold-loving species such as reindeer, woolly mammoths and woolly rhinoceros. By the same token, human occupation was not continuous and when the climate deteriorated, Britain may have been deserted for long periods.

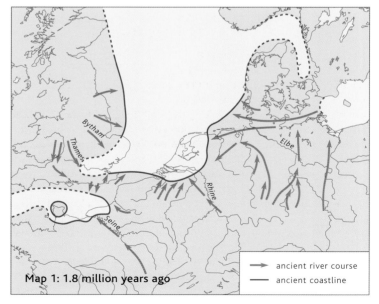

Map 1: 1.8 million years ago

ancient river course
ancient coastline

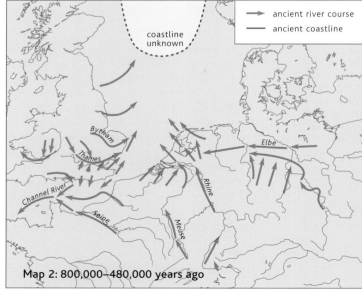

Map 2: 800,000–480,000 years ago

ancient river course
ancient coastline

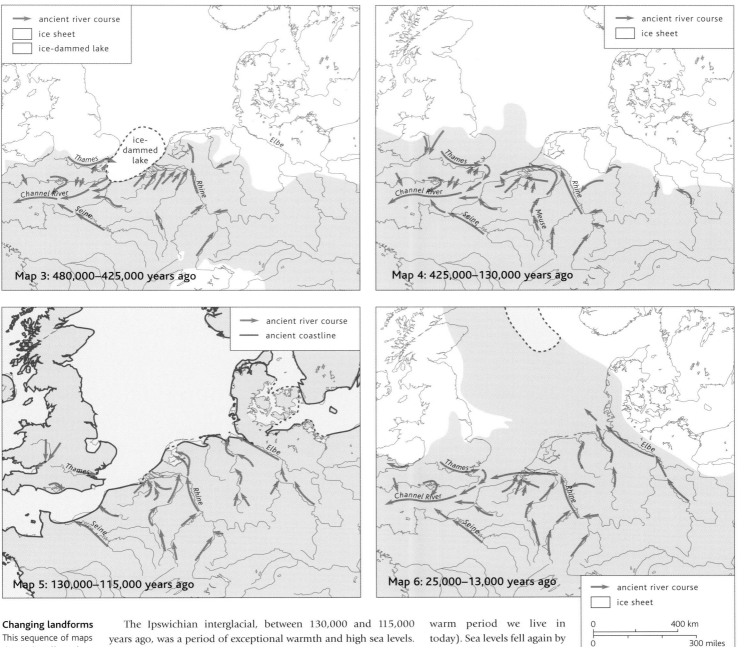

**Map 3: 480,000–425,000 years ago**

**Map 4: 425,000–130,000 years ago**

**Map 5: 130,000–115,000 years ago**

**Map 6: 25,000–13,000 years ago**

Legend (Maps 3):
→ ancient river course
◻ ice sheet
◻ ice-dammed lake

Legend (Map 4):
→ ancient river course
◻ ice sheet

Legend (Map 5):
→ ancient river course
— ancient coastline

Legend (Map 6):
→ ancient river course
◻ ice sheet

| 0 | 400 km |
| 0 | 300 miles |

**Changing landforms**

This sequence of maps shows the effect of climate and sea level changes on the rivers and landforms of north-western Europe during the Pleistocene.

The Ipswichian interglacial, between 130,000 and 115,000 years ago, was a period of exceptional warmth and high sea levels. Fossil beetles found in Britain suggest that average temperatures were 2–3°C higher than they are today. Animal species such as straight-tusked elephants, spotted hyenas, fallow deer, narrow-nosed rhinoceros and hippopotamus are common from this time. Hippo remains in particular have been found in London in ancient Thames gravels beneath Trafalgar Square and at Brentford, and as far north as Teesside and the North York Moors. Although climatic conditions at this time were suitable, early humans were completely absent; presumably the high sea levels prevented them from crossing from Europe. Indeed the coastline of Britain may have been similar to today for up to 60,000 years (see Map 5).

## THE LAST ICE AGE

Lasting from around 115,000 to about 13,000 years ago, the Devensian was the last glacial period before the Holocene (the warm period we live in today). Sea levels fell again by as much as 120 metres (394 ft) during the middle part of the period, re-establishing the land bridge with the Continent. However, the climate was not uniformly stable. Climate fluctuations lasting between 500 and 2000 years saw a shift in average temperatures of approximately 7°C and caused profound disruption to flora and fauna; many species became extinct. Beetle remains indicate that temperatures in July rarely exceeded 10°C, while winter temperatures were around –25°C in lowland parts of Britain. Fossils of several cold-loving species from this period have been found in the London area, including woolly mammoth and bison. The coldest point of the Devensian was reached around 20,000 years ago, with ice sheets covering Scotland, Wales and northern England (see Map 6). Britain would have been bleak, inhospitable and deserted.                    **DS/CJ**

# THE EARLIEST HUNTERS

From around 400,000 years ago, the London region was periodically occupied by several different human species, who shared the landscape with a wide range of animals.

Although there is evidence of early human presence in East Anglia from 700,000 years ago, the Thames valley does not seem to have been occupied until about 400,000 years ago. At this time, Britain had a temperate climate and the valley was home to large herds of straight-tusked elephants, horses and aurochsen, which grazed the river margins. In direct competition for prey with carnivores such as lions, cave bears and wolves,

## FLINT TOOLS

As well as the human skull fragments – and many animal bones – the Swanscombe site has also produced thousands of early flint tools. Similar tools have been found across the London region along former courses of the Thames and its tributaries. Many are carefully shaped flint hand-axes (see below left) often likened to modern Swiss army knives in terms of the range of functions they could have performed. However, most were probably used to skin and butcher animals. The manufacture and use of such hand-axes demonstrates that these early humans already had a detailed knowledge of raw materials and of the ways in which these could be transformed into effective tools.

Flint tools were often discarded after use, and sometimes the discarded tools were later swept into rivers by flash floods and transported for considerable distances downstream. However, some have been found where they were dropped, along with the

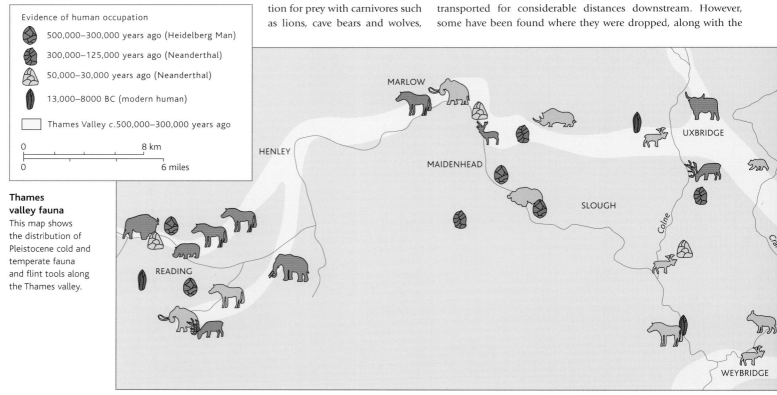

**Evidence of human occupation**

- 500,000–300,000 years ago (Heidelberg Man)
- 300,000–125,000 years ago (Neanderthal)
- 50,000–30,000 years ago (Neanderthal)
- 13,000–8000 BC (modern human)
- Thames Valley c.500,000–300,000 years ago

0 — 8 km
0 — 6 miles

**Thames valley fauna**
This map shows the distribution of Pleistocene cold and temperate fauna and flint tools along the Thames valley.

MARLOW
HENLEY
MAIDENHEAD
SLOUGH
UXBRIDGE
Colne
Cran
READING
WEYBRIDGE

***Flint hand-axe***
*Found near St Paul's Cathedral, this flint hand-axe dates from c. 400,000 BC.*

humans had already developed hunting techniques that allowed them to thrive at the extreme north-western limits of their range. Subsequent climate changes led to the appearance in Britain of animals that were adapted to glacial (cool) and interglacial (temperate) conditions (see map, above).

Although their stone tools are abundant, the physical remains of these early people have been rarely identified. However, three fragments of the same female human skull were found at Swanscombe in Kent in 1935, 1936 and 1955. Until recently, she was the oldest-known early human in Britain, but the discovery of other remains at Boxgrove in West Sussex in the 1990s are believed to date to 500,000 years ago. The Boxgrove finds, a shin-bone and some teeth, have been attributed to the species Heidelberg Man (*Homo heidelbergensis*) and indicate a robust individual around 2 metres (6 ft) tall. The Swanscombe skull, around 100,000 years younger, appears to represent a transitional form between *Homo heidelbergensis* and the early Neanderthals (*Homo neanderthalensis*).

remains of the animals upon which they were used. Cut-marks have occasionally been identified on animal bones and indicate how the carcasses had been skinned and butchered.

## THE NEANDERTHALS

The Neanderthals had evolved fully by 250,000 years ago. Compared to *Homo heidelbergensis*, Neanderthals were shorter and stockier, but possessed great upper body strength. Chemical analysis of their bones and teeth reveals that they were top predators, consuming large quantities of meat. However, their 'close encounter' style of hunting frequently left them with injuries and broken bones, similar to those seen in modern rodeo riders. They favoured open grasslands as their hunting grounds and would drive animals towards marshes or over cliffs in order to kill them. The faces of the Neanderthals were characterized by prominent brow ridges, broad noses and recessive chins. Although they are today often thought of as particularly well suited to cold climate

**Mammoth tusk**
*Found in Ilford, its owner died in a catastrophic flood c. 200,000 years ago.*

that they may have retreated so far into Europe because of the severe cold that they were not able to return before rising levels once again cut Britain off from the Continent during the Ipswichian. It was not until around 60,000 years ago that groups of Neanderthals returned to Britain, moving across the land bridge that re-emerged as sea levels fell again during the Devensian. At this time, Neanderthals were using small triangular hand-axes, a number of which have been found in the Thames valley.

The Devensian environment was treeless tundra that supported large herds of woolly mammoths, reindeer and horses, but with winter temperatures of around –10°C, Neanderthals may have stayed only during the short summers. At Lynford in Norfolk, there is evidence of Neanderthals butchering mammoth carcasses, after killing individual animals near a marsh. Similar activities no doubt took place in the Thames valley too, with Neanderthals regularly visiting favoured localities to hunt. **DS/CJ/AG**

conditions, evidence shows that they were equally at home in environments as warm as today's (and in some cases, even warmer).

Although hand-axes were still being made, Neanderthals had developed a method of producing multiple sharp flakes of predetermined shape that could be attached to wooden spears (see

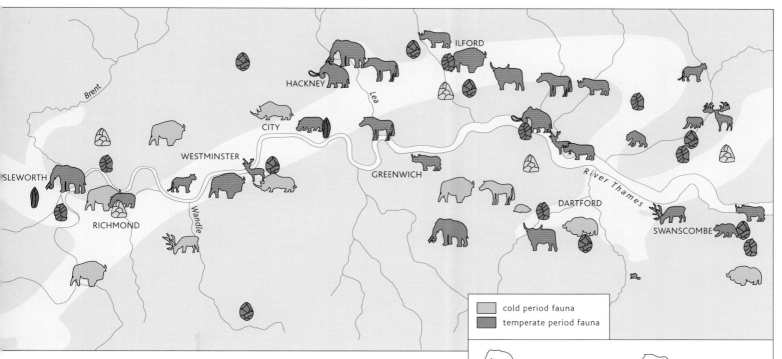

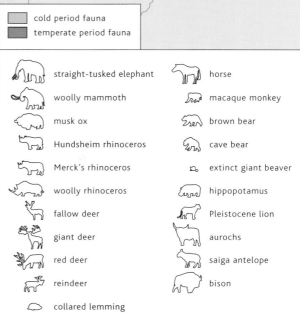

| | |
|---|---|
| cold period fauna | |
| temperate period fauna | |

| | straight-tusked elephant | | horse |
|---|---|---|---|
| | woolly mammoth | | macaque monkey |
| | musk ox | | brown bear |
| | Hundsheim rhinoceros | | cave bear |
| | Merck's rhinoceros | | extinct giant beaver |
| | woolly rhinoceros | | hippopotamus |
| | fallow deer | | Pleistocene lion |
| | giant deer | | aurochs |
| | red deer | | saiga antelope |
| | reindeer | | bison |
| | collared lemming | | |

**Flint spearhead**
*A flint spear head of a type made by early Neanderthals, 250,000 years ago.*

below left). Evidence of this technique has been found at Baker's Hole in Kent, where flake tools created from good quality flint nodules were found at the base of a chalk cliff.

Not all of the animals whose bones have been discovered perished at the hands of early human hunters, however. Many whose remains were found at Ilford seem to have drowned in a catastrophic flood around 200,000 years ago. They included many steppe mammoths (the ancestor of the woolly mammoth, see above), red deer, horses, aurochsen and lions, all species typical of rich temperate grasslands. At Aveley, a young straight-tusked elephant appears to have died from starvation having become stuck while attempting to cross a marshy stream channel; a woolly mammoth shared the same fate at the same spot a little later.

## DESERTION & RECOLONIZATION

Following a glaciation around 160,000 years ago, Neanderthals disappeared from Britain for close on 100,000 years. It is thought

# MODERN HUNTERS & GATHERERS

Anatomically modern humans first appeared in the Thames valley *c.* 40,000 BC. Around 13,000 BC they were present more or less permanently. Their camps were close to rivers, lakes and springs.

period is Heathrow, where a small hunting band left behind some flint tools that are uncannily similar to others from the period found in Eastern Europe.

Temperatures reached their lowest point around 20,000 years ago. As the climate gradually warmed up from around 13,000 years ago, the open tundra (mammoth-steppe) was successively colonized by low birch scrub, pine forest and finally broadleaf deciduous wildwood. People and animals returned by way of the land bridge to Europe.

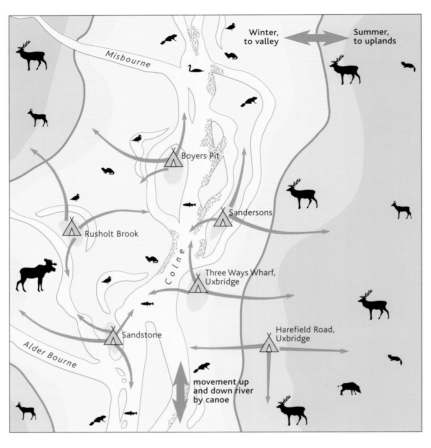

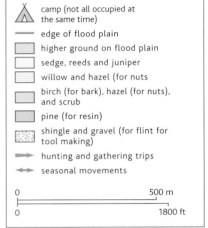

**Colne valley resources**
Valley floors and slopes provided mobile hunter-gatherer groups with a rich range of exploitable resources. Many of the locations on the Colne valley floor near Uxbridge appear to have been visited in the late winter or early spring. The summer was probably spent foraging in the woodlands on the higher ground of the interior.

## THE START OF SETTLEMENT

A series of camps across the London area help to illustrate what life was like for these colonizing hunter-gatherer groups. Most chose to settle close to rivers, although springs and lake margins were also favoured. More often than not, activities centred on hearths that provided both warmth and security. However, no convincing traces of any structures such as houses or windbreaks have yet been identified, even though examples are known for this same period from elsewhere in the British Isles.

Small temporary camps seem to have dotted the floor of the valley of the river Colne in the area around Uxbridge (see map above). Most were sited on low gravel ridges out of the reach of floods and appear to have been occupied in the late winter or early spring. The earliest was set within a landscape dominated by open steppe-tundra and was briefly occupied by a small hunting band around 12,000 years ago. The hunters used long robust flint blades skilfully struck from flint nodules picked up from the local riverbeds. These were used to butcher the carcasses of several reindeer and a horse. Having eaten and repaired their damaged tool kits, the band moved off along the valley in search of further game (see opposite top).

Anatomically modern humans (*Homo sapiens*) evolved in Africa more than 100,000 years ago. Groups moved out of Africa and gradually colonized the world, eventually replacing the existing populations of early humans in each area. Evidence of their distinctive technology and culture has been found in north-west Europe from around 40,000 years ago, and they seem to have replaced the Neanderthals. The reasons for this are unclear, but it may be that the newcomers were more numerous and simply better equipped to cope with rapid climatic change. In any event, the Neanderthals disappear from the archaeological record some 30,000 years ago.

Between around 26,000 and 13,000 years ago, ice sheets covered much of northern Europe, extending in Britain as far south as Cardiff. During this 'Last Glacial Maximum', the London area was a barren polar desert with annual temperatures around 16–17 degrees lower than today's. Sea levels were also around 100 metres (330 ft) lower. There is little evidence for a human presence in Britain at this time. One of the few localities in the London area that shows evidence of human visits during the earlier part of this

**Uxbridge camps**

*The earliest camps in the Uxbridge area were carefully sited so as to allow hunting bands to intercept the herds of reindeer during their annual migration up the valley, as shown in this illustration.*

Almost a thousand years later, a second larger group revisited the same spot. By now the climate had warmed up sufficiently to allow the growth of thick pinewoods on the valley slopes, though the valley floor was dominated by birch and hazel, with willow and sedge closer to the braided courses of the many streams. Up to twenty people gathered around a hearth to extract marrow and grease from a heap of red- and roe-deer bones stored since the previous autumn's hunt (see below left). Traces of wear on flint tools suggest that these people worked antler and animal hide on the site, while bones of swans, otters, beavers and pine martens show that the group was skilled at exploiting a wide range of local resources.

Around 8500 years ago, rising sea levels turned Britain into a group of islands. In the London area, river levels rose and many low-lying sites along the Thames and its tributaries were submerged. People were forced to move back up the valley slopes to new camp sites. Widespread evidence of burning here suggests that clearings were established in the tangled deciduous wildwood and that these were maintained by fire-setting. Animals lured out into the open to graze on the fresh young vegetation were easy prey for experienced hunters.            **AG/JFC**

**Hearth seating plan of c. 8500–8000 BC**
Evidence in Uxbridge shows a large group of hunter-gatherers, comprising one or more extended families, engaged in a series of tasks. It is likely that the hearth provided not only warmth and security but also a social focus for gossip and story-telling.

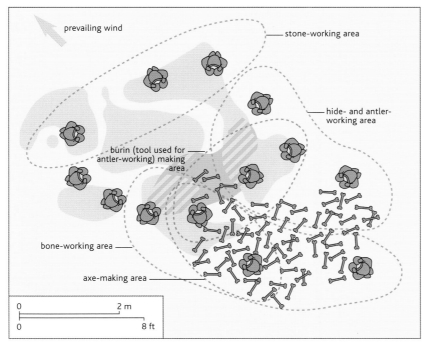

prevailing wind

stone-working area

hide- and antler-working area

burin (tool used for antler-working) making area

bone-working area

axe-making area

0 —————— 2 m

0 —————— 8 ft

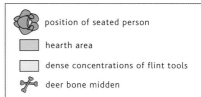

position of seated person

hearth area

dense concentrations of flint tools

deer bone midden

# CREATING A NEW WORLD

Domesticated plants and animals, pottery and new tools show settled life in the Thames valley, but it is earth and timber monuments that best characterize the 4th and 3rd millennia BC.

**Yeoveney Lodge**
*The large causewayed enclosure at Yeoveney Lodge, Staines, may have been built and used as a meeting place by scattered communities.*

**Staines Road Farm**
The Staines Road Farm site was constructed on a more modest scale, presumably to serve the needs of a single community. The spot was memorable enough to have acted as the focus of much later activities marked by a hearth, cooking pit and waterhole.

Traces of human activity dating to the early 4th millennium BC have been found along the floodplain of the Thames and the lower valleys of its tributary streams. Many localities continued to be occupied on a temporary, perhaps seasonal, basis. Occasionally, however, evidence of substantial buildings survives. At Runnymede

Bridge, at least one large rectangular timber house was erected beside the Thames between 3900 and 3500 BC. The area around it was strewn with broken pottery, discarded flint tools and cattle bones. Other isolated houses have been found near Staines and at Cranford Lane, near Harlington. Each was probably the home of an extended family group.

Such groups seem to have followed a semi-nomadic lifestyle of herding, supplemented by hunting and gathering. A cache of burnt wheat grains dated to between 3900 and 3300 BC found near Canning Town, however, suggests that at least one group was also growing crops. Not far away, the body of a young woman was discovered at Yabsley Street, Blackwall. She lay on her left side in a foetal position and had been buried with a pot and a flint knife. Dating to around 4000 BC or shortly after she is, in effect, our earliest modern Londoner.

## AN AGE OF MONUMENTS

One of the outstanding features of the mid- to late-4th millennium BC is the series of monuments of earth and timber built in areas cleared of woodland at various points along the valley. These include large circular causewayed enclosures, as at Yeoveney Lodge, Staines (see left), smaller circular and horseshoe-shaped enclosures, as at Horton, Ashford and Staines Road Farm, and long linear 'avenues' or cursus monuments, as at Stanwell. Many of these monuments lie in the Heathrow region of west London (see map opposite).

Some seem to have entrances aligned with the rising or setting sun; others are carefully placed so as to be visible from a distance. It is possible that the Yeoveney Lodge site was built as a place for scattered groups of local people to meet – other sites may have commemorated special events or marked the ownership of particular parts of the landscape. It is also likely that the construction of the largest monuments required the cooperation of many different communities. It has been estimated, for example, that a workforce of ninety-six could have built the 3.6-kilometre (2.2-mile) Stanwell avenue in around sixteen to eighteen weeks, although in practice it seems more likely that it was constructed in shorter periods of work spread over a number of seasons.

Finds recovered from the ditches of these monuments provide clues as to their function and significance. At Staines Road Farm (see left), deer antlers and the skull of a wolf had been carefully placed on the floor of the encircling ditch, along with cattle bones, flint arrowheads and several upturned pottery bowls. Two human burials had also taken place on the northern side of the ditch; one comprised the remains of a male torso, the other was the crouched body of a woman in her thirties (see opposite top). Scientific analysis of the woman's teeth suggests that she had grown up far to the north of the valley in which she was eventually buried. It seems likely that the open area enclosed by the Staines Road Farm ditch had been the scene of gatherings celebrated with food, music and dance. The site must have

---

*Map labels:*

Later Bronze Age features

'water hole'

rectangular pit

torso burial

hearth

inhumation burial

ditch

ditch

wolf skull

antler

mortlake bowl rim

antler

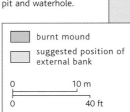

burnt mound

suggested position of external bank

0        10 m

0                    40 ft

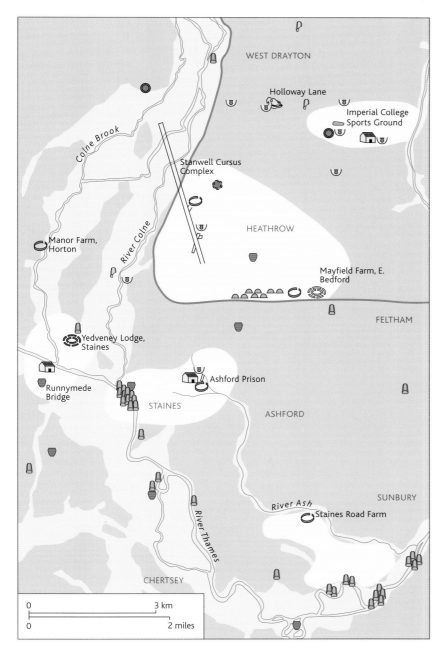

**West London monuments**
The number of monuments in the west London area suggests the presence of a sizeable local population.

**Young woman**
*Reconstructed from a skull buried at Staines Road Farm, this woman was in her thirties when she died.*

**Alder wood club**
*Over 5000 years old, this alderwood club found in the Thames at Chelsea would have been a dangerous weapon.*

**Bronze dagger**
*An early bronze dagger buried with the ashes of its owner beneath a barrow in Sandy Lane, Teddington.*

## THE SACRED RIVER

The Thames provided a wide range of natural resources, as well as being an artery of communication and a physical and psychological boundary. Increasingly, it seems to have been seen as a sacred river too, rather like the Ganges in India.

Offerings to its waters included human remains, pots, bone and antler tools and hundreds of flint and stone axes. Many of these axes were traded from distant places, such as the Lake District, Ireland, Cornwall and the Continent, which must have enhanced their value in the eyes of local communities. The largest and finest axes appear to have been deliberately chosen as gifts to the spirits of the stream.

## SOCIAL UPHEAVAL?

For close on a thousand years no new monuments were built along the Thames valley. Instead, offerings continued to be made to the river, while others were buried in small pits, often some way away from the old sites. The contents of these pits usually included pottery and flint tools alongside gathered autumnal foods such as crab apples, sloes and hazelnuts. One large pit contained the butchered remains of a young aurochs or wild ox, whose carcass was embedded with six flint arrowheads.

Changes in funerary rites around this time suggest wider changes in society. Previously the dead had been buried anonymously in the ditches of monuments, or placed in the Thames. By the mid- to late-3rd and early-2nd millennia BC, however, certain individuals were being buried beneath earthen barrows, with pots, archery gear and the earliest metal tools and weapons (see bottom right). It may be that these people were reaping the early benefits of alliances with distant suppliers of copper and tin – a trade that was to become increasingly important as time went on. **JFC**

lingered long in the memories of the people who lived in the area. For almost a thousand years later it provided a focus for cooking and feasting, which was centred round a small hearth and a rectangular boiling pit served by a deep waterhole.

This period was no rural idyll, however. Disputes over land and access to resources must have been common. Flint arrowheads seem to have been used as much against people as in hunting animals, for example, while several human skulls appear to have sustained probably fatal blows from blunt instruments. A heavy alderwood club found in the Thames at Chelsea and dated to around 3500 BC is just the sort of weapon likely to have been responsible for such injuries (see middle right).

# FIELDS & FARMS

Dramatic changes occurred from the early 2nd millennium BC as farming replaced herding. Land once dominated by monuments was now systematically cleared and divided up into hedged fields.

Changes in land-use across the London area in the early 2nd millennium probably reflected wider developments in society as trade in copper and tin intensified. Early beneficiaries of the trade were buried beneath circular earthen barrows built in prominent positions, often close to or overlooking the Thames (see map below). These barrows may also have been a deliberate reference on the part of local communities to the monuments of earlier times, in an appeal to custom and tradition. Pressure on land and resources intensified throughout the period as population levels increased.

Climate change was an important factor. In the valley floor, rising river levels drowned woodlands and led to the construction of brushwood trackways as people struggled to maintain access to traditional hunting and grazing grounds. Such was the pressure on land that attempts were also made to bring low-lying islands in the floodplain under cultivation (see opposite bottom); plough-marks dating to between 1520 and 1220 BC have been discovered in north Southwark, for example. Like the wooded river margins, these ploughed areas were finally drowned by the rising Thames.

As the river level rose, the position of its ever-fluctuating tidal limit may have held particular significance for local communities. The wooden 'bridge' or jetty at Nine Elms, Vauxhall, for example, was constructed close to the tidal limit in the mid-2nd millennium BC (see map opposite). It would have afforded access to a mid-stream island and a deep-water channel, and allowed local communities to make propitiatory offerings to the waters.

## OWNERSHIP & BOUNDARIES

Further back from the river, extensive field systems were laid out (see map below). Initially, the old monuments were respected, but as time went on they were ignored by farmers hungry for land. At Perry Oaks near Heathrow a series of up to seven individual landholdings has been identified. Served by a system of parallel tracks, each was subdivided into smaller hedged fields, some of which contained waterholes for cattle. Weaving gear in the form of spindle-whorls and loom-weights also suggests the presence of sheep flocks. To judge from the remains of seeds found in waterholes barley, wheat and flax were cultivated, while blackberries, sloes and hazelnuts were available in the hedgerows.

Such landholdings probably belonged to individual families or to extended families who lived in small settlements marked by fences or palisades out in the fields. These settlements were usually placed close to major tracks and were often divided into an inner domestic area and an outer compound, perhaps reserved for the livestock. The inhabitants cremated their dead and buried the remains in pots placed in small cemeteries situated away from the living areas. A number of these cemeteries have been found in

**High-status areas**
Many of the high-status settlements, cemeteries and metal hoards overlook the Thames or are associated with large field systems.

- island site
- possible island site
- circular enclosure
- large metalwork hoard
- small metalwork hoard
- barrow
- cremation cemetery
- large cremation cemetery
- main distribution of river-deposited metalwork
- extent of field systems
- gravel terraces

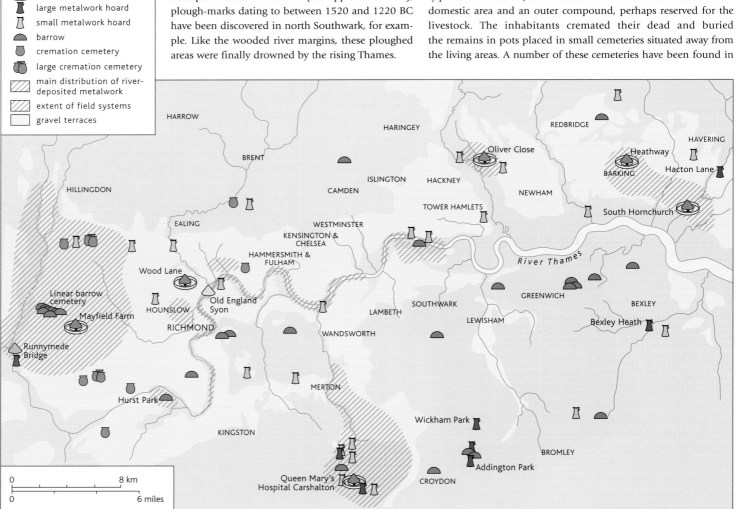

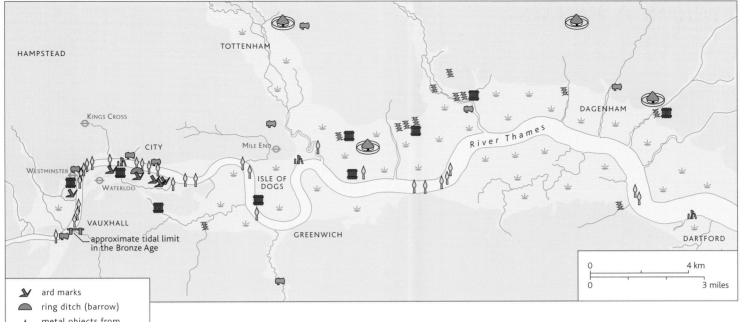

## Legend

- ![ard marks] ard marks
- ![ring ditch] ring ditch (barrow)
- ![metal objects] metal objects from Thames/flood plain
- ![wooden bridge] wooden bridge or jetty
- ![wooden structure] wooden structure
- ![trackway] trackway
- ![submerged forest] submerged forest
- ![settlement] settlement
- ![metalwork hoard] metalwork hoard
- ![wetland] wetland

west London, most of which contain up to thirty burials. Larger cemeteries have also been found at Ashford Common and in Hayes; it is likely that these were used by the inhabitants of more than one nearby settlement.

## A SOCIETY BASED ON PRESTIGE

Powerful individuals came increasingly to the fore again around 1100 BC, no doubt on the back of success in agriculture and the long-distance trade in copper and tin. These individuals advertised their wealth through feasting, patronage of skilled metalsmiths and the possession and disposal of fine objects. New settlements were established that speak of this interest in status and prestige. Upstream of the Thames's tidal limits mid-stream islands at Wallingford, Runnymede Bridge, and possibly Syon Park, provided the settings for large-scale feasting and trading as well as a wide range of high-status manufacturing activities, including metalworking. Thin-walled pottery jars, cups and bowls indicate the importance that was attached to the presentation and serving of food at this time. These vessels imitated metal forms, and buckets and cauldrons of sheet bronze were highly valued.

Similar activities appear to have taken place in a series of circular enclosures set back from the Thames. Their occupants probably traded commodities such as salt, quern-stones and metal goods along the Thames valley and beyond. One site, at Queen Mary's Hospital, Carshalton, dominated a zone of the North Downs where large hoards of metalwork had been buried. These must have represented considerable wealth, and it is surely no coincidence that they were found in an area of great agricultural productivity.

## RITUAL DEPOSITS

Ritual came to dominate all aspects of everyday life. Token deposits of human ashes were buried at house entrances aligned with the rising sun, pots containing food and drink were placed in waterholes, bronze weapons were offered to the river, while bronze tools were buried on land. Some of these deposits may have authenticated claims to land and resources, some may have sought to ensure the fertility of both humans and animals, while others may have been offered up as part of funerary ceremonies.

Bronze Age societies had always depended on supplies of copper and tin from distant sources and when these dried up – as they appear to have done around 800 BC – the whole system of carefully nurtured alliances collapsed. This had far-reaching consequences, not the least of which was the adoption of iron-working, which exploited local ores. **JFC**

**Thames flood plain**
Rising river levels drowned expanses of grazed and ploughed fields in the Thames flood plain, and necessitated the building of wooden trackways.

*Ploughing, Bermondsey*
*Demand for land now meant that low-lying islands came under cultivation.*

# MOVING BEYOND THE VALLEY

The centuries before the Roman conquest are often seen as a time of unremitting inter-tribal warfare, but most settlements were farmsteads and most people were farmers rather than fighters.

**Oppida and coin-using tribes**
Oppida plotted against coin-using 'tribal' groupings. Uphall Camp in Ilford falls just within the area of the Catuvellauni/ Trinovantes.

Map legend:

- oppidum
- possible oppidum

Coin-using areas, with associated tribal names
- Corieltauvi
- Iceni
- Catuvellauni/Trinovantes
- Cantiaci
- Atrebates
- Durotriges
- Dobunni

Map labels: Stanwick, North Ferriby, Dragonby, Old Sleaford, Ancaster, Leicester, Grim's Ditch, Cambridge, Salmonsbury, Baldock, Bagendon, Braughing, Camulodunum, Wheathampstead, Dyke Hills, Verulamium, Silchester, Uphall camp, Oldbury, Canterbury, Winchester, Loose, Bigberry, Hengistbury, Chichester Dykes

0 — 200 km
0 — 150 miles

**Wooden tankard**
*Found in the Thames at Kew, this bronze-bound wooden tankard had a capacity of four pints. It dates to the 2nd or 1st century BC.*

The disruption of long-standing bronze-trading networks meant that local communities were thrown back on to their own resources in the early 1st millennium BC. While the old circular enclosures lay abandoned, many of their fields remained in use, and new ones were occasionally laid out. The ancient tradition of depositing rich items in the Thames and in pits and waterholes continued, but on a more modest scale (see map right). People were clearly aware of the past and keen to emphasize their links with it. There is also some evidence of early iron-working at a settlement near Weybridge, where a series of smelting and smithing hearths have been found.

## SEASONAL SETTLEMENT

From the middle of the 1st millennium BC the landscape of the London region was dominated by hamlets lived in by single and extended families on a short-term, possibly even seasonal, basis. As before, house entrances were usually aligned with the rising sun. Consisting of several large round houses and associated granaries, the farmstead at Dawley near Heathrow is typical. It appears to have been occupied for several generations on at least two separate occasions between *c.* 500 and 330 BC. Another, slightly larger settlement at Perry Oaks was sited on common land between blocks of earlier fields. Most of these local communities practised a mixture of arable and pastoral farming, with some small-scale iron working, as well as spinning and weaving.

## THE WIDER WORLD

Links to the wider cross-channel world were gradually re-established. Coinage, in the form of imported Gaulish gold staters, was in circulation from the 2nd century BC, though the earliest British coins (the tin-bronze 'potins' of north Kent) appear a little later. Coin-using tribal elites began to emerge in parts of southern Britain at around this time too, and may have occupied 'enclosed oppida' (see map left). These were large enclosures surrounded by earthworks within which a wide range of prestige craft activities such as metal-smithing and glass-working were carried on.

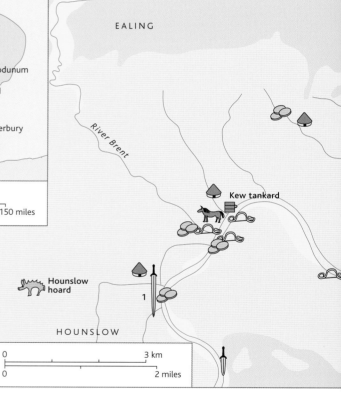

Map labels: EALING, River Brent, Kew tankard, Hounslow hoard, HOUNSLOW, 1

0 — 3 km
0 — 2 miles

The site at Uphall Camp on the river Roding near Ilford is the nearest that the London region has to one of these oppida. This huge enclosure was clearly a major centre, strategically sited to control the lower Roding valley. There were a number of substantial round houses associated with rectangular barns or outhouses and potin coins have been found together with good evidence for metal- and cloth-working. Quantities of charred cereals suggest that the site stored grain brought in from a wide area.

## CREATING NEW IDENTITIES

Some people in the south-east appear to have adopted new 'Roman' identities in the century after Caesar's expeditions to some of which continued in use into the Roman period. One or two, like Beddington and Keston, eventually developed into villas. Elsewhere, as at Perry Oaks, long-established fields were realigned.

## SACRED SITES

The Thames remained a place of pilgrimage and devotion, but it was perhaps now also a frontier between various distant tribal groupings. River offerings diminished in number but their prestige value increased, as fine individual pieces like the Kew Tankard (see opposite) and the Battersea Shield (see below right) show.

Away from the river, religious sites included the 'shrine' at Caesar's Camp, Heathrow (see left), and the rectangular enclosures at Rainham, Orsett and Gun Hill, Tilbury. These are similar in form to cult sites on the

**Caesar's camp**
The small rectangular 'shrine' at Caesar's Camp, Heathrow, was set within a large earthwork enclosure.

**Thames offerings**
The Thames continued to receive offerings of prestige objects like weapons, personal ornaments and feasting utensils, but less than in earlier times.

**Battersea Shield**
The Battersea Shield was a display piece. It dates to between 300 and 100 BC.

Britain in 55 and 54 BC. They espoused Roman ways of dressing, eating and drinking, and learnt to speak – perhaps even write – Latin, while some of the most ambitious aristocrats sent their sons to Rome to acquire a formal Roman education.

Roman influence in south-east Britain was felt through trade contacts with ports on the south coast and Essex; these increased after about 20 BC. (The Roman writer Strabo famously provided lists of British imports and exports at this time.) Products of this trade – wine amphorae and silver drinking cups among them – found their way into aristocratic graves in the areas north and east of London. Locally, the period from about 50 BC to AD 50 is characterized by a series of small enclosures and open settlements,

Continent and may have been the domain of religious specialists such as the druids. Once again, offerings were an important part of the ceremonies performed here, as the cache of iron spearheads deliberately buried in the ditches of the Orsett enclosure shows.

The effect of the Roman conquest on the London area is difficult to assess. There appears to have been no tribal centre on the site of Roman Londinium. Indeed the London region seems to have been peripheral to the politics of the period. It may be precisely because there was no strong pre-existing presence that the Romans chose to found London where they did. **JFC**

# ROMAN LONDON

The Romans created London. For nearly 400 years it was the largest city in Britannia, a province which was the northern outpost in an empire that encompassed the entire Mediterranean. This vast area was held together by laws, language and an evolving civil service. People travelled widely, trading in ideas no less than in goods. But the empire was far from uniform. Local customs persisted, and local communities governed themselves in towns that drew inspiration from numerous architectural models.

Londinium was built where the Thames was narrow enough to be bridged, yet was still tidal. Sea transport linked it to the rest of the empire, while roads radiated out to the other major towns in Britain. It began as a wooden frontier settlement but by the mid-2nd century sprawled for 2 kilometres (1.2 miles) along the north bank of the river and covered over 300 acres (121 ha) on that side alone.

London soon became the base from which the whole province was managed. An enormous basilica and forum catered for administrative, legal and commercial needs, while bathhouses and an amphitheatre provided entertainment. On both sides of the river were spacious temple precincts and elegant official residences. A high stone wall fortified the north-bank conurbation from the early 3rd century onwards.

Settlements sprang up along the highways leading from the city. Some were at major river crossings. Others were straggling groups of smallholdings or industrial units with no obvious centre. The countryside was intensively farmed, except for the densely wooded clay soil of north London. On the slopes of the North Downs sat the comfortable stone villas and bathhouses of the well-to-do.

Britain ceased to be a province early in the 5th century, and the Roman way of life disappeared within a generation. South-east England received no direct legacy in terms of culture, law or language. But the square mile enclosed by the Roman walls became the medieval city of London and remains to this day London's commercial centre.

***Londinium* c. AD120**
*The city was at its
maximum extent at this
time, with an estimated*

# LONDINIUM: CREATION & EARLY DESTRUCTION

London was founded soon after the Roman invasion of AD 43. It grew rapidly and had a cosmopolitan population. This thriving settlement was destroyed in the Boudican revolt of AD 60.

In the summer of AD 43 a Roman army of some 40,000 men landed in Britain. Their ostensible purpose was to reinstate a British chieftain, an ally of Rome, who had been driven out of his kingdom during an inter-tribal war. Their real purpose, however, was to win for their emperor, Claudius, a famous victory in a far-off land. This most unmilitary of emperors badly needed a prestigious campaign to tighten his tenuous grip on power.

The Romans started from Boulogne, armed with far more knowledge of their destination than Caesar had had when he set out for Britain nearly a century earlier. They would have known both the physical and the political geography from the reports of merchants who regularly traded there, and by questioning British nobles who sometimes attended the court in Rome. It is likely that the crossing – at least of the main force – was the shortest possible: to Richborough in Kent, where archaeologists have discovered Roman beach-head fortifications. Caught off-guard, the Britons did not oppose the landings. Regrouping, they made a first stand by a river, probably the Medway, and then a second at a point on the Thames where there was marshland that flooded at high tide. This cannot have been far from the future site of London. Both times they were initially successful but ultimately overwhelmed by Roman troops who swam across the rivers to attack them.

**Londinium before its destruction in AD 60**
Houses and shops clustered on the hill east of the Walbrook and along the main roads.

Now Claudius himself arrived to take command. The army was encamped by the Thames, and so the emperor, like millions of future visitors, may have reached the London area directly by ship rather than overland from the Channel ports. Heading north, he captured Camulodunum (Colchester), the seat of the most powerful British king, and accepted the surrender of many tribes. By early autumn most of south-east Britain was under Roman control.

## THE SITE OF LONDON

Roman strategy gave the future site of London a significance that it had not had before. One hundred kilometres (60 miles) to the north-east was Colchester: first a legionary fortress, then a colony for retired soldiers. Thirty-two kilometres (20 miles) to the north-west was Verulamium (St Albans), and 80 kilometres (50 miles) to the south-east, Canterbury. Both places were important tribal centres that became Roman towns. The highways connecting them had to cross the Thames, and London was where the river was narrow enough to be bridged yet had sufficiently high ground, especially among the marshes on the south bank, for the construction of approach roads. To this point too the Thames was tidal, enabling large cross-Channel ships to sail up-river, bypassing the Kent ports and delivering goods closer to where they were needed.

The Romans' original choice of crossing point may have been about a mile further west, for the Verulamium and Canterbury roads are aligned in the direction of Lambeth–Westminster (see pages 32–3). No bridge or harbour works have been found here, however, and the plan must soon have been abandoned. By AD 48, just five years after the invasion, construction was underway of the street that would form the east–west axis of Londinium, while on the south bank of the Thames, the incoming roads were being re-routed to cross near today's London Bridge.

## TOWN LIFE

The centre of the early town was on the north bank of the river, east of the Walbrook. Here, on the summit of the low hill overlooking the river crossing, a large gravelled courtyard was laid out. It may have served both as a market square and as

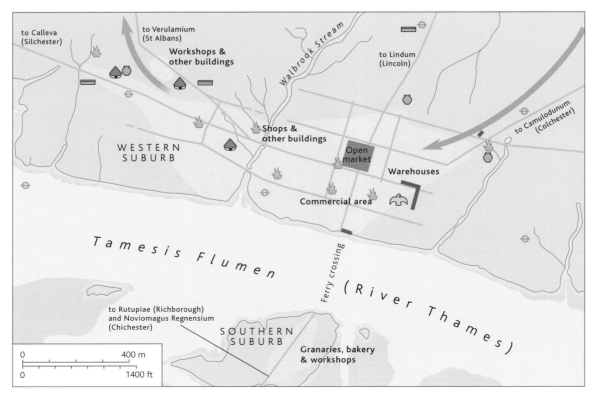

Map labels:
- to Calleva (Silchester)
- to Verulamium (St Albans)
- Workshops & other buildings
- Walbrook Stream
- to Lindum (Lincoln)
- to Camulodunum (Colchester)
- WESTERN SUBURB
- Shops & other buildings
- Open market
- Warehouses
- Commercial area
- Tamesis Flumen (River Thames)
- Ferry crossing
- to Rutupiae (Richborough) and Noviomagus Regnensium (Chichester)
- SOUTHERN SUBURB
- Granaries, bakery & workshops

Scale: 0 — 400 m / 0 — 1400 ft

Legend:
**Pre-Boudican London**
- main urban area
- road
- roundhouse
- cremation burial
- inhumation burial

**The Boudican revolt**
- advance of Boudican army, AD 60
- evidence of burning during Boudican sack of Londinium
- Roman defence works, AD 61
- possible area of Roman army base, AD 61

an assembly point for the military supplies and soldiers who were passing through in large numbers.

At this time, the Roman historian Tacitus says, London was 'crowded with merchants and goods'. A quayside wall of planks and staves was under construction in AD 52. Long, rectangular 'strip buildings' of clay and timber sprang up along the main streets to serve a cosmopolitan population that may already have numbered 10,000. These buildings had shops or workshops in the front and living accommodation behind. Archaeologists have identified a bakery, a pottery shop and a store containing grain imported from Turkey. Wine and olive oil were shipped from the Mediterranean in ceramic amphorae, along with glassware and fine pottery. Immigrant craftworkers made Roman-style pottery in the western suburb while, near the river crossing, an immigrant jeweller supplied gemstones for setting in signet rings. Outside the town, in Highgate and on the road to St Albans, industrial centres began to turn out kitchen pottery for the thriving new market.

West of the Walbrook, along the Silchester road, some people were living in circular houses of a type familiar in Britain for centuries before the Roman conquest. They used fewer Mediterranean imports than their neighbours to the east, and in one workshop broken Roman glass was re-fashioned into beads in a traditional British style. Were these people Britons, who had been forcibly settled here as a source of semi-skilled labour for the new town? Or had they come voluntarily, attracted by new opportunities for employment or the sale of farm produce?

## DESTRUCTION BY BOUDICA

During the summer of AD 60, thriving early London was destroyed completely. This catastrophe had its origins in a dispute more than 150 kilometres (100 miles) to the north-east, where the Romans had not conquered the powerful Iceni tribe but made a pact with their king, Prasutagus. This arrangement, which enabled the Romans to concentrate their army elsewhere, was tactically astute but strategically hazardous. When Prasutagus died, the Iceni assumed that the king's status as client ruler would pass automatically to his heir, Queen Boudica. The Romans saw client status as a temporary arrangement. Soldiers moved in to seize control, violating Boudica and her daughters, and soon the Iceni, with the Trinovantes, their neighbours to the south, had risen in revolt.

Boudica's army marched south, destroyed Colchester, and then turned on London. Populated by merchants and immigrants living in an overtly Mediterranean style, the town was symbolic of Roman imperialism. With the army campaigning elsewhere, Catus Decianus, the emperor's financial representative (procurator), had hardly any troops. He fled the country, and the entire town was burned to the ground. On nearly every site of this period, archaeologists have discovered layers of charred and vitrified debris up to a metre thick – even across the river, where shops and houses had flanked the road leading to the crossing. Only the British-style roundhouses in the western suburb escaped destruction.

Turning north-west, Boudica destroyed Verulamium, but early in the autumn her army was defeated by two Roman legions returning from campaigns in Wales. In London the soldiers took control, building a fortified compound between the gravelled courtyard and the river. A protective ditch and rampart incorporated dozens of large timbers charred in the burning of the town. By AD 63, work was underway on a new quay that would allow essential supplies to be imported safely again from the Continent.    **FG**

*Londinium on the eve of the Boudican revolt*
A view from the north-west, looking towards the main settlement on the far side of the Walbrook, drawn by Peter Froste.

*Bronze arm from an above life-sized statue*
This bronze arm was buried in damp conditions near the Walbrook stream in about AD 70. Did it come from a monumental statue of the despised emperor Nero, torn down when his memory was disgraced by the disaster of the Boudican revolt?

# THE ROMAN CITY AT ITS HEIGHT

Within fifty years of the Boudican revolt, London had become by far the largest city in Britain. Administrative, commercial and military zones developed around impressive major buildings.

**Bronze bust of the emperor Hadrian**
*A replica of a bust found in the Thames. Hadrian visited Britain in AD 122.*

**Londinium at its maximum extent**
Commercial and residential zones, and principal public buildings are shown.

It was over a decade after the Boudican sack before the rebuilding of Roman London began in earnest. Not only had the early town been almost totally destroyed but, in AD 68–70, civil wars between rival emperors had interrupted the development of new provinces such as Britain. Around AD 75, work commenced on the forum-basilica, the most important public building in any provincial town. Its large open piazza was surrounded by shops or offices, and a 50-metre long (164-ft) basilica, bigger than many of today's parish churches, lay on the north side.

On the steep hillsides down to the Thames, building platforms were levelled out and consolidated with timber or concrete retaining walls. Two such terraces south-west of the forum were the site of a large hall and ornamental pool, perhaps part of a public bathhouse or a government official's residence. On terraces west of the Walbrook, there were monumental buildings for public entertainment and religious ceremony, including a very large baths and, alongside it, a temple precinct. To the north, on poorly drained ground less suitable for private housing, stood an amphitheatre.

By AD 100, London had grown far larger than any other town in Britain and the Romans decided to rebuild it on a much grander scale. A vast new wing was added to the western baths and the amphitheatre was refurbished in masonry. But the most prestigious of these projects was a new forum. Its basilica exceeded in length most medieval English cathedrals. On the outskirts of the town a stone-walled fort was created, large enough to house at least a thousand soldiers who were seconded to the governor of Britain for ceremonial or administrative duties. Everywhere, the houses, shops and workshops of ordinary Londoners continued to multiply. Large courtyard houses began to appear, and humble 'strip buildings' were extended behind the street frontage, sometimes even decorated with mosaics. But in the AD 120s these developments were halted by another widespread fire, this time probably started by accident.

## A CITY BUILT ON WATER

Nowhere was London's growth and prosperity more evident than along the Thames. Massive oak baulks, often cut from trees nearly 200 years old, were used to build quays that stood a metre (3 ft) above the river at high tide. Behind them were warehouses for cargoes. These port works started at the mouth of the Walbrook and extended eastwards for half a kilometre (0.3 miles). Of the Roman bridge there is now little trace, although its position is indicated by street alignments and by the large numbers of coins that have been found in the riverbed. Was it intentionally or by accident that travellers across the bridge so often dropped their small change into the Thames? It is tempting to see a conscious continuation here of the long pre-Roman tradition of depositing precious metalwork in the river.

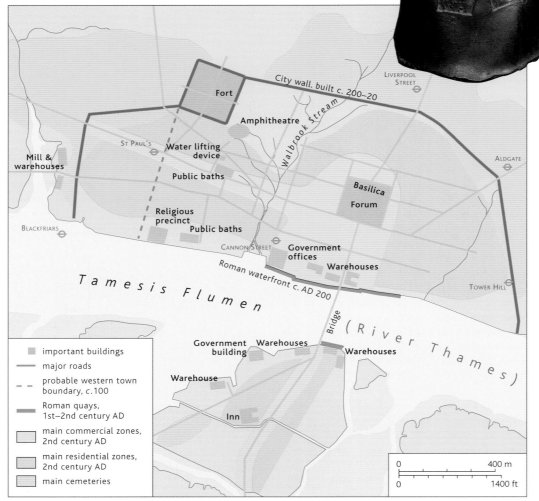

City wall, built c. 200–20

LIVERPOOL STREET

Fort

Amphitheatre

St Paul's

Water lifting device

Mill & warehouses

Public baths

Walbrook Stream

ALDGATE

Basilica

Forum

Religious precinct

Public baths

BLACKFRIARS

CANNON STREET

Government offices

Warehouses

Roman waterfront c. AD 200

TOWER HILL

*Tamesis Flumen*

Bridge

*(River Thames)*

Government building    Warehouses

Warehouses

Warehouse

Warehouses

Inn

- ▪ important buildings
- — major roads
- -- probable western town boundary, c.100
- — Roman quays, 1st–2nd century AD
- main commercial zones, 2nd century AD
- main residential zones, 2nd century AD
- main cemeteries

0    400 m
0    1400 ft

To the west of London was the Fleet, whose wide mouth provided additional anchorages, perhaps mainly for smaller boats working the upper Thames. At least one warehouse has been found here. The Walbrook was too small for shipping and its many small channels threatened to turn the northern part of the town into semi-marshland. Noxious, water-dependent industries like leather-working were sited here. Efforts were made to regulate the Walbrook by re-cutting and revetting its streams, and it powered a watermill, but gradually it silted up or was deliberately infilled.

Water for drinking and everyday use was distributed through ceramic or wooden pipes, but there is no evidence that London

the two roads approaching the Thames, was an industrial quarter with workshops both for bronze-casting and blacksmithing.

Major improvements came early in the 2nd century. A range of palatial rooms, including a baths suite and a barrel-vaulted hall painted in Italian style, was built overlooking the river. It may have served senior military personnel. Along the commercial thorough-fare, buildings at the northern end were converted or rebuilt in masonry to form covered ranges around an open market square. By contrast, a Thameside warehouse made entirely of oak and partly sunk into the ground was a more temporary structure. Built in AD 152–3, it lasted less than ten years. Meanwhile, at the southern

*Londinium, c. AD 120*

*A view from the south-east, with the fort and amphitheatre in the distance, drawn by Peter Froste.*

had an aqueduct. Instead, sophisticated bucket-chain machines lifted water from wells. The largest of these, south of the amphi-theatre, could supply up to 7000 litres (1850 gallons) per hour, but it is doubtful that they operated throughout the Roman period. Many Londoners collected water sufficient for their needs from small wells in the Walbrook valley, where the water table was high.

## THE SOUTH BANK SETTLEMENT

From the very beginning London was a town that spanned the Thames. The south bank settlement was confined to two of the islands that rose above the river channels, but even so it covered over 32 hectares (80 acres), not much less than the entire Roman town of Silchester. Timber revetments kept the land dry at high tide and the narrow channel between the islands was gradually infilled. Logs were laid horizontally on the mudflats as foundations for the sand and gravel embankments that carried the main roads.

The street leading to the bridge was the principal commercial thoroughfare. During the AD 70s, narrow timber-framed buildings sprang up along most of its length. One of these was a smithy. West of the street stood a large masonry building, possibly an inn. Its courtyard was open towards the street but enclosed on the other three sides by a corridor and rooms. Further west, by the lesser of

limit of the settlement, earlier structures were levelled to make way for a religious precinct, which contained at least two temples. Beyond it lay burial grounds, the grand monuments of which bear witness to the prosperity of this part of Londinium.          **FG**

*Water lifting machine*

*A modern life-size working replica of the largest of the bucket chain machines, based on evidence found at Gresham Street.*

# GREATER LONDON IN THE ROMAN PERIOD

Londinium was at the centre of a large hinterland, which was united by a radiating network of roads. Small towns served as local markets, while farms and villas developed in the countryside.

**Greater London in the Roman period**
Small roadside settlements grew up along the major roads that radiated from London, while the villa estates took advantage of the rich agricultural soils of the south-east.

Philologists believe the name 'London' derives from two ancient British roots: *plowo*, to do with ships, swimming or flooding, and *nida*, 'river'. If Tamesis (another ancient British name) denoted the entire Thames, Plowonida would be the wide, tidal section that could be negotiated only by boat. When Londinium was founded around AD 50, it lay well downstream of the tidal head, which at that time was at Westminster. Later, river levels dropped sharply and the tidal head shifted eastwards, making the city's quays less suitable for sea-going ships. Throughout the Roman period, the Thames both facilitated communication and hindered it, separating north from south and funnelling traffic towards a small number of bridges, ferries and fords.

## THE HINTERLAND OF LONDINIUM

The road network did not evolve from a system of Iron Age track-ways but was laid out with astonishing skill by Roman surveyors who combined point-to-point directness with respect for the land-scape. Many alignments remain in use to this day. Some roads, such as Ermine Street, ran up river valleys. Others, including the Canterbury and Silchester roads, followed the Thames itself but at sufficient distance to avoid the flood plain. Yet others, notably the St Albans road, could not avoid hills entirely and so were surveyed in sections. As on Brockley Hill, these sometimes ascended steep gradients before changing direction on the summit.

Pontes ('Bridges') was one of several roadside towns that sprang up at river crossings; Brentford, Old Ford and Noviomagus were others. No doubt they held markets for the produce of local farms, as well accommodating travellers. On the Ebbsfleet, Springhead became one of the most important shrines in Britain. As many as a dozen temples clustered around a pool fed by natural springs.

West of Londinium, well-drained gravel terraces near the Crane and Colne were intensively farmed. Large fields, for crops or livestock, were connected by trackways to the main roads. The well-wooded uplands of north London yielded plentiful supplies of firewood and clay, and so were ideal locations for making pottery and tiles. The kilns at Brockley Hill and Highgate may have been operated by itinerant workers who, like the farmers of west London, evidently lived in build-ings so simple as to have left no archaeo-logical trace. Only in the south-east, on the slopes of the Downs and along the Cray or Darent valleys, were there country estates with substantial stone-built villas. Although many had their own bath-hous-es, barns and agricultural facilities show that they were working farms as much as residences. **FG**

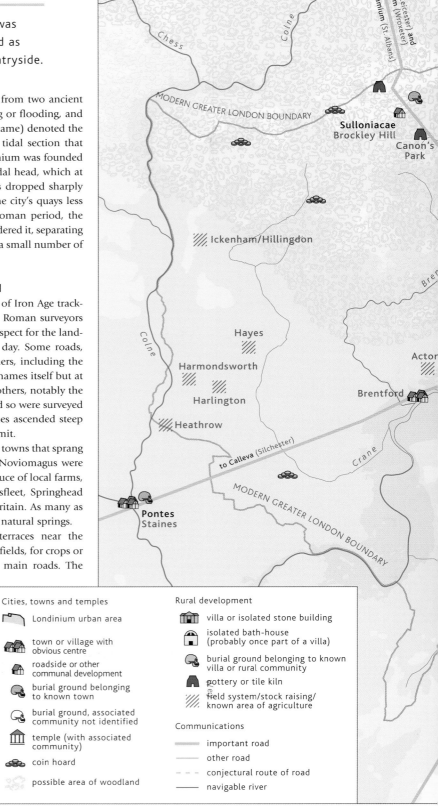

**Cities, towns and temples**

Londinium urban area

town or village with obvious centre

roadside or other communal development

burial ground belonging to known town

burial ground, associated community not identified

temple (with associated community)

coin hoard

possible area of woodland

**Rural development**

villa or isolated stone building

isolated bath-house (probably once part of a villa)

burial ground belonging to known villa or rural community

pottery or tile kiln

field system/stock raising/ known area of agriculture

**Communications**

important road

other road

conjectural route of road

navigable river

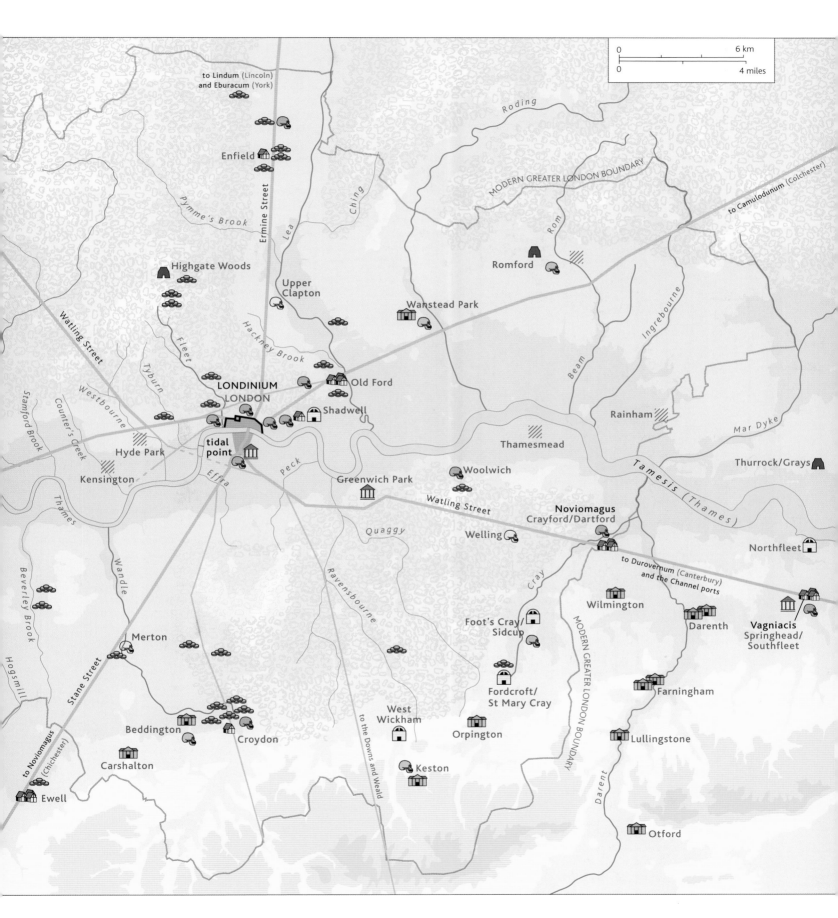

to Lindum (Lincoln)
and Eburacum (York)

Roding

MODERN GREATER LONDON BOUNDARY

to Camulodunum (Colchester)

Enfield

Pymme's Brook

Ermine Street

Lea

Ching

Rom

Ingrebourne

Highgate Woods

Upper Clapton

Hackney Brook

Wanstead Park

Romford

Beam

Watling Street

Fleet

Tyburn

Westbourne

**LONDINIUM**
LONDON

Old Ford

Shadwell

Rainham

Counter's Creek

Stamford Brook

Hyde Park

tidal point

Peck

Effra

Greenwich Park

Woolwich

Thamesmead

Mar Dyke

**Tamesis (Thames)**

Thurrock/Grays

Kensington

Thames

Wandle

Quaggy

Watling Street

Welling

**Noviomagus**
Crayford/Dartford

Cray

to Durovernum (Canterbury)
and the Channel ports

Northfleet

Beverley Brook

Ravensbourne

Wilmington

Darenth

**Vagniacis**
Springhead/
Southfleet

Hogsmill

Stane Street

Merton

Foot's Cray/
Sidcup

MODERN GREATER LONDON BOUNDARY

Fordcroft/
St Mary Cray

Farningham

West
Wickham

Beddington

Croydon

Orpington

Lullingstone

to the Downs and Weald

to Noviomagus (Chichester)

Carshalton

Keston

Darent

Ewell

Otford

# PUBLIC ARCHITECTURE

Major buildings were sited for maximum visual impact: the forum-basilica on a hill and the public baths on the riverbank. Sculpted blocks show how elaborately these were decorated.

**The Huggin Hill baths**
*This model is set around AD 120, showing the baths being extended with a second suite of rooms, some of which had hypocausts.*

southwards to the river crossing. The two met at right angles at the gate to the forum, the east–west street commanding the high ground on either side of the Walbrook. On the eastern hill there was a rectilinear street grid of unknown extent; on the western hill none at all. Here a second east–west street, roughly parallel to the first, followed a contour 2 metres (6 ft 6 in) from the summit of the hill before taking a vertiginous 1 in 10 drop to the Fleet. Nearby, on terraces along the Thames, a bathhouse and temple precinct provided an impressive spectacle for visitors arriving by water. The temple was on a north-east/south-west alignment and so pointed directly at the forum-basilica, from which – on the eastern hilltop – it would have been clearly visible.

## PUBLIC BUILDINGS

To visitors crossing the Thames from the south, the 2nd-century forum-basilica would have been an impressive sight, towering above them. Far bigger than any comparable building in Britain, the forum-basilica symbolized the ambitions of the fast-growing town. Its plan, however, was conventional. Originating in Italy as a loose arrangement of temples and council offices around a piazza, the forum-basilica had become a single building by the time urban ideas had spread across Gaul to Britain. It had a functional blueprint comprising a rectangular courtyard, a cross-hall and three ranges of porticoes, shops and offices.

The largest of London's bathhouses, in the south-west quarter, was no bigger than that of the average Romano-British town. A monumental public baths, commensurate with the forum-basilica, perhaps remains to be discovered. Perched on a Thameside terrace, the Huggin Hill baths began life in the AD 70s as a modest row of four or five rooms: unheated anterooms in the east, leading through to a hypocaust-heated hot room in the west. Fifty years later it was augmented with more impressive heated rooms, those to the east apparently forming a self-contained suite. Given that Roman ethics – and laws – specified that men and women bathe separately, it is curious that double bathhouses were exceptional in the empire rather than standard. Perhaps in London there were segregated facilities.

Except for the temple of Mithras, no complete temples have been excavated, but the limestone blocks from a monumental arch offer a rare glimpse of the magnificence of Londinium's religious architecture. Traditional Roman representations of Hercules and Minerva, together with more homespun portrayals of the Seasons, call upon the heavenly powers to protect Londinium and bring it prosperity.

The most distinctive characteristic of almost all Roman towns was a rectilinear street-grid. Londinium's plan (see page 30) displays elements of a grid but, at the same time, it shows a response to the geography of the site, with concern for sight lines and the positioning of monumental buildings. In this respect, London can be compared with the very grandest cities in the Roman Empire, where emperors or private benefactors commissioned building programmes of such magnitude as to extend over several blocks, or to open up previously vacant districts. Such projects may well have shaped Londinium, but in the absence to date of any written records we cannot be sure.

Two streets governed the layout of the north bank settlement and would have been the first to be surveyed: the mile-long street leading westwards to Newgate, and the short street running

**The forum-basilica**
*This model is set in the middle of the 2nd century. Seen from the south, it shows the monumental entrance (foreground), stalls in the forum (centre), and the basilica (top). Altogether this was one of the largest Roman buildings north of the Alps.*

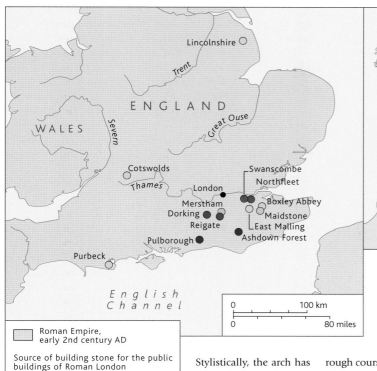

Lincolnshire
Trent
Great Ouse
ENGLAND
WALES
Severn
Cotswolds
Thames
London
Swanscombe
Northfleet
Merstham
Boxley Abbey
Dorking
Maidstone
Reigate
East Malling
Pulborough
Ashdown Forest
Purbeck
English Channel

0    100 km
0    80 miles

Roman Empire,
early 2nd century AD

Source of building stone for the public
buildings of Roman London

- chalk
- limestone
- marble & other decorative stone
- porphyry
- ragstone
- Reigate stone
- sandstone

London
Belgium
black marble
Rhine
EUROPE
Dnieper
Italy
Danube
Pyrenees
Black Sea
Greece
Anatolia
green porphyry
Mediterranean Sea
AFRICA
Egypt
red porphyry
Nile

**Sources of building stone**
Many building materials were available in southern Britain (left), and could be transported to London by boat. For the finest buildings marble veneer was imported from far-flung corners of the Mediterranean (right).

The nearest source of building stone was 48 kilometres (30 miles) away, near Maidstone. Kentish rag is durable, but cannot be worked to a smooth finish, still less carved to make a column capital or door frame. For such decorative elements, Lincolnshire limestone or Bath stone was often used, the walls themselves built in rough courses of Kentish rag alternating with horizontal courses of tiles. Such walls might be plastered and painted to simulate opulent stone facades or, in the most expensive buildings, veneered with marble. Marble was obtained from wholesalers, not directly from the quarry, and so fashions set elsewhere in the empire dictated what was available in London. White marble – at first mainly from Carrara in Tuscany, later from Proconnesus in Turkey – was more affordable than the Greek and Egyptian green or red porphyries, which were often simulated in paintwork.

Most of the town's ceramic building materials – including the thousands of *tegulae* (flat oblong tiles with raised edges) and *imbrices* (half-pipe tiles) required for roofing – were fashioned from local clay. Kilns have been discovered near Edgware and some of the bricks and tiles were stamped with the logo of the procurator. As the emperor's financial representative in the province, he may have helped finance the public works projects of the 1st and 2nd centuries. **FG**

Stylistically, the arch has more links with Germany or Gaul than with Italy, and the same is true of the distinctive 'Romano-Celtic' type of temple. The design – a square tower surrounded either by an enclosed ambulatory (walkway) or open portico – may have been influenced by native ceremonies involving procession around an icon housed centrally. Two such temples lay on the outskirts of the south bank settlement, beside the Canterbury road, where their towers would have welcomed travellers approaching Londinium from the Channel ports.

## THE BUILDING INDUSTRY

Londinium employed hundreds of workers, from unskilled labourers to skilled masons or joiners, and consumed vast quantities of building materials. Oak was the main timber used in construction. The gigantic baulks, often 0.185 metres square (2 ft sq), which made up the 1st-century quay fronts, came from very old trees that had been growing wild in forests prior to the Roman conquest. But by the 2nd century, oaks were being cultivated specifically to supply posts and planks for carpentry.

*Monumental arch*
*The original for this model of a monumental arch came from a religious precinct near Blackfriars. Over 30 huge limestone blocks remain from an arch that once symbolized the prosperity of London. One sculpture (far left) shows Mars and the shoulder of a second god, possibly Mercury, with a money bag.*

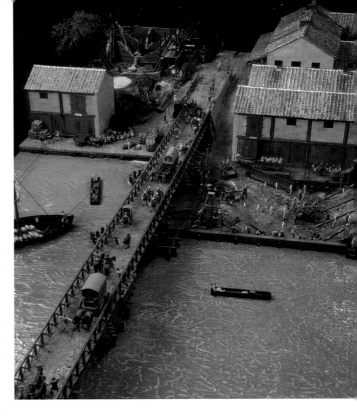

# THE PORT, TRADE & WORK

Roman London played a pivotal role in the developing province and its commercial success was reflected by the size of the port, the variety of imports and the service trades needed in a thriving town.

***Roman London's port***
*Quays north and south of the river were linked by a bridge, only marginally different in position to today's London Bridge.*

***Trades and industries***
Although polluting industrial processes were, by necessity, sited in areas unsuitable for habitation, food production remained a central activity.

Merchants in the Roman empire were always on the lookout for new markets, and London quickly became a vast emporium for the burgeoning province, importing merchandise and foodstuffs from all over the empire. The town's waterfront expanded rapidly, with timber revetments built out into the river and warehouses fronting the quayside. New crafts and craftsmen were required to service the needs of an ever-growing populace and areas of the town became the quarters for various specialist crafts and industries.

The modern roads Upper and Lower Thames Street reflect the line of the Roman quayside, where waterfront construction began as early as AD 52. What began as a simple revetment soon grew into well-constructed quays, constructed from massive oak beams. The quays and revetments stretched for over 650 metres (2133 ft) from modern Cannon Street station to east of the Custom House. Over time, however, as rising water levels dropped and quays silted up, new ones extended out into a river that was as much as 100 metres (328 ft) wider and shallower than it is today. From the mid 1st century onwards, a bridge connected the quays on the north with the southern settlement. The remains of two boats, preserved in the mud of the Thames, have been excavated. One, found at County Hall in 1912, was a Mediterranean-style ship with a deep keel that could have sailed the open seas. The other, uncovered at

Blackfriars in 1965, was of a flatter construction and was perhaps used for more local traffic. This boat had sunk in the 3rd century with its cargo on-board – Kentish rag, a building stone brought from the Medway area, primarily for use in public construction.

## IMPORTS & EXPORTS

A series of stone warehouses on the riverfront, open-fronted with wooden shutters, enabled goods to be stored in transit. Imports from all corners of the empire flooded into Londinium to satisfy the needs of the town's mixed population. Tableware of ceramics, glass and bronze came from the western provinces; exotic marbles for building from Greece, Turkey and Egypt; and large containers – wooden barrels of German wine and ceramic vessels containing olive oil (for cooking and lighting), fish sauce and wine – from Italy, Spain and southern France. Imports must have far outweighed exports, although Britain did export slaves, hunting dogs, oysters and metal ingots, in particular lead from the government-controlled mines in the Mendips.

Consignments were checked through customs and contents identified by painted inventories on the outside of the containers. Small lead seals, some belonging to customs officials and others to merchants, were attached to goods entering the country. Documentation was crucial; wooden tablets that once held writing on a thin layer of beeswax held detailed lists of goods. Surviving tablets testify to the buying and selling of goods, including slaves.

Goods were then loaded into carts or smaller boats to be transported to the rest of the province. Some goods were kept in the town; richer items were moved up the hill to the fashionable shops surrounding the forum, the hub of commerce and finance. Narrow

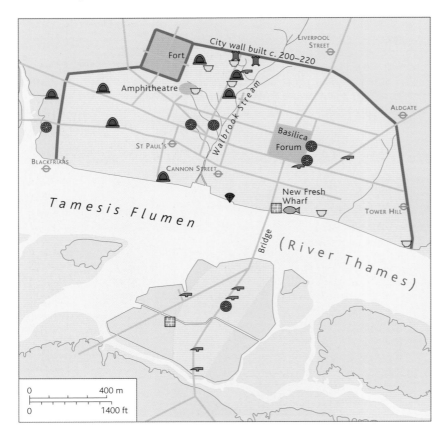

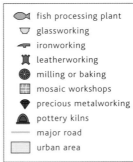

🐟 fish processing plant
🥛 glassworking
⚒ ironworking
🗡 leatherworking
⚙ milling or baking
🏢 mosaic workshops
🔻 precious metalworking
🔔 pottery kilns
— major road
▫ urban area

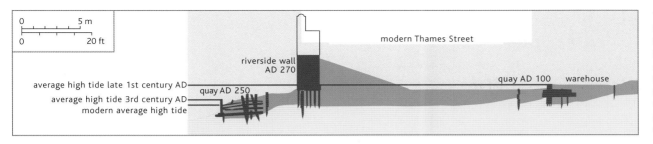

Mediterranean-style buildings lined the main roads, with shops and workshops facing the road. There Roman Londoners could purchase ready-to-use stoneground flour rather than having to grind it at home. Food shops, bakeries and fast food stalls all helped to feed the citizens.

## SERVICE TRADES

From Londinium's foundation, a myriad of local craftsmen were needed to service the new community – carpenters for building the timber-frame houses, leatherworkers for fashioning shoes, metalworkers and toolmakers, as well as such shopkeepers, grocers and bakers. The remains of workshops and rubbish dumps – off-cuts of wood and leather, tools stamped with the makers' names and a huge dump of glass ready for glassworkers to recycle – point to the presence of these craftsmen. Some crafts needed access to running water and tended to congregate near the Walbrook stream. The

malodorous tanning processes of leatherworkers, in particular, were positioned away from the main residential areas, in the north-west of the city.

Although the majority of Roman Londoners would have been working class – the craftsmen, shopkeepers and labourers who built and maintained the town – there must have also been a large mercantile class who created the town's wealth, enticing many entrepreneurs hoping to make their fortunes and bringing in foreign merchants on the look-out for new markets. Craftsmen with skills still unknown in Britain, such as mosaicists and wall painters who could command a higher fee than other craftsmen, were probably brought from the Continent to decorate the new public buildings until such time as local workers became experienced, combining a more British style with Romanized crafts.

**JMNH**

## FISH SAUCE

Evidence of foodstuffs rarely survives, but this Roman storage jar contained fish bones, the remains of fish sauce (*garum*). Moreover, the neck of the vessel had a painted inscription claiming that 'Lucius Tettius Africanus supplies the finest *garum* from Antibes' (in southern France). Fish sauce was a key ingredient in both sweet and savoury Roman dishes, essential for Roman Londoners used to a Mediterranean diet.

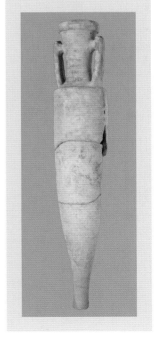

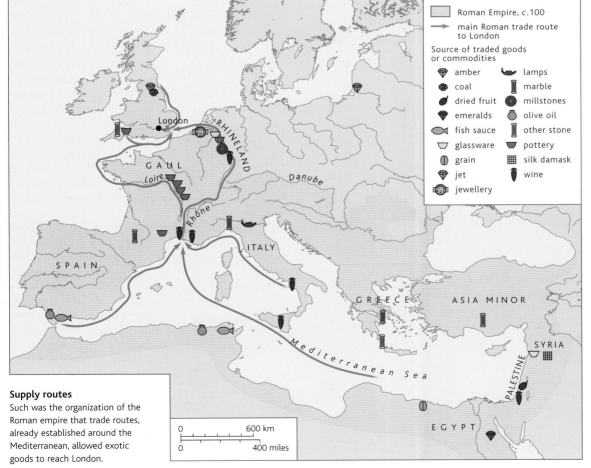

**Roman Empire, c.100**

main Roman trade route to London

Source of traded goods or commodities

| | |
|---|---|
| amber | lamps |
| coal | marble |
| dried fruit | millstones |
| emeralds | olive oil |
| fish sauce | other stone |
| glassware | pottery |
| grain | silk damask |
| jet | wine |
| jewellery | |

**Supply routes**
Such was the organization of the Roman empire that trade routes, already established around the Mediterranean, allowed exotic goods to reach London.

# THE PEOPLE OF ROMAN LONDON

Roman Londoners must have always been a changing racial mix, segregated by firm social divisions that separated men from women, rich from the poor and free citizen from the slave.

**Roman couple**
*This reconstruction is based on the evidence from two graves excavated from the Roman eastern cemetery, where jewellery as shown on the woman here and accessories were found that indicated the couple may have been German in origin. The reconstruction is by Derek Lucas.*

## CITIZENS & SLAVES

Slavery was crucial to the efficient running of the empire. A recovered funerary monument dedicated to a citizen of Londinium named Claudia Martina shows that she was the young wife of a provincial slave, Anencletus, who was presumably senior enough in the government administration to avoid the stigma of a female citizen marrying a male slave. A deed of sale written on black wax set in a wooden writing tablet found during excavations at Poultry records that Vegetus, an imperial slave whose abilities had allowed him to become a deputy-treasurer in the central administration, paid a high price for Fortunata, a female slave from northern Gaul, who was 'guaranteed healthy and not liable to run away'.

was of German origin, and the altar dedicated by Marcus Martiannius Pulcher, a 3rd-century governor of Upper Britain, whose family name, Martiannius, suggests a Celtic origin. Surviving tombstones also indicate the various ranks of military personnel (centurion, legionary soldier and military policeman) stationed in London. They were seconded from legions based in Britain but, following normal Roman practice, these legions themselves would have been recruited from outside Britain to reduce the possibility of support among soldiers for local insurrections.

Most Londoners, however, were not from the military. Evidence from cemeteries suggests that the town represented a balanced cross section of society. Information from the cemetery population has also made it possible to come up with the average physical statistics of Roman Londoners: men averaged 1.69 metres (5 ft 6 in) in height and women 1.58 metres (5 ft 2 in). Skeletal bones show that Roman Londoners were robustly built and ate balanced, healthy diets, with plenty of fruit and vegetables, and used honey as a sweetener. The shape of their skulls and facial bones corresponds to those of other Romano-British communities, which indicates that the majority were probably native Britons.

From its origins, Londinium maintained regular contact with the rest of the empire. Including the indigenous Britons, it was therefore a culturally and ethnically cosmopolitan town, with all social levels represented. Citizenship was gained originally only by birth into the elite families of Rome, but as the empire expanded a succession of emperors gradually widened the privilege, until in the early 3rd century all free men of the empire were granted citizenship. Male citizens proudly demonstrated their status with three Latinized names, often shortened to three initials, whereas women and freedmen had two names and slaves only one. The names of some Roman Londoners have survived either as stone inscriptions or as graffiti scratched on possessions. The manumission (ceremonial freeing) of slaves was not uncommon; such freed slaves often continued to work for their masters after their release.

## MILITARY & CIVILIAN

Evidence for the origins of London's ruling classes come from sources such as the tombstone memorial of the procurator Classicianus, who

## A CULTURAL MELTING-POT

The majority of Roman Londoners were shopkeepers, craftsmen and labourers. Some came from elsewhere in the empire, like Demetrius, the Greek owner of a lead amulet seeking divine protection from the plague, and Aulus Alfidius Olussa, possibly a merchant,

**Leather briefs**
*An unusual pair of leather briefs, possibly the uniform of a teenage acrobatic performer.*

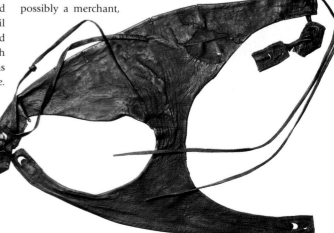

who was born in Athens. Tiberinius Celerianus, an important trader, and Gaius Silvius Tetricus, a travelling salesman in eye ointments, both hailed from Gaul, as did the female slave Fortunata. Aside from name origins, the identification of foreigners from excavated burials provides evidence for migration. DNA and isotope analysis of human remains make it possible for modern archaeologists to identify the genetic origins of some individuals, confirming Londinium's cosmopolitan mix of people.

Little evidence remains of the clothing of Roman Londoners, apart from the sturdy ankle boots and more ornate sandals made out of leather. Textiles seldom survive long-term burial but leather, if buried in damp or waterlogged conditions, can remain intact for archaeologists to examine. In addition to shoes, pairs of female leather briefs have been found from London, one possibly the costume of a young acrobat, although others may have been a form of female underwear. Roman fashion competed with native styles; leggings, tunics and woollen cloaks proved more practical in the British climate than the toga, which was the mark of a Roman citizen and was probably only worn by the higher classes on special occasions. Women wore long tunics with decorative brooches to fasten their dresses. Their long hair needed numerous hairpins to hold the style in place and those with leisure time on their hands and available cash were able to purchase a variety of cosmetic creams and pigments.

Small containers and glass flasks would have held coloured pigments for eye and face make-up as well as perfumed oils that tended to be olive oil-based but perfumed with flowers or aromatic spices. A unique tin canister was found to contain a face cream – something that was probably widely used but which rarely survives. Analysis of the still-soft cream ascertained that it was made of animal fat, starch and tin oxide, not dissimilar to the ingredients of modern face creams. All such beauty products for women were intended to keep up Roman appearances.          JMNH

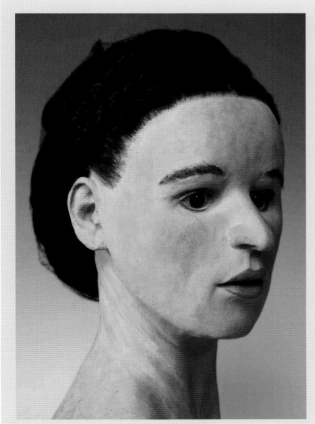

## A FACE FROM ROMAN SPITALFIELDS

The remains of one Roman Londoner found at Spitalfields provide a fascinating insight into the cosmopolitan nature of the city. A woman who died in her early twenties, she was a first-generation immigrant who came to live in late Roman Londinium as a young child. DNA and isotope analyses indicate that she came from either Italy, Spain or southern France.

This reconstructed head, based directly on the skeletal remains found in her coffin, gives as accurate an impression of her probable appearance as current forensic science allows.

Most unusually, textile fragments of damask silk, woven in a chequerboard pattern and decorated with gold thread, were found in her coffin with her remains. Silk thread from China had been woven into damask in the eastern Roman province of Syria, before being made into a garment worn in Londinium, at the other end of the empire.

*The reconstructed head of a young woman from Roman London.*

**Manicure set**
*As part of the cleansing programme, it was necessary to keep nails clean and trim and facial hair plucked. This bronze manicure set, originally brightly decorated with red enamel, would have hung from a belt at the waist for daily use.*

# HOUSES & LIVING CONDITIONS

As Londinium grew, houses and shops lined the main roads. The wealthy chose to leave the busy streets, and the numbers of villas around London may indicate their move to country estates.

Most of the population of Londinium was crammed into the centre of the city, where small, rectangular timber-framed buildings lined the main east–west road. These basic dwellings housed the working population. They were long strip buildings, similar in layout, style and construction to Mediterranean buildings, either

*A wealthy dining room*
Part of the inner city improvements of the 3rd century led to the building of spacious stone town houses with mosaic floors and underfloor heating.

with side corridors linking the rooms that ran from the front to the back of the house, or central corridors leading to rooms on either side. Most of these houses would have been single storey, perhaps with under-the-eaves storage.

Research shows that these houses were prefabricated off-site; the ground was prepared and levelled, and the main frame was then installed on-site. There were no foundations and the walls were either woven twigs and clay or built from clay-mud bricks. Walls were then given a coat of plaster, inside and out, and the roofs would have been either thatched with straw or planked with wood. Rising damp must have been a constant problem and the houses must have needed replacing every ten to fifteen years. Inside, conditions were basic, with earthen floors and hearths set in clay-lined hollows in the floor or as brick-built structures against the wall. These hearths were used both for cooking and to heat the room. Sleeping mattresses would have been brought in at night.

In the early years of the city's development, and on its outskirts during later periods, excavations have also revealed a number of native-style round houses. These houses, which were used for living accommodation and workshops, suggest that some people in Londinium preferred the old ways to the new. Inhabitants of one series of round houses excavated in Gresham Street in the City, for example, were using fragments of Roman glass to manufacture beads in a pre-Roman style.

## WEALTHIER HOUSES

Living conditions for the ordinary people of Roman London must have been hard, and living beside the main road would have been particularly noisy, dirty and damp. Houses in the centre of the city were cramped, divided by narrow alleys and with small backyards where animals were often kept and rubbish of all kinds was dumped. There was no provision for toilet facilities inside and the contents of jars and buckets would have fouled these areas. Domestic wells were frequently located too close to rubbish, which caused contamination and health hazards.

It is hardly surprising, therefore, that wealthier houses started to be built away from the busy main roads in quieter districts, although they were still integrated with shops and workshops. The houses of the better off in the 1st and 2nd centuries were built in a similar manner to the poorer houses: they were constructed as timber-frame houses on one or more floors, but with the addition of shallow foundations and an element of internal flooring. This might have consisted of a thick, hard-wearing layer of mortar mixed with crushed tile or, in the more prestigious rooms, decorative mosaic panels set in plain tessellated floors. Internal walls were painted with decorative panels, the owners obviously wishing to impress visitors. Early fashions were for brightly painted wall panels set above a dado, with a painted marble effect below. Before the introduction of under-

*A poorer lifestyle*
Inner-city living – most houses had basic, multifunctional rooms. Cooking was done on the hearth set into the floor.

floor heating, heat was provided by fires set in metal braziers on the floor. Larger houses of this type in Londinium may have been rented out as apartments.

## INNER CITY REGENERATION

During the 2nd and 3rd centuries some central areas of the city were cleared, and more solidly built houses with stone walls and tiled roofs were erected. At the same time, some of the earlier wooden houses received extensions at the back built of stone. Many of these new houses had underfloor heating and fine mosaic floors in the main rooms. Some of these later buildings may even have had a private bathhouse attached, the owners no longer wishing to fraternize with ordinary people in the public baths.

Local craftsmen were now skilled enough to introduce painted scenes to wall panels in these houses. Mythological scenes were common, and typically were carefully chosen: Bacchus, the god of wine, partying with his entourage, was probably a popular subject for a dining room, while sea creatures would have been more likely in a bathhouse. Improved glass technology led to larger windows, leading in turn to a fashion for lighter and more detailed wall paintings. **JMNH**

**A wealthy kitchen**
*Reconstructed view showing a kitchen from a wealthy house of Roman London. Cooking would have been done on grills over embers, reminiscent of the modern barbeque.*

## URBAN DEVELOPMENT AT NO. 1 POULTRY

Excavations at Poultry and the surrounding area in the modern City of London have provided evidence for over seventy buildings spanning 350 years of Roman occupation. This area in the heart of Roman London reveals the cramped nature of inner-city living during different periods. Early buildings fronted on the main east–west road through the city (the Via Decumana), and later 1st-century buildings respected the building lines of structures destroyed in the Boudican fire of AD 60/61. However, major site clearance in the 3rd century led to a change in the character of the area with larger upgraded buildings. A possible temple was constructed to the south of the intersection.

timber building
stone building
drains
road

**Central development**
London's main street (*Via Decumana*) over time. Slum clearance changed the nature of the inner city.

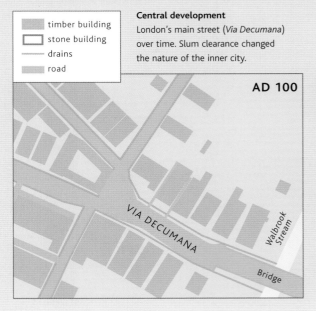

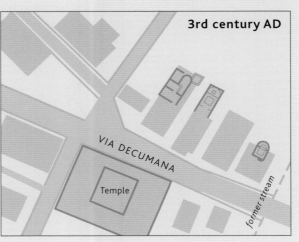

# BATHS, THE AMPHITHEATRE & ENTERTAINMENT

Public baths in Roman London were the leisure centres of their day, allowing people to relax and socialize as well as keep clean. Public entertainment was provided in a smart amphitheatre.

**Huggin Hill public baths**
The major baths, conveniently sited beside the river to dispose of dirty water, were extensively renovated in the late 1st century.

The Roman historian Tacitus credited his father-in-law Gnaeus Julius Agricola, governor of Britain in AD 78–84, with civilizing the province. A major element in this process was Agricola's view that bathing was an essential part of a civilized Roman life: a visit to the baths combined health and hygiene with a social event where one could meet friends, exercise and have something to eat.

Roman bathing involved passing through a series of rooms like modern saunas and Turkish baths, each warmer than the last, culminating in a hot, steamy room where the bather could sweat out the labours of the day. Sweat, dead skin and old oils were then scraped off the skin with a curved blade (strigil). Cold water from plunge pools was then

*Strigil and flask, used in bathing*
*The necessary requisites for a visit to the baths – a strigil for scraping oil and sweat from the skin and a glass flask for fresh, perfumed oil.*

splashed on the skin to close the pores, before fresh perfumed oils were applied.

The large public baths complex on the river was part of the late 1st-century building boom in Londinium. The baths were extended in the early 2nd century, but less than 100 years later the cost of the building's upkeep proved to be too onerous and it was dismantled.

Other public bathhouses may have taken its place, providing bathing for ordinary Londoners or for particular sectors of society, while the rich increasingly chose to build their bathhouses en suite. A new large bathhouse, recently discovered at Shadwell, just over a kilometre (less than a mile) east of the town, suggests that an exclusive bathing establishment may have been established outside the city.

## PUBLIC ENTERTAINMENT

A major form of entertainment was a visit to the amphitheatre. Built to the north-west of the main settlement, the amphitheatre was first built of wood in about AD 70. The arena was dug into the ground with an oval earth bank around it supporting the wooden tiers of seating. Estimates suggest that it could have seated as many as 7000 people. The sunken arena could become waterlogged, so a network of oak drains was installed. These covered drains were well maintained throughout the life of the amphitheatre.

Some thirty years later, parts of the building were renovated. The arena wall and main entranceways were rebuilt in stone and decorated with colourful plaster and Egyptian marble inlays, while the rest of the building remained in wood. The main entrances (to the east and west of the arena) were solely for those taking part in events in the arena. Entrance to the seating area was by stairs on the outside wall of the amphitheatre.

In the early 4th century, the amphitheatre fell out of use, in line with other known amphitheatres in Roman Britain. Maintenance of the drains was neglected, causing the arena to become damp and boggy. The arena itself may have become a slaughterhouse or the town's rubbish dump in the late Roman period. Entertainments in the amphitheatre must have relied on wealthy benefactors, and their demise may have been due to the decline of such sponsorship.

Direct evidence of the events staged in the amphitheatre in Londinium is limited, but one of the two small antechambers had evidence for a trapdoor leading out into the arena that could be raised to release penned-up wild animals. The animals were not the exotic types that were shipped to the Colosseum in Rome, but were more

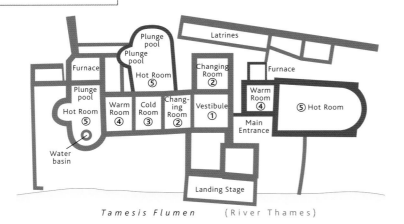

original bath house, c. AD 75

later additions

①-⑤ order in which rooms were used

Plunge pool
Plunge pool
Latrines
Furnace
Hot Room ⑤
Changing Room ②
Furnace
Warm Room ④
Plunge pool
Warm Room ④
Cold Room ③
Chang-ing Room ②
Vestibule ①
⑤ Hot Room
Hot Room ⑤
Main Entrance
Water basin
Landing Stage

*Tamesis Flumen* (River Thames)

**Public baths**
The earlier large establishment must have been a drain on public resources and funding and fashion gave way to private baths attached to wealthier houses or smaller commercial establishments.

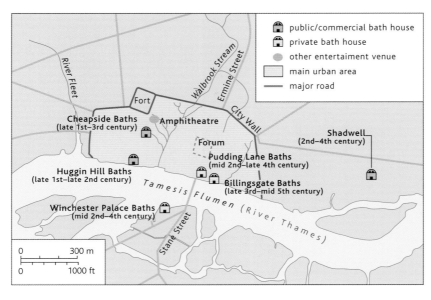

public/commercial bath house
private bath house
other entertainment venue
main urban area
major road

River Fleet
Walbrook Stream
Ermine Street
Fort
City Wall
Cheapside Baths (late 1st–3rd century)
Amphitheatre
Shadwell (2nd–4th century)
Forum
Huggin Hill Baths (late 1st–late 2nd century)
Pudding Lane Baths (mid 2nd–late 4th century)
Billingsgate Baths (late 3rd–mid 5th century)
*Tamesis Flumen (River Thames)*
Winchester Palace Baths (mid 2nd–4th century)
Stane Street

0 ———— 300 m
0 ———— 1000 ft

## ROMAN BOARD GAMES

Board games with sets of counters made of bone, glass or clay were popular Roman equivalents of games like backgammon. Roman dice, like their modern counterparts, had opposing sides that added up to seven. Dice games led to heavy betting, so much so that they were banned by the Emperor Hadrian. Alternative dice games must have been played with a word (made up of one to six letters instead of a number) appearing on each face and must have been part of a word game, yet to be identified.

*A throwing cup and dice from Roman London. One of the dice is marked with letters rather than numbers.*

likely to have been those native to Britain, such as bulls, bears and wolves. Gladiator shows must have been rare and popular spectacles when travelling bands of professional gladiators toured the empire. Gladiators were often put up against local volunteers, with almost inevitable consequences. The arena also provided a venue for the public execution of criminals as well as boxing, athletic, musical and even religious events.

Although the amphitheatre provided mass entertainment, like other towns in Roman Britain, Londinium probably had other venues for spectacles. There may have been a circus for chariot racing and events in both the amphitheatre and circus could have led to excessive betting on the outcome, as was the case in Rome. In addition, there may also have been a semi-circular theatre for dramatic performances, although no evidence has yet been found. Music would have been an important part of Roman entertainment and both wind and string instruments are known to have been used. Professional musicians would have been hired to play at musical events and to take part in funeral processions while music would also have been enjoyed in the home or in the local taverns. **JMNH**

**The amphitheatre**
Excavations in 1988 unexpectedly revealed the main eastern entrance and a portion of the curved arena wall of the amphitheatre. The damp conditions of the site preserved the extensive system of oak drains that kept the arena dry and clear of rubbish. The remains can be seen on display at the Guildhall Art Gallery.

Guildhall

Antechamber

Gate

East entrance

Guildhall Art Gallery

Antechamber

Guildhall Yard

The Mayor's & The City of London Court

St. Lawrence Jewry

Guildhall House

- ▬ excavated amphitheatre walls
- ▬ conjectural amphitheatre walls
- ░ excavated earth bank for supporting seating
- ▓ excavated arena/internal areas
- ── drains
- ── modern buildings

| 0 | | 20 m |
| 0 | | 70 ft |

# RELIGION IN
# THE ROMAN CITY

Religious observance was central to the lives of Roman Londoners, but was very varied. Temples and shrines existed throughout the city, with many dedicated to Eastern gods.

Worship, both formal with temple visits and informal by seeking the approval of the gods for every deed, determined every aspect of Roman life. As the Roman Empire swallowed up conquered territory into new imperial provinces, it recognized local religions as a unifying force. London must have been liberally sprinkled with formal temples dedicated to the classical deities while the style of other structures reflected Eastern or Celtic religions either brought to London by new settlers or included as native traditions, all of which, with the exception of Druidism, were accepted into Roman religious practice.

Roman gods like Jupiter may have been worshipped in classical-style temples, but other temples were dedicated to eastern deities such as Mithras, Isis and Bacchus. These gods and goddesses would have been worshipped in temples with Eastern-style architecture, whereas native deities were worshipped in Celtic-style temples. There is a great deal of evidence in Londinium of deities from the eastern part of the empire, whose cults may have been introduced by soldiers stationed in Britain, or merchants whose business put them in contact with eastern parts of the empire.

**Venus figurine**
*Cheap mass-produced figurines like this one were used as offerings in the local shrines.*

### EAST MEETS WEST

A temple dedicated to the god Mithras, excavated in 1954, lay close to the Walbrook stream. Mithras, originally from Iran, was a god of heavenly light, and his worship spread from the east across much of the empire; the cultured elite of Rome itself admired the high ideals of Mithraism. The mystic cult, modified through contact with Roman culture, became established during the late 1st century AD and spread quickly with the military as far as the empire's western reaches. Mithraism demanded honesty, purity and courage from its followers at a time when the empire was struggling to maintain its authority. The cult was male-orientated and was organized as a secret society.

The Walbrook temple, built in about AD 240, was a typical low sunken building intended to reflect the origins of Mithras, who was reputed to have been born in a cave. It remained in use as a Mithraeum for about 100 years before structural problems – and possibly a decline in numbers of worshippers – led to its conversion to a temple to the traditional Graeco-Roman god Bacchus (see the plans opposite).

**Mother goddesses**
*The mixed native and Roman cult usually displayed three deities. Here, the fourth may personify a deified empress.*

### NATIVE RELIGIONS

An excavation at Tabard Square in Southwark uncovered a site where two Romano-Celtic temples once stood, as well as statues to the gods standing in an open plaza. The style of these temples, with a walkway around a central room, is typical of the north-western provinces of the empire. The complex also had a guest house for visiting worshippers. One temple may have been dedicated to the Mars Camulus, the Roman god Mars combined with Camulus, a native god of northern Gaul (France).

A number of skulls have been found within the city itself, especially in the stream bed of the Walbrook. These skulls are discoloured, suggesting that they were exposed for some time after death. They are likely to be evidence of native British ritual

**Native temples**
Confined to the northern provinces of the empire, Romano-Celtic temples reflected the wide influence of northern religions.

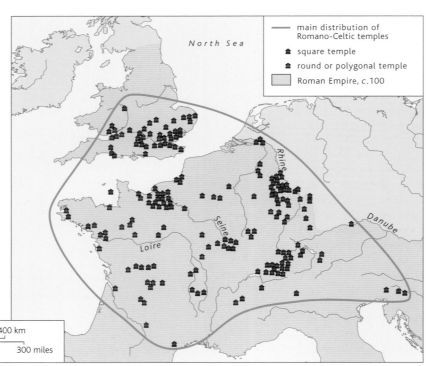

main distribution of Romano-Celtic temples
■ square temple
■ round or polygonal temple
▨ Roman Empire, c.100

North Sea

Rhine

Seine

Loire

Danube

0        400 km
0        300 miles

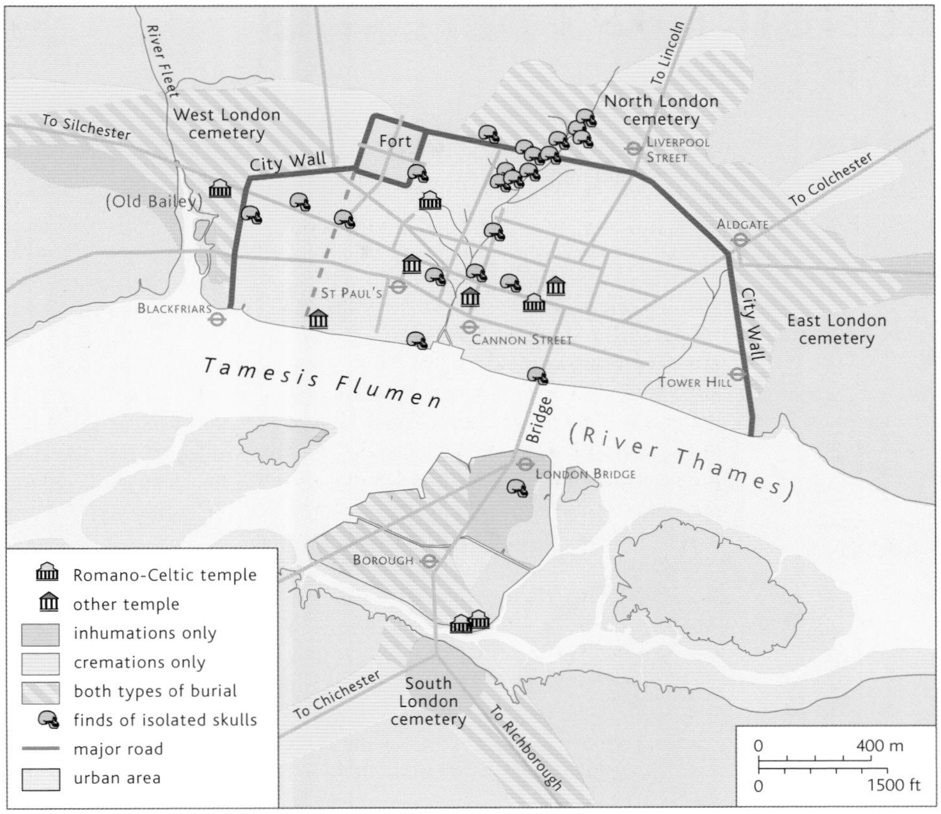

**London's religious structures**

London had numerous temples and shrines throughout the town whereas the cemeteries were, by law, confined to the outskirts of the town. The shifting cemetery areas reflect the growth or diminution of the settlements.

**Mithras**

*This Italian marble head would have formed part of a life-size portrayal of the god slaying the bull – the central belief of the cult.*

**An Eastern-style temple re-purposed**

The Walbrook temple of Mithras (upper plan), suffering from serious structural faults, was later extensively renovated as a temple to Bacchus (lower plan).

practices in which heads were deposited in the sacred stream as part of a votive rite. The practice was probably linked with an Iron Age funerary rite in which skulls, removed for separate disposal, were worshipped in their own right.

As well as temple visits on formal occasions, Roman religion involved many informal practices connected with what we would regard as superstitious belief. Roman Londoners sought the blessing of the gods for everyday events, which was obtained by placing or nailing up small votive offerings at temples and small shrines. It is likely that many shrines were sited along the Walbrook stream. The focus on water was an important part of ritual in both Iron Age and Roman religion. Water was regarded as a great source of sustenance and constituted a dwelling place of the gods.

Map legend:
- 🏛 Romano-Celtic temple
- 🏛 other temple
- inhumations only
- cremations only
- both types of burial
- finds of isolated skulls
- major road
- urban area

Map labels: River Fleet, To Silchester, West London cemetery, City Wall, (Old Bailey), BLACKFRIARS, St Paul's, Tamesis Flumen, Fort, North London cemetery, Liverpool Street, North to Lincoln, To Colchester, ALDGATE, City Wall, East London cemetery, TOWER HILL, CANNON STREET, Bridge, (River Thames), LONDON BRIDGE, BOROUGH, To Chichester, South London cemetery, To Richborough, 0 400 m, 0 1500 ft

## RITES OF PASSAGE

The dead of Roman London were buried beyond the lawful boundary of the city. Cemeteries sprang up around all the main roads that led out of town. Some burials were confined to special areas, for instance in designated family plots or within walled cemeteries, while others took place in overcrowded parts of a public cemetery. Most burials were marked by a tombstone or wooden marker, but the rich and powerful were entombed in the stone mausolea that lined the roads. Several instances of walled cemeteries have been found in Great Dover Street in Southwark and mausolea in Southwark and the East London cemetery, where it seems that certain areas may have been divided up into specific plots that may have been associated with burial clubs for groups of well-off Roman Londoners.

Cremation was the most common method of disposing of the remains of the deceased for the first 200 years of Londinium's history. Bodies were burnt in a burial pit in the cemetery and the bones were then ceremonially collected, washed and placed in containers, some in special urns and others in everyday cooking pots. As general fashions changed, bodies were more often interred in the ground, either placed straight into the ground or buried in wood or lead coffins or even stone sarcophagi, depending on the budgets of those burying the deceased.

Funeral rites included a procession and ceremonial rituals. Burials were often conducted in the evening and would have been accompanied by burning torches and incense, and a funeral feast.

Food and drink was also deposited in the tomb to feed the deceased on their journey to the underworld. Coins were sometimes included to pay the ferryman for the journey across the River Styx, the river that Romans believed separated the world of the living from the underworld. Some burials included grave goods chosen for their meaning rather than their value, while some burials had no personal possessions at all.                 JMNH

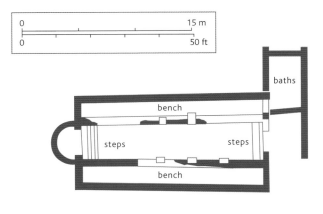

0 — 15 m
0 — 50 ft

(labels: baths, bench, steps, steps, bench)

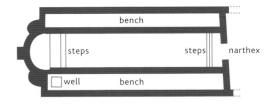

(labels: bench, steps, steps, narthex, well, bench)

# LONDINIUM'S DEFENCES

Roman London's main fort was in the north-west, away from the main area of habitation. As threats multiplied, a wall was built that defined and defended the city for 1500 years.

Roman military legions were never formally stationed in London but those soldiers in London were a mix of legionary (citizen) soldiers and auxiliary (non-citizen) soldiers, seconded from the British-based legions. Their purpose was to administer the province, acting as clerks or military police. However, there had been insufficient numbers of soldiers to defend the town when Boudica attacked in AD 60–1. To prevent further rebellions and to maintain order during the rebuilding, a temporary military base may have been established in the area of modern Fenchurch Street immediately after the uprising. Parallel ditches and a turf-faced rampart formed part of a military encampment and perhaps were linked to a section of defensive works on the waterfront to the south and with other ditches of the same period found further north.

A stone fort housing as many as 1000 soldiers and set away from the main settlement was built in about AD 120, possibly on the orders of the emperor Hadrian, who disap-

**Legionary helmet**
*A replica of a bronze helmet, possibly lost by a legionary soldier when crossing the Thames during the original Claudian invasion.*

***Roman Newgate***
*A reconstruction of Newgate, one of four city gates. It provided access to the main road leading to Silchester and the west.*

proved of soldiers living among civilians. The rectangular fort occupied an area of 5 hectares (12 acres) with a gate in each side. The walls, 1.2 metres thick (4 ft) and 4.5 metres high (15 ft), had corner watchtowers and small, square internal turrets to allow access to the sentry walk. Barrack blocks were ranged around a central block of administrative buildings and store houses.

The fort seems to have gone out of use some eighty years later, when a city wall was extended more than 3 kilometres (1.8 miles) from the site of the later Tower of London as far as Blackfriars, incorporating two sides of the pre-existing fort. For nearly 1500 years it limited the physical growth of the City of London.

## ON THE DEFENSIVE

In about AD 200, the construction of a city wall must have been a huge logistical task, requiring 86,000 tons of Kentish ragstone, which was shipped from the Medway, and taking two to three decades to build. The wall was constructed of squared blocks laid in courses, sandwiching a rubble and mortar core. Courses of flat, red clay tiles were interspersed at intervals to give the wall extra strength and stability. Complete with its battlements, the wall would have been at least 6 metres high (20 ft) and 2.7 metres wide (8 ft 8 in) at ground level. The external face of the wall was defended by a ditch cut about 4 metres (13 ft) from the wall itself, and surplus earth was banked up against the inner face of the wall for additional strength. City gates were erected at Bishopsgate, Newgate and Ludgate, where the main roads left the town, but an existing stone gate at Aldgate on the road linking London with Camulodunum (Colchester), was also incorporated in the wall.

### The Carausian rebellion
In AD 286 the later empire lost northern Gaul and Britain to Carausius and his successor, Allectus. London, finally retrieved by Emperor Constantius Chlorus with support from the fleet, may have paid the price for siding with the usurpers, while ever-increasing threats of Saxon raids necessitated south-eastern coastal fortifications.

Roman Empire, 286
held by Carausius, 286–93
held by Allectus, 293–6
mints of Carausius
Constantius's campaigns of reconquest
late Roman forts
sites producing *Classis Britannica* stamped tiles

## MILITARY LIFE AND DEATH

Roman soldiers paid dues to burial clubs to cover the cost of funerals and monuments and, therefore, most of the surviving tombstones are for military personnel. Vivius Marcianus, a centurion of the 2nd Legion Augusta, was probably seconded to work on the governor's staff in an administrative capacity. Although camp followers were an accepted part of military service, wives were not legally recognized in the army until AD197, when the emperor Septimius Severus allowed soldiers to marry. The inclusion of Marcianus's wife's name, Januaria Martina, on his funerary monument proves the legality of her title. Most military families, however, lived in settlements that grew up outside the forts until their menfolk retired from the army.

*Funerary monument to Vivius Marcianus.*

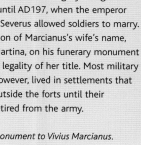

The settlement on the south bank of the Thames remained unfortified. It may be that there was a permanent military presence there anyway. A large public building, built by the army, perhaps housed an official contingent of soldiers during the 3rd century and after, and perhaps this was considered an adequate defence.

In the late 3rd and 4th centuries, the increasing threat of Saxon raids from across the North Sea – and the turmoil of events like the Carausian rebellion (see map, left), in which Londinium was for several years a stronghold of the usurper emperors Carausius and Allectus – led to the completion of Londinium's northern defensive circuit by the addition of a riverside wall north of the waterfront and the construction of at least twenty semi-circular towers on the eastern side of the landward wall. A new gate, Aldersgate, with twin roadways flanked by semi-circular projecting towers, was also built.

The riverside wall was less well constructed than the landward wall. In some parts it was clearly put up in haste, using large ragstone blocks rammed

into a clay base, or stone sculptured blocks taken from a nearby religious complex.

The east-facing semi-circular towers, probably 8–9 metres (26–29 ft) high and built of solid masonry recycled from funereal monuments at nearby cemeteries, provided an elevated platform for heavy catapults.

JMNH

### Walls and fortifications

The walls completely encircled the northern settlement while later towers, added to the eastern wall, provided an extra defence.

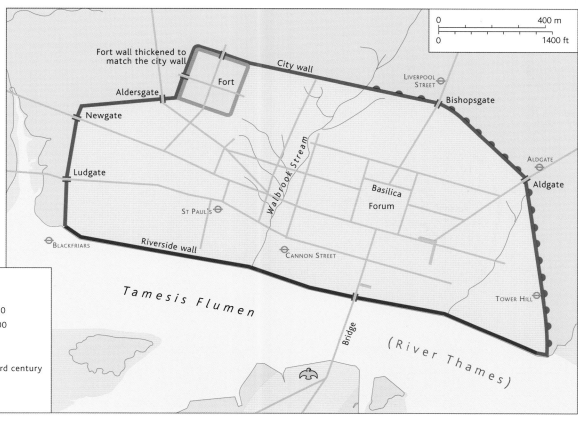

- defensive ditches, AD 61
- fort, built c. AD 110–20
- main city wall. built c. 200–20
- riverside wall, built c. 280–300
- bastion towers, built c. 350
- gateways
- possible legionary garrison, 3rd century
- major road
- urban area

# THE END OF ROMAN LONDON

Late Roman London declined as a commercial and administrative centre. As the population fell, houses became fewer but more luxurious. The city was abandoned once Roman rule ended.

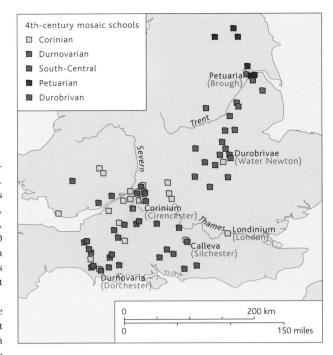

4th-century mosaic schools
- ☐ Corinian
- ☐ Durnovarian
- ☐ South-Central
- ■ Petuarian
- ☐ Durobrivan

**4th-century mosaics**
Produced by several workshops distinguished by style, the finest mosaics were laid in the Midlands and West Country. These were the most prosperous areas in the 4th century.

***Gold coin of Magnus Maximus, AD 383–8 (replica)***
*The mint mark is 'AVG', for Augusta, the 4th-century name for London.*

**Late Roman London**
The great public buildings of the 1st–2nd centuries were dismantled, and London became a small enclave on the hill east of the Walbrook.

For its first hundred years Londinium was a town of spacious public buildings but cramped, cheaply constructed houses and shops. For the next two hundred it was one of decaying public buildings but large, well-appointed private residences. In the forum-basilica, damage caused by fires and subsidence was sometimes patched up, but for long periods the main rooms lay neglected. By AD 200 both the small baths on Cheapside and the much larger Huggin Hill baths had been dismantled, and the fort decommissioned. Its north and west walls were later included in the city defences, but elsewhere its ditches filled with rubbish.

In the private sector, things were different. Workshops in the metalworking district on the south bank were regularly rebuilt. At the Walbrook crossing, shops and houses were refurbished with stone-built extensions containing baths and heated rooms. Fine mosaics were laid here at the turn of the 3rd and 4th centuries, almost certainly by a London workshop. Elsewhere – by the bridge at Billingsgate, for instance – were even larger stone houses built around courtyards. But in many areas there was nothing but the gardens that surrounded these residences of the well-to-do.

The enlargement and elaboration of small older houses also took place on country estates, especially those on the slopes of the Downs, south-east of the city. At Keston, a timber-framed house was replaced by a stone-built winged corridor villa. It also became common to bury the dead in imposing mausolea. Some small towns, such as Old Ford, expanded, though few achieved the sophistication of Shadwell, where large public baths were built.

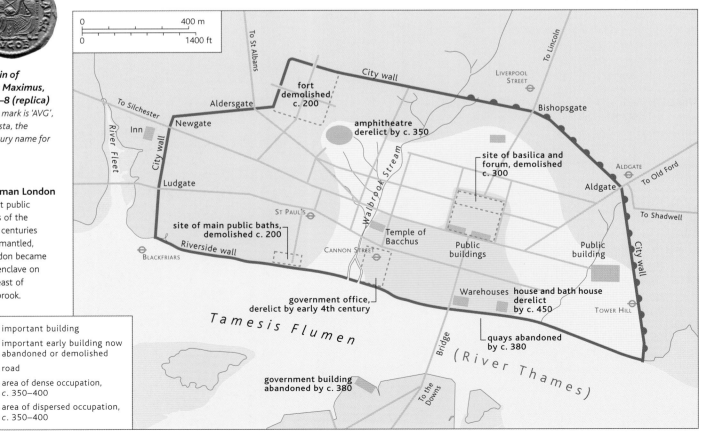

- ■ important building
- ⌐⌐ important early building now abandoned or demolished
- — road
- ▨ area of dense occupation, *c.* 350–400
- ☐ area of dispersed occupation, *c.* 350–400

*Reconstruction of Londinium in the 4th century*
A view from the south-east, with open space where the forum-basilica once stood (centre right). Few people now lived west of the Walbrook.

These changes resulted partly from London's decline as an administrative centre, once Britain had been divided into two provinces soon after AD 200. They were also a consequence of reduced commercial activity. Falling tidal levels required the quays to be extended ever further into the river, and with the army now mostly stationed around Hadrian's Wall, military supplies were increasingly imported through northern ports. During the civil wars raging in the empire in the 3rd century, rich citizens spent money on their own homes, whether in town or country, rather than on public buildings. Thoughts turned to security, and the city wall was by far the largest public building project of the 3rd century.

## REVIVAL & COLLAPSE

The earliest picture of London appears on a gold medallion of AD 296 (see right). In this work of official propaganda, a citizen kneels outside the gate, welcoming the emperor Constantius Chlorus, who has just overthrown the usurper Allectus. Allectus and his predecessor Carausius had minted coins in London, and their headquarters may have been near the former public baths, where foundations of a monumental building have been dated by tree-rings to AD 294–5. Constantius and succeeding emperors brought stability, so that much of Britain prospered as never before, but London did not share in this revival. Some country villas were reduced in size, and the forum/basilica was mostly demolished. On the south bank, people were buried where once there had been habitation. Well-appointed graves show that London still had wealthy citizens, but its status had again been reduced by dividing Britannia, this time into four provinces.

Soon afterwards, however, Londinium was re-named 'Augusta' (Imperial): this signified a decisive break with the city's past, and a new role. Late 4th-century emperors, threatened by rebellion and invasion, rarely resided in Rome but travelled from city to city, accompanied by their courts. Valentinian's representative, Count Theodosius, visited Augusta in AD 367–8, and a civil service handbook reveals that a senior treasury official resided there permanently. Archaeologists have found the grave of a more junior official, buried with the glittering belt that was his badge of office.

Augusta was a small enclave on the hill east of the Walbrook, but it had some magnificent new buildings. While heated rooms were added to old houses on the waterfront, the largest mosaic so far discovered in London – over 8 metres square (86 ft sq) – was laid to the north of the old forum. Elsewhere a grand basilica was built, at least as large as the old. Now that Christianity was the official state religion, could this have been a cathedral for the bishop of London? In the countryside, meanwhile, at Lullingstone villa in Kent a wealthy Christian owner built a chapel whose walls were painted with worshippers standing in prayer.

By 410, with the army withdrawn to the Continent, Britain ceased to be a Roman province. As public services failed and

*Gold medallion minted at Trier and found at Arras (replica)*
London welcomes Constantius Chlorus, mounted on horseback, while his army arrives by ship.

Late 1st century    3rd century    Early 4th century

*London as a provincial capital*
Britannia was originally one province (left). Around AD 200 it was split into two (middle), and around AD 300 into four (right).

buildings became unsafe, the city was abandoned within a generation. On rural estates life continued, however. Burials around Croydon, on the Downs and by Trafalgar Square reveal the arrival of Saxons, who soon mingled with the Romano-Britons to form a new population. Significantly, it was the ancient British name 'London' – not the new 'Augusta' – that survived.                    **FG**

○ Diocesan capital
○ Provincial capital

# EARLY MEDIEVAL LONDON

The period between the 5th and the 13th centuries saw London grow into the largest town, chief port and the capital city of a unified kingdom of England. Yet medieval 'Lunden' did not spring directly from its Roman predecessor Londinium. There is a gap of 200 years in the historical and archaeological record that reflects a time when London was largely deserted.

By the 6th century, small Anglo-Saxon kingdoms in the east of Britain vied for supremacy. The site of Roman London lay in the kingdom of the East Saxons when in 597 Christian missionaries arrived from Rome. It is in this period that London became a town again.

Along the Thames west of the former Roman site, in what is now the Strand, Aldwych and Covent Garden, a new settlement of craftspeople, farmers and merchants grew up. This town, identified only in the last twenty years, has been called Lundenwic by archaeologists – one version of its Old English name.

In the 9th century London suffered another setback. The Vikings sacked the town; their armies ranged over England, and Scandinavian settlers occupied the east and north. The town on the Strand was abandoned, and new streets were laid out inside the Roman city walls. The *Anglo-Saxon Chronicle* records that in 886 King Alfred founded Lundenburg' – but the foundation was surely a long drawn out one.

In the 10th and early 11th centuries, London was a stronghold in the wars that culminated in the accession of a Danish king, Cnut, to the English throne. But it was a new Anglo-Saxon king, Edward the Confessor, who founded a royal palace at Westminster, alongside his new abbey, which slowly became the centre of royal power. The growing distinction between a national government in Westminster and the commercial and industrial heart of the City is still reflected in the London's geography.

The Norman Conquest brought London within a different sphere of influence. People from the commercial cities of northern France, including many Jews, established homes and businesses; Churchmen maintained strong links with their European counterparts. A variety of languages could be heard, as merchants and seamen from all over northern Europe thronged the city's streets and quays.

London grew in population and extent. Royal castles threatened it on both sides. New monasteries, churches and hospitals were established. A great fire in 1087 provided the opportunity for the construction of a new cathedral church of St. Paul, which was to dominate the skyline until that other Great Fire of 1666. With a new stone bridge across the river, begun in 1176, London was taking a shape that is recognizable even today.

...M: HIC PORTA TVR:CORPVS:EADWARDI:REGIS:AD...

**The new abbey**
*The incomplete Westminster Abbey (centre), the destination for the funeral cortege of King Edward the Confessor (right), in January 1066. Its depiction in the Bayeux Tapestry – in this case, the 19th-century Reading copy – is*

# THE ANGLO-SAXON SETTLEMENT

Early Anglo-Saxon settlers around London mostly avoided the ruins of the Roman city – but the foundation of a cathedral there in 604 suggests that London was by then an East Saxon royal centre.

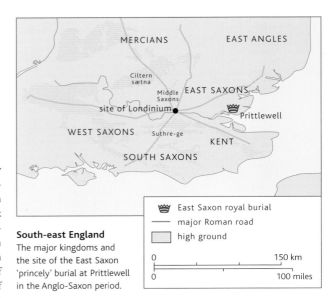

**South-east England**
The major kingdoms and the site of the East Saxon 'princely' burial at Prittlewell in the Anglo-Saxon period.

By the early 5th century, throughout Roman Britain, the urban way of life had collapsed, along with overseas trade, centralized authority and provincial administration – the main functions of Roman London. In spite of many years of intense archaeological work within the City of London, no evidence has been found of continued settlement within the Roman town walls. In the 5th century Angles and Saxons from northern Germany settled in eastern Britain. The fate of the indigenous population of Romanized Britons is not clear. They may have been driven off their land; they may have found themselves with new Anglo-Saxon landlords; or they may have intermarried with the newcomers. A new culture developed that was essentially Anglo-Saxon, with a Germanic language that its speakers called *Englisc* (English).

The new people were farmers who settled mostly in areas well away from the overgrown ruins of the Roman city. The old Roman roads continued to be used, but many of the early Anglo-Saxon settlements lay on the banks of the River Thames, or on tributaries like the Colne and the Wandle, which provided transport as well as

**Blue glass vessels, 7th century**
*Perhaps made in Kent, this pair of cups was among the array of rich objects buried in a grave discovered in 2003 at Prittlewell, Southend – perhaps that of an East Saxon ruler.*

serving as a source of fish for food. Most of these settlements seem to have been either single farmsteads or small villages made up of related families living in clusters of timber-built 'halls' and smaller single-roomed buildings with their floors dug below ground level. Excavations in west Middlesex have revealed the new field systems around these farms; many of them followed boundaries that were first laid down in prehistoric times.

## AN UNSETTLED TIME

In the London area, as elsewhere, most of our knowledge about the Anglo-Saxon way of life comes from their cemeteries and the objects, such as weapons and jewellery, that the Anglo-Saxons buried with their dead. Most burials have been found south of the Thames and in the Surrey hills around Croydon, but there has been little evidence of the settlements to which these burials belong. The weapons, brooches and jewellery found in these graves were made locally on the whole and their style and decoration

suggests links with other people in the Thames valley. Occasionally, precious objects with more exotic connections have been discovered, such as glassware from Europe. But generally the people in the London area seem to have been less wealthy than their neighbours in Kent, where the burials are much more elaborate.

Life at this time was unsettled, and men were typically buried with their weapons. Finds of weapons in the Thames may reflect clashes with neighbouring people, or perhaps – particularly in the case of the area around Brentford, where over forty spearheads have been found – offerings made to the gods. Place names reveal the existence of local peoples or 'tribes', such as the *Gillingas* of Ealing, the *Berecingas* of Barking and the *Stæningas* of Staines, and the *Gumeningas* whose 'high holy place' – *Gumeninga heargh* – gave its name to modern Harrow (see map, right).

## THE ANGLO-SAXON KINGDOMS

During the 6th century, a number of Anglo-Saxon kingdoms became established in eastern Britain, in areas such as Kent – Cantwarena or the land of the 'Kent-dwellers' – whose proximity to mainland Europe led to increasing contact with the Christian realm of the Franks.

The inhabitants of early Anglo-Saxon villages along the Thames used the river for transport and local trade; archaeology reveals no real differences between the peoples north of the river and those to its south. With the growth of more territorially-based kingdoms, however, the Thames formed a natural border. It separated Kent from East Sexena – the land of the East Saxons of 'Essex' – whose kingdom stretched westwards to the Colne, including the London area and what later became the county of Middlesex as well as part of later Hertfordshire. By the 8th century, this area fell under the domination of the powerful kings of neighbouring Mercia, lying to the north-west, and was separated from the control of the kings of Essex. Its people became known as the Middle Saxons.

South of the Thames lay the mysterious area known in the 7th century as the 'southern district' or Suthre-ge – modern Surrey. This area may at one time have been controlled by East Saxon kings, but by the 670s it was ruled by a 'sub-king' who owed allegiance to Wulfhere, king of the Mercians.

The origins and histories of these early kingdoms, their fluctuating borders and the claims they may have had in the London area, are all far from clear. It is possibly in this period that a number of large earthworks and ditches, perhaps intended to define boundaries, were built – the *Fæsten dic* on the east of the River Cray near Dartford, and Grim's Dyke near Pinner in Middlesex.

## ROYAL ESTATES

An Anglo-Saxon king would rule not from a single capital but from any one of the royal estates scattered around his kingdom, calling his council to meet wherever was convenient (this was a practice that continued well into medieval times). It is only when written records began to be kept in the 7th century that these royal centres or 'vills' can be identified with certainty. The East Saxon kings almost certainly had one such centre in the east of their kingdom, probably at Prittlewell (Southend) where in 2003 archaeologists uncovered a magnificent 7th-century burial (see map opposite). The elaborate tomb and the quality and number of objects buried with the dead man left little doubt that it was the grave of a member of the East Saxon royal family. Nonetheless, the East Saxon kings might well have had an estate in the west, in or near London.

In 604, the East Saxons were ruled by King Sæberht, nephew of King Æthelberht of Kent. When, on his uncle's advice, Sæberht received Christian missionaries, it was in London that a cathedral was built after the king's conversion, and it was there that the first bishop, Mellitus, made his base. This followed an established earlier practice – in Kent, cathedrals had been built in the old Roman cities of Canterbury and Rochester – but it also suggests there may have been a royal vill (estate) nearby. A few finds to the west of the Roman city, especially at the site of the later church of St Martin-in-the-Fields, suggest that an Anglo-Saxon settlement existed here from the 5th century. An East Saxon royal estate may well have formed the core of the Saxon town of Lundenwic that grew up here in the 7th and 8th centuries.
**JC**

**Silver brooch**
*Brooch made of gilded silver, 6th century, from the grave of a woman buried in an Anglo-Saxon cemetery in Mitcham, south London.*

**Greater London in the early Anglo-Saxon period**
The many cemeteries between Ewell and Croydon suggest that there were extensive rural settlements in this area that have not been found so far.

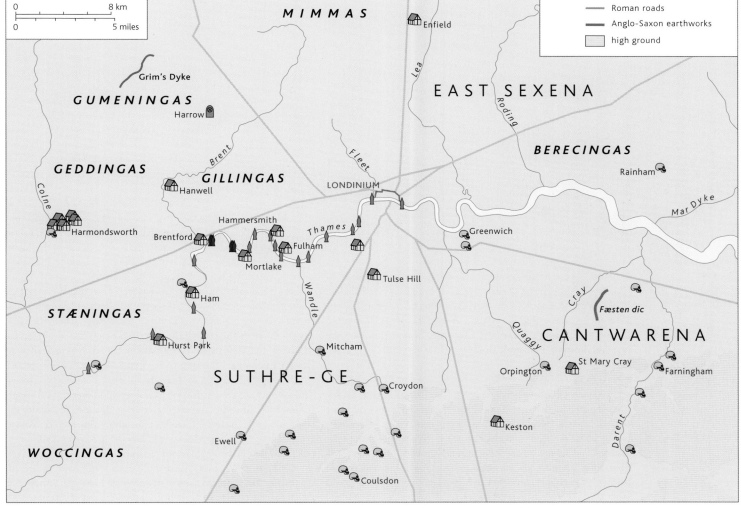

EAST SEXENA — Anglo-Saxon kingdom or sub-kingdom
*MIMMAS* — Anglo-Saxon people/tribe
settlement
burials
pagan shrine
Finds of spears in river
single
multiple
Roman roads
Anglo-Saxon earthworks
high ground

# THE SAXON TOWN & THE VIKING RAIDS

A trading town known as Lundenwic grew up on a site west of the ruins of Roman Londinium. Its wealth attracted Viking raiders, and in the late 9th century it was abandoned in its turn.

**Cooking pot, 8th century**
*This fine white pottery vessel was found in Lundenwic and comes from northern France.*

In 2005 to 2007 excavations under and around St Martin-in-the-Fields church, on the east side of Trafalgar Square, uncovered a late Roman burial and traces of buildings belonging to the very end of the Roman period. Saxon pottery dating to about AD 500 and rich Saxon burials of about AD 650 (see right) found on the same site suggest that occupation may have continued in this suburban area while the Roman city of Londinium to the east lay abandoned.

Although in 604 the cathedral of St Paul, the seat of a bishop for the newly converted East Saxons, was built within the walls of Londinium, it was in this western area that a new town was to grow up. The Anglo-Saxon historian Bede (*c.*673–735), writing in about 730, described London as 'the metropolis of the East Saxons' and as 'an emporium [market] for many nations coming by land and sea'. Archaeologists have discovered the site of Bede's London, lying in the area of modern Covent Garden, stretching west to Trafalgar Square and south to the river (as shown in the map below). Documents of the time refer to this town as Lundenwic – or rather 'Lunden wic', the ending 'wic', denoting a port or trading town, added to the root form 'Lunden'.

**The site of Lundenwic**
The new Saxon trading town grew up west of the River Fleet in the 7th century, as revealed by Saxon finds and excavations since the 1980s. A large minster church may have been founded at Westminster in the 8th century; Bermondsey Priory may have originated in the same period.

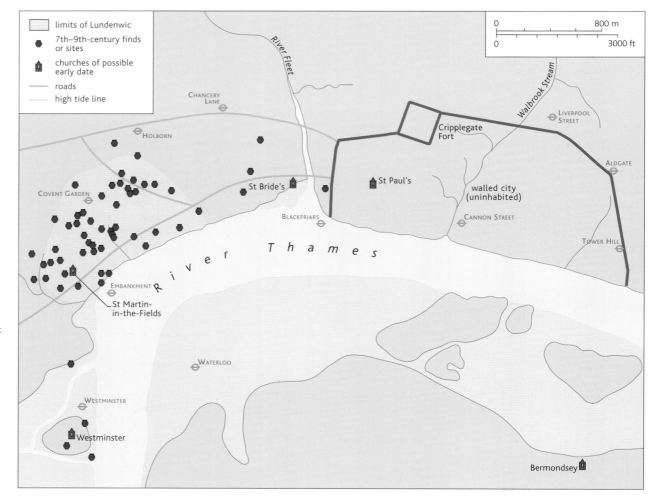

limits of Lundenwic
7th–9th-century finds or sites
churches of possible early date
roads
high tide line

0    800 m
0    3000 ft

River Fleet
CHANCERY LANE
HOLBORN
Walbrook Stream
LIVERPOOL STREET
Cripplegate Fort
ALDGATE
St Bride's
St Paul's
COVENT GARDEN
walled city (uninhabited)
BLACKFRIARS
CANNON STREET
TOWER HILL
EMBANKMENT
St Martin-in-the-Fields
River Thames
WATERLOO
WESTMINSTER
Westminster
Bermondsey

Lundenwic was not the only such 'wic'. Names such as Ipswich survive today, while Saxon Southampton was 'Hamwic', Anglian York 'Eoforwic'. These 'wics' or 'emporia' (to use Bede's Latin word) formed part of a network of such places, where not just local but international trade could be carried on and where kings could levy lucrative taxes on the trade. From Lundenwic ships carried cargoes and travellers to such destinations as Quentovic, near Étaples in France, Dorestad at the mouth of the Rhine, or Hedeby in Denmark. Silver coins minted in England (some from London) found on Continental sites and foreign coins found in England reflect this trade. English wool and woollen cloth were already an important export. Pottery, glass and metalwork from northern France and the Rhineland, millstones from Germany and amber from the Baltic have all been found in Lundenwic. It was almost certainly access to the easy sea route from the Thames to the Rhine and to the valuable trade it carried that in the 8th century led the kings of Mercia, in central England, to extend their influence south and to wrest control of London from the East Saxons.

However, Bede's 'many nations coming by land and sea' to the 'metropolis of the East Saxons' included people not just from overseas, but from the other Anglo-Saxon kingdoms of England. Kentish laws in the 7th century required people from Kent trading in London to report their dealings to the king's agent there. Pottery made in Ipswich and coins from Northumbria have been found in Lundenwic, while nearby smaller 'wics' such as Greenwich and Woolwich probably handled local trade along the Thames.

## THE TOWN OF LUNDENWIC

As a trading town, Lundenwic benefited from the surviving network of Roman roads that still converged on London, but like most of the other emporia its chief advantage was its position on a tidal river with easy access to the sea. The gently shelving Thames riverbank to the west of the River Fleet that gave its name to the Strand (literally the 'beach') provided good berths for the flat-bottomed ships of the Saxon period – far better than the ruined waterfront of Roman Londinium itself, cluttered with decaying timber wharves and collapsed stone walls. An excavation near Charing Cross at the west end of the Strand revealed a Saxon river embankment reinforced with timber, on which ships could be safely beached for unloading.

At its largest, Lundenwic spread over 55–60 hectares (136–148 acres); it was perhaps half the size of Roman Londinium. Excavations in Lundenwic, particularly around the site of the Royal Opera House in Covent Garden, suggest it was a crowded, busy, but well-organized place. It was probably laid out on a rough grid pattern with gravelled main streets leading northwards from the Strand. One street may have extended north to join the Roman road along the line of Oxford Street. There were houses and workshops along the main streets, well built of timber with walls made of wattle and daub or planks, with alleys and yards between them.

There is evidence of manufacturing, including weaving, bone-working and metalworking, and the many finds of imported material demonstrate the town's trade links with other ports on the North Sea. However, livestock were kept, and areas of the town may have been devoted to more agricultural activities.

Burials have been found, but no public buildings or church sites have yet been identified – although it is possible that Saxon churches preceded the present St Martin-in-the-Fields, St Mary le Strand and St Clement Danes churches on the Strand.

## THE COMING OF THE VIKINGS

Attacks on Britain and the northern coasts of Europe by Vikings, sea-raiders from Denmark and Norway, began at the end of the 8th century. North Sea trade was seriously disrupted, and the emporia that depended on that trade went into decline. Lundenwic itself was attacked by Vikings in 842, and again in 851. At first the raiders sailed from their home ports only in summer, but soon they were establishing winter bases in England. In 865 a 'Great Army' of Danish Vikings gathered in East Anglia and in a series of annual campaigns won control of the whole of eastern and northern England, overrunning the kingdoms of Northumbria, East Anglia and much of Mercia. The Danish army wintered in London in 871–2, but there is as yet no evidence for where their base was, nor whether they left a permanent garrison in Lundenwic. A 9th-century defensive ditch across part of the existing town plan, discovered during excavations at the Royal Opera House site, may relate to this period, as may a hoard of Northumbrian coins, perhaps buried by an owner who never returned. Lundenwic seems soon to have been largely abandoned.

By 877, only the West Saxons under King Alfred among the English kingdoms had retained their independence from Danish control. Alfred's subsequent victories over the Danes and his establishment of a fragile peace with them were to inaugurate a new phase in London's history. Only the name 'Aldwych', 'the old wic', was to survive to commemorate the site where London had stood for 250 years.                    **HS/JC**

*Iron sword pommel*
This sword pommel, set with silver plates showing intertwining serpents, was found at Chiswick. It dates from the period of Viking attacks on England after about 800.

*Aristocratic brooch*
This brooch, decorated with gold filigree work set with a mosaic of polished garnets from the mid-7th century, was found in the grave of a woman in Floral Street, Covent Garden. Such brooches were fashionable among aristocratic Anglo-Saxon ladies, particularly in Kent; the woman in the grave may even have been of royal birth.

*Gold pendant, 7th-century*
Set with glass, this gold pendant was found in a woman's grave on the site of St Martin-in-the-Fields church.

# ALFRED'S NEW TOWN & DANISH RULE

In the 880s, Lundenwic was abandoned, and the area within the Roman walls was reoccupied. New wharfs brought trade, but new Danish attacks put a Danish king, Cnut, on the English throne.

According to the *Anglo-Saxon Chronicle*, in 886, following the wars with the Danish invaders, King Alfred *gesette Lunden burg* – founded or settled the burh (fortified town) of London. At about the same time, a boundary was established with the lands ceded to the Danes in eastern England, the Danelaw. This boundary ran from the Thames up the River Lea, a few miles to the east of London, making London a strategic centre, so that strengthening it became vital to the defence of Anglo-Saxon England.

The realization in the 1980s that the Saxon trading town of Lundenwic lay not within the Roman city walls but to the west, while 10th-century archaeological finds were found inside the walls not outside, provided an obvious explanation of the puzzling statement in the *Chronicle*: Alfred had taken the decision to create a new town within the defensible perimeter of the surviving Roman fortifications. Yet there is some evidence that there were moves to settle inside the walls as early as the 850s, when London was still in the hands of the Mercian king Burgred. And Alfred's own special issue of silver coins with a monogram made up of the letters LVNDONIA – stressing his interest in the town – may have been minted in about 880 (see opposite).

## THE RESTORATION OF LONDON

Nor was the process of resettlement a rapid one. As late as 898, the year before he died, Alfred held a meeting at the royal estate in Chelsea to discuss 'the restoration of London'. But the main elements of Alfred's 'plan for London' are clear. He placed control of the city in the hands of his son-in-law, the Mercian noble Æthelred. A block of new streets was laid out east of St Paul's Cathedral, between the river and what is now Cheapside. The riverside, south of the now-crumbling Roman riverside wall, was embanked to provide berths for trading ships – particularly in the area that became known as Æthelred's Hithe (now Queenhithe), presumably named after the Mercian Æthelred. To encourage the re-establishment of trade along the Thames and overseas, interrupted by the Viking attacks and subsequent war, Alfred granted trading privileges in the port of London to leading members of his court, such as Bishop Wærferth of Worcester and Archbishop Plegmund of Canterbury. Beyond the planned streets lay open ground, still within the Roman walls, suitable for markets, pasturing livestock, small-scale farming and deploying troops – for the army of 'the men of London' was to play an important role in subsequent warfare.

Archaeological evidence suggests that a similar grid of streets in the eastern half of the city, at the head of London Bridge, was developed later, perhaps towards the end of the 10th century. South of the river lay Southwark, first mentioned as *Suthringa geweorche* (the fortified work of the men of Surrey) in about 915, one of a planned series of burhs or strongholds to defend southern England against further Danish inroads. Together with London it could guard the vital river passage against Viking fleets. If Alfred had followed the lead of his contemporary the Frankish king Charles the Bald, who constructed fortified bridges across rivers, linking strongholds on the banks to stop enemy ships, he might well have planned such a bridge to connect London and Southwark. Yet there is no evidence that the bridge itself, a great timber structure, was built before about 1000.

## THE WAR RENEWED

By this time London was once more the centre of warfare, as Scandinavian rulers, with the support of the people of the old Danelaw, attempted to wrest control of England from the

**Late Saxon London**
The site of Lundenwic had reverted to fields by the late Saxon period, and is only remembered in the name 'Aldwych' – the 'Old Town'.

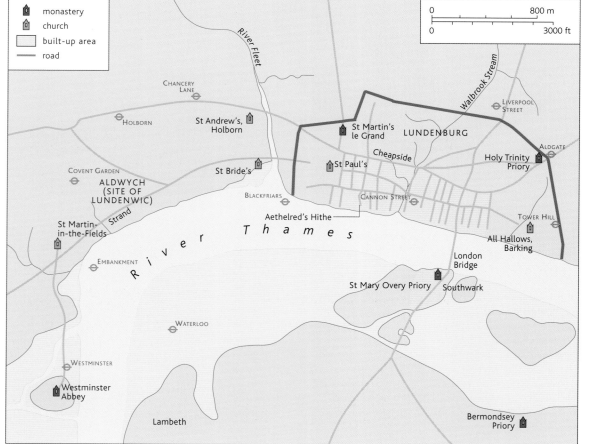

century, two larger monasteries, Holy Trinity Priory near Aldgate and St Martin's le Grand, north of St Paul's. Houses were built within the old Roman amphitheatre, along with cowsheds; some areas within the Roman walls continued in use as pasture. Evidence has been found for a number of industries including metalworking in iron, bronze and pewter, and the working of bone, antler, textiles, leather and stone. The export of English wool and woollen cloth through the port of London had revived, and imported goods show links with the Scandinavian world, of which England with its Danish ruler was very much a part. **JC**

*Alfred penny*
*Silver penny issued by King Alfred in about 880. On the reverse is a monogram of the letters LVNDONIA – the name of London in medieval Latin.*

Anglo-Saxon king. In 994, according to the *Anglo-Saxon Chronicle*, 'Olaf [Tryggvason, of Norway] and Swein [Forkbeard, of Denmark] came to London with 94 ships, and attacked the city continuously, and tried to set it on fire – but they suffered a worse defeat than they had thought any town garrison could have inflicted on them.' In a subsequent battle Olaf Haroldson (later King Olaf of Norway) contrived to pull down the bridge. In 1016 Swein Forkbeard's son Cnut found the bridge so well defended that he was forced to drag his ships around it through a channel dug to the south.

By the end of 1016, however, the English king Æthelred and his eldest son Edmund were both dead, and Cnut, with whom the Londoners had already bought a separate peace, was accepted as king of all England. During the wars the invaders had often been bought off by payments of Danegeld. Similar payments continued to the new Danish ruler, in the form of a regular tax to pay for a standing army and fleet. London's wealth at the time is indicated by the fact that in 1018 the city was taxed the huge sum of 10,500 pounds in silver. The rest of the kingdom contributed 72,000 pounds, showing that London was unquestionably the largest and wealthiest town in the kingdom.

The built-up area slowly expanded beyond the core of Alfred's planned town around Æthelred's Hithe, gradually stretching north of Cheapside, at the east end of which a cattle market had grown up. There were a number of small churches, and, by the mid-11th

**Danish grave slab**
*Grave slab, early 11th century (found in 1852 on the south side of St Paul's Cathedral). It probably marked the grave of a follower of the Danish king Cnut. It shows a Scandinavian-style lion fighting a serpent. On the left-hand edge is an inscription in Scandinavian runes, in Old Norse: 'Ginna and Toki had this stone laid'.*

**Sword from the Danish wars**
*This sword, dating from the early 11th century, was found in the Thames at Putney. The knicks in the blade are clear evidence that it saw use in the extensive fighting during the Danish wars in this period.*

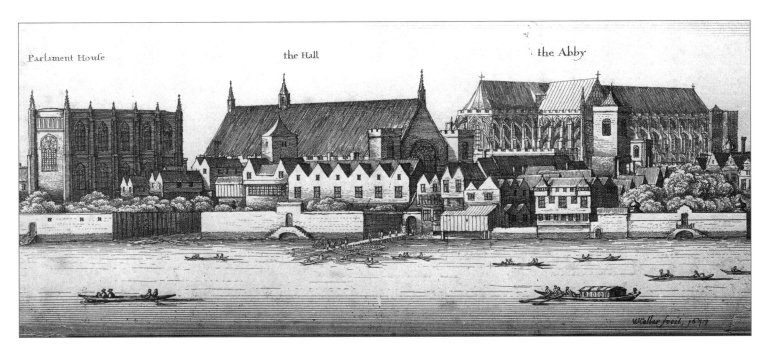

Parlament House     the Hall     the Abby

# THE GROWTH OF WESTMINSTER

From the llth century, Westminster grew around a nucleus of the existing abbey and a new palace. It became the focus of royal power, but its fortunes were always linked to those of London.

There was an abbey at Westminster by the 8th century, at the south end of Lundenwic, on an island where the Tyburn met the Thames. Possibly the first king to reside at Westminster was Cnut, in 1035. According to tradition, his famous demonstration of the limits of royal power by ironically rebuking the tidal Thames took place here. From the 11th century, this abbey was joined by a complex of royal buildings, which became the medieval Palace of Westminster; construction began under Edward the Confessor around 1052, when he also began to rebuild the abbey. The abbey church is depicted on the Bayeux Tapestry with a central tower and transepts, and fragments have been found beneath its successor, the present building. It was finished just before Edward's death in December 1065 and he was buried in front of the high altar. This is the origin of the tradition that kings and queens of England since William the Conqueror are crowned at Westminster Abbey.

At first, Westminster was one of several royal palaces in southern England, including Winchester and Gloucester. But in the 12th and 13th centuries, it became a permanent administrative complex, with government offices and the embryonic civil service, making it the political capital in place of the Saxon capital at Winchester.

Although Westminster Hall was impressive (both when it was built by William II in 1097–9 and rebuilt in 1394), the building that most represented royal taste was the abbey church as rebuilt by Henry III in 1240–72 to rival the new French churches at Reims, where French kings were crowned, and St Denis, near Paris, where

***City of London seal***
*This 13th-century seal shows St Thomas of Canterbury (Thomas Becket), one of the two patron saints of the City (the other was St Paul). Though the City continually proclaimed its independence, it was firmly linked to the Crown in many ways.*

the French monarchs were buried. Henry's palace also had gardens, a large fountain and an aviary.

The court buildings at Westminster generated artistic patronage and increased cultural contacts. Merchants and workshops played an important part in supplying the court. Courtiers and churchmen who served as high government officials needed residences near the court and built town houses (or 'inns'), particularly along the Strand, the main highway from London. Some of these were as elaborate as royal palaces, with gardens and private landing stages on the river, which was itself an important communication route. The land between Westminster and the City, formerly arable, began to be built up with new establishments like that of the Knights Templars, whose great house and round church (the 'New Temple') was built near the Thames in1185. The development of this area into a legal quarter followed in the middle of the 13th century.

Medieval Westminster existed largely to serve the abbey and the palace and was little more than a single street from Charing Cross to the palace and abbey gates, which were next to each other on today's Parliament Square. There were many taverns (three at the north end of Westminster Hall were known as Heaven, Hell and Purgatory, perhaps because two were former prisons), workshops of goldsmiths, couturiers and later, bookshops. William Caxton had a shop within the abbey grounds, where he set up England's first printing press in 1476. Westminster had two parish churches – St Margaret's and St Martin-in-the-Fields – both of which survive today, although the latter was rebuilt in 1728.

To the south lay fields, in what is now Pimlico and Belgravia. Westminster Bridge did not exist although from just before 1200 there was a ferry close to the royal palace that went to the archbishop of Canterbury's London residence, Lambeth Palace. On the

***The Palace of Westminster***
*One of the earliest detailed views of the Palace of Westminster, by Wenceslaus Hollar in the 1650s. The jetty into the Thames is today replaced by Westminster Bridge. The main buildings shown are St Stephen's Chapel ('Parliament House'), Westminster Hall, and Westminster Abbey, all in their medieval forms.*

outskirts of Westminster were a couple of religious houses. To the west, the hospital of St James for leprous women is mentioned in the middle of the 12th century. After the Dissolution of the Monasteries its site became St James's Palace. On the north side, at Charing Cross, the Hospital of St Mary Rouncivall was founded just before 1231; its site is now beneath Northumberland Avenue.

Only parts of the medieval royal palace still survive: Westminster Hall, the undercroft below St Stephen's Chapel and the Jewel Tower. More survives of medieval Westminster Abbey, including monastic buildings, such as the ruined infirmary c.1160, and the tombs of several medieval monarchs from the time of Henry III.

In contrast to the nearest Continental city of similar size, Paris, London (including Westminster) was first and foremost a trading city, with many Continental contacts; its role as a royal capital was secondary. The establishment of the royal palace at Westminster had a lot to do with its proximity to the city.      **JS**

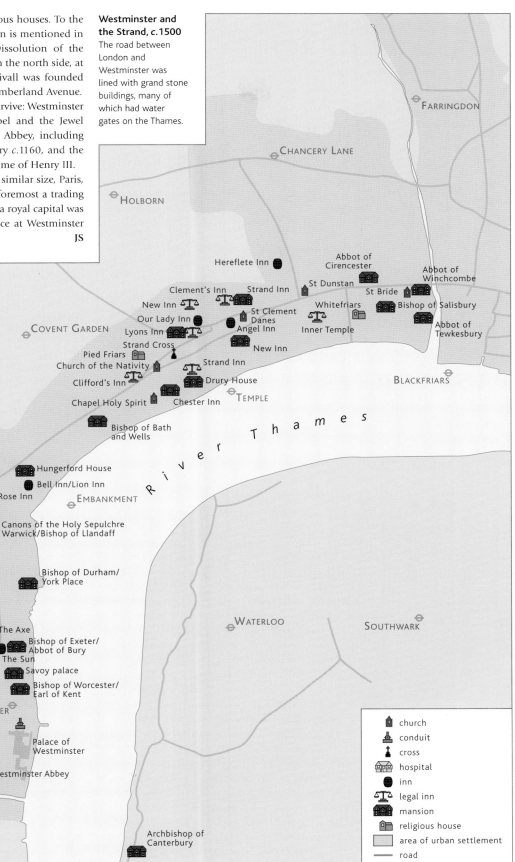

**Westminster and the Strand, c.1500**

The road between London and Westminster was lined with grand stone buildings, many of which had water gates on the Thames.

Legend:
- church
- conduit
- cross
- hospital
- inn
- legal inn
- mansion
- religious house
- area of urban settlement
- road

# THE SAXON & NORMAN CHURCH

By 1200 most of the City of London's 110 churches and their individual areas of authority or parishes had been established. A person walking across the City would pass sixteen of them.

After a serious fire in 1087, St Paul's Cathedral was rebuilt on such a grand scale that some doubted it would ever be finished. It was completed about 100 years later, and the nave stood until the Great Fire in 1666; but no trace remains of the choir, which housed the relics of St Erkenwald (an energetic 7th-century bishop of London).

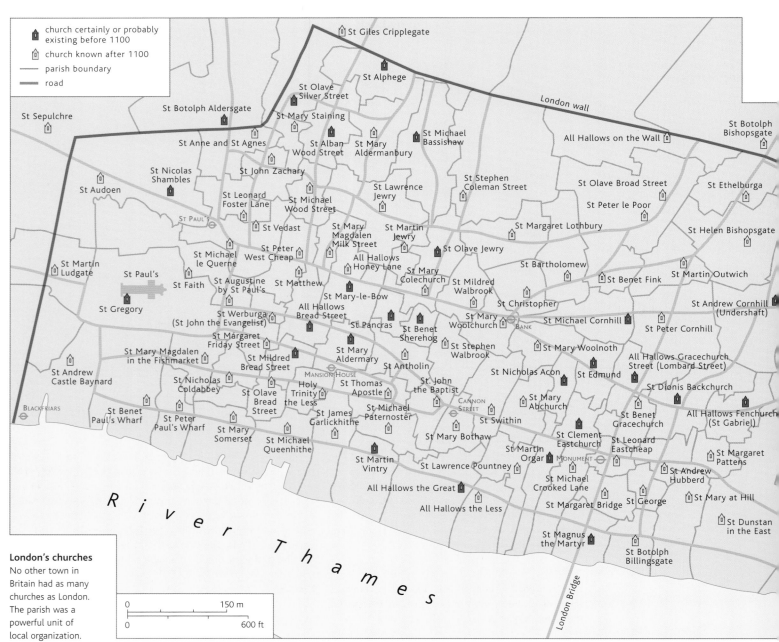

**Legend:**
- church certainly or probably existing before 1100
- church known after 1100
- parish boundary
- road

St Giles Cripplegate
St Alphege
London wall
St Olave Silver Street
St Botolph Aldersgate
St Mary Staining
St Sepulchre
St Botolph Bishopsgate
St Anne and St Agnes
St Alban Wood Street
St Mary Aldermanbury
St Michael Bassishaw
All Hallows on the Wall
St John Zachary
St Lawrence Jewry
St Stephen Coleman Street
St Olave Broad Street
St Ethelburga
St Nicolas Shambles
St Audoen
St Leonard Foster Lane
St Michael Wood Street
St Peter le Poor
St Vedast
St Mary Magdalen Milk Street
St Martin Jewry
St Margaret Lothbury
St Helen Bishopsgate
ST PAUL'S
St Michael le Querne
St Peter West Cheap
St Mary Magdalen Milk Street
All Hallows Honey Lane
St Olave Jewry
St Bartholomew
St Benet Fink
St Martin Outwich
St Martin Ludgate
St Paul's
St Faith
St Augustine by St Paul's
St Matthew
St Mary Colechurch
St Mildred Walbrook
St Christopher
St Michael Cornhill
St Andrew Cornhill (Undershaft)
St Gregory
St Werburga (St John the Evangelist)
All Hallows Bread Street
St Mary-le-Bow
St Mary Woolchurch
BANK
St Peter Cornhill
St Margaret Friday Street
St Pancras
St Benet Sherehog
St Stephen Walbrook
St Mary Woolnoth
All Hallows Gracechurch Street (Lombard Street)
St Mary Magdalen in the Fishmarket
St Mildred Bread Street
St Mary Aldermary
St Antholin
St Nicholas Acon
St Edmund
St Dionis Backchurch
St Andrew Castle Baynard
MANSION HOUSE
St Thomas Apostle
St. John the Baptist
St Mary Abchurch
St Benet Gracechurch
All Hallows Fenchurch (St Gabriel)
BLACKFRIARS
St Nicholas Coldabbey
Holy Trinity the Less
St Olave Bread Street
St Michael Paternoster
CANNON STREET
St Swithin
St Margaret Pattens
St Benet Paul's Wharf
St Peter Paul's Wharf
St James Garlickhithe
St Mary Somerset
St Mary Bothaw
St Clement Eastchurch
St Leonard Eastcheap
St Andrew Hubberd
St Michael Queenhithe
St Martin Vintry
St Lawrence Pountney
St Martin Orgar
MONUMENT
St Mary at Hill
All Hallows the Great
St Michael Crooked Lane
St George
St Dunstan in the East
All Hallows the Less
St Margaret Bridge
St Magnus the Martyr
St Botolph Billingsgate
London Bridge

*River Thames*

**London's churches**
No other town in Britain had as many churches as London. The parish was a powerful unit of local organization.

0 — 150 m
0 — 600 ft

**The choir of St Bartholomew the Great**

*This church in Smithfield was an Augustinian priory dating from 1123.*

From 1100, successive bishops acquired land and streets around the cathedral and filled in a great ditch on the west side to form the cathedral close where the deanery, bishop's palace and canons' houses could be laid out, as can still be seen at the cathedrals of Lincoln and Wells. The close had a wall around it and several gates that were locked at night. North of the precinct ran Paternoster Row, (named for the 'paternosterers', who made rosary beads).

To the north-east of St Paul's lay the large and wealthy religious house of St Martin's le Grand, now commemorated by a street

of citizens. During the 12th century a church would often pass into the ownership of St Paul's, Westminster Abbey or one of the religious houses, including those based abroad. This corporate ownership may account for the survival of so many small churches right up to the Reformation in 1536. The earliest surviving masonry in a London church is at All Hallows by the Tower (also known as All Hallows Barking, built in the 11th century), where there is an arch made of Roman bricks.

The dedications of these churches tell us about Londoners' favourite saints. From the Saxon period came St Ethelburga, St

**St Paul's Cathedral**

This hypothetical reconstruction shows the Norman cathedral in relation to Wren's cathedral, which stands on the site today. Around it were houses of the churchmen attached to the cathedral.

Legend:
- conjectured outline of Norman St Paul's
- modern St Paul's cathedral
- modern buildings

0 — 40 m
0 — 140 ft

cemetery

site of Saxon Folkmoot

nave | choir

parish church of St Gregory

precentor

site of Bishop's palace

chancellor

treasurer

St Augustine on the Wall

t Mary Axe

St Botolph Aldgate

ALDGATE

St Katherine Creechurch

All Hallows Colemanchurch

All Hallows Staining

St Olave Hart Street

TOWER HILL

All Hallows Barking

St Peter ad Vincula

The Tower

name. St Martin's may have been founded before the Norman Conquest and possibly represented a link with a former Saxon royal palace in this area.

Further north, St Bartholomew's priory was built on one side of Smithfield and the choir of its church, although now restored, is London's best example of Romanesque architecture from the period 1130–60. It has been used in several historical films. With the exception of the Tower, all surviving examples of 12th-century buildings in London are churches or parts of them: a crypt at St John Clerkenwell, the Temple Church and scraps of masonry at Southwark Cathedral. In the wider London area there are parts of Romanesque village churches at Harlington, Harmondsworth and East Ham.

### PARISH CHURCHES

By 1200, London boasted over 100 parish churches, more than almost every major town in Europe. Of these, over a quarter were established by 1100. Private churches were built by wealthy landowners or groups

Mildred and St Dunstan; from the 11th-century period of Viking influence and the Normans, St Alphage, St Martin, St Magnus and St Olave. Dedications to St Giles, St Dionys (Denis), St Sepulchre and St Thomas of Acon may point to further French connections and the Crusades.

### SCHOOLS

Twelfth-century London was an important centre of education, at a time when all formal education was run by the Church. The main schools were at St Paul's, St Mary le Bow, St Martin le Grand and Holy Trinity Priory. London was well connected with continental Europe, intellectually as well as by trade links. Thomas Becket was a pupil at St Paul's school in about 1127, before going on to the university of Paris. The cathedral and the monastic houses had libraries, and some produced notable scholars. But school life was not only about debating in Latin and harsh discipline; Shrove Tuesday (the day before the start of Lent, a period of abstinence) was celebrated with a cock fight in the morning, followed by a ball game, possibly football, in the open space at Smithfield, outside the wall of the City to the north-west. **JS**

# THE MEDIEVAL JEWISH COMMUNITY

In the 1200s London's money market was run by the Jews. They made fortunes, but as a group were despised and occasionally murdered. Few medieval Londoners respected Jewish culture.

A distinctive feature of the larger towns in medieval Britain, and especially London, was the presence of Jews. They came with William the Conqueror in the 11th century, and until 1140 seem to have stayed only in London. Thereafter they spread to other towns such as York, Lincoln and Canterbury. Their numbers were always low, perhaps 5000 at the most in England at any one time.

From the point of view of the Christian world in which they lived, the Jews had a very useful function in medieval society from the king downwards: they lent money (something that Christians were foresworn from doing). As collateral or surety, they could take movable goods, and in London they often acquired houses and land in the city. Prevented by law from following any other trades, they inevitably became rich, which caused resentment.

Jews were officially the property of the king and he was obliged to protect them. This did not, however, prevent violent anti-Semitic feeling flaring up at times, such as during the coronation of Richard I in 1189, when a riot led to arson attacks on Jewish houses in London. Jews were also massacred at this time in York and King's Lynn. In 1264 the followers of Simon de Montfort killed scores of Jews in London, including many of their leaders. These attacks were often motivated by the debts that Christians (often knights) owed to the Jews; their financial records in particular were sought out and destroyed.

Jews had their own cemeteries, and at first there was only one in England, in London outside Cripplegate. All English Jews had to be brought there for burial. In 1177 the Jews were allowed to establish burial grounds outside other towns, such as York.

## WHERE THE JEWS LIVED

There were no organized ghettos in English towns, but Jews tended to cluster in areas known as Jewries. The modern street name Old Jewry suggests that the main Jewish neighbourhood was in the City of London. In the 12th century this area moved to the west around Milk Street, and was bordered by Catte Street (now Gresham Street) on the north and Cheapside on the south. It spread over nine parishes, four of which were sometimes described as in the Jewry (such as St Lawrence Jewry, which was rebuilt by Wren after the Great Fire in 1666 and still stands today).

The Jewish community lived in the middle of town, well positioned for business. At least one Jewish house in the early 13th century occupied a

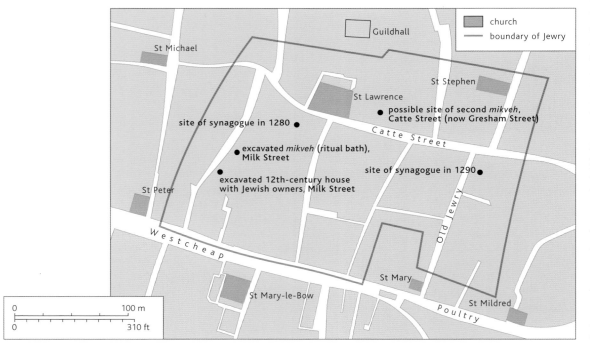

**London's Jewish area**
The Jewry of London was a specific part of the city just north of Cheapside (Westcheap). However, it was not exclusively Jewish or surrounded by a wall. Significantly, perhaps, it lay between the main market street and Guildhall, the centre of secular authority and power.

prominent site in Cheapside itself, at the corner of Ironmonger Lane. In 1246 seven Jewish householders in the Ironmonger Lane, including one woman, were criticized for having built pentices (covers for their windows or doors) into the street. The London Jewry, like those in other towns, was not demarcated by a wall or fence, and Christians also lived within it. However, it was a defined zone; in the 1270s Christians were fined if they were found there at night.

## SYNAGOGUES

We do not know accurately where the main synagogues were in London, but in 1212–13 a 'great synagogue' lay north of Cheapside and east of Old Jewry. A synagogue was burned down in the riots of 1264 and this may have been on the same site. Recent research suggests that a synagogue was formed out of a Jewish house opposite St Lawrence Jewry in 1280. After the expulsion in 1290, another syna- gogue in Coleman Street, temporarily occupied by friars, was incorporated into a mansion owned by Robert Fitzwalter. Several Jewish houses also contained private synagogues.

Most of the archaeological remains of the Jewry have now been destroyed by modern developments, but two cellar-like features have been found in the area. One, in Gresham Street, was a stone pit with steps leading down to it, which may have been a strongroom in an ordinary house; the other, in Milk Street, had a curved wall and was more probably a *mikveh* (ritual bath), although no inscription survives to confirm this.

## THE EXPULSION OF THE JEWS

Financial and other pressures on the Jewish community heightened during the long reign of Edward I in the 13th century. In 1278–9 over 280 Jews in London were hanged for allegedly clipping coins – that is, shaving off a small portion of the gold or silver from which coins were then made, to be collected and melted down later for profit. By the time all Jews were expelled from England in 1290, by royal command, there were perhaps only about 2000 left in the country. On 10 October 1290 the poorer Jews of London started on their way to the coast, carrying the Scrolls of the Law. Some richer families took passage on a ship, only to be marooned by the ship's captain on a sandbank at the mouth of the Thames, where they drowned. Others were left destitute on the coast of France. Eventually most found refuge among the Jewish communities of France, Italy and Spain. Jewish properties in central London were quickly taken over by other Londoners. For example, the house of Master Moses and his son Hagin near Cheapside became the store- house or 'wardrobe' of Henry de Lacy, Earl of Lincoln. This lay at the northern end of what is now Ironmonger Lane, where it meets Gresham Street. After 1290, there are records of a few Jews living in London, but their general return did not occur until after 1655.      **JS**

**A possible Sabbath lamp**
*This lamp was found in St Martin's le Grand. It may have been used by Christians, but probably originally belonged to a Jewish family, as a special lamp lit on the eve of the Sabbath.*

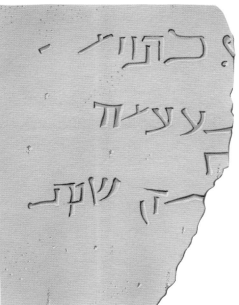

**Jewish ritual bath**
*An archaeologist excavates the remains of a Jewish ritual bath or* mikveh *in Milk Street. Jewish buildings are a very rare find in the City's archaeology. The remains of this* mikveh *have been removed from the site and preserved for safekeeping elsewhere.*

**Jewish tombstone fragment**
*This fragment of a Jewish tombstone, commemorating 'Nahum', was found in 1753, built into London's medieval city wall where it had been used to make a repair. Early chroniclers of London noticed other stones with inscriptions, which were often reused in this way.*

# LONDON'S CASTLES & THE CITY DEFENCES

Medieval London had three castles, initially built by the Normans to control the unruly city. The Roman wall also survived, with an extension to the west in the 1270s around a Dominican friary.

*London Bridge*
*London Bridge had two gates and a drawbridge that until about 1475 was raised to allow ships through to Queenhithe. In this detail (c.1540), we can see the outer gate with statues and the City arms, like the gates in many other European towns.*

The Tower of London was established by William the Conqueror to dominate the city, just as castles dominate many other towns in Britain. It was positioned at the seaward end of the riverfront, to control access to the sea and to repel invaders if necessary. Building began shortly after 1070, when an expert builder named Gundulf, who happened to be the Bishop of Rochester, was put in charge; tree-ring dating suggests that the first building, the keep or White Tower, was finished after 1100.

The Tower expanded into the great fortress we see today mostly during the reigns of Henry III (1216–72) and Edward I (1272–1307). By 1300 the whole complex looked like a larger version of one of Edward's castles in Wales. It was used as a palace and prison, and contained a mint and at some periods even a royal zoo. Overall, however, the Tower had little impact on the growth of medieval London, since there was no pressure for development around it until the 16th century.

London had two other Norman castles on the west side of the city, the sites of which are only approximately known: Baynard's Castle (certainly in existence by 1087) and Montfichet's Tower (by 1136). These seem to have been related fortifications, lying south-west of St. Paul's cathedral. They belonged to powerful nobles, however, not to the king. Baynard's Castle was destroyed in 1213 by command of King John after its lord, Robert FitzWalter, had taken part in a rebellion, and in 1276 the site – which probably included Montfichet's Tower as well – was given to the Black Friars (Dominicans) for a new religious precinct. The riverside area still bears its name today.

To the west, just outside the city wall, the street name Old Bailey suggests another, possibly royal, fortification, but there is no further evidence. Next to it on the slope down to the Fleet was a royal prison, called the Fleet Prison, which originated as a 12th-century castle-like complex on an island in the river Fleet itself.

## THE CITY WALLS

The Norman preference for castles as a means of control and defence – as well as residences for the king or nobility – did not mean that London's existing city walls were allowed to decay. The walls had been formidable enough to discourage William I from a protracted siege in 1066. During the turbulent reign of King John (1199–1216), concerns about the defence of London led to the taking of stone from Jewish houses for repair work to some of the interval towers in the wall, particularly those on the west side of the city, a system of towers only half completed by the Romans. The Roman wall along the Thames bank, however, had long been left to decay and parts had fallen into the river. By 1200 this wall had been removed completely above ground and its foundation had been put into use as the front wall of stone houses built on newly reclaimed land south of the old alignment, as the waterfront pushed out into the water. This helped to establish Thames Street for the first time, running from Blackfriars to the Tower, and connecting the important markets of Queenhithe and Billingsgate with London Bridge. The riverside wall thus disappeared, but the city wall otherwise proved a significant barrier to expansion of the built-up area of London until the 16th century.

### REDECORATING THE TOWER: UNDER ROYAL ORDERS

Henry III was fastidious about his royal palaces; he wanted them just so when he stayed in one. In 1240 he ordered that at the Tower, 'the queen's chamber [is] to be panelled and entirely whitewashed inside and newly painted with roses; a partition wall of panelling to be made between that chamber and the garderobe thereof and the same to be tiled outside. Our great chamber to be whitewashed and painted and all its shutters to be remade with new wood, new catches and hinges, to be painted with our arms and newly barred with iron. Also all the glass windows in the chapel of St. John the Baptist are to be repaired, and the windows in the great chamber towards the Thames, and in the corner of the same chamber a great round tower to be made so that its lowest chamber goes down into the Thames ...'. Today these gaily painted chambers and decorations have to be imagined, as most of Henry's buildings have not survived, although the chapel of St John is still one of the architectural gems of the Tower.

During the Middle Ages the city wall was significantly modified in two places. At the south-east corner, the expansion of the Tower of London in the 13th century erased part of it; and in 1278 the wall south of Ludgate was extended to a new course beside the Fleet, taking in the new estate of the Black Friars.

The wall had seven gates, all but one of which was built on the sites of their Roman predecessors. They were removed in the 18th century, but their names can still be found in the streets where they stood: from west to east, Ludgate, Newgate, Aldersgate, Cripplegate (now under the Barbican), Moorgate (the only new medieval gate, built in 1415), Bishopsgate and Aldgate. There were also two gates and a drawbridge on London Bridge, the main road to the south.

The gates of Roman London mostly had two equal arches, but by the 13th century they had been rebuilt with a single arch for carts and a smaller pedestrian arch. The rooms above the gates were let out to public officials; Aldgate was let in 1374 to Geoffrey Chaucer, a royal servant and author, on the condition that he would vacate the premises in time of unrest. The City authorities also tried to use the gates to control access, for instance preventing the entrance of lepers.

## STRONGHOLDS IN THE COUNTRYSIDE

As a great medieval city, London needed walls and gates for its defence, although it was never seriously besieged. Most of the smaller towns in the London region were not walled, and there were few castles in the immediate vicinity. At small towns such as Ruislip or Chipping Ongar, now in the London suburbs, the outline of a Norman castle can still be traced, and there are larger castles further afield at Guildford, Rochester, Canterbury and Colchester. When they were first built, these strongholds, held by the king or his close and trusted associates, made the clearest statement that the Norman Conquest would not be reversed. They were truly colonial buildings as much as the forts of the Romans before them, and as much as the fortifications in foreign lands which became the basis of the British Empire in later centuries.        **JS**

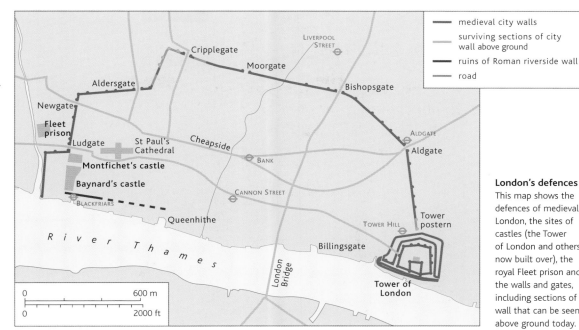

*City wall tower*
*A tower on the city wall near the Barbican. The stonework is mostly medieval; the brickwork dates from much later, when the tower formed the base of a Victorian warehouse that was destroyed in the Blitz. Below ground, the city wall running behind the medieval tower is a surviving fragment of the original city wall of Roman Londinium.*

**London's defences**
This map shows the defences of medieval London, the sites of castles (the Tower of London and others now built over), the royal Fleet prison and the walls and gates, including sections of wall that can be seen above ground today.

Legend:
- medieval city walls
- surviving sections of city wall above ground
- ruins of Roman riverside wall
- road

# LATER MEDIEVAL LONDON

By the 13th century, the topography of London was well established: the walled city north of the Thames, suburbs in Southwark and along the Strand, and a ring of monasteries and hospitals. Small enough to walk across in twenty minutes, London housed a population of over 80,000 people by 1300 – making it one of the largest cities in northern Europe.

London had a mayor from the late 12th century; over the next 200 years city government became increasingly complex. Local administration and justice was in the hands of the powerful aldermen. A Court of

Common Council provided opportunity for wider discussion of city affairs. The regulation of trade and industry was left to the guilds, and their influence grew. Their stormy relationship with the city authorities and each other became a feature of local politics, while relationships with the royal court were not always amicable.

The urban area had its own problems. One of the earliest recorded measures of the first mayor, Henry Fitz Ailwin, was a set of building regulations intended to prevent fires. Markets were controlled; staple foodstuffs were inspected for quality and price; rubbish was

regularly cleared; drinking water was piped
from springs to the west of the city.

London was sorely tested in the 'calamitous'
14th century. Famines throughout northern
Europe after 1315 killed the poor and the weak,
and the war with France drained men and
money. The Black Death of 1348–9 may have
reduced London's population by half. There
was civil disturbance, and London became the
target of the Peasants' Revolt in 1381.

But the horrific toll of the Black Death had
had unexpected results. With a reduced
population, London soon flourished again.

Trade and industry revived as wealth was
concentrated in fewer hands. The city's
power was reflected in grand public buildings,
churches and fine town houses. The city's
wealth and influence extended well beyond
its built-up area, and it drew on a large region
for food and supplies. By the late Middle Ages,
England's capital dominated the nation in
a way not matched anywhere else in Europe.

# THE CENTRE OF POWER & FASHION

The largest and wealthiest city in medieval England, London became home to an increasingly centralized national government in Westminster, as well as a centre of fashion and display.

**England and Wales in the 14th century**
London was by far the largest and wealthiest city, and the centre of a network of major roads.

'Let us go to the King – he is young – and show him how we are oppressed … And when the King sees and hears us, he will remedy the evil.' These words inspired the rebellious peasants of Kent and Essex to march on London in the summer of 1381 – though their trust was betrayed when their leader, Wat Tyler, was killed at Smithfield by members of Richard II's entourage. With the royal court at Westminster, London was by this time the centre from which the kingdom of England was ruled, while the riches and power of London itself were a magnetic attraction for anyone in search of a better lot. Although the concept of a 'capital' city is a modern one, London, according to the historian and monk Matthew Paris in about 1250, was *le chef d'angleterre* (the 'chief city' – that is, the largest, richest and most famous – of England) long before it became a capital in the modern sense.

London was already the most populous city in England by the end of the Anglo-Saxon period. At its peak, at the beginning of the 14th century, with a population of more than 80,000, it was probably four or more times the size of its nearest rivals, such as York. The difference in spending power was even greater. In 1334 London's taxable wealth was assessed at £11,000; that of the second wealthiest city in the kingdom, Bristol, was £2200; London's wealth alone exceeded the combined total of that of Bristol and the next eight wealthiest towns.

Some of this wealth was generated by the presence of the royal court. Edward the Confessor had built his palace at Westminster, but he and his Norman successors had travelled the kingdom, summoning the court to meet wherever was convenient. Westminster, like its early rival Winchester, was at first just one of those places. But the presence of the wealthy, influential and independent-minded city of London a mile away was to make Westminster more and more the natural home of the king and his court.

Simon de Montfort's 'Parliament' of 1265 and Edward I's so-called 'Model Parliament' of 1295 both met in Westminster, although thereafter the medieval Parliament was sometimes summoned in other places, such as York. From 1339 to 1377 Parliament met consistently in Westminster, but there remained occasions on which it was called elsewhere right up to the Stuart period. In the 14th century Westminster became the permanent home of an increasing number of departments of government. The royal courts of law, which previously had followed the king about the kingdom, became based in Westminster. The Court of Common Bench met in Westminster Hall from the 1350s; the

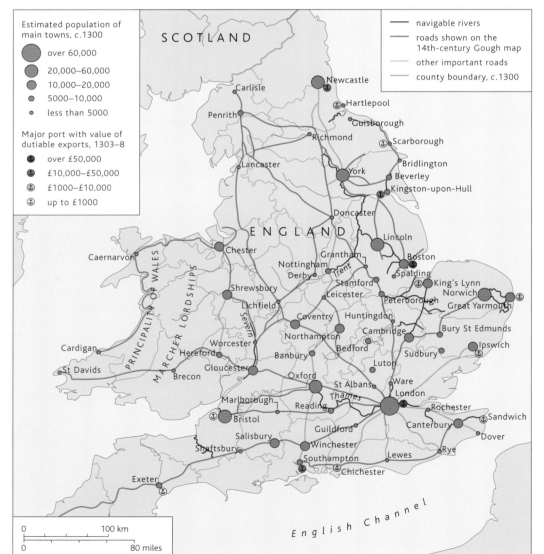

Estimated population of main towns, c.1300
- over 60,000
- 20,000–60,000
- 10,000–20,000
- 5000–10,000
- less than 5000

Major port with value of dutiable exports, 1303–8
- over £50,000
- £10,000–£50,000
- £1000–£10,000
- up to £1000

navigable rivers
roads shown on the 14th-century Gough map
other important roads
county boundary, c.1300

SCOTLAND

ENGLAND

PRINCIPALITY OF WALES

MARCHER LORDSHIPS

Carlisle
Penrith
Newcastle
Hartlepool
Guisborough
Richmond
Scarborough
Lancaster
Bridlington
York
Beverley
Kingston-upon-Hull
Doncaster
Lincoln
Chester
Grantham
Boston
Caernarvon
Nottingham
Derby
Spalding
Trent
Stamford
King's Lynn
Shrewsbury
Leicester
Norwich
Lichfield
Peterborough
Great Yarmouth
Coventry
Huntingdon
Severn
Northampton
Cambridge
Bury St Edmunds
Cardigan
Worcester
Bedford
Ipswich
Hereford
Banbury
Sudbury
St Davids
Gloucester
Luton
Brecon
Oxford
Ware
St Albans
London
Marlborough
Thames
Reading
Rochester
Sandwich
Bristol
Guildford
Canterbury
Salisbury
Dover
Shaftsbury
Winchester
Lewes
Rye
Southampton
Exeter
Chichester

English Channel

0    100 km
0    80 miles

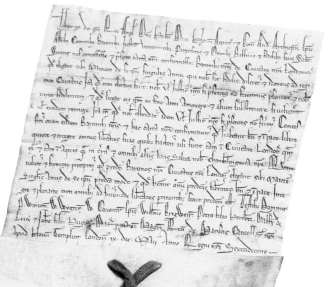

King's Bench increasingly met there after 1365. Most important, perhaps, the Exchequer (the royal treasury), which had formerly moved around and had been based in York since Edward I's wars in Scotland, finally settled in Westminster under Edward III in 1339.

## SPLENDOUR & PAGEANTRY

Leading English nobles and churchmen acquired fine houses in London or along the Strand, which they occupied when attending the royal court. At other times, their agents used these London properties as bases from which to purchase goods to supply their rural estates from London merchants, craftspeople and suppliers, because luxury goods were more readily available in London than elsewhere. Supplying the royal court itself was an even more lucrative business. People like Richard Whittington made fortunes selling luxuries like imported textiles to the king – he was owed £1000 by Richard II when the king was deposed in 1399. Near St Paul's after 1361 stood the King's Great Wardrobe, a central warehouse filled with goods supplied by Londoners for royal use or imported through the port of London. Other members of the royal family at times also had their own wardrobes; in 1331, for example, certain houses known as 'La Riole' in College Hill, off Cannon Street, were acquired by Edward III as the Queen's Wardrobe for his wife.

Royalty and nobility brought visual splendour and pageantry to London. Noble cavalcades passing through Cheapside on their way

**Leather shoes, late 14th century**
*The longer shoe, a fashionable 'poulaine', has its toe stuffed with moss to stiffen it.*

to or from Westminster or the Tower always attracted onlookers. Geoffrey Chaucer's idle apprentice Perkyn Revelour in the *Canterbury Tales* would leave his work and rush to see any 'riding in Cheap'.

The fine clothing worn by the nobility was in itself a status symbol. Attempts were made to restrict its use by legislation, decreeing the types of fabric and fur that could be worn by different classes of men and their wives, and even restricting the wearing of gold and silver jewellery. Despite this, Londoners seem to have followed courtly fashions as far as they were able. Cheap dress fittings and jewellery made of brass and pewter followed the contemporary styles in gold and silver. 'Poulaines', the exotic and impractical pointed-toe shoes of late 14th-century high fashion (see below), are more commonly found in archaeological excavations in London than in other English towns. And they reappeared a hundred years later, in spite of a law of 1465 forbidding 'beaks or pikes of shoes or boots' over 2 inches (5 centimetres) long 'upon pain of cursing by the clergy' and a fine of 20 shillings.

## A TRANSPORT HUB

A 14th-century map of England now in the Bodleian Library, known as the Gough Map, shows in red a network of routes radiating from London, linking the city with other important towns. Medieval roads were busy but notoriously bad, particularly in winter weather – in the winter of 1294, for example, it took nine days for a convoy carrying royal treasure to travel the 185 kilometres (115 miles) from Westminster to Norwich. In more normal conditions this same journey took three or four days for a cart – the time taken by the carrier from Norwich who arrived once a week at the Rossamez Inn in St Lawrence's Lane. Such regular carrier services were provided by two-wheeled carts hauled by three or four horses, and they took consignments of goods, parcels, letters and even passengers. Even long-distance routes had their regular carriers; for example, in 1484 William Naynow, then aged 61, declared that he had been driving the London–Exeter route for over 35 years.

For those on horseback, travel was much faster: London to York, for example, took four and a half days. The road from London to the Channel port at Dover – also used by pilgrims as far as Canterbury – was served by 'hackneymen', who hired out horses in Southwark and the towns along the route. In 1396 the hire of a horse cost 12 pence for the journey from London to Rochester, 12 pence on to Canterbury, and 6 pence for the shorter leg from Canterbury to Dover. Few Londoners could afford such an expense; most of those who travelled did so on foot. JC

# WEALTH & CIVIC PRIDE

As London's economic and cultural dominance grew in the 13th century, it acquired civic buildings like the Guildhall, houses of a high standard, and piped water sooner than most European cities.

By 1300, London was the largest city in Britain, whether measured by population or by wealth. In 1340 the citizens of London were forced to lend King Edward III £5000 to pursue his war against France. The names of the 232 Londoners who contributed to the loan are recorded. Most gave £5 or £10. By this reckoning, the richest man in London in 1340 was William de Caustone, a mercer, who contributed £400 – several hundred thousand pounds in modern terms.

London was different from other towns not only in scale, but also in kind. It was a place to make your fortune, then retire back to the provinces; but the City of London was also a community of traditions and groups that ran themselves. A fierce civic pride shows in the City's organization and in its standards of living, hygiene and building. The superior lifestyle of Londoners was shown by their urban environment, houses and public facilities.

By 1300, a range of different types of houses could be seen on London streets. Rich merchants, lords and religious leaders could afford large courtyard houses, which resem-

**London wealth**
A tax on citizens who were not clergy in 1332 reveals City wealth by ward. The richer wards were in the centre, poorer areas on the suburban margins.

bled the manor houses with gardens and stables still found in the countryside today. Between these larger houses and the streets were smaller houses, of either one room or two rooms on each floor, with jetties (overhangs) on the upper storeys. The vast majority of houses were timber-framed, although some had vaulted cellars of stone (one of about 1375 survives at Merchant Taylors' Hall in Threadneedle Street). In the commercial districts and in the Jewry

north of Cheapside (see pages 74–5) there were probably a higher proportion of houses completely made of stone.

London houses were probably of a higher standard than elsewhere: many had individual privies and a well, and (at least by 1500) a high proportion of heated rooms. Archaeological work on waterfront structures demonstrates that carpentry became more sophisticated during the 13th century, enabling the building of houses with more storeys, which would generate more rent and house more people. London's population burgeoned during this century and the volume of buildings grew not only across the landscape but also upwards.

**Goldsmith's Row**
*Goldsmith's Row in Cheapside, built 1491, decked out for the coronation procession of Edward VI, 1547.*

## CIVIC GRANDEUR

London had a range of public buildings: a town hall (Guildhall), several specialized market buildings and two main landing places on the river front. The first city halls in north European towns were built in the 12th century, and that of London was probably among them. The earliest mention of the London Guildhall is shortly after 1100, and by 1200 it is likely there was a stone building for the civic leaders; it lay on top of the embankment of the destroyed and forgotten Roman amphitheatre, although this is probably a coincidence. The present Guildhall is largely a creation dating from between 1411 and 1430 by the mason John Croxton; in size and grandeur it rivalled the king's Westminster Hall, which had just been rebuilt. The porch had statues of civic virtues, four of which can now be seen in the Museum of London. In 1440 Croxton was

---

— boundary of ward

Vintry name of ward

Mean lay wealth per taxpayer by ward, 1332

- more than £8
- £6 to £8
- £4 to £6
- £2 to £4
- less than £2

Cripplegate
Aldersgate
LIVERPOOL STREET
Bishopsgate
Farringdon
B.
CS.
Broad Street
Portsoken
ALDGATE
Cheap
BANK
Ch.
LS.
Aldgate
Castle Baynard
BS.
Cd.
W. CANNON STREET
CwS.
L.
BLACKFRIARS
Queenhithe
Vintry
Dowgate
Br.
Bg.
TOWER HILL
Tower

0 — 600 m
0 — 2000 ft

River Thames

BS.  Bread Street
Cd.  Cordwainer
B.   Bassishaw
CS.  Coleman Street
W.   Walbrook
CwS. Candlewick Street

Br.  Bridge
Ch.  Cornhill
Bg.  Billingsgate
L.   Langbourn
LS.  Lime Street

also working on Leadenhall, a market complex on Cornhill. This was a quadrangle of warehouses on stately arcades, with an adjacent chapel and a school. Parts of this complex survived into the 19th century (one piece of walling until 1984) and the Victorian market of Leadenhall now covers the site. Other medieval markets were held in streets or by the main landing stages for goods at Queenhithe and Billingsgate. A stone building used by fishmongers and other traders, called the Stocks, was located at the end of Cheapside where the Mansion House now stands (and where it is commemorated by a Blue Plaque).

## PUBLIC PROVISION

The development of public services is one sign of a maturing sense of civic responsibility. In 1236 the city authorities acquired rights to springs by the Tyburn stream, close to modern Bond Street station, and began to lay lead pipes to convey drinking water to London, nearly 5 kilometres (3 miles) to the east; the work may have taken twenty-five years before the pipeline was complete. In the 1440s the supply was supplemented from more distant sources at Bayswater. This may have been one of the earliest medieval city water systems in Europe. The main conduit-heads were called 'standards' and were of some architectural note: they were in Cheapside from 1381, in Cornhill soon after 1378, and in Fleet Street by 1471. Many households had wells, but water could also be obtained from these conduits or directly from the Thames. Water-bearers, both men and women, carried water for a fee to houses from the conduits, in large containers on their backs.

By 1212 London had laws that governed the construction of buildings, trying to prevent the spread of fire, which was a constant hazard in a city built of timber. Street cleaners and other officials attempted to keep the urban environment free of rubbish, trade waste (especially offal from the butchers) and roaming animals. There was a clear desire to keep the city a wholesome place to be proud of. With its unrivalled concentration of people, trading links and money, London was an advertisement for modern, urban standards of living.

At the same time, neighbours often complained about each other's building works. Walls of timber and loam were very liable to penetration by water, and drainage by guttering and downpipes had not yet been developed. Privacy was jealously guarded and windows could not overlook a neighbour's property on the ground floor or below a height of 4.8 meters (16 ft). Sewage from privies sometimes leaked; firewood was stacked against walls and got in the way. Old buildings leaned and prevented new building by a neighbour; stone walls were sometimes condemned as dangerous to passers-by. Encroachments into the street, by steps, pentices (roofed shelters over windows or doors, as in premises used as a shop) or structures such as forges, were controlled by either the city authorities or royal justices, since the streets belonged to the king. But too often the encroachment was allowed on payment of a fine, thus making the street-line irregular over time. Some of the religious houses consolidated their precincts by absorbing existing lanes, despite local opposition. Thus their gardens overlay previous housing, as also happened at several Oxford colleges. **JS**

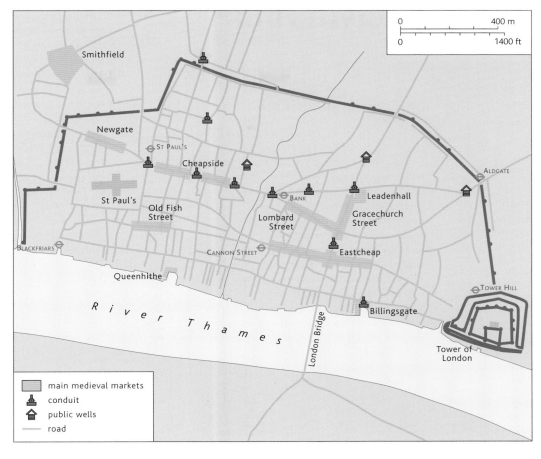

**Conduits and wells**
By 1450 London had a system of conduits and public wells (probably more than those shown here, which reflects current knowledge) both in market areas and in side streets.

**The Guildhall**
A reconstruction of the medieval Guildhall in the late 15th century. Unlike those of other towns, this centre of civic power and law was not in the main market street, but behind Cheapside in a quieter area.

# LONDON'S RELIGIOUS PRECINCTS

Large areas of medieval London were given over to monasteries, schools, hospitals and friaries. At the centre of the city was the medieval cathedral of St Paul's.

**Religious precincts**

Medieval London supported a great range of religious houses. They occupied large areas of the city and suburbs, and all were private precincts with walls and gates.

London must have been a living pattern book for fashionable styles in architecture. During the 12th and 13th centuries, many new monasteries, hospitals and friaries were established in and around the City and in Southwark. A small number found locations inside the city walls, but the majority were situated on the edges of the settlement or in the fields beyond. Although they probably began as simple timber buildings, they soon attracted funding and were transformed into large stone complexes, each with a church, buildings for eating, sleeping, meeting and storage, and up-to-date plumbing. By the end of the medieval period London (including Westminster and Southwark) had at least twelve hospitals, six for the sick and six for the poor.

Among the earliest monasteries were several Augustinian houses, one inside the walls (Holy Trinity Priory Aldgate, 1108) but the others outside, especially to the north-west and north-east, such as St Bartholomew Smithfield (a joint priory and hospital, 1123), St John of Jerusalem in Clerkenwell (about 1145), St Mary Spital (1197) and St Mary Bethlem (1247), which by 1403 had become a hospital for the insane. A priory was established in Southwark (now Southwark Cathedral) in 1106, followed by St Thomas's Hospital in 1213. Beyond to the south-east lay the large precinct of Bermondsey Abbey, founded by 1100 and at that time well out in the countryside. In the other suburbs were three hospitals founded by the French Cluniac order, and leper houses, placed further out on the main roads. London had more monasteries and hospitals in its suburbs than any other town in Britain, underlining its role as the most important place in the land by 1200.

**Smiling nun**

*A stone head-stop, or decoration from the meeting point of two arches, probably from a London church.*

## THE FRIARS

From about 1220, a new wave of religious houses

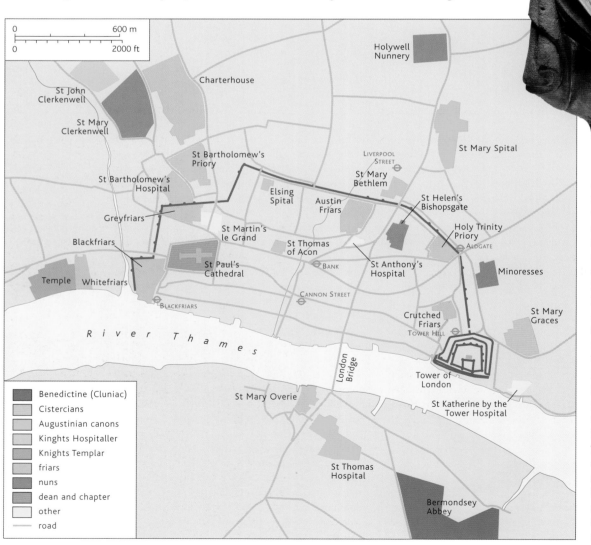

emerged – the friaries. These mendicant ('begging') orders were supposed to survive by serving townspeople directly, and not by accumulating town or country estates. By the end of the 14th century, London had five major friaries: the Dominicans or Blackfriars (1221, moved site 1275), the Franciscans or Greyfriars (1222), the Carmelites or Whitefriars (1247, south of Fleet Street), the Austin Friars (1253) and the Crutched Friars (before 1269). It is significant that all these names can still be found on the street map today. There were also some lesser orders (such as the Minoresses) and the large Carthusian Charterhouse, north-west of the city, founded in 1371, which survives as a historic complex of buildings. The medieval

*Map legend:*
- Benedictine (Cluniac)
- Cistercians
- Augustinian canons
- Kinghts Hospitaller
- Knights Templar
- friars
- nuns
- dean and chapter
- other
- road

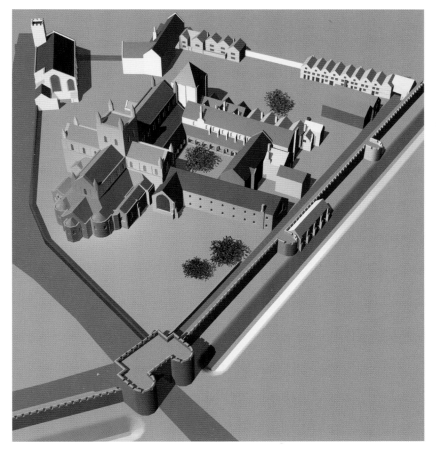

*Holy Trinity Priory, about 1500*
A reconstruction of one of London's greatest religious houses, founded in 1108 inside the city wall near Aldgate (foreground). By this date, the priory contained many prestigious stone buildings.

*The 'New Work' at St Paul's*
We know of the appearance of the eastern extension of St Paul's only through this engraving by Wenceslaus Hollar in 1657, long after its heyday.

areas throughout medieval Europe, and the friars associated with middle ranking and poorer people; their churches were meant to be austere. In London, however, the friaries also became favourite burial places for royalty and the nobility.

A further group of religious orders grew out of the Europe-wide passion for the Crusades from the late 11th century. In London both the Knights Hospitaller and the Knights Templar were represented (see map opposite). Their establishments were perhaps the most ostentatious in the 12th century, and the Templars eventually became too powerful for some of Europe's rulers. They were suppressed in 1314. The Knights Hospitaller survived.

## THE 'NEW WORK'

The largest church in medieval Britain was St Paul's Cathedral after it was extended (the 'New Work') in the period 1250 to 1314. The nave of about 1190 stood until the Great Fire in 1666 and the central tower had a tall wooden spire added by about 1240. The New Work involved the rebuilding and extension of the choir, a large rectangular building similar to those of the same period at Ely and Lincoln. As at these other great churches, the aim was to provide a suitably magnificent setting for the shrine of the local saint, in London's case St Erkenwald, the 7th-century bishop of London reputed to have converted the East Saxons to Christianity. The style of the architecture was international. A rose window in the east gable, the largest in Britain, may have been a conscious echo of the rose window in the south transept of Notre Dame, Paris. This was the most ambitious part of the New Work and it faced Cheapside, the secular centre of the city. Visible all over London, this impressive facade must have had a similar impact to those today of York Minster or Lincoln Cathedral.    **JS**

buildings of all the other friaries have disappeared, with the exception of a couple of fragments within modern offices.

## A WORLD APART

The monasteries, hospitals and friaries of the period 1100–1350 in London formed self-enclosed, walled enclosures of considerable size. Intended as islands of sanctity and contemplation, these monastic houses were normally out of bounds to ordinary citizens and, with their dazzling rich architecture and comfortable lifestyle, were worlds apart within the medieval city.

Today this can best be appreciated by exploring the surviving fragments of the monastic buildings of Westminster Abbey. The present chapter house and cloister date from the 13th and 14th centuries, and are partly the work of architects in the royal service such as Henry Yevele. Other buildings that can be seen include the abbot's house, the undercroft of the dormitory (now a museum) and the site of the monastic infirmary, now a garden.

Despite their exclusive nature, there were often close bonds between individual religious houses and the citizens. Some children of merchants or tradesmen became monks or nuns. There was a particularly high regard for the Carthusian order, represented in London by the Charterhouse. Many merchants arranged to be buried in a monastic house, and accordingly bequeathed money to the institution of their choice. In general, the monasteries belonging to important or fashionable religious orders were closely associated with the privileged or wealthy, and sought patronage among royalty and the nobility or the more important officials. Friaries were established as a matter of policy in poorer, typically urban

# IN POVERTY, SICKNESS & DEATH

Giving alms to the poor and caring for the sick were medieval Christian duties, but London's physicians could not cure the Great Pestilence that devastated Europe in the mid-14th century.

**St Mary Spital**
*A reconstruction of medieval London's largest hospital, on the road out of the city outside Bishopsgate.*

**Glass urinal, 15th century**
*Holding such a vessel to the light, a physician diagnosed illness by the condition of the patient's urine.*

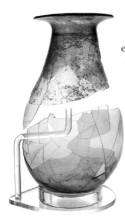

A few of its people shared in the wealth for which London was famous, but there was dire poverty as well. By 1300 the population of London may have exceeded 80,000, many of whom were ill-fed and ill-housed. Excavations in the graveyard of the medieval hospital of St Mary Spital (illustrated above) have revealed a large number of burial pits, each containing up to forty bodies. Many of these pits can be dated to the 1250s – a period we know from contemporary accounts was marked by appalling weather conditions, failed harvests and consequent mass starvation and disease. One writer recorded that 'In London alone 15,000 of the poor perished; in England and elsewhere thousands died.' Later, between 1315 and 1322, a calamitous series of harvest failures caused by cold and wet weather led to famine throughout Britain and northern Europe. In London, grain prices – and with them bread prices – were suddenly double what they had been in even the worst of previous years. A disease struck cattle at about the same time, worsening the situation. In Europe as a whole, as many as one in ten people died of starvation or disease in this eight-year period. According to one London chronicler, 'the poor people ate cats and horses and hounds … and stole children and ate them'.

At daybreak on 3 July 1322 'a great multitude of poor people' gathered at the gate of the friary of the Black (Dominican) Friars, where alms were to be distributed, a bequest by the charitable citizen Henry de Fingrie. When the gate opened there was such a rush that over fifty people were crushed to death. Most of the dead were never identified.

Poverty was seen as inescapable. When John le Stolere was run over by a water cart in Cheapside in 1339, the coroner's record described him as 'a pauper and beggar'; he was just seven years old.

The giving of alms to the poor was a Christian duty and many wealthy Londoners, like Henry de Fingrie, included bequests in their wills. Some, during their lifetimes or through their wills, established almshouses or hospitals. In 1329 William de Elsyng founded a hospital near London Wall to house blind people, later known as Elsingspital; a hundred years later Richard Whittington's executors established an almshouse for thirteen poor men called 'Whittington College'. Such homes or hospitals were not intended for the sick and provided no medical care. The presence of priests with a duty to pray for the soul of the founder reflects the ulterior motive some benefactors may have had.

## HOSPITALS & HEALTH CARE

Two 11th-century bishops of London had died of leprosy. Lepers (including misdiagnosed sufferers from a variety of skin diseases) were outcasts, forced to beg for their food. In about 1276 a London ordinance decreed that 'no leper shall be in the city, nor come there, nor make any stay there by night or by day'. Already a number of leper hospitals or 'lazar houses' providing refuge had been established outside the city. The earliest was that founded in about 1117 by Queen Matilda, wife of Henry I, at St Giles-in-the-Fields. Its rural site beside a main road along which lepers banished from the town might travel was typical of such foundations, like the hospital of St Mary and St Leonard (the Lock Hospital) at the edge of Southwark beside the Dover road, and St James's, on the site of the later palace.

Individual benefactions supported other hospitals, some of which, like St Bartholomew's in the city and St Thomas's in Southwark, are familiar even today. Some hospitals acquired a reputation for dealing with particular conditions; for example, St Mary Bethlehem (Bedlam), on the site of modern Liverpool Street station, looked after people who 'had fallen out of their wits'.

The hospital of St Mary without Bishopsgate ('St Mary Spital') was established in 1197 at the cost of a prominent Londoner, Walter Brunus, and his wife Roisia. With initially sixty beds, and later ninety (and in times of need several people in each bed), it was the largest hospital in medieval London, and one of the largest in England. Run by Augustinian monks, it took in pilgrims and travellers, the poor and the sick. It provided care for pregnant women and for the child if the mother died.

In excavations on the site between 1982 and 1991, several distinct groups of burials were uncovered. West of the 13th-century hospital building lay what was probably the main graveyard for hospital inmates at this time. Most were men who had died under the age of thirty; the condition of their bones shows they had suffered from illness in childhood, and had undertaken heavy manual labour from an early age. Some perhaps had been poor migrants seeking work in London. By contrast, burials in the hospital chapel, those of the clergy and wealthy patrons, reflect longer life and better health and nourishment.

## THE BLACK DEATH

Even in St Mary Spital the poor could expect little medical care; the wealthy sought the aid of physicians and were nursed at home. Both rich and poor relied on prayer and the intervention of saints. But neither physicians nor saints seemed able to help when in

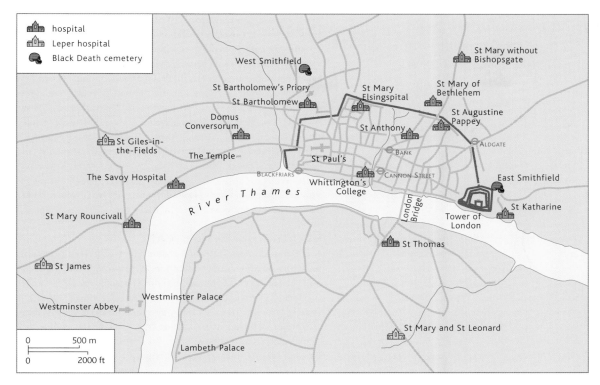

hospital
Leper hospital
Black Death cemetery

West Smithfield
St Bartholomew's Priory
St Bartholomew
Domus Conversorum
St Giles-in-the-Fields
The Temple
The Savoy Hospital
St Mary Rouncivall
St James
St Mary Elsingspital
St Anthony
St Paul's
BLACKFRIARS
Whittington's College
BANK
CANNON STREET
St Mary without Bishopsgate
St Mary of Bethlehem
St Augustine Pappey
ALDGATE
East Smithfield
St Katharine
London Bridge
Tower of London
River Thames
St Thomas
Westminster Palace
Westminster Abbey
Lambeth Palace
St Mary and St Leonard

0    500 m
0    2000 ft

**Hospitals and Black Death cemeteries**

Medieval 'hospitals' included both establishments for the care of the poor sick, like St Bartholomew's Hospital, and homes for the elderly, like Whittington's College. Beyond the outskirts of the city were the leper hospitals.

*Plague victims*

*The remains of victims of the Black Death uncovered during excavations at East Smithfield. Although these bodies lie in a mass burial trench, it is clear they were placed with care and respect despite the frightening circumstances of an epidemic that might soon also claim those responsible for burying them.*

1346 rumours began to reach England of a horrifying disease that had broken out in Asia, killing thousands. No one knew what caused it or how it spread. Today it is known as the Black Death; then it was called simply 'the Great Pestilence'.

The conventional identification of this disease as bubonic plague has recently been questioned, but whatever it was, it spread rapidly across Europe and the death toll was immense. The Black Death reached London towards the end of 1348. Over the next eighteen months perhaps as many as half of all Londoners died. At Westminster Abbey the Abbot died, together with twenty-six monks, half of the establishment. Graveyards filled and two emergency cemeteries were opened. Excavations in one of these, at East Smithfield near the Tower of London, took place between 1986 and 1988. Although many burials had been placed in individual graves, there were also three large burial trenches, one of them over 125 metres (400 ft) long (illustrated right). The bodies had been laid in these up to five deep, but some were in coffins and all had been carefully placed. Despite the terrible circumstances, the authorities still ensured the proper disposal of the dead.

The worst was over by the end of 1350. Those who survived faced changed economic and social conditions. Churchmen complained of a moral collapse and a breakdown of respect for religion and the law. Young people were dressing in extravagant fashions and ignoring the advice of their elders and of the Church. There was a shortage of skilled labour; prices and wages both rose, in spite of government legislation. The population of London did not rise again to the sort of level it had reached at the beginning of the 14th century for 150 years. But in a less crowded city there was more for everyone to share. The poor remained, but the mass starvation of 1315 did not recur. There were bad harvests from 1437 to 1440, but careful management of London's grain supply kept bread prices reasonable. Although one London chronicler recorded that 'the poor Commons were fain to make bread of

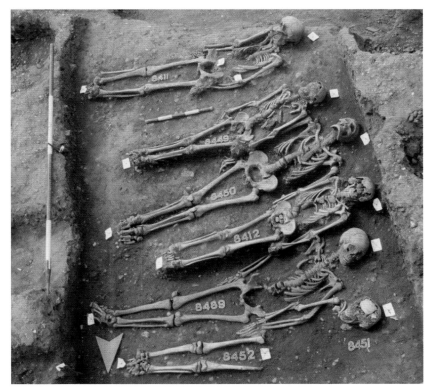

barley or beans, peas and vetches etc', this time there were no reports of people eating cats, dogs and children. In the 14th century London and its people survived the worst suffering that nature could inflict. The feeling that death, sudden and gruesome, was ever present was to make its mark on society, on culture and on art throughout the later Middle Ages. **JC**

# A CITY OF IMMIGRANTS

Medieval Londoners were extremely xenophobic, but from the 12th century onwards immigrant communities from Europe established themselves, however precariously, in the city.

In 1300, the population of London and its suburbs (without Westminster) was probably in the region of 80,000 people; smaller than that of Paris or Milan, but larger than Cologne or any other city on the other side of the North Sea. For most of the Middle Ages, however, the city's death rate exceeded its birth rate, and new immigrants were always needed. Although London was by far the largest town in England, it was comparatively isolated; the nearest towns were 60 kilometres (37 miles) away. But the city survived, and grew, by sucking in immigrants from the countryside and from overseas; then as now, there was no shortage of people hoping to make a new life for themselves in the city streets.

Some of the leading families of 13th-century London can be traced for two or three generations, but otherwise there were no long-lived dynasties in the capital. Many men who rose to be city leaders came originally from the provinces as young men: Richard Whittington came from Gloucestershire, and his contemporary Simon Eyre, who built Leadenhall Market in the 1440s, from Suffolk. Studies of surnames that might relate to their place of origin show that apprentices in London came in the early 1300s from the Home Counties and the East Midlands (Cambridgeshire to Suffolk), and in the 15th century from Yorkshire. The evidence suggests that, like more recent London immigrant communities, many newcomers settled in that part of the city nearest to their counties of origin; not only was this the part of London they first encountered, but it was the nearest to their relations in the countryside. There was also a large transient population: traders, carriers and butchers, among others, regularly moved between town and country. During the 15th century especially, the centralizing of goods for export through London rather than other ports must have meant that many people in the cloth industry, for instance from towns in Yorkshire, had knowledge of and probably did business in London.

## RESIDENT ALIENS

Foreigners tended to stick together. Groups of foreign merchants had their own establishments on the waterfront; some may have been at Dowgate before the Norman Conquest. In 1304 'aliens' included Gascon wine merchants and merchants from Spain and Picardy (northern France) living in the streets around this same area. The most distinctive compound of foreigners, however, grew into the Steelyard in Thames Street, which housed about thirty German merchants in 1304.

Although some merchants from overseas became citizens of London, there were also periods of tension and xenophobia in

*The Steelyard,* as shown by Wenceslaus Hollar in 1647, little changed from its rebuilding in about 1475. The Steelyard was the London depot of Hanse merchants from Cologne and Lübeck, the most important enclave of foreigners in medieval London.

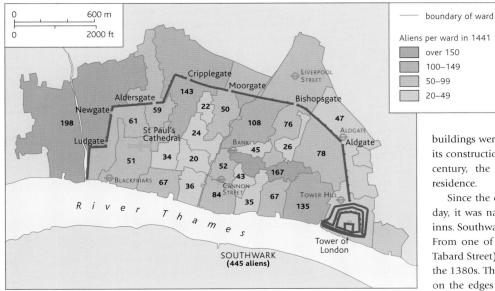

**Numbers of aliens by ward, 1441**

Foreigners were resident in all parts of the City in the 15th century: London was already cosmopolitan.

Map legend:
— boundary of ward

Aliens per ward in 1441
- over 150
- 100–149
- 50–99
- 20–49

Map labels: Cripplegate, Moorgate, Liverpool Street, Aldersgate, 143, 22, 50, Bishopsgate, 59, 47, Newgate, 61, 198, St Paul's Cathedral, 24, 108, 76, Aldgate, Ludgate, 45, 26, 78, Bank, 51, 34, 20, 52, 43, 167, Blackfriars, 67, 36, 84, Cannon Street, 35, 67, Tower Hill, 135, River Thames, Tower of London, SOUTHWARK (445 aliens)

Scale: 0 – 600 m; 0 – 2000 ft

In the 1320s, Edward II had a royal house called the Rosary built opposite the Tower on the Southwark bank of the Thames, although he did not enjoy it for long during his brief reign. The Rosary may have reinforced a trend for the establishment of mansions of secular lords or nobles in Southwark. There had been at least one, belonging to the powerful Warenne family, in the 12th century; high-quality stone buildings were found on the site of London Bridge station during its construction in the 1830s. Next to the Rosary, in the following century, the famous soldier Sir John Fastolf built a palatial residence.

Since the city gate on London Bridge was closed at dusk each day, it was natural for travellers to stay in the suburb outside, at inns. Southwark's main street had at least twenty-two inns by 1381. From one of them, the Tabard (its site now a mere memory in Tabard Street), Chaucer's pilgrims set out in his *Canterbury Tales* of the 1380s. The larger inns would have functioned like bus stations on the edges of towns today, with wagons going in and out on many routes.

JS

which foreigners suffered. In the 13th century there were periodic attacks on merchants in the city from Italy and central France (notably those from Cahors), as well as on the Jews. The Italian community had been caught up in financial problems with the king in the 14th century, but about fifty men and a few women of Italian origin lived around the Austin Friars in the north-east of the city. The Peasants' Revolt in 1381 was accompanied by assaults on foreign communities, and over a hundred Flemings and Lombards (from north Italy) were killed by mobs. The Flemings had taken refuge in two churches, which must indicate their neighbourhoods at the time: St Martin Vintry (by the waterfront) and the Austin Friars church (where a Dutch congregation, established much later in 1550, still worships today).

## SOUTHWARK & THE DUTCH

After 1400 the largest influx of foreigners to London came from Flanders, Holland and Zeeland; they were lumped together in the popular mind as 'Dutch'. Many settled in Southwark and some in Westminster, where they prospered by making beer (with the new ingredient hops, which made it last longer and therefore more transportable), brass items, bricks and by working leather. In 1440 there were 445 Dutch taxpayers in Southwark, carrying out forty different occupations; fifty of these households had servants. They were a cohesive group and lived together in the parish of St Olave, Tooley Street. They preserved their language, while learning English to survive, and were subject to extra taxation and discrimination in the local courts. As one historian has commented, 'they were poor, numerous, and foreign; classic targets for discrimination'. East Southwark, by the 16th century, was an industrial zone largely occupied by the Dutch immigrants, producing clothing, beer, pottery and glass; they were also dyers, leatherworkers, builders, joiners, cobblers and shoemakers.

Southwark had always been a place of contrasts. In the 12th century the small settlement around the foot of London Bridge (in whatever form it took before it was rebuilt in stone in 1176) included the large mansions of religious leaders such as the Bishop of Winchester (the gable from his 14th-century hall survives as a monument) or the Abbot of Battle, from the monastery in Sussex.

### IMMIGRANTS IN LONDON IN 1483

A tax on foreigners in 1483–4 reveals people of many nationalities in London. They mainly came from Flanders and Germany; there were clusters of people (several taxpayers) from Haarlem, Gouda, Dordrecht and Bruges. Here are some of them, all identified as 'German' unless indicated otherwise.

| Name | Occupation |
|---|---|
| Anthony Kelle | merchant, importing and exporting |
| Adrian Water | servant of Robert Tate (mayor 1488–9) |
| Cornelius Johnson | basketmaker |
| John Gayle | weaver |
| Simon Herman | beer brewer |
| Thurstan Grysley *Icelander* | servant of William Heryet (mayor 1481–2) |
| John Evynger | beer brewer, with eleven servants or workmen, all 'German' |
| Gerard Godfrey | bricklayer |
| John Sewell *French* | servant of Vincent Toteler, a 'German' armourer |
| James Dunton | servant of Robert Westwode, blacksmith |
| Alexander More *Scottish* | porter |
| James Ramsay *Scottish* | surgeon |
| Louis Hunsan | instrument maker |
| Henry Hunderpound | goldsmith |
| John Letowe *Lithuanian* | printer |
| William Ravenswalde | printer |
| Benedict Calaman *Indian* | not stated |
| Augustine Bowyne | locksmith |
| John Nele | mariner |
| John Wright *Scottish* | carpenter |

# THE PORT OF MEDIEVAL LONDON

Much of medieval London's riverfront was given over to wharves and warehouses, handling both local and overseas trade. The bridge carried essential traffic, but obstructed the river-users.

From its origins in the foundation of Lundenburg by King Alfred and the embanking of the Thames to provide berths for shipping at Æthelred's Hithe (Queenhithe), the medieval city's waterfront reflected its dependence on river traffic and the trade it brought. Between the 10th and 15th centuries, a large area of land south of Thames Street was gradually reclaimed from the river for new wharves and warehouses – extending as much as 100 metres (100 yards) in the central area between Queenhithe and London Bridge.

The first embankments appear to have been made of brushwood, with clay and gravel on top, reinforced at the front with low revetments of timber posts and planks or wattlework. The shallow-draft ships of late Saxon and Norman times could be beached on the open foreshore where they were unloaded and loaded over the sides; in some cases plank trackways were laid on the foreshore to give better access. Gradually shipbuilding and harbour construction developed, side by side. Seagoing vessels became larger with higher sides; waterfronts became taller and more solid, with increasingly sophisticated forms of support.

A series of archaeological excavations along the City waterfront between the 1970s and 1990s chronicled these developments. Dendrochronology allowed the close dating of the timbers, and demonstrated how quickly timber structures became dilapidated. The areas of timber covered and exposed twice daily by the tides rotted quickly, and required replacement within thirty years or so. It was much easier to build a complete new revetment in front of the old one and fill the intervening space with soil and rubbish than to replace individual rotten timbers. In some cases the ground gained between successive revetments was only two metres (6 ft), and the rebuilding can hardly have been motivated by a wish to extend the property.

Yet such motivation did exist. In 1244 the city authorities confirmed that it was permissible for wharves to be 'lengthened and extended towards the current of water', since this protected the land 'against the sea rising and falling by day and night'. In 1345 Gilbert de la Brewere, Dean of St Paul's, began extending the 'kaium' (quay) near Woodwharf, south of the cathedral, 'to enlarge and improve the property' – much to the annoyance of his neighbour Elizabeth de Montacute, against whose wall the new quay was being erected and who complained to the local alderman.

The first embankments at Æthelred's Hithe (Queenhithe) were probably built as part of Alfred's plan for London, by royal authority and at public expense. Queenhithe was to remain a public wharf. At the other end of the city, at Billingsgate, an 11th-century document records the royal dues payable on ships coming to port and goods being unloaded, not just on goods from overseas but on fish, on baskets of chickens and eggs, and on butter and cheese. But the space between these 'hithes' gradually filled with privately-owned wharves – some like Asselyn's Wharf taking their names from their owners, others such as Woodwharf

*Riverside revetment*
*This front-braced oak structure, built around 1220 and 2.3 metres (8 ft) high, was revealed in 1982.*

named after the goods they handled. Between them public lanes led down to the waterfront for those who needed to reach the river for transport, to fetch water or to wash clothes, although a survey in 1343 revealed how frequently these had been blocked or narrowed by encroaching buildings on either side.

Certain parts of the waterfront (see map, left) had special functions. Wine Wharf and the Vintry were the centre of the wine trade. London's first dockside cranes, powered by treadwheels, were erected here to lift barrels from ships' holds, and appear in the earliest illustrations of the Thames waterfront. The Steelyard, beside Dowgate, was the London headquarters of the powerful merchants of the German Hanseatic League. Further east, Custom House, on Wool Quay, was from at least the early 14th century the place where wool was weighed and the royal customs duty on its export levied.

**The medieval riverfront**
Public and private wharves and quays stretched east and west from London Bridge.

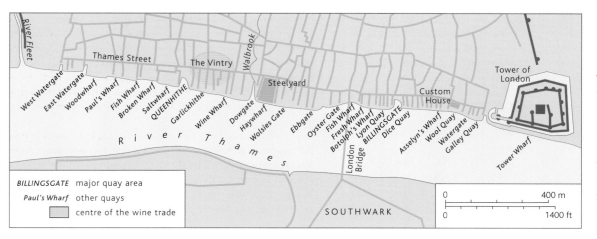

BILLINGSGATE  major quay area
Paul's Wharf  other quays
centre of the wine trade

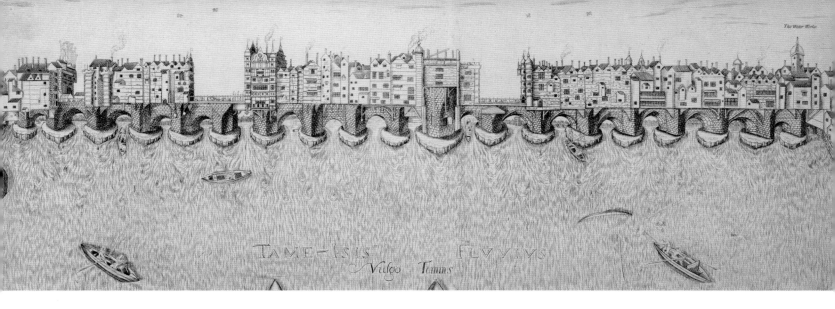

The Water Works

TAME-ISIS FLVVIVS Vulgo Temms

## LONDON BRIDGE & NEW WHARVES

*London Bridge*
*The bridge in about 1600, seen from the downstream side. River craft try to pass through the narrow arches; a capsized boat can be seen in the right foreground.*

Dominating London's port was London Bridge, the stone bridge begun in 1176 and complete by 1209. Over 270 metres (900 ft) long, with its chapel of Thomas Becket and the houses, shops and fortified gates that surmounted it, the bridge was a wonder to foreign visitors. There was a drawbridge allowing larger vessels to pass upstream to Queenhithe and the Vintry. Records in the year 1381–2 show an average of seven vessels passing through each day – up to twenty-five a day in the busiest month, June. But navigation was difficult. The narrow arches obstructed the river, causing a powerful and dangerous tidal flow through each of them. As ships grew larger even the drawbridge was too small to allow them access upstream. By the end of the 15th century, it was no longer in use and the largest ships were confined to the area of the port east of the bridge, the later 'Pool of London'.

The upkeep of London Bridge was a public duty. The Bridge Wardens, with income from tolls, rents and private bequests, employed a permanent workforce to keep it in good repair.

Unlike the bridge, the building of new riverside works was a piecemeal process, dependent on the enterprise of individual property owners. Wharves were erected and extended at different times; neighbouring properties show different qualities of construction and timberwork, some employing the best craftsmen and materials, others erected hastily, with revetments of reused timbers and ships' planking. But many show expert carpentry. From the 12th century onwards, timbers, formerly used in the round, were squared, allowing more complex joints to be used. Vertical revetments were supported by diagonal braces, at first from the front, or river, side (see illustration opposite).

In the 14th century a new technique was invented: revetments were retained by strongly-fastened braces running back into the fill of soil and rubble behind them, leaving the front unimpeded and more convenient for mooring ships.

In 1384 Richard Willysdon and his wife Anneys acquired the lease of a property with a wharf near Billingsgate. Under the terms of the lease they were required, within ten years, to extend the wharf 'stretcchyng in the themesward' by 1.2 metres (4 ft), with a wall built of 'Maidstone stone'. Such river walls of masonry became the norm during the 15th century; although they were much more expensive to construct, they were excellent investments, requiring far less maintenance and far less frequent replacement than the earlier timber structures.

No longer would the London waterfront advance steadily into the Thames as successive new timber revetments were built. Apart from some rebuilding after the Great Fire and the construction of a new river wall for the Blackfriars Underpass in the 1960s, the modern riverfront from Blackfriars to the Tower of London remains more or less on the line established by the end of the Middle Ages. **JC**

### EXOTIC CARGO

This is a selection of the goods noted by port officials in the hold of the Venetian galley of Bernard Bondymer, which came to London in June 1481. They are listed under the names of the Italian merchants who consigned them to London.

| | |
|---|---|
| Alesio Summa | 1 barrel soap |
| Damyan Pastrovichio | 2 barrels of oil; 12 carpets |
| George de Camsa | 3 pairs small cor8al beads; 1 great sack of sponges; 1 barrel of oil; 5 carpets; 2 chests of pepper; 1 fardel (pack) of silk |
| John de Bodna | 2 apes |
| Leonard Purveour | 1 firkin (small barrel) of raisins of Corinth |
| Ralph de Sancto George | 1 barrel treacle |
| Nicholas Dedo | 1 barrel frankincense; 4 loads of brazil wood [to make red dye]; 1 chest with 20 pieces of camlet [rough cloth made of camel or goat hair]; black and green satin; 4 pomanders [balls of aromatic herbs to ward off infection] |
| Cosma Spenelli | 9 bales Moorish wax |
| Jeronimo Teople [Typolo] | 1 box borax [used in metallurgy]; 1 case powdered sugar; 28 cases Messina sugar; 1 barrel mace; 6 barrels green ginger; 4 bales of silk |
| Peter Pastrovichio | 300 bocals [glass bottles or jugs] |
| Paul Fustaryno | 60 carpets |
| Stephen de Sancto Nicholo | 1 bag of shears; 1 barrel of glass beads and shears; 1 bag soap; 5 glass pots; 1 'griffin's egg' [a vulture's egg, perhaps made into a novelty goblet] |

# A PLACE OF TRADE & INDUSTRY

Throughout the Middle Ages, Londoners amassed real wealth by commerce, not from land. The power and influence of London grew with its national and international trade.

**London's economic hinterland**
Medieval London's trade wealth was founded on the market centres within its orbit – a large consumer base as well as a supply region for the city.

Trade with other English towns formed the bedrock on which medieval London's international trade was founded. London was a major trading centre for ports on Britain's east coast and for an increasingly large hinterland in south-east England. This hinterland not only supplied the city with grain, meat, produce and wood for fuel, but was also a large and relatively wealthy market for goods manufactured in London or imported by its merchants. This consumer base increased as new towns were established in the population boom of the 12th and 13th centuries; new roads were built and many were improved with new or rebuilt bridges.

Flanders, in the 1270s, Italian traders moved in and helped make London the principal place of export for English wool, and later finished cloth, to the Mediterranean and the Middle East.

By 1300, London was England's greatest port, for both imports and exports. Inwards came wine, spices, dyes, fine cloths and furs; the main exports, apart from English cloth, were raw materials such as wool, other animal products, tin, pewter and sea coal. During the 14th century goods manufactured in the Low Countries poured into London as the Hanseatic League created an efficient economic zone throughout the North Sea. By the 1480s, port records show that ships came to London from all round the Baltic, the Dutch and French coasts, northern Spain and Portugal. The Italian trade was declining, but in 1481 a Venetian galley came into the port, bringing spices, wine, soap, expensive textiles, carpets and other luxuries of enormous value.

## MANUFACTURING

London was also the largest manufacturing centre in the kingdom. More than a hundred distinct occupations are mentioned in taxation documents of 1332, although up to 80 per cent of the workforce remained unrecorded and is thus invisible to us. The main industries were food and drink, such as bakers, vintners and

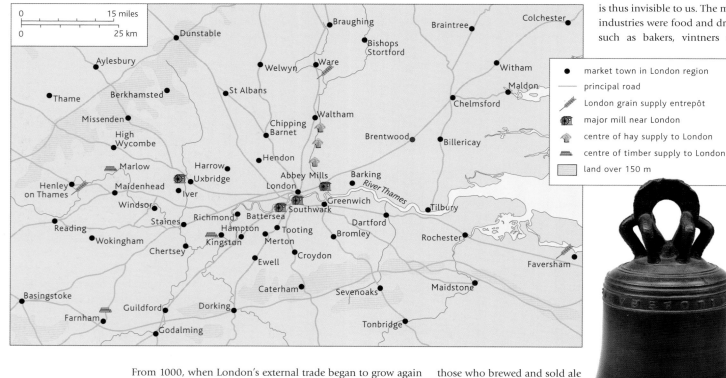

<table>
<tr><td>●</td><td>market town in London region</td></tr>
<tr><td>—</td><td>principal road</td></tr>
<tr><td></td><td>London grain supply entrepôt</td></tr>
<tr><td></td><td>major mill near London</td></tr>
<tr><td></td><td>centre of hay supply to London</td></tr>
<tr><td></td><td>centre of timber supply to London</td></tr>
<tr><td></td><td>land over 150 m</td></tr>
</table>

**Bells of London**
*This church bell of about 1340 is inscribed 'PETRVS: DE: VESTON: ME : FECIT' ('Peter de Weston made me'). Peter de Weston was one of London's leading bell-founders, with a foundry just outside Aldgate.*

From 1000, when London's external trade began to grow again after the turmoil of the Viking wars, documents tell of merchants from France, Germany and the Low Countries coming to London to buy and to sell. International commerce was directed through markets and entry points such as the wharf at Billingsgate, so that it could be controlled and tolls paid to the city and to the king. Foreigners were restricted to the waterfront, where groups of German traders, for example, had their own establishment near Dowgate by the 12th century. The wine trade was particularly important and the traders in wine, some from Gascony, gave their name to their section of the waterfront, Vintry. (Wine traders were called 'vintners'.) After a major dispute between English wool producers and their most important customers, the cloth traders of

those who brewed and sold ale (that is, beer without hops).

As in other English and continental towns, specific local resources and economies of scale had ensured by around 1300 that particular industries were concentrated in different areas of the city, but these were not sharply defined: consumers, and the streets favoured by shoppers, shifted around the city over time. Metalworkers produced lots of smoke and noise, sometimes in large workshops, and therefore tended to be located on the outskirts of the built-up area, either just inside the north city wall near St Margaret Lothbury (where there is still a Founders Court), or around Aldgate, particularly outside the wall, where bell-founders congregated in the 14th century. Some craft halls were in areas directly associated with their trade.

Medieval London's most important manufacturing area was in Southwark, outside the regulatory reach of the city. The making of cloth, hats and caps, and tailoring were particularly widespread. Flemish craftsmen treated leather and made shoes and saddles, the tidal streams running into the Thames proving useful for tanners. They acquired their raw material from the butchers who served the city across the bridge.

In the wider London area, there was substantial production of grain and timber for the London market. Mills existed on the Thames, at Battersea by 1086 and in Southwark by the 12th century. Upriver, Kingston was a source of timber and pottery by the 13th century, producing much of London's pottery for table and larder. Like the major rivers of Europe and America today, the Thames was a commercial highway.

Over the last thirty years many thousands of medieval artefacts have been dug up on archaeological sites in the City and its

**Markets and manufacturers**
Although London's markets changed with time, Cheapside remained the most important commercial axis. Craftworkers and manufacturing became concentrated in certain areas of the medieval city.

## CRAFTS AND TRADES, 1374–1486

Occupations listed in 4516 wills made in London church courts between 1374 and 1486 give us a glimpse of the range and proportion of crafts and trades in the city during this period:

| Trade | Percentage of workers |
| --- | --- |
| Victuals | 22% |
| Mercantile | 14% |
| Metalwork | 13% |
| Clothing | 12% |
| Leather | 11% |
| Building | 6% |
| Textiles | 5% |
| Wood | 3% |
| Transport | 2% |
| Chandlery | 2% |
| Armaments | 1% |
| All other trades | 9% |

The victualling and provisioning trades (vintners, bakers, butchers) provided occupations for the largest proportion of workers, followed by mercantile trades (grocers, haberdashers), metalworking (including goldsmiths) and clothing.

**Venetian glass beaker**
*This decorated Italian beaker belonging to an inhabitant of Tower Street was found in 1989. Glassware was not made in medieval England: its presence is evidence of international trade in luxury items.*

environs, although no group of objects from a single, individual household has yet been identified. There is do doubt that overall standards of living were improving during the Middle Ages. There may even have been, in London, the seeds of an economic revolution that is normally placed much later, in the 18th century: consumerism, and a real market for mass-produced personal and domestic items. **JS**

# MEDIEVAL & EARLY TUDOR GREATER LONDON

Medieval London's influence spread over much of southern and midland England, but it was most powerful in the immediately surrounding region, the area that is today Greater London.

**Medieval and early Tudor greater London**
By the late Middle Ages, London dominated its immediate surroundings, where many settlements remained small.

Everywhere in today's Greater London was within half a day's horseback ride of the medieval city, or not much longer by cart or on foot. A network of roads around London carried local as well as long-distance traffic; most of them are still major roads.

The upkeep of these roads was the responsibility of the local landowners, and they were poorly maintained. The road out of London into Essex presented a particular problem, where it crossed the marshes and streams of the lower Lea valley. Between 1110 and 1118 Matilda, queen of Henry I, ordered the building of a causeway and bridges over the main channels. This new route crossed the river at the place still called Old Ford.

The Thames itself was crossed not only by London Bridge, but by bridges upstream at Kingston (by 1219), Chertsey (after 1300) and Staines (by 1222). Other bridges spanned the larger tributaries; elsewhere ferries or fords sufficed.

Barges carried grain down the River Lea from the farms of Hertfordshire to mills at Stratford to feed London's population; improvements to the waterway were made in the fifteenth century, and the first double-gated pound lock was installed at Waltham in 1577. Most other Thames tributaries, such as the Wandle, were obstructed by watermills and by fishing weirs, making them unsuitable for river traffic.

## THE DEAD HAND OF LONDON

London's social and economic power discouraged independent urban development in its near vicinity. Middlesex was wholly dominated by the capital. It had only one substantial town – Uxbridge. At the crossing of the River Colne, Uxbridge was the first stopping point on the road from London to Oxford, Gloucester and the West Midlands, with many inns catering for travellers. The town had two weekly market days and two annual fairs, and a corn-milling industry on the river. Elsewhere in Middlesex there were very few settlements that could boast even a weekly market. South of the Thames, the picture was much the same – the exception was Kingston upon Thames, with a first royal charter granted by King John in 1208 and borough status confirmed by Edward IV in 1481. Although most of the settlements whose names are familiar on a modern London map already existed in the Middle Ages, many of them were no more than hamlets or groups of scattered farmsteads. **JC**

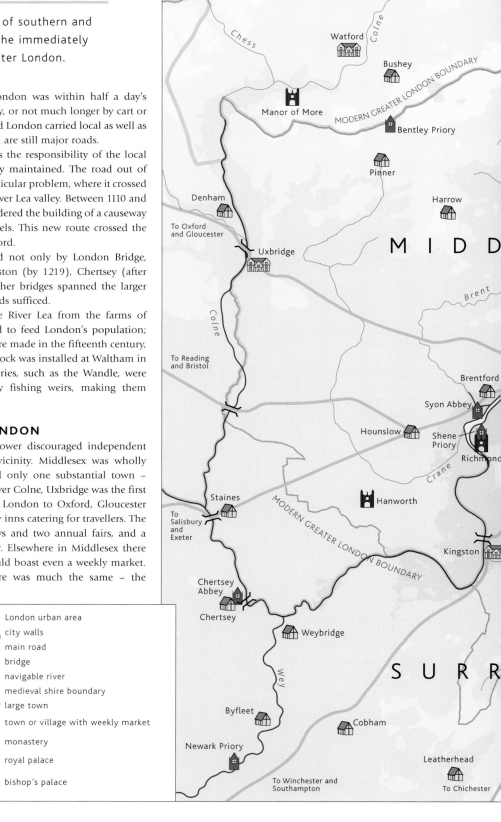

Legend:
- London urban area
- city walls
- main road
- bridge
- navigable river
- medieval shire boundary
- large town
- town or village with weekly market
- monastery
- royal palace
- bishop's palace

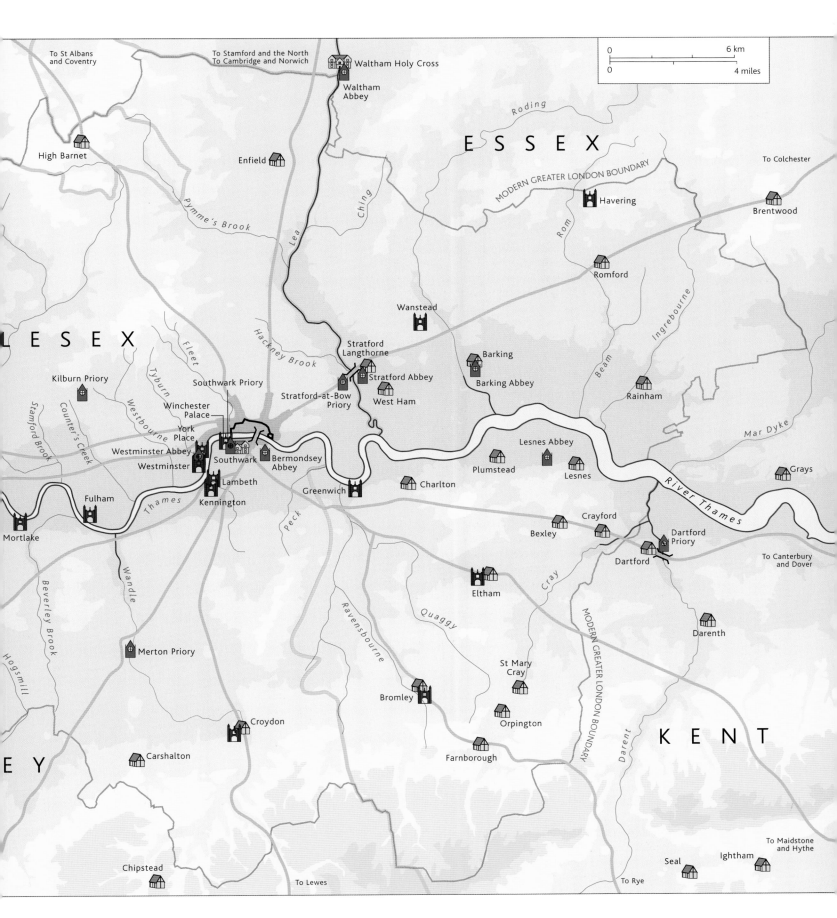

To St Albans
and Coventry

To Stamford and the North
To Cambridge and Norwich

Waltham Holy Cross

Waltham
Abbey

E S S E X

Roding

MODERN GREATER LONDON BOUNDARY

To Colchester

High Barnet

Enfield

Havering

Brentwood

Pymme's Brook

Ching

Lea

Rom

Ingrebourne

Romford

Beam

Wanstead

Hackney Brook

Stratford
Langthorne

Stratford Abbey

Barking

Rainham

D L E S E X

Fleet

Tyburn

Kilburn Priory

Southwark Priory

Stratford-at-Bow
Priory

West Ham

Barking Abbey

Mar Dyke

Westbourne

Winchester
Palace

York
Place

Stamford Brook

Counter's Creek

Westminster Abbey

Westminster

Southwark

Bermondsey
Abbey

Lesnes Abbey

Plumstead

Lesnes

Grays

Fulham

Lambeth

Greenwich

Charlton

River Thames

Mortlake

Thames

Kennington

Peck

Crayford

Bexley

Dartford
Priory

Wandle

Beverley Brook

Ravensbourne

Eltham

Cray

Dartford

To Canterbury
and Dover

Merton Priory

Quaggy

St Mary
Cray

Darenth

Hogsmill

Bromley

Orpington

MODERN GREATER LONDON BOUNDARY

Darent

K E N T

Croydon

Carshalton

Farnborough

Chipstead

To Lewes

To Rye

Seal

Ightham

To Maidstone
and Hythe

# TUDOR & EARLY STUART LONDON

For Londoners, the Tudor and early Stuart period was a time of political turbulence and Civil War, huge redistribution of wealth, and a remarkable growth in London's size and power, both at home and, increasingly, abroad. The Dissolution of the Monasteries (1535–40), which started experimentally in London in 1532, brought about violent changes to the character and appearance of London. It must have been a liberating time for many. The religious precincts in the urban centre and their widespread rural estates were carved up, pulled to pieces and enjoyed by hundreds, if not thousands, of new owners.

At the same time, London attracted immigrants from other parts of Britain and abroad, and the population (both City and suburbs, with Westminster) grew from perhaps 150,000 in 1580 to at least 500,000 by 1660.

Overcrowding led to inadequate sanitation, and occasional food shortages and diseases contributed to high death rates. Plagues in 1563 and 1603 killed many, the latter claiming about a fifth of the population, mostly from suburbs outside the walls.

People required housing and feeding, and fields around the City soon sprouted streets and courts of houses, often badly built. Crime and begging increased. In London the very wealthy began to drift west, towards Covent Garden and Westminster. Increased overseas trade promoted the development of suburbs along the Thames waterfront downstream of the City, on both banks, where shipwrights worked and sailors lodged. It became more noticeable that rich and poor lived in separate areas.

Only in London, with its heaving, restless population craving stimulation, was the flowering of the Elizabethan and Jacobean theatre possible. Londoners used the comedies and tragedies of Shakespeare, Marlowe, Webster and others to make sense of their new urban and overseas world. By the 1630s, that expanding world of connections and possible fortunes included America and the Caribbean.

*The Copperplate map (detail), c. 1559*
*This etched bird's-eye view of London (reversed in this image so it reads correctly) shows Bishopsgate (bottom right) and the suburban street outside. In the fields women lay out clothes to dry and bleach. To the north are windmills. Only three plates of an original total of fifteen for the whole map are known.*

# DISSOLUTION & REFORMATION

The Dissolution of the Monasteries brought perhaps the largest upheaval in London's economic history. The new private owners of monastic estates led the way in a booming, expanding city.

*St Paul's Cathedral, 1559*
*Shown here from the Copperplate map, St Paul's lost its spire, one of the highest in Europe, when it was destroyed in a lightning strike in 1561.*

The Dissolution of the Monasteries and the Reformation of the English Church between 1530 and 1570 transformed London's religious and social history. The medieval city's religious precincts were claimed for secular use, and parish churches were radically modified to suit new Protestant ways of worship. An enormous amount of land went onto the property market just as London took in many thousands of immigrants, both from other parts of England and from abroad.

The religious changes that convulsed England between about 1530 and 1558 had two quite separate causes: the financial and

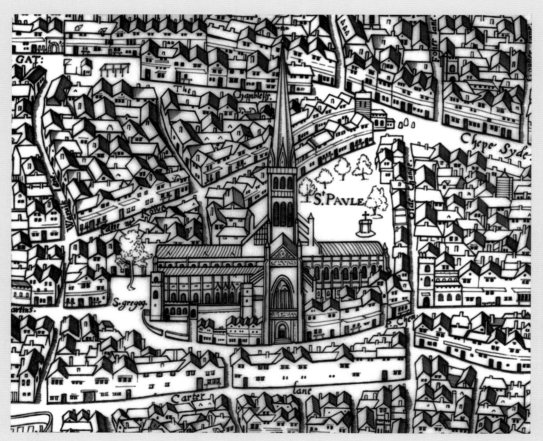

marital problems of Henry VIII and the Protestant Reformation, which spread from towns in continental Europe, disseminated by the new technology of printing. London's role as a centre of religious radicalism and debate was already well established. In the centuries before newspapers, it was in parish churches that people met to discuss news – and religion. The spiritual unease and thirst for change they sensed from events abroad made them look anew at the religious buildings around them.

The Dissolution also altered the topography of large parts of London, both in the central urban area (where there were over twenty monastic houses and hospitals) and in the countryside around the capital. Although a few churches, such as St Bartholomew Smithfield, St Helen Bishopsgate and Greyfriars, re-emerged as parish churches (and two other religious buildings were used by immigrant communities), most religious precincts were sold or given away to royal favourites, initially to become the sites of urban mansions. A second use was as royal depots for munitions or pageant decorations. St Mary Graces, east of the Tower, became the site of a yard providing provisions for the Tudor navy, as the nearby riverside developed into an area for building and repairing ships.

The mansions carved out of religious precincts were the urban contemporaries of the innovative Elizabethan country houses that have survived today, and it is likely that these now lost London houses were the models followed elsewhere in England for their architecture and features such as large glass windows and classical details. By the 1570s, however, the brief era of these great houses had passed and most former precincts began to fragment into smaller housing and industrial units. Fashion and the Court began to crystallize around the palace at Westminster and, from the 1630s, around Covent Garden and Queen Street (now west of Kingsway, just south of Holborn).

Although the majority of religious properties passed into secular hands and many people profited from dealing in land, the leaders of the community also used the changes to establish charitable institutions and schools. By 1600 London had three hospitals and an orphanage run by the City, all based on former monastic sites. Prominent members of livery companies or, sometimes, pious individuals with fortunes, established almshouses – small courtyards enclosed by dwellings for the retired – on the fringes of the built-up area and increasingly in nearby villages such as Islington, Hoxton, Acton and Greenwich.

## ST PAUL'S CATHEDRAL

In the heart of the city, St Paul's Cathedral survived, but in a decaying and dilapidated state; the spire was hit by lightning in 1561, after which it was taken down and not replaced. Many of the cathedral's monuments, including the shrine of St Erkenwald, were demolished or damaged by religious zealots. Perceptive churchmen had predicted that the invention of printing would bring about the downfall of the established Church, because they would no longer have a monopoly on the interpretation of the Bible. And so it turned out to be; St Paul's Churchyard, around the cathedral itself, became the national centre of the book trade by 1550. Between 1633 and 1642 a classical portico was added to the west end, paid for by Charles I and designed by Inigo Jones. Fragments of the columns came to light for the first time in excavations in 1996;

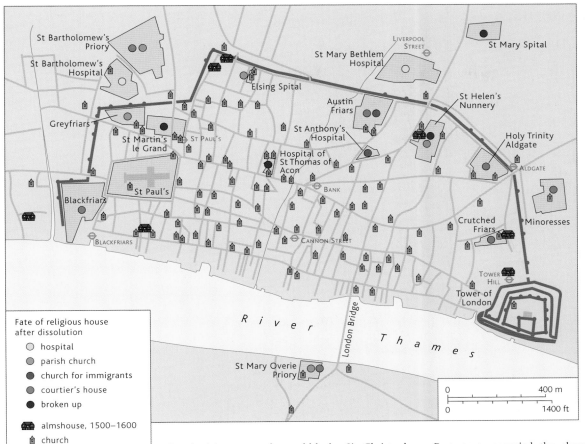

**Fate of religious house after dissolution**
- ○ hospital
- ◔ parish church
- ● church for immigrants
- ◕ courtier's house
- ● broken up
- 🏠 almshouse, 1500–1600
- ⛪ church
- — road

Map labels:
St Bartholomew's Priory
St Bartholomew's Hospital
Greyfriars
St Martin's le Grand
St Paul's
Blackfriars
Elsing Spital
St Mary Bethlem Hospital
Austin Friars
St Anthony's Hospital
Hospital of St Thomas of Acon
St Paul's
Bank
Cannon Street
Blackfriars
Liverpool Street
St Mary Spital
St Helen's Nunnery
Holy Trinity Aldgate
Aldgate
Crutched Friars
Minoresses
Tower Hill
Tower of London
London Bridge
River Thames
St Mary Overie Priory

0 — 400 m
0 — 1400 ft

## Priory developments

St Bartholomew's Priory, Smithfield was developed after 1560 and several courtiers' grand houses (nos. 1–6) were carved out of its stone buildings; to the east, several streets, which still survive today, were laid out over the priory's grounds. Here Bartholomew Fair was held, the subject of Ben Jonson's play of that name. The large priory church was cut in half; its choir survives today as St Bartholomew the Great parish church.

**London after the Reformation**
Most of the religious houses in and around the city were destroyed or became courtiers' houses. A few were partly reused for new parish churches.

debating how to repair it; Wren wanted to build a dome on to the existing central tower. His friend Robert Hooke, meanwhile, was using the old tower for experiments, perilously picking his way between decayed beams to measure atmospheric pressure, because it was the highest building in London.

## IMMIGRANTS

From the 1540s, London attracted refugees and minority communities who wished to have their own places of worship. When the Dutch congregation was recognized in 1550, it was granted the nave of the former Austin Friars church in Broad Street (where the Dutch church remains today). French

they had been reused as rubble by Sir Christopher Wren in the foundations of the south-west tower of the present cathedral. In 1642 the cathedral was closed by Cromwell's government, and used as stables for soldiers; the roof of the south transept caved in because scaffolding had been sold off and removed. St Paul's Cross, where the works of Martin Luther had been burned in front of Cardinal Wolsey, was taken down.

Attitudes changed with the Restoration of the monarchy in 1660. Four months before the Great Fire in 1666, a commission that included Wren himself as a young scientist, was

Protestants occupied the chapel of St Anthony's Hospital in Threadneedle Street. By the mid-17th century London was also a major focus of Nonconformist activity. The Quakers met in several places from 1654 and acquired their own burial ground at Bunhill Fields, north of the City, in 1661. In 1655 Oliver Cromwell allowed the Jews to return to England; they established themselves and their synagogues around Aldgate, sparking their long and enduring association with the East End of London.    **JS**

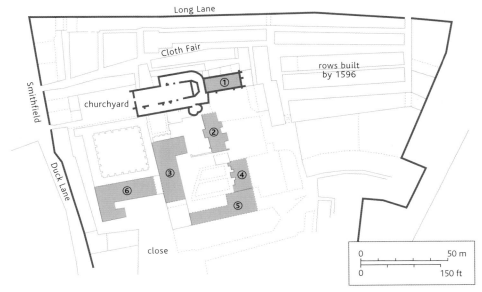

**courtiers' houses created from former monastic buildings**
① Sir Percival Hart
② Mr Jarvis
③ Lord Abergavenny
④ Sir Edward Barrett
⑤ Sir Henry Carey
⑥ Sir Walter Mildmay, then Sir Thomas Neale
— precinct boundary

Map labels: Long Lane, Cloth Fair, rows built by 1596, Smithfield, churchyard, Duck Lane, close

0 — 50 m
0 — 150 ft

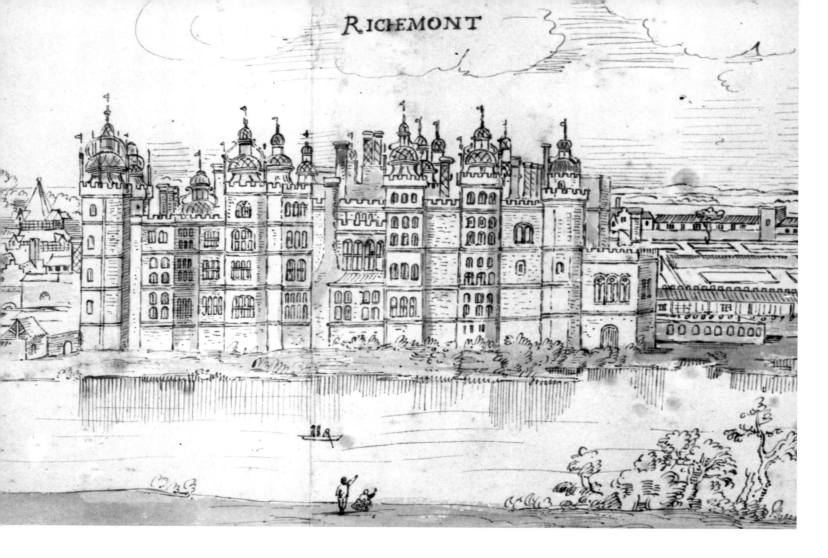

# ROYALTY & ROYAL HOUSES

Henry VIII became the most prolific palace-builder in British royal history. Many of his most important new, remodelled or newly acquired palaces were in London or its immediate vicinity.

**Richmond Palace**
*This view of Henry VII's palace at Richmond, by A. van den Wyngaerde, c.1558–62, is from across the Thames. Little more than the gatehouse now remains. Henry's daughter Elizabeth I died here in 1603. Most of the palace was later destroyed by Oliver Cromwell.*

London has always been a focus for royalty and the Court. In the Tudor period, one of the ultimate expressions of royal power and magnificence were the monarch's houses, particularly during the reign of Henry VIII (r. 1509–47). Little remains today of his building obsession apart from Hampton Court, St James's and Eltham, but in these great edifices we can still catch a glimpse of his passion for architecture and magnificence.

As well as extending and improving palaces he already owned, Henry accumulated new properties throughout his reign, either through the Dissolution or from unwilling courtiers. By his death in 1547 he possessed over fifty houses, more than any other monarch before or since, with twenty-one in the London area. They provided the setting for many major political events and acted as a playground of the favoured aristocracy. Henry's expenditure on building was enormous – but many of his houses were sold off or given away after his death by his children and other subsequent monarchs.

It may have been Henry's father who encouraged his passion for architecture. Henry VII (r. 1486–1509) rebuilt some of the medieval houses that he had gained on his accession, spending at least £20,000 on creating an elegant palace at Sheen (renamed Richmond), the design of which was influenced by the grand castles he had stayed in while an exile in France. He also renovated large parts of Greenwich Palace, including the construction of an impressive river frontage. This palace went on to become one of the favourite residences of Henry VIII and his daughter Elizabeth I.

## BRIDEWELL

At the start of Henry VIII's reign, Westminster Palace was the seat of royal power. However, a fire in 1512 destroyed most of the king's lodgings there, leaving him without a residence in London. Soon after this, he began to build a palace in the City at Bridewell, near the River Fleet. Construction was finished in 1522, in time for the visit of the Holy Roman Emperor Charles V. Charles's entourage stayed in Bridewell, while Charles himself lodged at Blackfriars next door. The two buildings were linked for the duration of the visit by a gallery that stretched between them across the Fleet.

Bridewell was also the place where Henry began his attempts to divorce his first wife, Catherine of Aragon, in 1528. However, the palace later fell from favour, particularly after plague broke out nearby. Finally, Henry's son Edward VI gave it to the City of London as a workhouse for the poor in 1553.

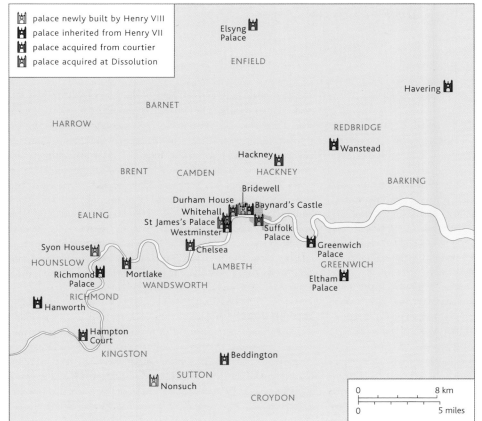

## WHITEHALL

Two of Henry's greatest acquisitions were the spoils derived from the fall from power of his chief minister Cardinal Wolsey in 1529 – York Place and Hampton Court. York Place was the traditional London seat of the archbishops of York, near Westminster Palace. Wolsey's five-year rebuild had made it one of the most sumptuous in London. Henry seized and extended the palace and it became his main residence. He changed its name to Whitehall.

The muddled appearance of Whitehall's exterior belied the richness of its interior. It was awkwardly divided by King Street, which ran from Charing Cross to Westminster, but the two sides were linked by two gateways. The principal royal lodgings were on the Thames side, and Henry – a keen sportsman – built a large leisure complex to the north of the road, consisting of tennis courts, bowling alleys, a cockpit and a tiltyard for jousting. Inside, the palace was richly decorated with coats of arms, tapestries, elaborate painting and gilded ceilings.

## NONSUCH

Another of Henry's passions was hunting and he enclosed huge areas of land around many of his houses to provide hunting parks. Large palaces like Hampton Court were surrounded by lodges for use as temporary accommodation on hunting trips. Henry spent thousands of pounds altering and enlarging these lodges.

The most spectacular hunting lodge was Nonsuch in Surrey. Begun in 1538, its name means 'none like it'. Building work involved demolishing the entire village of Cuddington and the destruction of Merton Priory nearby, to provide stone – 3648 cartloads were used in the foundations. The house consisted of two courts. The north court was of traditional Tudor design of brick with stone facings, but the south court was very different. Its upper two storeys were timber-framed, making it the largest timber-framed house ever built in England. Panels of moulded stucco depicted classical figures; on the timber frames were carved and gilded slates decorated with roses and Renaissance motifs.

An army of workmen was needed to build this stunning house, and many were pressed into service from other parts of the country. Others were foreign; pieces of slate found during archaeological excavations on the site have instructions in French scratched on the reverse. The craftsman responsible for the slate work was an Italian, Nicholas Bellin of Modena, who had worked for Francis I, the king of France, one of Henry's arch rivals.

Despite the enormous expense (over £24,000), Henry's descendants rarely visited this exquisite building. In 1556 Mary I gave Nonsuch to the Earl of Arundel, whose family lived there until they returned the house to Elizabeth I in 1580. Eventually it passed into Stuart hands; Charles II gave the house to his mistress the Duchess of Cleveland in 1669. She demolished it in 1682 and sold all the materials. The only surviving record of the house was a small number paintings made at the time until its site was excavated by archaeologists in 1959.

## HENRY'S LEGACY

The rest of Henry's palaces suffered similar fates. Many were given away or allowed to fall into disrepair. Others flourished, depending on the whim of subsequent monarchs. Elizabeth I (r. 1558–1603) favoured Greenwich, Whitehall and Hampton Court. but built no new residences. She preferred to lodge with chosen courtiers in the course of her celebrated progresses around the kingdom, and defer the expense to them – an honour that could bring the unlucky subject to the brink of bankruptcy. **MJ**

**Map legend:**
- palace newly built by Henry VIII
- palace inherited from Henry VII
- palace acquired from courtier
- palace acquired at Dissolution

ENFIELD
Elsyng Palace
BARNET
HARROW
Havering
REDBRIDGE
Wanstead
Hackney
HACKNEY
BARKING
BRENT
CAMDEN
Bridewell
Durham House
Whitehall
St James's Palace
Westminster
Baynard's Castle
EALING
Suffolk Palace
Greenwich Palace
Syon House
Chelsea
GREENWICH
HOUNSLOW
LAMBETH
Richmond Palace
Mortlake
WANDSWORTH
Eltham Palace
RICHMOND
Hanworth
Hampton Court
KINGSTON
Beddington
SUTTON
Nonsuch
CROYDON

0 — 8 km
0 — 5 miles

# TRADE & INDUSTRY IN TUDOR & STUART LONDON

From the mid-16th century a growing demand for manufactured goods led to the creation of new industries in London. London merchants also began to seek markets further afield.

Although woollen cloth remained London's principal export well into the 17th century – between 1503 and 1609, seventy-two of the ninety-seven Lord Mayors of London made their money in cloth – the nature of the trade changed. Heavier cloths exported to northern and eastern Europe were replaced in importance by lighter-weight woollens going to southern Europe. London remained the main English hub of the trade. Provincial cloth merchants brought their goods from the Cotswolds, Somerset, East Anglia and Yorkshire to Blackwell Hall on Basinghall Street for inspection, after which they were ready to be purchased for export by one of the London cloth dealers. Most of this trade went through Antwerp, the most important European port for English ships until the mid-16th century. Ships returned with linens, silks, wines, spices, sugar, dyes and iron. From 1496, the Company of Merchants Adventurers held an effective monopoly of English trade with Antwerp. The company had been founded in 1407 and was re-chartered in 1564. It was largely controlled by the Mercers, and included many of the wealthiest merchants in London. Its power increased with the expulsion of the Hanseatic League from London in 1598, only diminishing with the rise of the Levant Company in the mid-17th century.

From the mid-16th century, war, the stagnation of the northern European cloth market and an increased access to international markets led to a change in London's axis of trade. New mercantile trading companies allowed London merchants to deal directly with foreign traders, cutting out European middle-men. These companies were also a means of financing England's fledgling colonies and were set up by royal charter, which granted them a monopoly on trade with a particular country or region. The companies were financed by private investors who purchased a share of the joint stock. After the Merchants Adventurers, the first chartered company was the Muscovy or Russia Company in 1553, followed by the Spanish Company (1577), the Levant Company (1581), the East India Company (1600), the Virginia Company (1606), the French Company (1611) and the Providence Island Company (1629), among others. The most successful was the East India Company, which monopolized trade between England and the Far East for over 200 years. It operated from several sites in the city, initially in Philpott Lane, then Bishopsgate, before leasing Lord Craven's house in Leadenhall Street, which became the site of East India House. A new shipyard and wet dock was built for the company at Blackwall, and when the New Exchange was opened on the Strand in 1609, members of the royal family were presented with goods from India and China.

**Tin-glazed earthenware plate, 1600**
*This plate, possibly made at Aldgate, is the earliest-known dated piece of English delftware. The central scene is generally considered to be a visualization of the City, or the Tower, of London.*

**Venetian glass**
*This optic-blown bowl, decorated with applied blue glass trails, is an example of the high-status, fine glass vessels that were imported from Venice.*

## NEW TRADE NETWORKS

By the mid-17th century, the nature of London's trading networks and markets had changed dramatically. Virginia tobacco had replaced tobacco from the Spanish West Indies, and sugar from the British West Indies had replaced imports from Brazil through Portugal. Pepper, long imported from India through Europe, was now brought directly to London by the East India Company, along with indigo, saltpetre and, by the late 17th century, cheap textiles. By 1700, a third of all England's imports were from Asia and America. Many of these commodities were then re-exported to continental Europe. At the same time, however, new markets in the south and west of England were opening up, gradually leading to the end of London's complete dominance of English trade.

The 16th and 17th centuries also saw changes that made maritime access to London easier. In 1517 Henry VIII established Trinity House, which supplied pilots to help guide ships along the coast and the Thames. Advancements in map-making meant that by the late 17th century these waters were better charted. The growth of trade meant that a bewildering number and range of vessels now docked in London, often making the collection of duty difficult. Concerns over the latter, and also about smuggling, led to the establishment of twenty 'legal quays' in 1558. These all lay along the north bank of the Thames between London Bridge and the Tower. Goods had to be unloaded and checked at these quays and duty collected – customs revenue doubled after their establishment. The 17th century also saw the growth of London's eastern suburbs, close to the deep-water port and docks at Blackwall. Trades such as map-making and shipbuilding became established here and existing settlements such as Wapping, Limehouse and Ratcliff grew, while new ones, such as Shadwell, were established.

## IMPORTING SKILLS

Domestic trade continued much as before. Food such as butter, cheese, grain and livestock mainly came from the surrounding counties, but also from further afield. From the 16th century, market gardening was increasingly popular and local produce replaced imports from Holland and France. Wood for fuel was also sourced locally, as was much of the pottery used in London, while coal was still imported from Newcastle.

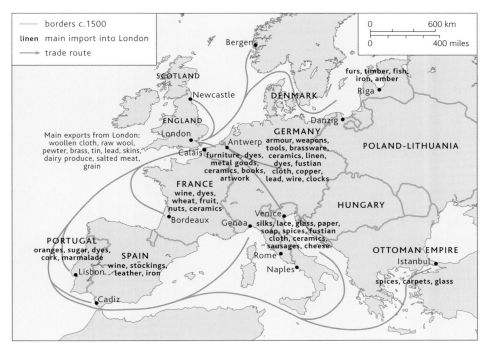

a group of German sword-smiths arrived and set up a workshop in Hounslow, producing swords for military and private purchase. Fine glassware was formerly imported from Venice, but in 1567, Jean Carré set up a glassworks in the former priory of the Crutched Friars near the Tower; a Venetian, Jacobo Verzelini, took over the works in 1572. In the 1580s, Guido Andries and Jacob Janssen set up the first tinglaze (Delftware) pottery in London in the priory buildings of Holy Trinity, Aldgate, and by 1612 tin-glazed wares were also being produced at kilns in Southwark and Lambeth. By the late 17th century, there were some 721 different occupations in the City of London alone. **JK**

**Tin-glazed tiles, c. 1570–1650**
*These are typical of the tiles that were either imported directly from the Low Countries or produced at kilns in London.*

**London's trade c. 1450–1500**
London's trade (left) stretched as far as Scandinavia in the north and Turkey in the southeast.

**London's trade c. 1660**
London's trade (right) was now worldwide, with flourishing links with the Americas, West Africa, India and the East Indies.

From about 1600, a host of new crafts and industries flourished in London. The first patent was granted in England in 1552, and some 200 were granted during the reigns of Elizabeth I and James I – many to foreigners on condition that they pass on their skills to local workers. Religious unrest in mainland Europe meant that many craftsmen were eager to travel to England. It is estimated that from 1550 to 1585 40,000 to 50,000 Huguenots may have arrived from the southern Netherlands. Henry VIII brought over skilled Italian armourers in 1515 and established a Royal Armoury in Southwark, moving to Greenwich in 1520, where armourers from northern Germany were employed. In the 1630s,

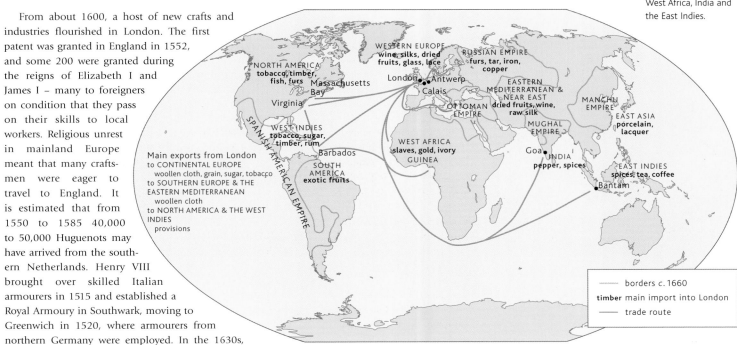

# THE SCHOOLS OF TUDOR & STUART LONDON

The education available to the citizens of Tudor and Stuart London was the best in the country. As a consequence, Londoners enjoyed the highest rates of literacy.

**Greek grammar**
*A Greek grammar compiled by William Camden, headmaster of Westminster School, and published in 1598.*

At the beginning of the Tudor period, a school education was largely the preserve of upper- and middle-class boys, despite the fact that many schools were free. The vast majority of girls did not receive any formal instruction. By the end of the 17th century, however, education had improved considerably – there were more schools, a greater variety of subjects being taught and literacy had increased dramatically for both men and women.

In 1179 Pope Alexander III had made it obligatory for cathedrals and monasteries to maintain schools. In the early 16th century, most London schools were still run by the Church, although a few had been set up by individuals or city companies. The Dissolution threatened an educational crisis but, in the event, many schools were re-established, either by City companies or by the Crown. St Peter's School at Westminster was re-founded in 1543 as 'the King's Grammar School at Westminster'.

The monastic school of the Hospital of St Thomas of Acon on Cheapside became the Mercers' Chapel Grammar School. Old monasteries were also turned into new schools. Henry VIII gave the house of the Greyfriars near Newgate to the City of London, which opened it as an orphanage called Christ's Hospital in 1552. The orphans, both boys and girls, were taught as well as housed and the school quickly developed a good reputation.

## TYPES OF SCHOOL

A 'petty school' was where children learnt the alphabet and the Lord's Prayer, but not writing. These schools were often no more than informal arrangements between pupils and teachers, and a licence to teach was easily obtained. Educational manuals of the time boasted that tailors, weavers and shopkeepers could use them to teach 'the petties' while they worked. Elementary teaching was often done by invalids and paupers as a means of support.

Grammar schools for boys were common. Their founders and teachers, such as John Colet, founder of St Paul's School (see right) in 1509, established curriculums that were followed with little change into the Victorian age. 'Grammar' meant learning Latin, Greek and, in some cases, Hebrew – not English. Most grammar schools in London were free and in theory were provided for the poor boys of the parish. All, however, levied certain charges, which would have deterred truly impoverished parents. At St Saviour's Grammar School on Bankside, boys had to pay a one-off entrance fee of two shillings and sixpence, and two pence a quarter for 'rods and brooms'. They also had to supply a pound of candle wax every winter. At the Merchant Taylors' School, 250 boys were

**London schools**
London schools, including Inns of Court and Chancery, in the 16th and 17th centuries.

Map legend:
- Church grammar schools
- Livery company schools
- other schools
- Inns of Court with date of earliest record
- Inns of Chancery with date of earliest record
- major road
- built-up area

taught free, 50 had to pay two shillings and two pence per quarter and 100 had to pay five shillings per quarter. All boys were expected to give money to the master on special occasions, to cover the cost of feasts and prizes.

City companies provided several grammar schools. St Paul's School and the Mercers' School on Cheapside were run by the Mercers, the Merchant Taylors ran a school on Suffolk Lane, and the Coopers' Company one on Schoolhouse Lane in Ratcliff, from 1540. Robert Aske, a member of the Haberdashers' Company, founded a school in Hoxton in 1690; the Brewers ran Owen's School in Islington from 1613 and the Drapers had their Greencoat School on modern Greenwich High Road from 1685.

## PRACTICAL EDUCATION

A grammar school education was almost entirely based on the 'classics' but there were schools that taught more practical subjects. At Owen's School and St Olave's in Southwark boys learnt the 'casting of accounts', a useful skill for would-be apprentices. Children could also go to Bridewell, a workhouse in Henry VIII's old palace near Blackfriars, to learn trades, spinning, weaving and tapestry. A Mathematical School was founded by Charles II at Christ's Hospital in 1673, for training forty boys in navigation and arithmetic before being apprenticed into the navy or onto merchant ships. For other specialist subjects, adults could attend lectures at Gresham College, founded by Sir Thomas Gresham in 1575, and held at his house in Bishopsgate Street from 1596. These were free public lectures on Divinity, Astronomy, Music, Geometry, Law, Physic and Rhetoric and paid for by revenue from the Royal Exchange.

Students of law went to the preparatory schools of the Inns of Chancery before studying further at the Inns of Court. By 1600 the educational role of the Inns of Chancery had diminished and students began to enrol directly to the Inns of Court where their legal education would last for seven to eight years. Here they would hear lectures given by senior barristers as well as learning

history, music and dancing to prepare them for the social circles in which they would move once they were qualified.

Throughout the Tudor and Stuart period, opportunities for women to learn increased, though school fees were often high. From the late 16th century, foreign women escaping religious persecution in Europe came to London and set up small schools. Anness Deger worked as a French teacher in Tenter Alley, Southwark, in 1618 and Marry Lemaire from Antwerp kept a school in Glean Alley, Southwark, from 1578 to 1618. In the 17th century, gentlewomen went to private schools in the suburbs where they learnt reading, writing, music, dancing and housewifery for around £20 per year. By 1690, the proportion of literate London women had increased from 16 per cent in the late 1500s to 48 per cent. From 1698, the Society for Promoting Christian Knowledge began to set up free charity schools that also accepted girls – by 1705 there were fifty-six of these schools in London, in places such as Lewisham, Spitalfields, Whitechapel and Wimbledon.

London was at the forefront of a trend towards increased availability of education that was spreading across England. By the end of the 17th century, many London parishes had a free boys' grammar school and there were many freelance teachers. But it was only with the foundation of charity schools that education became more available for the poor. Children were still trained only for their expected position in life – poor boys and girls left school early and were apprenticed into trades. Wealthy boys went to university and their sisters were 'finished' in suburban schools before being married. Today's concept of a basic academic education for all was not considered desirable in Tudor and Stuart Britain. **MJ**

# PRINTERS & BOOKSELLERS

London was the national centre of the book trade; there were more bookshops in the city per capita than in any other part of the kingdom.

**Heart of the book trade**
*The north transept of St Paul's Cathedral, with bookshops crammed between the buttresses. Painted by John Gipkyn in 1616.*

One surprising outcome of the spread of literacy in Tudor London was the removal in 1599 of the 'common privy' in St Paul's Churchyard to make way for a new bookshop. The invention of the moveable-type printing press in the mid-15th century brought books to a wider audience and at a price many could afford, but improvements in literacy and education had come about slowly. When William Caxton (*c.* 1422–91) established his press, the first in London, 'at the sign of the Red Pale' in Westminster in 1476, he had little competition. Within a few years, another press had opened in Dowgate (near modern Cannon Street station), and after Caxton's death there were several printing presses operating in London, mostly in Fleet Street and at several locations in the parish of St Dunstan's in the west. By 1500, the printers were part of a community of some 300 craftworkers employed in the making and selling of books in the capital, and London had become the leading centre of the book trade in Britain.

The precincts of St Paul's Cathedral and its immediate environs had long been the nucleus of the book trade, and many of the sheds, stalls and shops in the churchyard and neighbouring lanes were occupied by stationers, booksellers and bookbinders. This location offered distinct commercial advantages. Many of the city's scholastic and educational institutions were located nearby, including St Paul's School and the grammar schools in St Martin le Grand and St Mary-le-Bow. Doctor's Commons, the 'common house' of the civil lawyers, stood in St Paul's Churchyard, and a little further afield were the legal scriveners in Holborn and Chancery Lane and the Inns of Court. This concentration of traders specializing in different aspects of the same business was also convenient for the book buyer, who could stroll around the area making choices from the huge variety of specialist texts on sale, in many different languages.

## THE RISE OF ENGLISH

Partly as a result of Caxton's determination to publish texts in the vernacular, English became standardized and was gradually adopted as the language of choice in the printing industry. The spread of Renaissance humanism and the Reformation also contributed to the demand for books in English, and a growing number of people shared Montaigne's view that 'learning cannot be too common, and the commoner the better'. Latin, however, remained the international language of scholarship, science and philosophy and when William Salisbury visited the bookshops around St Paul's in 1550 to look for a book in English on the spheres and heavens, he could not find one. Having tried many bookshops in the churchyard, he then 'returned backe even the same way … and asked agayne for the same workes in laten, wherof there were .iii or .iiii of sondrye Aucthoures brought and shewed unto me'. During

**St Paul's Churchyard in 1600**
Thos plan shows the concentration of bookshops. 'Right round the church dwell the booksellers and binders where all manner of fine books may be had for sale.'

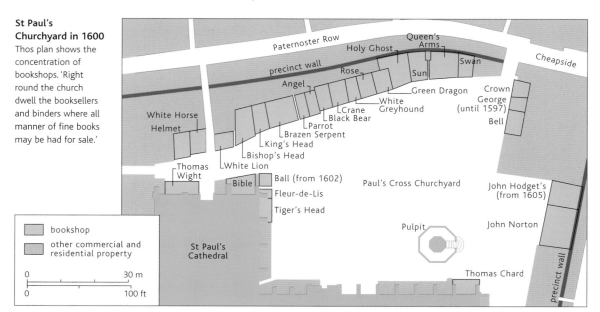

94

and businessmen frequenting the taverns and, from 1652, the coffee houses, clustered around the Exchange. Among the more important works published and distributed from these shops was Shakespeare's *Love's Labours Lost* in 1598 and in the same year *A Survey of London* by John Stow, the first real guidebook to London. **HF**

Elizabeth's reign, a growing pride in the richness of the vernacular found expression in the publication of the first English grammar in 1586, and English translations of foreign texts were much in demand.

By 1600 some London book dealers and traders had started to move away from St Paul's Churchyard, setting up shops in Holborn and the Strand, and in particular in the area around the Royal Exchange in the heart of the City. Here, specialist books and pamphlets were sold to serve the needs of the mercantile community and those engaged in international trade. Almanacs, travel books, guides, maps, information and news items found a ready market among the traders

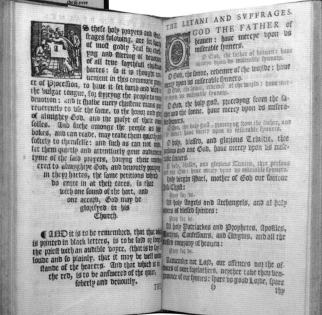

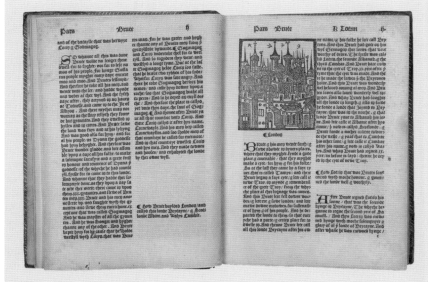

**The Chronicles of England, 1497**

*Originally compiled by William Caxton in 1480, this chronicle gives an account of the history of England from the time that the legendary 'Albyne with his susters entred into this isle' until the accession of Edward IV. The work was in constant demand and was regularly reprinted; this edition was printed in 1497 by Caxton's successor, Wynkyn de Worde.*

## A BESTSELLING LIST

The aptly named Wynkyn de Worde was the most prolific printer and publisher of early Tudor England. A native of Worth (the real origin of his familial name) in Alsace Lorraine, de Worde came to England in 1496 to work with William Caxton at the Sign of the Red Pale in Westminster. Following Caxton's death in 1491, de Worde took over the business and expanded its operation, acquiring additional premises in the neighbourhood. For the next few years he continued to use Caxton's impress and issued a number of reprints of popular works such as the *Golden Legend* and *The Chronicles of England*.

But de Worde had spotted a gap in the market and he was soon issuing romances, devotional works, instructional aids and manuals, books on husbandry and household management, children's books, books on marriage guidance and medical treatises. Realizing that he would attract a broader range of customers if he relocated nearer the City, de Worde moved to Fleet Street in 1500/1 and opened up new premises at the sign of the Sun, in the parish of St Brides. By 1509, he had acquired another retail outlet at the very centre of London's book trade in St Paul's Churchyard, and it was here at the sign of Our Lady of Pity that de Worde kept a close eye on his competitors and began to issue a range of educational books and spiritual works for London's religious houses. Wynkyn de Worde died in 1534/5, a respected entrepreneur and leading member of the international book trade, with over 800 titles to his credit.

# DOMESTIC WEALTH & POVERTY

London in 1600 offered huge contrasts. Alongside former church palaces and repurposed monasteries were industrial works and older houses. It was not a Renaissance city like Paris or Rome.

Rich and poor lived in close proximity in Tudor and early Stuart London; there was not yet any move to the suburbs where richer people would try to be separate (that would come after 1630). Houses were built of timber and brick, with an occasional stone wall from long ago surviving, often along a property boundary. Gardens were widespread but small. Along major streets, houses reached five or six storeys; flat lead roofs and balconies appeared at these dizzy heights, where people conversed with neighbours or played music. From about 1600 it seems likely that well-to-do house interiors in London looked like those we know from Dutch paintings by Vermeer or de Hooch. Provision of water was still an acute problem; the larger houses had lead cisterns to collect rain water, and all sizes of house shared wells with neighbours, either in a yard or sometimes intentionally placed in a boundary wall between properties.

Although there was much subdivision of properties and subletting, the idea of the flat or apartment, in which one tenant or family occupied all the rooms on one floor, does not seem to have been current in London at this time, apart from the rooms of lawyers at the Inns of Court. Everybody preferred to have a front door facing the outside world, usually on the ground floor, though it might be to an alley or yard rather than to a street.

The largest houses, as shown in the reconstruction here, were carefully arranged sequences of spaces, with trade rooms towards the street (right in the illustration) and private rooms to the rear; the most private space, furthest from the street, was the garden. At this level the house was a community of family and servants, the building full of mixed uses. In the grandest merchant houses, men and women servants slept in different wings of the house, though there might only be one chamber for each sex. By 1600 some of these mansions had a

## Treswell plan

*An original plan by Ralph Treswell of a group of old timber-framed houses. Treswell (1540–1616/17) was a prolific surveyor of houses and estates, whose clients included Christ's Hospital (as in this example) and the Clothworkers' and Leathersellers' companies.*

## Key

1. Paved passage from Pancras Lane (just off the drawing to the right)
2. Central yard, with entrances to cellars below the hall (open to the sky)
3. Hall, with main fireplace and largest window
4. Main stair to upper floors
5. Parlour, with a window overlooking the garden
6. Garden, recently reduced in size due to division of the large property
7. Kitchen and butteries
8. Second stair to upper floors
9. Warehouse
10. Second warehouse
11. Buttery for the hall, to store drink and drinking vessels
12. Small light well open to the sky

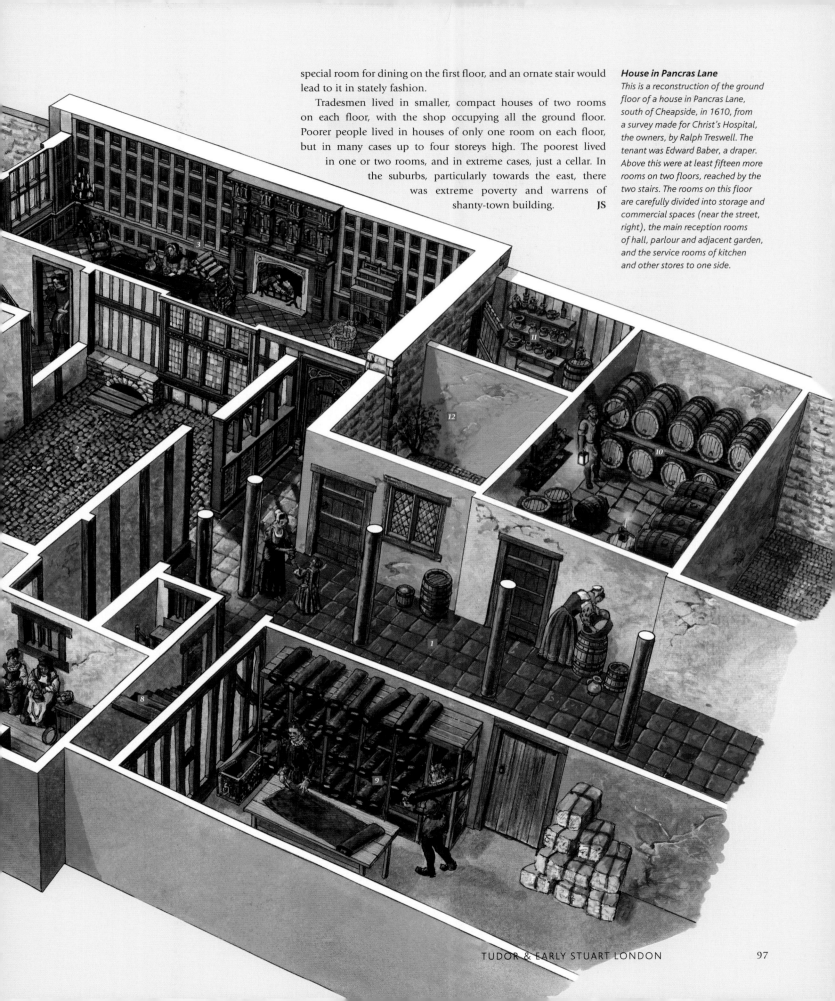

special room for dining on the first floor, and an ornate stair would lead to it in stately fashion.

Tradesmen lived in smaller, compact houses of two rooms on each floor, with the shop occupying all the ground floor. Poorer people lived in houses of only one room on each floor, but in many cases up to four storeys high. The poorest lived in one or two rooms, and in extreme cases, just a cellar. In the suburbs, particularly towards the east, there was extreme poverty and warrens of shanty-town building. **JS**

### House in Pancras Lane

*This is a reconstruction of the ground floor of a house in Pancras Lane, south of Cheapside, in 1610, from a survey made for Christ's Hospital, the owners, by Ralph Treswell. The tenant was Edward Baber, a draper. Above this were at least fifteen more rooms on two floors, reached by the two stairs. The rooms on this floor are carefully divided into storage and commercial spaces (near the street, right), the main reception rooms of hall, parlour and adjacent garden, and the service rooms of kitchen and other stores to one side.*

# THE TUDOR THEATRES

With six or more permanent playhouses and play performances every day but Sunday, London provided a new form of popular entertainment both for court circles and for the general public.

The late 16th century was a seminal period in English drama, with the first construction of purpose-built theatres in which new drama was performed for profit by professional actors to public audiences. Plays were written specifically for these theatres, and the physical appearance of the theatres influenced how the plays were presented and interpreted. In this short period play-writing became the highest form of English literature.

This theatrical development was a London phenomenon. Only the capital could provide the court patronage and audiences of sufficient size to support professional theatres. William Shakespeare (1564–1616) was a key part of the London theatrical world. The most popular theatres were the outdoor playhouses, of which eight were built. The size, shape and nature of these playhouses were for many years the topic of much modern debate. Three of these theatres have now been located through archaeological excavation and, in the case of one, the Rose, its plan almost completely revealed. With a working replica of the Globe theatre built near to its original site on Bankside we now have a better understanding than ever before of the theatre of Shakespeare.

## THE ORIGINS OF PROFESSIONAL THEATRES

London's theatres have a complex origin. In the Middle Ages, religious mystery plays and secular shows were performed in the open air on temporary stages. Plays were also performed in the great halls of the nobility and royalty, and sometimes in the courtyards of galleried inns. These locations provided the model for later purpose-built theatres. Circular or polygonal bear- and bull-baiting arenas provided a model for a new type of outdoor playhouse.

The professional theatre found itself in a peculiar position. The city authorities, seeing any gathering of people as a source of potential unrest, loathed the playhouses. New plays were regarded as an opportunity to challenge authority; a Master of the Revels was made responsible licensing theatres and censoring new plays. In 1574 a law forbade the construction of playhouses within the City of London, so that the first purpose-built public theatres were all in the suburbs. Support for the theatre came from the top and bottom of society: theatres were incredibly popular with average Londoners, but also received patronage and protection from Crown and Court. In this peculiar climate, they prospered. From the late 16th century until 1642, London never had fewer than six playhouses and four regular companies performing daily, except Sundays and during Lent, although the worst ravages of the plague did for a time stop performances.

The outdoor 'amphitheatre' play-houses, however, were a relatively short-term phenomenon. For a while these playhouses were truly democratic, performing the

**The Rose Theatre**
*This reconstruction of the Rose Theatre shows how it it may have appeared when it was first built in 1587, with room for up to 1100 spectators in the galleries and 500 more 'groundlings' in the yard.*

same plays for both court and commoners at affordable prices, comparable to other mass entertainments such as bear- and bull-baiting. Shakespeare was very much part of this movement. Criticized by the university-educated playwrights who were his contemporaries, he could write from first-hand experience as an actor. As the 17th century progressed, however, a class divide began to emerge between the outdoor playhouses and the indoor hall theatres.

as with most other buildings of the time, would have been half-timbered construction using laths (flat wood strips) and plaster as infill between the main frames.

All theatres were closed in 1642 because of the Civil War ban on mass gatherings and Puritan disapproval of popular entertainment. When the ban was lifted after the Restoration the outdoor playhouses did not re-open; it was the more exclusive indoor hall theatres that established the basis for modern theatre.   **HS/JC**

**Early theatres in and around London**
Outdoor playhouses, such as the Rose, were built in Shoreditch and Southwark; elsewhere plays were performed at inns and in private halls.

## HISTORY & REDISCOVERY

The first purpose-built outdoor playhouse, simply called the Theatre, was built in 1576 in Shoreditch. In 1577 the Curtain was built close by and another theatre was built at Newington Butts in Southwark. The first to be built on Bankside was the Rose (see left), constructed in 1587, followed by the Swan in 1595. The Globe theatre was built in 1599 using timbers from the dismantled Theatre. The last Bankside playhouse was the Hope, built in 1614 and designed to double as a bear-baiting arena. Another playhouse, the Fortune, was built in Cripplegate in 1600.

No physical evidence for the Bankside theatres was known until 1989, when the site of the Rose was excavated (see far left). Later the same year a small section of the Globe was uncovered and in 2001 foundations of the Hope theatre were also found. Until the discovery of the Rose, evidence consisted of a few contemporary drawings and panoramic maps. These showed the general shape of the theatres – but the excavation of the Rose has revealed a full working plan.

The Rose was polygonal, although the exact number of sides is not clear. The central area remained open to the sky. The walls were built on chalk foundations (see opposite, far left) with wooden sleeper beams carrying the main structure, which,

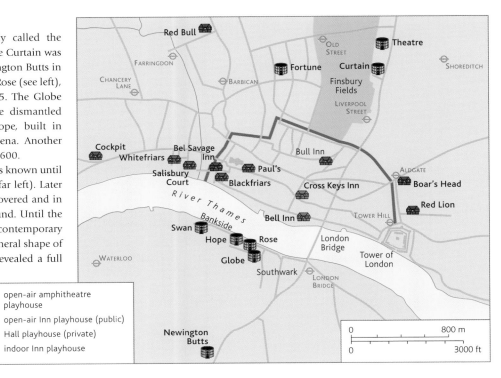

open-air amphitheatre playhouse

open-air Inn playhouse (public)

Hall playhouse (private)

indoor Inn playhouse

# 'A TOWN OF PLEASURE & JOY'

The sights and varied opportunities for entertainment in Tudor London brought visitors to the capital from far and wide. The first tourist guidebooks were produced to cater for them.

Many visitors took the short trip across the Thames to Bankside (see opposite bottom), the principal focus of popular entertainment in the city, with attractions to suit all tastes and budgets. There were playhouses, pleasure gardens, cock-fighting pits, bull- and bear-baiting arenas, taverns, alehouses and brothels – a fascinating mix of culture, vice and dissipation. The Paris Garden, densely planted with large shrubs and trees, was a delightful place during the day, though at night it was described as the 'very bower of conspiracy'. At the nearby Bear Gardens, bulls, bears and other

Byrsa Londinensis *vulgo* the Royal Exchange,

***Royal Exchange, Cornhill***
*Tourist souvenirs, knick-knacks, guidebooks and luxury goods were sold in 150 small shops on the upper floor of the Royal Exchange. This view of the inner court of the Royal Exchange was engraved by Wenceslaus Hollar.*

During the 16th century the cultural advantages of travel became an accepted and valuable part of a gentleman's education. Atlases of cities were published, and travellers began to record their observations in journals and diaries. On the European tourist itinerary, London was regarded as one of *the* places to see. According to the Swiss student Thomas Platter, 'he that sightsees London … may assert without impertinence that he is properly acquainted with England'. Although this view was not shared by all, visitors from home and abroad were struck by the range of attractions available in the capital. London guidebooks appeared for the first time in the 1590s and the major landmarks and places of entertainment became part of the tourist trail.

The Thames was considered one of the 'great singularities' of London, and travel by water was the easiest and quickest way to get around town. Passenger wherries with upholstered seats, embroidered cushions and protective awnings could be hired for a day or evening cruise, darting 'hither and thither across the river, according to the whims of those inside'. London Bridge, with its buildings and narrow arches, was a spectacle to behold, and many visitors admired the swans, the royal barge house and the palaces and gardens along the north bank between the City and Westminster.

animals were baited, and the great English mastiffs that were set upon them, some 200 or so, were trained in public view on Sunday afternoons. Visitors paid two pence to stand and four pence for a seat at the bear-baiting; these spectacles were so popular that over 1000 people sometimes crowded in for a performance. On 13 January 1583 one of the stands collapsed, 'many being killed thereby, more hurt, and all amazed'. The Bear Gardens were closed by Act of Parliament in 1642, but cock-fighting remained popular.

## GARDENS & OPEN SPACES

The open spaces – 'wild areas and pleasure grounds' – surrounding the metropolis were especially appreciated as the city expanded. Gardens and summer houses were created in Finsbury Fields to the north of the City, and the semi-rural taverns and alehouses of Bankside, Deptford, Hackney, Holloway and Chelsea were particularly popular in the spring and summer months. Some proprietors offered special foods or a particular brew to entice customers, such as Lambeth ale and Islington cheesecake. Others provided bowling alleys or a large garden with benches for drinking out of doors. Hyde Park, opened to the public in the early 17th century, offered open spaces for promenades, carriage races, fireworks and bowling;

the Spring Gardens in Westminster, which also opened in the early 17th century, had archery butts, a bathing pond and a water feature attached to a sundial. One visitor recorded that when the gardener observed strangers peering at the dial, he turned a tap to 'plentifully sprinkle those that are standing around'.

## SIGHTS OF THE CITY

One of the most important and popular tourist destinations in the City was the Tower of London. It was an impressive structure, 'a citadel to defend or command the city', but it also served as a royal palace 'for assemblies or treaties [and] a prison of state for the most dangerous offenders'. Encircled by a moat, the Tower housed the state records, a magnificent armoury, the Crown jewels, the royal mint and the royal menagerie. Conducted tours were given by a Yeoman of the Guard and the Master of the Jewel House.

Another magnet for tourists was the Royal Exchange (see left), which opened for business in 1571. Here visitors could watch merchants trading in the morning and evening and browse around 150 shops on the upper floor that sold a wide range of knick-knacks and fancy goods, including books, maps and guides to the city.

Foreign visitors to London were particularly impressed by Cheapside, the City's principal thoroughfare, and Horatio Busino, chaplain to the Venetian ambassador in 1617–18, noted that 'inexpressibly great treasures and vast amount of money may be seen there'. This wide street contained four large fountains or conduits, taverns, merchants' mansions and luxury shops. The goldsmiths' shops at the west end of the street were especially remarkable, 'exceedingly richly furnished continually with gold and silver plate and jewels' and, according to one visitor, surpassing in magnificence those of Florence and Paris.

Just to the north of Cheapside stood the Guildhall, the centre of civic government, where visitors could see the famous statues of the two legendary giants Gogmagog and Corineus (later known as Gog and Magog) that had been paraded in civic pageants and processions since at least the early 15th century. Further to the west loomed the great cathedral of St Paul's. Although it was severely damaged by a lightning strike in 1561, the cathedral's roof walk was open for visitors to enjoy a fine view of the city. The tombs and monuments were a source of wonder, and tourists were amazed by

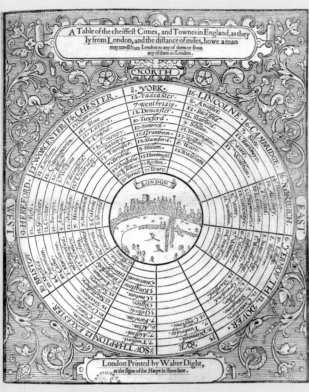

the so-called 'Pervyse of Paul's', a plain middle aisle used between 1550 and 1650 as a common thoroughfare where fashionable young men could idle away the hours, lawyers could meet their clients and people of all sorts could congregate to exchange news.

## A TRIP TO WESTMINSTER

No visit to London was complete without an excursion to Westminster. A penny could buy 'an earful of a most eloquent oration upon our English Kings and Queens', and visitors were encouraged to see the 'marble throne of the Kingdom of Scotland' in the royal chapel. They could also pick up a guide to the 'very splendid monuments' and effigies in the abbey.

The neighbouring galleries, courtyards, gardens and elaborate furnishings of Whitehall Palace were also open to the public; English and foreign tourists alike were mesmerized by the Queen's bath, with water spouting from a grotto of oyster shells and rocks, the great rib bone of a whale in the grounds and the park with deer and other exotic beasts.

The capital had so many delights that it is no wonder that in 1657 James Howell's book *Londinopolis* stated, 'For healthful corporal Recreations, and harmless passe-timmes, London may go into the Van[guard], to any place.' **HF**

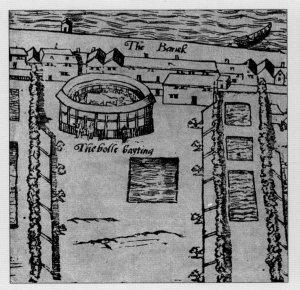

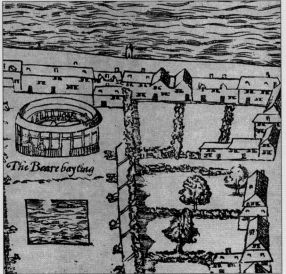

# 'ENDLESS INNS & EATING HOUSES'

London's many and varied catering outlets offered the choicest foods and the widest dining experience in the country, and in some areas one house in five was licensed to sell beer or wine.

**The Ape & Apple from Philip Lane**
*Some tavern keepers spent as much as thirty or forty pounds on the 'gorgeousness' of their signs to promote their business and emphasize their wealth and status in the community.*

When Robert Burton published his discourse *Anatomy of Melancholy* in 1621, he suggested that 'immoderate drinking' was one of the prime causes of unhappiness, and noted with dismay that Londoners flocked 'to the tavern as if they were born to no other end but to eat and drink ...'. Parliament had tried to limit the number of licensed premises in the capital, but by 1618 Londoners were complaining that many of the 'better sort of houses' had been acquired by vintners and converted 'into taverns … to the great inconvenience and disquiet of the neighbours'. A few years later, there were 400 taverns and 1000 alehouses in the City alone. But the situation was worse in the suburbs: in Kent Street, Southwark, 228 alehouses were competing for custom. By the 1660s the proportion of officially licensed premises was as much as one for every five households in certain areas of the city.

Some Londoners felt that the spread of 'tippling houses' posed a threat to social stability, but for others they were the focus of social life, providing food and drink in convivial and often very comfortable surroundings. Alehouses were scattered throughout the city, but the taverns, fairly select establishments licensed to sell wine, were located along the principal thoroughfares with particular concentrations near Whitehall and in the commercial and mercantile areas of the City.

These premises varied in size, from single rooms in a cellar or above a shop to multiple-roomed dwellings occupying a substantial plot with a yard, outhouses, gardens and bowling greens. The fashionable taverns of King Street, Covent Garden, Cheapside and Cornhill were particularly grand, with private dining facilities and a range of comfortable rooms for hire. Equally impressive were the inns on the major axial routes out of town, which provided accommodation for the carriers and travellers arriving from all parts of the kingdom (see map, opposite). A list compiled 'with tedious toyle' in 1637 suggests that the

**Tabard Inn, Southwark**
*The Tabard, later known as the Talbot, was already a famous inn for travellers in the time of Geoffrey Chaucer. It is shown here shortly before its demolition in 1876.*

carriers chose inns en route to their homes; so that every Friday night the carriers from St Albans lodged at the Peacocke in Aldersgate Street, while those from Aylesbury stayed at the George near Holborn Bridge, the Swan in the Strand, the Angel behind St Clement's church and the Bell in Holborn.

## PROTOTYPE GASTRO-PUBS

From the early 17th century, the alehouses and taverns provided a greater choice of food and drink, and some began to gain a reputation for their fine cuisine and varied menus. The Ship tavern in Old Fish Street was famed for its Friday night suppers, the Crown in Leadenhall Street for pies and the Saracen's Head in Islington for cream and cheesecakes. But others were known for serving meagre portions and bad food at high prices. Locket's Tavern in Charing Cross was infamous for '20 shillings worth of sauce upon ten pennyworths of meat'. Some taverns offered an 'ordinary', or fixed-price meal, in addition to their normal menus, possibly at special tables, but the term 'ordinary' also applied to separate eating-houses such as Pontack's in Abchurch Lane, which specialized in French food and wines. Prices varied enormously from sixpence at the Black Eagle in Holborn for 'stale batchelors [and] thrifty attorneys' to the extremely expensive ordinary at Shaver's Hall in Charing Cross, which charged as much as six shillings per meal.

## COOKSHOPS & FAST FOOD

The other specialized eating-house in London was the cookshop, which played a crucial role in the diet of Londoners by offering quickly prepared hot meals for those without cooking facilities or the time and inclination to cook for themselves. Cookshops supplied roast meats and pies as well as partly cooked and ready-to-eat convenience foods to take home, and because the demand for these establishments was considerable they were scattered around the capital with particular concentrations near Westminster Gate, Cookes Row in the Vintry, Eastcheap, Bread Street and around Smithfield. The cookshops of Pie Corner, Giltspur Street and Cock Lane catered for the market traders and visitors to the annual Bartholomew Fair, whereas those in Chick Lane served

**Southwark inns and taverns c.1550**

This map shows just how many hostelries, taverns and alehouses catered for travellers arriving in or leaving London by the road to the south. Only the George survives today, though it was rebuilt in 1676 and partly demolished in 1899.

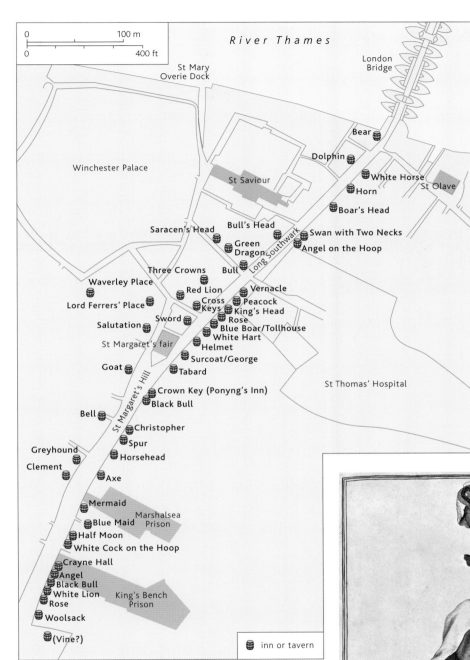

0    100 m
0    400 ft

*River Thames*

London Bridge

St Mary Overie Dock

Bear

Dolphin

White Horse

St Olave

Horn

Boar's Head

Swan with Two Necks

Angel on the Hoop

St Saviour

Winchester Palace

Saracen's Head

Bull's Head

Green Dragon

Bull

Three Crowns

Waverley Place

Red Lion

Vernacle

Cross Keys

Peacock

Lord Ferrers' Place

Sword

King's Head

Rose

Blue Boar/Tollhouse

White Hart

Salutation

St Margaret's fair

Helmet

Surcoat/George

Goat

Tabard

St Thomas' Hospital

Crown Key (Ponyng's Inn)

Black Bull

Bell

Christopher

Spur

Greyhound

Horsehead

Clement

Axe

Mermaid

Marshalsea Prison

Blue Maid

Half Moon

White Cock on the Hoop

Crayne Hall

Angel

Black Bull

White Lion

King's Bench Prison

Rose

Woolsack

(Vine?)

🛢 inn or tavern

*Long Southwark*

*St Margaret's Hill*

***Tankard***
*Londoners preferred to drink from pewter. This mug is inscribed with the name and address of the tavern proprietor 'Walter Barden att ye Hole in ye Wall in Pearle Street Near king Street Wapping/1706' and the words 'Stop Thife'.*

Londoners liked to go to the hamlet of Pimlico on Sunday afternoons for pudding pies and hot pies; gingerbread and nuts were sold from the stalls on Fleet Bridge. Pancakes were a speciality of Rosemary Lane and pies were also sold at The Farthing Pie House in Marylebone Fields.        **HF**

'measly pork and neck beef' disguised by carrots and marigold leaves, which was nonetheless consumed with relish by the carriers and drovers with 'fat [dribling] down from the corners of their mouths'. Although they were popular, cookshops had a rather unsavoury reputation and many contemporaries complained about the quality of the food and the standards of hygiene and service.

In addition to the foods provided by the main catering establishments, Tudor and Stuart Londoners could also buy from transient retailers and hawkers who sold shellfish, nuts, fresh fruit and cheap hot snacks. Certain localities specialized in particular types of food: Lambeth was noted for its apple tarts, The Lodge in Hyde Park was famed for its syllabubs, sweetmeats, cheesecakes and fresh cow's milk, and Islington, Hackney, Holloway and Deptford all had a fine reputation for cheesecakes.

***Street hawker***
*'Hot Bak'd Wardens', or stewed pears, were especially popular in winter. This engraving by Marcellus Lauron comes from his Cries of London series (c.1687).*

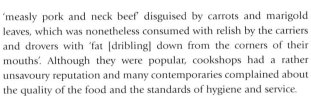

**Westminster Hall,
1097–1401**
*Westminster Hall is the
main medieval survival
of the royal Palace of
Westminster. The lower
parts of its walls date
from 1097–9, but it
was rebuilt in 1394–
1401. This is the north
end, which was
originally adorned
with many statues.*
Underground:
Westminster

**The Banqueting House, Whitehall, 1619–22**
*The Banqueting House is the first great architectural work in
central London by Inigo Jones. It was to be part of a larger royal
palace, never built. King Charles I stepped on to the scaffold
from one of its windows in January 1649.*
Underground: Westminster or Charing Cross

# SURVIVALS
# MEDIEVAL & TUDOR

**St Ethelburga
Bishopsgate, c. 1400**
*This tiny medieval
church survived the
Great Fire of 1666 and
the Blitz, but was badly
damaged by an IRA
bomb in 1993. It has
since been rebuilt to
look as it was before
the blast, and now
serves as a Centre
for Reconciliation
and Peace.*
Underground:
Liverpool Street

**The Queen's House, Greenwich, from 1617**
*Also by Inigo Jones, the Queen's House is an Italianate villa
in Greenwich Park. It was ready in 1637 for Henrietta Maria,
the queen of Charles I. The colonnades that approach
it from both sides date from 1807–16.*
Rail: Greenwich

**The Tower of
London, from
c. 1097**
*Royal fortress,
armoury, menagerie,
prison and place of
execution, home of
the Crown Jewels –
the Tower has a long
history. This image
shows medieval and
Tudor outer walls,
refurbished in the
19th century.*
Underground:
Tower Hill

**Staple Inn,
Holborn, 1586**
*This part of the Inn
was radically restored
in 1894 to look like
a Tudor building in the
popular imagination.
It is, however, our
best example of what
many buildings in
Shakespeare's
London looked like.*
Underground:
Chancery Lane

**Prince Henry's Room, Fleet Street, c. 1610**
*This house was also called the Prince's Arms. It has been moved back several feet to widen the roadway, and restored. The attic storey has a balustrade to the street, a feature of many Tudor houses.*
Underground: Temple

**The Guildhall, 1410**
*The medieval building at the core of the City's government can be seen behind its porch, originally of the same date but refaced in the 18th century with unusual elements derived from Indian architecture.*
Underground: Bank

**Westminster Abbey west front**
*The porch is originally of 1338–43, the west front above of the 16th century and capped by Hawksmoor's towers of 1735–45. The porch lost many of its statues, perhaps in the 16th century; these were replaced in 1989–98 by statues of four Virtues at the sides and ten 20th-century martyrs above, chosen from every continent.*
Underground: Westminster

**Lambeth Palace gateway, 1490**
*This is the gate to the palace of the Archbishop of Canterbury, built by Archbishop John Morton. Though restored, it still shows some of the original diapering, the diamond-shapes in burnt brick that are a feature of palaces of the time.*
Underground: Westminster or Lambeth North

**St Helen Bishopsgate, c. 1500**
*This view of the west front shows the unusual two naves; on the left was the nave of the nunnery church, on the right the nave of the parish. This is still an active parish church in the City of London, restored after damage in an IRA bomb of 1992.*
Underground: Liverpool Street

# LATER STUART LONDON

Since the Middle Ages, successive kings and queens had needed London to be on their side for the monarchy to exist. In 1642 the Londoners demonstrated so forcefully against Charles I that he left town. Fatally, he resigned the assets of London to his opponents: the Tower, the militia, money and materials. During the Civil War of 1642–9 London, on balance, suffered economically. But even this was not without odd benefits. John Evelyn, an early campaigner against air pollution in London, noted that when the supplies of coal from Newcastle, for thousands of domestic hearths, were interrupted by the war, orchards and gardens in the centre of London bore 'plentiful and infinite quantities of fruits'.

By 1650, one adult in six in England had direct experience of London life, either by being born there, moving there or dying there. Much of the City of London was destroyed in the Great Fire of 1666, but it was rebuilt almost totally on the same pattern as before. By 1700, London as a whole was probably the largest city in Europe, with nearly 600,000 inhabitants in the metropolitan conurbation. The City of London was where the money lay, and increasingly the hub of a new commercial and overseas empire; but Westminster, around the royal court, was the centre of fashion and politics even more than it had been in the time of Henry VIII. Especially after the Restoration of Charles II as monarch in 1660, the West End of London became a national epicentre of manners and taste. The existence of great estates owning much of the land around Westminster led to the development of 'squares', that is areas of residential development controlled by one noble or institutional owner, giving exclusive character to an area.

There were also changes in the way people thought and acted. Age-old values were being replaced by more individual thinking. New groups were breaking away from traditional society. Consumption habits became more fluid, and by 1700 people were indulging more than before in consumer goods.

**The Great Fire, 1666**
This view of the Fire, by an unknown Dutch artist,
shows the evening of Tuesday 4 September. The
details of many buildings are accurate, showing
that the artist had local knowledge.

# FROM CIVIL WAR TO RESTORATION

A Parliamentary stronghold in the Civil War, London was the scene of intense political and religious debate, regicide, Commonwealth rule and the coronation of the new king.

London had a strange Civil War. The city was hugely important as the political capital and because of its wealth and population, and arguably the war began in London with the demands of Parliament and the hasty withdrawal of King Charles I from Whitehall, first to Hampton Court and then to Oxford in January 1642. However, London was not the scene of any fighting. The closest it came to witnessing hostilities was in November 1642, when the Royalist army, having just taken Brentford, turned back at Turnham Green in the face of a much larger force made up of regular Parliamentarian troops under the leadership of the Earl of Essex and the capital's own Trained Bands (local militia). The Royalists withdrew to Hounslow, and then eventually to Oxford, which became the Royalist capital. This proved a turning point in the war. Parliamentary control of London was not threatened again, and without London the Royalists could not win the war.

The London 'mob' of hostile crowds had been instrumental in Charles' flight from the capital. While the City leaders had remained pro-Royalist in the approach to war, ordinary Londoners had mostly taken the side of the Parliamentary opposition; rumours had circulated that the king was plotting a pro-Catholic coup But the masses, including the hordes of apprentices, did not stay universally loyal to Parliament, and in 1643 demonstrations for peace had to be broken up by soldiers. A weak economy, political unrest and the attempt to impose new religious controls led to further disturbances.

London played a crucial part in funding the Parliamentary cause. This was not only because of the city's size and wealth; it also became proportionately more important because it was difficult for Parliament to raise taxes or funds in Royalist areas of the country. The loans of city financiers were also crucial; among other things, these paid for the formation of the New Model Army, a volunteer citizens' army. As things turned out, the greatest fear of civilian populations – occupation by armed forces – befell London only after the end of the war, when the New Model Army was garrisoned there in 1647 and again in 1648. However, the troops appear to have been relatively well ordered in both cases.

## DEFENDING THE CITY

The most obvious physical impact of the war on London's topography was the circuit of defensive works that was constructed between the autumn 1642 and the spring of 1643. Erected with the support of specialist engineers from Holland and a voluntary labour force of men, women and children from every part of London, these works were the longest continuous defensive circuit to be built in Britain since Roman times. The defences consisted of 18 miles of linked trenches known as 'lines of communication', encircled by earthworks and a ring of twenty-four forts (see the map on this page). Although the defences were never put to the test, they did provide a formidable barrier and enabled the authorities to control the traffic of goods and people into and out of the city. Much of the circuit was dismantled in 1647, but some of earthworks and forts survived

**London from Civil War to Restoration**
The line of Civil War defences protected the entire city, far beyond the old circuit of the medieval wall.

Map labels:
0 — 1.5 km / 0 — 1 mile
Fort New River Head
Fort Kingsland Road
Fort Hackney Road
EUSTON
OLD STREET
Batteries 'near Bedford House' (Great Ormond Street)
Fort or battery Brick Lane
Jan. 1661: exhumed body of Oliver Cromwell hanged and decapitated at Tyburn
CHANCERY LANE
4 Jan. 1642: five MPs fleeing royal arrest take refuge in the City
LIVERPOOL STREET
Fort or battery Whitechapel Road
Forts and batteries Great Russell Street, Wardour Street
HOLBORN
ALDGATE
1642–3; City wall reinforced
St Paul's
CANNON STREET
Battery 'Oliver's Mount' (Mount Row)
COVENT GARDEN
BLACKFRIARS
River Thames
London Bridge
Tower of London
Fort or battery Wapping
Forts Hyde Park Corner
30 Jan. 1649: execution of Charles I, Whitehall Palace
EMBANKMENT
Southwark
July 1642: Royalist Lord Mayor imprisoned in the Tower
WATERLOO
WESTMINSTER
Westminster Abbey
Jan. 1649: trial of Charles I, Westminster Hall
Fort Blackman Street
Battery Tothill Fields (Millbank)
Fort St George's Fields (Imperial War Museum)
Fort Kent Street (Old Kent Road)
Fort Vauxhall
28 Oct. – 6 Nov. 1647: Putney Debates

Legend: Lines of Communication / built-up area / major road

**Pikeman's helmet**
A Civil War-period helmet, of the type worn by the relatively well-equipped London Trained Bands.

until the end of the 18th century. No contemporary maps have survived, but written descriptions, sketches, place names and other contemporary accounts give some indication of the circuit's structure and extent.

## THE COMMONWEALTH & PROTECTORATE

During the war, London attracted refugees from other parts of the country, and became a centre for political and religious debate. Pamphlets and tracts were published in vast numbers expressing bitterly contrary views. Most radical of the agitators were those know as the Levellers, who met in small groups in London taverns and organized public petitions. They had strong influence in the ranks of Oliver Cromwell's New Model Army. So it was under the auspices of 'the agents of the five regiments of horse, and since by the general approbation of the army' that in October 1647 there appeared *An Agreement of the People for a Firm and Present Peace upon Grounds of Common Right and Freedom* which set our proposals for a fully democratic parliament. From 28 October to 9 November 1647, soldiers and officers of the New Model Army and civilian representatives met in St Mary's church, Putney, to debate formulations for the future constitution of England (the 'Putney Debates'). Although it was a platform for ordinary soldiers and citizens, the debate was inconclusive.

Taken prisoner first in 1647, Charles I was brought to London in January 1649 to face trial for high treason in Westminster Hall. He was executed by beheading on a scaffold in front of the banqueting house of Whitehall Palace on 30 January.

In 1653 Cromwell dismissed Parliament to rule as Lord Protector – king in all but name – making Whitehall Palace his headquarters. Cromwell died in 1658, and was buried in Henry VII's chapel in Westminster Abbey. London diarist John Evelyn described his funeral as 'the joyfullest funeral that ever I saw, for there was none that cried but dogs'. Cromwell was succeeded briefly by his son Richard, but a new Parliament entered into negotiations with Charles I's son, in exile in Holland, to pave the way for his return as king.

### RESTORATION

Charles II returned to England in 1660. He entered London on 29 May, and was publicly acclaimed rightful king at the Royal Exchange. The surviving 'regicides', those who had signed the death warrant of his father Charles I, were arrested and tried for treason. Twelve were condemned to death, and hanged. In January 1661 the body of Oliver Cromwell was exhumed, hanged and decapitated at Tyburn.

On 22 April 1661 the new king processed through London, passing through a series of specially constructed triumphal arches, from the Tower of London to Whitehall, before his coronation at Westminster the following day. A witness records that 'Infinite and innumerable were the acclamations and shouts from all the parts as his Majesty passed along, to the no less joy than amazement of the spectators, who beheld those glorious personages that rid before and behind his Majesty.' Staunchly Parliamentarian at the start of the Civil War, Londoners turned out in force to welcome their returned king.

HS/JC

**Cromwell's death mask**
*After the Restoration, Cromwell's body was exhumed, hanged and decapitated by the Royalist authorities.*

**Bust of Oliver Cromwell**
*Cromwell as Lord Protector, memorialized by Edward Pierce.*

**Charles II enters London, April 1661**
*The king's procession through City of London on 22 April 1661, the day before his coronation, winds through the specially erected triumphal arches. Painting by Dirck Stoop.*

# THE GREAT PLAGUE

*The outbreak of plague in 1665 was a disaster of the first magnitude for London. By the end of the year some 100,000 inhabitants had died, livelihoods were lost and trade suffered.*

**The Great Plague**
*A detail from a plague broadside by John Dunstall showing 'the Greatness of the Calamity and the Violence of the Distemper' in 1665. 1. The sick at home; 2. Shutting up the houses; 3. Fleeing London by boat; 4. Fleeing London by land; 5. Carrying the corpses; 6. Carrying the dead in carts; 7. Burying the dead; 8. Funeral procession; 9. Return to London.*

At the end of December 1665 a small volume appeared in an Aldersgate bookshop entitled *London's Dreadful Visitation: or, a Collection of all the Bills of Mortality for this Present Year*. This compilation of the weekly lists of the dead in each of the 130 parishes of the City charts the progress of the last major outbreak of plague in London and the last epidemic of the disease in England.

In seven months, the bustling city had been transformed into a place of 'dismal solitude' and, according to one eyewitness, 'every day looks with the face of a sabbath-day … shops shut, people rare, very few places to walk about insomuch that the grass begins to spring up in some places … no rattling coaches, no prancing horses, no calling customers, no offering wares, no London cries …'. By the end of the year over a fifth of London's population had died and every town and village within a ten-mile radius was affected.

The plague, primarily a disease of the black rat (*Rattus rattus*), is caused by the bacillus *Yersina pestis*. It is transmitted between rats by fleas, and humans are infected in three main ways: by flea bites; by an open wound contaminated by direct contact with plague-infected material; or (occasionally) by infected breath. After an incubation period of two to six days, victims typically experience flu-like symptoms and discomfort under the arms and in the groin. Swellings or buboes appear with localized inflammation and sub-cutaneous bleeding, accompanied by high fever. Contemporaries record that death typically followed in two to three days. As an epidemic develops, the bacillus becomes more virulent and the pneumonic form of the disease more common. Patients die within a matter of hours, before the more obvious symptoms appear.

Plague was an ever-present threat in medieval and early modern London, but few citizens were prepared for the onslaught of 1665. One noted that 'it kills where it comes without mercy … suddenly [and] sometimes within a few hours after its first approach'. It began just before Christmas 1664, when two men died of a 'spotted fever' in Drury Lane. No further cases were reported for six weeks, although the death rate rose considerably. At the end of February plague began to be reported in the western and northern suburbs and in Southwark. William Boghurst, a physician in St Giles-in-the-Fields, claimed that it began in his parish 'upon the highest ground about London, and the best air.' From the western suburbs it then spread to Holborn and the Strand, with a simultaneous outbreak in the very heart of the City in the parish of St Mary Woolchurch. By the middle of May, the Reverend Thomas Vincent commented that the 'disease begins to so much increase and spread' and in the following month, plague victims appeared in many parishes within the City walls.

As the plague took hold, those who could afford to do so left the capital. Within weeks, trade began to decline and the highways were thronged with refugees. Those who remained behind carried

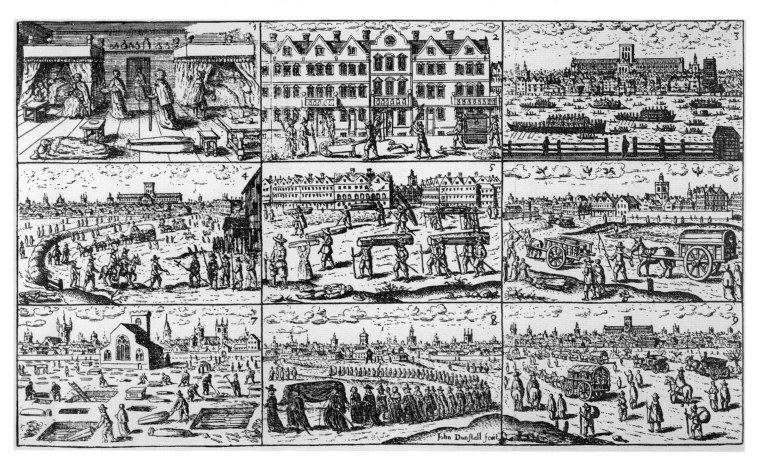

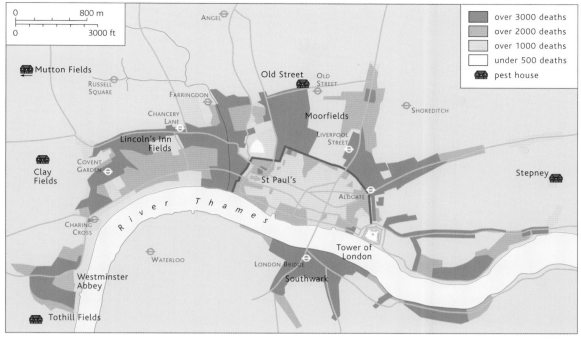

*Map legend:*
- over 3000 deaths
- over 2000 deaths
- over 1000 deaths
- under 500 deaths
- pest house

Map labels: Angel, Mutton Fields, Old Street, Russell Square, Farringdon, Shoreditch, Chancery Lane, Moorfields, Lincoln's Inn Fields, Liverpool Street, Clay Fields, Covent Garden, Stepney, St Paul's, Aldgate, Charing Cross, River Thames, Waterloo, London Bridge, Tower of London, Westminster Abbey, Southwark, Tothill Fields

**The Great Plague**
The impact of the plague was heaviest in poorer areas of the city, where people could not afford to escape to the country.

shared use. Burial grounds were established north of the City wall in Moorfields, Finsbury Fields, Goswell Street, Bishopsgate, Shoreditch and Stepney. The ground surrounding the City pest houses was also used, and it was only after vehement complaints that the authorities enclosed the sheds and graves in Tothill Fields with a protective wall and ditch.

Although the Bills of Mortality underestimated the numbers of plague victims, they do show that the progress of the disease was different in each parish. In most, however, -mortality rates followed a standard pattern, reaching a peak, declining and then rising again before finally subsiding to normal levels. Survivors and returning citizens were encouraged to suck lozenges for three or four weeks and to fumigate their homes with lighted tapers, aromatic pastilles, herbs, resin and sulphur. The King returned to London in December, but Parliament did not reconvene until the following spring. **HF**

bunches of rue and wormwood, sucked lozenges, swallowed tinctures, wore amulets and pomanders and smoked tobacco to protect themselves from infection. Victims were shut in their homes, and a red cross with the words 'Lord have mercy upon us' was daubed on the doors. Watchmen stood guard and citizens passed with 'fearful looks'. By the end of July most parishes both within and without the walls were affected; Thomas Vincent, who remained in the city throughout, commented that death rode 'triumphantly on his pale horse through our streets and breaks into every house almost where any inhabitants are to be found'.

## EMERGENCY MEASURES

Seventeenth-century Londoners knew that the disease was infectious, but attributed plague to miasmas and noxious vapours from the earth, to divine retribution for wrongdoing and to unfavourable conjunctions of the planets. The authorities tried to stop contagion by segregating those affected in so-called 'pest houses', located in the fields and open spaces. In Westminster, a pest house was erected in Tothill Fields (now Vincent Square) to house sixty patients. For the parishes of St Martin's, St Clement's, St Paul's Covent Garden and St Mary Savoy, 2 hectares (5 acres) of ground called Clayfield in Soho Fields (now Golden Square) were used, and a pest house was also built in Mutton Fields in Marylebone, despite local objections. The City pest house was located on isolated ground near Old Street (now off Bath Street), and plague victims from east London, Tower Hamlets and the Tower of London were taken to the pest house in Stepney. As the plague spread, the pressure on burial sites grew. During the peak of the epidemic, between mid-August and mid-September when 7165 died in a single week, traditional burial practice broke down and common graves were dug within the churchyard. Since the outlying parishes had more land, special burial grounds were set up for

*Plague handbell*
*Such bells were rung to announce the collection of deceased plague victims.*

*A Bill of Mortality*
*Each of the City parishes supplied a weekly list of deaths to Parish Clerks' Hall for printing. In 1665 the rise in deaths from plague was horrific.*

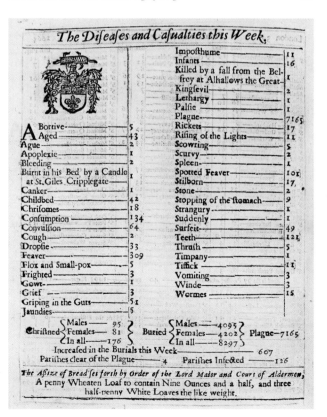

The Diseases and Casualties this Week.

| | |
|---|---|
| Abortive — 5 | Imposthume — 11 |
| Aged — 43 | Infants — 16 |
| Ague — 2 | Killed by a fall from the Belfrey at Alhallows the Great — 1 |
| Apoplexie — 1 | Kingsevil — 2 |
| Bleeding — 2 | Lethargy — 1 |
| Burnt in his Bed by a Candle at St. Giles Cripplegate — 1 | Palsie — 1 |
| Canker — 1 | Plague — 7165 |
| Childbed — 42 | Rickets — 17 |
| Chrisomes — 18 | Rising of the Lights — 11 |
| Consumption — 134 | Scowring — 5 |
| Convulsion — 64 | Scurvy — 2 |
| Cough — 2 | Spleen — 1 |
| Dropsie — 33 | Spotted Feaver — 101 |
| Feaver — 309 | Stilborn — 17 |
| Flox and Small-pox — 5 | Stone — 2 |
| Frighted — 3 | Stopping of the stomach — 9 |
| Gowt — 1 | Strangury — 1 |
| Grief — 3 | Suddenly — 1 |
| Griping in the Guts — 51 | Surfeit — 49 |
| Jaundies — 5 | Teeth — 121 |
| | Thrush — 5 |
| | Timpany — 1 |
| | Tissick — 11 |
| | Vomiting — 3 |
| | Winde — 3 |
| | Wormes — 15 |

Christned { Males — 95, Females — 81, In all — 176 }
Buried { Males — 4095, Females — 4202, In all — 8297 } Plague — 7165
Increased in the Burials this Week — 607
Parishes clear of the Plague — 4    Parishes Infected — 126

The Assize of Bread set forth by Order of the Lord Maior and Court of Aldermen; A penny Wheaten Loaf to contain Nine Ounces and a half, and three half-penny White Loaves the like weight.

# 'AN INFINITE GREAT FIRE'

The Great Fire of London in 1666 destroyed 436 acres of the capital and made thousands of people destitute. It is an event that has remained in the consciousness of Londoners ever since.

***The extent of the Fire's devastation***
*An engraving by Wenceslaus Hollar (1607 – 77) showing the area of the City burnt by the Great Fire.*

The Great Fire began early on Sunday morning on 2 September 1666 in Thomas Farriner's bakery on Pudding Lane. By 7 a.m. Samuel Pepys' maid reported that 300 houses had burnt down. The fire raged for four days, finally being extinguished on the morning of 6 September. By this time, 13,200 houses, eighty-seven churches, St. Paul's Cathedral, the Guildhall and fifty-two livery company halls had been destroyed. The cost of the damage was estimated at around £10 million, an almost unimaginably large sum by the standards of the day. Although fewer than ten people died, around 100,000 Londoners were now homeless, their lives and businesses shattered.

London in 1666 was a tinderbox, ready to ignite at any time. The City had experienced a very dry summer. It was crowded with timber houses, which often leant far out into the narrow streets, making it easy for flames to jump between buildings. A very strong easterly wind fanned the fire relentlessly. Pudding Lane was near the river, where warehouses stood along the north bank, full of

combustible products such as oil, pitch and hemp. There was no coordinated fire service at the time – instead, each parish had fire-fighting equipment, such as axes and hooks to pull down buildings to create firebreaks, and buckets for water. Local people were supposed to band together to put out fires, but most Londoners felt the situation was hopeless and concentrated their efforts on escaping with as many belongings as they could carry. Many fled to the river, cramming their possessions into boats, or fought their way through the crowded streets to escape out of the City gates.

Some Londoners watched in fascinated horror as the flames claimed swathes of the City. Thieves took advantage of the chaos and looted abandoned homes. King Charles II even resorted to touring the city on his horse, handing out money to persuade people to stop and fight the flames. At first the Lord Mayor was reluctant to order the pulling down of houses, for fear of compensation claims from the owners; this delay probably exacerbated the effects of the fire.

## THE FIRE'S PROGRESS

Once the fire got hold of the riverside warehouses, the wind blew it further into the City, where it consumed street after street with terrifying speed. Tuesday 4 September was described as the worst day of the fire. It engulfed all of Cheapside, the City's principal street, in a matter of hours and then moved on to the heart of London – St Paul's Cathedral, where the wooden scaffolding for the cathedral's repair work caught alight. John Evelyn described the stones of St Paul's exploding like grenades and the melted lead from its roof running down the street like a stream. From here the fire continued westwards beyond the City walls towards the Temple, and northwards up to Cripplegate.

Throughout the Great Fire, people had endeavoured to pull down houses in order to create firebreaks, which should have stopped the fire spreading. However, the mayor, Thomas Bludworth, complained that 'the fire overtakes us faster than we can do it'. The wind propelled the fire over any gaps created. A quicker way of demolishing houses was to blow them up with gunpowder, but this technique was not used until the third day of the fire. Fire posts, each manned by 130 men, were established around the City to fight the blaze.

On Tuesday night the wind dropped, and on Wednesday and Thursday the flames were finally dowsed. The last recorded outbreak was at Bishopsgate, at 6 a.m. on Thursday, where Samuel Pepys organized sailors and locals to help extinguish it.

### 'HER GLORY LAID TO DUST'

The fire had reduced four-fifths of the City of London to a blackened ruin. For days afterwards the ground was too hot to walk on: both Pepys and Evelyn wrote in their diaries that they had burnt their feet. Lacking familiar landmarks, people became lost among the rubble. Londoners who had fled the flames in large numbers were now camped in the fields around the city, surrounded by their salvaged belongings. Some gradually moved back and set up temporary shelters on the sites of their former homes. Thousands faced months of hardship and destitution, with no protection against the freezing winter other than tents.

Charles II used a series of proclamations to order relief to the suffering Londoners. Bread was brought in to feed the refugees, other towns were required to take in the homeless and allow them to practise their trades. A national fast took place on Wednesday 10 October, when around £12,000 was collected in aid – though this was very little compared to the scale of the disaster. The Lord Mayor distributed the money to those most in need, although it did not go very far. A widow, Elizabeth Peacock, was typical: She had spent £800 on her house before the Fire and when it was burned she was unable to rebuild without assistance. She was granted £10 from the relief fund.

### WHO WAS BLAMED?

Many people, including the king, believed that the Great Fire was an act of God. Preachers wrote books and pamphlets blaming the sins of Londoners. One of the sins pinpointed was that of gluttony – on the basis that the fire had started in Pudding Lane and had stopped at Pye Corner (it actually spread further than this).

At the time of the Great Fire, England was at war with France and the Netherlands. There were several occasions during the fire where rumours of a French invasion circulated, leading to widespread panic. Mobs prowled the streets looking for any foreigners, attacking them and looting their homes.

There was a general feeling among many people that the Fire was started as part of a Catholic plot to destroy London, a Protestant city. After the fire an official parliamentary enquiry was set up to investigate the cause. The resulting reports contain endless stories of neighbours' gossip and accusations against suspected Catholics, who had apparently hinted that a fire was imminent. The enquiry concluded that the fire was an accident ('the hand of God'), although this did not prevent years of speculation afterwards about a plot.

Thomas Farriner, the baker in whose establishment the fire had first started, managed to escape blame. The scapegoat for the disaster was an unfortunate Frenchman called Robert Hubert. Hubert seems to have suffered from mental problems and confessed to starting the fire deliberately; he was tried and hung for the crime in October 1666. However, it was later discovered that his ship had arrived in London after the fire started. Experts have recently been investigating what may have started the fire and have concluded that, despite his denials, Thomas Farriner probably neglected to extinguish his oven fully on the night before the fire started. A bakery containing spare fuel and combustible flour was the kindling that led to such devastation.　MJ

**The spread of the Great Fire**
The Fire burned for four days, spreading through the City. An East wind accounts for the westward extent of the burnt area.

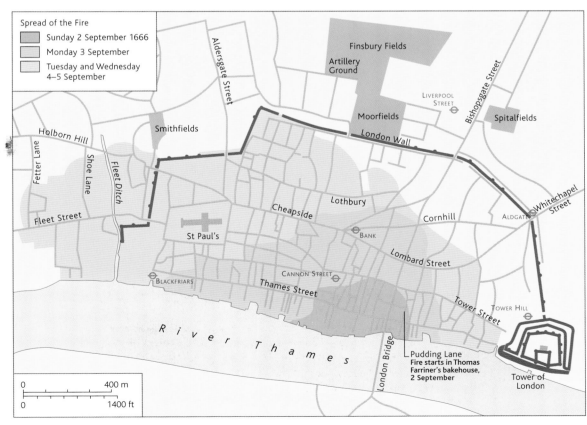

Spread of the Fire
- Sunday 2 September 1666
- Monday 3 September
- Tuesday and Wednesday 4–5 September

Aldersgate Street
Finsbury Fields
Artillery Ground
Liverpool Street
Bishopsgate Street
Spitalfields
Moorfields
London Wall
Smithfields
Holborn Hill
Fetter Lane
Shoe Lane
Fleet Ditch
Lothbury
Cheapside
Cornhill
Whitechapel Street
ALDGATE
Fleet Street
St Paul's
BANK
Lombard Street
BLACKFRIARS
CANNON STREET
Thames Street
TOWER HILL
Tower Street
London Bridge
Pudding Lane
Fire starts in Thomas Farriner's bakehouse, 2 September
Tower of London

River Thames

0　400 m
0　1400 ft

# REBUILDING: IDEAL PLANS & SOBER REALITY

Many believe that Wren's grand Baroque rebuilding scheme was thwarted by City interests. The truth is less dramatic, but shows the determination of Londoners to choose their own way.

one by a Captain Valentine Knight. Not all of these plans have survived. The most interesting schemes were those put forward by Wren and Evelyn, and a plan now attributed (although not conclusively) to Hooke.

Wren proposed several long, straight streets using London Bridge, Ludgate and Newgate as the main entry points to the City. The new streets radiated from circular or semi-circular piazzas, or formed a regular grid. The new Royal Exchange and the new cathedral were prominently displayed.

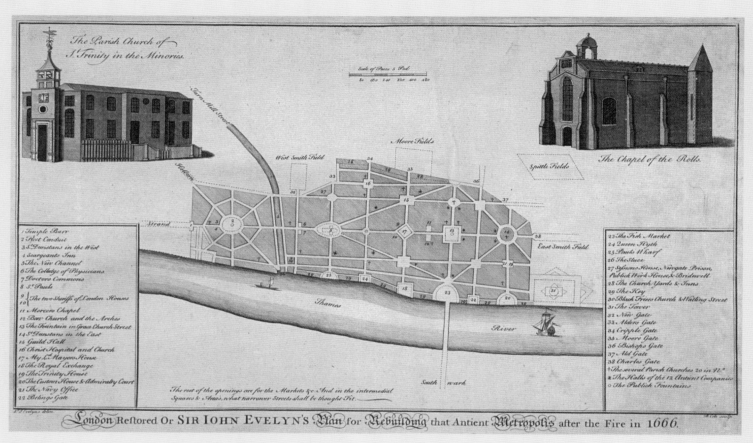

London Restored Or SIR IOHN EVELYN'S Plan for Rebuilding that Antient Metropolis after the Fire in 1666.

**John Evelyn's plan for London**

*One of three successive plans by John Evelyn, engraved in 1748. Piazzas would be used as market places and the city would be crossed by stately diagonal roads.*

Immediately after the Fire, several individuals put forward schemes for rebuilding the devastated area of the city. These plans reveal how the central part of London might have been rebuilt to match other cities across Europe at the time. Many people, from the king downwards, realized that the Fire had given London a chance to rebuild itself as a new and better city, avoiding many of the accumulated problems of the medieval city: narrow, dangerous and unsanitary streets, an unfashionable old hotchpotch of buildings with few squares or boulevards, and no canals. For five months, until February 1667, there was intense debate.

At first, King Charles and his advisers thought that an entirely new ground plan for the burnt area was practicable; the city authorities had asked for this as early as 8 September, only three days after the fire had ended. Christopher Wren (1632–1723) submitted a plan direct to the king on 11 September, while the cellars of the city were still smouldering. John Evelyn (1620–1706) came up with three versions as his ideas developed; other plans were produced by Robert Hooke (1635–1703), by the city surveyor Peter Mills, two by the cartographer Richard Newcourt (c. 1610–79), and

Evelyn's plan was initially similar, although as it developed the old pre-Fire street plan began to reappear, as if he was responding to the actual rebuilding already taking place on the initiative of the citizen themselves. Evelyn also incorporated many of the existing, – though damaged – churches and Christ's Hospital school, in the former Greyfriars buildings; these, being of stone, had partly survived the Fire. He proposed moving the Exchange to the riverside and put a fountain on the old site. Like Wren's, Evelyn's plan featured straight avenues and circular piazzas, reflecting recent trends in Rome and Paris.

Hooke's plan, which was preferred by the city authorities above that of their own surveyor Mills, has not certainly survived, but a plan that may be his has been found as an inset in a Dutch engraving of the fire-damaged city dating to about 1670. This plan is influenced by that of an ideal city published in 1615 by Vincenzo Scamozzi, an architectural writer known to Wren and Hooke.

A bizarre plan put forward by Valentine Knight included a 9-metre (30-ft) wide canal, which looped through the city from Billingsgate, through Cripplegate, to join the Fleet River.

None of these plans was implemented; the problems of compensating all the landlords and tenants must have been too great, and there was a great pressure to rebuild. There were many small improvements, such as the widening of streets and the raising of Thames Street; and one new street was created running while this space was largely cleared, individual property boundaries still crossed it, defeating the overall purpose of the scheme. The quay owners needed to erect sheds, cranes and warehouses, and the idea was soon abandoned. There was virtually no new reclamation into the river after the Fire.

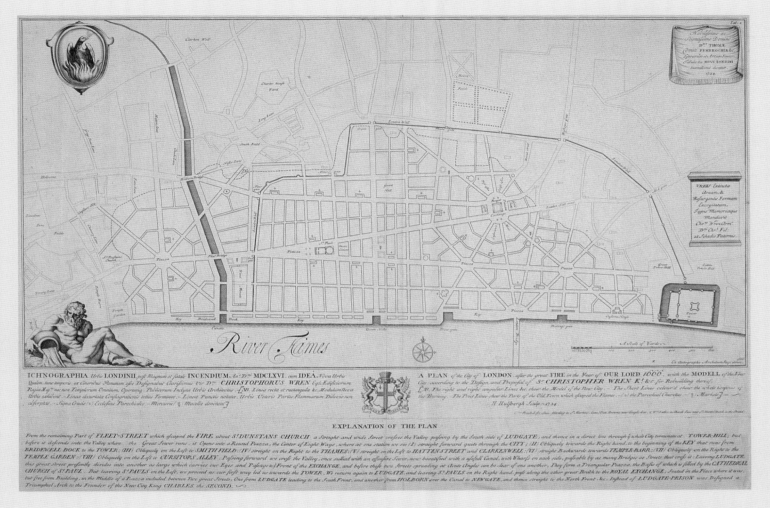

ICHNOGRAPHIA Urbis LONDINII, post Magnum et fatale INCENDIUM, An.° D.ni MDCLXVI. cum IDEA Nova Urbis Quæ, tunc temporis, ex Genvino Senatus usu, Designabat Clarissimus Vir D.nus CHRISTOPHORUS WREN Eqs Ædificiorum Regiæ Maj.tis nec non Templorum Omnium, Operumq. Publicorum Insignis Urbis Architectus.

A PLAN of the City of LONDON, after the great FIRE in the Year of OUR LORD 1666, with the MODELL of the New City according to the Design, and Proposal of S.r CHRISTOPHER WREN K.t &c.r for Rebuilding thereof.

EXPLANATION OF THE PLAN

from Guildhall to the quay. But this street, and the Monument which now stands to commemorate the Great Fire, were not features of these ideal plans.

## ACTUAL IMPROVEMENTS

Two schemes for the River Fleet and the Thames waterfront were, however, adopted by the authorities, with mixed results. The Fleet below Holborn Bridge was canalized – that is, the banks were straightened and heightened by building brick vaults along them for storing merchandise. These vaults formed the base of streets along the canal, and smart buildings soon rose at the rear. This scheme was designed by Wren, Hooke and John Oliver, but as a commercial venture it failed, and the Fleet below Holborn Bridge was arched over in 1766, to form the present New Bridge Street.

The City authorities had similar plans for the mile-long north bank of the Thames between Blackfriars and the Tower, all of which had been destroyed. An open space 12 metres (40 ft) wide was to be cleared from the river end, to provide a wharf suitable for a European capital. Ogilby and Morgan's map of 1676 shows that

For some time, the Fire-damaged area resembled the bombed parts of British and German cities during World War II, with crumbling ruins, very few inhabitants apart from a small number of the poorest former householders living in tents, and mountains of rubble. When he had to walk across the area at night, the diarist Samuel Pepys kept his sword drawn.

It quickly became clear that rebuilding on the old foundations was the only practical solution. Many landlords and tenants argued about responsibility for rebuilding individual properties. The City set up the Fire Court – a panel of judges – to deal swiftly with these cases. Although these judges heard arguments from all parties, their overriding wish was to see the City rebuilt as quickly as possible, and they made prompt decisions in hundreds of cases. The speed and efficiency of the Fire Court is one of the main reasons that London was rebuilt so quickly; and this in turn is one reason why the post-Fire boundary walls of so many buildings sat on their medieval – sometimes even Saxon – predecessors. Within a few years, the determination of Londoners to restore a functioning city had taken precedence over the ideals of the planners. **JS**

*Christopher Wren's plan for London*
Wren's plan for the new city, engraved in 1724. The wavy edge shows the extent of the Fire; to the north and east, the old city remained. The plan makes no provision for growth.

# THE REBUILDING OF LONDON

Changes brought by the Great Fire have been exaggerated. Many public buildings were rebuilt in modern styles, but timber buildings continued to house most Londoners for generations.

**The post-Fire Royal Exchange**
*Designed by Edward Jarman and finished by Thomas Cartwright in 1668, the Royal Exchange is seen here from Cornhill. It perished in another fire in 1838.*

By the time of Ogilby and Morgan's detailed map of the city in 1676, the area of London destroyed or damaged by the Great Fire had been almost completely rebuilt, apart from a few churches and their towers. Such recovery within a decade was remarkable. Many streets were slightly widened and public buildings in stone, such as the Royal Exchange, a repaired Guildhall and some new markets, now adorned the city. The international wharves were now even more concentrated below the Bridge, but the capacity of their warehouses had been significantly increased.

The new public buildings, livery company halls and churches were designed by a small number of London-based architects and surveyors, with (as far as we know) almost no foreign involvement: men like Robert Hooke, Edward Jarman, Peter Mills and, above all, Sir Christopher Wren. They took stylistic ideas from France, The Netherlands and (somewhat more rarely) from Baroque buildings in Italy.

Thirty-six parish churches that had been damaged by the fire were not replaced; instead, their parishes were joined with others. Fifty-two churches, however, were rebuilt, to the designs of Wren and his colleagues (and it seems that Hooke also designed several). Thirty-nine of these survive today – buildings of historical importance on a European scale. In most cases the design of a new church was influenced by the partial survival of the pre-Fire church it was intended to replace, very often in the form of a substantial

**Fresh Wharf, near London Bridge**
*Wren's St Magnus the Martyr church stands next to the bridge, rebuilt in this form in 1759. In the foreground is a fragment of the New Quay of the 1670s. The painting is by William Marlow, about 1762.*

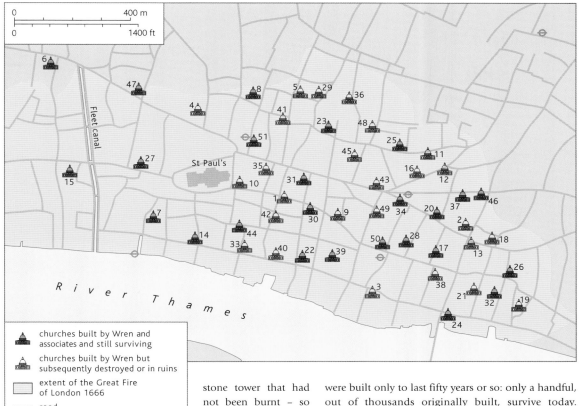

**Churches rebuilt by Wren and his associates after the Fire**

Several have succumbed to demolition in the 19th century or damage in World War II. The map also shows the Fleet Canal, an unsuccessful venture of the period.

1.  All Hallows Bread Street
2.  All Hallows Gracechurch Street (Lombard Street)
3.  All Hallows the Great
4.  Christ Church Newgate Street
5.  St Alban Wood Street
6.  St Andrew Holborn
7.  St Andrew Castle Baynard
8.  St Anne and St Agnes
9.  St Antonin
10. St Augustine by St Paul's
11. St Bartholomew
12. St Benet Fink
13. St Benet Gracechurch
14. St Benet Paul's Wharf
15. St Bride
16. St Christopher
17. St Clement Eastcheap
18. St Dionis Backchurch
19. St Dunstan in the East
20. St Edmund
21. St George Botolph Lane
22. St James Garlickhithe
23. St Lawrence Jewry
24. St Magnus the Martyr
25. St Margaret  Lothbury
26. St Margaret Pattens
27. St Martin Ludgate
28. St Mary Abchurch
29. St Mary Aldermanbury
30. St Mary Aldermary
31. St Mary le Bow
32. St Mary at Hill
33. St Mary Somerset
34. St Mary Woolnoth [later rebuilt by Hawksmoor]
35. St Matthew Friday Street
36. St Michael Bassishaw
37. St Michael Cornhill
38. St Michael Crooked Lane
39. St Michael Paternoster
40. St Michael Queenhithe
41. St Michael Wood Street
42. St Mildred Bread Street
43. St Mildred Walbrook
44. St Nicholas Coldabbey
45. St Olave Jewry
46. St Peter Cornhill
47. St Sepulchre
48. St Stephen Coleman Street
49. St Stephen Walbrook
50. St Swithin
51. St Vedast

Map legend:
- churches built by Wren and associates and still surviving
- churches built by Wren but subsequently destroyed or in ruins
- extent of the Great Fire of London 1666
- road

stone tower that had not been burnt – so most of Wren's church towers are at heart medieval. Many London churches had contained galleries since the 1580s, so the provision of galleries in several of the new churches was not an innovation either.

## BUILDING REGULATIONS

Historians once thought that the Great Fire of London had an important effect on the future design of streets, buildings and services in London and other British towns. But destructive though the Fire was, it devastated only about one third of the city then standing. Within the immediate area of the fire, a new city of brick and (occasionally) stone arose, but around it a larger area remained timber-framed for decades to come. Much has been made of the apparent newness of these houses, and the related phenomenon of residential squares (see pages 126–7), but in fact neither the design of the houses themselves nor the fact that they were sometimes built in rows and squares was really new. The arrangement of rooms had not changed; neither had the shape of houses, except for some regulation concerning their height. They were probably more sanitary, and timber fronts with protruding storeys had been banned, but in many ways the new houses were no more than the various existing forms of Elizabethan and Jacobean city houses reclothed in brick. Shops were still shops, and for several decades after 1666 they were allowed to have projecting signs outside just as they had before the Fire. Although a move to the fashionable west, around the Court at Westminster, had started well before the Fire, the City was still full of people. The great majority of buildings after the Fire had the same functions as before.

We cannot even say for certain that the new houses were necessarily better constructed, since especially in the squares they were built only to last fifty years or so: only a handful, out of thousands originally built, survive today. Nonetheless, replacement of the lost old houses by new construction did represent something of a fresh start for City inhabitants – bringing a consciousness of sophisticated urban living for many. The rebuilt area inside the City now resembled more closely the new streets laid out in Westminster and the better suburbs, which meant that the distinction between the old City and its suburbs was further blurred.

The great majority of the rebuilding was over by 1670; life was returning to normal. Streets and other public places were newly paved; business started again. The press of carts passing over London Bridge required the appointment in 1670 of what must have been the first regular London traffic policemen. At that time they directed traffic to keep to the opposite side of the road from today's rules.

## ST PAUL'S CATHEDRAL

London's most important single building standing today dates from these years. The new St Paul's Cathedral was designed by Christopher Wren and built between 1675 and 1714. It stands on the site of its medieval predecessor; and much of the stone from the previous cathedral was used as rubble in the lower walls of Wren's building. The cathedral quickly became a national mausoleum for heroes (Nelson and Wellington are buried here) and a place for royal occasions and national celebrations. It can still be seen today from distant parts of London such as Highgate Hill or Greenwich, due to laws that have preserved vistas through the clumps of modern buildings. Wren's sumptuous masterpiece would have crowned the Stuart City even more grandly than it does the City of today. **JS**

# NEW SQUARES, GRAND HOUSES & INNS

By 1700 London was becoming the hub of one of the greatest empires the world had ever seen. Its status as a metropolis was reflected in the grand buildings and squares of the new West End.

A fashionable movement westwards from the city accelerated in the 17th century. Squares and streets of sophisticated housing filled the fields between the city and Westminster. As London grew spectacularly in population, the suburbs expanded in all directions. Even more than before, London became the hub of Britain and galleried inns sprang up to profit from the new level of traffic between the city and the provinces.

In 1700, London's development had resulted in areas of great contrast, from east to west and from north to south. Strype's 1720 map of London and Westminster (see opposite) shows a single conurbation stretching from Westminster to the east of the rebuilt City, and a rapid expansion of streets and buildings in Southwark.

Fashionable squares were first laid out in the fields west of the City with Covent Garden in the 1630s and Lincoln's Inn Fields in

**Covent Garden**
*Laid out in 1631 by Inigo Jones for the Duke of Bedford, whose house bordered the square on the south, Covent Garden is an early example of a private estate.*

## RICH & POOR IN KENSINGTON

Beyond the built-up area of London there were fields, farms and hamlets. We can reconstruct the inside of houses here from inventories made on the death of the owner. Here are two from the 1670s for Kensington, then a small hamlet.

Phillipp Coleby (died in 1672) had a mansion with a hall, two parlours, a dining room, several bedrooms and two chambers for women servants. In the hall were maps and eleven pictures; several of the other rooms also had pictures, including portraits of a dozen English monarchs and princes since the time of Queen Elizabeth. Books included Luther and Calvin. All the main rooms and bedchambers were hung with fabric or tapestry. Coleby's cutlery included eighteen silver spoons, three silver wine cups and two small forks, then coming into fashion. His total movable wealth amounted to £509 18 shillings.

By contrast, Alexander Bean (died 1674), had a house of three rooms and a stable – probably two rooms downstairs and a single bedchamber upstairs. In the kitchen were two tables and three old chairs. In the chamber was a fireplace with three old leather chairs and two stools. The assessors found an old horse in the stable, along with a cart and a pair of wheels. Bean's wealth totalled £14 2 shillings, one thirtieth of Coleby's.

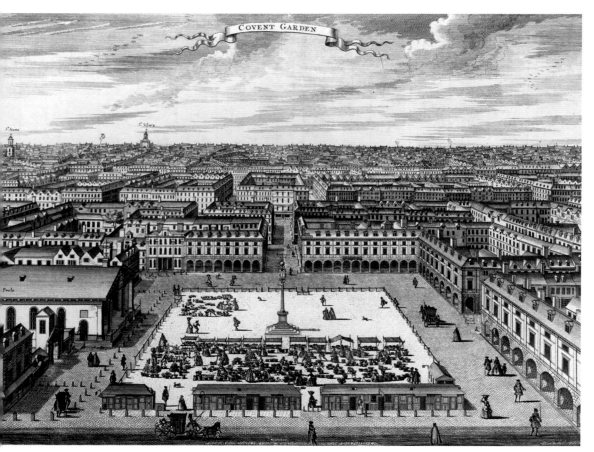

COVENT GARDEN

were other speculators too, often London craftsmen and builders.

Bloomsbury Square dates from 1665; St James's Square, 1667; Leicester Square, 1671; Soho (originally King's) Square, 1681; Golden Square, 1688; Grosvenor Square (its gardens on the site of one of the Civil War forts), 1695; Red Lion Square, 1698. The squares often had a large noble house occupying one side, as at Bloomsbury and Leicester Squares, to set the tone of the new area.

This idea of developing a complete unit comprising a square, secondary streets, market and perhaps a church had begun with the Earl of Bedford's house on the south side of Covent Garden in the 1630s. Two sides of this square were built with fashionable housing above arcades, the fourth side being occupied by a new parish church, St Paul's Covent Garden, designed by the court architect Inigo Jones (1573–1652).

Strype includes Hanover Square, then just completed, and the first developments north of Oxford Street on the Harley-Cavendish estate, then being built. This would produce Harley Street and Cavendish Square, by 1717. The building developments of the 17th century also had lasting effects on later ones: the squares

the 1650s. Noble landlords made substantial amounts of money by financing developments on their land on London's outskirts (often acquired at the dissolution of the monasteries), but there even further west after 1760, north of Oxford Street as far as Marble Arch, were determined and constrained by streets extending from their predecessors.

**The City and Westminster in 1720**
*In John Strype's map of 1720 the medieval city is hardly recognizable. The expansion of Southwark to the south and Westminster to the west was about to start in earnest.*

The dukes who owned large areas of the former fields kept their ownership and were thus able to determine the social, architectural and economic character of complete neighbourhoods. The squares were exclusive; Bedford Square, built in 1776, had five gates with lodges and gate-keepers, who kept out flocks of sheep, carts, empty cabs, exercising horses or funerals.

On the Bedford estate, the houses could only be used for gentlemen's private residences, and many trades were banned. A house could not be converted into a school, concert hall, police station, hospital, shop or brothel. This is one reason why Bedford Square is today the only intact 18th-century square remaining in London.

## NEW SUBURBS

East and north-east of the city, beyond the now redundant city wall, new suburbs were growing fast. The Huguenot community had settled in Spitalfields and all kinds of shipping and nautical suppliers, as well as sailors, lived in Wapping and other former hamlets on the bank of the Thames downstream of the Tower and of the Pool of London (the Elizabethan port had been established east of London Bridge in the 1550s, and this is why most warehouses in the city lay in the east half, well into the 19th century). Beyond Whitechapel, in 1600 though not for much longer, were open fields, into which the new docks would be later inserted.

Across the river in Southwark, the medieval suburb was beginning to grow as a centre of manufacturing, particularly of pottery, and as the site of several breweries using imported hops. Southwark had its own widespread fire in 1678, but many

buildings built there afterwards were still of timber construction. Here also, were many coaching inns, the successors of the Tabard in Chaucer's time, forming the city end-points of transport routes into much of south-east England, like the railway stations that have now replaced them, and in almost the same spot. The inns were meeting places and showrooms for men of business on the move, not unlike today's cafes and bars.          JS

**Bloomsbury Square**
*This detail from John Rocque's map of 1747 shows Montague House and Bedford House on the north side of Bedford Square.*

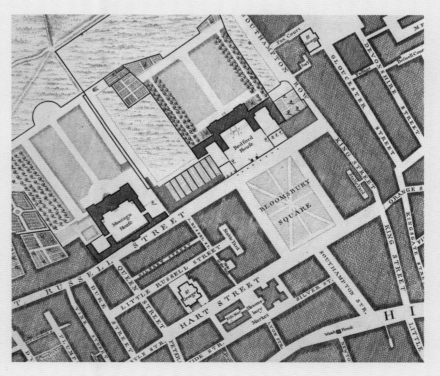

# THE NAVY IN LONDON

The Royal Navy was closely associated with London. In the 17th century its administration, the Admiralty, and its facilities at Deptford, Woolwich and Greenwich saw major reforms.

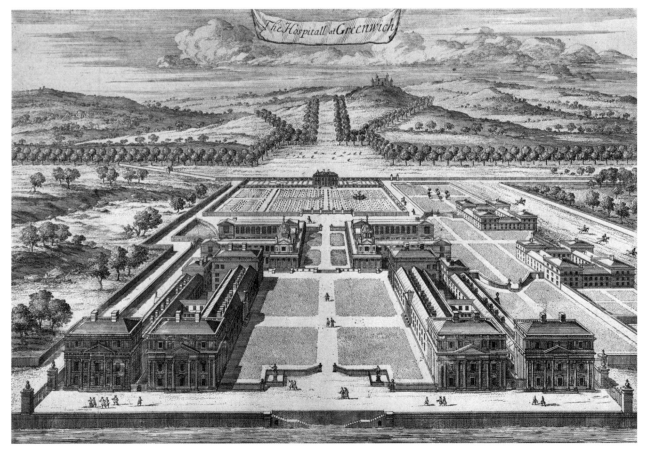

The 17th-century Admiralty consisted of two bodies, the Court of Admiralty (judicial) and the Navy Board (administrative), both based in London. The Court of Admiralty met at St Margaret's Hill in Southwark, before moving in 1676 to the hall of Doctors' Commons on St Benet's Hill in the City. It heard maritime cases and adjudicated on prizes won during wartime.

The Navy Board was the body in charge of shipbuilding and repair, management of the docks and clothing, victualling and wages for seamen. It was set up by Henry VIII in 1546 and had its main office in Seething Lane. The Victualling Office stood on Tower Hill near the storehouses and slaughterhouses that supplied the Navy. The Navy Board worked closely with the Board of Ordnance, which made and supplied the Army and Navy with munitions. Their offices and stores were at the Tower of London.

Samuel Pepys (1633–1703) began his involvement with the Navy as Clerk of the Acts to the Navy Board. A natural administrator, Pepys spent his working life in naval reform, promoting proper recordkeeping and financial control, improved standards for the construction of ships, victualling, discipline, seamen's welfare and training of officers. In 1673 King Charles II appointed Pepys as secretary to the Privy Council's Admiralty committee. This gave Pepys a great deal more power to push through reforms. In 1677 he established an examination system for lieutenants, and set standards for certain jobs, such as pursers and surgeons. He also oversaw the construction of thirty new ships from 1677, many of which were built in London's royal dockyards. His role increased further in 1684 when the King made Pepys Secretary for Admiralty Affairs, a hugely important post.

## TRINITY HOUSE

Trinity House was the public authority responsible for looking after waterways. It also licensed pilots and watermen. The Navy Board relied on Trinity House to examine sailing masters, recruit seamen and hire merchant vessels. Its headquarters were in Water Lane, although there were two subsidiary bodies – Trinity House in Deptford and another in Trinity Lane, Ratcliff. Samuel Pepys was a member and became Master in 1675–6. He reorganized the office's record system during his time as Master. He also arranged for Trinity House to undertake the examination in navigation of boys from Christ's Hospital mathematical school.

Trinity House also maintained almshouses and a hospital for retired mariners and their families. From the early 16th century, it had almshouses near the Royal Dockyard at Deptford, later called

**The Royal Hospital for Seamen, Greenwich**
*The naval hospital opened in 1705. The architects, Christopher Wren and Nicholas Hawksmoor, produced a divided design that preserved the vista from the Queen's House (centre background) to the river (foreground).*

Rose Cottages. In 1670 Trinity Hospital was built on Church Street in Deptford, with fifty-six almshouses. A further set of almshouses was built on Mile End Road in 1695 with accommodation for twenty-eight retired masters and commanders, or their widows.

## PAY & CONDITIONS FOR SAILORS

Pay and conditions for sailors in the 17th-century were very poor. Often they were not paid at all at the end of a period of service, particularly during wartime when money was extremely tight. Sometimes they were paid with vouchers that could only be redeemed at the Navy Pay Office, in Tower Hill. Whether they would receive the full value of these vouchers depended on the Navy's finances at the time.

While Pepys worked hard to stamp out fraud in the Navy, it was difficult to stop pursers (officers responsible for food, drink and clothing) from swindling the seamen. As a consequence, sailors lived in a semi-starved state and frequently fell ill. The fate of sick and injured seamen was an unenviable one. During wartime their care was organized by the Sick and Wounded Board, first set up under the Commonwealth government during the First Dutch War in 1653. The Board was temporary, existing only in wartime. Its first office was in Little Britain, near the hospital of St Bartholomew. It was common practice for seamen to be treated at the ports where they landed, but accommodation was always a problem. Seamen were also brought to London for treatment, and space was reserved for them in the hospitals of St Bartholomew, St Thomas in Southwark, the Savoy on the Strand and Ely House. Reservation of beds in these hospitals was greatly resented by Londoners, especially as many seamen had long-term medical problems and disabilities as a result of their injuries. There was a desperate need for a naval hospital.

John Evelyn, a commissioner on the Sick and Wounded Board from 1664, campaigned for the establishment of a naval hospital, but there was never enough money to build one. In 1690 the Sick and Wounded Board consulted Dr. Richard Lower, who suggested building a hospital with 500 beds at Greenwich, and in 1691 Queen Mary II gave permission for this to be established on the site of the old royal palace. It was for 'the reliefe and support of Seamen ... belonging to the Navy Royall ... who by reason of Age, Wounds or other disabilities shall be uncapable for further service ... And for the Sustentation of Widows and the Maintenance and Education of the Children of Seamen happening to be slain or disabled.' The hospital (see opposite) opened in 1705.

## LONDON'S ROYAL DOCKYARDS

Two of the most important royal dockyards in Britain were Deptford and Woolwich, with their strategic position on the Thames, their facilities and their proximity to the markets and labour available in London. Both had been set up by Henry VIII in 1513. Although they were supervised by the Navy Board – Pepys even instituted surprise inspections – the dockyards were rife with corruption by the 17th century. Clerks and badly paid labourers falsified records, siphoned off goods from the stores and generally cheated the system as much as they could. Pepys tried to combat this corruption with new systems of recordkeeping and checks, but many of the abuses continued into the 19th century. Nonetheless, some of the 17th century's greatest ships were built at the London royal dockyards, such as the 1500-ton *Sovereign of the Seas* by the master shipwright Phineas Pett and his son Peter, at Deptford. Private dockyards also existed, such as the East India Company's facility at Blackwall, where the merchant ships known as 'East Indiamen' were built for trade with India and China.       MJ

*Prospect from Greenwich, 1620s*
*Deptford is on the river bend in the left centre; Greenwich borders the river right centre. Above Greenwich, the ships mark the East India Company dockyard at Blackwall. In the distance on the left is London.*

*Samuel Pepys (1633–1703)*
*Pepys' tireless work to reform the Navy helped to develop it into the professional force it remains today.*

# MEDICINE, SCIENCE & NATURAL PHILOSOPHY

London saw great scientific advances in the 17th century. Home to the Royal College of Physicians and the Royal Society, it was thronged with medical practitioners, from physicians to quacks.

***Robert Hooke (1635–1703)***
*Hooke was 'curator of experiments' of the Royal Society. This painting, by Mary Beale in 1674, has recently been identified as his portrait.*

***A lantern clock of about 1680***
*This clock was made by Joseph Knibb at his workshop at The Dial in Fleet Street. The work of such London craftsmen was key to the scientific advances of the period.*

At their headquarters in Warwick Lane, the Royal College of Physicians (established in 1518) regulated medical practice within a seven-mile radius of the City of London. They examined and licensed physicians and punished those who practised illegally or incompetently. Many of their views were very traditional and were beginning to be challenged by 'new scientists' who questioned ancient theories on how the human body worked and how it could be treated. Nicholas Culpeper (1616–54) was a physician and apothecary who treated the London poor at his premises in Threadneedle Street. In 1649 he enraged the College of Physicians by publishing an unauthorized English translation of the College's Latin *Pharmacopoeia*, which contained details of the drugs they used and how these were made. Then in 1653 Culpeper wrote *The English Physician Enlarged*, describing over 500 plants. He felt that the high fees physicians charged were un-Christian and that by producing texts only in Latin, the College was infringing the liberty of ordinary citizens. From around this time medical books were written in English.

## MEDICAL PRACTITIONERS

Doctors were men who had practical training, usually by apprenticeship. They set bones, healed injuries and bled patients. Physicians were distinct – they had degrees in physic from universities and advised on diet, exercise, and drugs. Their treatments involved purging, bleeding and sweating to restore the balance of a patient's body. They were expensive, and indeed beyond the purse of many Londoners, charging between 10 and 20 shillings in fees. Many physicians were based around Fleet Street, such as Richard Lower (1631–91) who worked at Salisbury Court. Lower became famous for performing the first successful blood transfusion in 1665, between two dogs.

Most of the population would visit a barber for day-to-day medical treatments. As well as cutting hair and shaving, barbers were also permitted to draw teeth. From 1540 to 1745 surgeons and barbers were members of the same organization, the Barber-Surgeons' Company, though there were frequent disputes between the two professions as their practices overlapped. It was common for barbers to bleed patients (a treatment used for many medical complaints) although strictly speaking this was a job for surgeons. Samuel Pepys's barber was Richard Jarvis of New Palace Yard,

Westminster. Pepys visited Jarvis for haircuts and to be shaved, but was bled by his surgeon, Thomas Hollier, who had successfully removed Pepys' bladder stone. Hollier worked at St Thomas's Hospital in Southwark and St Bartholomew's Hospital in Smithfield, although he visited Pepys at home.

Medicines were sold by apothecaries, the equivalent of modern pharmacists. Originally apothecaries were members of the Grocers' Company, as they sold spices, herbs, perfumes and drugs – all part of the Grocers' trade. By the mid-16th century, however, apothecaries had become specialists who prepared and sold substances for medicinal purposes. In 1617 the Worshipful Society of Apothecaries was established. Their hall still stands on its original site at Blackfriars.

Most medicines were derived from herbs, plants and vegetables, so in 1673 the Apothecaries started their own Physic Garden in Chelsea. There was a cluster of apothecaries' shops in the area of Bucklersbury in the City of London. The apothecaries had a long-running dispute with the Royal College of Physicians over who should prescribe medicines. The physicians felt that the apothecaries should only dispense to prescriptions drawn up by physicians, not on their own account. The College had its own official dispensary, with two branches, at St Martin's Lane in Westminster and St Peter's Alley in Cornhill. These sold medicines at cost price; in the year 1703 they made up about 20,000 prescriptions at around a penny a dose for basic drugs.

## QUACKS

A large number of 'quacks', or unlicensed medical practitioners, operated in London, peddling supposed miracle cures for all kinds of diseases, particularly for the more embarrassing conditions such as syphilis. The gates of St Bartholomew's Hospital were a popular haunt for quacks, such as William Salmon, who sold an 'Elixir of Life' and an antidote against the plague. Anne Laverenst ran a business in Arundel Street off the Strand where she treated 'Morbus

**Urethral syringe**
Syringes like this were used in the 17th century for administering mercury to treat syphilis.

Gallicus' ('the French disease', or syphilis) and removed women's bladder stones (a service advertised by a red cloth covered in the stones of previous patients).

Quacks also sold their products through London's increasing number of coffee houses, whose walls were covered in advertisements for cures. 'Fletcher's Powder' was sold at Newman's Coffee House in Gracechurch Street; it was claimed to be effective 'against all diseases but against death'. 'Sovereign julep' for consumption and other chest problems could be bought at Morandi's Chocolate House in Drury Lane, for half a crown per bottle.

## HOSPITALS

Most medieval hospitals, run by the Church, were closed during the Dissolution of the Monasteries, although some were re-founded by Henry VIII and his successors. Hospitals were often described as 'for the relief of the poor' – they were mainly where the poor and destitute took shelter, rather than where the general population went for medical treatment. Some had a specific purpose, such as St Mary Bethlehem, which was for 'lunatic people'. St Thomas's in Southwark was established for the 'sick and aged'. Here patients were expected to pay for their upkeep if they were able, but the poor were provided with food, bedding, clothes and three pints of ale per day. St Bartholomew's Hospital employed some distinguished physicians, such as William Harvey, who published his book on the true nature of the circulation of blood and the action of the heart as a pump in 1628. His theories overthrew medical beliefs that had been held for centuries, and were met with much opposition.

*Tin-glazed drug jar*
Inscribed 'C. RVTAE', this 17th-century drug jar was used to hold a compound of the plant rue, particularly favoured as an emetic and an antidote for poison and the plague.

## MEN OF SCIENCE

London was home to many of the greatest scientists of the 17th century, whose discoveries were vital in the development of physics, mathematics, astronomy and medicine. The astronomer Edmund Halley (whose name was later given to a comet he had observed in 1682) lived at Winchester Street. John Flamsteed, another famous astronomer, worked at the Royal Observatory in Greenwich (opened 1676) making detailed observations of the heavens and cataloguing stars. Sir William Brouncker (first president of the Royal Society) and Sir Jonas Moore, (surveyor general of the ordnance at the Tower of London) were renowned mathematicians. London physicians such as Thomas Willis, who wrote the first comprehensive book on the brain and the nervous system, contributed important new work, published in London. Sir Isaac Newton himself moved from Cambridge to Jermyn Street in 1695

*An instrument for surveyors*
A 'circumferentor', used for measuring angles, made by Henry Sutton of Threadneedle Street in 1658.

and worked for the Royal Mint, significantly improving its production of coins.

The Royal Society was established in 1660. Its Fellows met weekly at Gresham College to discuss natural philosophy, medicine, mathematics and physics, and to watch experiments. Charles II granted the society a charter in 1662. From 1665, it published its *Philosophical Transactions*, containing scientific papers. After the Great Fire in 1666, the society moved to Arundel House on the Strand, as Gresham College was taken over by the City authorities. Fellows of the society included Christopher Wren, Samuel Pepys, John Evelyn, Robert Boyle and Isaac Newton. Their first curator of experiments was the scientist Robert Hooke (see opposite). His most famous work, *Micrographia*, was published in 1665 and featuring extraordinarily detailed drawings of tiny organisms like fleas made with the help of a microscope.

Such scientific advances depended on London's craftsmen. Vital to Hooke's work were instruments made by the London clock maker Thomas Tompion at his shop on Water Lane. Spectacle makers such as John Marshall and John Yarwell of Ludgate Street ground lenses for telescopes and microscopes. Glass blowers produced clear, inert glass for experimental equipment.

In the 17th century, London was the birthplace of much of the new thinking in science and medicine. Nonetheless, while important advances were made, healthcare did not significantly improve; many Londoners still turned to quacks for treatment.    MJ

# GEORGIAN LONDON

Eighteenth-century London was Europe's
most phenomenal city, a disorderly yet
dynamic boom town, unprecedented in its size
and social diversity. Between 1700 and 1800
London grew from a city of 600,000 people,
somewhat overawed by its Dutch rivals,
to a metropolis of over a million people,
the largest city in the world, eclipsing all other
European capitals in its network of commercial
and military interests stretching around the
globe. Protestantism and capitalism were the
roots of London's growth, but its energy came

from its free market. Services, goods, people
and materials could all be bought and sold
more or less without restraint. Entrepreneurs
flourished on the right and wrong sides of the
law. Pickpockets sold on gold watches; ship-
owners sought out investors to take shares in
cargos of West Indian sugar. To the religious,
such uninhibited moneymaking turned
London into a modern Babylon, a symbol of
mankind's greed and moral failure, exemplified
in particular by the issue of slavery. To the more
secular minded, London stood for new forms

of freedom, a place of intellectual stimulation where everything conspired to 'agitate, amuse and elevate the mind'. The writer James Boswell was one of many magnetically attracted to the British capital. Boswell's blood 'thrilled with pleasure' at what London had to offer and he associated the city with happiness. London also held out the prospect of misery. The sheer size of the population overwhelmed the old medieval systems for relieving distress. London was notorious across Europe for the numbers of prostitutes in the streets, and the feral children who darted through the crowds. Such a large concentration of human beings in one place was beyond experience; the city seemed sometimes on the verge of chaos. Its citizens had the finest consumer goods in Europe at their disposal but formed the unruliest crowds: the city could conjure up a mob as well as a regiment of foot soldiers. London had clubs and societies for all beliefs; hundreds of shopkeepers and merchants; thousands of servants and streetwalkers buying and selling themselves. London was out of control.

# TOWNHOUSES & COUNTRY HOMES

The new streets and squares of Westminster represented new ideals for fashionable living. Entrepreneurial aristocrats were quick to exploit the potential for profit.

London's house-building boom depended on a new system of property ownership: 'leasehold'. As pioneered by the Earl of Southampton for Bloomsbury Square in the 1660s, this enabled aristocrats to turn property-developers at little financial risk. The landowner granted parcels of lands to a leaseholder – sometimes a building tradesman, sometimes a financial speculator – allowing them to erect houses at their own expense. Houses were then leased or sold to an occupier who might then sublet to tenants. Everyone in the chain made money.

The aristocratic entrepreneurism that lay behind this method of development left its mark in the names of streets and squares. The Grosvenor, Curzon and Berkeley estates north of Piccadilly were built over in the first half of the century. Above Oxford Road (today's Oxford Street), the Portman and Portland estates were laid out in new streets, including Devonshire Place, from the 1760s. North of Oxford Road, the Bedford Estate, was developed from the 1770s.

*Devonshire Place and Wimpole Street*
*An engraving of 1799 of recently built streets on the Portland Estate, looking south from the New Road.*

Who populated these new residential quarters? During the 18th century, London's population almost doubled to just under one million, 20 to 30 per cent of which, it has been estimated, were from the upper and middle classes – a higher proportion than in any other European capital. London's growing middle classes included government office holders, physicians, bankers, brokers, lawyers, army and navy captains alongside wealthier shopkeepers and master-craftsmen. All desired the social advantages that went with a fashionable address. Sprinkled among the new streets and squares were palatial town houses for the nobility – Devonshire House (begun 1734), Norfolk House (1748) and Apsley House (begun 1772). 'A good lodging in a good part of the town is absolutely necessary. These are very dear' lamented the writer James Boswell. 'None proper for me can be had under two guineas or a guinea and a half.' Boswell ended up in Downing Street with three rooms for £40 a year.

## CITY FASHIONS

Appearance was all-important for these new buildings. A classical architectural style was compulsory. For those master-builders who had not been to Italy to study it first-hand, newly published builders' pattern books taught them how to replicate Palladian or neoclassical detail. The straight lines of the classical style made the builder's task easy, but the results were not to everybody's taste: '… Yet this metropolis of fashion, this capital of the capital itself, has the most monotonous appearance imaginable', complained

former marshlands of the Minories, where the surveyor George Dance laid out London's first two curved, terraced developments, called simply the 'Circus' and the 'Crescent'. The novelty of curved streets caught on fast, and by 1800 several more rounded features had appeared on London's street map.

Further afield, pockets of smart Georgian housing began to line the main roads out of London, joining up the surrounding, once-separate villages; Kensington, Chelsea, Pimlico and Knightsbridge, for example, all began to merge. Hackney, Finsbury and outlying villages as far as Walthamstow were all altered significantly in appearance by the arrival of new terraces and villas. These suburban properties had no need of imported sheep to create the illusion that they were in the country.

Perhaps it is no accident that the most spectacular failure of London's Georgian building boom was a development that made no concession to rural picturesqueness. This was the Adelphi, the project of Robert (1728–92) and James Adam (1730–94), the fashionable country house architects who had recently erected Kenwood House on Hampstead Heath for the Earl of Mansfield. The Adelphi was altogether more urban. Building on the wasteland and mudbanks between the Strand and the river, the Adam brothers laid out a number of streets culminating in a palatial terrace of eleven extraordinarily lavish houses, built above a working wharf and warehouses. In the wrong part of town and a little too close to commerce, the Adelphi did not become fashionable and almost bankrupted the Adams, only ever attracting grudging praise: 'To whatever criticism it may be liable in point of architecture' said a guidebook of 1794, '[it] is the admiration of foreigners.' **CR**

Robert Southey. 'The streets are perfectly parallel … you would suppose them to be hospitals, arsenals or granaries.' By 1807, when this comment was made, picturesque informality was in fashion, which gave a new importance to the gardens laid out in the centre of the squares. Some were gently landscaped; and Cavendish Square even had a flock of sheep, imported to cast an air of rural charm over the urban surroundings.

Inside these town houses, appearance was also important. A fashionable household no longer lived in one room, but had a decorated salon for civilized pastimes such as conversation and music. In William Hogarth's *Marriage à la Mode* sequence of paintings (1743), the cramped and plain quarters of the unfashionable City merchant is contrasted with the more spacious salon of 'Earl Squanderfield', its walls crowded with paintings and plasterwork. Even in the smaller middle-class house, there might be separate rooms for dining, a study and a library. The colourman (paint merchant) John Middleton lived above his shop on St Martin's Lane, but nevertheless furnished his home fashionably (see his family portrait above).

## RURAL AIRS

This was all very far from the narrow, dark lanes and odd-shaped building plots of the City. Traditionally, City merchants had lived over their shops, but now commuting from a more comfortable home elsewhere became more usual. Broker John Angerstein was typical in having a smart new villa built for himself at Blackheath in 1774. In the City itself, the Corporation erected a new, fashionably styled town house for the Lord Mayor, the Mansion House (1739–53), but this was more of an official palace than a modern home. A few Westminster-style speculative building developments occurred on the City's fringes, notably on the

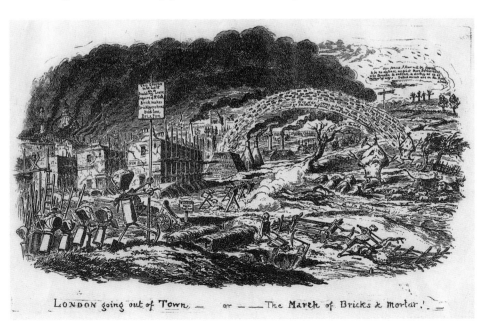

LONDON going out of Town. — or — The March of Bricks & Mortar.

# STOCKS, SHARES & SPECULATION

By the late 17th century, London had become a centre for the trade in money, stocks and shares. Key venues were the Bank of England, the Royal Exchange – and a network of coffee houses.

The Bank of England was created by Act of Parliament in 1694. Funds were urgently needed to pay for the war against France (1688–97), and the Scottish financier William Paterson (1658–1719) came up with the idea of the Bank. Its initial capital of £1,200,000 was subscribed by a group of wealthy City financiers and merchants. The Bank transferred this capital to the government in return for an interest of 8 per cent per annum. The Bank had its offices in Grocers' Hall in Princes Street.

A new opportunity for stock speculation occurred in 1711, when the South Sea Company was established. This company took on the government's short-term war debt in return for a trading monopoly with the Spanish colonies of South America. Although its trade activities performed poorly, the company took on further government debt in 1719 and 1720. Its finances were questionable and some of its leading government supporters were bribed. Nonetheless, as its stock began to rise, a frenzy of buying took place. South Sea stock rose higher and higher, sucking in more and more investors. When the bubble burst, many were ruined; the Bank of England had to intervene to calm the market.

In 1734, the Bank moved to a large new building in Threadneedle Street, opposite the Royal Exchange. The new building – London's first purpose-built bank – suited its expanding role as sole manager of the national debt. Fifty years later, staff numbers had risen to over 350 as its business grew in managing government stock, annuities and lotteries. An army of clerks was required to keep the books, take in subscriptions and pay out interest.

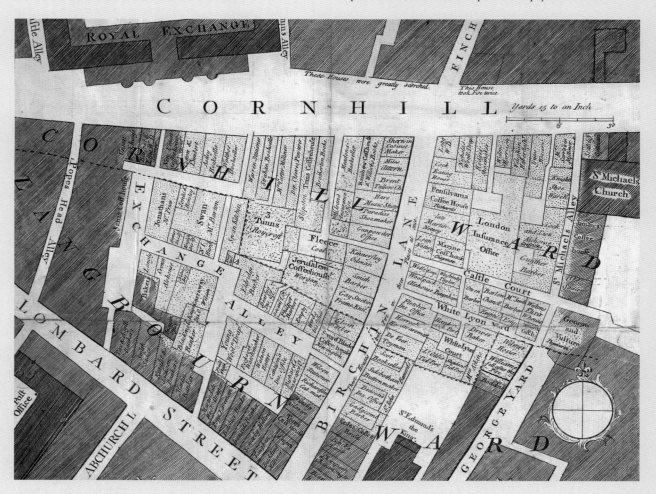

**Exchange Alley**
*The City's leading coffee houses and taverns are all marked on this plan, concentrated around Exchange Alley. The lighter area in the map records fire-damage. The blaze broke out in the powdering room of Mr Eldridge, a wig-maker, in the early hours of Friday 25 March 1748.*

For a time, the Sword Blade Company in Birchin Lane threatened the Bank's power and influence. It had received a charter in 1692 with further rights to own property and issue stock, and its land, bank and stock business expanded rapidly. In 1697, however, the Bank of England's charter was renewed and a further Act in 1708 limited other banking operations to a maximum of six partners. This curtailed all major competition.

## THE ROYAL EXCHANGE

Across the street, the Royal Exchange was the main public meeting place for business people. It had been rebuilt rapidly after the Great Fire and had reopened in 1669. The plan of the old building had been followed, with an open courtyard surrounded on four sides by a covered arcade, with shops on the upper floors. Statues of royalty were placed in niches on the first floor, facing the courtyard. The street elevations were even more impressive, especially that fronting Cornhill, which had a pair of large Corinthian columns each side of the entrance, supporting semi-circular pediments, and a three-storied tower topped by Gresham's grasshopper weather vane.

The Exchange was open six days a week, although business was limited to two sessions a day, between 11 a.m. and 12 noon in the morning and 5 and 6 p.m. in the evening, one hour later in the summer. The floor of the Royal Exchange was arranged into sectors or 'walks' frequented by different nationalities, merchants, ship-owners, factors and brokers. In the south-east corner, for example, Jewish merchants gathered; the south-west corner was divided between the New England, Carolina and Virginia merchants. Notices were fixed to walls and pillars announcing the latest bank-ruptcies, ship arrivals and departures, and daily stock and commodity prices. The central courtyard was unroofed, and when it rained the piazzas provided shelter. The Royal Exchange was not, however, the only place in London to meet and do deals.

## A PROFUSION OF COFFEE HOUSES

Opposite the Exchange's main entrance was Exchange Alley, opening into a warren of small passages and alleys around Birchin Lane and Lombard Street. Here there were coffee houses and taverns much used by City merchants. Exchange Alley became the haunt of stockbrokers and stockjobbers trading in government, East India Company and South Sea Company stock. The market congregated particularly in two coffee houses: Garraway's and Jonathan's. By 1691, Edward Lloyd's coffee house in Lombard Street, near the General Post Office, was providing captains, ship-owners and merchants with the latest shipping news. His coffee house soon became the principal market for marine insurance.

Unlike the taverns or the Royal Exchange, coffee houses provided a congenial and comfortable environment for doing business and obtaining the latest information. Merchants announced that they were 'to be found' at a particular coffee house. A one-penny entrance fee allowed unlimited time for business. There were simple wooden benches and tables, and fires to provide warmth in the winter. Coffee and other beverages were served and daily newspapers were available. Foreign visitors remarked on the atmosphere and pungent smell of tobacco.

Individual coffee houses were often named for a specialist area of commerce or trade, such as the Marine, the Amsterdam, the East India, the New England and the Jamaica. Coffee houses were also used as sales rooms for ships, commodities and goods of all types, and sometimes eve-n for the display of curiosities. In 1728, an advertisement announced the sale of 'a Negro boy, aged eleven Years' at the Virginia coffee house, and a few years later the same establishment hosted the display of 'the largest rattle snake ever seen in England – recently arrived from Virginia'. Competition was as fierce among coffee-house owners as it was in the financial community. The profusion of coffee houses in the City reflected London's growing status as a world financial centre.        AW

*The inside of the Royal Exchange, 1788*
The second Royal Exchange, in Cornhill, operated from 1669 until it burnt down 169 years later in 1838.

# THE SPREADING CITY

London's built-up area spread into the surrounding countryside as two new bridges opened up land south of the river. New roads and housing developments permanently changed the city's map.

'The figure of London is very irregular' lamented a guide-book writer in 1787, 'being stretched out in buildings at the pleasure of every undertaker, for conveniency of trade or otherwise; whereas Rome was round with very few irregularities.' What the ragged oblong of London represented, however, was not the tight controls exercised by the planners of Roman cities but rather the dynamism of a city erupting into a new phase of growth.

The growth of Westminster was the main cause of London's extended oblong shape, swelling up on the western side of the City as a kind of burgeoning new town, its stone and brick-built houses and regular squares setting new standards for fashionable town living. The scale of building was remarkable. 'I am credibly informed,' said the author Tobias Smollet in 1771, 'that in the space of seven years, eleven thousand new houses have been built in one quarter of Westminster'.

The Westminster model spread like wildfire, and versions of its terraced streets and planned squares began to erupt in all

**The 18th-century building booms**

Two major building booms in the Georgian period saw a dramatic expansion in the built-up area of London.

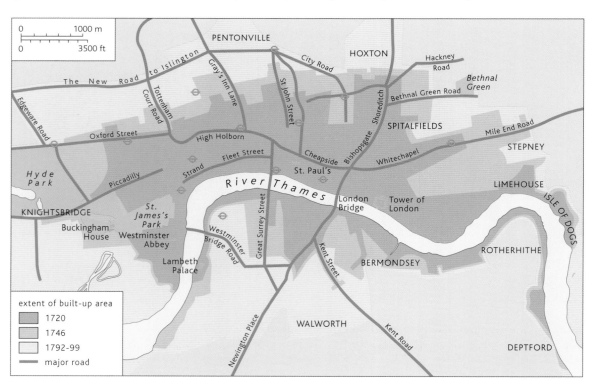

directions. Two separate building booms, the first ending in 1730 and the second in 1760, pushed London's boundaries further into its rural surroundings. By the end of the century the medieval settlements of the City and Southwark were loosely encircled by a ring of Georgian suburbs, whose brick-built terraces and detached villas proclaimed themselves the epitome of the modern way of living: half in the town and half in the country.

## ROADS TO THE NORTH

London's growth into Middlesex and Essex owed much to improvements in the major roads. Turnpike trusts became the favoured way of financing road repair and construction. Under the terms of an Act of Parliament, trusts were empowered to borrow money against the expected income from tolls collected from road users at toll gates. Most of the major roads into London were turnpiked, and toll gates became familiar landmarks – notably those at Hyde Park Corner, Mile End and Islington.

Turnpiking meant better roads as the trusts set about draining and gravelling the highways. Better roads meant more vehicles. The hay wagons, carts, stagecoaches, post-chaises and aristocratic carriages that poured into London along the new turnpikes added further congestion to London's already crowded streets.

Better roads also opened up areas for property development. The capital's most significant road-construction project was the New Road, the 18th-century equivalent of modern London's North Circular road, built in 1750s across open land to the north to link the City with Westminster. The new road brought two new planned suburbs. Pentonville was laid out from the 1770s on land owned by Henry Penton. Further west, Somers Town was laid out by Lord Somers from the 1790s.

Pentonville was the link in the chain that joined the former Middlesex village of Islington to the metropolis. Islington had seen pockets of smart terrace housing in the 1730s, but by the end of the century it was London's boom suburb with new terraces appearing in Highbury and Canonbury. Over the next decades all the land south of Pentonville Road would be built over, making Islington into an outlying district rather than an independent centre.

## BRIDGES TO THE SOUTH

The city's southward spread took off with the construction of an additional two bridges over the Thames. Until 1750 the capital's sole crossing point was London Bridge, but in that year Westminster Bridge opened, after a long and troubled construction history. As the name suggests, the bridge was designed to serve Westminster. Its construction had been opposed by the City Corporation, which in 1769 retaliated with a new bridge of their own, Blackfriars Bridge.

These two bridges helped to create new residential quarters in Surrey. The districts of Newington Butts, Kennington, Walworth and Camberwell all began to develop as a mosaic of terraces, villas and crescents. Nearer the river, houses even began to be built on Lambeth Marsh, a low-lying, poorly drained area, criss-crossed with ditches and dikes and liable to flooding.

**Mogg's London in Miniature, 1809**
*Mogg's map shows a London that had expanded dramatically after the two building booms of the 18th century.*

The approaches to the new bridges came together at St George's Circus, a road junction completed in 1771 to link the new roads to the older roads into Kent and Surrey. A stone obelisk was placed at the centre of the circus to mark the achievement.

## THE NEW DEVELOPMENTS MAPPED

Edward Mogg's map of 1809 (see above) shows London at the end of its 18th-century building booms. Two new bridges have opened up the land south of the river, but the three Regency bridges (Waterloo, Southwark and Vauxhall) are not yet built. To the north, a new west–east route has opened, along which the developments of Pentonville and Somers Town are just starting to take shape.

Other relatively new London landmarks visible in the Mogg map include the pleasure gardens at Vauxhall, Westminster's genteel squares and regular streets, and St George's Circus in Southwark. The shape of things to come for London's port is also visible at the new London Dock in Wapping, the second of the new docks developments.

Mogg was a cartographer who published a series of popular maps of London from the 1790s, selling them from his shop in Great Newport Street. This map was entitled *London in Miniature* and it promised users 'an entire new plan' showing all the improvements both present and intended, the whole 'laid down from the best authorities and carefully corrected'. **CR**

# MADE IN LONDON

London became the largest manufacturing centre in Britain in the 18th century, with small workshops and skilled labour making luxury goods, as well as having larger factories and mills.

London had three major advantages as a manufacturing centre. It was the country's largest consumer market. It was the largest port, enabling raw materials and finished goods to be transported with ease. London also had Britain's largest pool of skilled labour, its workforce including many European craftsmen, drawn by the relative freedoms England had to offer.

The main drawbacks of manufacturing in London were that land and coal were expensive. London's industrial character thus tended to favour goods that could absorb high overheads. The more expensive end of the glass industry thrived in London where glass decorators and glass cutters could match their products to changes in fashionable taste. Basic window glass was far cheaper to make in the north-east, where coal was cheap. Much of the glass used in London's 18th-century building boom was shipped to the capital from glasshouses on Tyneside and Wearside.

Those large manufacturing concerns that did thrive in the capital made goods for a mass market, including food and drink. London's breweries were among the largest in the country. Samuel Whitbread's at Chiswell Street opened in 1750 and in 1796 became the first brewery to record production of 200,000 barrels of beer a year. Vinegar-making, tanning, glue- and paint-making were also pursued in relatively large-scale manufactures.

## POTTERY & PORCELAIN

Potteries making tin glazed earthenware were long-established on the south bank of the Thames between Southwark and Vauxhall, and stoneware was made in Fulham. Eighteenth-century potter-entrepreneurs were driven by the quest to find a way of replicating the fine stoneware and blue and white porcelain imported from the Far East, to satisfy the demand of the tea-drinking upper classes. An early experimenter was Nicholas Sprimont who in the 1740s opened a porcelain works in Chelsea, designed to supply wealthy customers. Charles Gouyn's short-lived 'Girl in a Swing' factory in St James's targeted the same market.

A more functional range of porcelain wares was produced by Thomas Frye and Edward Heylin's factory at Bow, known as 'New Canton'. This factory was modelled on a Chinese prototype and employed about 300 workers at its height. It was commercially very successful, selling to the middle classes. There were other porcelain works at Limehouse, Vauxhall, and Isleworth. The ceramic industries also supported a number of finishing workshops devoted to decorating plain wares, sometimes made outside London. The best known of the independent decorators was James Giles, who ran premises in Kentish Town, retailed in fashionable Soho and Charing Cross, and decorated for the Worcester porcelain factory.

## A SPECIAL COACH

The Lord Mayor's Coach shows the high-quality craftsmanship that London could offer. Designed by the architect Sir Robert Taylor from a commission by the Lord Mayor elect, Sir Charles Asgill, this eye-catching vehicle had its first outing at the Lord Mayor's Day procession in 1757. Previous Lord Mayors had made do with hired carriages.

The construction of the coach was overseen by Joseph Berry of Leather Lane, Holborn, whose bill amounted to £860. Berry would have subcontracted a range of specialist craftsmen: among them carpenters, wheelwrights, wood carvers, iron founders, leather harness makers and an upholsterer, for the silk and velvet interior. The external panels were the work of Giovanni Cipriani, a painter who had arrived in London from Rome two years earlier. Cipriani's allegorical paintings

**Industrial Southwark**
By the 1790s large-scale manufactories, particularly breweries, had started to dominate Southwark.

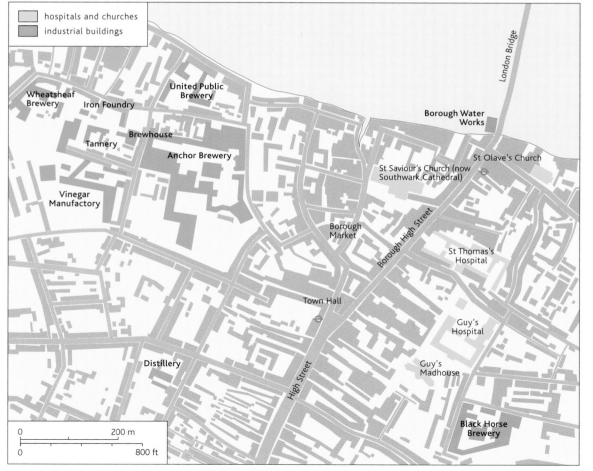

- hospitals and churches
- industrial buildings

Wheatsheaf Brewery
Iron Foundry
United Public Brewery
Borough Water Works
London Bridge
Brewhouse
Tannery
Anchor Brewery
St Olave's Church
St Saviour's Church (now Southwark Cathedral)
Vinegar Manufactory
Borough Market
Borough High Street
St Thomas's Hospital
Town Hall
Guy's Hospital
Distillery
Guy's Madhouse
High Street
Black Horse Brewery

0        200 m
0            800 ft

**The Lord Mayor's Coach**

*The elaborate and highly ornate Lord Mayor's Coach was built in London in 1757. It combined French rococo style with the latest coachbuilding technology.*

represent London's mercantile might, as 'the genius of the City', receiving exotic goods from around the world and mingling with the gods. The exuberantly carved shells, tritons and sea serpents refer to London's maritime interests.

The Lord Mayor's Coach would have been viewed at the time as an ultra-fashionable, modern and European vehicle. The rococo style of the design was distinctly French, and had come to London with migrant craftsmen. Besides its Italian paintings, the coach was of a modern, light 'Berlin' type, rather than the heavier and more formal state coaches traditionally seen in England.

## FASHIONABLE FURNITURE

London's cabinetmakers remained at the forefront of their craft throughout this period, supplying wealthy customers the length and breadth of the country. With better transport links and greater availability of printed information, many developed sophisticated trading networks through the publication of pattern books. Thomas Chippendale (1718–1779) was one of the best known of London's cabinetmakers; his *Gentleman and Cabinet Maker's Director*, published by subscription in 1754, provided patterns for provincial craftsmen to copy. Chippendale supplied a great range of goods from his Cabinet and Upholstery Warehouse in St Martin's Lane. Some workshops employed specialist craftsmen such as carvers, gilders and upholsterers; others subcontracted to firms in nearby Soho, with neighbouring trades interdependent on each other's skills.

### CLOCK- & WATCHMAKING

London clock- and watch-makers enjoyed an international reputation for their good value and reliability. Technological advances in watchmaking in the 17th century had introduced new tools and 'engines' and this labour intensive industry was one of the first to demonstrate the economic advantages of division of skills and mechanisation.

At least 5000 men and women outworkers were employed by the master clockmakers based in the area north of the Strand and Fleet Street. Later in the century, watchmakers moved away from the retail shops, settling in Clerkenwell, which remained the focus of the industry for two hundred years. A great variety of watches were made, from basic brass timepieces to finely chased and enamelled gold watches, incorporating the more accurate horizontal or cylinder escapement invented by George Graham in 1725.

### SPITALFIELDS SILK

The London silk industry was boosted by the influx of large numbers of Huguenots, protestant refugees escaping persecution in Northern France. By the early 1700s the colony in Spitalfields had established a viable alternative to the fashionable silks made in Lyon. By 1750 there were 500 master weavers in Spitalfields, with 15,000 looms at work.

The Spitalfields weavers produced work of great technical and artistic quality. Amongst the better known are weavers from Huguenot families, including Christopher Baudouin and James Leman, who specialized in supplying fashionable designs to master weavers. Tissues woven with gold and silver thread for royalty and the aristocracy, as well as velvets, damasks, taffetas, satins, and other plain silks were all made. The exquisitely patterned silks made by the 'Flower'd Branch' of the industry produced a great variety of surface textures and patterns. The technical possibilities were exploited to the full in the 1740s by Anna Maria Garthwaite, whose intricate floral designs were charming and botanically accurate.

*A piece of silk woven in London, 1707.*

Despite the efforts of the Weavers' Company to protect the interests of its members, weaving was vulnerable to economic change. The poorer silk weavers were notorious for outbursts of violence; their protests were often directed at 'Calico Madams', who wore gowns of printed cotton, a cheaper imported alternative to patterned silk.

By the end of the century, London's industrial dominance was waning as mining and the new textile mills were beginning to create independent centres of growth in the Midlands, the North, south Wales and Scotland. Many expert trades such as shoemaking and silk weaving migrated to other centres where labour was cheaper. The high quality of surviving artefacts made by the artisans and industrial entrepreneurs of Georgian London testify to their extraordinary skills, which began to decline only with the onset of mass production. **JL**

# STRANGERS & FOREIGNERS

Eighteenth-century London was a city of migrants. Thousands made their way to the capital from other parts of Britain, Europe or further afield and swelled all levels of society.

**May Morning, c.1760**

*John Collet's painting shows a group of London artisans, including a black servant, celebrating May Day in the traditional way by a noisy street parade.*

A record of patients at Westminster General Dispensary between 1774 and 1781 shows that out of 3236 people, only 25 per cent (824) were born in London: the majority, 58 per cent (1869) were born elsewhere in England: 9 per cent (281) in Ireland, 6 per cent (209) in Scotland and 2 per cent (53) in 'foreign countries.' By the end of the century, London's population of just under one million, included 15–20,000 Jews and 5–10,000 black and Asian people.

Only a few groups were large enough to put their stamp on an area. London's 'Little Dublin' was the parish of St Giles in the Fields. The Irish who settled there tended to be migrant workers.

Unskilled, poor and Catholic, they were often treated with hostility. Brawls between English and Irish labourers were common. In the Gordon Riots of 1780, several Irish public houses were sacked on the grounds that 'there had been an Irish wake in the houses, they were Irish Roman Catholicks and the house must come down'.

Two other groups put down roots in particular districts. The French Huguenots, who had fled to London as Protestant refugees, colonized two areas – Spitalfields, to the east of the City, and Soho. By 1700, there were nine Huguenot places of worship around Spitalfields and fourteen in the West End. The Jewish presence also grew more visible as their numbers swelled from 1000 in 1700 to 15–20,000 by 1800. The eastern edge of the City became the most visible centre of London's Jewish life. London's earliest synagogue had been erected at Creechurch Lane in 1657 and a second followed at Duke's Place in Aldgate (1690). During the 18th century, these were joined by three more: at Bevis Marks (1701), the new 'Hambro' (or Hamburg) synagogue in Fenchurch Street (1725) and the 'New Synagogue' in Leadenhall Street (1761).

The community's 18th-century growth reflected the arrival of Ashkenazi Jews from central Europe, following the Sephardic Jews from Spain and Portugal, attracted to the relative freedom of London. As numbers increased so London's Jewish quarter spread eastwards to Aldgate and Mile End, where two Jewish burial grounds had been established by the mid-18th century. Like the Huguenots, Jewish craftsmen also moved with the fashionable drift westwards, creating the nucleus of a Jewish community in Soho. The Western Synagogue opened in 1791, in premises off the Strand previously occupied by the Royal Academy.

## BLACK LONDONERS

Both Huguenot and Jewish communities were sufficiently large and mature to develop their own charities, schools and institutions. Without such communal support, members of other communities had to rely on their own wits. One such was Ignatious Sancho, an African who was brought to England as a child slave, but who rose to become a writer, composer and wealthy tradesman. In 1774, he opened a fashionable grocery store in Charles Street, Westminster, allowing him to become, as a male Anglican property owner, one of the few known black people in 18th-century Britain to possess a parliamentary vote.

Sancho's experience was not typical. Growing numbers of Lascar seamen (from India and Asia), destitute former servants and beggars were found in London's poorer areas, such as St Giles and St George in the East. Their numbers were swelled by former slaves who had fought for Britain in the American War of Independence (1775–83). It was partly this influx and partly the plight of the Lascar seamen that led to the formation in 1786 of the Committee for the Relief of the Black Poor. By this time slavery had become the most pressing moral question of the age. Former slaves such as Olaudah Equiano, Ottobah Cugoano and James Albert Gronniosaw were key figures in London's anti-slavery campaign;

their presence brought a degree of compassion to the way in which London's black poor were sometimes seen, although this could be sentimentalized: 'Forlorn wretches – in a strange land, cold, hungry, naked, friendless' as one appeal described them.

## OUTSIDERS

Black and Asian foreigners were visibly different in 18th-century London but white-skinned strangers were also marked out by appearance, accent or dialect. Difference could lead to hostility, as James Boswell witnessed at Covent Garden theatre in 1762. 'Just before the overture began to be played, two Highland officers came in. The mob in the upper gallery roared out, "No Scots! No Scots! Out with them!" hissed and pelted them with apples. My heart warmed to my countrymen, my Scotch blood boiled with indignation … The rudeness of the English vulgar is terrible. The liberty which they have [is] the liberty of bullying and being abusive …'

The hostility of the London mob toward foreigners was infamous. In 1701, Daniel Defoe wrote a scathing satire reproaching 'the true born Englishman' for despising others. As the English were themselves a 'mongrel half-bred race', argued Defoe, they had no grounds for superiority: 'an Englishman of all Men ought not to despise Foreigners as such … since what they are today, and we were yesterday and tomorrow they will be like us … We are really all Foreigners ourselves.'

**CR**

**Omai, c. 1774**
*Omai was a Tahitian who came to England on the* Adventure, *the sister ship to Captain Cook's* Resolution. *He spent three years in London, during which he was taken up by fashionable society and treated as an exotic prince.*

**Immigrant London**
Areas of 18th-century London were identified with particular groups of 'strangers'.

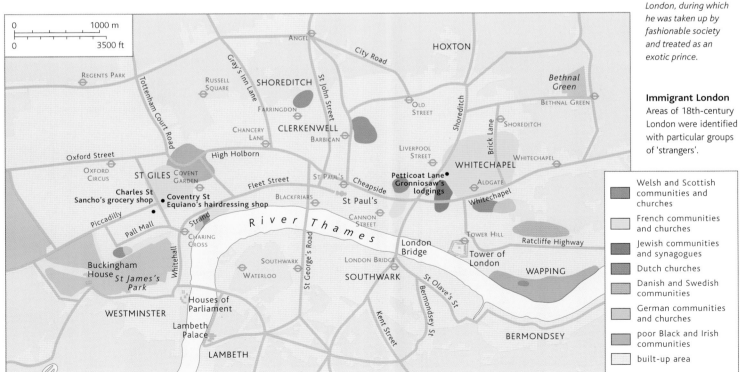

| | |
|---|---|
| | Welsh and Scottish communities and churches |
| | French communities and churches |
| | Jewish communities and synagogues |
| | Dutch churches |
| | Danish and Swedish communities |
| | German communities and churches |
| | poor Black and Irish communities |
| | built-up area |

# LONDON, SUGAR & SLAVERY

The West Indies trade brought wealth to London and moral outrage. How could a Christian country justify profiting from the systematic use of African slave labour on its plantations?

London's 18th-century wealth was partly built on Caribbean plantations and the slave trade. The fashion for drinking sweetened tea and chocolate created a huge demand for sugar. Goods such as textiles, beads, gunpowder and guns were shipped to Africa to exchange for men, women and children who were then transported to the Caribbean as slave labour for the sugar plantations. Sugar, coffee and tobacco were then brought back to England, making huge profits for captains, plantation owners and traders.

London played a central role in this triangular transatlantic trade. Its merchants dealt in sugar and tobacco. London financiers funded and insured the ships and cargoes, and the South Sea Company had its headquarters in the capital. London shipowners were engaged in the slave trade. Between 1698 and 1809 more than 3000 ships sailed from London ports to transport over 740,000 enslaved Africans to the plantations in the New World.

## THE CLAPHAM CONNECTION

**Clapham in the 1780s**

In the late 18th century, Clapham was home to a group of evangelical Londoners prominent in the movement to abolish slavery.

William Wilberforce (1759–1833) is synonymous with the campaign to abolish slavery. He was visible in Parliament, as the MP for Hull and later Yorkshire, but was just one part of the campaign to bring an end to slavery; other Members of Parliament such as James Stephen, Henry Thornton, William Smith and Charles Grant also campaigned for a change in the law.

Together, these men formed part of an influential group of social reformers known as the Clapham Sect. The name developed because most of them lived or worshipped in Clapham, south London. The sect's members were mainly prominent and wealthy evangelical Anglicans who shared political views on the liberation of slaves, the abolition of the slave trade and the reform of the penal system. Other members included the Reverend Henry Venn (the founder of the group) and his son John Venn, who were both rectors of the Holy Trinity Church, and banker John Thornton and his son Henry Thornton. Also members were Zachary Macaulay, who had been an overseer on a Jamaican plantation, and John Shore, Lord Teignmouth, who was the influential Governor-General of India. The group was sometimes called 'The Saints'.

They joined forces with a Quaker campaign for the abolition of the slave trade. Working with them was Granville Sharp, who subsequently became leader of the Clapham Sect itself. In 1772, Sharp had successfully challenged English law with the case of James Somerset, an enslaved African who had been brought to England. Somerset had escaped but had been recaptured and abused by his master, who imprisoned him on a ship bound for Jamaica. Sharp argued that although colonial law allowed slavery, the same law did not apply in England and that as soon as a slave set foot in England he became free. The judgement confirmed that it was illegal to forcibly enslave a person in Great Britain.

Sharp continued to campaign for other enslaved Africans and, in 1787, established the Society for the

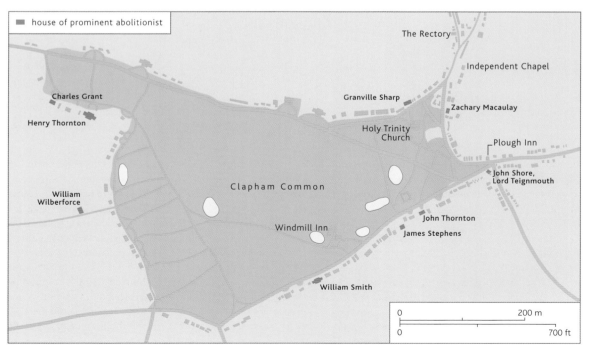

- house of prominent abolitionist

The Rectory

Independent Chapel

Charles Grant

Granville Sharp

Zachary Macaulay

Henry Thornton

Holy Trinity Church

Plough Inn

John Shore, Lord Teignmouth

William Wilberforce

Clapham Common

John Thornton

Windmill Inn

James Stephens

William Smith

| 0 | 200 m |
| 0 | 700 ft |

Abolition of the Slave Trade with fellow campaigner Thomas Clarkson. Wilberforce and other members of the Clapham Sect joined the society and instituted a series of meetings and rallies in London and across the country; they distributed pamphlets and presented Parliament with petitions against the trade signed by thousands of people.

The group was also instrumental in the foundation of a settlement in Sierra Leone, created as a new colony for freed slaves. In 1791 the Sierra Leone Company was founded, with Granville Sharp as president, Henry Thornton as chairman and Charles Grant and William Wilberforce as directors. There were, however, many years of difficulty before the community established itself. In

travelled to London, where he lived for several years in between further spells at sea. In 1759 he was baptized a Christian at St Margaret's Church in Westminster. In the 1760s he was apprenticed to a hairdresser in Coventry Court, off the Haymarket. By this time Equiano had become involved in the abolition campaign. He was a commanding and popular speaker, campaigning throughout England. He was actively involved with the Sierra Leone project, becoming Commissary in 1787, although he was later sacked after exposing corruption within the venture.

In 1789, Wilberforce's first bill to abolish the slave trade failed. In the same year, Equiano was persuaded to tell his story, and in London he published *The Interesting Narrative of the Life of Olaudah*

*The Rev.ᵈ Mr Kicherer.*     *Mary.*     *John.*     *Martha.*

Pub. by T. Williams, Stationers Court, 1. Jan.ʸ 1804.

the late 1790s, with Zachary Macaulay as governor, the settlement finally prospered. The Sierra Leone Company became a chartered company and in 1808 Sierra Leone became a Crown colony.

## AFRICAN VOICES

The Clapham Sect, and Granville Sharp in particular, highlighted the horrors of slavery by working with men like Olaudah Equiano, a former enslaved African. Equiano is thought to have been born around 1745, into the Igbo tribe in Benin (now Nigeria), West Africa. While still a child, he and his younger sister were abducted from their home, separated, transported to the Caribbean and sold as slaves. After being sold to a number of different owners, Equiano was able, at the age of twenty-one, to purchase his freedom. He

*Equiano or Gustavus Vassa the African.* The book was the second to be written by a former slave and laid out a number of religious and economic arguments for abolition. It helped to raise public awareness of the campaign, and nine different editions were published before his death in 1797. John Wesley, clergyman and leader of the Methodist movement, read the book and urged Wilberforce to use it in his campaign against slavery in the House of Commons.

The Abolition of the Slave Trade Bill was passed in 1806. The Act banned all trading of slaves within the British Empire and stopped all slave ships from leaving Britain after 1 May 1807. Many campaigners, the Clapham Sect included, believed that the Act did not go far enough and pushed for the abolition of slavery itself. Parliament finally passed the Slavery Abolition Act in 1833. **AE**

# THE RIVER & PORT

London was Britain's largest and most congested port. Its medieval quays were increasingly unable to cope with the huge volume of shipping the city was attracting by the 18th century.

By 1700, London was the most important port in Britain. At the beginning of the 18th century about 7000 ships were entering the port each year, carrying goods and produce from around the coast and cargoes from the growing number of overseas colonies. Before the end of the century, the number of ships had nearly doubled and the tonnage of cargoes had grown by more than 300 per cent. The port's facilities, however, failed to develop at the same pace.

Since 1588, all cargoes entering the port had to be discharged at the designated 'Legal Quays' close to the Customs House in the Pool of London. These quays, lining the north bank of the river between London Bridge and the Tower of London, consisted of twenty individual wharfs totalling 432 linear metres (1420 ft). As London and its colonial commerce expanded, additional wharfs, known as the 'Sufferance Wharves', were established on the south bank of the Pool. These additional facilities, however, did little to ease the port's congestion.

## PRIVATE INTERESTS

The port's problems stemmed from the fragmented ownership of the Thames-side quays. Botolph's Wharf, for example, originally consisted of Hammond's and Botolph's Wharfs and Lyon Quay. These were acquired piecemeal by the wealthy London merchant Sir Josiah Child, who was also a governor of the East India Company. He was therefore able to ensure that his wharfs handled much of the Company's profitable trade. Even the huge mooring chains slung across the riverbed, on which those ships able to make their way into the Pool were moored, were privately owned.

Such private interest hampered any strategic development of the port itself. Part of the problem lay in the fact that the port's operation was controlled by the City Corporation. Bound by centuries of tradition and very much City-focused, the Corporation treated the port as just another income-generating activity, rather like its numerous markets, and there was little understanding or appreciation of the complex needs of a growing international port.

The riverside area itself was virtually unchanged from the medieval period, with narrow streets largely inaccessible to carts.

*Congestion on the Quays, 1757*

This satire on the English taste for French luxuries was published during the Seven Years War. The scene is set on Custom House Quay with the Tower of London and a forest of ships' masts in the background.

**London, 1746**
This detail from John Rocque's map of London shows the city's sufferance wharves lining both sides of the Thames.

Although the destruction caused during the Great Fire of 1666 offered a unique opportunity for redeveloping the riverside wharfs – and the City Corporation approved a design for a 24-metre wide (80-ft) quayside lining the north bank of the Pool – plans did not reach fruition. By the beginning of the 18th century, the quaysides were once again a congested clutter of narrow streets and makeshift buildings, still adhering largely to the medieval street plan.

## THE PORT IN CRISIS

By the last decade of the 18th century, the port was in crisis. Discharging ships was becoming prohibitively costly. In 1793, after the outbreak of war with Revolutionary France had led to the reintroduction of the convoy system, the merchant William Vaughan described the Legal Quays as, 'A space, so exceedingly inadequate to the Business of the Port of London that it is not uncommon to see the Wharfs universally encumbered with Piles of costly Goods, exposed to every Risk of Weather and Plunderage.' Furthermore, he observed, 'the largest and deepest laden ships find it not safe to advance higher up the river than Deptford; the greater number do not moor within one Mile and a Half of the nearest legal quays; and few or none can be laid along-side the Wharfs'.

Vaughan's complaints were typical. It was not unknown for a ship to wait three months to be discharged – a particular problem for the West India merchants because imported rum not cleared through customs within a statutory thirty-day period was subject to seizure by customs officers. The risk of fire, to both ships in the crowded Pool and goods on the quaysides, meant that the cost of insurance rocketed and the cartel of wharf owners were able to extort ever-increasing rates for the use of their facilities. Simple overcrowding led inevitably to collisions, with resulting damage to both ships and cargo. The problem was illustrated bluntly, in retrospect, by Patrick Colquhoun in 1800: 'No more than 879 Ships and Vessels can be easily accommodated in the Harbour: yet, it frequently happens, when the Fleets arrive together, that from 13 to 1400 Vessels, including Coasters, are in Port at the same time.'

In addition to this, the state of the river itself was giving increasing cause for concern. Waste material from the city's growing population was pouring into the water, increasing sedimentation and encouraging the development of dangerous shoals on which numerous ships were wrecked. Furthermore, a shortage of deep-water anchorages meant that at low tide there was a real danger of ships being holed by their own anchors.

Exasperated by the state of the port, the city's merchants – especially those involved in the profitable West Indies trade – began campaigning for improvements. In response, in 1796, the government set up the first of a series of select committees to enquire into the state of the port. Their investigation led to the West India Dock Act of 1799: London's port was at last set for redevelopment.   **TW**

# MARKETS & FOOD

Several of London's food markets were enlarged in the 18th century to meet new scales of demand. Eating-houses reflected new fashions and more cosmopolitan tastes.

During the 18th century, Londoners' palates developed a taste for new and diverse foods. While beef, a wholesome symbol of English cuisine, would remain the most popular dish, food staples such as bread, cheese and fish were now joined by more exotic imports from across the world. Items such as tea, coffee and tobacco were no longer seen as luxury goods, and numerous cookery books were published listing Indian, Turkish and French recipes. By 1773, establishments such as the Norris Street Coffee House in the Haymarket were serving curry to their customers.

## LONDON'S MARKETS

London's large bustling markets provided the city with foodstuffs and necessities. The markets were defined by the type of wares they sold, the most famous being Covent Garden, situated on the site of the original convent garden of the monks of Westminster Abbey. Between 1631 and 1639 Francis Russell, 4th Earl of Bedford, employed Inigo Jones (1573–1652) to design a three-sided piazza on the site, and in 1670 the 5th Earl of Bedford obtained a royal charter to establish a market there for fruit, vegetables and flowers on weekdays. By the turn of the century, Covent Garden (see

below) had become the city's main provider of fruit, vegetables and flowers. Most of the produce sold in the market was grown in the market gardens located around the edge of the city.

The demolition of Bedford House and the building of Tavistock Row in 1705–6 enclosed the piazza, moving the market into the centre. By 1748, it had been completely remodelled, when it was rebuilt with 106 new shops and 229 stands. As the gentry had moved to the west of the city, artists, writers and shopkeepers took up residence in the area around the piazza.

London's other main fruit and vegetable market was the Stocks Market, established in the 13th century adjoining St Mary Woolchurch. In 1737, it was moved from its original site to permit the construction of the Mansion House and re-established in Farringdon under the name of Fleet Market.

**Covent Garden, c. 1770**
*Covent Garden was the largest and most famous of London's produce markets in the 18th century.*

London's fish market was situated at Billingsgate, one of the city's main wharfs since medieval times. In 1698, an Act of Parliament declared it a 'free and open market for all sorts of fish', breaking the monopoly of a group of fishmongers. Billingsgate was notorious for the bad language employed by the fishmongers and fishwives as they touted their wares, in large baskets balanced on their heads. Nearby, the market shrimp girls and oyster sellers sold their wares from barrows.

The city's largest meat market, Smithfield, was named after the site on which it stood, originally a grassy 'smooth field' outside the city walls. Smithfield market had been held weekly since medieval times, trading in cattle and livestock, but it was not until 1638 that the City of London Corporation formally established a cattle market on the site. The animals came from the Midlands and Welsh borders to be fattened in the Home Counties; from there they were driven to Islington, where London drovers took them to the market and finally to the Shambles, the slaughterhouse area on Newgate Street. Leadenhall Market on Gracechurch Street was the main poultry market, but was also known for selling leather and wool. It was named after a large lead-roofed mansion built on the site in the 14th century.

## STREET FOOD & EATING-HOUSES

Bartholomew Fair, which was held at Smithfield for three days in August, was famous for its hot food stalls. Hot sausages were cooked over glowing charcoal fires and pie men and gingerbread sellers mingled with the crowds. These food stalls had been on the city's streets for centuries. Many Londoners had limited access to cooking facilities and bought cheap bread, pies and puddings sold from barrows and kept warm by compartments full of hot charcoal. Cookshops also provided inexpensive food and cheap cooked cuts of meat, which could be eaten on the premises or taken away. 'Pottage Island' was a group of cookshops in the slum area between St Martin's Lane and the Strand.

For those with more money to spend, there were various other options. Chophouses had become popular in the 17th century, with waiters and waitresses serving customers seated on benches with partitions in between. One of the most famous was Dolly's in Paternoster Row, which was also renowned for its beefsteaks.

Coffee shops, taverns and alehouses also offered hot food, and pleasure gardens such as Vauxhall and Ranelagh served tea and supper. One of the city's most exclusive dining establishments, The City Tavern in Bishopsgate Street, opened in 1768. The building contained purpose-built banqueting rooms and an imposing ballroom, all of which could be hired out for functions. The City Tavern gained such note that in 1783 a group of publishers produced a ghostwritten recipe book, *The London Art of Cookery*, under the name of John Farley, the head cook of the City Tavern.

Confectioners' shops were also extremely popular, offering expensive sweets and pastries, which could be consumed on the premises or taken away, often by female clientele. Sophie von la Roche, a visitor to London in 1786, noted on her visit to a pastry shop, that it contained 'all kinds of preserved fruits and jellies … pyramids of small pastries and tartlets and some larger pastries with sweetmeats; wine glasses of all sizes, with lids to them and full of liqueurs of every conceivable brand, colour and taste'. Von la Roche was one of many visitors from abroad who marvelled at London's variety of foodstuffs and the many eating experiences offered by the city.                                                                OC

# PLEASURE GARDENS & OTHER ENTERTAINMENTS

*Vauxhall Pleasure Gardens, 1740s*
*A general panorama showing the grand walk,*
*the orchestra pavilion and supper boxes.*

The rise in popularity of public pleasure gardens in the early 18th century popularized smart London's new code of fashionable behaviour. Public sociability was à la mode.

In 1789 the German writer Baron von Archenholz recorded his observations of Londoners' social habits. He noted: 'They take great delight in public gardens near the metropolis, where they assemble and drink tea together in the open air. The number of these gardens … is amazing and the order, regularity, neatness and even elegance of them is truly admirable.' These public so-called 'pleasure gardens' were the social arena in which to be seen in Georgian London.

Although many London parks had been open to the public for promenading and the taking of air since the early 17th century, it was the opening of the New Spring Gardens at Vauxhall in 1732 that heralded the transformation of urban cultural life. Vauxhall Gardens, where stunning and varied architectural, musical and visual displays could be enjoyed for only a shilling, inspired similar venues across Europe, as well as the creation of hundreds

of smaller-scale London gardens and spas catering for the new demand in open air entertainment.

The gardens were planted in the undeveloped spaces to the north and south of the City by entrepreneurs and by investors anxious to open up new ground away from the regulations, high prices and increasing squalor of jostling central London. Well over 600 were established or improved during the period. These varied in scale from the splendour of Vauxhall's 12 acres (5 ha), where the Prince of Wales was entertained by the finest musicians of the day, to the more modest attractions of bowls and trap-ball at the Adam and Eve Tea Gardens in Tottenham Court Road.

Many of the smaller rustic north London gardens, such as Sadler's Wells in Clerkenwell, had been promoting the healing properties of their waters since the 17th century. These spas were the main public healing places in an era when the curing of illness was largely left to the individual, and the commercial exploiters of mineral springs quickly embraced the new trend by adding attractions to existing gardens. With the restorative powers of nature widely extolled in contemporary literature, Londoners increasingly desired an escape to the delights of a quasi-rural retreat. Pleasure gardens created the required idyll (albeit in a suitably manicured

version) in which to refine jaded urban sensibilities on the doorstep of the city.

It was twenty-one-year-old entrepreneur Jonathan Tyers who masterminded the transformation of Vauxhall from a simple country house garden, described in the 1660s by John Evelyn as merely 'a pretty, contrived plantation'. The sumptuous imitations that followed at Ranelagh, Cupers and Marylebone created fierce competition. When Ranelagh Gardens opened in Chelsea in 1742, Horace Walpole wrote: 'It has totally beat Vauxhall … You can't set your foot without treading on a Prince or Duke of Cumberland.'

## EXCITING ENCOUNTERS

This new-found enthusiasm for outdoor socializing was certainly not the result of a radically different London climate; events were frequently rained off. Nor was it restricted to the aristocratic classes, who had long enjoyed the grand scale of their private gardens. Many Londoners were benefiting from unprecedented prosperity as a result of thriving trade and a stable government. Ordinary merchants, professionals and their families now had time and money for leisure as never before. The grand gardens allowed them access to magnificent surroundings that had previously been the preserve of the aristocracy.

This intermingling of social classes created an entirely new public juxtaposition of respectability and dissipation. The dark groves of Vauxhall provided ample scope for social and sexual excitement – so much so that they were lit in the 1750s by order of the magistrates. Advertisements for Cupers Garden in 1749 ended with the line 'N.B. Great Care will be taken to keep out Persons of ill Repute.' Watchmen and 'vigilant officers' were in attendance to keep order and exclude 'undesirables'.

The reputations of individual gardens were crucial in determining their success. When George II's daughters the princesses Amelia and Caroline created a vogue for taking the waters at Islington Spa in 1733,

fashionable society flocked there. At the high point of its history over 1600 people took the waters daily. But as the status of the spa's clientele gradually fell, so did its reputation, until it finally closed in 1810.

By the late 18th century, going to gardens was in decline as London's fashionable elite sought new venues for their diversions. The Adam and Eve's clientele became 'a motley crew of highwaymen, footpads and low women'. Its skittle yards were razed in the early 19th century by magistrates and it reopened as a tavern. Ranelagh's distance from London's centre became a drawback, and its great rotunda was demolished in 1805. Vauxhall's fortunes waxed and waned, but eventually its demise was proclaimed in 1859 in a series of flyers announcing 'positively the last night ever'.

The gardens had prospered as a result of shrewd entrepreneurship that both provoked and responded to the desire for a new public arena. They created a stage for the display of the fashionable as never before, but – most importantly – it was a democratic stage, reflecting wider changes in Georgian society. Almost everyone other than the very poor could emulate high society when promenading the grand walks at Vauxhall, and in doing so they could assert their newly powerful position in the national economy of Georgian Britain.                                                                      **ES**

# PRINTING & PUBLISHING

London was the printing capital of Europe. Hundreds of printing presses published broadsides, pamphlets, books and newspapers, spreading ideas, news and opinions.

The term 'Grub Street' came into use in 1755, with its inclusion in Dr Johnson's *English Dictionary*: 'Originally the name of a street in Moorfields in London, much inhabited by writers of small histories, dictionaries, and temporary poems; whence any mean production is called grubstreet.' The term points to a real social phenomenon in London (and indeed wider British) society: the emergence in the course of the 18th century of a true print culture that was both widespread and effectively uncontrolled. The ending of censorship with the Glorious Revolution of 1688 and the lapsing of the Licensing Act in 1695, which ended the monopoly of the Stationers' Company over publishing, had made both printing and publishing in effect free markets. The annual number of new publications increased prodigiously in the 18th century, from about 21,000 in 1710 to some 56,000 in the 1790s (compared to perhaps 6000 in 1620) – the vast majority produced in London.

### GRUB STREET

As Johnson observed, the expression had its basis in a real street, and later a more general area, of London. Grub Street itself dated back to the medieval period, its name being derived from 'grube' – a drain or a ditch. The term was applied, however, not only to this single street, but to most of the area of the surrounding ward of Cripplegate, which encompassed, as a contemporary writer noted: 'Fore Street, Postern-Street, Back-Street, Little-Moorfields, Moorlane, Grub-street, Whitecross-Street, Redcross-street, Beech-Lane, Golden-lane, Barbican, Jewen Street'. The actual street no longer exists; it was renamed Milton Road in 1830, most probably after the poet John Milton who had lived in Grub Street in 1661–2, and is now lost beneath the Barbican development.

The parish of St Giles Cripplegate was renowned for its poverty and incipient criminality before it became associated with hack literary production – even its church was named for the patron saint of beggars. It remained an area of severe poverty throughout the 18th century. The parish contained two workhouses and two hospitals for mental illness (the latter, St Luke's and the infamous Bedlam, were adjacent). Its streets consisted mainly of narrow courts and alleys, which gave rise to numerous lurid contemporary accounts of the thieves' dens and brothels hidden within it.

The area's notoriety as a general area of disrepute dates from the 17th century. Its position just outside the City walls placed it outside the immediate jurisdiction of the City; it was not only one of the earliest London suburbs, but also a haven of criminality.

The association of Grub Street with hack literary production came about because its cheap rents attracted struggling writers and printers. In the 18th century, it even hosted the Moorfields Academy, a prolific training ground for hacks, run by John Eames.

One of the best contemporary descriptions of Grub Street is contained in John Hawkins's *Life of Samuel Johnson*, written in 1787:

> Mention is often made, in the *Dunciad*, and other modern books, of Grub-street writers and Grub-street publications, but the terms are little understood: the following historical fact will explain them: During the usurpation [that is, the Civil War and Commonwealth], a prodigious number of seditious and libellous pamphlets and papers, tending to exasperate the people, and encrease the confusion in which the nation was involved, were from time to time published. The authors of these, were, for the most part, men whose indigent circumstances compelled them to live in the suburbs and most obscure parts of town; Grub Street then abounded with mean and old houses, which were let out in lodgings, at low rents, to persons of this description, whose occupation was the publishing of anonymous treason and slander.

### BOOKS & NEWSPAPERS

Behind this huge rise in literary production were the newly-powerful booksellers, who were also publishers in today's sense. James Lackington, owner of a celebrated cheap bookshop in Finsbury Square, claimed in 1792 to have an annual turnover of over 100,000 volumes; he was also the inventor of 'remaindering' – that is, boosting sales of books near the end of their print runs by selling them off cheaply. Daniel Defoe

**An Englishman's Delight**

*A comment on the appetite for news that spawned a new, thriving printing and publishing industry in 18th-century London.*

AN ENGLISHMANS DELIGHT OR NEWS OF ALL SORTS.

All Englishmen delight in News
In London there's enough to chuse
Of morning papers near a Ream
Fill'd with every kind of theme
At Noon there's such a duced Clatter
Strangers must wonder what's the matter
And E'en that day the Lord hath blest
Is now no more a day of rest

Forth from the Press the Papers fly
Each greedy reader to supply
Of battles fought, and numbers slain,
Of Towns besieg'd, and prisoners ta'en
Ecche from Aldgate to the Strand
Hail! happy land, sure none's so blest
With News to comfort every breast.

*Published as the Act directs 30 Dec.r 1780 by W. Richardson N.o 68 high Holborn.*

identified booksellers explicitly as 'the Master Manufacturers or Employers', and the writers, copyists and editors as 'workmen'. While a few such workers in print were able to profit from this new relationship (thanks in part to another publishing innovation, the advance paid to an author for a book not yet written), most – including Defoe himself – struggled to support themselves by adapting their talents to any opportunity available.

Among such opportunities, the 18th century also saw the emergence of scores of examples of two new print media: the journal and the newspaper. The former included Daniel Defoe's *Review*, Richard Steele's *Tatler* and the *Spectator* of Steele and Joseph Addison, and many others. Newspapers had existed before the 18th century, but their total circulation numbered only a few thousand; in the course of the century they saw an explosion, in both London and the provinces: by 1801, London had twenty-three newspapers, and national circulation had reached sixteen million.

These media created a huge demand for copy – and were responsible for the creation of a new trade, that of the professional journalist. Market forces ensured that the less successful proponents of this new trade were exploited and ghettoized in the shady world of Grub Street.

## HIGH & LOW LITERATURE

Johnson had noted the common metaphorical usage of 'grub-street,' but the area's literary infamy was spread above all by the satirical attacks of the age's greatest writers, Alexander Pope, Jonathan Swift and Johnson himself. These writers, who occupied the heights of English literature in the 18th century, made much of the differences between their world and that of Grub Street. Their most stinging attacks were on the pretentious less-talented proponents of serious literature who monopolized public literary life in London – and the association of such writers with the world of Grub Street was the perfect weapon to use against them.

Perhaps the most famous literary satire of the age is Pope's *Dunciad*, first published in 1729. In this, one of the greatest of all London poems, his mock-heroic couplets revel in plunging his opponents, the 'Dunces' (among whom the chief is Colley Cibber, the Poet Laureate) into the very lowest depths of Grub Street:

Not with less glory mighty Dulness crown'd,
Shall take thro' Grub-Street her triumphant round;
And her Parnassus glancing o'er at once
Behold an hundred sons, and each a Dunce.

Pope's image of the epic triumph of ignorance, vapid modernity and talentless pretension ('Dulness') in London society is one of the most powerful in Georgian literature. A visual counterpoint is provided by William Hogarth's *The Distressed Poet* (painting *c.* 1735, print 1736–7), showing a young writer whose illusions keep his wife and family in rags (see above). Above his head is a carica-

ture pinned to the wall depicting Pope, the scourge of such fools.

Jonathan Swift's *Tale of a Tub* and Samuel Johnson's *Life of Mr Richard Savage* followed the attacks of the *Dunciad*, and a satirical periodical, the *Grub-street Journal*, edited by Pope, ran to 418 issues between 1730 and 1737. The *Journal* in particular sustained throughout its existence a mocking attitude towards the world it supposedly represented, passing up no opportunity to satirize the venality, shallowness and pretension of Grub Street, as in this couplet of 28 October 1731:

Grub Street, renown'd in old and modern times,
The venerable seat of prose and rhimes.

Despite such deliberate high irony, there remains nonetheless a certain conscious ambiguity in the attitude of these high literary authors. For one thing, they were themselves scarcely removed from the world they affected to despise: Pope was the son of a modest bookseller, while Johnson's labours on his *Dictionary* involved him in long years of anxious and resentful toil not much different from the careers of the hacks. For another, the traditional literary world of leisure and aristocratic patronage that they implicitly championed was fast becoming an anachronism. The future belonged to those bestselling authors, like Defoe, Addison and the historian Edward Gibbon, who embraced with skill and enthusiasm the opportunities that the commercial world of Grub Street had to offer. **MB**

**The Distressed Poet, 1736**
*William Hogarth's image satirises the deluded ambitions of the hack writer.*

**A bookseller's tradecard**
*James Buckland's tradecard, c.1750. Paternoster Row was the centre of London's book trade.*

# THEATRES & OPERA HOUSES

Theatre was central to the ferment of ideas that made Georgian London Europe's most uninhibited city. As the capital grew larger and noisier, every aspect of its theatre world expanded.

Theatre was the classic boom-or-bust business of the 18th century, making fortunes for some entrepreneurs and leaving others bankrupt. It created celebrities of the best actors and actresses: this was the era of David Garrick, Colley Cibber and Sarah Siddons. The less fortunate led a hand-to-mouth existence that left some actresses as little more than prostitutes.

In 1700, the London stage was still emerging from the shadow of Puritanism. Although the Restoration had seen the flourishing of a new generation of playwrights, London audiences had a choice of only two theatres. The Theatre Royal at Drury Lane and the smaller theatre at Lincoln's Inn Fields were both 'patent' theatres, operating under a royal monopoly. The loosening of such controls helped usher in a new era of theatre-building by entrepreneurial actor-managers. Substantial new theatres were erected in central London, along with smaller playhouses in fashionable suburbs such as Greenwich, Hampton Court and Richmond. Stage and music performances also spread to smaller venues such as 'Great Rooms', tavern booths and coffee houses.

London's first major new theatre was built in Haymarket in 1705. Designed by John Vanbrugh, this 'Queen's Theatre' soon acquired a reputation for a fashionable new performance form – Italian-style opera. Handel's *Rinaldo* had a sell-out run in 1711. By mid-century, the new house had become known as the King's Opera House. A second new theatre opened in 1732 in Covent Garden. The businessman behind it was John Rich, who had already tasted financial success with a production of *The Beggar's Opera* in 1728. Rich courted a popular audience, including in his programmes not only the standard Shakespearean repertoire but also modern comedies and pantomimes. A sensation of Rich's period was the actress Peg Woffington, who in 1740 confirmed the views of those who thought that the stage was the work of the Devil by playing a male role in *The Constant Coup*.

Covent Garden and the older Theatre Royal in Drury Lane dominated London's theatrical world throughout the century. The latter was run by a succession of actor-managers and from 1747 by David Garrick, under whom it flourished. Garrick brought a serious eye to the productions, pioneering regular rehearsals, better lighting and closer attention to the text. Drury Lane continued to attract royal patronage, with both George II and George III regular visitors. After damage to the building in the 1780 riots, a company of guards was detailed to stand outside during evening performances, a custom that survived until 1896.

Covent Garden Theatre and the Theatre Royal were both rebuilt towards the end of the century to accommodate ever-larger audiences. Covent Garden received in 1784 a new auditorium and space for 2500; seven years later Drury Lane was rebuilt to accommodate 3600. The Opera House in the Haymarket also ended up with capacity for an audience of 3000. The larger theatres brought new income, but also complaints from regulars that the 'vast void' of the new spaces destroyed the intimacy of performances. Actors had to work hard to project their voices and to exaggerate gestures and facial expressions.

Performances always had an edge of anarchy. Evening shows generally began at 6 p.m. but the doors opened at 4 p.m., for audiences to bag their unreserved seats in the pit, gallery or boxes. Seats were plain wooden benches, although more expensive boxes provided chairs. Lighting was provided by large rings

**Covent Garden Theatre, 1802**
Entitled 'A peep behind the scenes', John Nixon's watercolour shows the stage from the wings with actors waiting their turn.

**Key**
1. Stage
2. Pit
3. Basket boxes
4. Dress Circle
5. One Shilling Gallery
6. Scene painters' workshops
7. Dressing rooms
8. Saloon

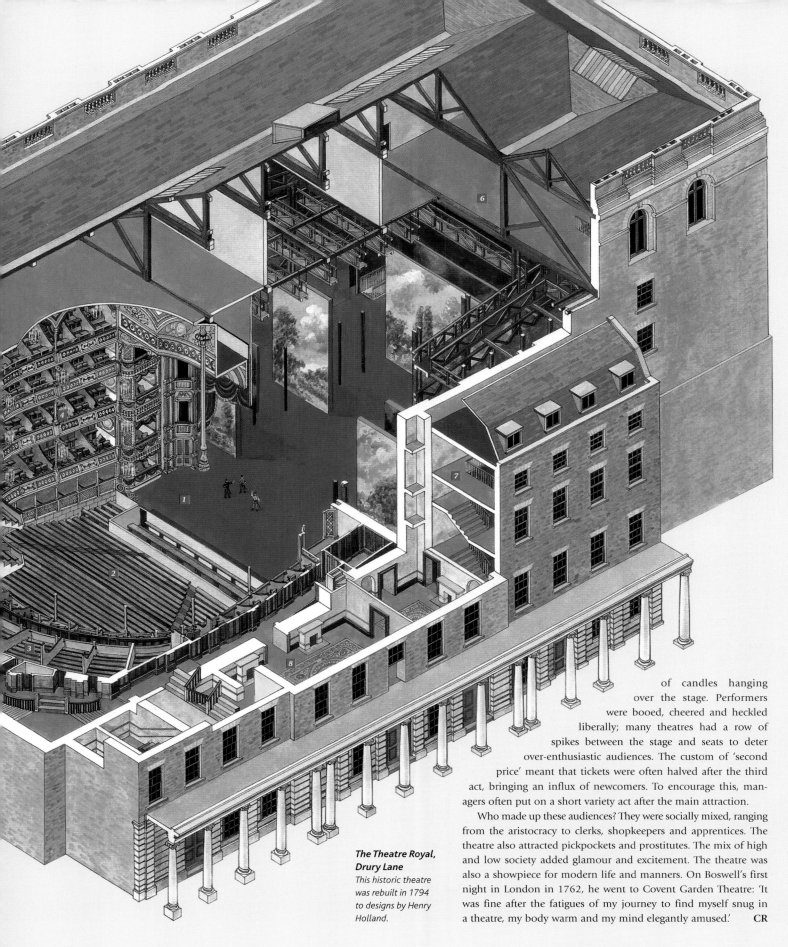

of candles hanging over the stage. Performers were booed, cheered and heckled liberally; many theatres had a row of spikes between the stage and seats to deter over-enthusiastic audiences. The custom of 'second price' meant that tickets were often halved after the third act, bringing an influx of newcomers. To encourage this, managers often put on a short variety act after the main attraction.

Who made up these audiences? They were socially mixed, ranging from the aristocracy to clerks, shopkeepers and apprentices. The theatre also attracted pickpockets and prostitutes. The mix of high and low society added glamour and excitement. The theatre was also a showpiece for modern life and manners. On Boswell's first night in London in 1762, he went to Covent Garden Theatre: 'It was fine after the fatigues of my journey to find myself snug in a theatre, my body warm and my mind elegantly amused.' **CR**

**The Theatre Royal, Drury Lane**
*This historic theatre was rebuilt in 1794 to designs by Henry Holland.*

# GEORGIAN ART & ARTISTS

The 18th century saw the rise in social status of artists as painting became associated with civilized behaviour. Artists moved west to newly fashionable Westminster.

**The Royal Academy, 1787**
*Royal patronage ensured that the Academy's exhibitions at Somerset House were society affairs. Here the Prince of Wales is seen admiring the dense hang.*

Compared to that of many other European cities at the turn of the 18th century, the London art market was relatively underdeveloped and still largely reliant on the traditional patronage of royalty and landed gentry. The mercantile patronage that did exist centred on the City, where money and wealth was created.

In the course of the century, however, a larger social and geographic change saw the merchants move to fashionable new developments in the West End, and this was reflected in the movement of artists themselves. The City remained the centre of the financial world but, importantly, not the social world, which the merchants now wished to conquer. With their growing social aspirations came the desire for increased cultivation, a key to London society. This more widespread knowledge of the arts, and the desire of merchants to have their likenesses realized in portraiture, led to a new level of patronage for artists. Fashionable portraits demonstrated the worldly success of their sitters, but also alluded to civic duty and charitable works – allusions intended to allay the vulgar associations of 'trade'.

## MOVING WEST

Covent Garden and Leicester Square emerged as two important centres of artist settlement in the 18th century. Covent Garden had been developed as a high-class suburb as early as the 1630s; for 18th-century artists it became the area where art was discussed, made and sold, as well as providing rich material for subject matter. On the whole, London's artists lived and worked at home; the taverns and coffee houses that proliferated around Covent Garden acted as meeting places, giving artists the opportunity to discuss ideas and learn from their fellow artists as well as meeting connoisseurs, collectors and potential clients. However, it was not solely the piazza itself that supported artists; the square boasted leading names such as Richard Wilson (*c.* 1713–82) and Johan Zoffany (1733–1810) among its residents. The side streets around Covent Garden were also populated by many artists, particularly

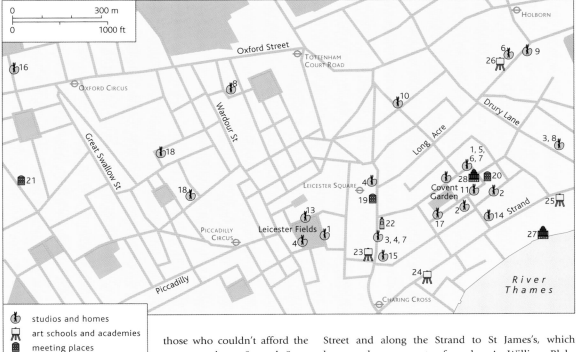

**Artists in the West End, 1700–1800**
Over twenty artists lived and worked in the small area of Covent Garden and Leicester Square, including Hogarth, Kneller and Lely.

Map legend:
- studios and homes
- art schools and academies
- meeting places
- recurrent London subject in art of the period
- artists' supply shop

1. William Hogarth,
NE corner of Covent Garden Piazza, 1729–33
The Golden Head, Leicester Square, 1733–64
2. Samuel Scott
4 Tavistock Row, 1718–47
2 Henrietta Street, 1747–65
3. Francis Hayman
104 St Martin's Lane, 1753
Craven Buildings, Drury Lane
4. Sir Joshua Reynolds
104 St Martin's lane
46 Great Newport Street, 1754–60
47 Leicester Square, 1760–92
5. Sir Peter Lely
NE corner of Covent Garden Piazza, 1662–80
6. Sir Godfrey Kneller
NE corner of Covent Garden Piazza, 1682–1702
55/56 Great Queen Street, 1709–1723
7. Sir james Thornhill
104 St Martin's Lane
Covent Garden Piazza, 1718–34
8. George Michael Moser
King Square Court
Craven Buildings, Drury Lane
9. Thomas Hudson
Great Queen Street, 1746–61
10. Joseph & Alexander van Aken
King Street, 1720s–56
11. Richard Wilson
Covent Garden Piazza
12. Johann Zoffany
Covent Garden Piazza
13. Edward Fisher
36 Leicester Square
14. Hubert François Gravelot
Southampton Street
15. François Robiliac & Nicholas Read
Peter's Court, St Martin's Lane
16. John Vanderbank
Hollis Street
17. James Macardell
The Golden Ball, Henrietta Street
18. Paul Sandby
38 Great Pulteney Street, 1753
Dufour's Court, Broad Street, 1763
19. Old Slaughter's Coffee House
74/75 St Martin's Lane, 1692–1843
20. Tom's Coffee House
Russell Street
21. Kings Arms
New Bond Street
22. John Middleton
80/81 St Martin's Lane
23. St Martin's Lane Academy I&II
St Martin's Lane, 1735–67
24. Society of Arts
Durham Yard, 1754–
25. Royal Academy Schools
Somerset House, Strand, 1774–1836
26. Great Queen Street Academy
55 or 56 Great Queen Street, 1711–15
27. Somerset House
Royal Academy of Arts, 1774–1836
28. Covent Garden Piazza

those who couldn't afford the centre, such as Samuel Scott (*c.* 1702–72), an important painter of London and the Thames, who lived at 4 Tavistock Row from 1718 until 1747, before moving to a larger home at 2 Henrietta Street (1747–65).

Though Covent Garden's fashionable piazza offered salubrious homes for artists, it was also an area where all levels of society could avail themselves of its market and entertainments, including seamier diversions like drinking and prostitution. William Hogarth's image *Morning* (painted in 1736, printed in 1738) famously depicts drunken rakes and prostitutes outside St Paul's church, Covent Garden, in the early hours of an icy winter's day. Hogarth (1697–1764) lived in Covent Garden until 1733, when he moved further from the city's centre to the Golden Head at Leicester Square, a sign of his rise up the social ranks. Leicester Square was a growing area of status, reflected by the residence of the Royal Academy's first president, Sir Joshua Reynolds (1723–92), who lived there between 1760 and 1792 in a 'a superior mansion' at 47 Leicester Fields.

## THE PRINT TRADE

Along with the movement of London's artists and merchants westward came a burgeoning print trade. By the end of 17th century, a large number of print shops were firmly established in London around St Paul's Church Yard and Fleet Street, alongside the publishers and booksellers. Peter Stent (*c.* 1642–65) and John Overton (1640–1713) were two of the most important printers of the period. Overton's great rivals were the Bowles family, whose business based at St Paul's Church Yard survived into the mid-19th century. Prints were part of London's blossoming consumerism and shops gradually appeared up and down Fleet

Street and along the Strand to St James's, which became the new centre for sales. As William Blake noted in 1800: 'There are now I believe … as many Printshops as of any other trade. We remember when a Printshop was a rare bird in London.' Prints played a vital part in 18th-century London's visual culture and brought images ranging from fine imported art to native satire to a widening audience. Satire pilloried all aspects of society, as well as occasionally providing a forum for artistic criticism, as seen by Paul Sandby's visual attacks on William Hogarth, and Hogarth's own insistence on the strengths of native British art.

## THE ROYAL ACADEMY

The London art world changed radically in the latter half of the 18th century with the death of Hogarth in 1764 and the establishment of a recognized professionalism, as manifested in the Royal Academy of Arts, in 1768. The Royal Academy held its first summer exhibitions at Pall Mall (1769–79) before shifting to the Great Room of Somerset House on the Strand in 1780. Westminster was the new artistic centre of the 18th century, the home of a growing number of gallery developments. The homes of the new members of the Academy, too, remained outside the bounds of the City, as Giles Walkeley noted in his authoritative survey of artists' houses in London: 'No less than 33 [of 36] of the founder members [of the Royal Academy] lived in London in 1769, the distinct majority of them collecting in Westminster. More exactly, most resided between Green Park and Lincoln Inn's Fields. Soho and the vicinity of Cavendish Square accounted for two other roughly equal portions.' The vibrant culture of Covent Garden and the fashionable, refined Leicester Square reflected the changing position of artists in London society.
**MB**

# RELIGION & DISSENT

Georgian London enjoyed a greater degree of religious toleration than other European cities. However non-Anglicans, including Catholics, Dissenters and Jews, were denied full civil rights.

To the French philosopher Voltaire, visiting the London Stock Exchange in the 1720s, London was a paradise of religious tolerance. 'There a Jew, a Mohammedan and the Christian deal with each other as if they were of the same religion, and give the name of the infidel only to those who go bankrupt; here the Presbyterian trusts the Anabaptist, and the Anglican honours the Quaker promise. On leaving these free and peaceful assemblies some go to the synagogue, others to drink … others go to church to await the inspiration of God; and all are content.'

**Dissenters in 1740s London and Southwark**
The City was riddled with meeting places, often located in alleys and yards, away from the main streets.

Compared to other European countries, England had indeed made the most progress in officially acknowledging religious plurality, through the Tolerance Act of 1689. However, it was not entirely true that 'all are content'. Non-Anglicans continued to be treated as second-class citizens, their civil rights restricted by law. Doctrinal differences, even within religious groups, continued to incite heated debate.

Religion was central to London's development as a metropolis of free thought and openly expressed ideas about individual rights.

Not only was London's huge population able to sustain sects and congregations of every persuasion, its metropolitan middle class also included a substantial body of Dissenters (Protestant but non-Anglican) to whom civil disabilities and legal discrimination were unacceptable. The campaign to repeal the Test and Corporation Acts, under which all holders of public office had to conform to the rites of the Anglican Church, was founded in the City in 1732 by a group of Protestant Dissenters, among them gentry, physicians and lawyers. The campaign almost achieved success in 1789 but foundered in the climate of fear generated by the French Revolution. Radical Dissenters, such as Richard Price, a Presbyterian minister from Stoke Newington, were among the most prominent supporters of the Revolution.

All three branches of 'Old Dissent' – Presbyterians, Baptists and Independents – were firmly established in London from the beginning of the century, with a strong presence in and around the City. There were said to be thirty-one Baptist groups in London by 1740. John Rocque's map records twenty Independent meeting houses and thirty Presbyterian meeting houses around the same time. The number of congregations was almost certainly higher than the number of buildings as each meeting house supported a number of groups, sometimes with different doctrinal beliefs.

Some congregations met in secular spaces, including livery halls, taverns and, in one case, an abandoned Roman Catholic chapel. John Wesley's followers created their first meeting house in a disused cannon foundry to the north of Moorfields.

The presence of Nonconformists in the City also owed something to the tradition of outdoor preaching at Moorfields and Smithfield, as well as at the unconsecrated burial ground at Bunhill Fields, which had provided a final resting place for Dissenters and Quakers since the 1660s. Further north, the villages of Hackney and Stoke Newington were notorious dissenting enclaves, the latter containing a celebrated Presbyterian Academy that counted the writer Daniel Defoe as one of its famous pupils.

## QUAKERS & JEWS

Amongst the City's commercial elite, however, the two most prominent non-Anglican groups were not from Old Dissent. Under the law, Quakers and Jews were treated separately from Dissenters. In the case of Quakers, civil restrictions were less burdensome in that they were allowed certain special privileges and could sit in Parliament; in the case of Jews the legal burdens were more severe in that they were still considered 'aliens'. An Act allowing the naturalization of the Jews of Britain in 1753 had to be hastily repealed because of public opposition.

Rocque's map records only eight Quaker meeting houses and three synagogues in 1740, but Quakers and Jews in the City were far from hidden. From their counting houses in Lombard Street, the great Quaker banking dynasties of Barclays and Lloyds kept capital circulating throughout the country. London's three large breweries – Whitbread's in Chiswell Street, Thrale's in Southwark and Truman's in Spitalfields – were all Quaker concerns.

in London. These were soon joined by the purpose-built Tabernacle erected in Moorfields by Wesley's fellow preacher, the more evangelically minded George Whitefield (1714–70).

Although Wesley (1703–91) regarded Methodism as compatible with mainstream Anglicanism, the movement's 'enthusiastick practices' alarmed Church leaders. Nonetheless, its intense fervour, particularly in Whitefield's more evangelical version of the movement, proved irresistible to a popular audience and in the 1750s Whitefield built a larger tabernacle in Tottenham Court Road, where crowds flocked to experience the love of God as dispensed by charismatic preachers.

## PRAGMATIC PLURALITY

The religious variety that London offered was one of the aspects of the capital particularly noted by the young wood engraver Thomas Bewick, who arrived from Newcastle in 1776. Bewick was a conforming Anglican, but was curious to broaden his mind: 'I believe I did not miss hearing any of the popular preachers in London. For many years after I left London I still kept on in the same way and went occasionally to hear the preachers of various persuasions and attempted to find out the general Character of their several Congregations.'

If the City was naturally favourable to religious diversity, it was also the cause of a notorious episode of civil 'persecution'. In a shameless ruse to raise money, the City Corporation elected a number of elderly but wealthy Dissenters to the office of sheriff, knowing that the compulsory oath of allegiance to Anglican doctrine would force them to refuse, thus allowing the Corporation to impose a heavy fine. Many Dissenters paid up rather than make a fuss, but the matter was taken to the law and the City was eventually condemned for effectively levying a tax on religious belief. It is said that the £30,000 cost of building the Mansion House came entirely from fines imposed on Protestant Dissenters.

## METHODISM

Methodism, a breakaway branch of the Anglican Church, was also in part a product of the City. The movement was founded in 1738 by John Wesley, when his heart was 'strangely warmed' as he attended a meeting of the Moravian sect in Aldersgate, and underwent a spiritual epiphany. By the time John Rocque's famous map was published in the 1740s, there were five Methodist meeting houses

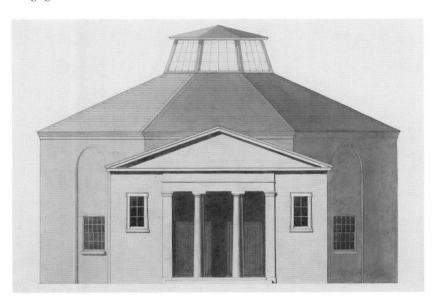

### ANGLICAN CHURCHES

Religious toleration led to Anglican fears. Were Londoners turning away from the established church to the detriment of the old systems of parish government? In 1711 the London Church Building Act assigned Coal Tax revenues to fund the building of fifty new churches. These large new buildings would provide capacity for the future and proclaim, by their physical presence, the power of the established church.

In the event only a dozen or so were built, but they include some striking London landmarks. The architect Nicholas Hawksmoor designed three great churches to serve the new industrial population in the East: Christ Church in Spitalfields, St George's at Stepney; and St Anne's in Limehouse. In Westminster, three new churches were erected south of Holborn: St Martin-in-the-Fields, St Giles-in-the-Fields and St Mary in the Strand.

In London, Bewick thought the Catholics perversely attached to old customs, the Methodists 'mostly unintelligible', the Quakers too sombre and the Unitarians 'well informed … not bewildered by dogmas and creeds'. As a man of modern sensibilities, he saw religious plurality as nothing more than common sense: 'There can be no objections to the religion of a virtuous man.'

In its daily life, 18th-century London had come to embody this plurality, its pace of change outstripping the British state's slow move towards separating civil rights from religious beliefs.   **CR**

# CRIME & PRISONS

Ineffective policing, corrupt prisons and a punitive system of justice did little to reduce London's lawlessness. Calls for reform increased as the 18th century progressed.

**Execution outside Newgate Prison, 1806**
*Thomas Rowlandson's record of the crowd at a public hanging includes all types: from ballad sellers and beggars to coach-owners.*

One of the consequences of London's population explosion in the 18th century was an increasingly anonymous and crowded city. This led to a rising fear of crime. Inadequate policing and an unreliable system of justice heightened the perceived threat to the homes of the burgeoning middle classes.

Henry Fielding (1707–54), the novelist and reforming magistrate, captured this spirit of apprehension: 'The cities of London and Westminster, with … the great irregularity of their buildings [and] the immense number of lanes, alleys, courts and bye-places … in which a thief may harbour with as great security, as wild beasts do in the deserts of Africa or Arabia.' As a result, vigilante groups like Hoxton's 'Military Association' of 1792 were established 'for the protection of their persons and properties against attacks of ruffians'.

Parts of the city were virtual no-go areas, such as Southwark and Alsatia (the area between Fleet Street and the Thames), notorious as being the dangerous haunts of criminal gangs. The perception grew of London teetering on the brink of complete lawlessness. Shortcomings in crime detection meant that the symbols of justice assumed powerful significance. Incarceration in the famously grim Newgate Prison or death on the gallows at Tyburn were highly visible symbols of the justice system's theatre of retribution, designed to provoke fear and secure obedience.

## A PUNITIVE SYSTEM

Despite widespread notions of a growing 'professional' criminal underworld, crime was often committed by the ordinary labouring poor or the unemployed. Criminal activity increased principally due to fluctuations in trade and the frequent harvest failures. The major difficulty in crime prevention was the lack of an effective, centrally organized police force. Patrolling the streets was the job of unpaid, part-time constables and amateur parish watchmen, a total force of only 3000 unarmed men. The system frustrated magistrates, who found it impossible to track crime across parish boundaries, and proved incapable of dealing with major civil disorders like the Gordon Riots of 1780 (see pages 162–3). Corruption riddled every level of the system. Magistrates taking bribes and 'thief-takers' like the infamous Jonathan Wild (who set up a business selling stolen goods back to their owners) further exacerbated the general lack of faith in the authority of law.

Public humiliation was widely used as a punishment for non-capital offences such as riot and fraud. Being dragged through the street on a hurdle and shackled in a pillory placed the convict at the mercy of verbal assault or rotten food hurled by passers-by. Fines, whipping, flogging, birching, branding and pressing (if a defendant refused to plead) were also administered. The

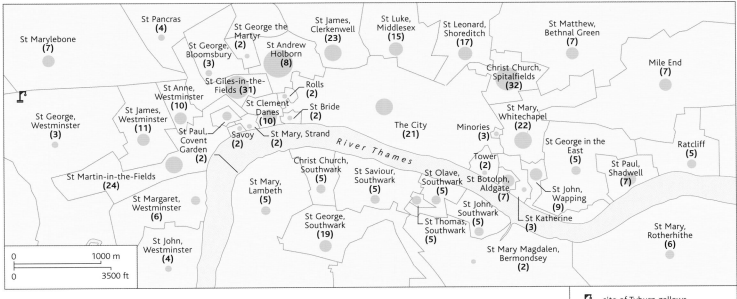

**Hangings in 18th-century London**

St Marylebone **(7)**
St Pancras **(4)**
St George the Martyr **(2)**
St George, Bloomsbury **(3)**
St Andrew Holborn **(8)**
St James, Clerkenwell **(23)**
St Luke, Middlesex **(15)**
St Leonard, Shoreditch **(17)**
St Matthew, Bethnal Green **(7)**
Mile End **(7)**
Christ Church, Spitalfields **(32)**
St Giles-in-the-Fields **(31)**
St Anne, Westminster **(10)**
Rolls **(2)**
St Clement Danes **(10)**
St Bride **(2)**
St James, Westminster **(11)**
St George, Westminster **(3)**
St Paul, Covent Garden **(2)**
Savoy **(2)**
St Mary, Strand **(2)**
The City **(21)**
Minories **(3)**
St Mary, Whitechapel **(22)**
St George in the East **(5)**
Ratcliff **(5)**
St Paul, Shadwell **(7)**
St Martin-in-the-Fields **(24)**
St Margaret, Westminster **(6)**
St Mary, Lambeth **(5)**
Christ Church, Southwark **(5)**
St Saviour, Southwark **(5)**
St Olave, Southwark **(5)**
St Botolph, Aldgate **(7)**
St John, Wapping **(9)**
Tower **(2)**
St Katherine **(3)**
St John, Southwark **(5)**
St Thomas, Southwark **(5)**
St John, Westminster **(4)**
St George, Southwark **(19)**
St Mary Magdalen, Bermondsey **(2)**
St Mary, Rotherhithe **(6)**

*River Thames*

0 — 1000 m
0 — 3500 ft

site of Tyburn gallows
ward or parish boundary
**15** number of hangings in the 18th century known to have originated in ward or parish
number of hangings relative to population of ward or parish

**Hangings in 18th-century London**
Over 340 people were hanged in London over the century: an average of approximately one every three to four months.

*Jack Sheppard, 1724*
*London's most notorious criminal of his day, sketched just before his execution by hanging. A thief and a highwayman, Sheppard was also famous for his escapes from Newgate.*

transportation of convicts to the Americas and later Australia provided a release valve for the overcrowded prison system until 1868.

Crimes against property were punished with the greatest severity; coiners and forgers were shown a particular lack of mercy. Phoebe Harris was convicted of 'high treason' in 'coining silver' in 1786. She was burnt to death – a practice finally abolished in 1790. The death penalty was applicable to no fewer than 200 offences by the end of the 18th century, and the vast majority of those hanged were convicted of theft. The anomalous nature of this system was clear, so judges and magistrates often granted pardons. The total number of convicts hanged did not increase in the period despite record numbers of offences on the statute books.

## PRESSURE FOR REFORM

With prisons privately owned and run for profit, corruption and deprivation were widespread. The incomes of gaolers came from the profits of selling goods to the prisoners, a situation that reformers argued 'doth notoriously promote and increase the very vices it was designed to suppress'. Blackmail and torture were endemic despite periodic inspection. Savage whipping of both sexes was common, and starvation frequent. Conditions were universally appalling in all of London's prisons. From the floating prison ships ('hulks') moored at Woolwich to the 'tomb for the living' that was Newgate Prison, death from cholera, typhoid and dysentery probably killed more prisoners than the gallows. While wealthier prisoners could rent better rooms and even entertain, poor convicts fell on the mercy of their relatives or charitable donations, or were permitted to beg outside the prison.

The grisly spectacle of execution at Tyburn and Newgate appeared to have the opposite effect on the public from that intended by the lawmakers. The vast drunken crowds who followed the processions made popular heroes of the condemned and treated 'Tyburn Fair' as a holiday. Critics like the philosopher and reformer Jeremy Bentham (1748–1832) began to see the process as counterproductive, and there is little evidence that this punitive regime was successful in deterring crime mainly caused by desperation and poverty. The voices of penal reformers gradually grew stronger in the late 18th century. John Howard devoted nearly twenty years of his life to an unprecedented systematic examination of prison conditions across Britain and Europe, demonstrating a multitude of abuses and failings in *The State of Prisons* (1777). Crime was beginning to be perceived as a social problem rather than simply the moral failing of individuals, but the era of prisons as agents of reform was still many years away. **ES**

# MOLLY HOUSES & MACARONIS

Georgian London supported a well-established gay subculture, with its own meeting places and manners. But moral disapproval was strong, and buggery was a capital offence.

**Ganymede and Jack Catch, 1771**
*This print portrays convicted sodomite Samuel Drybutter ('Ganymede') as he escapes being hanged. The hangman ('Jack-Catch') says 'Damme Sammy you'r a sweet pretty creature & I long to have you at the end of my string.' Drybutter coyly replies 'You don't love me Jacky.'*

At the beginning of the 18th century, the streets of London were teeming with what was considered to be low life. Bawdy houses and brothels were many, and petty crime was rife. Homosexual practice was also perceived to be on the increase, with 'He-Strumpets', 'He-Whores' or 'sodomites' frequenting the streets, parks and theatres. A moral crusade against such developments was also underway.

To the Society for the Reformation of Manners, founded in 1690, debauchery, profanity and 'unnatural practices' – as sodomy was termed – had to be exposed and prevented, especially among the lower classes. The society, founded by the Reverend Thomas Bray and a group of puritanical Christians, set up a network of 'guardians', placing stewards in each ward of the city. By 1701, there were nearly twenty in the capital. A committee gathered the names and addresses of offenders and gay meeting places by using agent provocateurs and informers. The society's aim was to bring prosecutions and to 'cleanse' the streets.

The public was scandalized by the trials that ensued, and the capital's printing presses ensured that they were able to read about them. At this time homosexuality was still a capital offence, a crime punishable by the pillory or the death sentence. Nonetheless, a homosexual subculture definitely existed. Its members often conducted themselves in a carefully codified way; men seeking sex with other men were identifiable by their elaborate dress and their feminine behaviour and way of speaking.

## MOLLY HOUSES

London offered a range of environments both indoor and outdoor that presented opportunities for sexual encounters. The first gay cruising grounds included the Royal Exchange and the area of Moorfields, north of the City. St Clement's and St Paul's church-yards were also popular with men seeking same-sex encounters. The theatre, long associated with liberalism and louche and radical behaviour, was a frequent haunt for gay men, and the coffee houses and areas around Covent Garden, such as the Piazza, Seven Dials and the Three Tobacco Rolls, were known as good pick-up points.

In 1701 alone, the Society for the Reformation of Manners had entrapped nearly 100 gay men, although not all were tried. For self-preservation, and to escape the risk of prosecution, members of the gay subculture began to form associations in less public places. Institutions known as 'Molly houses' sprang up around the city, catering to a range of homosexual proclivities. Molly house culture mimicked the affectations and manners of the aristocracy. It was also commonplace for their members to dress as women, to use female names and to imitate female behaviour. A Molly house might adjoin a tavern or private house, often with guarded rooms, and provided an environment in which gay men could meet for drinking and entertainment, and engage in sexual acts, behind closed doors. One Molly house, at the Royal Oak on the corner of St James's and Pall Mall, had a private chapel for gay marriages.

One of the most infamous Molly house trials of the day, at the Old Bailey, was that of Margaret Clap of Field Lane, Holborn. In 1726 she was indicted for keeping a house in which she procured persons to commit sodomy. After being found guilty, Mother Clap stood in the pillory at Moorfields along with six others, was fined twenty marks and suffered two years' imprisonment. To stand in the pillory while the mob hurled faeces, rotten produce and eggs was a horrific punishment; it could end in mutilation, blindness or even death, usually from suffocation. Others who were implicated in the Clap trial were even less fortunate: Gabriel Lawrence was hanged for his part in the case.

## THE MACARONI CULTURE

The term 'Maccaronie' had come into common usage in the late 17th century, and featured in many satires. It is said to have been derived from the aristocratic practice of going on a Grand Tour to Italy. 'Maccaronies' were young men, fops or dandies with affected mannerisms, who returned home from the Grand Tour with a taste for other men. Long ponytail hairstyles became their trademark. There is no evidence that a specific 'Macaroni Club' ever existed, but the term was certainly used to indicate the homosexual subculture of the period. The story went that at a Newmarket club young gentlemen ordered a dish of macaroni every time they dined together, showing that they were all 'travelled' individuals as a kind of code for their homosexual proclivities.

also engaging in sex. The clients were from working-class trades and most of them were also married. The trial of the 'Vere Street Coterie', as they came to be known, resulted in severe punishments for the eleven men convicted, including the pillory and two year's imprisonment. For Thomas White, a drummer aged sixteen, and John Newbolt, an ensign aged forty-two, the sentence was to be hanged.

By 1810, however, nearly all of London's Molly houses had been closed down in raids instigated by the Society for the Reformation of Manners.

## PROSECUTIONS CONTINUE

Eighteenth-century London had undergone considerable expansion, and with the growth of the city came a greater degree of anonymity, enabling men to move between places, classes and identities. The Vere Street case scandalized polite society, particularly because it revealed the ability of ordinary men to subvert conventional society relatively unhindered. A new bill was passed in Parliament in 1828, intended to make convictions for sodomy easier by reducing the burden of proof. (Hitherto, the Crown had had to prove that both penetration and ejaculation had taken place.) The foundation of the Metropolitan Police Force in 1829 by Robert Peel (1788–1850), together with this change in the law, saw a marked increase in arrests for sodomy, many being made around St Paul's, Bishopsgate, the river and the City of London.

During the period from 1800 to 1834, eighty men were hanged in England for sodomy. This punishment continued to be meted out as late as 1835, when John Smith and James Pratt were the last two men hanged for the offence. It was not until 1861 that the death sentence for sodomy was finally abolished. **SG**

**How D'ye Like Me, c.1772**
*A stereotypically simpering Macaroni with powdered wig and fashionable dress.*

Samuel Drybutter, who kept a trinket- and bookshop in Westminster Hall, was considered the leader of the Macaronis in the 1770s. He was no stranger to the Old Bailey, where he appeared several times. Committed to the Tothill Fields Bridewell prison in 1770, he suffered the pillory in 1771 for an incident with a grenadier of the Horse Guards, and in 1772 he managed to escape apprehension for sodomy with a Captain Jones, an event that gained him some notoriety. Acquitted for sodomy in 1774, he is said to have been pilloried for selling adapted homoerotic copies of *Fanny Hill* in 1775. Drybutter suffered several homophobic attacks. He attempted in 1777 to pick up a man in St James's Park, a renowned cruising ground, but was apprehended by two soldiers and released to a mob, which brutally attacked him. He escaped home, but the mob chased him there and the crowds were only dispersed by the military. It was Drybutter's last escape: he died five days later of his injuries.

By far the most notorious case of gay subculture in late Georgian London came in 1810, when a group of around thirty men were arrested at the White Swan, a male brothel in Vere Street, near Clare Market. There gay marriages were performed and consummated in front of other men or couples

**London's gay areas**
Areas associated with homosexual activity, as revealed mainly through Old Bailey prosecutions.

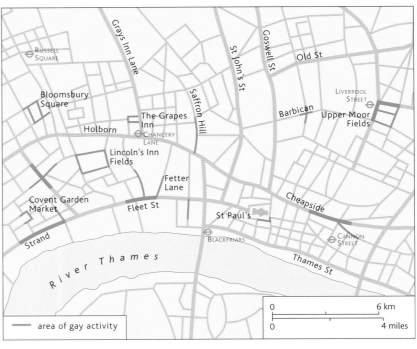

— area of gay activity

# STREETWALKERS & STRUMPETS

Prostitution was highly visible in 18th century London. Thousands of women solicited for sex in the city's public places. A few were attached to organized brothels but most operated on their own.

**'Light, your honour?', 1772**
*The boy's seemingly innocent enquiry contrasts with the diseased face of the woman's client.*

When the young Newcastle woodcarver Thomas Bewick arrived in London in 1760 he noticed differences between the capital and his home town: '...the first of these [matters] that struck me & what constantly hurt my feelings', he noted, 'was the seeing of such a number of fine-looking women engaged in the wretched business of *Street Walking'*.

In the 1790s it was claimed that 50,000 women were working as prostitutes in London. Although the number was probably exaggerated, there is no doubt that tens of thousands of women were involved. Typically, prostitutes were from a poor background and in their late teens and early twenties. Some were out-of-work servants; others women who had been seduced and abandoned – thus rendering themselves unmarriageable in 'polite' society. Many were using sex as one way among many to make a living in London's underworld. Records of Old Bailey trials show that 'common whores' were as likely to be prosecuted for theft as vagrancy. Daniel Defoe's heroine Moll Flanders saw her chance when a client fell asleep after sex in his coach. 'I took this opportunity to search him to a nicety. I took a gold watch, with a silk purse of gold, his fine full-bottom periwig and silver-fringed gloves, his sword and fine snuff box, and gently opening the coach door...I got softly out, fastened the door again, and gave my gentleman and the coach the slip both together, and never heard more of them.'

**A Harlot's Progress, 1732**
*The first in Hogarth's famous sequence of prints shows the country lass Moll Hackabout received in London by a bawd, recognizable as the real-life Mother Needham.*

## BRUTES & PENITENTS

Moll was a picaresque character, but prostitution was generally a grim business. The radical artisan Francis Place described low-life prostitutes in St Catherine's Lane, during the 1780s. 'Most of them had clean stockings and shoes, because it was to them the fashion to be flashy about the heels, but many had ragged dirty shoes and some no stockings at all … many of that time wore no stays, their gowns were low round the neck and open in front to expose their breasts. … many hung down in a most disgusting manner,

their hair among the generality was straight and "hung in rats tails" over their eyes and was filled with lice.' Place also noted that drunkenness and fighting were common 'and black eyes might be seen on a great many'. John Collett's picture of female 'bruisers' (see opposite) shows two women, recognizable as prostitutes by the amount of leg they are showing, supposedly fighting over a client. These women are portrayed not as creatures to be pitied, but as base and brutish in themselves, dangerous carriers of disease and social degeneration.

The view of prostitutes as victims gained ground in the second half of the century. In 1758 the philanthropist Jonas Hanway founded the Magdalen Hospital for the reception of penitent prostitutes. This provided a refuge and the means of rehabilitating 'fallen women' through instruction in useful trades. Another new charitable institution was the London Lock Hospital, which opened in 1747 for the treatment of venereal diseases. Gonorrhoea and syphilis ('French Pox') were constant hazards for both prostitutes and their clients. The belief that syphilis could be cured by mercury ointments was equally dangerous, leaving sufferers with distinctive deathly-white skin.

## BAWDY HOUSES

The majority of London's prostitutes worked for themselves on the streets. Certain districts became notorious for the trade, due to their combination of cheap lodgings and a plentiful supply of male clients. In Westminster, the red light area was Drury Lane, Covent Garden and the Strand. The City equivalent was the large ward of Faringdon Without, stretching from Fleet Street to Smithfield. East of the City, Whitechapel and Aldgate drew clients from the growing industrial suburbs of the east. London's pleasure gardens and public grounds all had their share of prostitutes, often strolling in pairs. Theatres were also notorious pick-up places.

Once a gentleman had been secured, the encounter would take place in a tavern backroom, or the women's own lodgings. At night, any narrow alley would do (see opposite above). The male client in this print is shown with a white face, indicating that he has almost certainly already contracted syphilis.

Brothels, or Bawdy Houses, operated in central London, some masquerading as taverns or bagnios (exotic bath houses). In these cases there was a degree of organization, with the brothel keepers enforcing control through the provision of clothes, board and lodging. Whippings or beatings to enforce control were not unknown. In 1752 the Disorderly Houses Act brought in new laws, but enforcement was lax. In 1749 a brothel in the Strand had been at the centre of a serious outbreak of disorder when a group of sailors had run riot after being robbed on the premises.

Despite legal restrictions, moral disapproval and humanitarian sympathy, prostitution was engrained in London's daily life. 'As I was coming home this night,' wrote James Boswell in March 1763, 'I felt carnal inclinations raging through my frame. I determined to gratify them. I went to St James's Park, and … picked up a whore.' Although this was a matter-of-fact encounter for Boswell, he did feel a twinge of pity. 'She who submitted to my lusty embrace was a young Shropshire girl, only seventeen, very well-looked, her name Elizabeth Parker. Poor being, she has a sad time of it.'  **CR**

**The Female Bruisers,** *1768*
*In John Collet's painting, the two low-life women wear the prostitute's usual costume of exaggerated flounces with ankle-revealing skirts.*

**Beauties of Bagnigge Wells,** *1778*
*Robert Sayer's satirical print shows a fashionable woman (almost certainly a prostitute) flirting with a rake at the notorious pick-up spot.*

# GIN LANE & THE WORKHOUSE

Cheap gin, crime and poverty combined to make conditions in the poorer parishes of 18th-century London particularly harsh. Effective reforms were very slow to emerge.

While London became ever more fashionable for a wealthy elite, the divisions between rich and poor widened. As wealth moved west, so poorer parishes entered a downward spiral of poverty, child mortality, disease and lawlessness.

The physical deterioration of London's poor districts was particularly marked. Areas such as Holborn and St Giles retained their essentially medieval layout with mazes of alleys and courts threaded between ramshackle buildings, their bricks held together with ashes and dirt. They were dangerous places, where 'falling houses thunder on your head' wrote Samuel Johnson in 1783. As seaborne trade expanded, districts near the river such as Wapping and Limehouse were given over to cheap lodging houses and dirty industries. It was in the poor districts that the metropolis's 'nuisances' took place. In Smithfield the odours of refuse, sewers, cesspits, burial grounds and dunghills mingled with the waste from the cattle market, tripe dressers and slaughterhouses. The effect on the poor was cumulative. Improvements could only be financed by local inhabitants, and large projects, such as the provision of clean water, street paving and street lighting, fell beyond the means of the poorer parishes.

As the physical environment deteriorated, so did the social character. Houses were subdivided into tenements; lodging houses let out leaking cellars and drafty garrets; and overcrowding was rife. As the wealthy moved out, street sellers, casual labourers and the very poor moved in. So, too, did criminals. The parish of St Giles was particularly known for its high incidence of poverty, alcoholism, prostitution and crime. It was the setting for Hogarth's *Gin Lane*, his famous polemic against the 'idleness, poverty, misery and distress' caused by 'the deadly draught'.

**Gin Lane, *1750***
*William Hogarth's campaigning print was designed to demonstrate the social degradation caused by cheap gin. The scene is set in St Giles, a notoriously gin-soaked area of town.*

***Westminster workhouse, 1809***
*Westminster had some of London's largest and most crowded workhouses, including those in the parishes of St Martin and St Giles-in-the-Fields.*

## THE GIN EPIDEMIC

Gin-drinking was London's most serious social problem in the 18th century. The appetite for gin was whetted early in the century, after the government had strenuously promoted the distilling industry, recognizing 'Madam Geneva' as a highly profitable outlet for the corn surplus. Distilleries were built, accompanied by legislation allowing the sale of spirits without a licence – suddenly, gin was everywhere and dirt cheap: 'Drunk for a penny, Dead drunk for two pence, Clean straw for nothing' reads the gin shop sign in Hogarth's print. In St Giles's, every fifth house was a gin shop, some doubling as brothels; the spirit could also be bought at chandlers, grocers, barbers, market stalls and from street sellers. More readily available than clean water, gin was consumed by men, women and children. It was estimated that by 1723 London was consuming the equivalent of a pint of gin per person per week.

Distilling was essentially a London trade and by 1723 the 375 million gallons of spirits distilled in England were largely consumed in London. To many at the time, the gin-drinking epidemic threatened the city itself: according to Henry Fielding, the inventor of gin was 'the poisoner of a fountain whence a large city was to derive its water'. Outcries against the unlicensed trade led in 1721 to the first of a series of government investigations into the effects of spirit consumption. Its findings threw up some horrific examples of the effects of addiction, including the infamous case of Judith Defour, who killed her baby in order to sell its clothes for gin money. Eventually the Gin Act of 1736 introduced a £50 licence for those wishing to sell spirits, and subsequent Acts helped at last to raise the price and curb the epidemic. Nevertheless, by the end of the century, it was still estimated that an eighth of all deaths in adults over the age of twenty was caused by drinking spirits.

## POVERTY

The gin epidemic diverted attention from the other problems faced by London's poor parishes, especially the surging numbers of destitute people. From the end of the 16th century, individual parishes had been responsible for providing relief for orphans, the aged and the infirm. The standard method was to offer 'indoor relief' through a poorhouse, in which conditions were usually harsh

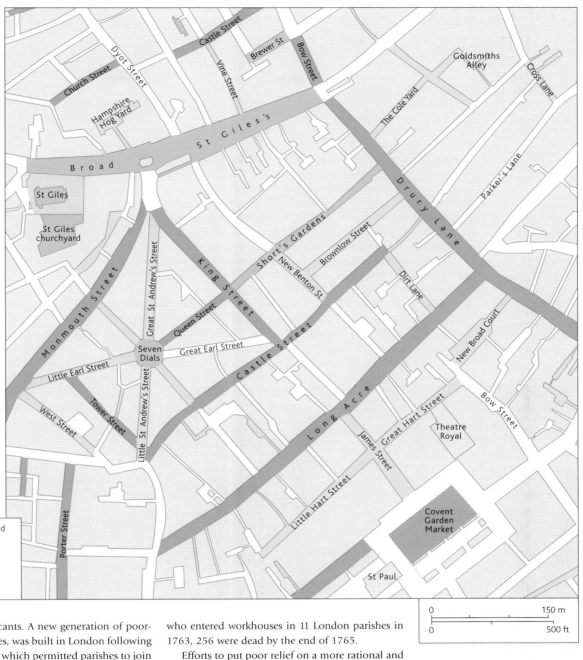

Number of criminal trials associated with each named street

- 1–8
- 9–22
- 23 or more

0    150 m
0    500 ft

as a deliberate deterrent to applicants. A new generation of poorhouses, now known as workhouses, was built in London following the Work House Test Act of 1723, which permitted parishes to join together to build larger institutions. The new workhouses soon gained reputations as filthy, overcrowded prison-like institutions with scandalously high mortality rates. Jonas Hanway, a tireless campaigner against the evils of workhouse regimes, called the Bloomsbury and St Giles workhouse 'the greatest sink of mortality in these kingdoms, if not on the face of the earth'.

Inside, inmates would work for twelve hours a day on unrelenting jobs such as spinning yarn or making shoes, stockings or seamen's caps. Punishments were frequent and brutal. An account of a workhouse in Holborn in 1732 records how swearing was punished in the stocks and brawling by twenty-four hours in the 'dungeon'. One campaigning pamphlet, *The Workhouse Cruelty*, describes a woman who starved to death during her 'correction' in the 'dark hold'. Child mortality was high. Of the 291 children

who entered workhouses in 11 London parishes in 1763, 256 were dead by the end of 1765.

Efforts to put poor relief on a more rational and humane basis were particularly aimed at 'parish children'. By the end of the century, parishes were being actively encouraged to send children under the age of six to country nurses or as apprentices to factories in the north of England. In the 1740s, Thomas Coram established his pioneering Foundling Hospital in Coram's Fields, just to the north of St Giles. Another philanthropist, Jonas Hanway, was involved in the Committee for the Relief of the Black Poor set up in the 1780s in response to the increasing numbers of black beggars – the 'St. Giles black birds' – on London's streets. Efforts to find an alternative to the workhouse led to the idealistic but ill-fated Sierra Leone expedition that attempted to settle former slaves and Lascars on the west coast of Africa. Two ships set sail from London in 1787 with 441 black emigrants and their wives aboard. Many died, and the experiment was not repeated.    **AL**

**London's most dangerous area**
The parish of St Giles, just to the north of Covent Garden. The worst of Georgian London's gin-consumption, poverty and criminality was concentrated here.

# HOSPITALS & HEALTH CARE

In 1700, London's provision for health care had not grown much beyond its medieval origins. By 1800, however, the map of institutional health care had become more recognizably modern.

At the beginning of the 18th century, London had four major hospitals – St Bartholemew's, Christ's, St Thomas's and Bethlem – all of which could trace their foundations back to the monastic 'hospices' built just outside the walls of the City. By the end of the century there were over twenty hospitals, including seven general hospitals for the sick poor. Hospital buildings now encircled Westminster as well as the City. Seventeen public dispensaries supplied medicines and diagnoses to up to 50,000 Londoners a year. There was also a thriving network of apothecaries, physicians, chemists, quack doctors, private asylums and boarding houses serving those who could afford to pay.

This growth in institutions reflected the inability of the older hospitals to keep pace with urban change. As London's population rose and its buildings spread, so too did the visible evidence of ill health and disease. This was particularly true of Westminster, the squares and terraces of which were far from the old royal hospitals of the City but dangerously close to the 'bad air' of the Thames marshes. The new hospitals also reflected the new moral and civic sensibilities of the age. Whereas the older hospitals were associated with royal patronage and financed by wealthy endowments, the

**Old and new London hospitals**
At the beginning of the 18th century, London had four hospitals. By 1800, there were a further seventeen, as well as nineteen additional almshouses and private asylums and hospitals.

new institutions were 'voluntary' and financed by subscriptions, a method of raising money more usually associated with commerce. The entrepreneurs behind them were merchants, gentry and bankers, to whom health care was not just a matter of Christian philanthropy but also humanitarian and civic good sense.

The five major new institutions that emerged from the voluntary hospital boom were the Westminster Infirmary, (founded in 1719), Guy's Hospital (opened 1725), St George's Hospital (1733), The London Hospital (1740), and the Middlesex Infirmary (1745). Only Guy's was like its endowed predecessors in that it was financed from a single bequest, that of Thomas Guy, a printer who had made a fortune from the South Sea Bubble; the others were financed by subscription. The London Hospital began life in a house in Moorfields. Within a year it had moved to larger premises in Aldgate, and in 1757 it moved again to a new purpose-built hospital on a greenfield site at Mile End. Becoming a subscriber was an attractive proposition for many London tradesmen in that it brought with it the right to recommend a person for admission, thus adding a very practical incentive to the charitable impulse.

## GENERAL HEALTH CARE

Health care provided in the hospitals was rudimentary by today's standards. 'Physic' and 'Surgery' were the two branches of professional medicine and in the days before anaesthetics, surgery was confined to simple operations such as amputations or the removal of gall stones. Although in theory anyone with a letter of recommendation could be admitted to a general hospital, in practice admissions were strictly controlled. People with infectious

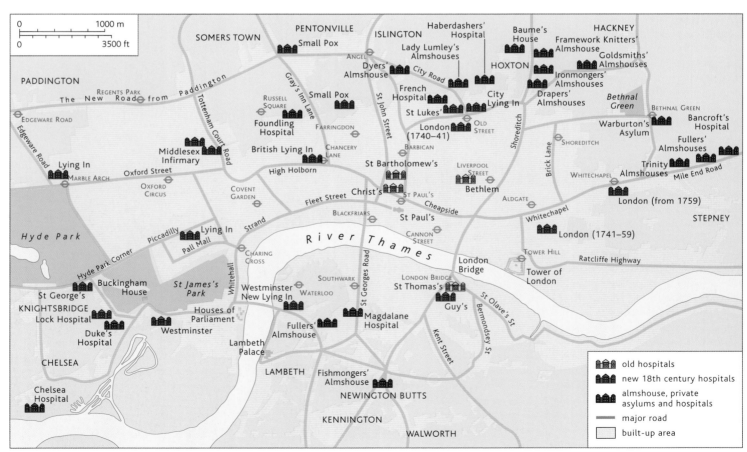

*A ward in the Middlesex Hospital, 1809*
Founded in 1745 as one of the new wave of voluntary hospitals, the hospital by 1809 had several new wards endowed by philanthropists such as the brewer Samuel Whitbread.

diseases were excluded, as generally were pregnant women. Hospitals concentrated on those who would respond to treatment. The 'incurables', a category that included the old, disabled or chronically ill, were left to the mercies of almshouses, or to the parish, which looked after sick paupers and bore the costs of burial. Despite a more humanitarian outlook, religion was never very far away. The Westminster Infirmary discriminated against Roman Catholics. At Guy's, respectful listening to Sunday Bible-reading was compulsory and 'if any person shall be observed to mock or scoff at these or any other religious directions, such persons shall be immediately discharged'. The London Hospital was relatively enlightened in admitting Jewish patients.

## SPECIALIST HOSPITALS

Specialist hospitals accommodated some categories of patients turned away from the larger institutions. The 'lying-in' or maternity hospital became a favourite medical charity of the 18th century, with five in London by 1800. From 1746 sufferers from venereal diseases could apply to the London Lock Hospital, and small-pox victims found care at an isolation hospital on the city's northern edge. St Luke's, founded in 1751, provided London with its second hospital for the mentally ill. The first was, of course, Bethlem, or 'Bedlam' – famous in the 18th century for the practice of exhibiting its inmates to visitors. Intended to stimulate charitable feelings, the practice was seen as inhumane by Bethlem's critics.

Some of London's 'hospitals' were in effect almshouses rather than medical institutions. The almshouse had been the favourite charity of the 17th century and the tradition continued into the first half of the 18th, with new almshouses built typically to the north and east of the City. The French Hospital, founded at Old Street in 1718 for infirm Huguenots, was part of the concentration of almshouses in and around Hoxton. The explanation for this concentration was partly Hoxton's proximity to the City but also land tenure in the eastern parishes, which tended to be in the form of small freeholds rather than the large estates of the west. The same factors may well explain the establishment of private 'mad houses' in Bethnal Green and Hoxton throughout the century.

For many 18th-century Londoners, health care was largely a matter of making do, relying on folk cures as much as medicines, and self-help as much as hospitals. The range of 'incurable' complaints was large, and illnesses were still seen as reflecting a spiritual as much as a physical condition. An alternative to the physic and surgery provided by the hospitals were the potions and powders sold commercially by chemists, apothecaries and quack doctors: men such as 'Dr Frederick', who promised 'no cure no pay'; or Joshua Ward who claimed to perform marvellous cures 'on persons pronounced incurable in several hospitals'. In an age when most babies born in London died before the age of five, the most common institution for health care remained the family. **CR**

*St. George's Hospital*
St. George's Hospital was founded at Hyde Park Corner in 1733 to benefit from the 'healthy air' of the then village of Knightsbridge.

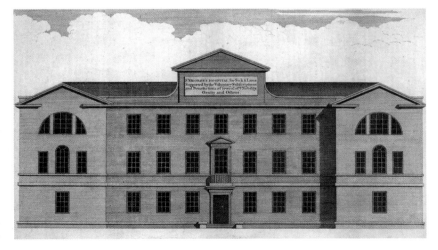

# RADICALS & RIOTS

Serious disorder seethed beneath the surface of late Georgian London. In 1780 the Gordon Riots brought the city perhaps as close to full-scale revolution as it has ever been.

**The Gordon Rioters outside Newgate Prison, 1780**
*This print shows the burning of the furniture and belongings of Richard Akerman, the keeper of Newgate Prison.*

The London mob was a powerful force, and in times of civil unrest the metropolis became a difficult city to govern. The reaction of the crowd could be unpredictable. Whether it was unemployed sailors, striking coal-heavers, weavers or just the unruly mass of London's underclass, a small dispute could often erupt into a full-scale riot. Sometimes the discontent of the city's large electorate, which included property-owning shopkeepers, tradesmen and merchants, was supported by working people such as shoemakers and tailors, who did not have the vote.

Often the army had to be called out if the local constables were unable to keep order. A magistrate had to be found to read the Riot Act and one hour was given for the crowd to disperse. Failure to comply was a capital offence and the troops could charge or open fire on the mob if necessary. Such circumstances led to uncomfortable stand-offs between the civilian population and the military.

After the defeat of the Jacobite Rising (1745–6) and the triumphant national successes in the Seven Years' War (1756–63), the popular Whig government of Pitt the Elder collapsed, and the power and influence of the new king, George III, and his Tory supporters under Lord Bute grew. Many Londoners felt that corruption and inefficiency were beginning to reach unacceptable levels in the new administration. In 1762, John Wilkes, a radical young Middlesex MP, had begun to use his weekly satirical journal *North Briton* as a vehicle for increasingly savage attacks on members of the Bute ministry, on their perceived Scottish bias, on the hated Treaty of Paris that had ended the Seven Years' War, and even on the king himself. Londoners rallied to Wilkes's support when he was tried for seditious libel, believing that their rights as freeborn Englishmen were under attack. 'Wilkes and Liberty' became their general rallying cry on the streets.

**A radical punch bowl, 1760s**
*The slogan 'Wilkes and Liberty' celebrates John Wilkes, London's best-known radical politician of his day.*

## THE CATHOLIC RELIEF ACT

In 1778, anti-Catholic sentiment in London was inflamed by the passing of the Catholic Relief Act, the main aim of which had been to reinforce Britain's army by removing the restrictions on Catholics becoming soldiers. Catholicism, however, was identified with the Jacobite rebellion, with Britain's French and Spanish enemies – and with allegiance to the Pope. On the hot summer day of Friday 2 June 1780, some 50,000 members of the Protestant Association, a campaigning group for the repeal of the Act, gathered in St George's Fields, Lambeth. Their leader, the unbalanced Lord George Gordon, MP for Ludgershall in Wiltshire, addressed them, urging them to remain orderly and peaceful in

their behaviour as there had been rumours that Catholic troublemakers were hoping to provoke a violent confrontation. His earlier speeches, however, had already whipped them up into an anti-Catholic passion.

As they marched through the streets of London with their blue cockades and 'No Popery' badges, further supporters joined them along with more unruly individuals looking for a fight. By the time they reached Parliament, the crowd thronged all the approach routes and as the MPs and peers arrived they were jostled and verbally abused. Their carriages were attacked and a few unlucky peers, such as the Duke of Northumberland, whose black costume was mistaken for a Jesuit's, were forced out of their carriages and threatened by the protesters.

Inside, Gordon laid their petition of 44,000 signatures before the House of Commons. From time to time, he left the chamber and spoke to the crowd, keeping them abreast of the debate. When the motion to repeal the Act was put to the vote, it was rejected by the House, by 192 votes to 6. The crowd then turned violent. When the Foot and Horse Guards arrived to disperse the mob, they were pelted with stones. Finally, a brave justice of the peace addressed the crowd and told them he would order the troops to disperse if they would break up peacefully. A cheer went up and slowly the protesters began to drift away from Palace Yard and the surrounding streets. However, this was by no means the end of the matter.

## THE GORDON RIOTS

For the following week, London descended into a state of anarchy, controlled by the mob. Property identified as being Catholic or foreign was attacked, including the Bavarian embassy and a Sardinian chapel. A feature of the assaults was the stripping of the fixtures and fittings of the buildings; everything was carried out into the street and burnt. Roman Catholics were targeted throughout London, and Irish property was subjected to some of the worst attacks. Fearing that their houses might become targets, some people tried to persuade the mob of their allegiance to the cause by shouting 'No Popery' from their windows or chalking the

slogan on their front doors. Rioters demanded money from house-holders and from people in the street. Fear gripped the city.

The army was powerless as the magistrates refused to read the Riot Act for fear of their own safety and of their houses being burnt. The mob ridiculed the soldiers as they stood impassively.

The attention of the rioters moved on to places identified with law and order. The prisons became their main objective: Newgate, supposedly an impregnable fortress, was besieged by a crowd that included the future poet and artist William Blake, its doors and entrances broken open with crowbars and sledgehammers. The rioters freed all the prisoners and then set the prison ablaze. Other jails such as the King's Bench, the Fleet, the Clink and Bridewell, were also set on fire and their inmates released. The houses of several magistrates were also broken into and a bonfire was made of their belongings.

During the final days of the riots, the mob's attention shifted again, to the City of London, and especially the Bank of England. Here, the rioters met very fierce resistance from City volunteers. The defence was well organized, with leaders including John Wilkes himself. Meanwhile the king, frustrated at the apparent inactivity of the London magistrates, authorized troops to take all necessary steps to restore order without first obtaining permission from the magistrates. Militias and regular military forces converged on London in large numbers, quickly quelling the riot.

## REVOLUTION AVERTED

The authorities arrested the supposed leaders of the riots, though many of the ringleaders were believed to have died in the final attack on the Bank. Altogether some 450 arrests were made, with 160 rioters indicted for their part in the events and 21 publicly executed at the locations in the city where they were proven to have committed offences. Lord George Gordon, with whom the disturbances have become permanently associated, was tried for high treason but found not guilty. He subsequently converted to Judaism, and died in prison in 1787 after being convicted of a libel against the queen of France, Marie Antoinette.

The six days of rioting represented Georgian Britain's most severe outbreak of mob violence, and caused damage to property in London not seen again until the Blitz of World War II. Nonetheless, given that the city had effectively been at the mercy of the large mob for a week, surprisingly little permanent destruction resulted. The rioters had concentrated their efforts on particular targets (even using fire engines on their own initiative to ensure that neighbouring properties were not set alight), and had studiously avoided the deliberate taking of human life. Of the 700 or so fatalities, not one was a Catholic: all the dead were rioters, killed by the military or meeting accidental death through fire or the collapse of buildings – particularly after the mob had looted several distilleries.

Many aspects of the Gordon riots remain unclear, not least the true motivation of the rioters. Rumours that foreigners and 'well-dressed' figures had been seen directing the final assaults have never been substantiated, but the deliberate targeting of prisons and the Bank of England suggest that the instinctive anti-Catholicism and xenophobia of 18th-century Londoners does not provide a full explanation. In fact, the remarkable similarities between the riots and events in Paris nine years later – including the organized assault on the city's most notorious prison – raise the interesting possibility that London in 1780 may narrowly have avoided an even more serious upheaval.          AW

**The Gordon Riots, 1780**
The army was mobilized in response to the rioting.

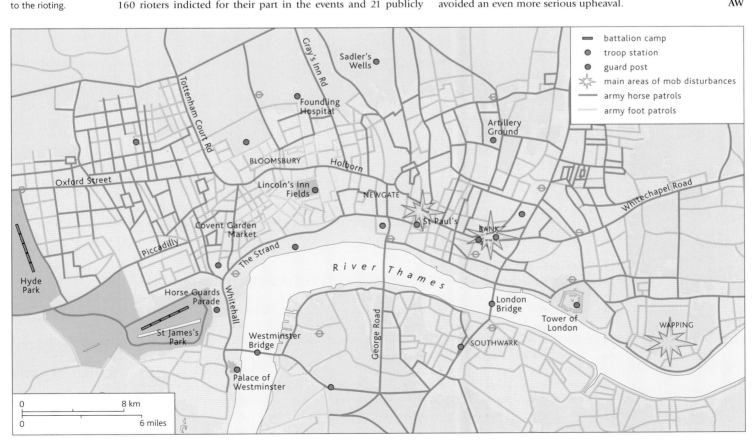

# REGENCY LONDON

Regency London saw the end of the long struggle between Britain and France, Europe's two superpowers. Victory over Napoleon left its mark on the capital with a new generation of place and street names: Nelson, Trafalgar, Wellington and Waterloo. The building boom that followed the end of the wars also saw a new mood. Churches, monuments and statues brought classical styles to the streets, linking modern civilization with the democracies of ancient Greece. Roads were widened and old buildings demolished. Science brought more improvements: gas-lighting, iron water pipes, and even a tunnel constructed under the Thames.

Regency London was less tolerant of disorder than its Georgian predecessor. An embryonic police force appeared. Streets became cleaner and paved in stone. The city's most ambitious improvement was a vast new docks complex to the east, providing modern and efficient shipping facilities on the Isle of Dogs, at Wapping and at Blackwall in place of the congested Pool of London.

The centre of London also changed as the 'West End' developed a distinctive sense of place, mixing conspicuous consumption with public fashionability. This was a place to see and to be seen. The Prince Regent reasserted the Crown's influence on London by becoming

the West End's main property developer. Regent's Park, Regent's Street, Piccadilly Circus and Trafalgar Square gave Londoners a network of new public spaces in which to parade their wealth and indulge in the new London habit of shopping. By the 1820s London's shopkeepers had spread out from the City along the Strand and Holborn to new shopping areas around Regent Street, Piccadilly and Bond Street.

Bazaars and arcades sprang up as new types of retail premises. Plate-glass shop windows, dressed with goods from around the world, were one of the sights of Regency London. 'I was still more astonished at the opulence and splendour of the shops,' wrote Robert Southey's fictional Spanish visitor, Don Espriella, in 1807. 'Drapers, stationers, confectioners, pastry-cooks, seal-cutters, silversmiths, book-sellers, print-sellers, hosiers, fruiterers, china-sellers, – one close to another without intermission, a shop to every house, street after street and mile after mile; the articles themselves so beautiful, and so beautifully arranged … Nothing which I had seen in the country had prepared me for such a display of splendour.'

# METROPOLITAN IMPROVEMENTS I

Crown patronage and the architect John Nash were behind
the development of London's most imposing new development,
a grand north–south route through Westminster.

The Regency period gave London what were to become its
most famous public spaces: Piccadilly Circus, Trafalgar Square
and Regent Street. Boldly imposed on the existing streetscape,
these dramatic metropolitan improvements gave Westminster a
new vertical spine, with two splendid new circuses, a crescent,
a quadrant, a marble arch and a square.

**The Quadrant,
Regent Street, 1822**
*John Nash's curved
colonnade was
designed to offer
genteel shoppers
protection against the
weather. It was taken
down in 1848 following
complaints from the
shopkeepers that
it cut out light and
encouraged vice.*

The new street plan marked the re-emergence of the monarchy
as a shaper of London. The city had never had a strong court
culture, and by the end of the 18th century the stubbornly
unfashionable George III (r. 1760–1820) was overshadowed by his
aristocratic grandees. The future George IV (r. 1820–30), Prince
Regent from 1811, brought a different tenor to the role of the
Crown. Fashionably urbane, he needed little persuading that
improvements to his capital city reflected his own status as the ruler
of Europe's most powerful country – since the Napoleonic Wars,
superior not just economically, but also in military and naval might.

## A PRINCELY PARK

The first improvement undertaken by the Crown was the
redevelopment of Marylebone Park, an area of heathland north of
the Oxford Road. What was to become Regent's Park began as a
property speculation of fashionable housing, laid out by the architect John Nash (1752–1835), for the Prince Regent. Responding
to criticisms that the enclosure of the park for private housing

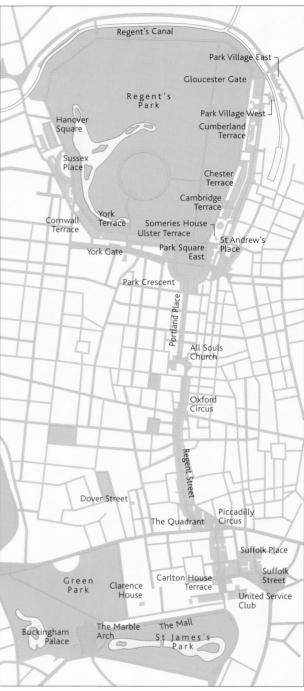

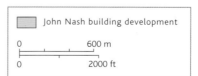
John Nash building development

0 — 600 m

0 — 2000 ft

**The New West End**
The new public park
and streets were built
on crown-owned land in
the early 19th century,
between 1810 and 1830.

went against the spirit of the age, Nash re-presented his proposal
in a manner that was flattering to his patron. This was not just any
property speculation: it was a magnificent public ornament 'in
every respect worthy of the nation and of the metropolis'.

The scheme proceeded in conventional fashion, with building

leases being let to speculators. Park Crescent, the great set piece at the Park's southern entrance, was begun in 1812; a start was made on the scattered detached villas inside the grounds in 1817; and the first of the large perimeter terraces, York Terrace on the eastern edge, was begun in 1820. The resulting mix of informally landscaped park and picturesque architecture gave London a new look, halfway between the 18th-century pleasure garden and the late 19th-century garden city. Genteel Londoners wandered this new precinct 'in perpetual transport at … every varying delight'.

## THE ROYAL WEST END

Regent Street was also designed to provide income for the Crown. The lack of a good north–south road in Westminster had long been noted, and the creation of the Park provided the opportunity to link the Prince Regent's home, Carlton House in Pall Mall, with his new creation. As with the Park, Nash produced a self-consciously picturesque development, a stage set of a street broken up by two circuses and an arcaded quadrant. The sinuous curve of Regent Street was, however, less to do with aesthetics than with property values: the street carefully separated the new first-rate houses to the west from the unimproved properties to the east.

Nash's reworking of central London continued when his royal patron, from 1820 King George IV, moved from Carlton House to the grander surroundings of Buckingham House. Nash's expensive improvements to the new palace included new wings, new facades and a theatrical marble arch in front (Marble Arch was moved to its present location later in the century). On the site of the Regent's old home, Nash built Carlton House Terrace, and conceived the idea of a large open space linking Pall Mall and Whitehall with the British Museum and the Strand. His vision began to take effect with the demolition of the Old Royal Mews in 1825. A new geometric street plan was laid over the old muddle of streets and alleys, and white classical terraces began to appear.

For these Strand developments, picturesque buildings gave way to classical sobriety. Dignity and symmetry were also the hallmarks of the National Gallery, begun in 1832 on the north side of the new square, and the British Museum, rebuilt on its Bloomsbury site in the 1820s. These institutions were part of London's new sense of itself as a modern European capital, a new Athens of enlightened values rooted in the cultural traditions of classical civilization.

Although the cycle of improvements had begun with royal patronage, it ended with a broader sense of nationhood. The National Gallery marked the first real intervention of the government into what had been a Crown undertaking. It was also Parliament's decision that the new square should contain a monument 'which may reflect honour on the patriotism and taste of the country'. It was given the name Trafalgar Square around 1830 and Nelson's Column emerged as the winning entry in a competition to create a monument to Britain's naval hero of the Napoleonic Wars. Its military hero, the Duke of Wellington, had fared far better for public memorials: he and his famous victory were commemorated in a number of monuments, streets and places in central London, including Waterloo Bridge. By 1840, the names of national heroes were dotted throughout the improved West End, expressing a far more complex mix of cultural forces than the self-interested speculation that had first covered the ground with buildings.          **CR**

*Hyde Park Corner and Constitution Arch, c. 1833*
*The two arches, both designed by Decimus Burton, juxtapose royal power and that of the people. Erected in the 1820s they marked the entrances to Buckingham Palace on one side and Hyde Park on the other.*

# RIVER CROSSINGS

The growth of south London was closely linked to the building of three new bridges in four years. London Bridge was also rebuilt and a tunnel under the Thames begun in the Regency period.

For centuries, Old London Bridge had provided Londoners with road access to Kent, Surrey and southern England. But by the late 18th century population and trade had both grown, creating a greater need for roads to transport people, commodities and food. Additional bridges (Westminster Bridge in 1750 and Blackfriars Bridge in 1769) had been built across the Thames in the 18th century, but because of their locations, these did little to ease congestion around London Bridge.

In 1801 the City Corporation came under renewed pressure to rebuild London Bridge as part of the agitation to improve London's port. The project began in earnest in 1823, with the passing of an Act of Parliament, and the new bridge was opened by King William IV in 1831 to great festivity. Constructed alongside the old medieval bridge, which was demolished as soon as the new one opened, the five stone arches carried a 15-metre (49-foot) wide road, immediately criticized for being too narrow. The whole project cost a colossal £2 million, including compensation to property owners whose buildings were swept away to clear the sites for new approach roads.

This was the third Thames bridge associated with the Scottish engineers John Rennie, father and son. The elder Rennie (1761–

1821) had prepared the designs and the younger (1791–1866) was the supervising engineer. By the time the new London Bridge opened in 1831 three additional bridges had appeared, all drawing on the Rennies' expertise, and all using new technologies, particularly cast-iron construction. The three newcomers, at Vauxhall, Waterloo and Southwark, were all toll bridges financed by private money, organized in large joint-stock companies.

## VAUXHALL

The first of these enterprises was the Vauxhall Bridge Company, which hoped to profit from the new developments by driving a road directly from Hyde Park across the river to Kennington and on to Greenwich. The company obtained an Act of Parliament in 1809 and engaged John Rennie to build a stone bridge. Within months, however, the project had run into financial difficulties and construction had to be continued in cheaper cast iron. Several months later, dissatisfaction with Rennie's design finally brought building work to a complete halt. A new design for a nine-arch bridge by Sir Samuel Bentham was accepted by the company, and Rennie's work was demolished. Doubts over the suitability of the design emerged once more, and in 1813 the company commissioned a third design, this time by James Walker. Walker's bridge, the first iron bridge over the Thames, was opened in June 1816.

## WATERLOO

Simultaneously, the Strand Bridge Company obtained an Enabling Act in 1809 to build a bridge and road crossing from the Strand to join up with St George's Circus. John Rennie was again appointed to design and build the bridge. Rennie's design envisaged a flat

***Waterloo Bridge, 1817***
*This view of the opening day of Waterloo Bridge contrasts the new bridge's level road with the humped profile of old London bridge in the background.*

**The Vauxhall Cast Iron Bridge, 1818**
Vauxhall Bridge, built in 1816, was London's first cast-iron bridge across the Thames.

rather than humped bridge across the river, which meant that long approach roads had to be constructed. The acquisition of the necessary land, especially on the south side where the approach road was more than twice as long (218 metres/716 ft) as on the north, proved complicated and costly. The Strand Bridge Company was forced to seek additional Acts of Parliament to enable them to raise further funding to complete the bridge. In June 1816, in the same month that the Vauxhall Bridge opened, the Strand Bridge Company reorganized its finances, and the bridge was renamed Waterloo

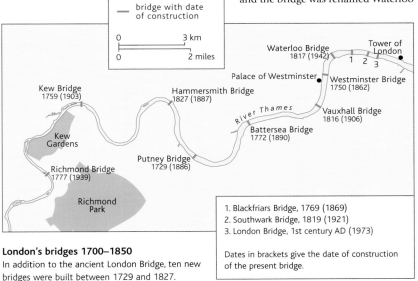

London's bridges 1700–1850

In addition to the ancient London Bridge, ten new bridges were built between 1729 and 1827.

1. Blackfriars Bridge, 1769 (1869)
2. Southwark Bridge, 1819 (1921)
3. London Bridge, 1st century AD (1973)

Dates in brackets give the date of construction of the present bridge.

Bridge, in honour of the Duke of Wellington's victory over the French in the previous year. The bridge itself opened a year later, on the second anniversary of the battle.

Waterloo was considered to be John Rennie's finest bridge. Its remarkable level roadway was much admired. So, too, was its granite stone: London's earlier bridges were faced with pale Portland stone; Waterloo used Cornish granite with Aberdeen granite for the balustrades. The grandeur, magnificence and solidity of Waterloo drew widespread praise, the Italian painter Canova calling it 'the noblest bridge in the world'.

## SOUTHWARK

The third bridge to be built during the Regency period, Southwark Bridge, was also constructed by a private company, but its Enabling Act was not passed until May 1811. This delay was the result of considerable opposition from the City Corporation, which objected

strongly to the fact that the second bridge linking the City to the south bank was to be a toll bridge, while the Corporation remained responsible for maintaining the more expensive and toll-free London Bridge. The Thames Conservancy, which considered that the position of the bridge, between London and Blackfriars bridges, would be a further hazard to navigation on the river, also raised objections. As a result, Rennie, who had once again been appointed to work on the bridge, designed a structure that bridged the river in three great arches, allowing more than 200 metres (660 ft) of navigable river beneath.

The bridge eventually opened with a dramatic midnight torch procession in March 1819, but within a year the company that had financed it was in financial difficulties. Again, the critical factor was the connecting roads. The position of the bridge had been determined by the availability of land and an approach road on the north side, in the City. On the south side, however, the land had already been built up. The construction of a road from the bridge to the hub at St George's Circus required the demolition of a large number of existing buildings, and the authority to do so was obtainable only piecemeal. As a result, the Southwark and Southwark Bridge Road took a meandering route north from St George's Circus to the bridge, while the bridge itself had to be steeply humped to accommodate Rennie's design.

## THE TUNNEL

Regency London also constructed the world's first underwater tunnel. The idea for a tunnel beneath the Thames had been around since the early 1800s when Cornish mining engineers had made several unsuccessful attempts to burrow from Rotherhithe to Wapping. Work started in earnest in 1825, with a scheme devised by a French engineer, Marc Isambard Brunel, who had invented and patented an ingenious 'tunnel shield' specifically for the purpose. By the 1830s his son Isambard Kingdom Brunel had joined him as resident engineer on the project.

The experimental nature of the tunnel proved difficult to finance and work stopped between 1828 and 1835. However, government funds were found and the tunnel opened in 1843. It only accommodated pedestrians, who could promenade the length of the tunnel by the light of hissing gas lamps.

A triumph of civil engineering, the tunnel proved a boon for souvenir sellers. The American writer Nathaniel Hawthorne, visiting in the 1850s, complained that the entire length was filled with market stalls selling fancy ware and 'multifarious trumpery'. 'There are people who spend their lives there, seldom or never, I presume, seeing any daylight.' In Hawthorne's view, beyond being a novelty place to visit 'the tunnel is an entire failure'. **TW**

# TRADE & INDUSTRY

London played a full part in the Industrial Revolution sweeping Britain in the 19th century. Large-scale brewing and shipbuilding in particular emerged alongside established specialties.

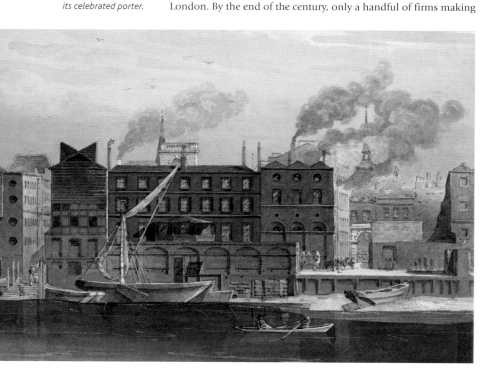

London remained one of the Britain's major manufacturing centres throughout the 19th century despite growing competition from the industrializing north of the country, making everything from marine engines to postage stamps. In contrast to other regions of Britain, no one industry or group of industries dominated early 19th-century London: its manufacturing base was notable both for its diversity and for its specialization.

Small factories and workshops predominated, especially to the north and the south of the City. 'Workers in metal, workers in glass and in enamel, workers in wood, workers in every substance on earth, or from the waters under the earth that can be made commercially valuable,' was how novelist George Gissing (1857–1903) described the labour force of Clerkenwell. Men toiled for long hours at the lathe or the workbench producing high-quality small items such as watches and clocks, jewellery and precision instruments. Young girls and women were employed more frequently in the less skilled trades. They might find work, for example, in an artificial flower workshop, bending and shaping wire, cutting, sewing and gluing the fabric and paper; or in a hat factory, picking out defective fibres of fur and adding the trimmings to hats.

Some traditional London industries declined in the early 19th century, such as silk weaving, which was centred largely in Bethnal Green and Spitalfields. The silk weavers and their families found it increasingly difficult to compete with foreign imports and with regional production centres such as Macclesfield. In the 1830s, there were perhaps seven or eight thousand weavers at work in London. By the end of the century, only a handful of firms making

***Calvert's Brewery, c. 1820***
*The site in Upper Thames Street had been a brewery since the 15th century. In the 18th century, under the ownership of the Calverts, the brewery grew massively, using steam power to brew its celebrated porter.*

specialist silk fabrics were still in operation, employing only a few hundred men and women.

The economic pressures on the larger manufacturers in the metropolis were considerable, including the relatively high wages paid to their workers, expensive property and the cost of fuel and raw materials. Industries in the Midlands and the north-east could produce goods far more cheaply. The key economic reason for locating a business in London was its proximity to the world's single largest market place for manufactured goods. This advantage became less significant as national transport and communication links were improved during the course of the century with the growth of the railway network, the establishment of fast, reliable coastal steamship services and the introduction of the electric telegraph. Nonetheless, a considerable number of major industries remained in London and the surrounding region.

## BREWING & DISTILLING

Among such industries was Barclay and Perkins' 'Anchor' brewery in Southwark, which was the largest in the world. It occupied a site of roughly 4 hectares (10 acres). A serious fire destroyed many of the buildings in 1832, but the brewery was rapidly rebuilt on an even larger scale. Because of its size, it became a famous landmark of London, with visitors marvelling at the enormous vats in the great brewhouse, the quantities of malt and hops stored in the adjoining warehouses, the pipes, pumps and steam engines, the large coppers and the mashing machines.

Barclay and Perkins was not the only major brewer in London. Truman and Hanbury's Brick Lane brewery was only slightly smaller in size, and another dozen or so brewers, including Whitbread's, Reid, Combe, Calvert (see left) and Meux, were about half the size but could still be considered as some of the largest undertakings in the capital. Many had sunk their own artesian wells to maintain a constant supply of fresh water; Barclay and Perkins, however, continued to draw large quantities of water directly from the Thames at Southwark.

Other trades in which London had a dominant role included distilling, rectifying – the conversion of the plain spirit from the distilleries into gin and cordials – and vinegar- and wine-making. These industries occupied premises usually alongside or close to

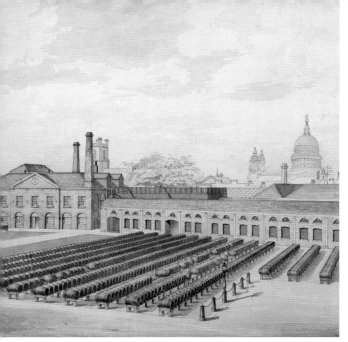

solutions of oak bark or tan until, over a length of time, they were transformed into leather. Specialist firms such as Bevington's Neckinger Mills made and dyed morocco leather from goat skins; this high-quality, soft leather was used for coach linings and chair covers, and for fine bookbinding.

## ENGINEERING & SHIPBUILDING

In the first half of the 19th century, Maudslay and Field of Lambeth was London's most innovative engineering works. Many of the greatest engineering entrepreneurs spent time working there under Henry Maudslay before setting up their own businesses. These included James Nasmyth, who invented the steam hammer, and Joseph Whitworth, who introduced mechanized screw-cutting machinery. By the 1830s, specialist engineering firms in Southwark and Lambeth were making precision engineering machinery for the printing trade and for the docks. A large number of marine engines and boilers were also produced here for Admiralty-commissioned steamships and merchant vessels under construction at London shipbuilding yards.

*Potts' vinegar manufactory, Bankside, 1840s*
*Potts' was one of the largest vinegar makers in England, its London location here emphasized by the dome of St Paul's in the background. This view shows the factory yard when 'fielding' was in progress: the exposure to the air of barrels of spirit for acetic fermentation.*

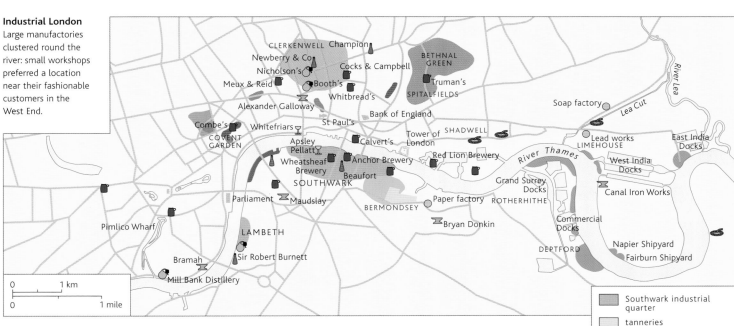

**Industrial London**
Large manufactories clustered round the river: small workshops preferred a location near their fashionable customers in the West End.

| | |
|---|---|
| | Southwark industrial quarter |
| | tanneries |
| | leather working |
| | coach building |
| | timberyards |
| | silk working |
| | furniture-makers |
| | clock- and watchmakers |
| | Soho light industrial quarter |
| | potteries |
| | shipyards |
| 🍺 | brewery |
| 🍶 | vinegar-maker |
| 🍶 | distillery |
| ⚒ | iron works |
| 🍸 | glass works |
| 🐛 | rope walk |
| ⦿ | other industry |

the river; many were in Southwark and Lambeth, others in Pimlico and Stepney. Each of the four London vinegar-makers had a large open area of ground where their casks were 'fielded', or left exposed to the air for about a month or so to allow acetification to occur (see the image above). In the 1840s, they together produced about a million and a half gallons of vinegar a year, representing more than half the country's total production.

## THE LEATHER INDUSTRY

The Bermondsey area had been the traditional centre of the country's leather industry for at least three centuries. The many tidal streams of the area were used by tanners and leather dressers to wash the foul and evil-smelling residue of their trade into the Thames downstream from the main inhabited areas. London harness- and saddle-makers, shoemakers, hatmakers and glove-makers obtained most of their leather from Bermondsey. The tannery yards still contained pits where hides were steeped in

The links between engineering and shipbuilding were particularly pronounced in the capital, as London was above all a port. In the mid-1830s, two shipbuilding yards were established at Millwall, on the Isle of Dogs, to produce iron ships. William Fairburn and David Napier (the latter another of Maudslay's pupils) were at the forefront of this new marine technology. Scottish shipwrights were recruited to work at the yards (a small Presbyterian chapel they constructed for worship still stands in West Ferry Road). Just as London-built wooden ships had a reputation for quality, so between the 1830s and the 1860s were London's iron-built ships considered to be at the cutting edge of new ship design. By mid-century, London was producing over a quarter of the country's tonnage of new-built merchant ships, the famous shipbuilders including Samuda, Young, Somes, Green, Wigram and Mare. **AW**

# BANKING TRANSFORMED

The rapid growth of London as a centre of world finance – and of financial speculation – in the 19th century brought dramatic changes to the appearance of the old City.

The City of London underwent a dramatic transformation during the 19th century. For many centuries, the 'square mile' had been the country's leading commercial and financial district. In 1845, the Bank of England and a brand new Royal Exchange stood at its centre, facing the Lord Mayor's Mansion House. Merchants who had once met in coffee houses to trade in commodities now gathered in purpose-built exchanges and salerooms. There were a few exceptional large banking and trading firms in the City, such as Overend, Gurney & Company, Barings and Rothschilds, as well as the offices of the fire insurance companies, which included such famous names as the

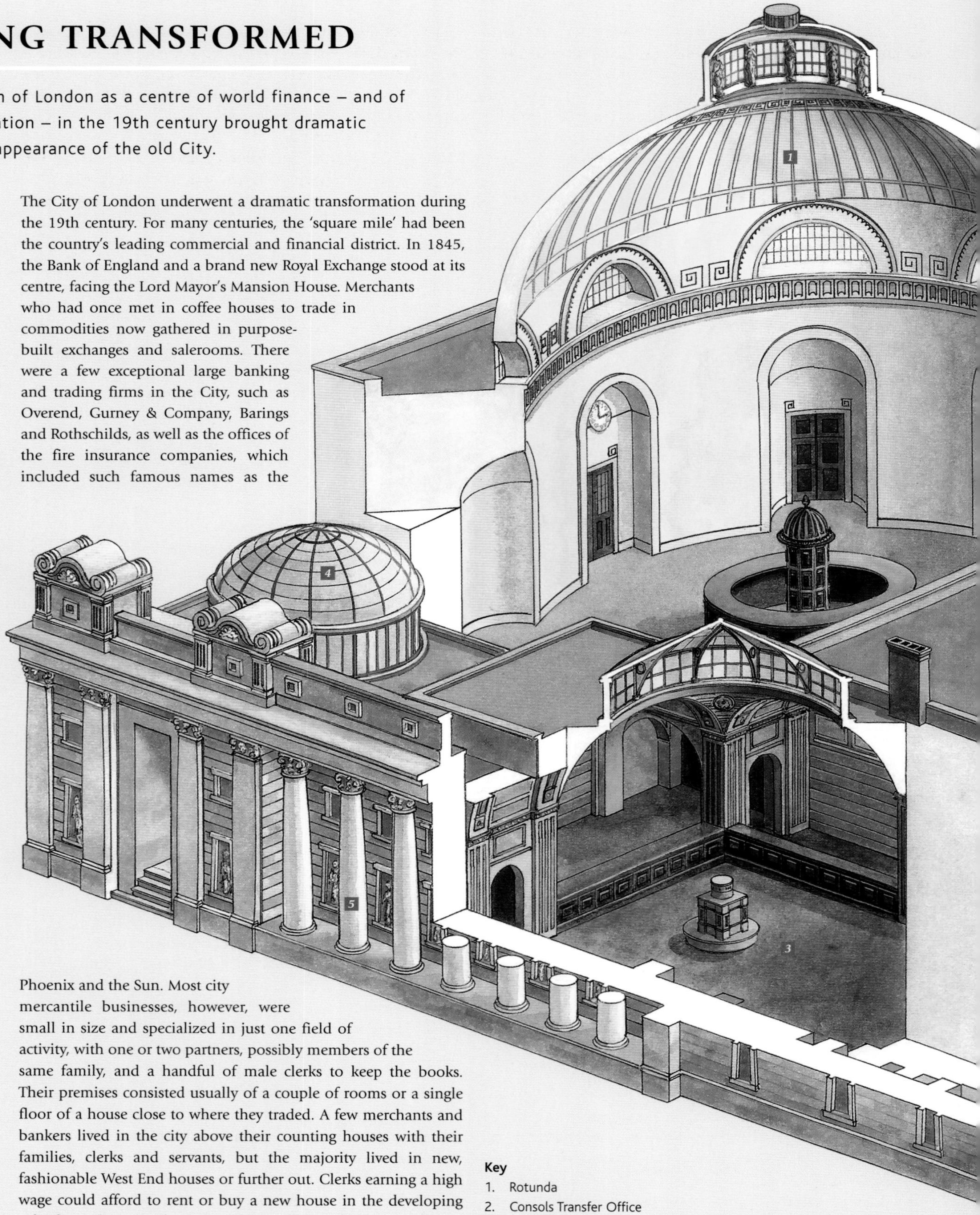

*The Bank of England*, c.1830
*Between 1788 and 1830 the bank's interiors were completely remodelled by the great architect Sir John Soane. Behind a long windowless wall, Soane created a series of airy, domed spaces for public banking halls, each devoted to different types of financial transaction. This shows the Five Per Cent (later the Colonial) Office.*

Phoenix and the Sun. Most city mercantile businesses, however, were small in size and specialized in just one field of activity, with one or two partners, possibly members of the same family, and a handful of male clerks to keep the books. Their premises consisted usually of a couple of rooms or a single floor of a house close to where they traded. A few merchants and bankers lived in the city above their counting houses with their families, clerks and servants, but the majority lived in new, fashionable West End houses or further out. Clerks earning a high wage could afford to rent or buy a new house in the developing suburbs such as Camberwell and Islington, while those on lower salaries lived within walking distance, in places like Finsbury, Southwark and Lambeth.

**Key**
1. Rotunda
2. Consols Transfer Office
3. Bank Stock Office
4. Vestibule
5. St Bartholomew's Lane colonnade

Gradually, the appearance of the City changed. The old brick buildings were demolished and new purpose-built offices were constructed in their place. These tall and impressive premises had many windows and were usually faced with Portland stone. The new banking halls had a feeling of solidity and permanence with stone floors, marble columns, and long mahogany counters. As financial organizations increased in size or amalgamated, they began to offer a variety of services to their clients. They required ever-larger offices to house a growing army of clerks.

The City's financial activities continued to grow in importance. Funds were needed to build factories, railway lines, docks and ships, not only in Britain, but around the world. The City became the world's leading investor, making large and profitable capital investments throughout Europe and America. The Bank Charter Act and Joint Stock Banking Act of 1844 had laid the foundation for the country's modern banking system, with the Bank of England and the City's private and joint-stock banks at its heart. The principal aim of this legislation was to curb inflationary trends by controlling the issuing of bank notes. During the century, the cheque replaced the bill of exchange.

## FINANCIAL CRISES

Financial crises did occur during the ensuing years, usually sparked by bad harvests, unwise investments and over-speculation. The railway mania of 1845–6 was an example of the latter, catching up the whole country in a frenzy of speculation. Everyone with money to invest was drawn into buying railway shares, including country parsons, widows and orphans who depended on their regular secure income. The Stock Exchange expanded to deal in the shares of the new joint-stock railway companies, benefiting the stockjobbers and stockbrokers as well as all those involved with promoting the new undertakings. An Act of Parliament was

***Cheque – Messrs Gosling
& Sharpe – 1840s***
*Writing a cheque, the new method
of transferring money, replaced
the old-fashioned 'bills of exchange'.*

required before construction work could begin on a railway line, and detailed plans had to be submitted for consideration by Parliament. In 1846, no fewer than 1263 railway bills were presented in a mad rush, many on the last possible day for submissions. When the bubble burst, share prices fell sharply and many investors found that they had lost all their money. It took some years for the market to recover and for confidence to return. **AW**

# REGENCY SHOPPING

The glittering and competitive new shops of Regency London pioneered many modern retailing strategies, including window-dressing, departments, advertising and sales.

***Interior of Harding & Howell's, 1809***
*Harding, Howell & Co, a drapers in Pall Mall, opened in 1796. Its large windows and spacious displays marked it out as a smart, modern shop.*

By the early 19th century, London's retailers had spread out from the City along the Strand and Holborn to create a new shopping centre in the West End. Its principal streets were Oxford Street, Regent Street, Piccadilly and Bond Street. The redevelopment of Regent Street (1816–c.1824) as one of London's foremost shopping streets was a key element in John Nash's metropolitan improvements. The street intentionally separated the wealthy and aristocratic quarter of Mayfair from the busy workshops and slum dwellings of Soho. At its southern end, Nash constructed the Quadrant, which led into Piccadilly Circus. It was lined with buildings designed with uniform facades whose ground and first floors were occupied by shops. Customers and passers-by were protected from the weather by arcades that projected across the pavement, forming London's first boulevard.

## BAZAARS & ARCADES

Two new types of retail outlet appeared in this period: the bazaar and the arcade. Both brought together a range of retailers under one roof. London's first arcade was the Royal Opera House Arcade, which opened in 1817. The architects John Nash and George Repton designed it as the entrance to the Royal Opera House, with a single row of shops.

***Burlington Arcade***
*The prestigious Burlington Arcade (opened 1818) combined luxury shops with the latest in retail design.*

Burlington Arcade, designed by Samuel Ware, opened the following year. The longest arcade in Britain at 178 metres (583 ft), it featured bow-fronted shops with living quarters above that lined both sides of the covered street, which was lit with large skylights. It occupied a choice retail location running parallel to Old Bond Street. In 1828, the fifty-five shops included milliners, hosiers, linen shops, shoemakers, hairdressers, jewellers, hatters, tobacconists and florists. Also in occupancy were an optician, a wine merchant, a pastry cook, a shawl seller, an ivory turner, a goldsmith, a glass manufacturer, a bookseller, a stationer, a music seller and an engraver. This range of shops was echoed in other streets in the area, where luxury goods mixed in with food shops including butchers, bakers and dairies.

Bazaars offered entertainment as well as shopping, setting retail space alongside conservatories and exhibition galleries. John Trotter opened the Soho Bazaar in Soho Square in 1816. The bazaar occupied two floors of an existing building, with mahogany counters set up in a series of open-plan rooms selling mainly millinery, gloves, lace, jewellery and potted plants. The counters were rented out to female traders on a daily basis. Two of the ground-floor rooms, named the Grotto and the Parterre, were decorated with climbing plants. Another innovative feature was the provision of a ladies' dressing room. To ensure the respectability of his establishment, Trotter employed porters to discourage unseemly behaviour, and insisted that the traders dressed plainly and sold their goods at fixed, marked prices. His success prompted the establishment of other bazaars such as the Western

Exchange in Old Bond Street (opened in 1819–20) and the Pantheon in Oxford Street (1834).

## ATTRACTING THE CUSTOMER

The 18th-century retail market was very competitive and the most ambitious and successful shopkeepers invested money in both the interior and exterior of their premises, with up-to-date lighting and glazing, and a high level of customer service. Visitors from overseas, like the German Sophie von la Roche who visited London in 1786, marvelled at the city's shops. In Oxford Street, 'behind the great glass windows absolutely everything one can think of is neatly, attractively displayed, and in such abundance of choice as almost to make one greedy'.

Lighting was particularly important in a city polluted by smoke and plagued by fog in the winter months. Richard Rush, the US ambassador, recorded that on New Year's Eve 1817 the fog was so dense that the shops in Old Bond Street had lit their lights before noon. The Argand light, which was patented in 1784 and emitted as much light as seven candles, was the most effective form of lighting in this period. The change in street lighting from wall-mounted oil lamps to gaslights mounted on metal posts set into the pavement made shopping in the central districts a safer and more pleasurable activity.

Retailers advertised their establishments and goods with trade cards, flyers and catalogues. Trade cards, engraved with the shop's name, address and services, doubled as invoices. Magazines and periodicals wrote articles about the latest and most fashionable shops. In March 1809, Rudolph Ackermann's *Repository of Arts, Literature, Commerce, Manufactures, Fashions and Politics* featured a description and coloured print of the interior of Harding, Howell & Company's Grand Fashionable Magazine at 89 Pall Mall, which had opened in 1796 (see above). The ground floor was separated by glazed mahogany partitions into four departments. These sold fur and fans; dress fabrics, haberdashery, lace and accessories; millinery and dress; and lastly jewellery, ornamental pieces in ormolu, French clocks and perfumes. Furnishing fabrics were sold on the first floor and there were workrooms above. Forty people were employed on the shop floor and in the workrooms, with men serving in the shop. The same issue of the *Repository* included

four swatches of dress fabrics available from the shop. These included an Anglo-Merino shawl cloth woven in Norwich and silk woven in Spitalfields in the East End of London.

In 1823, Ackermann featured Blades' ornamental glass showroom on Ludgate Hill, the approach to St Paul's Cathedral. Although the West End was now the main shopping centre for fashionable goods, Blades' was typical of a number of exclusive shops that maintained luxurious premises in the City, selling expensive – often imported – manufactures. They included several mercers and shawl shops whose establishments became a byword for luxury. The City also remained an important centre for menswear, of all qualities.

## DISCOUNT & SALE SHOPS

Those Regency Londoners on low incomes bought from local shops, markets and street traders. Although the poor relied heavily on second-hand goods, some neighbourhood shops sold seconds and discounted damaged goods alongside cheap ready-made textile items, clothes and accessories. Temporary sale shops were also established in working-class areas to sell off outmoded stock. The anonymous author of *Reminiscences of an Old Draper* (1876) remembered that the best-selling lines in the shop in Colt Lane, Limehouse, that he managed were men's ready-made blue check and striped cotton shirts, children's socks, men's and women's stockings and 'other useful goods'.

One of the best days for trading was Sunday when the shop, like local public houses, opened from 8 a.m. until church time, to meet the needs of customers whose wages were paid on Saturday evening. **EE**

*Blades' glassware showroom, 1823*
Located in the less fashionable City, this Ludgate Hill shop was nevertheless near its suppliers: the Whitefriars glass house and a network of glasscutters' workshops in Holborn and Clerkenwell.

*The Haberdasher's Dandy, 1818*
This scene is a satire on London's shop assistants, whose fashionable chit-chat hides poor service.

# THE NEW DOCKS

The West India Dock Act of 1799 heralded a huge change in the riverside landscape to the east and south-east of London. On both banks, vast new docks were created.

Pressure for the establishment of new dock facilities in Regency London came principally from traders with the West Indies. Initially, they proposed a new general dock facility at Wapping.

Wapping was, however, densely occupied by housing, as engineer Daniel Alexander reported: 'the number [of houses] necessary to be purchased … is One thousand Four hundred and Thirty … It will be necessary to pull down for the Docks about Eight hundred houses' (Report to Select Committee, 1796). By 1798, therefore, the West Indies lobby had turned their attention instead to a low-lying area of marshy land at the north end of the Isle of Dogs. This location had the advantages of being further downstream, where the river was deeper, and of saving ships the passage around the Isle of Dogs itself. Excavation began on two large dock basins and entrance locks in July 1800. Massive new warehouses were incorporated to house the produce from the West Indies plantations, and tight security was provided by walls, ditches and the West India Dock Company's own police force. The financial viability of the new dock was secured by the grant to the company of a monopoly on London's West Indies trade for twenty-one years.

The exclusive nature of the new docks meant that the main port of London remained overcrowded and, in 1800, a London Dock

*The opening of the St Katharine Dock, Wapping, 1828*
*The maritime parade was led by the* Elizabeth, *an East India trader.*
*The second ship, the* Mary, *carried fifty veterans of the Battle of Trafalgar.*

Act was passed, enabling a newly-formed London Dock Company to proceed with the original scheme for docks at Wapping. Both schemes overcame serious opposition from the City Corporation and those with commercial interests near the old Pool of London.

## THE NORTH BANK

Work began on the London Dock in 1801 under the supervision of the architect Daniel Asher Alexander (1768–1846), although much of the work on the basins was done by John Rennie. Within a year the company was in financial difficulty. The cost of clearing existing housing had proven much greater than estimated, and renewed war with France had led to inflation and labour shortages. The company's financial security depended on a monopoly over tobacco, rice, wine and brandy imports – but the resumption of war had hit this trade hard. It was forced to seek additional capital, until it had raised over three times the original estimates.

The initial building phase included an entrance lock and basin from the river at Wapping leading into a large dock (the Western Dock). Simultaneously, land was acquired and cleared for a further extension eastwards, consisting of a link-dock (later known as Tobacco Dock), constructed between 1815 and 1820, and an Eastern Basin, completed by 1831. Meanwhile, in 1812, the Regent's Canal Company excavated a dock at Limehouse to give its new canal access to the Thames. This dock was enlarged some eight years later to admit seagoing ships.

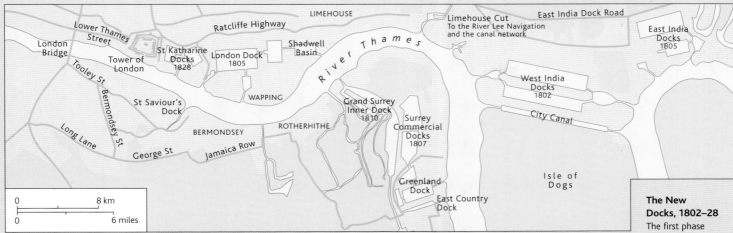

The New
Docks, 1802–28
The first phase
of dock-building
colonized both sides
of the River Thames,
providing greater
capacity for London's
huge and growing
shipping trade.

The initial success of the West India and London docks soon prompted the East India Company to review its facilities. Its ships already used the Brunswick Dock at Blackwall for fitting out and repairs, but this was unsuitable for cargo. An East India Dock Company was quickly formed to extend it. The new East India Dock, opened in August 1806, had few warehouses as all goods were transferred immediately to the company's warehouses in the City. Private toll roads (the Commercial Road and its eastward extension the East India Dock Road) were constructed to carry this traffic from both the East and West India docks.

## THE SURREY DOCKS

On the south side of the river, developments took a much more confused course. During the 1790s, several schemes for canals and dock basins on the Rotherhithe peninsula had been considered. None was accepted, but in 1801, a Grand Surrey Canal Company was created to build a canal that would ultimately link the Thames with Portsmouth, via Surrey. Work started in 1802, but difficulties quickly arose in purchasing land along the proposed route. The plans included an enlarged canal entrance basin, the Grand Surrey Outer Dock.

By the time the first ship entered the Grand Surrey Outer Dock in 1807, rival companies had bought up the land to the north of the new dock and the existing canal. The Commercial Dock Company had begun to develop the extant Greenland Dock, and the East Country Dock Company had started to build an additional dock between the Greenland Dock and the canal.

Two years later the Baltic Dock Company acquired much of the remaining land between the canal and the river to build docks and storage ponds for its imported timber. By the mid-1820s, the eastern side of the Rotherhithe peninsula had become a patchwork of eight docks, hemmed in by the Grand Surrey Canal and owned by three different dock companies.

## THE END OF THE DOCK BOOM

The last phase of dock building during the Regency period was also the most controversial. In 1824, in the light of the imminent expiry of the West India and London Dock companies' monopolies, a St Katharine Dock Company was incorporated, with a scheme for building a dock in the small area of land between the Tower of London and the London Dock. The proximity of the proposed site to the City was one of its main attractions, but the area was already densely packed with houses. Demolition of these houses was costly, and the project included the controversial destruction of the medieval hospital of St Katharine, but nevertheless the scheme went ahead. The engineer Thomas Telford came up with an ingenious plan for the limited land available – but the dock was simply too small to take the ever larger steam-powered vessels now beginning to dominate trade. Within five years the demand had fallen away: the dock boom was over.                                    TW

Plan of the West
India Docks, 1802
Ralph Walker's
plan of the new
complex includes
the unsuccessful
canal built by the
City Corporation
as a shortcut across
the Isle of Dogs.

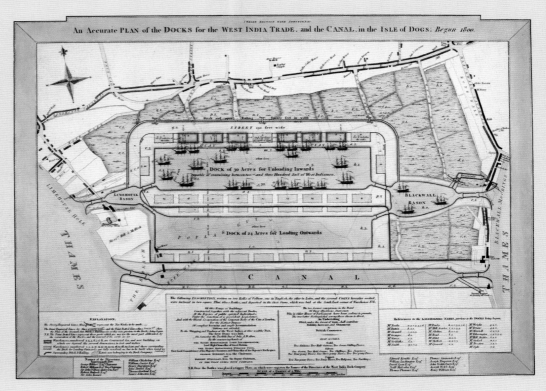

# LEISURE IN THE CITY

Early 19th-century London offered a wide range of opportunities for entertainment, both high-life and low-life. The Regency added a new sense of style to leisure.

**The licensed Victuallers' Fete,** *1831*
*The Victuallers' Association opened a charity school at Kennington in 1803. The annual fete, held at the Eyre Arms Tavern in St John's Wood, raised money for the school and provided a festive day out for members.*

Leisure in London changed during the Regency period. Style and leisure became more obviously connected in the popular imagination, particularly through the fashionably urbane Prince Regent. The archetypal figure of style in Regency London was the witty and stylish dandy, the gentleman of leisure. In popular print and literary culture, tales of rakish behaviour and the excesses of men of leisure were avidly consumed. Such popular accounts reveal the geography of pleasure in the Regency metropolis and give first-hand accounts and intimate details of the social ritual and mores of the age.

The most famous and popular account of leisure in this period is in Pierce Egan's *Life in London, or The Day and Night Scenes of Jerry Hawthorn Esq. and his Elegant Friend Corinthian Tom*, serialized between 1820 and 1821 and richly illustrated with caricatures by George and Robert Cruikshank (see right). It was so popular that it resulted in a continued series of books, several stage versions and a variety of merchandise including Tom and Jerry silk handkerchiefs. The rambling tale narrates the journey through the high and low life of London of Corinthian Tom and Bob Logic in their initiation of Jerry Hawthorn into urban lifestyle and manhood.

## BLOOD SPORTS & GAMBLING

Among men of all levels of society, the 'gentlemanly' pursuits of sports and gambling were enormously popular. For the fashionable and the wealthy, this meant the exclusive clubs of London's most fashionable district, such as Brooks's and Crockford's in St James's. Gambling was not, however, exclusive to high society; low gaming houses including Boodle's and White's, which provided for a more mixed clientele. Gambling was also central to the blood sports enjoyed throughout the metropolis. Ratting, cock-fighting and dog-fighting were commonplace in purpose-built arenas attached to inns and taverns, although the foundation of the Society of the Prevention of Cruelty to Animals in London in 1824 reflected a changing attitude to such sports. In *Life in London*, the protagonists visit the Westminster Pit to see a dog fight against a monkey: '[The monkey] with his teeth, which met together like a saw, made a large wound in the throat of the dog, as if done with a knife; and from the great loss of blood the dogs in general sustained, who were pitted against JACCO MACACCO, several of them died soon afterwards.'

**Low-life at Max's, 1820–1**
*Tom and Jerry admire the 'jigging' in a sailors' tavern, along with 'Lascars, blacks, jack-tars, coal-heavers, dustmen, women of colour old and young'.*

Pugilism and prizefighting attracted some of the heaviest gambling. The long rounds, before the Marquis of Queensberry's rules of 1886, meant that boxers regularly suffered severe injuries, their faces smashed beyond recognition. Within St James's, pugilism was practised and watched by gentlemen at establishments such as Gentleman Jackson's training rooms at 13 Bond Street, visited by Tom and Jerry, who went to meet 'this celebrated teacher of the Art of Self-Defence'. Tom Cribb's tavern in Panton Street, also visited by the protagonists of *Life in London*, was frequented by working-class, professional boxers and upper-class patrons.

## THEATRES & MEETING PLACES

London's theatres were at the centre of the city's leisure life and many were expanded and redesigned in the early 19th century. The King's Theatre (or the 'Italian Opera House') was, as its alternative name suggested, the centre for Italian opera and French ballet. By contrast, Covent Garden, 'the seat of Cyprian indulgence', had much lower associations. As the theatres grew to allow for larger audiences, spacious saloons were created; these became known as areas of sexual assignation.

Assembly rooms, by contrast, provided highly respectable places for public gatherings outside the family home. These were ideal venues for procuring marriage arrangements. They were designed with separate rooms for the types of leisure that they provided: a ballroom for dancing and entertainment; a card room for games; and a refreshment room. Almack's Assembly Rooms of King Street, St James's, was the most exclusive venue in London in the early 19th century, as Hermann von Pückler-Muskau noted in his 1827 *Tour*: 'Almack's balls in London are the resort of people of the highest rank during the season, which lasts from April to June; and five or six of the most intensely fashionable ladies … who are called Patronesses, distribute the tickets.'

The 'lowest life in London' according to Egan, was found in taverns such as Max's (see above). 'It required no patronage; a card of admission was not necessary; no inquiries were made; and every cove that put in an appearance was quite welcome: colour or country considered no obstacle …' Riotous behaviour features largely in *Life of London*, whether it be taunting the nightwatchmen or cavorting with prostitutes. Alcohol was the fuel for rakish behaviour in the St James's club as much as the gin shop.

## ART GALLERIES & EXHIBITIONS

Another kind of leisure, overtly associated with style and cultivation, expanded in Regency London: the public art gallery. The National Gallery, established on the north side of Trafalgar Square in 1832–8, vied with the once-exclusive Royal Academy (founded in 1768) and its popular Summer Exhibition, held annually at Somerset House from 1780 to 1836.

Exhibitions of curiosities and spectacular inventions appealed to a broader audience. These included everything from performing flea exhibitions and ballooning to panoramas. Among the latter, the Diorama in Regent's Park, the Cosmorama in Regent's Street and the Apollonicon in St Martin's Lane were notable.

The new image of leisure in the sophisticated metropolis was summed up in a song in *Life in London*:

> LONDON Town's a dashing place
> For ev'ry thing that's going.
> There's fun and gig in ev'ry face,
> So natty and so knowing.

MB

**High Life at the Royal Academy, 1820–1**
*Tom and Jerry mingle with High Society.*

# POLICING & PUNISHMENT

A centralized, professional police force for London was created only in 1829, despite the city's lawless reputation. It owed much to the vision and energy of the Home Secretary, Sir Robert Peel.

**Robert Peel (1788–1851)**
*The Home Secretary created London's first official police force and inspired their nicknames: 'peelers' or 'bobbies'.*

In 1841, the novelist Charles Dickens (1812–70) described his reasons for writing *Oliver Twist*: 'It appeared to me that to draw a knot of such associates in crime … to paint them … in all the squalid poverty of their lives; to show them as they really are … with the great black, ghastly gallows closing up their prospects; it appeared to me that to do this would be an attempt to do something which was greatly needed and which would be a service to society.'

Dickens began writing *Oliver Twist* in 1837, but he drew heavily from his own childhood experiences in the 1820s. He vividly describes the criminal underworld that thrived in London during the first half of the 19th century. Crimes such as house-breaking and pickpocketing plagued the city, and magistrates were notoriously corrupt and inefficient. The parish-based law enforcement agencies still lacked the organization required to tackle disorder and struggled to cope with increasing lawlessness.

Despite the need for action, there was widespread opposition from the public to the idea of a centralized police force. Londoners felt that law and order should be the responsibility of local areas and feared the use of force in suppressing protests. Paris was renowned for its paid police force, but because Britain had been at war with France from 1793 to 1815, many people disliked the idea

of a French system on principle. One option for controlling the unruly city was to improve the street lighting. The first general use of gas street lighting in London came in 1814 in Pall Mall. By 1823, nearly 40,000 lamps had been installed across 346 km (215 miles) of London streets. But lighting alone was not enough to stem the rise of crime.

## WATCHMEN & MAGISTRATES

In 1792, seven Public Offices were established in Middlesex, each with three magistrates and six constables. They had the power to arrest 'ill disposed and suspect persons'. These offices caused resentment among parish constables and watchmen, who perceiving them as interfering with local policing. However, the local watchmen themselves generally had a poor reputation among the public. In a satirical sketch *c.* 1795, the artist Thomas Rowlandson illustrates the inefficiency of traditional parish law enforcement. He depicts a scruffy-looking watchman yawning as he patrols the streets with his lantern and cudgel, while in the background two burglars brazenly go about their business (see left). Many watchmen were believed to be in league with criminals. By the early 19th century, the slang nickname for a watchman – a 'charley' – gives some indication of the lack of respect the public had for them. Later, the nickname became a general term for a fool.

In addition to the watchmen, the Bow Street Horse patrols (by a troop of former cavalry troopers) watched over the main routes out of London from 1805. They were the first law officers to wear a uniform and carry arms. Other parts of London, however, were still at risk of becoming no-go areas.

## A PROFESSIONAL POLICE FORCE

In 1812, 1818 and 1822, Parliamentary committees were appointed to investigate crime and policing. From 1822, Sir Robert Peel (1788–1850), the Home Secretary, lobbied for the establishment

**Watchman, by Rowlandson, c.1795**
*Thomas Rowlandson's satirical portrait of a slow-witted 'charley'.*

of a professional London-wide police force under central control. His vision and determination led to a complete overhaul of the antiquated criminal code and finally, in 1829, to the creation of a centralized police force, the Metropolitan Police Force. The new force operated initially within a 6- to 11-kilometre (4- to 7-mile) radius of Charing Cross; ten years later, this zone was extended to a 24-kilometre (15-mile) radius.

alarmed by such a move, maintaining that being spied upon infringed on their traditional personal liberty. Plain-clothes policemen were initially called 'Divisional Detectives'. Two officers per police division were allowed to go undercover and they had to make themselves known when arresting a suspect by showing a symbol of authority such as a tipstaff (a wooden staff tipped with metal, from which the policeman's truncheon evolved).

**Inside a watchhouse, 1822**

*From a comic series,* Fashion and Folly: *here, the two heroes, Dashall and Lubin, 'object to the restraints of the Charleys'.*

Once the force was established, Peel appointed the first police commissioners. His choice of Charles Rowan, who had led an infantry regiment at the Battle of Waterloo, and Richard Mayne, an Irish lawyer, was inspired. Their complementary skills in law and order helped create a police force run on a military model; they remained in joint control for over twenty years. In 1829, Mayne wrote: 'The primary object of an efficient police is the prevention of crime; the next that of detection and punishment of offenders if crime is committed. To these ends all the efforts of police must be directed.' Recruits were to be 'young, strong men of good intelligence and with a written recommendation as to good character' – a marked improvement on the previous law enforcers.

The force was initially based in a private house, 4 Whitehall Place, backing onto Great Scotland Yard, giving the police headquarters the name by which it is still known today. London was divided between seventeen police divisions and the parish watchmen were everywhere disbanded. The only part of London outside the control of the new Metropolitan Police was the City of London but, in 1839, the City established its own police force on similar lines to the Metropolitan.

In the 1840s, it was decided that police officers occasionally needed to work undercover in plain clothes. The public was at first

At first there was considerable hostility towards the new constables, with their truncheons, blue coats and top hats. But soon many Londoners began to feel safer with their presence on the streets. In 1833, a riot at Cold Bath Fields in Clerkenwell saw three policemen stabbed and one killed. But police charges broke up the riot without anyone in the crowd being seriously injured and the public's fears that the police would be oppressive and violent were quelled. Almost overnight the police went from being feared to being admired, now known by the more affectionate nickname of 'Peelers' or 'Bobbies' after their founder. The original 1000 officers had grown to 3300 by 1839 and the service needed to develop fast throughout the 19th century in response to new threats and an increasing stratification of crime. **ES**

**Policeman's rattle, c.1840**
*Rattles were used to raise the alarm before the introduction of whistles in 1884.*

# RADICALISM & REFORM

Regency London was no hotbed of radicalism, but pressure for Parliamentary reform was growing. The 1832 Reform Act met some demands, but did not satisfy most activists.

'London differs very widely from Manchester, and, indeed, from every other place on the face of the earth. It has no local or particular interest as a town, not even as to politics. Its several boroughs in this respect are like so many very popular places at a distance from one another, and the inhabitants of one of them know nothing, or next to nothing, of the proceedings in any other, and not much indeed of those of their own.' (1840)

This is how the Charing Cross tailor and veteran radical Francis Place described London and its disjointed politics in the first forty years of the 19th century. In contrast to the large provincial cities like Manchester and Birmingham, London never witnessed a high general level of agitation for political reform. This was due, in part, to the sheer size of the city and the variety and relative small scale of its many industries. Essentially artisans, Londoners were not subjected to the dramatic fluctuations in employment experienced by the factory workers of the north. Popular political activity in London remained comparatively uncoordinated, typified by isolated outbursts such as the Cato Street Conspiracy of 1820, when a group of radicals led by Arthur Thistlewood were arrested for plotting to assassinate the entire cabinet. The conspirators were hung and beheaded.

## THE GREAT REFORM ACT

Large-scale radical action was more evident in England's provincial cities, but the working-class movement was nevertheless to some extent centred on London – if for no other reason than that London was the home of Parliament. Furthermore, the need for electoral reform was nowhere more marked than in London before the Great Reform Bill of 1832; before the Bill, London was home to the most under-represented urban population in Britain in relation both to its wealth and to its numbers.

Electoral reform was the galvanizing issue for radical political movements – both working class and middle class – challenging the exclusiveness of the existing political system and campaigning for universal male suffrage. The level of parliamentary corruption before 1832 was exemplified by the 'rotten boroughs'.

These were ancient boroughs that had dwindling and minuscule populations, but could still return members to Parliament: for example, the constituency of Old Sarum in Wiltshire represented only eleven eligible voters. By contrast, London, with a population of some 1,878,000, returned only ten MPs: four for the City and two each for Westminster, Southwark and the County of Westminster. Furthermore, London's electoral process, based on public hustings, had become notorious for riotous behaviour, bribery and corruption.

The people of London stirred themselves in 1831, when the terms of the first Reform Bill were published in March. When the second Bill was defeated in the House of Lords in October 1831,

*Spirit flask, 1831*
*Made by Doulton & Watts of Lambeth, this gin flask celebrates Lord Chancellor Henry Brougham, a hero of the reform campaign.*

riots ensued in several British cities; widespread support for the protests in London led to the formation of the National Union of the Working Classes (NUWC) and an equivalent middle-class lobby for reform, the National Political Union (NPU). The former radical John Cam Hobhouse recalled: 'In Bond Street I saw a large placard with this inscription: "199 versus 22,000,000!" [a reference to the opposition of the government to the will of the country as a whole] and I went into the house to persuade the shopman to take it down.'

The campaign raged throughout 1831, and the so-called 'Great Reform Act' was finally passed in 1832; it was the first major reform of the representative system since the time of Cromwell. About 7 per cent of the adult male population of Britain – those with property worth £10 or more – was now eligible to vote, and the political map of London was effectively redrawn: in addition to the existing ten MPs, another twelve were granted through the creation of new constituencies – Finsbury, Marylebone, Lambeth and Tower Hamlets – each with two MPs, and a further four representing Greenwich and other parts of Kent and Surrey now joined to the metropolis.

## THE FAILURE OF REFORM

The Reform Act of 1832 had been devised to address the most obvious failings of the existing system, but by no means was it intended to meet the demands of the most radical reformers. In fact, its sponsor, Lord Grey, had specifically seen it as an opportunity to divide the 'respectable' middle-class reformers from their working-class allies by overtly favouring their interests. The Act therefore did not satisfy most of the reformers, and there was general disillusionment across the country with the process of reform. London was still very under-represented with twenty-two MPs for a population of 1,900,000, whereas Cornwall, with a population of only 300,000, still returned forty-four.

Two other great 19th-century Reform Acts, in 1867 and 1884, followed the Act of 1832 in extending voting rights to new categories of men, but universal adult suffrage – including votes for women – was not finally achieved until the 20th century. **MB**

*An eclipse over London, 1832*

*This is a satire on the Duke of Wellington's unsuccessful attempt to form a government. Wellington (in the sun) is eclipsed by Lord Grey, holding the Reform Bill, and Henry Brougham (in the moon).*

*Crowds at the Westminster Hustings, 1818*

*The poll for Westminster's two MPs took place in front of St Paul's church, Covent Garden, the candidates addressing the unruly crowds from a stand, or 'hustings'. The event was famously boisterous.*

**New London constituencies**

The new London Parliamentary constituencies as proposed in 1831 in the Great Reform Bill, passed in 1832.

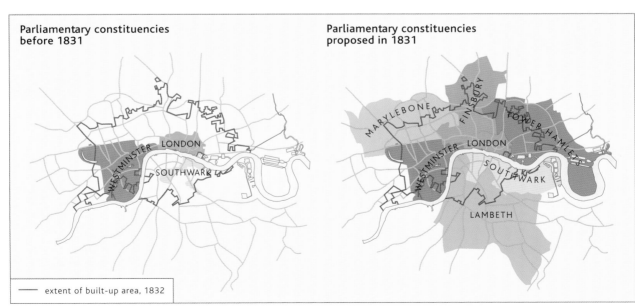

Parliamentary constituencies before 1831

Parliamentary constituencies proposed in 1831

— extent of built-up area, 1832

## The Mansion House, 1739–52
The official residence of the Lord Mayor of London, the Mansion House is still used for ceremonial state and civic occasions. The architect was George Dance the Elder.
Underground: Bank

# SURVIVALS
# GEORGIAN & REGENCY

## The British Museum, 1823–47
The British Museum is a grand, classically-styled replacement for Motague House which had housed the British Museum's collections since the mid-18th century. The architect was Sir Robert Smirke.
Underground: Holborn

## Dulwich Picture Gallery, 1811–14
Designed by Sir John Soane for Dulwich College to house its collection of paintings, this was one of the earliest purpose-built public art galleries in London.
Rail: West Dulwich

## The Theatre Royal, Drury Lane, 1810–12
Designed by Benjamin Wyatt, this was the fourth theatre on this site: previous buildings had burnt down. The porch was added in the 1820s.
Underground: Covent Garden

## The Royal Society of Arts, 1772–4
The Royal Society of Arts was founded in 1754 to encourage invention, arts and commerce; it was designed by Robert Adam.
Underground: Embankment

**Regents Park, 1812–28**
The new park transformed what had been rough heathland. It was laid out by John Nash, who also designed the grand terraces and picturesque villas around the edges.
Underground: Regent's Park

**The Ledger Building, West India Quay, 1827**
Originally the dock office for the West India docks, the Ledger Building was remodelled as a ledger office by the engineer John Rennie. It adjoined the row of massive warehouses along the north side of the dock.
Docklands Light Railway: West India Quay

**St Paul's Cathedral, 1675–1711**
The current cathedral, designed by Sir Christopher Wren, was finally completed in the early Georgian period.
Underground: St Paul's

**St Paul's church Deptford, 1712–30**
St Paul's was one of the 'Coal Tax Churches', intended to provide Anglican churches in populous parts of London. The architect was Thomas Archer.
Rail: Deptford or Greenwich

**St Bartholomew's Hospital, 1730s onwards**
The ancient hospital was expanded in the 18th century with a new extension by James Gibbs.
Underground: Barbican

**Lock & Co., c. 1810–20**
Lock & Co., hatters, have occupied this premises in St James's Street since 1765. The shop front dates from the early 19th century
Underground: St James's Park

# EARLY VICTORIAN LONDON

By the mid-19th century, London was a confident, expanding metropolis. Railways and steamships were helping to speed the city's economic growth. The Great Exhibition confirmed it as the capital of the most powerful nation of the industrial age.

Population growth was speeding up. Between 1831 and 1871 London's population doubled from 1.6 million to 3.2 million. Many of the new arrivals crowded into the old city-centre housing stock. Cholera killed many.

It became clear that the city's endemic problems of disease and sanitation would never be solved by the old parish-based systems of government. Opinion turned decisively towards new city-wide authorities, sponsored by national government. The new metropolitan police force was followed by a Metropolitan Board of Works, charged with improving roads, buildings and sanitation.

London still felt chaotic. The main roads into the city had been much improved by the late 1830s. Hundreds of stagecoaches arrived and departed each day, carrying passengers, packages and the Royal Mail. The streets were filled with the clatter and smell of horse-drawn vehicles even after the coming of the railways, with Joseph Hansom's famous cab introduced in 1835.

This was the London Charles Dickens knew. 'What inexhaustible food for speculation, do the streets of London afford!' wrote the young reporter in 1836.

**Trafalgar Square by Moonlight, 1861–7**
*Henry Pether's painting captures London's grand
new public square, an expression of the capital's
mid-century confidence. Nelson, the hero of the
Battle of Trafalgar, keeps watch over Whitehall and
the newly built Palace of Westminster in the distance.*

# PARLIAMENT & THE VOTE

London remained a centre of political unrest after the Reform Act of 1832. The Chartists demanded further reform, including votes for working men. Parliament was rebuilt on a grand scale.

In early Victorian London, a man's right to vote was linked to the property that he owned or leased. The Reform Act had set a minimum annual value of £10. Small properties in the metropolitan seats were more numerous and more highly valued than in other parts of the country, where voters were typically landed gentry; this gave London a relatively large and diverse electorate. Radicals were regularly elected to Parliament with little or no allegiance to the dominant aristocratic political parties.

Some MPs representing rural constituencies could be considered as Londoners, as they lived and worked in the metropolis. These included wealthy city bankers and merchants who had acquired large estates in the country. They kept a watchful eye over the government's fiscal and colonial policy, as many of them had interests in the East and West Indies.

Charles Barry and A. W. N. Pugin were its principal architects and designers. London's finest Gothic Revival building – a marvel of sculpted stonework on the exterior and carved woodwork and elaborate painted panels on the inside – took over twenty years to complete. Its historicist style came to symbolize the perceived traditions of the British Parliament.

The Palace of Westminster became one of the sights of the metropolis, a testament to British constitutional and artistic excellence. Intense popular interest surrounded the giant clock tower and its chime of bells. The first bell cast for the purpose cracked and the metal was re-cast at the Whitechapel Bell Foundry in east London. The massive clock with its 7-metre (22-ft) diameter face finally started to tick in 1859. After installation, the second bell also cracked, and it took a further three years to repair it in situ. Big Ben, as the clock was popularly known, marked time for the entire British Empire.

## THE CHARTISTS

Dissatisfaction with the Reform Act of 1832 – even after the Act, only about 7 per cent of the adult male population of London had the vote – was expressed politically through Chartism, a movement of essentially working-class and metropolitan origins.

**The Houses of Parliament from Millbank, 1861**
*David Roberts' painting shows the shimmering new Palace of Westminster rising above the ramshackle buildings and barges at Millbank.*

The aristocrats who dominated London's political life occupied all the high offices of state. They owned and maintained large London town houses in which they lived during the 'Season' and the parliamentary term. The House of Commons and the House of Lords at Westminster were the centres of government in Victorian Britain, although real political patronage and power was often determined in the gentlemen's clubs of St James and Pall Mall.

## THE NEW PALACE OF WESTMINSTER

The old Palace of Westminster was destroyed in a spectacular fire in 1834, so a new parliamentary complex needed to be built. Sir

Chartism was the first attempt to create a mass political movement representing the interests of working people. It originated with the London Working Men's Association, founded in 1836 with headquarters in Gray's Inn Lane. Like similar groups founded at the same time in much of Britain, the London organization was created from the remains of the earlier radical campaigning organizations for political reform. The basic demands for reform had been formulated in the 1780s, but in May 1838 the Association took the formal step of publishing them as a 'People's Charter', compiled by William Lovett with the help of Francis Place and John Roebuck.

The Charter's six points were:

1. Every man over twenty-one should be entitled to vote.
2. Voting should be by secret ballot.
3. MPs should not be required to be property owners.
4. MPs should receive a salary.
5. Each constituency should have an electorate of equal size.
6. There should be annual parliaments.

Nationally, the stated objective of the new movement was to have their charter made the law of the land – 'peaceably if we can, forcibly if we must', according to one of the movement's slogans. The Chartists quickly built up a mass following, but their movement was hampered from the start by its need to address a wide range of different grievances among working people. In London, where skilled artisans predominated, the movement emphasized self-help and political education, in contrast to the more class-based activism of the northern cities. Support for the movement also waxed and waned with prevailing economic and political conditions: activity peaked in periods of economic depression in 1839 and 1842, then again in 1848 in a time of recession and revolution in Europe.

## PUBLIC DEMONSTRATIONS

Large Chartist meetings were held in the capital with delegates attending from all over the country. Several national petitions, signed by millions of people, were presented to Parliament (and rejected each time).

The London authorities feared such large demonstrations in the metropolis, and the army was often put on alert in case of trouble. Trafalgar Square, with its proximity to the clubs, the Palace and the new Parliament building, became the preferred new venue for political protest, replacing the traditional gathering places for mass political meetings at Smithfield, Clerkenwell Green, St George's Fields and Hyde Park.

The most famous of these mass rallies took place at Kennington Common on 10 April 1848. The government took elaborate precautions for the capital's security. Special reserve constables were recruited in case of trouble and a large military force was made ready to defend the approaches to Westminster and the West End. A crowd that was much smaller than expected turned up for the rally. The intention was to march from Kennington to Parliament, where a petition containing supposedly six million signatures was to be presented. In the end, the rally dispersed peacefully, and only a handful of Chartist delegates delivered the petition to the House of Commons – where it was again rejected.

The 1848 demonstrations marked the end of Chartism as a mass political movement. Relative economic prosperity after that date, combined with concern at the upheavals in other European countries, led to a loss of popular support; it survived only as a movement promoting education, temperance and reform in local government. Twenty years later, the 1867 Reform Act extended the parliamentary vote to some male householders. But the Chartists' six demands still remained unmet. **AW**

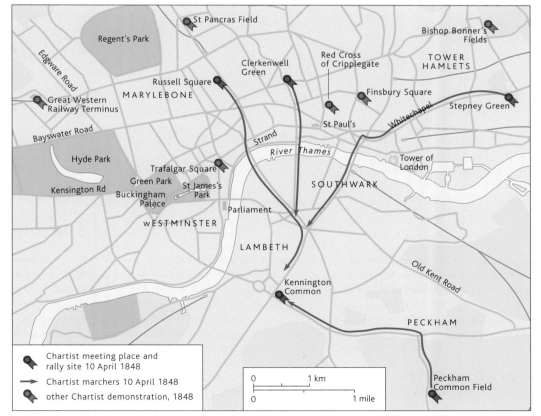

Chartist meeting place and rally site 10 April 1848

Chartist marchers 10 April 1848

other Chartist demonstration, 1848

# THE GREAT EXHIBITION

The Great Exhibition proclaimed Britain's industrial might as 'the workshop of the world'. It was a great spectacle, attracting thousands to its Hyde Park site.

On 1 May, 1851, Queen Victoria opened the world's first great international exhibition in Hyde Park. Housed in a glittering glass palace, the exhibition symbolized Britain's commercial and industrial supremacy, and was intended to promote the nation's leading role in technological progress. The exhibition was conceived by Prince Albert and Henry Cole as a way of stimulating British manufacture and design, educating the public and increasing cooperation and understanding between nations. No government money was used, and funding was raised by subscription. An astonishing array of raw materials and high-quality manufactured goods from around the world were on show. London became a focus for tourism on an unprecedented scale as thousands poured into the city to view the exhibition.

The building (main illustration) was designed by Joseph Paxton, head gardener at Chatsworth House in Derbyshire, based on designs for conservatories that he had created there. The huge glass,

**The Crystal Palace 1851**
*A reconstructed external view of the vast glass palace designed by Joseph Paxton to house the Great Exhibition in Hyde Park.*

**Key**
1. Boiler house
2. Statue of Richard I
3. Western nave – British exhibits
4. Eastern nave – foreign exhibits
5. South entrance
6. Vaulted transept with crystal fountain and trees
7. Machinery in Motion display
8. Refreshment room

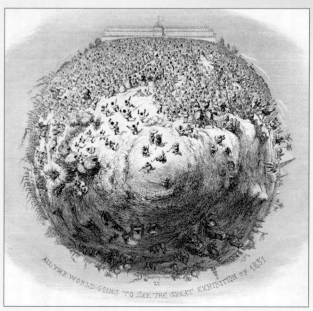

**All the world going to see the exhibition of 1851**
*George Cruikshank's humorous vision of the Exhibition's world-wide fame shows visitors coming from all corners of the globe.*

iron and timber structure was erected in just seven months; the *Illustrated London News* gave weekly progress reports. By December 1850, 2000 workmen were on site daily. Standardized components were used, with iron castings and glass panels made in the Midlands and transported to London by railway and horse-drawn wagons. Glaziers fitted over 300,000 panes of glass. Hollow cast-iron columns and 48 kilometres (30 miles) of guttering carried away rainwater and condensation, while huge panels of cotton cloth shielded visitors and exhibits from the sun.

Paxton's original design was modified to include a vaulted transept 30 metres (104 ft) high to accommodate three huge elm trees growing on the site. Overall, the structure was over 560 metres (1800 ft) long – more than three times the length of St Paul's Cathedral, and more than six times its floor area. Nicknamed the 'Crystal Palace' by the satirical magazine *Punch*, it was widely regarded as the most revolutionary building of its age.

The palace housed over 100,000 exhibits displayed on 16 kilometres (10 miles) of stands. They were divided into four categories: raw materials, machinery, manufactures and fine arts.

**Colonial
Produce, 1851**
*Sugar cane from
Trinidad and produce
from other colonized
countries were
included in the Great
Exhibition displays.*

north bank of the Serpentine, despite fears that the glass palace
would be shattered by the noise. During its six-month run, the
exhibition drew over six million visitors. For many people it was
their first trip to London, and guidebooks were produced for these
new tourists. Extra omnibuses and cabs were laid on. Railway
companies cooperated to provide transport at special low fares.
The demand for accommodation in London was so great that
temporary dormitories were set up, but lodgings were still scarce.

Visitors came from all sections of society. Admission prices
were kept down to encourage those on low incomes to visit.
Almost 800,000 visitors were season ticket holders, averaging
thirty return visits each; Queen Victoria visited on many occasions.
Refreshment rooms and public toilets were provided – the first
modern public toilets in London. Official catalogues were on sale,
along with commemorative medals, but no other souvenirs. Many
canny Londoners, however, made a tidy profit from memorabilia
for tourists, including mugs, vases, toys and games.

Profits from the exhibition were used to acquire a long stretch
of land south of Hyde Park, between Kensington Gardens and
Cromwell Road. A number of museums, concert halls, colleges
and schools were built here, including the Royal Albert Hall and

Many represented Britain's empire. Other exhibits came from other
parts of Europe, Africa and Asia. The three largest foreign
exhibitors were the USA, the German Zollverein and France.
Representatives of countries and exhibiting firms were on hand to
explain the displays and offer advice on purchasing the goods on
show, as they could not be bought at the exhibition itself. Some
commentators criticized the British content, believing that the
quality of some foreign exhibits showed Britain lagging behind
its competitors.

The opening ceremony on 1 May, 1851 was watched by a crowd
of 300,000. To announce the opening, guns were fired from the

Imperial College. The Albert Memorial was erected in Kensington
Gardens, with a statue of Prince Albert carrying a copy of the
official exhibition catalogue. The palace itself was dismantled after
the Exhibition (it was always intended to be recyclable) and
re-erected in Sydenham, Kent, opening in 1854. Here, visitors
could enjoy art exhibitions, concerts and firework displays. The
Crystal Palace was destroyed by fire on 30 November 1936.  **KF**

# WATER & DISEASE

Cholera outbreaks made public health early Victorian London's most urgent problem. Recognition of the link between sanitation and epidemics led to major reforms in both care and prevention.

**The 'Silent Highway' Man,** *1858*
*A* Punch *cartoon, drawn in the year of the 'Great Stink', offers a pointed comment on the River Thames as a carrier of pollution and disease.*

Early Victorian London was overcrowded, dirty and unhealthy. Its population swelled by almost a fifth each decade, and as it grew, the elements necessary for good public health – sufficient housing, efficient sewage disposal and a clean water supply – became inadequate. Infectious diseases such as typhus, typhoid, tuberculosis, measles, dysentery, smallpox, scarlet fever and, from 1832, cholera, took hold. London had a notably higher mortality rate and a lower life expectancy than the surrounding areas.

Infectious diseases were a fact of life for all, but it was the poor who were hardest hit. In slum areas like St Giles-in-the-Fields, Shoreditch and Bethnal Green, thousands of people lived in overcrowded, damp and filthy dwellings with inadequate sanitary provision and with access to water only from street pumps or, if they were lucky, from pipes turned on for brief periods each day. Weakened by a poor diet, terrible working conditions and long hours, they were especially vulnerable to disease. In St Giles, for example, one child in three failed to reach its first birthday. In Bethnal Green in 1843, a gentleman's life expectancy at birth was forty-five; that of a labourer was sixteen.

**London's new sewage system**
The new infrastructure of sewers and pipes was installed by the Metropolitan Board of Works, under its chief engineer, Joseph Bazalgette.

## CHOLERA

As long as infectious diseases affected mainly the non-voting poor, politicians had little incentive to call for sanitary reform. When cholera hit London in February 1832, however, political opinion began to change. Cholera is contracted by drinking water contaminated by infected faeces (a fact not demonstrated until Dr John Snow's work in Soho during the cholera outbreak of 1853–4, and not accepted by the medical profession until a decade later), and London's water supply made it particularly vulnerable. The

THE "SILENT HIGHWAY"-MAN.
"Your MONEY or your LIFE!"

city's cesspits overflowed and leaked their contents into the surrounding subsoil, contaminating nearby wells. Water closets, which had become increasingly popular since the late 18th century, improved sanitation for their well-off owners, but deposited waste directly into London's main water source, the Thames. From there it was pumped back and delivered in drinking water to Londoners. Although cholera killed far fewer than other infectious diseases, its mode of transmission did not discriminate between rich and poor. Calls for action increased.

A further reason for these calls was the financial burden of the new Poor Law system. Investigations into the sanitary conditions in the originating areas of workhouse inmates were published in the Poor Law Commissioners' fifth annual report in 1839. It contained graphic descriptions, of which that of John's Passage in Bethnal Green was typical: 'In the middle of the street is a large gutter always full of filth … and the noxious matter is with difficulty kept from flowing into the houses.' If London's sanitation could be improved, the Commissioners argued, disease would be reduced, and with it the number of workhouse inmates.

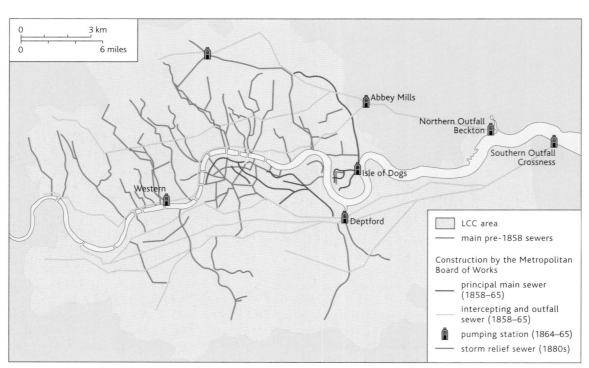

0 — 3 km
0 — 6 miles

Abbey Mills
Northern Outfall
Beckton
Southern Outfall
Crossness
Isle of Dogs
Western
Deptford

| | LCC area |
| --- | --- |
| — | main pre-1858 sewers |

Construction by the Metropolitan Board of Works

| — | principal main sewer (1858–65) |
| — | intercepting and outfall sewer (1858–65) |
| 🏭 | pumping station (1864–65) |
| — | storm relief sewer (1880s) |

## SANITATION & SEWERS

Several official reports between 1842 and 1845 highlighted the need for a single unified body to deal with London's drainage as a first step in improving sanitation. The Metropolitan Commission of Sewers, appointed in 1848 (and responsible for London outside the City), and the City Commission of Sewers went some way towards this. However, these commissions at first concentrated on building new sewers to improve the efficiency by which London's waste was washed into the Thames, thus unwittingly exacerbating a further cholera epidemic in 1848–9.

had opened in 1828, and in 1837 this became the Royal Free Hospital. General provision expanded, for example with St Mary's, Paddington, founded in 1845. Reflecting increasing medical knowledge, specialist hospitals – a London hallmark today – also proliferated. By 1860, there were at least sixty-six specialist hospitals and dispensaries in London, including the Brompton Hospital (founded in 1841), the London Chest Hospital (1848), the Hospital for Sick Children, Great Ormond Street (1852) and the world's first specialist cancer hospital, Marsden's Free Cancer Hospital (now the Royal Marsden Hospital, 1851).

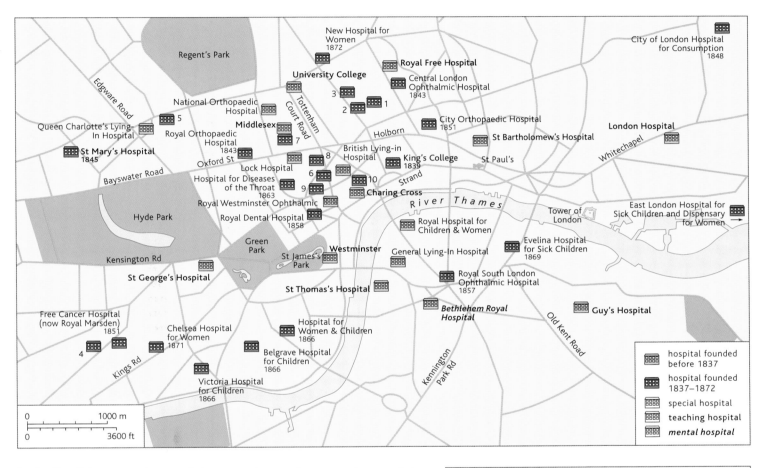

**London Hospitals**

The mid-19th century saw a proliferation of new hospitals in London, many offering specialist care.

The commissions spent the next six years arguing over designs for London's sewers, and in 1855 a Metropolitan Board of Works was established in their place. The new Board made little progress, however, until the 'Great Stink' of the summer of 1858 when politicians, directly affected in their offices by the stench arising from the Thames, voted to give the Board the resources it needed. Work began on an extensive new network of intercepting sewers designed by the Board's Chief Engineer, Joseph Bazalgette (1819–91), which discharged London's waste downriver from the city. In 1866, a fourth and final cholera outbreak was largely confined to areas where the network was incomplete. After completion of the whole in 1875, cholera never returned to London.

## NEW HOSPITALS

While the government was for the first time involving itself in public health, medical men and philanthropists continued to work to provide better treatment in London. The first free dispensary

1. Hospital for Sick Children, 1852
2. London Homeopathic Hospital, 1849
3. National Hospital for the Paralysed & Epileptic, 1859
4. Hospital for Consumption & Diseases of the Chest (Brompton Hospital), 1841
5. Western Ophthalmic Hospital, 1856
6. St John's Hospital for Diseases of the Skin, 1863
7. National Hospital for Diseases of the Heart, 1857
8. Hospital for Women, 1843
9. French Hospital and Dispensary, 1867
10. St Peter's Hospital for Stone & other Urinary Diseases, 1860

Although much work remained to be done to improve the health of Londoners, the first essential steps had been taken. Although the scientific causes of epidemics were still hotly disputed, the link between sanitation and disease – particularly cholera – had been recognized. Snow's insight and Bazalgette's engineering genius had given the city a sewer system fit for purpose. The long process of sanitary reform had begun. **JH**

# METROPOLITAN IMPROVEMENTS II

Newly-created centralized bodies targeted some of the capital's problems, but housing provision in early Victorian London remained a matter of philanthropic or private effort.

The Metropolitan Police and the Metropolitan Commission for Sewers, founded in 1848, had given London a model of how city-wide bodies might work. With the help of new laws, they tackled urban problems much more effectively than the former mosaic of parish authorities. The most significant new city-wide body to emerge in the early Victorian period was the Metropolitan Board of Works (MBW), established in 1855. The MBW initially took responsibility for the sewers, but this was soon extended to road building, drainage and clearing of 'nuisances' in the capital. Its power was bolstered by new public health laws, all intended to stem the city's descent into squalor.

The road construction, street-widening and clearance schemes of the MBW followed the precedent established by the Commissioners of Woods and Forests, who had built New Oxford Street (1847) and Victoria Street (1851). The appearance of central London was gradually transformed by MBW improvements; early new highways included Garrick Street and Southwark Street, followed by Clerkenwell Road, Charing Cross Road, Great Eastern Street, Hyde Park Corner and Shaftesbury Avenue. Many of the widening schemes remain in place today: for example, at High Holborn and Kensington High Street. The Corporation of London was also involved with road improvements at Cannon Street and Farringdon Road. Its most ambitious scheme was the Holborn Viaduct (1869), a raised road crossing over the River Fleet, which had been enclosed in the 18th century. It ran east to west and created a new route between the City and the West End.

The main aim of these works was to improve the road system in the capital, but an equal objective was to clear away some of the worst slum areas. Little thought was given, however, to where the displaced population would be forced to move. Karl Marx (1818–83) described from first-hand experience how these improvements and 'every sanitary measure' hunted 'the labourer from one quarter to another, by demolishing uninhabitable houses', serving 'only to crowd them together yet more closely in another'. Finally in the 1870s, such schemes were governed by limiting powers which enforced the Metropolitan Board of Works to provide alternative accommodation if more than fifteen houses occupied by the working classes were to be destroyed.

## EMBANKING THE THAMES

Perhaps the most impportant road improvement carried out by the MBW was the building of the Victoria, Albert and Chelsea Embankments between 1868 and 1874. Many previous schemes had been proposed for embanking the Thames. The foul-smelling mud, debris and sewage exposed at low tide were seen as a danger to health. The opposition of manufacturers and wharf owners along the river was now overruled as the benefits to London and Londoners were shown to be many, including a new road and a number of new public gardens.

The Victoria Embankment, on the north side between Westminster and Blackfriars Bridge was the more complicated to construct as it included three tunnels, one for the low-level northern sewer (see page 192), one for the new Metropolitan District Underground Railway and one for gas and

*The Thames Embankment works*

*Working labourers and piles of timber line the shore between Waterloo and Blackfriars Bridges during the construction of the Victoria Embankment in 1865.*

*New Oxford Street, 1875–80*

*Oxford Street was driven through the slums of St Giles in 1847 as part of a new east–west route through London.*

These small-scale initiatives scarcely dented London's housing problems. The arrival in 1862 of the US philanthropist George Peabody gave a new impetus to the idea that decent housing could be built and managed economically. The first 'Peabody Block' opened in 1864 in Spitalfields. It fronted onto Commercial Street, a new road built by the MBW in 1858.

*Peabody Square, Westminster, 1869*
*These buildings are a typical example of the estates funded through the Peabody Trust to alleviate the living conditions of the poor.*

## FIREFIGHTING

Firefighting within the metropolis had long been the responsibility of the private fire insurance companies. Each had its own firefighting service, charged with protecting only those properties insured with it. In 1832, a group of fire insurance companies agreed to merge to form the London Fire Engine Establishment. James Braidwood was appointed as its superintendent, with

water pipes and telegraphic cables. Once the Embankment was completed, the river appeared much narrower. Initially, road traffic was light, but gradually the new road came to be used as a fast route between Westminster, the West End and the City.

## MODEL DWELLINGS

Working-class housing was early-Victorian London's second most critical issue, after health. Lodging houses were notorious. 'In London fifty thousand human beings get up every morning not knowing where they are to lay their heads,' wrote the young German Friedrich Engels in 1845. 'The luckiest of this multitude … enter a lodging house … where they find a bed. But what a bed!

These houses are filled with beds from cellar to garret, four, five, six beds in a room, as many as can be crowded in. Into every bed four, five or six human beings are piled, as many as can be packed in, sick and well, young and old, drunk and sober, men and women, just as they come, indiscriminately.'

Housing reformers sought to encourage builders to provide more and better-quality rented housing. The Metropolitan Association for Improving the Dwellings of the Industrious Classes, founded in 1841, led the way in erecting model dwellings. Isolated blocks appeared in St Pancras, Bloomsbury and Pentonville. For the Great Exhibition, Prince Albert designed a small model cottage, later re-erected in Kennington Park.

*The Great Fire in Tooley Street, from Nicholson's Wharf, 1861*
*Six warehouses and the life of Superintendent James Braidwood were lost to the mighty flames of the blaze.*

seventy-seven men and fourteen fire engines kept at thirteen stations around London, all under his control. As the number of large buildings increased, the number of men under his command nearly doubled, with a similar rise in the number of fire stations. His team fought many serious fires at theatres and manufactories, becoming very skilled in firefighting.

Unfortunately, in 1861 a huge fire broke out in Tooley Street that was too much for Braidwood's men and equipment. It had started when a cargo of jute caught alight in a riverside warehouse close to the southern end of London Bridge. The fire raged for four days and nights, destroying six large warehouses. Braidwood lost his life while leading the efforts to bring the blaze under control. As a result of his courageous actions he became one of London's most famous popular heroes. The insurance claims that arose as a consequence of the Tooley Street fire were of such unprecedented scale that the London fire insurance companies considered disbanding the firefighting service. The government was forced to intervene, placing the service under the control of the Metropolitan Board of Works. In 1866, it was renamed the Metropolitan Fire Brigade, with Captain Massey Shaw as its first Chief Officer. **AW**

# COSTERMONGERS & COCKNEYS

London's crowds of street hawkers, market-traders and makeshift scavengers were described by journalist Henry Mayhew. His vivid account brought the streets of the capital to life.

The streets of mid-Victorian London provided the venue for an extraordinary variety of economic enterprise. Few people enjoyed regular earnings all their working lives, and many turned to the streets for subsistence. Some inherited their professions, but most were forced onto the streets by unemployment, illness, having too many children to support, or intemperance. The seasonal nature of some trades created underemployment.

For those facing destitution, the streets provided a last-ditch means of avoiding the discipline of the workhouse. After the new Poor Law in 1834, no person capable of work could receive help from the Poor Law authorities except within a workhouse, where they were forced to carry out menial tasks to pay their way.

In total only around one-fortieth of Victorian London's working population made a living on the streets, but they were highly visible and figured prominently in the public consciousness. The publication of Henry Mayhew's monumental *London Labour and the London Poor* between 1851 and 1862 heightened awareness of their plight. Mayhew devoted three volumes to street folk, visiting some of the most deprived parts of the city to interview them.

Street trading required little capital outlay, but the profits were generally low; most traders could never hope to lift themselves out of poverty. Many hawkers congregated around the city's street markets, while others tramped for miles through residential areas, whatever the weather. The majority were costermongers – sellers of fruit, vegetables or fish. Mayhew estimated that there were around

**Covent Garden Market** *(detail), 1864*
*Phoebus Levin's painting evokes the bustle of the market at dawn, as street traders and customers engulf the Piazza.*

**The Crossing Sweeper,** *1858*
*Rich appears to meet poor in William Powell Frith's painting as a young road-sweeper encounters a well-dressed woman as she crosses the street.*

30,000 of them mid-century and that their numbers were increasing yearly. Most bought their supplies from the wholesale markets. Up to 4000 costermongers were reckoned to purchase their fruit and vegetables from Covent Garden market on a busy Saturday, and they bought as much as half of all the fish sold at Billingsgate.

Costermongering was in part a hereditary occupation, and entire families – including women and children – were often

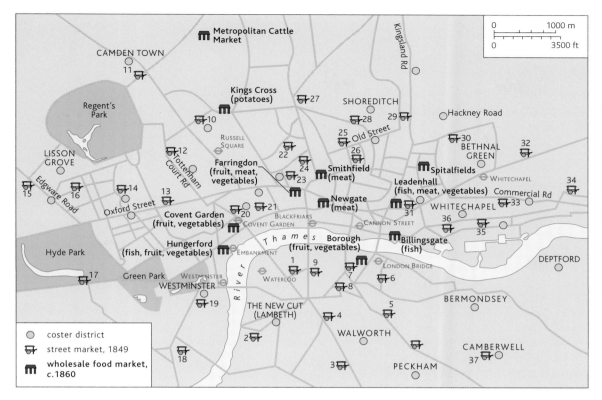

**London's markets and costers in the mid-Victorian period**
Sellers scattered themselves throughout the city meeting local demand in residential areas as well as centrally.

Street markets, with numbers of costermongers
1. New Cut, Lambeth (300)
2. Lambeth Walk (104)
3. Walworth Road (22)
4. Newington (45)
5. Kent Street, Borough (38)
6. Bermondsey (107)
7. Union Street, Borough (29)
8. Great Suffolk St (46)
9. Blackfriars Rd (58)
10. Brill & Chapel Street, Somers Town (300)
11. Camden Town (50)
12. Hampstead Road & Tottenham Court Road (333)
13. St George's Market, Oxford Street (177)
14. Marylebone (37)
15. Edgware Road (78)
16. Crawford Street (145)
17. Knightsbridge (46)
18. Pimlico (32)
19. Tothill Street & Broadway, Westminster (119)
20. Drury Lane (22)
21. Clare Street (139)
22. Exmouth Street, & Aylesbury Street, Clerkenwell (142)
23. Leather Lane (150)
24. St John's Street (47)
25. Old Street (St Lukes) (46)
26. Whitecross Street, Cripplegate (150)
27. Islington (79)
28. City Road (49)
29. Shoreditch (100)
30. Bethnal Green (100)
31. Whitechapel (258)
32. Mile End (105)
33. Commercial Road (East) (114)
34. Limehouse (88)
35. Ratcliffe Highway (119)
36. Rosemary Lane (119)
37. Camberwell (15)

engaged. According to Mayhew, around half inherited their profession, while those new to the trade were poor Irish, Jews, unemployed mechanics and tradesmen. Some costermongers had fixed stalls, while others had rounds of up to 16 kilometres (10 miles). Occasionally, country rounds would take them 160 kilometres (100 miles) or more outside the city. They used baskets, barrows or donkey- (or pony-) carts for their goods. Good business could be done at street markets like Brill in Somers Town on Saturday nights, after workers had received their wages.

The hereditary nature of costermongering meant that costers lived in close-knit communities. They typically lived in courts and alleys near street markets, in recognized 'coster districts'. Few coster couples married, and they were mostly illiterate, with a fondness for drinking and gambling. They were noted for their cockney slang, almost incomprehensible to outsiders, which enabled them to evade police and outwit rivals. Community life centred on beer shops, dancing rooms, theatres and penny gaffs. Gambling at cards was a popular pastime, as were skittles, shove-halfpenny and boxing. 'Twopenny-hops' offered dancing, often for whole families, until the early hours of the morning. They enjoyed sports like rat-killing, dog-fighting and pigeon-racing.

## OTHER STREET PROFESSIONS

There were innumerable other street professions. Many street sellers dealt in food and drink, including fried fish, ham sandwiches, hot green peas, plum duff, ginger beer and asses milk. The provision of ready-cooked food was vital to working-class families who either lacked facilities or could not afford the fuel for cooking. Other vendors dealt in manufactured articles, from matches, razors and tea trays to dog collars and birdcages, as well as live animals and street literature. Some specialized in cheap, second-hand goods like clothes and crockery. Street artisans and pedlars made or repaired articles like chairs, kettles and clocks, while others made items for sale, including clothes pegs, dolls, caps and rugs. Not all street people sought to sell: some bought goods that had a resale value, such as hare skins, old clothes, waste paper or dripping.

Performers and showmen provided cheap street entertainment. Italian organ grinders and German brass bands were welcomed in poorer districts. Acrobats, sword-swallowers and fire-eaters were common, and crowds gathered for dancing dogs, wise cats or industrious fleas. There were peep shows and travelling waxworks, and exhibitions of physical oddities like giants or pig-faced ladies.

At the bottom of the pile were the scavengers, those who picked up whatever they could find to eat or sell in the streets, on the river foreshore or in the sewers. Every scrap had a value – including pieces of metal, coal, wood, old rope, rags and bones. Pure pickers lived by gathering dog dung, known as 'pure', for sale to tanning yards, and cigar-end finders or 'hard-ups' collected the butts of smoked cigars, dried them, and sold them as tobacco to the very poor. Mayhew estimated that there were between 800 and 1000 bone grubbers in the 1850s, all old and mostly ex-labourers. They searched narrow back streets where rubbish accumulated, filling a sack with anything that might be saleable. They could travel twenty-five miles a day, sleeping at night in cheap lodging houses.

Within fifty years of Mayhew's work, many of London's street characters had disappeared, although their decline was slow and varied from one trade to another. Welfare initiatives such as the Education Act of 1870 took people off the streets, while competition from new retail outlets made some trades untenable. The arrival of motor transport by the end of the century changed the character of the city's streets for good. **KF**

# GETTING AROUND THE METROPOLIS

New horse-drawn vehicles updated travel in London. Omnibuses were a runaway success, ousting the old hackney coaches. The cabriolet, or 'cab', was reinvented as the hansom cab.

**Shillibeer's Omnibus, 1829**
*This was London's first regular horse-drawn omnibus service; it ran between Bank and Paddington. Passengers paid a shilling fare.*

**Transport in London**
This map shows the routes taken by the omnibus services on land and steamboats on the Thames.

George Shillibeer had pioneered the omnibus in London in July 1829, having seen its potential in operation on the streets of Paris. The first service ran between Paddington Green and the Bank. Up to twenty passengers sat facing each other on two benches inside a long, shoebox-shaped vehicle drawn by three horses. The omnibus proved to be very successful, especially after 1832, when the hackney coach monopoly was abolished in the central area. This allowed omnibuses to set down or take up passengers in the main shopping and business area of the city. Unfortunately, Shillibeer was unable to compete with rival operators and went bankrupt.

Omnibus design gradually evolved in the second half of the century; improvements included brakes and 'knife-board' or back-to-back seats on top of the bus, which increased the number of passengers that could be carried as well as lowering the ticket price. At first, access to the roof was by either iron rungs or a steep ladder but, by the 1880s, some omnibuses had a curving flight of stairs up to the top deck with forward-facing 'garden' seats, making it more accessible to women travellers. Along the upper length of the omnibus, 'decency' boards were fitted to conceal the passengers' legs as well as to offer them some protection from the weather; these carried brightly painted advertisements.

The number of horses used to pull this extra weight of passengers was reduced to two, and regular changeover points were needed to replace them with a fresh team. The working life of a London omnibus horse was estimated at about four years. An omnibus driver had to work very long hours, from 8.30 in the morning to 11.15 at night, with an allowance of twelve breaks of ten to fifteen minutes each, at the end of each journey. (The relatively late start reflected the fact that most passengers were middle class; the working day began much earlier for most working-class Londoners.) Wages for omnibus drivers, at thirty-four shillings a week, were considered to be good.

Visitors to London were faced with a confusing range of different shaped and coloured omnibuses, although the wheels were always painted yellow. The lack of final destination boards made it difficult to work out the direction of travel from the route boards, especially for those unfamiliar with the geography of the metropolis. Nevertheless, many tourists took advantage of the top deck, finding it an excellent way for seeing the sights of London. Omnibuses became one of the most popular forms of transport in the London area during the late Victorian period. They offered a convenient mode of travel for the middle classes in the city and outlying areas, complementing rather than competing with the railways.

## CABS, GROWLERS & TRAFFIC CONTROL

'The appearance of the first omnibus,' wrote Charles Dickens, 'caused the public mind to go in a new direction and prevented a great many hackney coaches from going in any direction at all.' Omnibuses

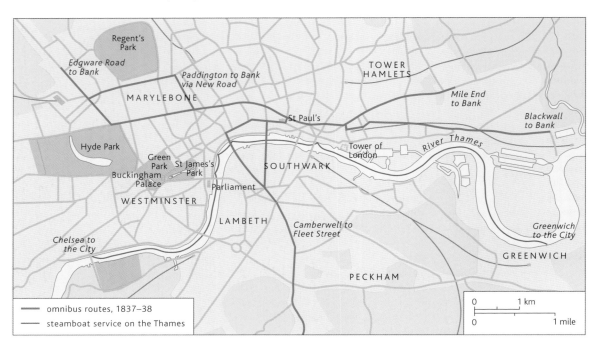

Regent's Park
Edgware Road to Bank
Paddington to Bank via New Road
TOWER HAMLETS
MARYLEBONE
Mile End to Bank
St Paul's
Blackwall to Bank
Hyde Park
Tower of London
River Thames
Green Park
St James's Park
SOUTHWARK
Buckingham Palace
Parliament
WESTMINSTER
LAMBETH
Camberwell to Fleet Street
Greenwich to the City
Chelsea to the City
GREENWICH
PECKHAM

— omnibus routes, 1837–38
— steamboat service on the Thames

0    1 km
0    1 mile

**Street scene with two omnibuses, 1845**
*By the mid-1840s London's streets were full of competing omnibuses. Here an E. and J. Wilson vehicle leads the way from Hornsey to Chelsea.*

offered a faster and more reliable means of transport than sailing vessels. As the frequency and regularity of services developed, competition between rival companies became fierce and the river was, at times, dangerously congested.

Day trips and excursions to seaside resorts on the Kent and Essex coast became a popular and affordable form of recreation for many Londoners. Commuters also used steamboats. In 1861, Henry Mayhew explained that 'the class of persons travelling by these steamboats is mixed. The wealthier not infrequently use them for their excursions up and down the river; but the great support of the boats is from the middle and working classes, more especially such of the working class (including the artisans) as reside in the suburbs, and proceed by this means of conveyance to their accustomed places of business.'

Accommodation on board offered high standards of comfort with 'handsome sofas', mahogany tables and large mirrors. Food and drink were served in the saloons and passengers were provided with playing cards and draughtboards. On-board entertainment was also supplied by a musical band or an orchestra. AW

sounded the death knell of the hackney coaches, which had been trundling round the city streets since the 17th century.

Hackneys also suffered competition from the lighter two-wheeled *cabriolet de place* or 'cab'. The cab, which was designed to transport one person at a time, was reinvented in 1834 as the hansom cab. A larger version, the four wheeled 'growler', which accommodated two people, also appeared.

At the time of the Great Exhibition in 1851, there were over 1200 omnibuses operating in London, many owned by the London General Omnibus Company, which owned nearly half the city's fleet by 1900. By 1860 there were also 4000 hansoms on London's streets.

The management of traffic in London was greatly improved by the Metropolitan Streets Act of 1867, which forced the omnibuses to stop on the near (left) side of the road within a 6-kilometre (4-mile) radius of Charing Cross, rather than drop passengers on whichever side of the street they pleased.

## STEAMBOATS

Steamboat services for passengers were introduced on the Thames in 1815. They

**Vessels in the Pool of London, 1840**
*Steamboat services add to the bustling Thames traffic alongside Fresh Wharf and New London Bridge.*

# THE COMING
# OF THE RAILWAYS

The railway boom of the 1840s strengthened London's role as national capital. New railroads between London and provincial cities transformed journey times.

In 1846, a parliamentary committee decided that no new surface railways should be permitted within the central London area south of the New Road (now known as the Marylebone and Euston Road) and west of City Road, Finsbury Square and Bishopsgate. The railway companies saw their main business as the long-distance transport of goods and passengers to other parts of Britain, and did not initially object to this restriction. Their great termini, bridges, tunnels and viaducts introduced a new form of architecture to London's streets and were hailed as an architectural and engineering triumph, but the real impact of railways on London itself was not yet felt. Only a few lines, such as those terminating at London Bridge and Fenchurch Street, carried daily commuters, who totalled only about 27,000 in the mid-1850s; most Londoners still walked or used the omnibus to get to work.

Nonetheless, by the 1850s, London was at the heart of a flourishing national rail network. Rail travel revolutionized the transportation of goods, the supply of food and the movement of people. By stagecoach, the journey from London to Birmingham took fourteen hours; by rail the same journey took just over five hours. Rail travel altered perceptions of space, geography and time, and the need to implement strict railway timetables resulted in the adoption of Greenwich Mean Time across the whole country, ending variations in local time.

**London's railway lines up to 1850**
Rail companies built their own separate tracks and stations in and around the capital.

London's first railway opened in 1836 between Bricklayer's Arms in Southwark and Deptford, carrying passengers along a continuous brick-built viaduct of some 878 arches; it was rapidly extended to London Bridge and Greenwich. In the following ten years, railway lines proliferated: the London and Birmingham Railway, terminating at Euston; the London and Croydon Railway, sharing the London Bridge terminus; the Eastern Counties Railway, terminating at Shoreditch; the London and South Western Railway to Nine Elms (and soon to Waterloo); and Brunel's Great Western Railway linking London to Bristol with a terminus at Paddington.

Railway development was both rapid and, at times, devastatingly destructive as neighbourhoods were swept aside to make way for track, stations and yards. The construction of the London to Blackwall line in 1836, for example, brought the demolition of 2850 houses along its route. Areas around the railway lines soon became associated with urban squalor and dereliction for, as a resident of east London commented in 1846, 'a viaduct would not be tolerated in a respectable neighbourhood and undoubtedly renders a bad one worse'.

## CLASS DISTINCTIONS
Rail travel reinforced the Victorian preoccupation with class. From the beginning, rail companies made separate provision for different classes of traveller, and eventually they even offered

**View of the London and Croydon Railway, 1838**
The new railway, opened to passengers in 1839, is seen here running along the deep cutting at New Cross. Trains ran hourly.

**Railway Bridge over Westminster Road, c. 1850**
High-level bridges and viaducts intruded into the capital's streetscape as part of the new railway age. High levels supposedly reduced the inconvenience of smoke and noise.

much slower than those carrying passengers who had paid more for their journeys.

Recognition of the value of railways for excursion travel was one of the factors that helped make rail travel a mass phenomenon. From 1844, railway companies were required to run at least one train a day in each direction at a fare not exceeding one penny per mile. By 1850, however, excursion trains were available to all classes. As well as offering Londoners the chance to escape the city, these services also enabled provincial dwellers to experience the thrills of the capital. The millions of passengers who travelled by rail to the Great Exhibition the following year reinforced the significance of the excursion train as an affordable and convenient form of travel for all.                                        **BC**

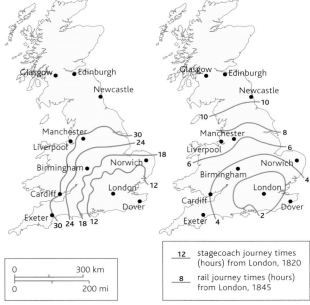

stagecoach journey times (hours) from London, 1820

rail journey times (hours) from London, 1845

services 'for the convenience of the poor'. Travellers were often segregated at the terminus, with first- and second-class passengers having separate entrances, refreshment rooms, lavatories and waiting rooms. First-class railway carriages were fitted with cushioned seats, glass windows and lamps for night travel. Second-class travel was a good deal less commodious, with wooden benches and carriages often open to the elements. Third-class trains either consisted of completely open low-sided wagons without seats or closed 'box-cars' without windows.

Ultimately, passengers of different classes were even accommodated on separate trains, with the third-class trains usually being

**Journey times from London in 1820 and 1845**
A clear reduction in hours was made possible with the advent of rail travel.

## THE CONSTRUCTION OF THE LONDON TO BIRMINGHAM RAILWAY

One of the most ambitious civil engineering projects undertaken in London during the early years of the railway age was the building of the London to Birmingham Railway, the first phase of which opened in 1837. To commemorate the first line to connect the capital city with the Midlands and the North, the railway company built an imposing Doric gate at the entrance to the Euston passenger terminus (demolished in 1961–2). Known as the 'Gateway to the North,' the gate came to symbolize the power and magnificence of the railways.

The building of the London to Birmingham Railway devastated the north London area of Camden Town and made many families homeless. In *Dombey and Son* (1846–8), Charles Dickens compared the building work to 'the shock of a great earthquake':

> Traces of its course were visible on every side. Houses were knocked down, streets broken through and stopped; deep pits and trenches dug in the ground; enormous heaps of earth and clay thrown up.

The early railways were constructed by the muscle power of horses and men. Labourers were usually itinerant workers who had come to London from other parts of Britain to work specifically on the railways

Building the Stationary Engine House at Camden Town, *28 April 1837. At this point on the London and Birmingham railway, two winding engines added extra power to haul trains from Euston uphill into Camden.*

and moved from site to site, often living and sleeping beside the railway tracks on which they worked.

# PENNY POST & TELEGRAPH

Victorian London became a remarkably efficient communications hub – the centre of a national postal service and a high-tech international network of telegraph cables.

**Penny Black stamp on a letter from the Duke of Wellington's house, 1840**
Penny Blacks were replaced in 1841 by Penny Reds. The new stamps showed up cancellation marks and made fraudulent re-use more difficult.

**Illustrated songsheet**
'The Telegraph', written and sung by George Leybourne, c.1863 was a popular tune. A female operator 'tap taps' to send a customer's telegram.

A 'penny post' had served London since the late 17th century, when the state-run Post Office acquired its monopoly on the delivery of letters. Traditionally, either the sender or the receiver could pay for the delivery and the charge varied according to distance and the number of sheets sent. Payment on delivery was an inefficient and much abused system. Furthermore, by the early 19th century, postage was expensive; for example, a letter delivered to Birmingham from London cost 9d.

In the 1840s, the postal service improved dramatically when the standard penny post rate was introduced for the carriage of letters anywhere in Britain. The scheme was ably conceived and implemented by Rowland Hill and his assistant Henry Cole. The first Penny Black stamp was sent on 6 May 1840. Stamps with a sticky solution on the back were bought from post offices or receiving houses, as they were known, and stuck onto the top right-hand corner of envelopes. Although this is a familiar practice today, this was a novelty in the 1840s.

Letter boxes were fitted to houses and letter collection points known as 'pillar boxes' (first proposed by the author Anthony Trollope) became a feature of the streets of London by the mid-1850s. Letters posted in London were sorted and then carried speedily across the country by the railways and mail coaches, and overseas by fast steamships. So great was the number of letters sent within London, added to the fact of the metropolis's size, that ten separate postal districts were created. During each day there were on average twelve collections and between three and five deliveries, depending on the area. In 1898, the cost of sending a letter from London

**THE TELEGRAPH.**

**GEORGE LEYBOURNE.**

to almost anywhere in the British Empire was reduced even further by the establishment of the Imperial penny post. The main exception was Australia, which continued with the 2d rate until 1905.

## THE ELECTRIC TELEGRAPH

The electric telegraph was first developed to provide an efficient communication and signalling system for the expanding railway network. By 1848, 1600 kilometres (1000 miles) of railway were equipped with telegraphic wires transmitting messages and Greenwich Mean Time to over 200 of the country's principal towns and cities. Lineside wires became a familiar feature of the landscape. In *Hard Times* (1854), Charles Dickens wrote of Mrs Sparsit observing the electric telegraph wires ruling 'a colossal strip of music-paper out of the evening sky'. Working together, the steam engine and the telegraph formed a formidable partnership and were referred to by *Punch* magazine as 'the two giants of the time'.

London dominated the new industry of telegraphic cable manufacture, with works such as Henley's at Silvertown, Bullivant's at Millwall, Hooper's at Millwall Dock and William Siemens' at Charlton. The latter grew to a vast size, employing thousands of men and women, making a range of electrical and related products.

Early messages were prone to faulty recording. The telegraphic likeness of 'one' and 'hog' could sometimes cause amusing results, such as the message 'Expect some hog to dinner.' Female telegraphists were trained in the manual transmission ('sending') and visual reception ('reading') of Morse signals using the single-needle instrument.

The development of the electric telegraph meant that information could be sent with great speed between one place and another. Baron Julius de Reuter was the first business man to exploit this new form of communication. In 1851, he established a twice-daily service of the latest Bourse and Stock Exchange prices for subscribers in Paris and London respectively. He made use of the telegraphic cable that had been successfully laid between Dover and Calais. In times of war and crisis, such a service was invaluable to governments. Also, it allowed financiers to trade in stocks in advance of others. The City of London, as the world's leading financial and commodity market, was prepared to pay highly for such information.

By the 1860s, London was telegraphically linked to all the world's major centres. Overland networks that could be unreliable as messages were copied from one telegraphic station to another were replaced with undersea cables, such as that laid in 1866 between Aden and Bombay. Henry Collins, a Reuters employee, wrote how 'the result of the English Derby reached Reuters's Office at Bombay within the short space of four minutes'.

Artist George Hicks (see below) captured the chaotic rush to catch the last Friday post at the General Post Office in St Martin's-le-Grand in the City – a regular event that attracted sightseers.

wider. Letter-writing soared in popularity as Londoners from all backgrounds took the opportunity to send news, gossip and sentiments to each other. With daily deliveries in the metropolis, the penny post changed the way people kept in touch with each other.

A good example of a letter-writing Londoner was Amelia Roper, the daughter of a Walthamstow undertaker who in 1857 married Tom Pyle, a butcher, and moved to Hackney. Amelia was a regular correspondent, writing regularly for much of her adult life to her close friend Martha Busher, a maid, who lived first in Sevenoaks and later in Woolwich.

With the introduction of the Penny Post in 1840 and the removal of the stamp tax on newspapers both encouraging the growth of a cheap daily press, the quantity of material sent by post grew enormously. On the right of Hicks's painting, a cluster of newspaper boys bundle papers into the post room. For its Victorian viewers, Hicks's painting represented the ever-increasing pace of the modern city, and a sense of London's growing communication links with places elsewhere.

The new system not only gave England a single postal rate, but also a relatively cheap one. Before its introduction, much had been made of the benefits to business. In fact the impact was much

In July 1857, one of her letters to Martha described the thrill of her first visit to the theatre:

… Mr and Miss Whitaker, Fanny and I all went to the Olympic Theatre last Monday fortnight and it was most lovely. I can't describe it to you I wished you could have been with us, they were all quite amused to see my 'greenness'. I couldn't keep from saying 'oh my!' now and then and it was most affecting in some parts. We went full dress. I had a low body on. We felt quite screamers I can assure you.

**AW**

# LATE VICTORIAN LONDON

By the late Victorian period, London was beginning to look like an imperial capital, with grand new government buildings to match the completed Houses of Parliament. In the 1860s, some thought the city 'shabby' compared to Paris. By the end of the century the British government operated from stately, modern offices, from which they ran the largest empire the world has ever known.

In the 1890s, London's population passed the four million mark, an increase felt in all parts of the metropolis. The fastest growing areas were the new working- and lower middle-class suburbs. Shops, markets, schools and churches spread among these suburbs. Only the poorest and the wealthiest lived in the centre.

The City become a daytime commercial and financial district. Retailing and entertainment districts grew in the West End; some department stores absorbed whole city blocks. Growing affluence led to a surge of theatre construction in the 1880s and the 1890s, particularly along Shaftesbury Avenue.

But new fears loomed. The public health reforms of the previous generation had not solved the city's social problems. Simmering unease about 'outcast London' brought new ideas for breaking the cycle of poverty and unemployment that afflicted low-paid workers as well as the very poor. Many came to believe that a more radical politics was needed to represent the working classes. The city's first socialist party, the Social Democratic Federation (SDF), was founded in the early 1880s and played a key role in mass demonstrations by the unemployed in the West End in 1886 and 1887.

London began to embrace the idea of municipal self-government, run for the people by the people. In 1888 the Metropolitan Board of Works was replaced by an elected body, the London County Council (LCC). Its first, progressive administration promised 'High rates and Healthy Cities'. In 1899, twenty-eight metropolitan borough councils were created in place of the old parishes and district boards in the hope that they would exert a restraining influence on the LCC. A modern secular society was emerging.

**From Pentonville Road**
**_looking west: evening, 1884_**
_John O'Connor's atmospheric view of the busy
metropolis, looking from Angel, Islington, towards
the imposing Midland Railway Hotel at St. Pancras._

# GOVERNMENT BUILDINGS & ROYAL JUBILEES

A growing government precinct in Whitehall expressed London's imperial role. Royal jubilees added popular patriotism and spectacle to the capital.

*Queen Victoria's Golden Jubilee, 1887*
*Crowds in Trafalgar Square celebrate the Queen's fifty-year reign. W. Hardy includes a turbanned figure, a nod to Victoria's imperial title of Empress of India.*

Late Victorian London was the capital of a worldwide empire. Over a quarter of the earth's surface and over a fifth of its population were governed from Westminster and Whitehall. In the course of the 19th century an ever-expanding empire and increasing state involvement in matters previously reserved for private and local interests, such as poor relief and sanitation, had created new government departments. The number of civil servants required to staff these had grown accordingly from about 19,552 in 1851 to over 49,000 in 1901.

By the early 1850s, the cramped, insanitary and expensive rented houses that government departments had hitherto occupied around the streets of Whitehall and Pall Mall had become unsatisfactory, and there were calls to move the departments into new purpose-built offices. Concentrated near the Houses of Parliament, these would enable civil servants to work more efficiently: communication within and between departments and with the Houses of Parliament would be improved, there would be no waste of room, and employees would be healthier.

Many wanted to restrict expenditure on the proposed new offices, arguing that they should be functional but not palatial. The prevailing view, however, was that London's government buildings should proclaim Britain's imperial power and wealth, and rival those of other European cities like Paris, Berlin and Vienna. As public money had to be found, land bought and – as was usual for grand public buildings – competitions held to choose architects, a progressive development of offices was proposed.

## WHITEHALL GRANDEUR

The first buildings completed were the Foreign Office and the India Office in 1868, both fronting St James's Park south of Downing Street. The 1857 competition to design the Foreign Office, which was eventually won by George Gilbert Scott, had sparked a fierce public debate about whether the Gothic or classical architectural style was most appropriate for national buildings.

The debate, known as the 'Battle of the Styles,' was won by the classical, and Scott's Italian classical design for the Foreign Office – with its grand romantic ornament – set a precedent for the new offices. Its magnificent State Stair and ornate reception and conference rooms decorated with marble, murals and ornately carved ceilings was fit to receive dignitaries from Europe and the Empire. The richness of the India Office, designed by Matthew Digby Wyatt with Scott after the British government took over the administration of India from the East India Company in 1857, was described as an 'Indian palace'. In 1878, grand new Colonial and Home Offices were completed along Whitehall to the east of the Foreign and India Offices, followed in the 1880s and 1890s by major extensions to the Admiralty on the north-west side of Whitehall.

The new government offices were designed to provide as much internal air and light as possible. Rooms were spacious and had windows, vital at a time when much government work involved reading and copying handwritten documents and when candles were expensive and gas gave off excessive heat and smells.

In 1899 grand new government offices along Great George Street, designed by J. M. Brydon, were begun, and in the same year a baroque-style War Office, designed by William Young, rose up on the east side of Whitehall with about 1000 rooms and two and half miles of corridors. With both buildings due for completion in the next decade, Whitehall's imperial silhouette had been cast.

## THE GOLDEN JUBILEE

As London's new government buildings proclaimed the capital's imperial might in stone, Queen Victoria's Jubilee celebrations in 1887 and 1897 broadcast it to the nation and the world. The year

*Whitehall c.1880*
*This early photograph shows the wide thoroughfare of Whitehall running between the Houses of Parliament and Trafalgar Square.*

pre-1864 government building

buildings and streets added 1864–1914

Victoria Embankment 1864–70

**Expansion and town planning around 19th-century Whitehall**

The creation of the grandest new government office buildings in Whitehall shaped the area as we know it today.

1887 saw the fiftieth anniversary of Victoria's reign. Against a background of economic depression, unemployment and instability in London, her Golden Jubilee was an opportunity to stimulate the patriotism of Londoners and visitors alike and to reinvigorate the popularity of the monarch.

The main focus of the Golden Jubilee celebrations was a magnificent procession through the streets of London on 21 June as Victoria proceeded from Buckingham Palace to a service of thanksgiving at Westminster Abbey. Crowds thronged the streets, windows, balconies and rooftops to watch the procession, which included members of royal families from throughout Europe, Indian princes, the queen of Hawaii and princes from Japan, Persia (Iran) and Siam (Thailand). The attendance of Victoria's children and grandchildren, now married into Europe's leading royal families, emphasized her role as the matriarch of Europe. The Queen, who had been persuaded with some difficulty to celebrate her Golden Jubilee, did not wear her robes of state, but chose instead a black satin dress and black satin bonnet with white feathers.

The following day Victoria attended a magnificent party in Hyde Park for an estimated 30,000 London schoolchildren. Toys, Jubilee mugs and medals were handed out and food and drink consumed. Entertainment was laid on and a hot air balloon with 'Victoria' emblazoned on it was released.

For the next four weeks celebrations continued in London with receptions, concerts and parties, a review of 28,000 military volunteers in Hyde Park, and beacon fires lit across the capital. Local groups and councils throughout the city erected statues and monuments commemorating the Jubilee. London retailers commissioned popular commemorative objects like ceramic mugs, cups and plates.

## THE DIAMOND JUBILEE

Victoria's Diamond Jubilee celebrations in 1897 were even more glittering. Three million people visited London for the celebrations, causing several commodities to run short and enabling servants to demand exorbitant raises. On 22 June the Queen rode in procession from Buckingham Palace to St Paul's Cathedral. Troops and dignitaries from Britain, Canada, the Caribbean, New Zealand, Africa and India paraded with her, followed by Indian princes and members of the royal family. As in 1887, every street, square, balcony and rooftop was full. Private rooms and balconies en route were rented out for enormous sums.

As the procession neared St Paul's, 'cheers broke into screams, and enthusiasm swelled to delirium'. About 15,000 people crowded around St Paul's to watch the thanksgiving service held on the cathedral steps. After the service, the procession passed Mansion House, London Bridge and along the south bank of the Thames through Southwark and the Borough so that poorer Londoners could see the Queen.

Again the streets of London, and in particular the West End, were magnificently decorated. St James's Street, for example, had Corinthian columns, potted palms, flower boxes and evergreen festoons. London again heaved with commemorative souvenirs, monuments, thanksgiving services, parties and concerts. The Princess of Wales, Princess Alexandra, organized Diamond Jubilee Feasts for 400,000 poor people across London.

Although they were criticized by some, Victoria's jubilees were high points in the capital's life during the 1880s and 1890s, symbolizing for many all that was magnificent and powerful in late Victorian London. **JH**

# THE GROWTH OF VICTORIAN SUBURBIA

London's ever-expanding railway network created a new ring of working-class and lower middle-class suburbs. The garden suburb ideal spread.

A home in the suburbs had long appealed to London's middle class as a retreat from the demands of inner-city living. A spacious, comfortable, newly-built villa in a semi-rural location provided a domestic ideal for those whose public lives were linked to the centre of the city, but who desired a more peaceful, private life away from its corruptions and overcrowding. The suburbs promised a healthier, more balanced and more ordered lifestyle and, most importantly for middle-class Londoners of the 19th century, the opportunity to enjoy greenery and gardens.

An early example of the self-conscious, progressive garden suburb was Bedford Park in Chiswick, laid out in the 1870s. Its promoter aimed to create an artistic as well as healthy community and its buildings included an art school alongside orchards and tennis courts. Early inhabitants included writers, barristers and architects.

While the impetus for suburban development derived from middle-class values and views on domesticity, life in the suburbs also appealed to working-class Londoners desperate to escape the overcrowded slums. The emergence of working-class suburbs was linked to the introduction of cheap trains run by railway companies such as the Great Eastern. Working-class suburbs like West Ham, which by 1901 had a population of 257,000 people, often provided local employment in chemical or other hazardous industries, in gas manufacture and in the docks.

**Infill in East Dulwich, 1880s**
These maps show Norland House and its grounds in East Dulwich before and after its sale in in 1877. The Worlingham Road houses were built from 1881–7.

## PIECEMEAL DEVELOPMENT

Most Victorian suburbs developed piecemeal, without planning. Planned estates such as Bedford Park were rare; most homes were constructed by small firms, often building fewer than six houses at a time. Fragmented development meant that gaps were left

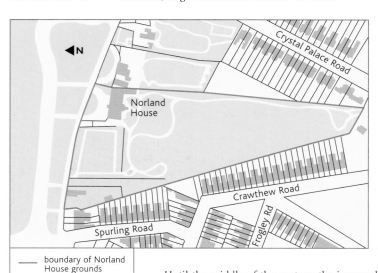

boundary of Norland House grounds

0 ——— 150 m
0 ——— 500 ft

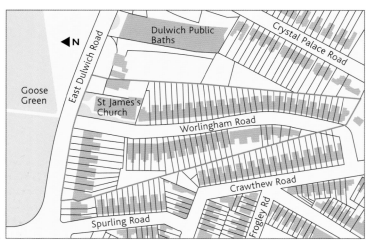

Until the middle of the century, the inner suburbs still retained an idyllic, insular character. In 1862, for example, George Rose Emerson described Hackney as 'one of the handsomest suburbs of London' with 'an old-fashioned air'. By the 1880s, however, an ever-increasing London population and the conversion of many buildings from residential to commercial use was placing tremendous pressure on the overcrowded central area, forcing future expansion outwards.

between housing developments, and streets, drainage and sewage systems were often uncoordinated. Most people rented rather than owned their homes and, gradually, poor Londoners spread into the suburbs, renting and overcrowding houses originally intended for single middle-class families. As a result, suburban slums soon emerged – such as Campbell Road in Finsbury Park, which by 1900 had become one of the most notorious and undesirable areas in London.

***Bedford Park, Turnham Green near Chiswick, 1882***
*A view of Tower House and Queen Anne's Grove, emphasizing the aesthetic qualities of the new garden suburb, with Japanese-style cherry blossom and tasteful architecture.*

As poverty encroached upon the suburban ideal, many middle-class families began to move further out. As the writer and social commentator Charles Booth noted of the northern part of Southwark in 1889, 'the rich have already left, the fairly comfortable are leaving and the poor and very poor remain and will remain until they are evicted'.

Suburban snobbery developed. As William Birt, general manager of the Great Eastern, noted, working-class passengers had a way of 'taking a train over', making life 'unpleasant' for others using their stations. He commented that they spat, used foul language, bothered young women, smoked 'noisome' pipes, cooked herrings in the waiting rooms and tried to evade payment. Edmonton, Stratford and Walthamstow, he claimed, had been 'spoilt for ordinary residential purposes'.

## THE SUBURBAN IDEAL

The suburban ideal helped create a new type of London district: the London County Council (LCC) cottage estate. The LCC's first housing projects had been inner-city blocks of flats. In 1903 it opened its first suburban cottage estate at Totterdown Fields, Tooting. Some cottages had indoor toilet and bathroom facilities and the estate was served by an electric tram system that reached central London in forty-five minutes for two pence return. Other estates followed, establishing a blueprint for public housing that gathered pace throughout the first half of the 20th century.

The new suburbs quickly developed a character of their own, independent of central London. Although many suburban workers commuted into the City and West End, others found local employment servicing the needs of their own communities, working in schools, hospitals and shops. For critics, a suburban lifestyle implied a retreat into an insular, private world that could encourage prejudice and repression. But the suburbs also had the potential for creating a new, more spacious and comfortable style of living for those who wished to distance themselves from the dirt and racket of the inner city.

By 1906, up to a quarter of a million people were commuting daily into central London, benefiting from an increasingly electrified public transport system that significantly reduced journey times. In 1861, only 400,000 Londoners lived in the outer suburban ring; by 1911, this figure had increased to 2.7 million. The significance of suburban growth was not lost on contemporary observers and, in 1903, the journal *Building News* announced that the speed, scale and impact of the expansion of the late Victorian suburbs constituted 'one of the social revolutions of the time'. **BC**

*A council estate, 1903*
*The London County Council promoted Totterdown to respectable workmen and their families. Features included nearby trams, cheap shops and schools.*

## BURROUGHS LODGE

Burroughs Lodge in Hendon combined all the ideals of middle-class suburbia, including a beautiful garden. In 1887, the Lodge was home to Mr and Mrs J. Crawford Bromehead. Mr Bromehead was a barrister, magistrate, local Conservative party president and vicar warden. Mrs Bromehead undertook charitable work and was treasurer of the Maternity Club. They had no children. Mr Bromehead lived in the property until his death in 1902. In the 1920s the Lodge was demolished and replaced by a row of modern detached and semi-detached properties.

*A tennis party at Burroughs Lodge, Hendon (1887), shown in a watercolour by Howard Gull Stormont.*

# CHARLES BOOTH'S LONDON: LIFE, LABOUR & POVERTY

Charles Booth's survey of London's life and labour was a landmark of social investigation. Booth set out to map scientifically the true extent of poverty in the capital.

**Over London by Rail,** *1872*
*Gustave Doré's dramatic engravings in* London: A Pilgrimage *created a new awareness of the density of the capital's housing.*

The 1881 census showed that Victorian London's population stood at nearly four million. That many hundreds of thousands lived in poverty was indisputable. But exactly how many, and how they worked and lived, was a matter of guesswork.

By the mid-1880s, a trade depression had led to mass unemployment in London. Dock workers struggled to feed and house their families, and a City committee had been set up to raise funds for the alleviation of poverty and starvation in the East End.

It was against this backdrop that Charles Booth (1840–1916), a partner in a Liverpool firm of merchants and shipowners, funded a private research project into the condition of the London poor. Booth was caught up in the ferment of ideas about metropolitan poverty. This was an area of intense debate and public emotions stirred up by writers and artists. In 1872 the publication of *London: A Pilgrimage* with prints by Gustave Doré (see above) gave the public yet more shocking images of the decay at the heart of the imperial capital. 'Here civilisation makes its miracles,' cried the accompanying text 'and civilized man is turned back into a savage.'

Booth's aim was to bring a scientific approach to the debate. 'The impulse came neither from politics nor from philanthropy but from scientific curiosity,' noted his collaborator Beatrice Webb, 'from the desire to apply the method of observation, reasoning and verification to the problem of poverty in the midst of riches.'

## BOOTH'S GREAT SURVEY

In 1886, Booth began by investigating poverty in London's East End. He chose the East End because 'it is supposed to contain the most destitute population in England and to be, as it were, the focus of the problem of poverty'. For this first survey Booth pioneered the method for which he became famous, combining a statistical framework with personal observations made by researchers and experts. This mixture of quantitive and qualitative data-gathering set a model for many subsequent social surveys. Booth's ambitious plan was to gather information about every family that had children. The records kept by London School Board visitors were used to classify each family into one of eight

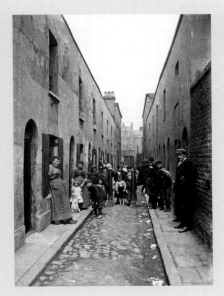

***Little Collingwood Street, c. 1900***
*According to Booth's survey, the people living in this Bethnal Green street included costers, fish curers, and child-thieves.*

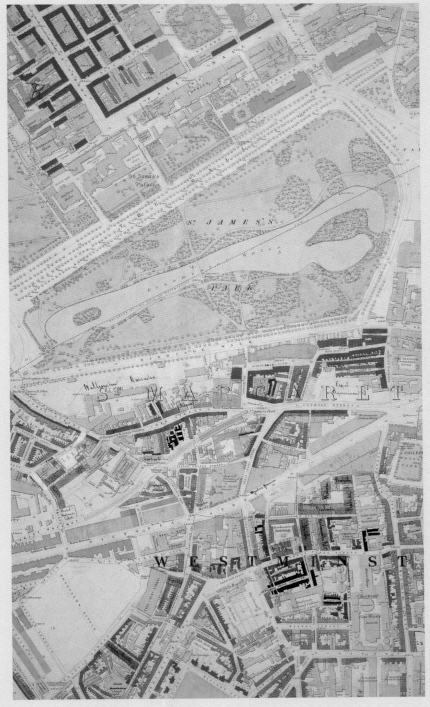

**Charles Booth's original Map of Poverty (detail), c. 1888–9**
*This section shows St James's and Westminster, an area with a characteristic mix of social classes, as reflected in the colouring on the map.*

social classes. Booth's team also consulted other experts such as local parish officers, charity workers, police constables, priests and their district visitors. After a few areas had been surveyed, he decided to speed matters up by gathering data on a street-by-street basis.

Booth published the first volume of his *Life and Labour of the People in London*, the definitive record of his survey, in 1889; it would ultimately run to seventeen volumes. The first volume was accompanied by a single-sheet map of the East End with streets coloured according to a six-colour code (black standing for the lowest class through to red for the middle class). This map, the *Descriptive Map of East End Poverty, Compiled from School Board Visitors' Reports in 1887*, was the first version of a series of maps that were to become famous.

As the survey grew to include wealthier areas of the city, a new colour, yellow, was needed to distinguish this category. For the resulting city-wide *Descriptive Map of London Poverty 1889*, published in 1891, the following seven-colour code was established:

| COLOUR | SOCIAL CONDITION |
| --- | --- |
| Black | 'Lowest class. Vicious, semi-criminal.' |
| Dark blue | 'Very poor, casual. Chronic want.' |
| Light blue | 'Poor. 18s to 21s a week for a moderate family.' |
| Purple | 'Mixed. Some comfortable, others poor.' |
| Pink | 'Fairly comfortable. Good ordinary earnings.' |
| Red | 'Well-to-do. Middle class.' |
| Yellow | 'Upper-middle and Upper classes. Wealthy.' |

Also in 1891, accompanying the second volume of the survey, Booth published a true 'poverty' map, the *Map Shewing Degrees of Poverty in London for 1889–1890*. In this map, London was divided into 134 areas, each tinted using seven shades from blue to purple; the lightest were those with the lowest levels of poverty and the darkest those with the highest. In 1902, he published a revised and larger version of the 1889 *Descriptive Map*, entitled *Map Descriptive of London Poverty 1898–9*, using the same colour coding. This was the culmination of an extended and revised street survey. Comparison of the two maps made it possible to trace social change in the areas mapped.

Booth's aim had been to provide a better understanding of 'not only where poverty exists in London and in what degree, but also something of its relation to industry and of the manner in which it is affected for good or evil by existing social action'. His survey showed that 30.7 per cent of London's population was living in poverty, for which the main causes were low wages and insecure employment, not moral weakness. He found that existing charitable effort was ineffective. Although 'Conservative in politics and strongly anti-socialist in temper and economic views', Charles Booth concluded that some degree of state intervention was essential: the state should provide for 'the helpless' and 'those who are not competent to provide for themselves'. **AW**

# TRAINS, TRAMS & THE UNDERGROUND

London's railway system extended further, over and under ground. In inner districts, horse-drawn trams brought a new form of cheap transport for workers.

By the middle of the 19th century, the centre of London was encircled by more railway stations than any other city in the world. Nonetheless, in 1851 only the Greenwich line, and its terminus at London Bridge, carried significant numbers of daily commuters. Then, in the 1860s, railway bridges were built across the Thames, serving new terminus stations at Cannon Street and Blackfriars in the City, and Charing Cross and Victoria in Westminster – stations sited specifically for their convenience for city workers. These new termini – and the explosive growth of the outer suburbs caused in part by the railways themselves – created a new class of London commuter and a second boom in railway construction.

The impact of this new railway building was felt especially by the London poor. When the Midland Railway cut a swathe through the area around St Pancras in the mid-1860s, an estimated 4000 houses disappeared and 32,000 people were displaced. Inner-city areas became more congested as the poor were forced to find new housing nearby, close to their places of work, in what soon became slums. It was not until 1885 that new legislation forced railway companies to rehouse those made homeless by railway construction. Overall, between 1850 and 1900, as many as 100,000 Londoners lost their homes to rail construction.

## THE UNDERGROUND

By the 1850s, road congestion in central London had become a major problem. The solution adopted was the creation of the world's first underground railway. The term 'underground' perhaps overstates the nature of this new railway. A large part of its route ran along open cuttings just under the streets. The construction method, known as 'cut-and-cover', involved opening up a roadway, moving all the gas, water and sewer pipes along its path and levelling the ground so that a track could be laid. This was then covered over with a continuous brick archway and the roadway remade on top to allow street traffic to resume. The only really deep tunnel was at the Clerkenwell end of the new line, at Mount Pleasant.

The Metropolitan line opened on Friday 9 January 1863, with the first paying passengers travelling the following morning between Paddington and Farringdon Street. Initial fears that the build-up of smoke would cause asphyxiation and the risk of fire in

**Map of London, 1882**

*This map shows the railway network (in blue), along with proposed extensions, other rail lines and routes (in red) of connecting trams and omnibuses.*

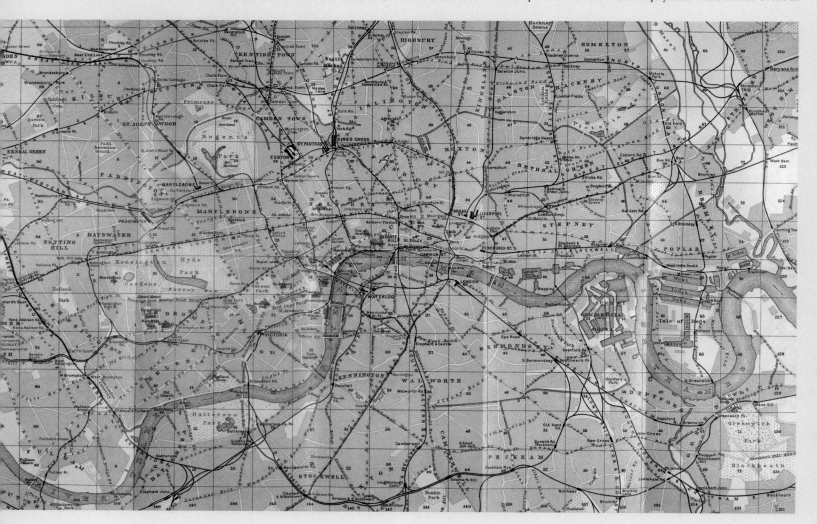

**Charing Cross Station interior, 1864**

*Charing Cross Station, seen here in its opening year. The original wrought iron roof collapsed in 1905.*

the tunnels proved unfounded. *The Times* reported that the line could be 'regarded as the great engineering triumph of the day'. Its success can be measured by the fact that nearly ten million passengers were transported underground in the first year of operation. Another railway company, the Metropolitan District, obtained an Act of Parliament in 1864 to extend the line to Notting Hill Gate, Gloucester Road and then eastwards to the City, looping back to rejoin the Metropolitan Line in an 'Inner Circle'. Some 2000 men, 200 horses and 58 steam engines tunnelled under terraces, streets and squares. By 1870, the extension had reached Blackfriars, but it took another fourteen years for the circuit to be completed.

Other lines were built to connect with the Metropolitan and District railway lines. Routes to Hammersmith, Richmond, Ealing Broadway and Wimbledon fed into the District Line. The Metropolitan and St John's Wood Railway joined Baker Street to St John's Wood Road and then on to Hampstead. The line extended to Swiss Cottage in the late 1860s and by the 1880s had reached West Hampstead, Willesden Green and Harrow.

## TRAMS

Horse-drawn trams were essentially omnibuses with iron wheels that ran along a grooved iron track. Although they were widely used in the USA, trams did not gain favour in London until the Tramway Act of 1870. An American, George Francis Train, had tried to demonstrate the benefits of tramways to Londoners by setting up three trial lines in 1861, the first of which ran along the south side of Bayswater Road. There was vociferous public opposition and they were quickly removed. Like the railways, the trams were not permitted to extend into the central parts of city. It was feared that they would make congestion worse and be a danger to pedestrians and to other horse-drawn transport, as well as reducing property values in the areas through which they passed.

The first successful tramways were developed along the main roads to the suburbs in south London and east of the City. One line ran from the south side of Westminster Bridge to Kennington, another from Blackheath through New Cross and on either to Elephant and Castle or Camberwell and Kennington. The East End was served by a tramway linking Whitechapel with Stratford.

Trams could easily be pulled by just two horses and could carry around fifty passengers at a time. This made them the cheapest form of transport in the capital. By 1875, there were 348 trams, and about 100 km (60 miles) of track, carrying around 49 million passengers annually. Trams ran frequently, roughly every three to four minutes. On board they were more comfortable and much less bumpy than the omnibuses. The services started in the early morning, making them a popular form of transport for the working classes for journeys between home and factory, shop or office. It was the trams, rather than the overground or underground railway, that allowed Londoners to travel cheaply and rapidly around town. By 1895, when the London County Council took over the tramways in its central area of jurisdiction, about 280 million passenger journeys were being taken each year along the 160 or so kilometres (100 miles) of city tramway lines. **AW**

**'Dipping' under Blackfriars Bridge, c. 1869**

*Henry Flather was commissioned to photograph the construction of the Metropolitan District Railway's underground lines. This photograph shows work under way at Queen Victoria Street and New Bridge Street.*

# SWEATED TRADES & LABOUR MILITANCY

London's vast workforce of casual labourers, unskilled hands and home workers came into the public eye in the late 1880s. New and well-organized unions gave workers a voice.

**'The Sweater's Furnace', 1888**
*A Punch cartoon depicts the cheap clothing trade as sacrificing human lives in the interests of profit.*

**Trade Union banner**
*Commemorating the foundation of the Stevedores' Union following the Great Dock Strike of 1889, this banner shows a stevedore and Australian 'wharfie' shaking hands, in honour of Australia's financial support of the strikers.*

The essence of the sweating system was twofold: first, the division of the production process into stages, with each task done by a separate individual; and second, subcontracting the supply process. This meant, for example, that instead of a suit being made by a single skilled craftsman, it would now be made by a team of unskilled workers, each carrying out a simple task like sewing button holes or pressing cloth. The customer would no longer buy the suit direct from the tailor, but from a shop that had bought it from a 'sweater', the middleman who employed or commissioned the unskilled workers.

By subdividing the making of an item into single repetitive tasks that were easy to learn, sweating opened the doors to an inexhaustible supply of workers, including women and children, men laid off from dwindling London trades, and immigrants. The introduction of the sewing machine and bandsaw in the 1850s further eased the way for unskilled workers.

Intense competition among sweaters meant that in the busy season workers were forced to work long hours for poverty-level wages. In 1888 Solomon Rosenberg, a boot finisher in the East End, was working seventeen to eighteen hours a day for fifteen shillings a week, far below Charles Booth's definition of 'chronic want'. In the slack season workers had little or no work.

The sweated trades required little space or equipment and East End tailoring and bootmaking workshops were crammed into every back room, garret and cellar, far away from the gaze of factory inspectors. Meals were eaten at workbenches, there was often no natural daylight and up to twelve people worked in a cramped space, often in high temperatures.

It required few skills to obtain sweated work and few resources to set up a workshop. Thousands of Jewish immigrants were sucked into the East End's sweated trades. Their willingness to accept long hours, low pay and poor conditions fuelled complaints that aliens were taking jobs from British-born workers.

Thousands of 'sweated' workers toiled in grinding poverty to produce the cheap goods demanded by London's growing middle and lower-middle classes. Sweating, a system characterized by long hours, low pay and poor working conditions, was central to many small industries. Common in matchbox-, brush- and artificial flower-making, it was most apparent in the clothing, footwear and furniture industries which, by the 1880s, were largely confined to Stepney, Whitechapel, Spitalfields and Bethnal Green in the East End.

Sweated trades were not new, but public opinion became increasingly alarmed by tales of their evil. In 1888 a House of Lords enquiry heard powerful evidence of the human cost of slop-clothing. Homeworking and sweaters' 'dens' slipped past new laws regulating conditions in factories. The problem was mainly associated with London, where thousands of unskilled men and women made a makeshift living at the mercy of sharks and middlemen.

## THE NEW UNIONISM

While the evils of sweating got worse and economic depression fuelled riots in the West End by the unemployed, the late 1880s saw a seismic change in the position of London's unskilled workers. Motivated by a new determination, led by largely self-educated leaders from within their own ranks, and helped by

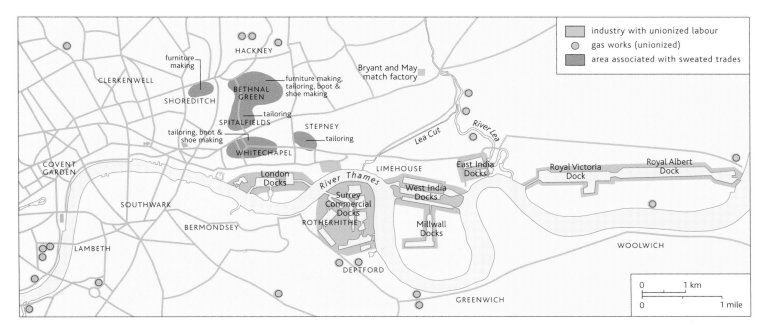

On the map:

industry with unionized labour
○ gas works (unionized)
area associated with sweated trades

furniture making
HACKNEY
CLERKENWELL
SHOREDITCH
BETHNAL GREEN
furniture making, tailoring, boot & shoe making
tailoring
SPITALFIELDS
STEPNEY
tailoring, boot & shoe making
WHITECHAPEL
tailoring
Bryant and May match factory
River Lea
Lea Cut
COVENT GARDEN
LIMEHOUSE
East India Docks
Royal Victoria Dock
Royal Albert Dock
London Docks
River Thames
West India Docks
SOUTHWARK
Surrey Commercial Docks
ROTHERHITHE
Millwall Docks
BERMONDSEY
LAMBETH
WOOLWICH
DEPTFORD
GREENWICH
0   1 km
0   1 mile

**Unions and sweated labour**
London's sweated industries were concentrated in the East End, The unionized docks and gas works provided a powerful alternative vision of the future of labour relations.

middle-class socialists, they organized to fight for labour rights. London trade unionism changed from being the preserve of skilled craftsmen into a 'new unionism', a militant, aggressive movement uniting ever-increasing numbers of unskilled workers.

The vanguard of the new unionism was the strike by the match girls at Bryant & May's match factory in Bow during the summer of 1888. After three weeks on strike, supported by much of the press and the public, the match girls won their demands. Less than a year later, in March 1889, Will Thorne, a stoker at the Gas Light and Coke Company's works at Beckton in East Ham, assisted by Ben Tillett of the Tea Operatives' and General Labourers' Association, formed the National Union of Gasworkers and General Labourers. They immediately campaigned for and won a reduction of the gas workers' day to eight hours.

Later the same year one of the most momentous events in 19th-century labour history took place when London's dockers went on strike. For years casual dock labourers had endured the degrading practice of the 'call-on', in which men fought at the dock gates often for a couple of hours' work, for which they would earn as little as 5d an hour. On 14 August a minor dispute at the South West India Dock escalated into an all-out strike across the Port of London. Led by Ben Tillett, Tom Mann, Tom McCarthy (secretary of the Stevedores' Union) and John Burns, trade unionists steeped in the socialist principles of the Social Democratic Federation, they organized themselves with skill and no little foresight.

A strike committee was set up and a strike fund collected. With a deliberate eye to public and press goodwill, as well as their own morale, the dockers marched daily 'with the regularity of a cathedral service' through the City of London to the dock companies' headquarters in Leadenhall Street. Impressing all who saw them with their dignity, the dockers received financial support from all over Britain, the United States and Europe. A large donation from Australia enabled them to continue their strike into September.

Finally, on 5 September, the dock companies gave in to the dockers' demands. Their most famous demand, pay of 6d per hour, immortalized in John Burns's phrase as 'the full round orb of the docker's tanner', was realized. By the end of the year, membership

of the Dockers' Union (formerly the Tea Operatives' Union) had risen from a few hundred to 18,000 and over the next few years many new unions emerged.

Although the fortunes of London's trade unions fluctuated over the next decade, the tide of labour change had turned irreversibly in favour of the capital's unskilled workers. By the mid-1890s, union membership in London had doubled from its level in 1888. The events of the late 1880s had sown among London workers a new confidence, determination and self-awareness, and a new understanding of their power to bring about change. The foundations of 20th-century labour reform had been laid.    **JH**

### ANNIE BESANT & THE MATCHGIRLS' STRIKE

In June 1888 the social reformer Annie Besant (1847–1933) published an article in the socialist journal *The Link* entitled 'White Slavery in London'. The article exposed the terrible conditions and low pay endured by the workers at Bryant & May's match factory at Fairfield Works in Bow. Working fourteen hours a day for less than five shillings a week, they were fined for offences like talking or dropping matches. Many of the women had been poisoned by the phosphorous used to make the matches and suffered from yellowing of the skin, hair loss and 'phossy jaw', a form of bone cancer. Bryant & May's response to the article was to sack the three women who had spoken to Besant.

The whole workforce went on strike, demanding the reinstatement of their colleagues and better pay and conditions. Together, the match girls and Annie Besant organized the strike with determination. They set up headquarters in Bow Road, created a strike fund, appeared before Parliament and held marches and rallies in Regent's Park, Victoria Park and Mile End Waste as well as in the West End. An appeal was launched in *The Link* and supporters wrote articles in newspapers in support.

After three weeks, Bryant & May agreed to all demands. The match girls formed the Union of Women Match Workers (later the Matchmakers' Union), with Annie Besant as the first secretary.

# PUBLIC HOUSES & MUSIC HALLS

A lively entertainment network of pubs and music halls grew up in Victorian London's working-class areas. Witty, verbal and boisterous, cockney culture thrived.

*'The Modern Plague' 1880s (detail)*
*A piece of temperance propaganda, showing all the public houses on a map of London, as listed in trade directories.*

Victorian London was a city of entertainment and pleasure. For those too poor to venture into the West End, the local pub, music hall and street entertainers offered a welcome diversion from the wretched realities of poverty and slum accommodation. There was often little distinction between organized indoor entertainment and spontaneous outdoor revelry. After spilling out of the pubs and music halls, Londoners could prolong an evening's entertainment by visiting late-night markets, where street entertainers and organ grinders offered their interpretation of music hall songs.

## THE LONDON PUB

Throughout the 19th century the pub and the temperance movement competed for the loyalty of London's working classes. Pubs were prolific in working-class areas and were held responsible for the poverty, misery and wickedness blighting the lives of the poor. Soho in the 1890s contained 357 pubs and beer houses and 192 off-licence premises while, in East London, one mile of the Whitechapel Road from Commercial Street to Stepney Green contained 48 drinking places. Pubs could remain open all day from 6 a.m. until 12.30 a.m. providing the working man with refreshment on his journey both to and from work.

By 1900, however, public houses played a broader role in the community than simply as drinking establishments for working men. A public house building boom in the late 19th century had introduced imposing, comfortable and highly decorative public

---

## ALBERT CHEVALIER: MUSIC HALL SUPERSTAR

Albert Chevalier (1861–1923) was a straight theatre actor who turned to variety after fourteen years in the profession. His first music hall performance was at the London Pavilion, Whitechapel, in 1891. He became the first and most famous of London's so-called 'coster comedians', who adopted the humour and cockney rhyming slang of London's barrow traders to sing of poverty and the realities of working-class life. His long career brought him great success both in London and abroad.

With his brother Charles Ingle (Auguste Chevalier), Albert wrote many favourite music hall songs including 'Knocked 'em in the Old Kent Road' and 'My Old Dutch', composed one foggy summer night as he made his way to Collins's Music Hall. This poignant song expressed a costermonger's love for his ageing wife as they were separated at the workhouse door; 'Dutch' is rhyming slang for 'wife', a shortening of 'Duchess of Fife'.

*Albert Chevalier at the height of his career.*

houses with dining areas, billiard tables and meeting rooms that could be hired out for political and educational purposes. Pubs were becoming more respectable and beginning to attract a wider clientele. As Charles Booth noted in the 1880s, 'young people do their courting in public-houses, since both sides are rather ashamed of their homes, and like to make themselves out a class above what they are'.

## THE RISE OF THE MUSIC HALL

From the pubs and penny gaffs evolved the music hall. By the 1860s, there were over 200 small music halls in London and over 30 larger establishments holding up to 2000 people. Many, such as 'The Old Mo' (Middlesex Music Hall) in Drury Lane, were originally small singing rooms attached to a pub. Music halls and prostitution proved, from the outset, to be complementary forms of entertainment. At Wilton's Music Hall in the East End, the gallery could only be entered through a brothel, while the large promenade at the Empire, Leicester Square, was notoriously filled with loitering prostitutes.

Despite opposition from moral campaigners, music halls continued to flourish, and the mass appeal of variety entertainment soon created superstars of performers such as Marie Lloyd, Dan Leno and Albert Chevalier. The East End accommodated more music halls than any other part of London, with up to 150 venues offering affordable entertainment to a predominantly local working-class audience. Purpose-built halls such as the Hackney Empire, which opened in 1901, resembled comfortable, modern theatres with rows of tip-up fixed seats, large stages and orchestra pits. These buildings also hosted cinema shows, the fledgling silent movie industry not yet regarded by music hall proprietors as a threat to live performance.

From the end of the 19th century, London's entertainment industry was increasingly influenced by US popular culture. The opening of the large Earl's Court and Olympia arenas encouraged spectacular productions to cross the Atlantic. In 1887, Buffalo Bill Cody's Wild West Show caused a sensation at Earl's Court. Every night for five months, up to 15,000 Londoners witnessed re-enactments of the attack on the Deadwood Stage Coach, the activities of the Pony Express and of a buffalo hunt, together with a display of shooting by Annie Oakley. The impact of the show went far beyond Earl's Court, however. After their arrival at Gravesend dock, the entire company of cowboys, Native Americans, stagecoaches, horses and cattle travelled to London in a spectacular cavalcade witnessed by huge crowds; several weeks later, the showmen again rode through central London ahead of Queen Victoria's official Golden Jubilee procession.

In 1898, the Olympia arena played host to the equally spectacular Barnum and Bailey 'Greatest Show on Earth', enthralling Londoners with its three-ring circus and popular sideshows including a Museum of Living Curiosities. The climax of the show, 'Nero or The Destruction of Rome', was a sensational historical production with 1000 performers, chariot races and gladiatorial combats. With the cheapest seats priced at only one shilling, such shows attracted a wide and varied audience.

Victorian London embraced US culture, but popular entertainment was also influenced by those who had settled in the capital both from abroad and from other parts of Britain. From Irish comedians to Italian street musicians, from Scottish music hall singers to Yiddish theatre productions and Northern clog dancers, the diversity of London's population was reflected in the range of entertainment on offer to all its citizens. By the end of century, London was truly a world city for entertainment. **BC**

**Behind the Bar, 1882**

*A typical late Victorian public house, possibly in Old Street or on the Caledonian Road. The artist, John Henry Henshall, makes a moral comment by including children in the scene.*

# OSCAR WILDE'S LONDON

The trial of writer and wit Oscar Wilde in 1895 confirmed that male homosexual activity, though publicly denied, played a part in even the most exclusive of London social institutions.

Leisure in Victorian London offered a valuable escape from the claustrophobia of domesticity. The anonymity of the urban world offered a playground in which conventional social distinctions were blurred, and in which large numbers of men found an alternative life. London was full of mashers, fake swells, bohemians and flâneurs, all looking for a good time. And there were plenty of excuses for a good night out: from the West End theatre to the gentlemen's club, to the more risqué music hall entertainments, as well as bars, brothels and coffee houses for those who were slumming it. Alternatively, a gentleman could take a night-time stroll in a pleasure garden such as the Cremorne in Chelsea. The city's streets were teeming with nightlife, with an estimated 55,000 prostitutes working the streets and brothels.

Around the West End, new and fashionable hotels, cafes and restaurants were appearing, including the Savoy and the Ritz, and continental restaurants such as the Tivoli in the Strand and the Criterion in Shaftesbury Avenue. These places offered new experiences and excitement, though their cosmopolitan clientele gave them a dubious reputation.

**Portrait of Oscar Wilde, 1884**
*A caricature of the flamboyant socialite, created by Carlo Pelligrini and published in Vanity Fair's 'Men of the Day' series.*

**The Athenaeum**
*The entrance hall of the most intellectually elite of London's gentlemen's clubs, in Pall Mall.*

## AN UNDERGROUND SUBCULTURE

London also offered opportunities for same-sex activities that smaller towns and cities did not. Male homosexuality was illegal and regarded with abhorrence in respectable society, but an underground subculture for 'inverts' and 'Mary Annes' existed, with its own nuances, codes, pick-up places and haunts. The city provided many opportunities for upper-class men to cruise public spaces with men from other social classes. Piccadilly Circus and Oxford Street were notorious for cruising and renting, perhaps linked to the introduction of male urinals in the West End in 1860. Both St James's and Hyde Park had to be closed at night 'to prevent scandalous behaviour'. New hotels like the Victoria in Northumberland Avenue and Anderton's in Fleet Street became synonymous with gay liaisons.

The death sentence for sodomy was abolished in 1861, but penalties introduced in 1885 made 'gross indecency' – any sexual contact between men – punishable by two years in prison, sometimes with hard labour. Nonetheless, 19th-century London witnessed a succession of homosexual scandals.

In 1871, two men were arrested for dressing as women and mixing with prostitutes in Burlington Arcade, the Alhambra

in Leicester Square and Surrey Theatre. Ernest Boulton and Frederick Park, known as 'Fanny' and 'Stella', were arrested for soliciting gay sex, but were acquitted because the jury decided that their cross-dressing was a harmless sign of high spirits.

From the 1880s to 1890s, a number of cases featured middle-class men and working-class boys, soldiers or working men. In July 1889, police raided a male brothel at 19 Cleveland Street, and a number of youths were convicted of indecency. The press found evidence of prominent aristocratic involvement and a cover-up, and a scandal soon broke out. The case fuelled public concern that same-sex sexual activities were an 'aristocratic vice' corrupting working-class youths; the story dominated the press for months.

## CLUB SOCIETY

The gentlemen's clubs and bachelor chambers in Pall Mall and St James's flourished from the 1830s. With all the perks of a comfortable hotel, clubs came with or without private rooms, restaurants and meeting rooms. They catered to service, political, sporting, social, bohemian, artistic and theatrical interests, but most were social in function, with strict rules on membership and etiquette. They became refuges for husbands and bachelors escaping domestic ennui while maintaining the trappings of respectability. Clubs were places where gentlemen members could relax and network, and attracted the conventional as well as the eccentric.

The Café Royal, established in 1865 and providing a club-like atmosphere, was a celebrated late-night venue. It became a favourite of London's emerging bohemian culture, attracting musicians and intellectuals, artists and writers such as J. M. Whistler, Aubrey Beardsley and Oscar Wilde, earning it a reputation as the 'rendezvous of the famous'.

## THE WILDE TRIALS

Irish-born Wilde had been a star at Magdalen College Oxford, where he discovered the 'dangerous and delightful distinction of being different from others'. He came to London in 1879, married in 1884 and had two children; he also gained fame as a writer and brilliant wit. A flamboyant character and dresser, he could often be seen holding court at the Café Royal.

between 1891 and 1895, including the *The Importance of Being Earnest* with its coded references to homosexuality.

The Marquis of Queensberry, Bosie's father, strongly disapproved of their relationship, and on 18 February 1895 he visited the Albemarle, Wilde's London club. He left there an open visiting card accusing Wilde of 'posing as a somdomite' [sic]. Ignoring advice from friends, Wilde sued for criminal libel. His civil suit was defeated, and in April he was himself arrested on a charge of gross indecency, based in part on the evidence presented in court.

Wilde mounted a spirited and moving defence, but after a sensational trial he was sentenced to

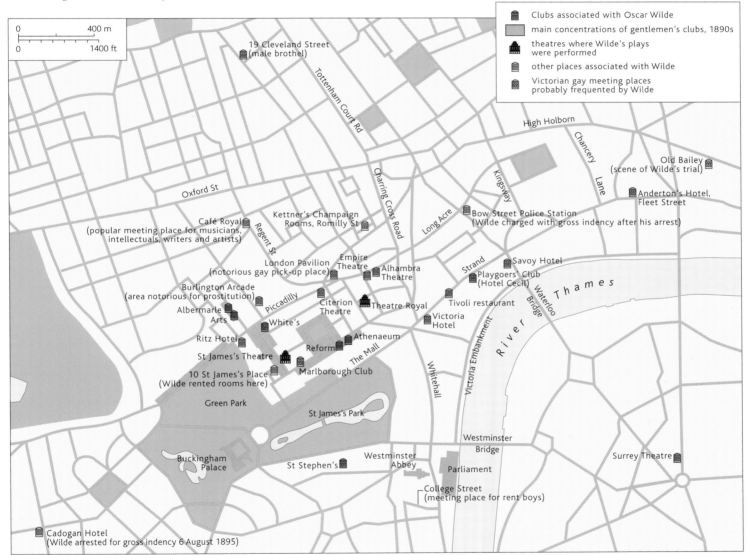

Despite his marriage, Wilde pursued a series of affairs with young men, many of whom he met through Alfred Taylor, a transvestite whose Westminster house he frequented. Wilde also kept chambers in St James's and often stayed at the Savoy.

In 1891 Wilde began an intense association with Lord Alfred 'Bosie' Douglas, which continued for nearly four years. The two embraced a promiscuous underground world in London, enjoying the high life as well as the company of working men and rent boys. Wilde's career was flourishing and his greatest plays were produced

two years hard labour, his career, reputation and family life irretrievably in ruins. He never saw his children again. He served six months at Wandsworth and the rest at Reading Gaol, and died a broken man in Paris in 1900.

By the end of the 19th century, homosexuality, 'the love that dare not speak its name', in Wilde's words, had been brought to public attention by his high-profile trials. Victorian society was forced to acknowledge homosexuality, and the first small steps had been taken in a movement for homosexual emancipation.   **SG**

**Oscar Wilde's West End**

Wilde's haunts included gentlemen's clubs and theatres as well as areas frequented by London's gay community.

# THE VICTORIAN ART WORLD

London strengthened its grip on the art world as the social status of artists rose. Some built grand studio-mansions in Kensington and St John's Wood.

**The Bayswater Omnibus, 1895**

*George William Joy's engaging view of modern life unites all types of people inside the horse-drawn omnibus, from City gent to poor milliner. Joy used his wife and daughter as models. He studied under Millais, Leighton and Watts at the Royal College of Art and the Royal Academy Schools.*

class. Perhaps more importantly, it also led to the enormous number of sales of prints from paintings, which were eagerly bought by those who could not afford originals. Paintings and their copyright were treated as two separate commodities, often sold separately. Artists reaped the financial benefits, indulging in ostentatious manifestations such as grand houses and a celebrity lifestyle that was eagerly reported by the journals of the day.

London was the centre of the Victorian art world, not only for annual exhibitions at the major institutions like the Royal Academy and the Grosvenor Gallery, but also for the communities of artists that developed throughout the city. Budding artists could begin at London's private art schools, in the hope of a successful transition to the Royal Academy schools. The Royal Academy of Arts, which moved to Burlington House in 1869, was at the apex of the artistic hierarchy. To become one of the privileged forty members was a guarantee of sales; it also ensured that an artist's paintings would be shown to their best advantage at the most prestigious and popular art event of the year, the Summer Exhibition. The Academicians' works were hung at eye level, or 'on the line', rather than high on the wall ('skied') or touching the skirting ('floored'), at a time when paintings were hung close together.

The desire to be in touch with art was no longer to the few, to the rare experts whose isolation in the Philistine world had been a pathetic feature of the previous period; on the contrary, every one began in greater or lesser degree to show that the new ideas and the more active aspirations had power to persuade them. Before long the reality of the change was beyond the possibility of doubt.

*The Studio, 1897, 'A Victorian Gallery'*

The popularity of art and artists became a defining characteristic of late Victorian Britain. Increased social mobility helped to foster the belief that art had an uplifting role for every member of society. In London, this belief led to the creation of galleries such as the South London Gallery, set up in the heart of one of the city's largest poor areas out of a philanthropic belief in the universal and improving value of art. Record numbers of visitors to the Royal Academy summer exhibition were recorded in the 1880s and 1890s, when the average attendance, from May to August, was 355,000.

For artists, the late Victorian era in London was a golden period. Through their work, they were able to reach the highest echelons of society. The popularity of their work led to record high prices for contemporary art, paid by the new industrial middle

## STUDIOS & SHOW HOMES

There were four main communities of artists in late 19th-century London: in Kensington, in St John's Wood, in Chelsea and in Hampstead. Artists of the period enjoying the financial rewards of their success had begun to create large 'palaces' that blurred the distinction between home and studio. These houses both displayed to the world the outward signs of their success and and helped create a fantastic and eclectic style that reflected their art itself. They were, in effect, show homes that advertised art, gave confidence to potential patrons and lived up to their owners' celebrity status. On 'Show Sundays', for example, artists opened their doors wider than to the regular visits of patrons, allowing the general public to tramp through their houses; the house of Luke Fildes (1844–1927) in Kensington, for example, received over 1000 visitors in a day.

## ARTISTS' COLONIES

Val Prinsep (1838–1904) and Frederic Leighton (1830–96) established purpose-built studios and homes in Holland Park. This area of Kensington became the heart of an artists' colony; Marcus Stone (1840–1921), Holman Hunt (1827–1910), Luke Fildes and William Burges (1827–81) all established themselves on the

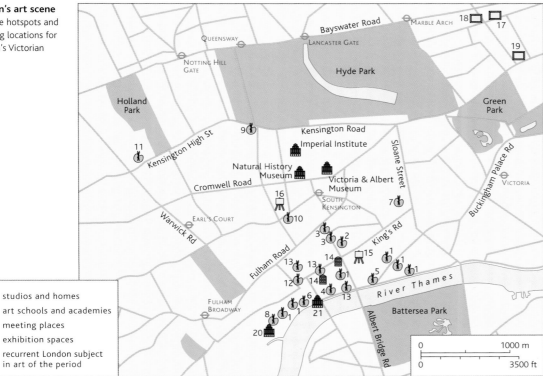

**London's art scene**
Creative hotspots and inspiring locations for London's Victorian artists.

- 🖌 studios and homes
- 🎨 art schools and academies
- 🏛 meeting places
- ▭ exhibition spaces
- 🏛 recurrent London subject in art of the period

Melbury Road, and Sir John Millais (1829–96) at Palace Gate. These artists, in most cases, were serious Royal Academy members, the leaders of the art establishment.

Fitzjohn's Avenue in Hampstead developed as an area of leading genre and historical painters. The maritime artist Clarkson Stanfield (1793–1867) lived here, alongside Paul Poole Falconer (1807–79), Henry Holiday (1839–1927), Carl Haag (1820–1915), Sir James Linton (1840–1916), Edwin Long (1829–91), Frank Holl (1845–88), John Pettie (1839–93), Kate Greenaway (1846–1901) and John Seymour Lucas (1849–1923).

Nearby St John's Wood, though similar to the artists' community in Hampstead, distinguished itself by being more overtly 'decadent' and showy than its neighbour. Its artist-residents included Sir Edwin Landseer (1802–73), George Dunlop Leslie (1835–1921), William Frederick Yeames (1835–1918), Philip Calderon (1833–98), Thomas Faed (1826–1900), Tissot (1836–1902), Lawrence Alma-Tadema (1836–1912), Briton Riviere (1840–1920), and Robert Little (c. 1855–1944). It also boasted the 'St John's Wood Clique', instigated in 1862 by David Wilkie Wynfield (1837–87), a society of narrative painters who were fascinated with re-enacting the historical in both their painting and their personal dress.

The exception to these communities was Chelsea, which was altogether more exotic. If Kensington, Hampstead and St John's Wood represented the intellectual side of the art world, Chelsea attracted a more bohemian set of artists. Number 16 Cheyne Walk was the home of Dante Gabriel Rossetti (1828–82), one of the founder members of the Pre-Raphaelite Brotherhood, whose house reflected a new aestheticism. Chelsea was also the home of the American painter James Abbott McNeil Whistler (1834–1903), after he had become a permanent resident in London.

The golden age of relative affluence and celebrity status for artists in the late Victorian period did not last. Widespread middle-class patronage dwindled and the hierarchical Royal Academy became less influential. In the Edwardian period, the taste for Victorian art waned to an all-time low. The proliferation of art schools and artists removed the urge toward artistic colonies and, with the development of modernism, London saw a new kind of artist emerge. Yet the late Victorian reverence for art and the belief that it could reach all levels of society remain influential to this day. **MB**

*Frederic Leighton, 1872*
*Watercolour by Jacques Joseph Tissot portraying the charismatic artist at one of his many social engagements.*

# THE JEWISH EAST END

Late-Victorian London experienced a huge influx of refugees. Over 150,000 Polish and Russian Jews arrived, mostly poor and many fleeing persecution by the Tsarist authorities.

**The Jewish East End, 1900**
Population density for the Jewish community centred on the area between Spitalfields and Whitechapel.

Between 1880 and 1914, London's small Jewish community was transformed by the arrival in Britain of 150,000 East European and Russian Jewish refugees fleeing economic hardship, the Russian pogroms and persecution. Up to 70 per cent of the new immigrants settled in the East End of London, swelling a well-established Jewish neighbourhood centred on the area between Spitalfields and Whitechapel. This area of London had long been associated with immigration, mainly because of its proximity to the London docks and Liverpool Street railway station, the point of disembarkation for those entering the capital via the port of Harwich. Often arriving with little more than the name of a relative or friend with whom they could find temporary shelter,

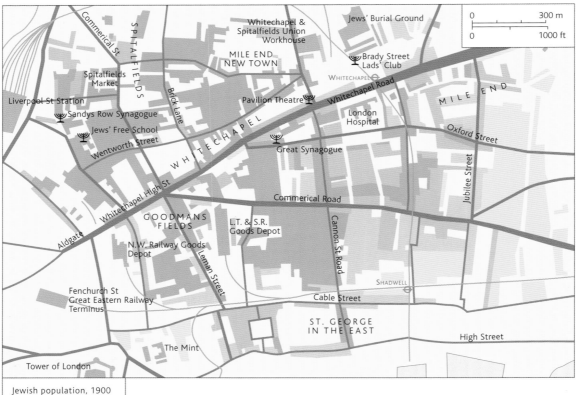

Jewish population, 1900

- 75–100%
- 50–74%
- 25–49%
- 5–24%

☪ Jewish cultural site

the new immigrants were encouraged to settle more permanently in the area by the availability of cheap housing and plentiful opportunities for work.

Many found employment in the clothing industry which, by the 1880s, was dominated by the 'sweating' system of small workshops and the subdivision of labour into unskilled or semi-skilled tasks. In 1888, Booth's survey of London counted 571 workshops making men's coats in less than one square mile in and around Whitechapel. Most employed fewer than ten workers, confined for long hours in cramped, damp and steamy workrooms, an ideal breeding ground for tuberculosis.

While the clothing trade dominated the Jewish East End, employing up to 70 per cent of its workforce, other immigrants found employment as local market traders and shopkeepers, providing services essential to the Jewish way of life. Jewish grocery stores, bagel bakeries and kosher restaurants thrived; by 1901 there were fifteen kosher butchers in Wentworth Street alone.

## A VIBRANT COMMUNITY

The Jewish East End was a vibrant, self-contained district. On weekdays community life focused on Wentworth Street (or 'The Lane') which resounded with the sounds and activities of Yiddish-speaking traders. On Saturday evenings social activity transferred to the wide pavements of Whitechapel Road as Jewish families celebrated the close of the Sabbath with 'The Saturday Walk'. Although Polish, Russian and Eastern European Jews were culturally diverse, the Yiddish language formed a common bond. The community was served by three daily Yiddish newspapers and Yiddish theatrical productions were regularly performed at the Pavilion Theatre in Whitechapel Road.

The immigrants maintained religious traditions by attending small, self-administered synagogues based on the old village communities of Eastern Europe. Initially meeting in homes and workshops, many of these smaller congregations amalgamated within the Federation of Synagogues – but the East End synagogues and shuls remained small in contrast to the larger cathedral-style synagogues preferred by the established Anglo-Jewish community.

Education was regarded as a means to economic and social advancement, and most Jewish parents applied to send their children to the voluntary aided Jews' Free School, established in the East End in 1817. Unsuccessful applicants went to local board schools like Commercial Street School, which, by the 1890s, was 90 per cent Jewish and closed on Jewish religious holidays. After school, children attended Hebrew classes and joined youth organizations such as the Jewish Lads' Brigade and the Brady Street Lads' Club, which aimed to bridge the divide between Jewish and English cultural traditions while ironing out the 'ghetto bend' in immigrant boys.

To outsiders, the area between Spitalfields and Whitechapel was an alien ghetto populated by 'strange exotics'. Their unfamiliar language, diet and religion could arouse suspicion and crimes that appeared to be 'foreign to the English style' – including the Jack the Ripper murders – were often falsely blamed on the Jewish community. Anti-Jewish sentiment found an official voice in the British Brothers League, an anti-alien pressure group established in 1901,

## THE FISZER FAMILY: JEWISH IMMIGRANTS IN SPITALFIELDS

The Jewish Fiszer family moved to London from Warsaw in Russian-controlled Poland in the early years of the 20th century. Juda Fiszer was a skilled umbrella-maker, and in 1907 he established an umbrella business in the heart of the Jewish East End at 45 Hanbury Street, Spitalfields. Although the family anglicized their name to Fisher soon after arrival in London, Juda and his wife Malka retained their Polish nationality.

During World War I, the Fishers moved to the more desirable area of Hackney, setting up home at 123 Victoria Park Road. Their son Morris Fisher continued the family business but, by the 1930s, the Hanbury Street shop had closed, the premises being taken over by a Jewish tailor. Reflecting the changing times, Morris switched from shop owner to market trader, operating a stall in the Whitechapel Road and selling – rather than manufacturing – umbrellas, walking sticks and handbags.

*The Fiszers outside their umbrella shop.*

but anti-Semitism was not a mass movement in the East End during this period. Most gentiles within the district accepted the ways of their Jewish neighbours.

### ANGLO-JEWISH HELP

The Anglo-Jewish population supported the new arrivals through charitable assistance and advice. Jewish immigrants received help from a network of relief agencies, including the Jewish Board of Guardians, which offered loans for the purchase of sewing machines, and the Poor Jews' Temporary Shelter in Leman Street, which offered board and lodging for the first two weeks of arrival.

Wealthy Anglo-Jewish families, including the Rothschilds, also supported the building of affordable accommodation for skilled Jewish workers. Administered by the Four Per Cent Company, the first tenement block built primarily for Jewish immigrants, the Charlotte de Rothschild Dwellings, opened in 1887 in Flower and Dean Streets. A second estate soon opened in Brady Street and the Nathaniel Dwellings, accommodating up to 800 Jewish workers, were completed in 1892. There was a strong sense of community within the Rothschild buildings and most residents enjoyed similar standards of living and shared ambitions. Many had young families and by the 1890s there was a birth in the buildings every nine or ten days.

The arrival of the Jewish immigrants invigorated the Spitalfields neighbourhood and transformed it from a slum into a cosmopolitan district filled with young families. For many who grew up in the Jewish East End, such as the playwright Arnold Wesker, the businessman Charles Clore, the artist Mark Gertler and the singer Bud Flanagan, the area provided inspiration for success in later life. Although economic progress enabled many Jewish families to relocate to the more affluent areas of Hackney, Stoke Newington and Stamford Hill, most retained close links with the Whitechapel and Spitalfields neighbourhood. Many continued to own factories and work in the area, while others returned regularly to go shopping in 'The Lane' or to visit elderly relatives in the Rothschild buildings. **BC**

*A Jewish couple celebrating the Jewish New Year in London, c.1900*
The banners surrounding the couple say 'Happy New Year' in Russian, Hebrew and English.

*The Pavilion Theatre on Whitechapel Road, c.1910*
The main London venue for Yiddish theatre during the early 20th century, the theatre hosted plays, concerts, boxing matches and political rallies until its closure in 1937.

# THE SCHOOL BOARD & EDUCATION FOR ALL

Education reform was Victorian London's great success story. The London School Board built new schools across the city, and great advances were made in technical and university education.

**Schools in Finsbury during the 1890s**
The geographical spread of School Board and voluntary school education in the area.

In 1870, a new chapter in the history of education in London opened. In that year, an Education Act was passed 'to provide for public elementary education' for the children of the lower classes not already attending voluntary schools. Such schools had, since the early years of the 19th century, been run by a range of religious, charitable and parish organizations to provide poorer children with

schooling. Others belonged to private individuals: for example, 'Dame Schools' were typically private schools run by old women. For the brief and frequently interrupted time that many children attended these schools, they received an education of varying quality. The better schools taught the 'three Rs' (reading, writing and arithmetic) and a useful skill such as needlework or bootmaking. Some Dame schools, however, acted as little more than childminders.

Under the 1870 Act, a School Board for London was created to build and run elementary schools for children in the metropolitan area. As was the case with the other new local school boards set up under the Act, these were to supplement, not replace, the voluntary system. The board was the first directly elected, London-wide body and was the largest and most powerful of the new boards in Britain. All London ratepayers could vote for the board and, significantly, it was one of the first public bodies to which women could be elected. It attracted many notable members including, in 1870, Elizabeth Garrett Anderson, England's first qualified female doctor, and in 1888 Annie Besant, the campaigner for women's rights.

As soon as the board took office, it embarked on an energetic school-building programme. It opened its first school at the end of 1872 in Berners Street, and by the end of 1874 it had built a further ninety-eight. Working from its purpose-built offices on the Embankment, it had by 1903 opened 500 new board schools: four to every square mile of London. These were usually three or more storeys high, and with their distinctive red bricks, Flemish gables, high chimney stacks and dormer windows – all features of the Queen Anne architectural style favoured by the progressive classes – they physically embodied the board's reformist ethos. They soon became, and still are, as much London landmarks as churches. Sherlock Holmes caught the mood of many when he remarked that such schools were 'Lighthouses, my boy! Beacons of the future! Capsules, with hundreds of bright little seeds in each, out of which will spring the wiser, better England of the future.'

## COMPULSORY ATTENDANCE

Board school pupils followed a standard curriculum that included Bible and religious study and the 'three Rs'. Older children also studied the history of England, elementary geography, drawing, and music and also drill. Other subjects, including science, were added in time.

Elementary school children by definition belonged to the poorest classes in society, and poverty meant that for many families the need to earn a living took priority over education. As a result, the board had to fight a constant battle against non-attendance. Even after 1876, when parents were obliged to ensure that their children received elementary education, and after 1891, when attendance was made free, non-attendance remained a problem. In 1899, for example, out of 112 Board schools, over 1000 children worked between 19 and 29 hours a week outside school, and hundreds worked more. Teams of 'visitors' were set up to trace children and facilitate their attendance at school. Parents who refused to co-operate could be prosecuted and their children could be removed to truant and Industrial schools. More often, teachers used treats and outings to encourage attendance. In 1887, the board started awarding medals for 'regular and punctual attendance.'

In the 1880s, rising levels of achievement led to increasing numbers of children staying on at school beyond the age of ten. To meet this demand, an additional year, entered by pupils at age thirteen, was added to the curriculum in 1882, and in 1887 the

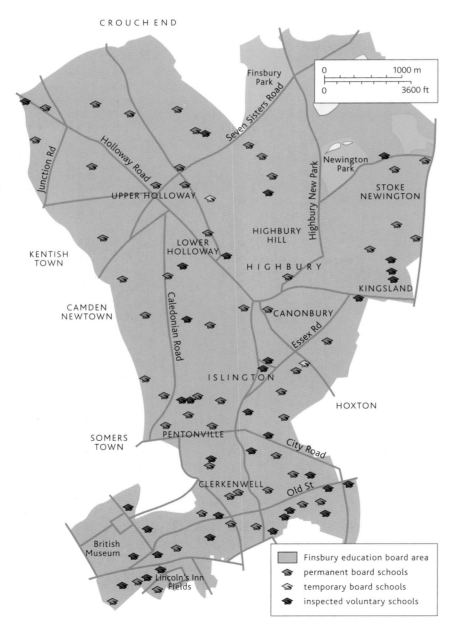

CROUCH END

Finsbury Park

Seven Sisters Road

Newington Park

Junction Rd

Holloway Road

UPPER HOLLOWAY

Highbury New Park

STOKE NEWINGTON

KENTISH TOWN

LOWER HOLLOWAY

HIGHBURY HILL

HIGHBURY

KINGSLAND

CAMDEN NEWTOWN

Caledonian Road

CANONBURY

Essex Rd

ISLINGTON

HOXTON

SOMERS TOWN

PENTONVILLE

City Road

CLERKENWELL

Old St

British Museum

Lincoln's Inn Fields

0     1000 m
0     3600 ft

Finsbury education board area
permanent board schools
temporary board schools
inspected voluntary schools

improve and support secondary and technical education in London. However, the London School Board's provision of higher grade and evening schools soon brought it into conflict with this new body. By the turn of the 20th century, it was clear that education at all grades in London needed to be provided for by a single body. In 1903, an Education (London) Act transferred all public elementary, secondary and technical education in London to the control of the London County Council.

## THE UNIVERSITY OF LONDON

It was also during the late Victorian period that university provision in the capital was transformed. In 1878, the University of London became the first university in Britain to admit women to degree courses. This led to the creation of dedicated women's colleges in the 1880s – Westfield College (1882) and Royal Holloway College (1886). By 1900, 30 per cent of all graduates of the university were women. During the same period science, economics and politics came into their own as university subjects with the creation of the Royal College of Science in 1881 (later part of Imperial College) and the foundation in 1895 of the London School of Economics and Political Science. At the same time, the university moved from being a purely degree-awarding body to being a teaching institution.

In a little over three decades, the education of Londoners had been transformed. At the upper end of the social scale, women theoretically now had access to education equal to that of men. At the lower end of the scale, people had access to a unified free education system that could take them from childhood to young adulthood. Science and technology were in the ascendant and Londoners were preparing for the technical and skilled jobs upon which the future of Great Britain would be built. **JH**

board created 'higher grade' or 'central' schools to teach pupils staying on between eleven and thirteen. By the end of the century, literacy in London had increased markedly, and the percentage of thirteen-year-olds remaining at school had tripled. Also during the 1880s, the board began running evening schools to provide recreational and vocational courses.

## TECHNICAL EDUCATION

The 1880s also saw the significant expansion of technical education in London, in response to a growing thirst for education among lower-class Londoners and a recognition in official and business circles that Britain needed to improve the technical skills of its workforce compared to those of foreign competitors. In 1882, the Polytechnic in Regent Street began providing working- and lower-middle class men and women with technical and recreational classes. City livery companies founded the City and Guilds of London Institute (1884), the East London Technical College (1896), and Goldsmith's Technical and Recreative Institute (1891). In 1891 the City Corporation and the London County Council (LCC) embarked on a joint effort to support further polytechnics and trade colleges across London.

In 1893, the LCC set up a Technical Education Board to

*School certificate*
*A School Board for London certificate awarded to Alfred Greenwood in 1883 for reaching the second standard in reading, writing and arithmetic.*

# OUTCAST & UNDERWORLD LONDON

Sympathy for the poor was combined with fear of a growing criminal underclass. Then, in 1888 the Jack the Ripper murders dramatized the terrors of London's dark side.

**A Poor-House, c. 1869**
*Gustave Doré's painting of the dimly-lit world of outcast London was based on his own observations. The poverty-stricken huddle together in a common lodging house or night refuge.*

The establishment of the Metropolitan Police in 1829 (see pages 180–1) brought with it annual returns of crimes committed and criminals apprehended from each district of London. Even though the figures only recorded reported crimes, they show a dramatic reduction in the metropolis from 1831 to 1892, which led the Director of Criminal Investigation to write in 1882 that the city was 'the safest capital for life and property in the world'. As in today's London, despite the statistics, the 1880s saw rising fear about criminal black spots. Novelists, newspapers and pamphleteers conjured up lurid tales of 'horrible London' where 'unspeakable horrors and abominations' were common. In 1883 a Congregationalist minister, Andrew Mearns, published *The Bitter Cry of Outcast London*, a polemic about poverty that fuelled fears of social degeneration. The belief grew that London's poor were 'sinking' downwards and mutating into a godless, criminal underclass.

## THE GEOGRAPHY OF CRIME

The areas of crime in late 19th-century London were the areas of crime that had existed for well over a century; they had, as Henry Mayhew noted, originally developed around the legal sanctuaries that had developed in the medieval and early modern city and around London's older hospitals. By the 19th century theatres and music halls were the magnets of criminal activity, particularly theft and prostitution. Known as 'Rookeries', the crime areas of the city were not only where crime was committed, but also where criminals resided and could disappear in a network of narrow streets and alleys. The area of St Giles had long been notorious. The construction of New Oxford Street had cleared some of the old slum properties but criminal associations remained. Nearby Wych Street and Hollywell Street became the centre of London's pornographic literature trade during this period.

Charles Booth's survey identified the 'dark borderlands' of the City as areas of crime. Hoxton, according to Booth, was 'the leading criminal quarter of London, and indeed of all England … Bad as things are in Hoxton itself, they reach an even more uniformly low level on the borders of Clerkenwell, which, if not more criminal, show at least a lower type of criminality.'

**Areas of criminal activity, 1880s**
Crime tended to cluster in areas that offered a combination of crowds, narrow alleyways and cheap property. Theatres were notorious magnets for prostitution.

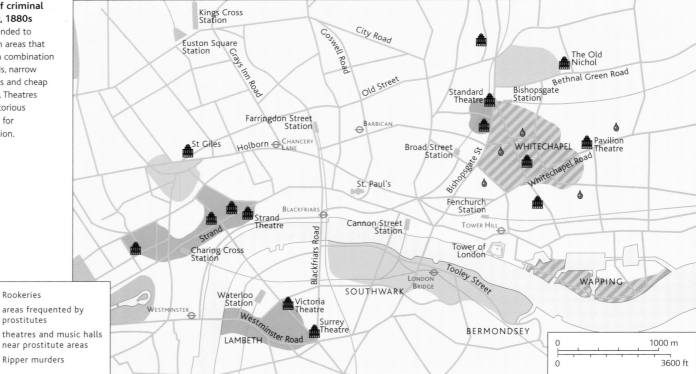

Legend:
- Rookeries
- areas frequented by prostitutes
- theatres and music halls near prostitute areas
- Ripper murders

**The Jack the Ripper Murders, 1888**
Whitechapel's most infamous crime scene, where six women were murdered in three months within a square mile of one another.

Map labels:
- 0  300 m
- 0  1000 ft
- Whitechapel & Spitalfields Union Workhouse
- Jews' Burial Ground
- 3 Hanbury St
- Spitalfields Market Place
- Brushfield St
- Brick Lane
- 6
- Commercial St
- Old Whitechapel Rd
- London Hospital
- Turner St
- 1
- Commercial Road East
- railway goods depot
- 4
- Berner St
- 5
- railway goods depot
- 2

◉ sites where Jack the Ripper's victims were found

1. 7 August: Martha Tabram's body found at George Yard Buildings (now Gunthorpe St)
2. 31 August: Mary Ann ('Polly') Nichols' body found at Buck's Row (now Durward St)
3. 8 September: Annie Chapman's body found at rear of 29 Hanbury St
4. 30 September: Elizabeth Stride's body found at the back of the International Working Men's Club in Berner St (now Henriques St)
5. 30 September: Catherine Eddowes' body found at 30 Mitre Square
6. 9 November: Mary Jane Kelly's body found at 9 Miller's Court, Dorset St

The most notorious of these borderland districts was 'the Nichol', a warren of cellar dwellings and ramshackle houses in around Old Nichol Street in Shoreditch. Here, crime was a way of life, as vividly described (under a fictional name) in 1896 by Arthur Morrison's popular novel *A Child of the Jago*. 'Cosh-carrying was near to being the major industry of the Jago,' Morrison informed his readers. 'The cosh was a foot length of iron rod, with a knob at one end, and a hook (or a ring) at the other'. Describing how women would lure drunken strangers to dark staircases where accomplices would cosh and rob them, Morrison blithely pointed out that 'this industry yielded a comfortable subsistence for no great exertion'.

By the time Morrison's book came out, the Nichol was being swept away by the London County Council (LCC) in its first major improvement scheme. In its place rose the showpiece Boundary Estate – providing rented flats for respectable workers, a statement of the LCC's intent to provide help for useful workers and let the underclass fend for themselves.

The Nichol's former inhabitants shifted into neighbouring districts, some continuing to operate on their own as petty criminals, others gathering into organized gangs. In the Edwardian period concern turned to the problem of young 'hooligans' and 'thugs', operating in gangs with distinct territories and turf-wars with their rivals. In the East End rival protection-racket gangs the Bessarabians and the Odessians fought for control of the Whitechapel streets.

## JACK THE RIPPER

The most notorious crimes of late Victorian London were the murders committed by 'Jack the Ripper'. In August 1888 the body of Martha Tabram, a woman working as a prostitute, was discovered on the landing of a tenement block in Whitechapel. She had been subjected to a frenzied knife attack. Over the next three months five other women were horribly murdered.

The case attracted unprecedented newspaper coverage. Journalists revelled in the gruesome details and stoked wild speculations about the murderer's identity. It is even possible that the name 'Jack the Ripper', supposedly the signature on a note sent to a press agency, was a journalistic invention. The police investigated many suspects in Britain and abroad but never caught the killer.

The Jack the Ripper case was a lightning conductor for deep-seated social anxieties about the mix of poverty, criminality and sexual promiscuity found in London's dark inner-city districts. Although, statistically, the Metropolitan Police had reduced crime over the previous half century, late Victorian London could feel like a city where sin and savagery were never far beneath the surface.                        **MoL**

***Crime reporting***
*Crowds gather around a newsagent's window to examine the gory pictures of the latest crimes in the* Illustrated Police News.

# POPULAR RELIGION & THE SALVATION ARMY

Evangelical Christianity swept through late Victorian London. Congregations flocked to hear charismatic preachers, and the Salvation Army emerged as a force for social reform.

As London's population increased, numbers regularly attending Church of England services fell. By the end of the 19th century, many Londoners had turned their backs on the established Church, finding alternative comfort in evangelical Christianity and the inspirational preaching of the Methodists, Baptists and Congregationalists.

London's evangelistic spirit was first awakened by Charles Haddon Spurgeon, who arrived in the city in 1854 aged nineteen to preach at a Baptist chapel in New Park Street, south London. His theatrical sermons soon attracted thousands of worshippers, prompting the playwright James Sheridan Knowles to observe 'I was once lessee of Drury Lane theatre; were I still in that position I would offer him a fortune to play for a season on the boards … Why, boys, he can do anything he pleases with his audience!'

By the end of the decade, Spurgeon had built the Metropolitan Tabernacle in Newington Butts, Southwark, a monumental building that held 6000 worshippers, referred to by *The Times* as 'one of the ornaments of the metropolis'. Beyond the pulpit, he established a boys' school and an orphanage where all children were enrolled in the 'Band of Hope' temperance union. Philanthropy and inspirational preaching proved a formidable combination and enabled Spurgeon to retain an influential presence in south London until his death in 1892.

In 1875, London experienced the spectacle of US evangelism when the American preacher Dwight Moody descended on the capital with his partner, the singer and composer Ira Sankey. Over 15,000 Londoners came daily to the Agricultural Hall, Islington, to hear Moody and Sankey's brand of evangelical Christianity during their ten-week residency. As Moody, the great storyteller, charmed the audience with his unfamiliar Americanisms, fiery sermons and humour, Sankey moved them to tears with his singing. Moody and Sankey's religious performances resembled a music hall act; they soon became superstars. Their popularity inspired the manufacture of souvenirs including Staffordshire pottery figures, commemorative photographs and penny song sheets, while Sankey's compositions such as 'The Ninety and Nine' and 'When the Mists have Rolled Away' were among the most popular street songs of the day.

The mass appeal of evangelism encouraged Moody and Sankey to establish the East London Tabernacle in Burdett Road, Bow. This gas-lit building with a galvanized iron roof and a sawdust floor held some 8000 worshippers, many drawn from the local working-class neighbourhood. As Henry Walker observed in the 1890s,

**Christian missionary and welfare activity in the East End in the late 19th century**
The charitable services focused on London's poorest regions.

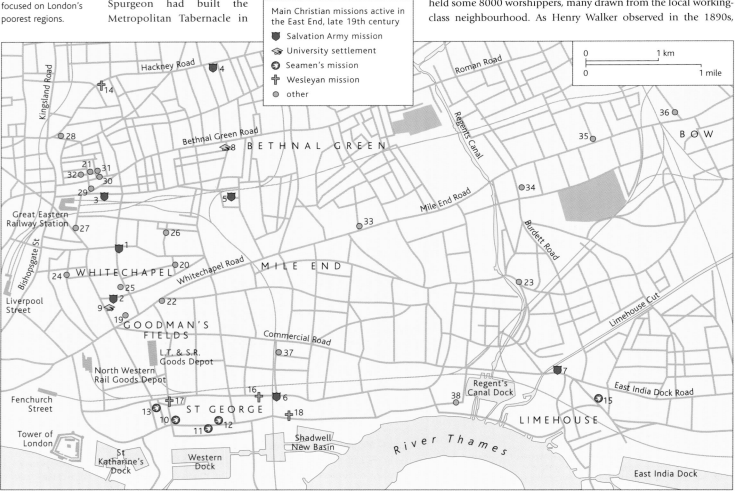

'Morning congregations in East London are almost everywhere at a minimum; yet here every Sunday is gathered, for the eleven o'clock service, a congregation of nearly two thousand persons.'

## THE SALVATION ARMY

Nonconformist religion was closely connected with the Victorian temperance and missionary movements. Philanthropic activity focused on areas of poverty, particularly the East End, and aimed to instill Christian values into poor Londoners while saving them from depravity and drunkenness. Missionary centres established by organizations like the London Congregational Union provided breakfast, clothing and holidays for poor children and sheltered accommodation and meals for the homeless. In the first nine months of 1891, Medland Hall in Limehouse, one of many shelters in East London, provided overnight shelter for 100,000 men. Of all the missions established during the late 19th century, however, the most famous and controversial was the Salvation Army.

The Salvation Army was founded on 2 July 1865 when William Booth (1829–1912) first preached his brand of evangelism to Londoners from a platform erected on the Mile End Waste. Booth originally marshalled his followers into the East London Christian Mission, which was renamed the Salvation Army in 1878, with headquarters in the Whitechapel Road. Support for the movement quickly grew, and in 1881 Salvation Army headquarters moved to a more imposing building in Queen Victoria Street, Blackfriars. Aiming to save bodies as well as souls, the Army maintained a consciously military ethos, engaging in what was seen as a war against sin and poverty. Members were organized into a military hierarchy

1. Salvation Army Rescue Home for Women, Hanbury Street
2. Salvation Army Slum Post, Wentworth Street
3. Salvation Army Slum Post, Sclater Street
4. Salvation Army Slum Post, Hackney Road
5. Salvation Army Slum Post, Tent Street
6. Salvation Army Slum Post, Cable Street
7. Salvation Army Slum Post, West India Dock Road
8. Oxford House University Settlement, Derbyshire Street
9. Toynbee Hall University Lay Settlement, Commercial Street
10. Seamen's Christian Friend Society, St George Street East
11. The Welcome Home for Sailors, St George Street
12. The Sailor's Rest, Betts Street
13. Sailors' Home & Church, Dock Street
14. Wesleyan Shoreditch Mission, Hackney Road
15. The Stranger's Home, West India Dock Road
16. St George's Wesleyan Chapel, Cable Street
17. Mahogany Bar Wesleyan Mission, Wellclose Passage
18. Paddy's Goose Wesleyan Mission, Ratcliffe Highway
19. George Yard Mission & Ragged School
20. King Edward Street Mission, Ragged Schools & Institutes
21. Old Nichol Street Ragged School, Mission & Chapel,
22. Whitechapel Mission for Destitute Boys, Whitechapel Road
23. Dr Barnardo's Edinburgh Castle Coffee House, Rhodeswell Road
24. Providence Row Night Refuge, Crispin Street
25. Christian Community Mission, Thrawl Street
26. Albert Street Mission, Albert Street
27. Bedford Institute, Headquarters of the Society of Friends' Home Mission to East London, Commercial Street
28. Shoreditch Tabernacle, Hackney Road
29. Miss Macpherson's Home of Industry for the Homeless, Bethnal Green Road
30. Mildmay Lodging House for Men, Church Street
31. Mildmay Mission Rooms, Turyville Street
32. Holy Trinity Church & Lodging House, Old Nichol Street
33. Tower Hamlets Mission, Mile End Road
34. East London Tabernacle, Burdett Road
35. Harley House, Bow Road
36. Clifton House Institute for Female Factory Workers, Fairfield Road
37. Ebenezer Mission Chapel & Hall, Watney Street
38. Medland Hall, shelter for homeless and destitute men, Medland Street

with General Booth at the top and newly arrived 'cadets' at the bottom. Field officers carried the message of salvation to the most deprived members of society through music, brass bands and the *War Cry* newspaper. The wearing of a distinctive uniform helped to give followers a sense of fellowship and commitment, and some elements of the uniform – such as the Hallelujah bonnet – became symbols for the Army. Developed by William's wife Catherine and a Salvation Army cadet, the milliner Annie Lockwood, the bonnet was 'cheap, strong and large enough to protect the heads of the wearers from cold as well as from brick-bats and other missiles'.

As Booth and his cadets targeted the sinners of East London they were regularly abused and attacked. On one occasion a group of Army women working in Whitechapel were roped together and pelted with burning coals. Their temperance work incurred the hostility of brewing companies and music hall proprietors, while their enthusiastic style of Christianity offended the Church of England hierarchy. The greater the abuse and disapproval they received, the more defiant they became and the louder they sang.

## WELFARE WORK

It was, however, the Salvation Army's social work rather than its religious message that had the greatest impact on London's poor. The Army quickly established a missing persons bureau, soup kitchens, night shelters for the homeless and even a clean, airy match factory that offered fair employment to young women. Booth's most controversial project, outlined in his book *In Darkest England and the Way Out*, was the establishment of Labour Homes and a Farm Colony in Essex, where unemployed London men could learn new skills like carpentry and brick-making, while being encouraged to convert to a 'changed life'. For those wishing to escape the poverty and desperation of the East End, the Army also assisted the destitute to emigrate and find work in the colonies.

At Booth's death in 1912, the Salvation Army was active in fifty-eight countries – and the General himself, who throughout his life had sought 'Heaven in East London for everyone' was considered 'the world's best loved man'. Over 65,000 mourners attended his funeral in Hackney, and his missionary and social legacy survives worldwide today. **BC**

*Night meeting at the Blackfriars shelter*
A refuge for the destitute was provided by the Salvation Army, close to their headquarters on Queen Victoria Street.

*Dwight Lynan Moody, c. 1875*
A souvenir pottery figure of the popular American preacher.

**Tower Bridge, 1886–94**
*Built by the Corporation of London and designed by their in-house architect Horace Jones, this was a state-of-the-art bridge in its day, with steam powered lifting machinery to raise the lower deck.*
Underground: Tower Hill

**Paddington Station, 1850–4**
*The London terminus for the Great Western Railway, Paddington (right) was designed by I. K. Brunel, the railways engineer, with architects M. D. Wyatt and Owen Jones, who devised the decorative scheme for the interior.*
Underground: Paddington

# SURVIVALS
# VICTORIAN

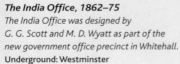

**Cleopatra's needle, erected 1877**
*A present from the Egyptian viceroy in 1819, the obelisk was transported to London after the construction of the Embankment in 1864–70. The bronze sphynxes were added in 1882.*
Underground: Embankment

**The India Office, 1862–75**
*The India Office was designed by G. G. Scott and M. D. Wyatt as part of the new government office precinct in Whitehall.*
Underground: Westminster

**'Gibson Hall' 1864–5**
*Formerly the head office of the National Provincial Bank, this was one of the most palatial banks in the City of London. Designed by John Gibson, it is surmounted by sculptures representing British cities.*
Underground: Bank

**All Saints Church, 1849–59**
*This richly decorated church (right) in Marylebone was intended to be a model church for the Ecclesiological movement. The architect was William Butterfield.*
Underground: Mornington Crescent

### Palace Theatre, 1888–91

A sumptuous new theatre built for theatrical impresario Richard D'Oyley Carte. It was designed by G. H. Holloway and T. E. Collcutt.
Underground: Leicester Square

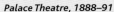

### Houses of Parliament, 1840–60

*The Houses of Parliament were designed by Sir Charles Barry to replace the old Palace of Westminster, which was destroyed in a catastrophic fire in 1834.*
Underground: Westminster

### The Natural History Museum, 1872–81

*Designed by Alfred Waterhouse to house the natural history departments of the British Museum, recently removed from the Bloomsbury site.*
Underground: South Kensington

### Leadenhall Market, 1880–1

*A market for poultry and produce had existed on this site in the City since the 14th century. The Corporation of London rebuilt the market in the 1880s to designs by Horace Jones.*
Underground: Bank

### The Midland Grand Hotel, St Pancras, 1868–74

*A large and impressive railway hotel built at the London terminus of the Midland Railway.*
Underground: King's Cross St Pancras

### Wigmore Hall

*A small concert hall in Marylebone, built as the Bechstein Hall in 1900. The portico was remodelled in 1904.*
Underground: Oxford Circus

# EDWARDIAN LONDON

L ondon generated many state-of-the-nation debates in the years before World War I, though cheering crowds expressed the popularity of crown and empire. Yet conditions in the East End continued to raise fears. The suffragettes moved their campaign to London in 1904, knowing that the capital offered the best stage for their confrontational 'deeds not words'.

The city kept on growing. Greater London's population reached 7.1 million in 1911, with 4.5 million packed into the inner core. No other British city topped the million mark and London still outstripped other European capitals. The only cities in London's league were across the Atlantic.

Managing this vast metropolis remained a Herculean task. The London County Council took over education in 1904 and began to tackle the huge persistent problems of malnutrition, vermin and disease among London's school children. Public bath-houses,

libraries and municipal electricity sub-stations appeared across the capital, as the twenty-eight metropolitan boroughs began to improve London at local level.

London's sheer size attracted new and ambitious commercial ventures. Impresarios turned music halls into lavish variety theatres. Mass-market newspapers appeared. The American Charles Yerkes led a transport revolution by burying 'tube' railways deep underground. The Hungarian Imre Kiralfy erected a giant Ferris Wheel at White City.

London was a city of the masses, an exuberant plebeian city as much as a sober imperial one. The London 'types' celebrated in word and song were costermongers, tram conductors, flower girls and policemen. But new lines were being drawn between outsider and insider as consciousness of 'aliens' grew, along with fears about the capital's 20th-century future.

# IMPERIAL CAPITAL

London's image as a great imperial city was expressed in its statues, monuments and urban set-pieces. Kingsway and the Mall added new grandeur to the city centre.

The coincidence of a new century, two coronations, twenty-eight new metropolitan boroughs and the empire at its height brought Londoners a new sense of their city's importance. London was an imperial capital, with world status. To Lawrence Gomme, chief clerk of the London County Council (LCC), the city could look back over its past with pride 'as Roman city, as city-state, as municipal city, as national city, as empire city'.

Two projects gave London the streets its status demanded. The Aldwych and Kingsway scheme, masterminded by the LCC, was opened in 1905. The Mall and Admiralty Arch scheme, opened in 1910–11, transformed the royal ceremonial route from Buckingham Palace to St Paul's, commemorating Britain's rise to world greatness under Queen Victoria. The scheme's architect, Sir Aston Webb, widened the Mall to create a more formal arrangement culminating in a new public space in front of Buckingham Palace. At the centre of this new area was Sir Thomas Brock's

**Coronation celebrations, 1902**
*Street decorations in central London marked the coronation of Edward VIII in 1902.*

monument to Queen Victoria, topped by a golden figure of Victory. It soon began to be described as 'the hub of Empire'.

At Whitehall, Webb erected Admiralty Arch to disguise the awkward angle where the Mall met the Strand. The arch was a powerful celebration of the maritime basis of Britain's imperial wealth. Its facade incorporated decorative stone sculptures of Navigation and Gunnery, again by Sir Thomas Brock.

The Aldwych scheme was less triumphal in style, speaking of civic, rather than royal, power (see below, right). There had long been calls for a new route between Holborn and Fleet Street; it was a classic 'improvement' with the added benefit of clearing slums at the east end of the Strand. Although modern in spirit, the scheme respected London's past. The new crescent was built around the historic church of St Clement Danes. Its Saxon-derived name, Aldwych, was chosen to reflect London's long history of settlement.

Kingsway, named in honour of Edward VII, ran north to Holborn. It was London's widest street to date, thoroughly modern in spirit, not least because a tunnel for electric trams ran beneath it. This was opened in 1908, three years after the street itself. The building plots on either side were leased to speculative builders in the hope of creating a new commercial district.

From the start, the new district had overseas associations. Aldwych's location on the royal route from the palace to St Paul's made it suitable for buildings associated with the empire. Australia

234

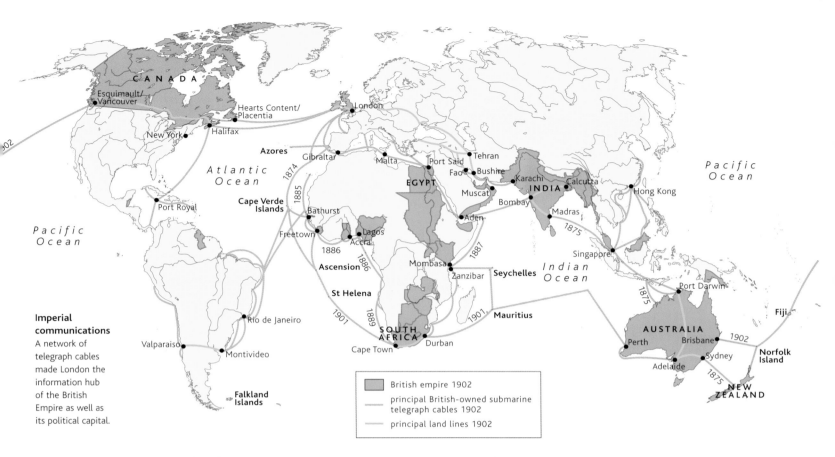

**Imperial communications**
A network of telegraph cables made London the information hub of the British Empire as well as its political capital.

British empire 1902
principal British-owned submarine telegraph cables 1902
principal land lines 1902

House, built in 1913–18, was the first of the large Dominion head-quarters in the area; it was followed in the late 1920s by India House. However, it was associations with the United States that came to predominate. The Waldorf Hotel, built on the north side of the crescent between 1906 and 1908, soon became a meeting place for Americans in London. Several US firms established their headquarters in the new office blocks along Kingsway.

## MONUMENTALIZING THE CITY

Elsewhere, the spirit of imperial pride spread through ornamental buildings and grand monuments. Department stores proclaimed London as the consumer capital of Europe. Harrods erected a terracotta palace in Knightsbridge between 1901 and 1905, but its title of largest department store in Europe was soon seized by the US-run Selfridges, whose huge classical block appeared on Oxford Street in 1907. The entrance to Waterloo Station was remodelled in lavish Beaux Arts style, but plans to rebuild Charing Cross Station and Hungerford Bridge were not realized. The new metropolitan boroughs erected town halls adorned with allegorical figures representing their aspirations: Justice, Science, Art and Literature in the case of Lambeth in 1911. Far grander was the headquarters of the LCC itself. The site chosen was the under developed Surrey (south) side of the Thames, opposite the palace of Westminster. Although the outbreak of war in 1914 prevented completion of the building, its design and scale were truly imperial.

A rash of new monuments and sculptures also expressed the city's greatness. A bronze Boudica appeared on Westminster Bridge in 1902, alluding to Britain's glorious history. A golden statue of the medieval Count Peter of Savoy was erected outside his name-sake hotel in 1904. A set of giant bronze women representing Agriculture, Architecture and other practical matters adorned Vauxhall Bridge, opened in 1906. Monuments to Edward VII included one in Whitechapel Road erected by the Jewish community in thanks for his support of refugees from Russian persecution.

London's new self-consciousness also produced a new society, a new museum and the Blue Plaque scheme. The London Museum opened in Kensington Palace in April 1912. The London Society was formed in 1912 to provide a forum for discussion of the city's buildings, streets and planning. The Blue Plaque scheme ensured that London's greatness as a place of individual achievement and effort was inscribed on its streets for all to see.    **CR**

*Aldwych, 1915*
*The grand buildings lining the west side of the crescent were completed by 1910. This view shows the New Gaiety Theatre in the foreground; the block containing the Waldorf Hotel, the Strand and Aldwych theatres is in the background.*

# COTTAGE ESTATES & EARLY FLATS

The London County Council's house-building drive got into its stride. Inner-city tenements and out-of-town estates provided healthy, clean homes for London's workers.

**New Homes in Catford, 1900**
*This advertisement shows a typical development of the basic suburban houses built by local builders to house commuters.*

Just as in the 19th century railways had helped London's bricks and mortar march into the countryside, so in the early 20th century the new electric trams and railways enabled commuter housing to spread yet further. The Edwardian house-building boom also saw a new player, the London County Council (LCC), which embarked on a vigorous programme of housing provision designed to rehouse London's workers in healthier homes – either flats in new inner-city blocks or cottages in new suburban estates.

LCC housing fell into two main categories: replacements for dwellings lost to slum clearance, and general housing for workers. Slum clearance was the most pressing concern. By 1900, the LCC had identified twelve inner-city areas that urgently needed to be cleared. Typical was the Union Buildings area in Clerkenwell, a patch of overcrowded tenements long identified as a health black spot by the medical officer for Holborn. The clearance was completed by 1907. The Union Buildings scheme displaced 1402 people and provided dwellings for 1414 in four large blocks. The associated Bourne Estate accommodated 2642 people, some displaced by the LCC's Strand and Kingsway project (see page 234).

LCC provision of general housing began in earnest in 1900, when legislation allowed councils to build on land beyond their boundaries. Seizing the opportunity to reduce overcrowding in the inner city, the LCC began to look further afield. By 1914, London was encircled by LCC 'cottage estates'. The first was begun in 1903 at Totterdown Fields in Tooting, where the council planned to accommodate 8788 people on a 15-hectare (38-acre) site. Totterdown was typical in that it was built at the end of an LCC

tramline, enabling workers to commute into central London. Similar cottage estates followed at Norbury in Croydon, Old Oak in Hammersmith and Tower Gardens in north London, the latter partly financed by the Jewish philanthropist Samuel Montague for Jewish workers from overcrowded Tower Hamlets. This development of 963 cottages became the southern part of the enormous White Hart Lane estate, a 91-hectare (226-acre) site acquired in 1901 to house up to 20,000 workers. The upper half of the estate was developed after 1919, by which time the street plan reflected the lower-density layouts preferred in the 1920s.

## THE GARDEN CITY MOVEMENT

For most commercial house-builders, new houses meant the type built in London for the previous fifty years: straight terraces with bay windows and little architectural flourishes depending on the market (see left). However, new housing slowly began to reflect the influence of the garden city movement and the value it placed on health, light and Arts and Crafts architecture. Much Edwardian housing had a vernacular, cottage feel, with red brick or tile-hung walls, tall Tudor chimneys, steeply pitched roofs and tree-lined avenues. Garden city ideals helped create small colonies of architect-designed detached houses in London's leafy suburbs, for example at Loughton near Epping Forest, or Parkside in Wimbledon. For the less affluent, a garden suburb provided the right feel on a more modest scale, for example at Brentham Garden Suburb in Ealing, begun in 1901, or Finchley Garden Village, developed in 1910.

London's most famous garden suburb was in Hampstead. The extension of the Northern line in 1906 brought a rush of developers keen to exploit the attractive land around the Heath. To control such development, the philanthropist Henrietta Barnett turned developer herself. Her Hampstead Garden Suburb, laid out to a plan by

**The Bourne Estate, Clerkenwell**
*This estate was built by the LCC to provide homes for people displaced by slum clearances.*

**Council Houses**

*This 1937 map includes post-Edwardian housing, but illustrates the LCC's strategy of building flats within its boundary and cottage estates without.*

Raymond Unwin, had picturesque groups of buildings along tree-lined, curving streets. The estate had overt social aims, being intended as a community where workers and the middle class lived side by side. These aims were never fully realized.

The marks of a modern house in the Edwardian period were its garden, its electricity, its bathroom and inside plumbing. For the really modern-minded householder there was even the possibility of buying. Cecil Rolph Hewitt recounted his family's move in 1910 to a rented house in Gowan Avenue, Fulham. They looked envious-ly at the new houses being built nearby and offered for sale at £300 with a £35 deposit. 'My parents and their intimates, I remember, thought these were totally impossible prices, putting house owner-ship far beyond the reach of such as they.' Their own house was a perfectly respectable Victorian terrace rented for sixteen shillings a week. It had no internal hot water or electricity, and water for washing had to be heated on the gas burner downstairs. Cecil recalled, 'I can't remember that any of this was regarded as in any conceivable sense a hardship.' **CR**

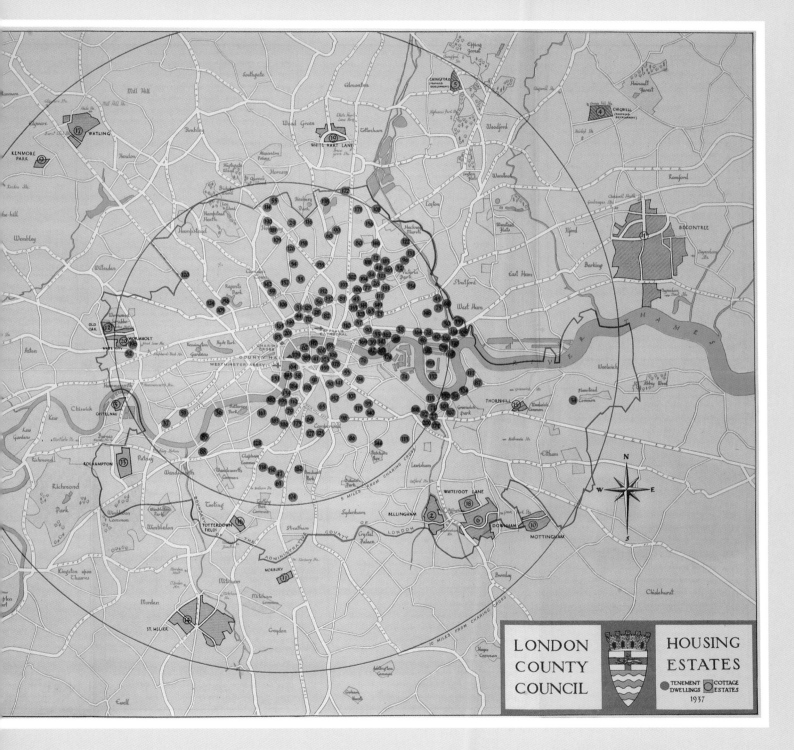

LONDON COUNTY COUNCIL

HOUSING ESTATES

● TENEMENT DWELLINGS ○ COTTAGE ESTATES

1937

# THE ELECTRIFICATION OF LONDON

Electricity began to change communications, lighting and public transport. The new fuel made underground trains and electric trams possible, but supply was patchy.

Electricity came of age in Edwardian London. It first made its mark in communication with the electric telegraph; by the second half of the 19th century a network of wires linked London to other British cities, and undersea cables provided similar links to Europe, the United States and the rest of the world. In 1880, the telephone, also powered by electricity, enabled Londoners to speak to each other from afar. Throughout the period, however, communication by telephone or telegraph was expensive and remained the preserve of government, businesses and the wealthy.

Electric lighting was first introduced in the late 19th century, but it did not become common until the 1920s. It was first trialled in 1878 along the Victoria Embankment but proved unreliable, and gas lighting was reintroduced. A year later, the British Museum installed internal electric lighting for use on foggy days and to extend the library's opening hours during winter. Four huge pendulum lamps in the Reading Room each supplied illumination equivalent to 3000 candles. In 1880, at the newly opened Royal Albert Dock, electric light enabled ships to be discharged and loaded at night. This was for many years the largest undertaking in London to be lit by electricity. The quayside and dock were lit by lamps suspended from 24-metre-high (80-ft) iron posts.

The most spectacular early use of electricity in the centre of the city was at the Savoy Hotel and Theatre, run by Richard D'Oyly Carte. In 1889, electric lighting was employed throughout the hotel. Much was made of the fact that it was possible for guests to turn out the lights from their bedsides. Lighting in the theatre could be brightened or dimmed by the turn of a handle. Over 800 'Swan' lights were directed at the stage and a further 150 lit up the auditorium. Electric light did not flicker as much as gas light and allowed the audience to see the faces of the actors and singers more clearly and to appreciate the sets and scenery better.

The history of Piccadilly Circus's famous illuminated advertising boards can be traced to the early 1890s, when a couple of 'sky-signs' were erected on the roof of buildings in Tichborne Street. It was not until 1908–10 that the first large illuminated signs appeared on the side of Piccadilly Mansions, a building on the north side of the Circus. These advertised Bovril and Schweppes, brands not directly linked to the businesses beneath them. More signs followed, and by the 1920s the north side of Piccadilly Circus had become a wall of illuminated signs.

## ELECTRIC TRANSPORTATION

Perhaps the most dramatic change that electricity brought was in transport. In 1890, the world's first electric underground railway opened in London. Electric-powered trains soon became the norm both above and below the streets (see opposite). Large power stations to supply the system were constructed, for example at Lots

Road in Fulham for the District Railway, and at Neasden for the Metropolitan.

Horse-drawn trams were also gradually replaced by electric trams. Some tram companies used overhead electrified wires, but the London County Council (LCC), which ran the largest tram network, employed a live rail underneath the road surface. A power station at Chiswick drove the London United Tramways system in west London and the LCC public tramways were supplied from the large Greenwich station. For a time it seemed as if electric automobiles would take over the streets of London, but their limited range meant that they lost out to petrol-powered vehicles.

Some electricity supply companies in the central city grew into large concerns. London local authorities also began to see the convenience of electricity; St Pancras adopted electric lighting to illuminate Tottenham Court Road in 1891. Many others followed, generating electricity municipally with profits benefiting ratepayers rather than private shareholders.

By the end of the Edwardian period, London's electric supply system was perhaps the least integrated of any major world city. Some sixty-five authorities ran seventy generating stations, many small and uneconomic, and several different voltage levels were in use. The metropolitan boroughs could choose either to provide their own supply or to license a private company. Generally, electricity in east London was supplied municipally, whereas in west London it was provided by private companies.

The new power source was promoted as odourless, smoke-free and clean for domestic use. In 1908, a model home at the Franco-British exhibition at White City showcased cookers, kettles, coffee percolators, heaters, refrigerators and even an electric 'sun bath'. In 1912, Tricity House opened in Oxford Street, with a showroom for a wide range of electric cookers. In the same year, Charles Belling patented his revolutionary 'Standard' electric heater. Despite such promotions, however, the domestic electric revolution for ordinary Londoners did not really begin until the 1920s and 1930s.   **AW**

*An early 'tube' map, 1907*
Produced by the Underground Group, which owned the new deep 'tube' lines and some of the electrified District railway. The Group's lines are shown in bold.

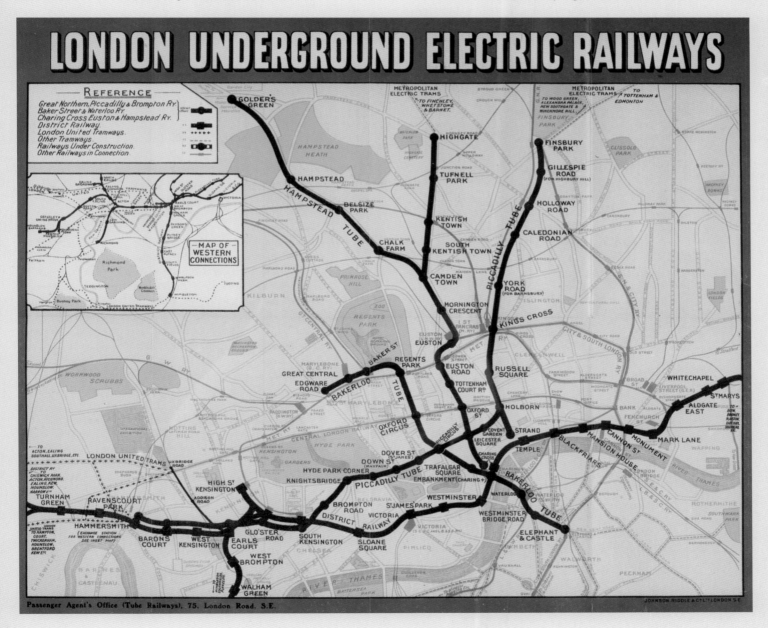

# THE HEYDAY OF FLEET STREET

A news revolution centered on Fleet Street. The district housed newly-launched, mass-circulation British newspapers and press agencies from around the world.

**A London News Boy**
*A poster image of a news boy from a 1919 series of 'London characters' produced for the Underground Group – hence the good news about trains.*

**Fleet Street, 1920s**
*The street's busy character owed much to the constant activity surrounding printing and newspapers.*

The abolition of the newspaper tax in 1855 began a period of unprecedented growth in the British newspaper industry. By 1900, titles had multiplied, readership had expanded and the industry was on the verge of a revolution from which would emerge the mass-market newspaper industry we know today.

A growing appetite for newspapers among an increasingly literate public and the growing ambitions of a new generation of press barons, most prominently the brothers Alfred and Harold Harmsworth, later Lord Northcliffe (1865–1922) and the first Viscount Rothermere (1868–1940) respectively, was to propel British newspapers into an era of unprecedented wealth and influence. The herald of this revolution was Alfred Harmsworth's *Daily Mail*, founded in 1896, the first British newspaper to achieve sales of one million. It was followed by Arthur Pearson's *Daily Express*, founded in 1900, and the Harmsworth brothers' *Daily Mirror* in 1908, the latter exploiting the developments in printing that enabled pictures to become crucial in news reporting. The *Daily Graphic* in 1891 can claim to be the first British newspaper to print a photograph, but it was the *Daily Mirror* that really established the importance of photo-journalism in the British press.

The heart of this revolution was Fleet Street in the City, which by the outbreak of World War I had become synonymous with the British press (see below). The location of a major manufacturing industry in the centre of London was on the surface an anachronism, but the raw materials Fleet Street needed were as much information and opinions as reels of paper and gallons of ink. Fleet Street was perfectly located to tap London's three sources of establishment news – government, City business and the law courts. It was proximity to the legal precinct of the Temple in particular that had established the trades of bookselling, printing and publishing in the area from at least the 17th century. More significantly for the newspaper revolution, Fleet Street was the location of the Press Association, founded in 1868 to supply news to the provincial press, using the then-new technology of telegraphy. While Reuters, the major press agency for foreign news, remained in its original premises at the Royal Exchange, by 1910 Fleet Street was home to many other smaller concerns, such as the London News Agency and the Universal News Agencies. It was these that made Fleet Street a magnet for journalists and newspapers.

## THE NEWSPAPER WORLD

By the outbreak of war, the buildings in and around Fleet Street contained a myriad of offices, sometimes just a single room, housing the London offices of virtually all the British provincial papers. The international press also had a strong presence, with London offices or press agencies for, in particular, publications from the colonies, such as the *Hong Kong Daily Press* and the *Calcutta Statesman*. US papers such as the *New York Herald* took up a sizeable proportion of Fleet Street's office space, as did the editorial departments of special interest publications such as the *Methodist Recorder* and *The Sporting Life*. A typical building was Byron House, 85 Fleet Street, which, according to the 1917 Post Office Directory, housed offices of twenty-nine South African publications, eight from New Zealand, two provincial English and two Irish

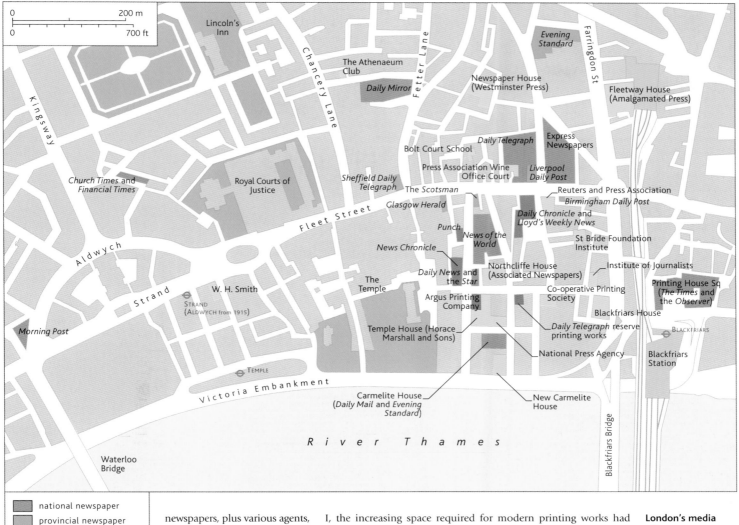

**London's media village, 1915**

The area around Fleet Street was dominated by newspapers, news agencies and the printing industry.

newspapers, plus various agents, advertising artists, 'newspaper representatives', paper agents, journalists and a phrenologist.

For publications printed in Fleet Street, space requirements were more than just an office and a telegraph. The building of the Embankment and the subsequent demolition of a City Corporation gasworks had opened up land to the south of Fleet Street, and it was here that the Harmsworth papers established a colony of printing works and editorial offices, moving to 24 Tudor Street in 1893. As their empire expanded, the Harmsworths expanded into Carmelite Street, where both the *Daily Mail* and the *Daily Mirror* were launched. The *Mail*'s immediate success led in 1899 to the opening of a huge new building, Carmelite House, which housed both offices and printing works, US-style, and incorporated the latest technology in the form of US presses for the printers and telegraphic rooms for the journalists. It was from Carmelite House that Alfred Harmsworth ran his publishing empire, which in 1905 expanded to include the *Observer*, and in 1908 *The Times*. *The Times* was typical of the older generation of British papers in that it was written and printed at single premises within the City, in this case Printing House Square in Blackfriars. By the outbreak of World War

I, the increasing space required for modern printing works had begun a process of separation, with printing migrating elsewhere. In 1912, Amalgamated Press, the periodicals branch of the Harmsworth empire, built a new editorial office in Farringdon Street, within reach of Fleet Street, but production was moved to a new printing works at Sumner Street in Southwark.

Fleet Street's dominance rested not just on newspapers and press agencies, but also on the host of supporting trades and services clustered around them: advertising agencies, printers, photographers, paper merchants, type-founders, and also cartoonists such as the Australian Will Dyson, whose powerful cartoons helped establish the left-wing *Daily Herald* in 1912.

Societies, pubs and clubs also formed part of the journalistic infrastructure, including the legendary wine bar El Vino, which opened at 47 Fleet Street in 1913. Perhaps the most significant of the supporting firms was the distributors W. H. Smith, which undertook to collect newspapers from the printers, parcel them up at premises in the Strand and deliver them by rail to a network of distributing centres. Equally significant were two technical education institutions, St Bride's Institute, founded in 1893, and the Bolt Court School, rebuilt in 1912. At a time of fundamental changes in printing technology, these schools equipped London's printers, engravers, compositors and typographers to keep pace with the transformation of their industry. **CR**

# LEISURE & THE WEST END

Better transport meant the West End widened its appeal. Women and men of all classes began to enjoy its variety theatres, department stores, cinemas and popular restaurants.

***Alhambra Theatre programme, June 1912***
*This large variety theatre in Leicester Square had begun life as a Victorian music hall. By 1912 it catered to a respectable West End crowd.*

Edwardian London lay at the heart of an empire at the height of its wealth and power. Imperial trade and administration had created tens of thousands of white-collar jobs, and with them a burgeoning middle class and a growing number of shop and office workers with middle-class aspirations. With more disposable income and leisure time, Londoners were eager to enjoy the good things in life.

Nowhere were good things more readily available than in the West End – which offered countless opportunities to consume and to be entertained. London's growing population provided a ready market, and a well-integrated transport system brought pleasure-seekers into the West End and took them safely home again.

It was the age of the great department store, and those of the West End embodied all London's confidence and prosperity. Some, like Harrods and Whiteleys, metamorphosed into purpose-built palaces, while others, like Swan & Edgar's, were embellished with extensive additions and alterations. With often over a hundred departments, these were vast emporia offering every item and service the middle classes could desire. Aimed particularly at women – and reflecting their increasing social emancipation – these stores were like female gentlemen's clubs, providing places where women could go out alone or meet friends.

The arrival of Selfridges on Oxford Street in 1909, with its US retail methods, revolutionized shopping in London. Goods were

**Theatres and cinemas**
The two traditional theatre streets were the Strand and Haymarket. Cinemas extended the entertainment district to Tottenham Court Road and Oxford Street.

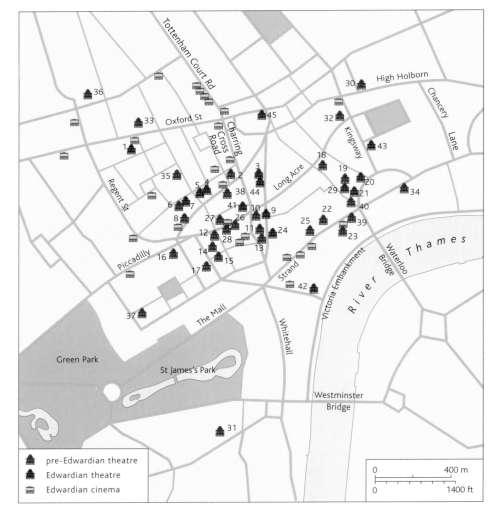

1. Palladium
2. Palace
3. Ambassadors
4. Queen's
5. Apollo
6. Windmill
7. Globe
8. Lyric
9. New
10. Wyndham's
11. Duke of York's
12. Prince of Wales'
13. Garrick
14. Comedy
15. Theatre Royal, Haymarket
16. Criterion
17. Her Majesty's
18. Royal Opera
19. Theatre Royal, Covent Garden
20. Aldwych
21. Waldorf
22. Vaudeville
23. Savoy
24. London Coliseum
25. Royal Adelphi
26. Alhambra
27. Daly's
28. Empire
29. Gaiety
30. Globe
31. Imperial
32. Kingsway
33. Princess's
34. Royal Strand
35. Royalty
36. St George's Hall
37. St James's
38. Shaftesbury
39. Terry's
40. Lyceum
41. London Hippodrome
42. Playhouse
43. Stoll Opera House
44. St Martin's
45. New Prince's

pre-Edwardian theatre
Edwardian theatre
Edwardian cinema

0    400 m
0    1400 ft

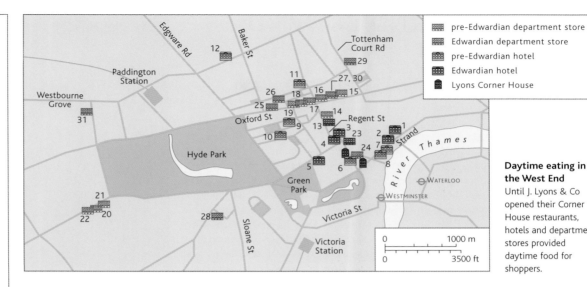

1. Waldorf Hotel, 1908/9
2. Strand Palace, 1909
3. Regent Palace Hotel, 1915
4. Piccadilly Hotel, 1908/9
5. Ritz, 1906
6. Carlton Hotel
7. Savoy Hotel
8. Hotel Cecil
9. Claridge's Hotel
10. Connaught Hotel
11. Langham Hotel
12. Great Central Hotel
13. Dickins & Jones
14. Liberty's
15. Bourne & Hollingsworth
16. Peter Robinson
17. John Lewis
18. D. H. Evans
19. Marshall & Snelgrove
20. Barker's
21. Derry & Toms
22. Pontings
23. Swan & Edgar
24. Burberry's, Haymarket, 1912
25. Selfridges, 1909
26. Debenham and Freebody's, 1909
27. Waring and Gillow's, Wigmore Street, 1909
28. Harrod's, Brompton Street, new building 1905
29. Heal's, Tottenham Court Road, rebuilt 1914–16
30. Mappin & Webb, 158–162 Oxford Street, 1908
31. Whiteley's, Queensway, new building 1911

**Daytime eating in the West End**
Until J. Lyons & Co opened their Corner House restaurants, hotels and department stores provided daytime food for shoppers.

displayed in well-lit, open displays with clear prices, and customers were encouraged to browse. Shoppers were welcomed to enjoy the warmth and atmosphere of luxury. Shopping as a leisure activity had arrived.

By day, shoppers and office workers were catered for by department-store luncheon and tea rooms and by tea shops like those of the ABC (Aerated Bread Company), the BTT (British Tea Table Company) and J. Lyons & Co. The first Lyons' Corner House restaurant opened in 1909, providing good-value light refreshments in surroundings where respectable women could eat unaccompanied (see below).

Eating out for pleasure became increasingly common, aided by a growing emphasis on the evening meal to suit changing work patterns, increased social freedoms for women, reduced space in mansion flats and less domestic help. Mixed dining out, and in particular supper parties in restaurants, took hold. The wealthy ate in grand establishments like Simpsons in the Strand and Pagani's in Great Portland Street, or in the new hotels, the Ritz and the Waldorf. Theatre restaurants such as the Criterion were also popular. European restaurants in Soho and the area north of Oxford Street provided for those of a more bohemian bent.

Great improvements in rail and sea transport had made travel – at least among the wealthy – increasingly popular. Visitors flocked to London, and hotels such as the Ritz and the Regent Palace, full of marble and crystal opulence, were built to satisfy their needs.

## THEATRES & CINEMAS

It was during this period that theatre-going, once the preserve of the wealthy, became affordable. 'Variety', a more respectable form of music hall, provided spectacular entertainment for the middle classes. Giant new 'palaces of variety' such as the London Hippodrome and the Coliseum joined converted music halls like the Alhambra and Empire in Leicester Square (see left).

Edwardian Londoners in search of a night out went to flamboyant new theatres around Shaftesbury Avenue and the Strand. With seats available for all pockets and programmes designed to end in

time for the last trains, they provided amusement for lords and shop girls alike. The West End had become 'theatreland'.

Cinemas too became an established feature of the West End. After their first appearance in London in the 1890s, moving pictures rapidly caught the public imagination. Purpose-built cinemas spread through the West End, particularly around Oxford Street and Tottenham Court Road. With tickets costing as little as threepence, cinemas provided entertainment for all in luxurious surroundings. Their appeal was shown by the number of new cinemas built in the West End between 1907 and 1914 – at least thirty-four.

By the outbreak of World War I, the West End we know today was established. It was no longer the focus of the aristocratic Season or a predominantly male preserve. It had become a Mecca of delights for all who had money and leisure time to spend. It was a place where the classes had begun to mingle, where all could find goods and entertainment to suit their pockets and where one man's – or one woman's – money was as good as the next's. **JH**

**Lyons Corner House**
*The first Lyons Corner House opened in 1909 in Coventry Street. The huge restaurant was instantly popular. A second opened in the Strand in 1915.*

# 'PAINT RUN MAD':
# MODERN ART

Avant-garde art movements caused sensations in Edwardian London. British artists looked for new subjects in the streets of Camden Town and welcomed the machine age.

At the turn of the 20th century, most Londoners had never come into contact with French Impressionism, let alone Post-Impressionism. Yet by 1914, all the avant-garde movements of the early 20th century art world had become widely known through a series of controversial exhibitions that had provoked extensive and often outraged press coverage. It was a period in which influences from Europe and the United States converged in London; where ragtime could be heard for the first time in England; and where the bohemianism of Europe was translated into the art societies, groups and clubs of London.

The New English Art Club (NEAC) had been formed in 1886, influenced by the forward-looking painters of France. More conservative in their approach than their French counterparts, the NEAC artists nevertheless referred to themselves as the 'London Impressionists' at a Goupil Gallery exhibition of 1889. A prominent member of the group, Walter Sickert (1860–1942), dissatisfied with the provincialism of the group, broke away to form the Fitzroy Street Group (1907–11) and subsequently the Camden Town Group (1911–14), both named simply by their locations – they rented studios at 19 Fitzroy Street and lived in Camden Town repectively. Their works, which used strong colour and explored the formal qualities of painting, were informed by the influences of both the Impressionists and the Post-Impressionists.

**Mornington Crescent, Camden Town Group**
*An impressionist view from the artist's window, painted by Spencer Gore in 1911.*

Impressionist artworks were first shown in London in 1905, but their impact was not widely felt until an exhibition entitled 'Manet and the Post-Impressionists' opened at the Grafton Galleries in the

winter of 1910. 'On or about December 1910 human character changed', wrote Virginia Woolf about the impact of the exhibition. The London press erupted in a series of bemused, outraged and derisory articles. 'There are more shocks to the square yard at the exhibition of the Post-Impressionists of France, at the Grafton Galleries', wrote a reporter in the *Daily Mirror*, 'than at any previous show in England. It is paint run mad.' The Chelsea Arts Club staged a satirical exhibition of pastiches entitled 'Septule and Racinists' to ridicule the movement.

## THE IMPACT OF FUTURISM

If the Post-Impressionists caused a stir in the sensibilities of the metropolis, the arrival of Filippo Tommaso Marinetti (1876–1944) and the Futurists at the Sackville Gallery in 1912 caused outrage. With radical images that extolled and celebrated a 'new machine age', performances of phonetic poetry and lectures by Marinetti, as Jacob Epstein recalled, 'with true Fascist impertinence they went from city to city spreading themselves and their silly gospel.' Cartoonists had a field day, papers and periodicals responded with outrage: 'The whole thing is so patently and pathetically misguided,' wrote C. H. Collins in the *Saturday Review*, 'that one simply does not know where to start.' Yet for all the outrage, many journals, such as *New Age*, explored the new movements seriously. Furthermore, Futurism influenced members of the growing London avant-garde, such as C. R. W. Nevinson, dubbed the 'English Futurist'.

**The New Bedford Music Hall**

*Painted by Walter Sickert in 1905. The dark palette and everyday, working-class subject matter gave Sickert's paintings a modern, ambiguous and controversial edge.*

The modern English artists who had orchestrated the exhibitions, Roger Fry (1866–1934) and Clive Bell (1881–1964), organized the Grafton Gallery and encouraged avant-garde influences from Europe. With other artists, including Duncan Grant, they formed the Bloomsbury Group, although their first formative group of like-minded artists named themselves the 'Neo-Primitives'. In 1913, the Omega Workshops were set up at Fitzroy Square by Fry and his co-directors, Grant and Vanessa Bell. Its aim was to create high-quality new design and to unite the English

*Blast* was called), 'LONDON IS NOT A PROVINCIAL TOWN. We will allow Wonder Zoos. But we do not want the GLOOMY VICTORIAN CIRCUS in Piccadilly Circus. IT IS PICCADILLY'S CIRCUS!'

World War I swept away much of the idealism of early Modernism, and Vorticism did not survive the conflict, which saw the death of its chief theorist, T. E. Hulme. Nonetheless, in the brief period leading up to the war, London had exploded with artistic radicalism, and joined the forefront of modern art alongside Paris and Rome. The effect of this radicalism was felt throughout the

**Artists' London**

Camden and Euston became artists' areas as painters found cheap lodgings and inspiration in their often dingy surroundings.

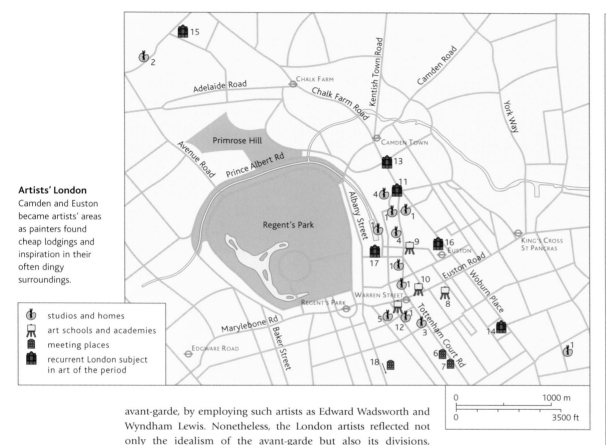

- 👤 studios and homes
- 🎨 art schools and academies
- 🏛 meeting places
- 🏚 recurrent London subject in art of the period

1. Walter Sicket
   6 Mornington Crescent, 1905
   8 Fitzroy Street, 1905–07
   247 Hampstead Road, 1908
   31 Augustus Road, 1909
   209 Hampstead Road, 1909
   Harrington Square, 1911–12
   24 Red Lion Square, 1914
2. Robert Bevan & Stanislawa de Karlowska
   14 Adamson Road
3. Harold Gilman
   14 Maple Street, 1908–12
4. Spencer Frederick Gore
   31 Mornington Crescent, 1909–12
   2 Houghton Place, 1912–14
5. Omega Workshop
   33 Fitzroy Street, 1913–19
6. Fitzroy Tavern
   16 Charlotte Street
7. La Tour Eiffel
   12 Percy Street
8. The Slade School
   University College, Gower Street, 1871–
9. Rowlandson House
   Sickert's Art School
   140 Hampstead Road, 1910–14
10. Euston Road School
    12 Fitzroy Street, 1937–38
    314/316 Euston Road, 1938–39
11. Mornington Crescent
12. Fitzroy Street
13. Bedford Music-Hall
    Camden High Street
14. Russell Square
15. Belsize Park
16. Euston Station
17. Cumberland Market
18. The Cave of the Golden Calf

0 — 1000 m
0 — 3500 ft

avant-garde, by employing such artists as Edward Wadsworth and Wyndham Lewis. Nonetheless, the London artists reflected not only the idealism of the avant-garde but also its divisions, spawning alliances, groups and coteries. Splits and division characterize the period from 1910 to 1914 and reflect real ideological uncertainty and the rapid pace of change in attitudes towards art.

capital and exercised a profound influence on taste and design for years to come. **MB**

## THE VORTICISTS

Led by Wyndham Lewis (1882–1957), the Rebel Art Centre was set up in opposition to the Bloomsbury Group, effectively ousting Fry as the prime mover in the London avant-garde. With the most radical British artists in support, Lewis positioned himself as leader of the Vorticist movement, centred in London. Formed in 1914, the Vorticists were the English response to the Futurism, Expressionism and Cubism of Italy, Germany and France respectively. Their bold machine aesthetic approached a new visual abstraction, in keeping with the pace and idealism of the modern world. This short-lived but influential movement organized an exhibition at the Doré Galleries, 35 New Bond Street, and produced two copies of a radical periodical, *Blast*, which included drawings by the artists and writing by Lewis, Ezra Pound and T. S. Eliot. 'WE WHISPER IN YOUR EAR A GREAT SECRET,' declared the puce monster (as

### THE CAVE OF THE GOLDEN CALF

The Cave of the Golden Calf was England's first 'Artists' Cabaret Club'. It opened in 1912 in the basement of a cloth warehouse off Regent Street. Its creator was Frida Strindberg, a wealthy bohemian, who wanted an avant-garde rival to the nearby Café Royal. She commissioned artists to decorate the room, among them Jacob Epstein, Eric Gill and Wyndham Lewis. The model was the Kaberett Fledermaus in Strindberg's native Vienna.

The Cave went into liquidation in 1914, but its influence lived on. It was a 'superheated Vorticist garden of gesticulating figures', remembered Osbert Sitwell, 'dancing and talking while the rhythm of the primitive forms of ragtime throbbed'.

# SUFFRAGETTE CITY

The Votes for Women campaign became centred in London in 1903. The suffragettes made headlines through spectacular staged parades and, eventually, militant action.

By 1900, women had been campaigning for the right to vote in parliamentary elections for over half a century. Fifty years of peaceful protest had, however, failed to arouse enough interest in the suffrage movement to provoke reform, and women, along with prisoners, the insane and less well-off, continued to be excluded from the parliamentary process.

In 1903, the 'votes for women' campaign was energized by the creation of the Women's Social and Political Union (WSPU). Founded in Manchester by Emmeline Pankhurst (1858–1928) and her daughters, the WSPU aimed to wake the nation to the cause of women's suffrage through 'Deeds not Words'. The decision to relocate the headquarters of the WSPU to London in 1906 transformed the movement and, for the next eight years, the fight to win the vote became a highly public and at times violent struggle.

The WSPU burst onto the streets of London at a time when women played little part in public life, their role being firmly centred on the home and family life. The Pankhursts stimulated a spirit of revolt that directly challenged this exclusion by bringing women to the forefront of public life. By taking their campaign to the streets the suffragettes attracted maximum publicity for their cause. (Supporters of the WSPU were known as 'suffragettes', while those who opposed militancy were 'suffragists'.) Recognizable by their purple, white and green colours, they became a familiar sight in central London. Street processions were announced by brass bands playing marching songs; meetings and events were publicized by poster parades and pavement chalking parties. The move to the political heart of the nation enabled suffragettes to maintain a constant presence in Whitehall, petitioning Downing Street, heckling MPs and chaining themselves to government buildings.

*Marches to Women's Sunday, 1908*
*A handbill issued by suffragettes to show the start points of the seven marches to Hyde Park (marked by letters) and the twenty platforms for speeches within the park.*

*Suffragette battles with police on Black Friday, 1910*
*Women in a deputation to the House of Commons were beaten and manhandled by policemen.*

A London base raised the campaign's international profile and provided opportunities for staging spectacular set-piece demonstrations. Women's Sunday, the first 'monster meeting' to be held by the WSPU, brought suffragettes from all over the country in June 1908 to march in seven different processions through central London to Hyde Park (see left and above right). Demonstrators arrived on specially chartered trains from over seventy towns and, on reaching Hyde Park, were addressed by more than eighty speakers. The highly choreographed demonstration attracted a crowd of up to 300,000, drawn by the spectacle of the delegates dressed in the suffragette tricolour and carrying some 700 embroidered banners. 'Never,' reported a *Daily Chronicle* journalist, 'has so vast a throng gathered in London to witness a parade of political forces.'

The coronation of George V (r. 1910–36) three years later

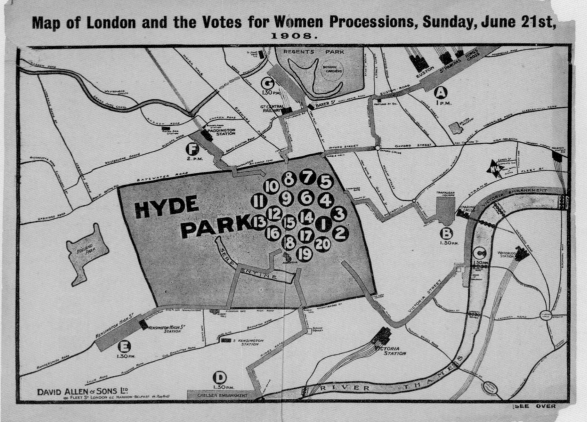

Map of London and the Votes for Women Processions, Sunday, June 21st, 1908.

inspired the WSPU to organize its own pageant. The four-mile-long suffragette Coronation Procession through central London culminated in a rally at the Royal Albert Hall and involved over 60,000 delegates from both regional and international suffrage groups dressed in national and historical costume.

The suffragette campaign was masterminded from WSPU headquarters, initially established at 4 Clement's Inn, the Strand, then from 1912 at Lincoln's Inn, Kingsway. Both salaried and volunteer office staff organized fund-raising events, public meetings and demonstrations and produced the weekly newspaper *Votes for Women*, which, by 1909, had a circulation of 22,000. The WSPU established ninety branches throughout Great Britain, but London remained the chief area of support with a total of thirty-four local offices.

In 1910, the publishing arm of the Union, The Woman's Press, moved to 156 Charing Cross Road, now the site of the Centrepoint building. The premises were chosen for their proximity to Oxford Street and included a shop selling a range of suffragette merchandise including badges, books, postcards and stationery. The commercial success of the business led to the opening of nineteen similar shops in the London area.

## A CHANGE OF TACTICS

The WSPU was a broad movement, but its most active members were young, single women with independent resources and few domestic responsibilities. Such women had more time to dedicate to the campaign as well as the courage and spirit necessary to undertake militant action that might lead to arrest. Over 1000 suffragettes, including Emmeline Pankhurst and her daughters Christabel, Sylvia and Adela, received prison sentences for their activism. Most were sent to Holloway Prison in north London where their protests continued as hunger strikes. The authorities responded with brutal force-feeding.

From 1912, the WSPU shifted the focus of its campaign to attacks on property and the disruption of public life. An organized window-smashing campaign by 150 suffragettes in May 1912 devastated London's shopping district and caused Emmeline Pankhurst to remark that the hour-long protest 'will long be remembered'. Suffragette attacks on works of art, including the slashing of the *Rokeby Venus* at the National Gallery, resulted in the closure of many London art galleries and museums to female visitors. Militancy often provoked confrontation with the police and public, undignified scuffles and abuse.

The outbreak of World War I brought an immediate suspension of action as the suffragettes threw themselves into supporting the British war effort. The tactics employed by the WSPU had failed to achieve parliamentary reform but, by taking their fight to the streets and making London the focus of their campaign, the Pankhursts had invigorated the movement and inspired in their supporters a confidence and independence that enabled them to challenge the male-run society in which they lived. Their work eased the way for women to take a more active and public role during the war – a role that was finally acknowledged with the grant of the parliamentary vote to propertied women over the age of thirty in 1918.

**BC**

*Women's Sunday, Hyde Park, Sunday 21 June 1908*
*Annie Kenney makes her way through the crowds to speak from platform no. 3.*

## THE 'YOUNG HOT BLOODS'

In 1907, a number of young suffragette militants fiercely loyal to Emmeline and Christabel Pankhurst formed a secretive group dedicated to carrying out 'danger duty'. These so-called 'Young Hot Bloods' (YHBs) were used to lead protests and organize parliamentary demonstrations and harassment of government ministers. Membership was limited to those under the age of thirty and included Elsie Howey, the daughter of a rector, Vera Wentworth, a former shopworker, and Jessie Kenney who, at twenty-one, had became the WSPU's youngest full-time organizer.

As career militants, the Young Hot Bloods regularly faced imprisonment and suffered with courage the pain and violence of force-feeding following hunger strikes. Many suffered long-term damage to their health as a consequence.

*Vera Wentworth and Elsie Howey, on their release from Holloway prison, September 1908.*

# LONDON AT WAR

World War I jolted London's sense of stability. Food shortages, aerial bombs and anti-alien feeling heightened fears and shook the capital's self-confidence.

**'Gunweek' in Trafalgar Square, 1918 (detail)**
*The Square was transformed into a mock battleground to raise funds for the war effort: Londoners were urged to 'Feed the Guns with War Bonds'.*

It is impossible to exaggerate the impact of World War I on London. 'The war to end all wars' diverted every aspect of the capital's life towards the war effort and left London a more self-consciously nationalistic city, but also a more cosmopolitan one. The war and its aftermath brought state regulations into daily life, working men and women into the electorate, new factory jobs and, less happily, Londoners' first experience of aerial bombing.

When war was declared in August 1914, Londoners displayed a genuinely popular enthusiasm for what was perceived to be a just cause. The central Recruiting Office at Scotland Yard was overwhelmed by volunteers, and by Christmas more than one million men had chosen to enlist. Most were in belligerent mood, believing that the Germans would soon be 'taught a lesson'. However, three years later, when the slaughter on the Western Front had cost many thousands of lives, London had become a city under martial law, its streets full of men in uniform, its night-time lights darkened and the sound of anti-aircraft guns constantly in the air.

War brought a new sense of Britishness, with dire consequences for London's long-established community of Germans. Before 1914, around 40,000 Germans lived in London, one of the largest foreign communities, particularly around Charlotte Street, north of Oxford Street, Leman Street in Aldgate and Peckham. German bakers, butchers and hairdressers were found all over London and the hotel orchestras in central London were largely made up of German musicians. On the outbreak of war, all Germans became 'enemy aliens' and the target for mob violence. German butchers in Smithfield market were attacked, bakeries had their windows smashed and worse. In Hammersmith, Cyril Rolph recorded: 'My brother Harold was chased home from a Fulham Palace Road bus-stop by an angry mob because he had tried, on his way home from school, to stop some children throwing lighted matches into the open basement windows of a German hairdresser's shop. Any firm with a name that was not obviously British was in danger

from the mob. Long-cherished names like Gluckstein were painted out and succeeded by impersonal ones like The Premier Stores.'

Anti-German feeling reached a peak in May 1917 with the sinking of the liner *Lusitania*, with heavy loss of life. In the East End, Russian and Jewish bakeries also came under attack, in the mistaken belief that they were connected with the hated 'Hun'. German men were interned at Olympia and Stratford as potential spies.

The other group of foreigners thrown into the spotlight by the war was the Belgians. At the start of the war, 400,000 Belgian and northern French refugees had fled across the Channel to London. Although the war was ostensibly being fought on their behalf, the refugees were not universally welcomed, again as Rolph reports:

> The custom grew quite rapidly of denegrating them as lazy, dirty, avaricious and immoral. … It was said above all that they would compete with the British in the labour market, which was odd since the British labour market seemed to need workers of every conceivable kind to replace the millions of young men being taken away for the armed forces.

Many found a more congenial welcome in Soho where the number of Belgian patisseries, cafes and bars tripled.

## THE HOME FRONT

Most aspects of daily life were affected by the all-embracing DORA (Defence of the Realm Act) regulations. Food rationing was not introduced until 1918, by which time the effects of the German U-boat blockade of shipping were beginning to be felt. Initially only sugar was rationed, but restrictions soon extended to meat and butter. Alcohol came under state control early in the war when restrictions on drinking hours in pubs were introduced. At Enfield, the location of London's most important munitions factories, the government took control of all licensed premises.

London's manufacturing capacity was almost entirely turned over to supplying armaments. The three royal ordnance factories – Woolwich, Enfield and Waltham Abbey – multiplied in size, Woolwich Arsenal's workforce expanding from 8500 to 75,000, making it the largest factory complex in Europe. By 1917, the Woolwich workforce included 24,719 women (before 1914 no women had been employed) and a football team, which moved from Woolwich to Highbury in Islington during the war years.

Elsewhere in London the war effort brought new industrial activity. At Chiswick the long-established Thorneycroft boatyard was adapted to make

**Zeppelin, 8 September 1915**
*A crayon drawing by Edwin Bale of the view from his window as he watched a Zeppelin airship caught in searchlights.*

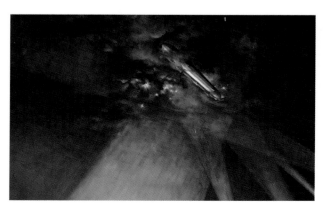

aircraft engines. At Silvertown in West Ham the chemical firm Mond Brunner took over a disused soda factory and transformed it into a production line of the high explosive TNT. The enterprise became notorious in the history of the local area in January 1917 when fifty tons of TNT exploded, destroying all the houses in the surrounding streets.

The demands of the war effort were dramatically underlined by the influx of women into factory jobs. By 1914, there were already three million women workers in industry, but this figure soared during wartime. Most noticeable were the women in visible jobs, such as bus conductors, railway workers and window cleaners. The London General Omnibus Company employed 226 women in 1914, but 2832 by 1918. The granting of the vote to women over thirty in 1918 was seen as a 'reward' for their war effort, though in fact most of the work had been done by younger women.

The most terrifying novelty of World War I for Londoners was aerial bombing. The Germans initially used Zeppelins, long cigar-shaped airships, to bomb the capital (see below and left). In the early part of the war, the Zeppelins could operate at altitudes beyond the reach of fighter aircraft, and were thus almost invulnerable. The first attack on London occurred late at night in May 1915, when a lone Zeppelin scattered incendiary bombs on Stoke Newington and other areas of the East End. Seven people were killed and the raid provoked another outbreak of anti-German rioting. From May 1917 onwards, fighter aircraft outclassed the slow-moving Zeppelins, and they were replaced by Gotha bombers; their bombs caused more damage, and they were more difficult for ground-based anti-aircraft guns to destroy. Bombs killed 600 Londoners during World War I, but for all Londoners the bombing created an unprecedented climate of fear.     **CR**

**The seven Zeppelin raids on London**
*This map was drawn for* Sphere *magazine in 1919 as a record of London's recent ordeal from the air.*

# INTERWAR LONDON

The end of World War I brought a new mood to London. This was the age of machines and modernity: wireless, jazz and mass democracy. Londoners began to glimpse a new vision for their city, a cleaner, more hygienic, more efficient London, scientifically planned to make all its citizens happy.

London became significantly larger, doubling in size as new roads and railways extended the built-up area well beyond the old LCC boundaries. This not only represented a population increase, to 8.6 million by 1939, but also a shift from the inner city to the outer suburbs. By 1939 London had in effect become Greater London.

Many aspects of life were better organized. The city's transport was brought together under a strategic authority. An automatic telephone system transformed the way Londoners communicated. Electricity, the fuel of the future, made an impact on the landscape with large power stations and lines of marching pylons.

London began to feel cautiously modern. It may have lacked New York's skyscrapers, but it had red public phone boxes and an efficient tube map. Democracy seemed to be steering it away from the extremes of Bolshevism and Fascism erupting in other European capitals. London's path to modernity was through evolution rather than revolution.

Despite the growing influence of America on cultural and economic life, London remained a self-consciously British capital. It was still the proud heart of empire, the hub of a trading and communications network that stretched round the globe, bringing prosperity to all the fortunate nations within the British 'common wealth': at least, in theory.

**Nerves of the World, by C. R. W. Nevinson, 1929**
*Nevinson's view of Fleet Street, its telegraph wires quivering with movement.*

**Winter, by C. R. W. Nevinson, 1928**
*Nevinson presents London as a somewhat dour working city,*
*animated by its links to the sea and maritime trade.*

# EMPIRE REDEFINED: WEMBLEY 1924

The British Empire began to market itself as a great, global trading family. A giant, state-sponsored exhibition was held at Wembley to promote empire products and trade.

The years after World War I saw the British Empire adjusting to very changed world circumstances. The major political debate was how to redefine the relationship between Britain and its dominions, colonies and protectorates. The Imperial Conference of 1926 created a new brand for empire – the British Commonwealth of Nations – to which the dominions were freely associated. But the new body added fuel to the campaign for home rule in the remaining colonies, spearheaded by figures such as the charismatic leader of the Indian National Congress, Mahatma Gandhi.

In central London the empire's new constitution was reflected in new buildings, mostly between Trafalgar Square and Aldwych. Australia House, on one end of the Aldwych island site, had been designed in 1912 and was finally opened in 1918. The pre-war vision of Aldwych as a home for Dominion buildings was strengthened in 1930 with the opening of India House at the other end of the island. Along the Strand were the smaller New Zealand House and various Australian and South African trade agents. The two largest Dominion buildings were Canada House and South Africa House in Trafalgar Square, opened in 1935.

Parallel to the political debate was an economic one. Should the empire seek economic self-sufficiency by trading freely among its own members but repelling outsiders through import tariffs? Preferential treatment for certain imperial imports began to be enshrined in British law from 1919; the resulting boost to empire trade was reflected in the ever-increasing capacity and profitability of the London docks. The new King George V dock opened in 1921, the first built by the Port of London Authority. It was smaller than some of its Victorian predecessors, but it could accommodate larger ships, even the giant *Mauretania*, which docked in 1939.

## THE EMPIRE EXHIBITION

More visible in daily life was the official encouragement to 'buy British'. In 1926 the Merchandise Marks Act made it illegal to display goods without giving their country of origin: 'British made' and 'foreign made' became familiar labels. The Empire Marketing Board (1926–33) mounted poster campaigns, shop displays, films, 'empire shopping week' promotions and publicity stunts. Perhaps most memorable, however, was the British Empire Exhibition at Wembley in 1924.

The 1924 exhibition was the first with an overall political purpose: 'To strengthen the bonds that bind the Mother Nation to her Sister states and Daughter Nations.' To this end, the 87-hectare

**Nevinson poster, 1924**
C. R. W. Nevinson's bus poster promoted the second season of the British Empire Exhibition in 1925.

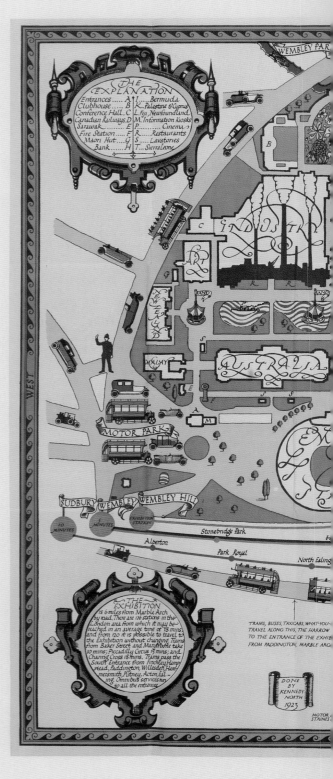

(216-acre) site housed pavilions from all countries of the empire, a British Government pavilion, palaces of Arts, Engineering and Industry, a Civic Hall and more. Popular attractions included a large amusement park and a huge stadium, far bigger than anything hitherto seen in Britain. The stadium was inaugurated with the 1923 FA Cup final; the size of the crowds astonished everyone. During the exhibition the

stadium hosted concerts, services, a torchlight tattoo and a rodeo. It was then given over to football and greyhound racing.

The 1924 exhibition was a popular triumph, attracting 6.5 million visitors by the end of the summer. Such was the success that it was decided to run a second season in 1925 (see left). The government also deemed it a success in modernizing the relationship between government and citizens. Apart from the boost it had

given to empire trade, the exhibition had also seen the release of the GPO's first pictorial commemorative stamps, the first royal wireless (radio) broadcast and the first concerted effort by the government to explain to its citizens exactly what it did. It had attracted worldwide publicity and visitors from over the globe. Despite its success, the exhibition did not, of course, silence the calls for political equality from the remaining colonies and dependencies. **CR**

*British Empire Exhibition*

This map shows the Wembley site in 1924 with its modern, efficient transport links.

# METROLAND: THE SPREAD OF THE SUBURBS

Suburban growth doubled interwar London's size. House builders, building societies and railway companies combined to create new places to live for modern-minded citizens.

**Laggard Leaves, 1925**
*A painting by Harry Bush of his back garden at Queensland Avenue, Merton. Known as 'the painter of suburbia', Bush exhibited this painting at the Royal Academy in 1925.*

**The birth of Greater London**
By 1939 London had spread far beyond the LCC boundaries, set fifty years earlier.

London's suburban growth between the wars was one of the most distinctive and debated aspects of the city's progress. It marked the city out from other European capitals and, for supporters like Harold Clunn, was a cause of pride: 'The suburbs of London can justly claim to be a hundred years ahead of those of the majority of the capital cities of the world. ... Those of Paris are commonplace by comparison.'

The scale of suburban growth was extraordinary. 'Ten of the districts in the outer ring of London have more than doubled their population since 1921', noted Clunn in 1935. 'Of these, Dagenham, which includes the district known as Becontree, easily tops the list; from a parish of 9,000 inhabitants in 1921 it has increased by 879 per cent and has blossomed into a great town of 100,000 inhabitants. Hendon follows Dagenham with an increase of 101 per cent from 57,529 to 115,682.'

The two districts mentioned by Clunn represent the twin engines of the boom. Becontree was the creation of the London County Council (LCC). This monster estate of 26,000 houses built on the Dagenham marshes represented a great leap forward in the LCC's drive to raise the standard of living of London's workers. Hendon represented the private developer: although it had an LCC estate at Burnt Oak, it was essentially a suburb of private housing.

Hendon was one of the north London suburbs that came to be broadly known as 'Metroland', even though, strictly speaking, the term only applied to those districts served by the Metropolitan railway. Metroland was created by a triangle of shared interests: those of house builders, building societies and transport companies. All three benefited from the spread of house-buying and commuting habits. Building firms like F&C Costain of Harrow and John Laing & Son of Mill Hill would buy plots of land and erect houses that would then be bought by London's families, using the new financial device of the mortgage.

By the late 1930s, Laing's had built nine estates in north London, and had a permanent 'new home exhibition' in Oxford Street and a full-size show home outside King's Cross station. Its cheapest houses, at Elstree, were priced at £545; the most expensive were at Hatch End, where the four-bedroom, detached 'Washington' type was priced at £1675. The Metroland model was followed in the Kent and Surrey suburbs served by the Southern Electric Railway Company. Southern Electric published an annual guidebook, *Southern Homes*, which described the delights of the southern commuter-belt districts, while advertisements from local firms such as George Wates of Streatham tempted prospective homebuyers.

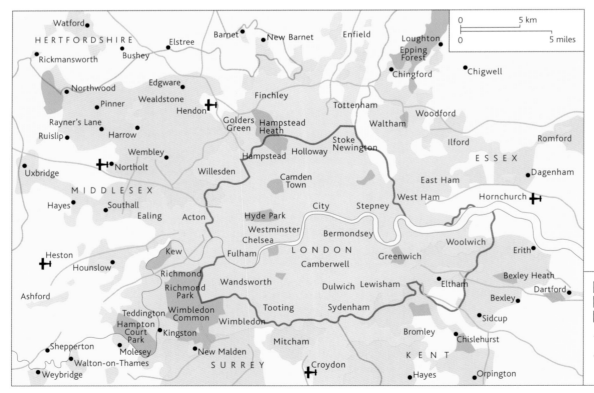

0 ____ 5 km
0 ____ 5 miles

|  | built-up area, c.1920 |
| --- | --- |
|  | urban expansion by 1938 |
|  | public open spaces |
|  | new arterial roads built 1918–38 |
|  | LCC boundary |
| ✛ | aerodrome |

## SUBURBAN LIVING

Good rail links to the City were a key factor in the location of the estates built by the developers. By contrast, the LCC's Becontree estate was badly served. Early newcomers found that what they had gained in standards of living they had lost in the inconvenience of travel. 'I ended up by cycling the fourteen-mile round trip to and from work', recalled one man whose job was on the Isle of Dogs. 'I had to get up at 5 o'clock in the morning every day and I didn't finish work until 9 o'clock at night, so it was quite an ordeal.' He, like many Becontree residents, eventually found work closer to home when the Ford Motor Company built its huge factory in Dagenham at the end of the 1920s.

In other ways, the Becontree housing was superior to the private schemes – or so claimed the LCC architects. They pointed to the generous layout of their developments, with broad avenues and parkways. Their houses were designed to look unpretentious, in contrast to the much derided half-timbering of the mass house builders. Inside, LCC architects kept faith with the Arts and Crafts ideal of the functional cottage. The main power was often coal rather than electricity, and the houses had sculleries and parlours rather than kitchens and lounges. However, they all had indoor plumbing, and to many new settlers the improvement was tremendous. 'As a child I used to read about pantries in books', recalled one Becontree resident. 'I remember I wrote to my friend back in Poplar. "We've got a beautiful house with flowers in the garden, and inside there's a bathroom and a pantry." It sounded so posh!'

In Metroland, electric appliances were part of the new lifestyle, as was modern, comfortable furniture. The ideal was an easily cleaned, modern room that reflected the taste of the owner. Manufacturers gaily plundered all styles of English design to meet the new demand. Arts and Crafts ideals turned into stained-glass windows with galleons; English Georgian into crinoline lady lampshades; Jacobean into 'Jacobethan' gate-leg tables and panelling. The new suburban householders bought them all, and by the late 1930s, even the rounded lines of machine-age modernism could be found in the front rooms of Wembley.

*Modern glass bowl, 1933*
Made at the Whitefriars glassworks in Harrow, this glass bowl cost 45 shillings, making it a smart but expensive purchase. It is typical of the clean, modern home furnishings seen as desirable for suburban living.

It was easy to ridicule the suburbs and their aspirations. The suburbanite became a new London type, middlebrow and unadventurous. 'Each house contains the same lounge hall', mused H. V. Morton in 1926, 'the same Jacobean dining-suite, the same (to all appearances) dear little wife.' It was even easier for disdain to become disapproval, on the grounds that suburban housing was a blot on the landscape and a threat to the countryside. Nevertheless, the growth of the suburbs helped redefine London as a city.  **CR**

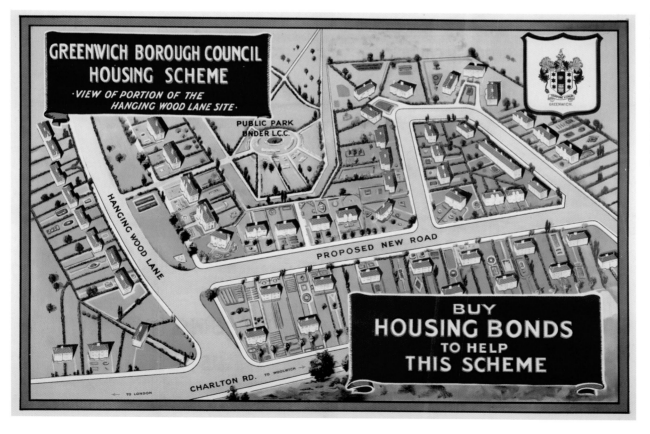

*Housing poster: plans for a council estate in Greenwich 1920*
This poster for a characteristic cottage estate scheme publicizes 6 per cent Housing Bonds, issued by the LCC in 1920 to raise funds for house building.

GREENWICH BOROUGH COUNCIL HOUSING SCHEME
·VIEW OF PORTION OF THE HANGING WOOD LANE SITE·

PUBLIC PARK UNDER L.C.C.

HANGING WOOD LANE

PROPOSED NEW ROAD

BUY HOUSING BONDS TO HELP THIS SCHEME

CHARLTON RD. TO WOOLWICH →

← TO LONDON

# ON THE TOWN:
# THE WEST END REVAMPED

As London expanded at the edges, its centre became more glamourous. Regent Street was rebuilt. Bright young things thrilled at the excitements of stage, screen and nightclub.

**The new West End**
The revamp brought bigger blocks, larger shops and new building types such as multi-storey garages.

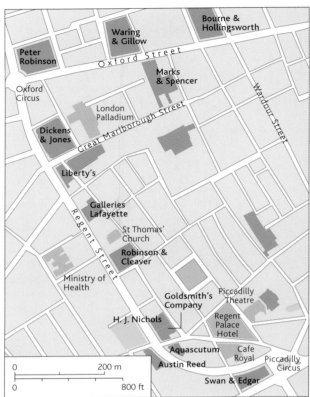

The West End began to reflect the Jazz Age. By day its buildings got more showy, to the despair of those who thought a capital city should display regularity and restraint. London had Roman trophies on its department stores, Egyptian palm trees on its cinemas and American zigzags on its office blocks. By night the West End was thronged with pleasure-seekers, more than ever before. Better transport drew audiences from all parts of London to the dance halls, super-cinemas and variety theatres.

The street that symbolized the West End's transformation was Regent Street, entirely rebuilt in the 1920s and formally reopened by George V in 1927. The old Regent Street was a creation of the early 19th century. Lined with shabbily picturesque stucco terraces,

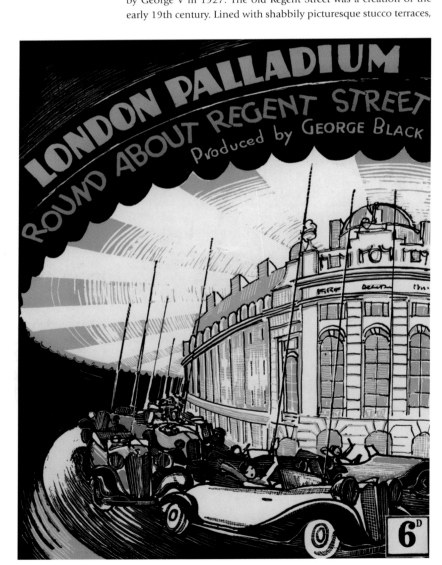

**Theatre programme, 1935**
Round About Regent Street *was a musical revue at the Palladium starring Teddy Knox.*

| | |
|---|---|
| | large stores |
| | cinemas & theatres |
| | new garages |

the domestic scale of its three- and four-storey buildings was inadequate for 20th-century shops. Modern retail demanded plate-glass windows, spacious showrooms and large eight-storey premises, preferably on an island block.

Rebuilding began in earnest in the early 1920s at the Oxford Circus end of the street. The land was owned by the Crown Estate, which laid down strict rules about the buildings to be erected. All were to have stone facings and be of a suitably dignified scale and style to match the street's overall scheme. The department store Liberty's obeyed the rules and rebuilt its Regent Street frontage with an imperial flavour, its facade topped by a frieze depicting Britannia receiving the glories of empire. Around the corner, the firm made a more defiantly English statement with a quaint, half-timbered 'Tudor' building.

The new Regent Street brought a sumptuous but democratic element to modern London. Traditional British retailers such as the men's outfitters Austin Reed were interspersed with US new-comers, such as the Ford Motor Company. The street retained its high-class shopping character, but the department stores and plate-glass window displays were free for all, and new developments included a 1400-seat cinema which opened in 1925. 'The new Regent Street', concluded the *Daily News* in 1927, 'does in a sense typify the spirit of the age – in its vitality and brilliance and audacity. It is more suited to the flashing bus and the rapid streams of polished motorcars than the old-fashioned coach and four.'

A year later, in December 1928, a magnificent tube station opened at the lower end of Regent Street. Designed to cope with

appeared in the West End before World War I but they now became larger in scale and far more extravagant. Unlike theatres, cinemas could flourish in the suburbs and attracting an audience into the West End meant 'super-cinemas' with something special.

The 2400-seater Regal at Marble Arch opened in November 1928 to gasps of astonishment at its fairyland interiors with glades of autumnal trees, Roman temples and starlit skies. It also had Europe's largest theatre organ and a carillon of bells. In the same month the old Empire Music Hall in Leicester Square reopened as the largest cinema in London with over 3000 seats and lavish interiors on a High Renaissance theme. The glossy all-black Odeon in Leicester Square, flagship of the Oscar Deutsch empire, opened in 1937 as a truly modernistic cathedral of dreams with its 27-metre- high (90-ft) tower and sensational interiors with mythical figures sweeping across the auditorium walls.

Despite competition from the silver screen, theatre continued to find an audience in the 1930s' West End. The Windmill Theatre in Soho unveiled its nude 'living statues'. The London Palladium stuck with variety (see left) and became the first home of Bud Flanagan and Chesney Allen's 'Crazy Gang' shows.

## NIGHTCLUB FRENZY

The changing character of London's West End continued into the night as Londoners of all classes danced into the small hours. The lifting of wartime restrictions through the replacement of the Defence of the Realm Act with the Licensing Act of 1921 led to what was described at the time as a nightclub frenzy. Many new clubs were opened in the West End, from the luxurious Ciro's, with its glass dance floor, to more bohemian affairs such as the Cave of Harmony, which was opened in Gower Street by the actress Elsa Lanchester. The Kit-Cat Club, 'the very stadium of nightclubs', in the Haymarket, had the largest dance floor and the most expensive cabaret shows: 'Everything is on the big scale. It is the dance club most favoured by Americans visiting London.'

The largest membership (over 10,000) was said to be at the London Club off Baker Street, which was where 'the big middle class goes to dine and dance and see a cabaret show and play billiards – girls as well as boys – on the club's forty tables.' The club was the brainchild of Scots entrepreneur Tom Gordon, who had been inspired to move into the London nightclub market by the thought of the hundreds of people in London who would like to have a night out but who could not afford an expensive club. 'He speedily discovered,' noted one commentator, 'that there are always new and undiscovered publics in this vast London of ours.'

Those who could not afford even the modest membership fees of the London Club also found entertainment in the new brighter West End. When the Welsh journalist Glyn Roberts came to London in the early 1930s he was struck by the crowds of largely Jewish young people sitting in Leicester Square's Corner House restaurant throughout the evening. 'I imagined when I first saw them that these people, so magnificently colourful and glossy and self-assured, must be very important and wealthy indeed – the women were so luxurious and the men so blasé. But I found out that they were really very poor; that they invaded the West End in their tens of thousands only twice a week or so; that they spent next to nothing.' London's West End had become a more truly democratic place, offering bright lights and glamour, cinemas, popular restaurants and dance halls to a wider range of Londoners than ever before. **CR**

**Tramway poster, 1927**
*Travel to and from the bright lights 'up West' was a common theme on transport posters. This one was designed by Leigh Breton Studios for LCC trams.*

fifty million passengers a year, the new Piccadilly Circus complex was a triumph of modern engineering, with eleven escalators, unprecedented in London's underground. It was also a triumphant expression of the new spirit of public service in transport provision in the world's wealthiest city. The station was lavish yet tasteful, with commercial window displays and educational elements in the form of a world map. It was luxuriously finished in marble, and followed the latest thinking on efficient design for public spaces.

## STAGE & SCREEN

The West End's glamour had always been tied up with its theatres. Now trams and trains could bring in new audiences from the suburbs, and theatrical impresarios began to think big. The 1920s began with the musical *Chu Chin Chow* breaking box-office records with an unprecedented five-year run. The showman Charles B. Cochran reinvented the revue and spared no expense on his annual shows at the Pavilion Theatre. Smart American musical comedies arrived along with American actor-stars. Tallulah Bankhead, Elsa Lanchester, Fred and Adele Astaire all added their celebrity to the West End's glittering appeal. By the 1920s glamour was moving from stage to screen. Purpose-built cinemas had

# NEW INDUSTRY
# & CORPORATIONS

London strengthened its position as Britain's centre of new industry in the interwar years. 'Made in London' now referred to modern household electrical goods as well as older products.

London was not immune to the depression that brought mass unemployment and real hardship to Britain between the wars, but it escaped relatively lightly. When unemployment peaked in 1932, London's rate was less than half the national average. Of the 3635 new factories that opened in Great Britain between 1932 and 1937, nearly half (1573) were located in Greater London. These factories accounted for two-fifths of all the new manufacturing jobs created in Britain over the period (see map, opposite).

London's ability to withstand hard times was explained by two things. First was the continued importance of imperial trade. This not only sustained the many commercial and manufacturing firms whose location depended on ease of access to London's docks, but also attracted US capital. The Ford Motor Company transferred its British manufacturing plant from Manchester to London in 1930 largely because of the ease with which it could enter, via London, Britain's overseas markets.

London's second advantage was its own large consumer market, the wealthiest in Europe. The house-building boom had created a new demand for modern domestic goods, and London consumers were eager buyers of the radiograms, electric kettles, vacuum cleaners and car accessories that flowed from production lines to the West End shops. London's share of British manufacturing grew during this period. 'London's great advantage' remarked one observer, 'lies in its possession of the lion's share of the expanding industries and practically none of the declining ones.'

## MOVING TO THE SUBURBS

The period saw a dramatic change in the industrial topography of the capital. As with housing, the overwhelming movement was outwards to the suburbs. In 1900, most of London's industry was found within a rectangle bounded by Camden, Stratford, Vauxhall and Greenwich. By 1939, the boundaries were Hayes, Dagenham, Enfield and Croydon. Within this outward spread, the boom area was west London. New road and rail transport gave this side of London an advantage in terms of distribution to the national consumer market. It also had space and clean air. Many of the new factories were built on greenfield sites and put into practice new ideas about healthy working conditions. The one disadvan-

*Magnet electric heater, 1920s*
*Electric heaters were one of the many domestic items that became popular after World War I. Although the British firm General Electric Company (GEC) which made this model manufactured in the Midlands, its head office and research laboratories were in London.*

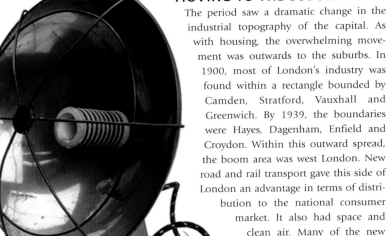

tage of west London was that London's main labour pool was in the east and south-east. 'But here,' noted the planner Patrick Abercrombie, 'modern city transport came to industry's aid and buses and electric trams brought the labour force to the factories from a wide area.'

Some of West London's new factories were built for new firms, many of which were American, and some for established London firms moving out of the inner city. Typical of the latter was the glass manufacturers James Powell & Sons, an old London craft firm that had been blowing glass on the riverfront site in the City it had occupied since the early 18th century. In 1919, the firm moved to a new purpose-built model factory in the semi-rural surroundings of Harrow and Wealdstone, a suburb in the north-west of London. Government grants made the move possible, and the firm took the opportunity of the move to modernize its production methods and overhaul its financial and ownership structure.

## STATE-OF-THE-ART FACTORIES

The new factories erected in west London were designed to proclaim the modern virtues of cleanliness, hygiene and efficiency. 'They afford a striking contrast to the dark and dismal factories erected no more than fifty years ago', said Harold Clunn. 'Many of them stand back some distance from the main road, amidst gardens, with frontages so ornamental that they might almost be mistaken by the casual visitor for large private mansions.' The factories Clunn had in mind were those on the Great West Road, built in the early 1920s as a bypass for Brentford and by the 1930s famous as the 'golden mile' of new industry. The two most spectacular were the Firestone Tyre and Rubber Company on the north side of the road and the Pyrene Fire Extinguisher Company on the south. Both were strikingly decorative and colourful. Further north, the Hoover factory added a jazzy flourish to Perivale's Western Avenue.

Park Royal, near Acton, grew to be the largest industrial zone in southern England during this period. The food manufacturer Heinz moved there in 1925, as did Guinness, whose huge brewery, erected in the mid-1930s, was the first to be built in London for thirty years. By 1939, Park Royal housed 256 firms, including Park Royal Vehicles, suppliers of bus bodies to London Transport.

In east London, industry tended to stick to its traditional areas along the banks of the Thames and its tributaries. The largest industrial newcomer on this side of London was the Ford motor car plant, built at Dagenham from the late 1920s and a sign to some that British industry as a whole was moving from north to south. Ford was typical of the riverside firms in relying heavily on water transport. The plant had its own docks and jetties for bulky raw materials – in Ford's case, coal and ore for the coke-ovens and blast furnaces. Many of Ford's cars were exported direct to overseas markets from the firm's own jetty.

Other new Thames-side factories included the state-of-the-art automated glassworks at Charlton built by United Glass Bottle Manufacturers Ltd from 1919 and the giant sugar refineries at Silvertown created by the merger in 1921 of the previously separate and competing firms belonging to Henry Tate and Abram Lyle. These two huge new firms also represented the tendency of businesses to amalgamate in the years following World War I. Automatic manufacturing needed larger capital resources, while global trading needed larger companies. Unilever, Imperial Chemical Industries, British American Tobacco and British Petroleum all assumed their modern shape during these years.

***Ford Model Y car, 1930s***
*Made at Dagenham, 'the Detroit of Europe', between 1932 and 1937, this light, affordable car, Ford's first design for the European market, swept to success in Britain.*

The new amalgamated firms and giant corporations also changed the landscape of central London. Large new office blocks appeared as these corporations created a market for prestigious head offices. In the City, Sir Edwin Lutyens designed a splendid new headquarters for British Petroleum in Finsbury Circus. Unilever's head office added a new landmark to the north end of Blackfriars Bridge. In Westminster, ICI and British American Tobacco located themselves in the mammoth new office development at Millbank erected in the early 1930s. Thames House and Imperial Chemical House were claimed to be 'the finest office building(s) in the British Empire', fully equipped with lifts capable of carrying passengers at 122 metres (400 ft) a minute. Their location, near the Palace of Westminster, underlined the importance of these new multinational corporations to the state as the British imperial project turned more wholeheartedly to matters of trade.

## A NEW TYPE OF CORPORATION

Another corporation that emerged in the period was the British Broadcasting Corporation. The BBC was constituted in 1927 as a new sort of body, a 'public corporation' operating with public ends in mind but outside state control. Its arm's length relationship with government was given physical meaning when the BBC located its head office in Portland Place, to the north of Oxford Circus

– a relatively neutral site in terms of state associations. The BBC also chose a modernist style for its new headquarters. Clean, white and functional, the building spoke of the new ideals of public service in a forward-looking city.

Central London's most controversial industrial building, however, was not clean and white. Battersea Power Station was built by one of the city's private electricity companies. Clean electricity came from its generators, but coal dust and smoke poured from its chimneys. To many, placing such a monster in the heart of London seemed like a throwback to Victorian days. But the power station was an apt symbol for a city where manufacturing provided jobs for 30 per cent of the workforce by the end of the 1930s. **CR**

**Interwar industry**
London's industry shifted westward but the east Thames corridor continued to attract large-scale endeavours.

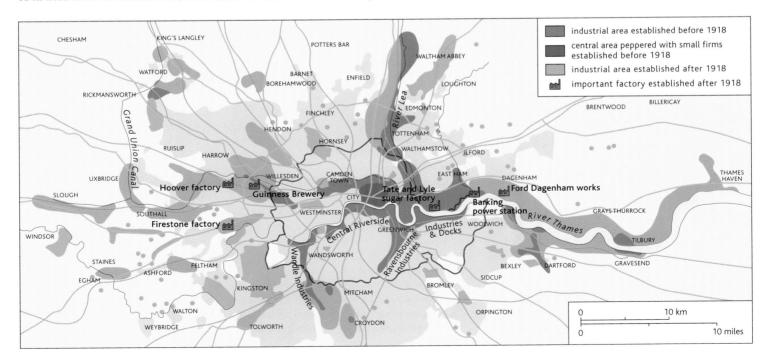

# MOTOR & AIR TRANSPORT

Petrol-powered cars and buses finally replaced horses in interwar London, bringing cleaner streets but more traffic and worse accidents. Regular passenger flights started up from Croydon.

independent buses racing to pick up passengers from crowded bus stops. Persistent roadworks, a street-widening programme and the rebuilding of Southwark and Lambeth bridges brought further disruption to London's road users. In 1926, one-way traffic systems were introduced at Hyde Park Corner, Trafalgar Square and Piccadilly Circus. Little, however, could be done to widen roads and improve congestion in the built-up central area and, by 1938, traffic speeds in the West End had dropped to below those of the horse-drawn era.

## NEW ARTERIAL ROADS

While traffic in central London continued to challenge planners, the suburbs provided an opportunity for a more systematic approach to road building. In 1918, the London Society had published a development plan for London that prefigured some of the major roads built by the Ministry of Transport in the 1920s. Of these the most significant was the Great West Road in Hounslow, opened in 1925 to provide access for a planned and orderly industrial development. The interwar road expansion programme also included the construction of the Great Cambridge Road in Enfield, the Eastern Avenue and Southend Road in east London and the North Circular Road from Woodford to Ealing, built as an unemployment relief scheme. The combination of new, wide roads and fast, modern motor lorries transformed London's economy, enabling industry to expand into the suburbs and allowing road transport to overtake railways as the preferred means of transporting goods because it offered the convenience of door-to-door deliveries.

For Londoners more familiar with the congested inner city, the new, arterial and bypass roads were a novelty. The Great West Road, wrote J. B. Priestley, 'did not look English. We might have suddenly rolled into California.' Leisure motoring became popular, as London's car owners took to the open roads at weekends to visit the surrounding countryside. Car dealer showrooms, petrol stations and garages soon replaced stables and coach houses.

*Charing Cross Road, 1935*
*Photographed in the smog by Austrian-born Wolf Suschitzky, the automated traffic light was a relatively new and welcome arrival to the junction on Charing Cross Road.*

By the end of the 1930s, motor vehicles reigned supreme on London's roads. Over 350,000 Londoners owned a car, and lorries dominated London's transport economy. Change had, however, occurred gradually; throughout the interwar period, horse-drawn vehicles and motor transport continued to jostle for position on London's streets, causing severe traffic congestion and chaos.

London's busiest road junction in the mid-1920s was Hyde Park Corner, with up to 51,500 motor vehicles and 3360 horse-drawn vehicles passing through each day. As in other parts of the West End, private vehicles competed for space with unregulated,

## ROAD SAFETY

Rising levels of motor transport led, inevitably, to an escalation in road traffic accidents. In 1930, over 7000 road deaths were recorded in the United Kingdom. Driving tests were not compulsory until 1935 and anyone over the age of seventeen could simply get in a car and drive away. From the mid-1920s, road safety became a government priority. In 1926, London's first traffic lights were installed at Piccadilly Circus. In the following decade the Ministry of Transport introduced road markings, road signs and pedestrian crossings lit by orange Belisha beacons. The Road Traffic Act of

WILLS'S CIGARETTES

DO NOT STEP FROM BEHIND ONE VEHICLE INTO THE PATH OF ANOTHER

WILLS'S CIGARETTES

PEDESTRIANS: USE RECOGNISED CROSSING PLACES

1930 defined a number of traffic offences, but the issue of 'dangerous driving' remained unresolved. In 1935 Lord de Clifford was charged with the manslaughter of Douglas Hopkins by driving in a reckless and negligent manner on the new Kingston bypass. He was acquitted for want of a legal definition of the offence.

As London's police became responsible for traffic regulations, they also faced the growing problem of car-related crime. In the late 1920s, the Metropolitan Police acquired motor vehicles to keep up with criminals who were increasingly using cars to make a getaway. Shops and jewellers were particularly vulnerable to attack by 'smash-and-grab' motor bandits such as Ruby Sparks from Camberwell and his female driver, the 'Bobbed-hair Bandit'. Incidents of car theft also rose and, in 1935, the police broke up a 'Great Car-Stealing Conspiracy' run by a south London gang with garages at the Oval and Camberwell.

By the end of the 1930s, motor transport had penetrated London's economic, social and cultural life, its growing influence symbolized by the new Ford factory dominating Dagenham in east London. Car manufacture had now come of age as a constant stream of mass-produced vehicles rolled off the assembly line. The dream of private car ownership was fast becoming an affordable reality for many London families. **BC**

*Road safety reminders, 1927*
*Cigarette cards in a 'Safety first' series were issued by Wills Cigarettes.*

## CROYDON: LONDON'S FIRST AIRPORT

Before 1914, air transport was primarily a spectator sport, with presentation air shows attracting large crowds anxious to view the exploits of the daring pioneer pilots. The war accelerated developments in aviation and facilitated the evolution of recreational passenger services.

London's first civilian airport opened in Croydon in 1920, on the site of two adjacent World War I airfields. The airfields were linked by a level crossing straddling a busy road and, as aircraft took off, traffic along Plough Lane was halted by a man waving a red flag. Regular scheduled flights carried passengers, mail and freight to France, Holland, Belgium, Germany and Switzerland. In the mid-1920s several aviation companies serving the airport merged to form Imperial Airways Limited, and the airport was developed to meet increased demand. Plough Lane was finally closed to traffic and a new comfortable passenger terminal building and hotel were constructed.

Air travel remained, however, an expensive luxury available only to the rich or glamorous – even though, once a passenger was in the air, the flying experience could be far from appealing.

As one noted, 'They put you in a box, they shut the lid, they splash you all over with oil, you are sick, and you're in Paris.'

*Croydon Airport, 1930s*
*The new terminal was completed in 1928.*

# THE DOCKS & THE PORT OF LONDON AUTHORITY

The quantities of goods passing through London's docks reached an all-time high in the interwar years. The Port of London Authority extended the Royal Docks and renamed Canary Wharf.

*London's Docks*
*This map from 1966 shows the full extent of London's dock system, including the main interwar additions. By the late 1960s only those areas shaded orange (with warehouses in red) were still in use.*

By 1939, London's port had grown into one of the biggest shipping and cargo handling facilities in the world. Under the management of a new governing body, the Port of London Authority, the docks had expanded to include 280 hectares (700 acres) of dock basins and 730 hectares (1800 acres) of dockside land.

From the mid-19th century, the dock companies had been locked in fierce competition; as a result, the dock system had expanded haphazardly. The first new docks, the Royal Victoria Docks, had been opened in 1855 by a group of entrepreneurs. Designed to take advantage of the new railways and hydraulic power, they had quickly drawn trade away from their rivals.

As profits began to fall, the older dock companies had begun a process of amalgamation and new dock building. The East and West India Dock Company had built the Millwall Dock in 1868 and the South West India Dock two years later. The London and St

Katharine Dock Company had responded with the Albert Dock in 1880, and the East and West India Company in turn with a new dock miles downstream at Tilbury in 1886.

By 1886, however, falling trade had led to a crisis that drove the East and West India Dock Company into receivership. In 1889, the Great Dock Strike had highlighted the poor management of the docks: at the height of Britain's imperial power, its greatest port had fallen into serious financial trouble. Many docks lacked access to railways, entrances were too small for steamships, and existing warehouses were inefficient. Furthermore, the private companies lacked capital for major improvements.

In 1900, a royal commission had identified a lack of coordination as the root problem. In 1908, the government finally set up a single management organization: the Port of London Authority (PLA). The PLA began an ambitious process of improvement, but financial strictures soon limited its activities.

The key was deepening the 80-km (50-mile) channel from the Thames Estuary. Dredging was to prove a continuous task: in 1963, tests showed that silt dumped at sea 48 kilometres (30 miles) beyond Southend was carried back up the river by the tide.

Demands for better facilities for increasing imports of fruit, coal, oil and refrigerated foods focused attention on the Royal Victoria and Albert Docks, and extensive improvements were undertaken. Central to this, however, was the building of a new dock – the King George V, at North Woolwich. Over 200 houses on

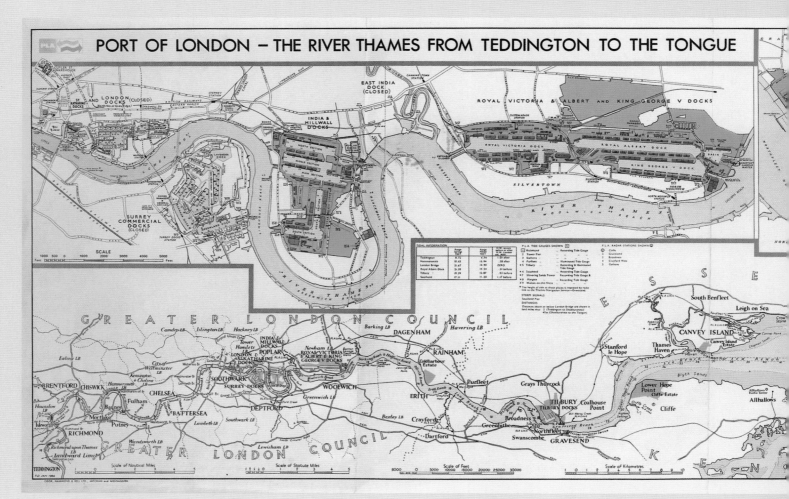

PORT OF LONDON – THE RIVER THAMES FROM TEDDINGTON TO THE TONGUE

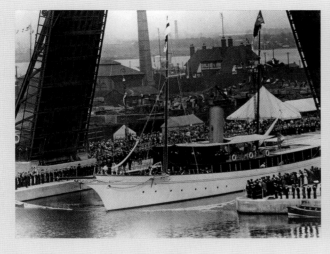

**The opening of the King George V Dock**
The King George V Dock opened in 1921. It had modern refrigeration facilities for cargoes of foodstuffs.

**Canary Wharf**
This view, looking east, shows the mid-1930s sheds that were built for the fruit trade.

the proposed site had to be demolished. Work began before 1914; by 1920, 3,823,000 cubic metres (5,000,000 cubic yards) of earth had been excavated; the dock was formally opened in 1921 (see above). In 1934, Silvertown Way was opened to provide access.

## BEYOND THE ROYAL DOCKS

The Royal Docks were not the only complexes to benefit from the planning vision of the PLA. South of the river, at the Surrey Commercial Docks, the expanding timber trade also required better facilities. The PLA responded in 1925 by building a range of new iron-roofed sheds with massive brick dividing walls designed to reduce the risk of fire. On the Isle of Dogs, entry to the West India Docks was improved by enlarging the western dock entrance. The PLA was also quick to transform misfortune to its advantage. When in 1935 a fire destroyed the old Rum Quay warehouses on the south side of the West India import dock, the PLA widened the quay and built modern transit sheds and warehouses for the fruit trade – to which it gave a new name: Canary Wharf (see above).

By 1939, the PLA had added 32 hectares (80 acres) of dock basin and 10 km (6 miles) of quayside to the port's facilities, and had completely dredged the river channel to allow the passage of modern ships. Such was the expansion that between 1920 and 1930 the volume of trade in the docks increased from three million to eight million tons, increasing by 50 per cent annually.

The development of the port received a devastating setback at the end of 1940. On Saturday 7 September, the Luftwaffe began its raids on London. From day one, the docks were a primary target, and the local communities suffered badly. At the West India Dock, incendiaries set fire to thousands of barrels of rum in the warehouses, and the flames quickly spread to stores of paint and rubber. The smoke was so dense that fighting the fires was almost impossible. South of the river, at the Surrey Docks, the PLA's attempts to provide fireproof warehouses proved fruitless in the face of bombing. The timber stacks ignited, burning for days and causing a colossal column of smoke and fire, which during the night could be seen as far away as Guildford. By December 1940, the dock facilities had been devastated. Some 30 per cent of the warehousing at the London and St Katharine Docks had been destroyed. **TW**

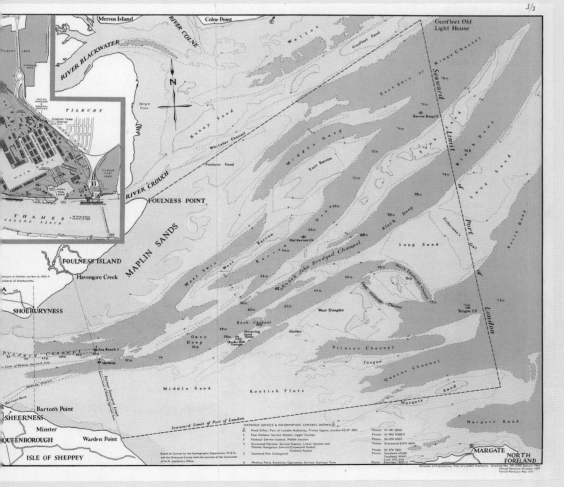

# LONDON POLITICS BETWEEN THE WARS

A new mass electorate made London's interwar politics more turbulent for both national and local government. Communists and Fascists took their politics to the city's streets.

London's political landscape was transformed in 1918 by the Representation of the People Act, the first and largest of the two steps that brought mass democracy to Britain. The Act enfranchised more people than the other three preceding Reform Acts put together and nearly tripled the electorate from 7.5 million to over 20 million people. Not only did it give women over thirty the right to vote, but it also enfranchised new swathes of Britain's men by cutting the centuries-old link between voting and property ownership. In London, the electorate rose from under 700,000 to over two million. In 1929, the second Representation of the People Act extended the vote to women between twenty-one and thirty, bringing London's electorate to an unprecedented 2.9 million people.

This great leap forward in democracy invigorated politics in the capital, not least by disrupting the old balance of power. In 1918 only two of the London boroughs' sixty-two Members of Parliament belonged to the Labour party: by 1935 Labour Members had risen to twenty-eight. The number of Conservative and Liberal MPs shrank accordingly, with the Liberal representation falling from fourteen to a single Member. As politics came to involve the masses, political parties began to discover mass marketing. The 1920s saw an outbreak of propaganda poster campaigns (see above) and the first election radio broadcasts. By 1930, the journalist H. G. W. Nevinson reflected that politics was now second only to sport in engaging the enthusiasm of the working man, a development he put down to the state's increasing intervention into matters of

**Election results**
Changes in support for political parties in London are shown by general election results for 1918 (below) and 1924 (bottom).

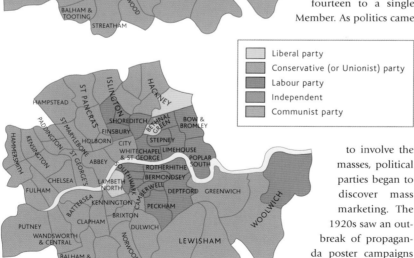

- Liberal party
- Conservative (or Unionist) party
- Labour party
- Independent
- Communist party

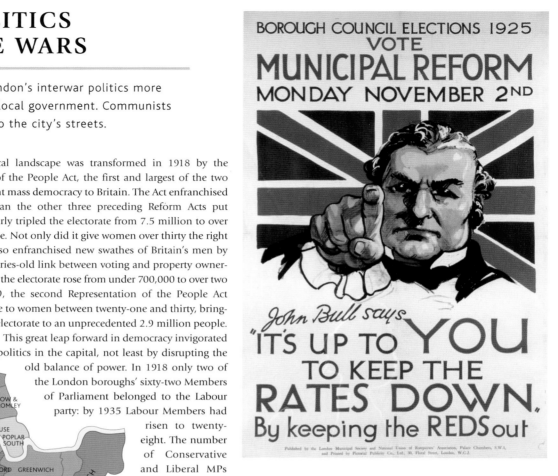

BOROUGH COUNCIL ELECTIONS 1925
VOTE
MUNICIPAL REFORM
MONDAY NOVEMBER 2ND

*John Bull says* "IT'S UP TO YOU TO KEEP THE RATES DOWN. By keeping the REDS out"

Published by the London Municipal Society and National Union of Ratepayers' Association, Palace Chambers, S.W.1, and Printed by Pictorial Publicity Co., Ltd., 30, Floral Street, London, W.C.2.

*Local election poster*
*The Municipal Reform party invoked John Bull, the national personification of Britain, in the 1925 London County Council elections to oppose high spending.*

daily life, as well as the new democracy. The turnout in parliamentary elections remained generally high in London during the 1920s, with the highest numbers, around 80 per cent, usually recorded in the two Woolwich constituencies.

## THE GENERAL STRIKE

The event that typified London's role as a stage for national politics was the general strike of May 1926. The strike grew out of a deadlock in Britain's coal industry: 'Not a minute on the day, not a penny off the pay' was the miners' slogan. Although the dispute concerned the mining areas in Wales and the North, it was in London that the trigger event took place, with the refusal of the *Daily Mail*'s Fleet Street printers to print a leading article attacking trade unions. It was also in London that the main events played out. A main aim of the strikers was to bring the capital to a halt and force the government to intervene on the side of the miners.

The strike call from the Trades Union Congress (TUC) took effect from the early hours of Tuesday 3 May. In London, the main groups of striking workers were the dockers, printers, power station workers, railwaymen and transport workers. The government immediately deployed the army to ensure that essential services continued and food supplies got through. Troops were dispatched to the docks and army barracks were set up in Hyde Park, which was turned into a milk and food depot. Although the government response was expected, the strikers were taken by surprise by the public reaction. Londoners who disapproved of the TUC 'holding a pistol to the nation's head' took action themselves, volunteering to work in place of the strikers. London's buses, trams, trains and delivery vans were kept running by a skeleton staff of non-unionized workers and university students. All in all, the event turned into a peculiarly British sort of muddle, rather than a dramatic clash of ideologies. The TUC called off the action on 12 May with the promise of new proposals for reorganizing the coal industry.

## STREET POLITICS

Establishment worries about the wisdom of placing voting power in the hands of the general population focused above all on the rise of the anti-democratic political ideologies of the interwar period. Communism and Fascism both established strong followings in London, as did the third of the alternative political creeds, Social Credit, which mustered many thousands of supporters among the unemployed in the 1930s. All three minority parties – and other smaller groups as well – reinforced London's role as a lightning conductor for national political ideas and a stage for political events, particularly demonstrations. Hunger marches from the North brought Welsh miners and Tyneside shipbuilders to the capital's streets; the publicity-minded 'Green Shirts' (Social Credit supporters) shot a green arrow into Downing Street and hurled green bricks into the Bank of England. The violence that accompanied Fascist rallies in London led to the Public Order Act, which forbade the wearing of military uniforms in peacetime – which the Green Shirts tried to circumvent by marching with their uniforms carried before them on coat hangers.

London provided fertile ground for all shades of political opinion. The Communist Party of Great Britain (CPGB) was founded in 1920 at a meeting held in the City of London. Like many minority parties, the CPGB was sustainable in the capital, where its core supporters covered the class spectrum, from dockers to intellectuals. In 1929, *The Times* reported that membership was 2000, of whom 900 came from the London district. The party had offices at King Street (Covent Garden) and Great Ormond Street, from where it published an impressive range of journals and newsletters. London also had one of Britain's two communist MPs.

Shapurji Saklatvala was elected as Member for Battersea North in 1922 and again in 1924. Saklatvala was one of the most charismatic figures of the period. An intense man of high principles, his presence in the House of Commons provoked fears not just about Communism but also about Indian nationalism, for which he was an eloquent advocate.

The British Union of Fascists also had a London support base. Founded in 1932 by the former Labour MP Oswald Mosley, it acquired notoriety with a rally at Olympia in 1934 where the violence directed by the black-shirted stewards against a few Communist protesters shocked the public. Under Mosley's militaristic leadership, the 'Black Shirts' cultivated an aggressive edge and their overt anti-Semitism provoked active opposition in the East End, London's main Jewish area. In 1936, the 'Battle of Cable Street' (see above) demonstrated that most East Enders wanted nothing to do with Mosley's creed of power through force. **CR**

### The Battle of Cable Street

In 1936, an historic clash took place when anti-Fascist crowds prevented the British Union of Fascists from marching through a Jewish area in the East End.

Anti-Fascists block the junction of Leman St and Commercial Road.

30,000–50,000 anti-Fascists gather at Gardiner's Corner and Leman St.

Anti-Fascists successfully resist police attempts to clear Leman St. The Fascist march is abandoned.

Anti-Fascists block Cable St. Police baton charges are repulsed by crowds throwing missles. Fascist march is diverted up Leman St.

Police clash with anti-Fascists blocking Royal Mint St.

Police force the anti-Fascist demonstrators back into Cable St.

Police cordon off Minories and neighbouring streets.

Fascists begin their march, under police protection.

A demonstration of 3000 Fascists gathers prior to march.

| | |
|---|---|
| ⊘ | meeting place of Fascist marchers |
| ✪ | meeting place of anti-Fascist demonstrators |
| ┈┈▶ | intended route of Fascist march |
| ➡ | actual route of Fascist march |
| ➡ | movements of anti-Fascist demonstrators |
| ✷ | clashes between police and anti-Fascists |
| ▤ | police roadblock |
| ▤ | anti-Fascist roadblock |

# ART & ARTISTS IN INTERWAR LONDON

As London artists pondered the stylistic challenges presented by modern art, a growing body of commercial artists found employment in the capital's fledgling creative industries.

**Artists' Hampstead**

In the 1930s Hampstead was a cell of European modernism, where London's main abstract painters and sculptors lived, alongside European refugee-artists.

London's interwar art scene was a diverse one as artists cast about for new forms of expression appropriate to the machine age. At the stylistically revolutionary end were those who saw meaning in the purity of abstract symbols. At the politically revolutionary end were the socialist realist artists of the AIA whose slogan was 'conservative in painting but radical in politics'.

Many artists drew inspiration from the city itself. C. R. W. Nevinson brought his pre-war Futurist style to bear on the postwar metropolis, producing meditations on a city heavy with tradition but quivering with rapid movement (see pages 250–1). Walter Sickert continued his fascination with London's everyday life. Anonymous commercial artists depicted Londoners at work and play for a variety of commercial purposes.

Despite their stylistic differences, however, London artists shared the same urban topography. The city's main reference points were the art schools that provided artists not just with social networks, but also with teaching work. By the 1930s, London had thirteen major art schools, offering a broad spectrum of courses. The Central School of Arts and Crafts, founded in 1896 by the London County Council, embraced what was later called industrial design. Strict 'fine art' training for painters was provided by the Royal Academy School, the Royal College of Art, the Slade School and a host of smaller private schools, such as St Martin's School of Art. Training in architecture was provided by the Royal Institute of British Artists and some of the smaller polytechnics. Many of these institutions admitted women, and the period saw a small but increasing number of women in the creative industries.

Studios and living spaces were still mostly in the cheaper areas of town. Sickert moved his studio from Camden Town to Islington in the 1920s, but the next generation of artists found Fitzrovia congenial. Fitzroy Street was a well-known source of cheap studio space, and many artists drank in the Fitzroy Tavern or ate in the cheap Charlotte Street restaurants. A colony of artists sprang up in Hammersmith, but the best-known artists' quarter of the period was Hampstead. A new 'London type' appeared, as personified by Ben Nicholson, described by the *Daily Express* in 1934 as 'the complete bourgeois conception of a Hampstead artist, vivid scarf, beret and all'.

- 🜊 studios and homes
- 🏛 meeting places
- 🏚 keynote architecture of the period

1. David Bomberg
   10 Fordwych Road, 1930–33
   66a Lymington Road, 1937
2. Naum Gabo
   Lawn Road flats, 1936–38
   101 Cholmley Gardens, 1938–39
3. Barbara Hepworth
   7 Mall Studios, Parkhill Road, 1928–39
4. László Moholy-Nagy
   Lawn Road flats, 1935
   7 Farm Walk, 1935–37
5. Piet Mondrian
   60 Parkhill Road, 1937–40
6. Henry Moore
   11a Parkhill Road, 1928–40
   7 Mall Studios, Parkhill Road, 1940
7. Paul Nash
   3 Eldon Grove, 1936–39
8. C. R. W. Nevinson
   Steele's Studios, Steele's Road
9. Ben Nicholson
   7 Mall Studios, Parkhill Road, 1936–39
10. Herbert Read (art critic)
    3 Mall Studios, Parkhill Road, 1933–37
11. Cecil Stephenson
    6 Mall Studios, Parkhill Road, 1929–40
12. Elleen Agar
    Steele's Studio, Steele's Road
13. Everyman Cinema
    1 Holybush Vale, est. 1933
14. The Isobar Club
    Lawn Road flats, est. 1937
15. 47 Downside Street
    Artists' Refugee Committee
    Home of Fred & Diana Uhlman
16. 47 Downside Street
    Meeting Place of the British Surrealists
    Home of Roland Penrose
17. Keats Grove
    Meeting place of the Hampstead branch of the Left Book Club
18. Lawn Road Flats
    Landmark modernist building, est. 1934
    Residents included Jack & Molly Pritchard, Walter Gropius, Marcel Breuer & Agatha Christie
19. 1–3 Willow Road
    Modernist houses designed and lived in by Erno Goldfinger, est. 1939

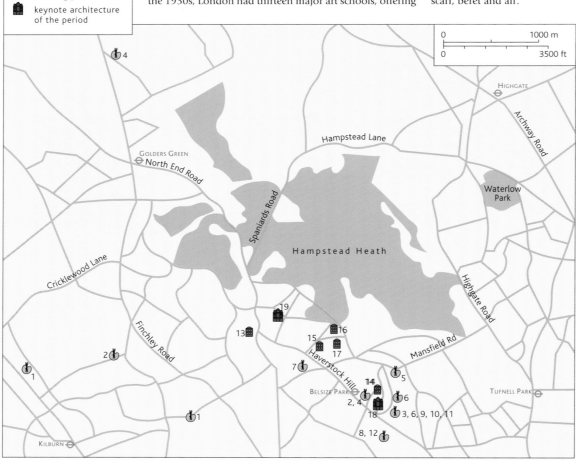

## HAMPSTEAD INTERNATIONALISM

Hampstead had always been regarded as somewhat bohemian, but in the 1930s it acquired a harder and more intellectual edge through its association with the European avant-garde. Part of Hampstead's attraction to artists was its purpose-built artists' studios. The Mall Studios in Parkhill Road, which were built at the turn of the century, housed a 'gentle nest of artists' by the 1930s – in fact the arch-proselytizers of abstraction, among them Barbara Hepworth, John Skeaping, Ben Nicholson and Henry Moore. The critic Herbert Read also lived in Parkhill Road, as did, from 1937, the Dutch abstract painter Piet Mondrian, a refugee from the Nazis. In nearby Steele's Road was the studio of the surrealist painter Eileen Agar.

Further north, on Downshire Hill, the home of Diana and Fred Ulman also housed the Artists' Refugee Committee, set up to help European artists fleeing the Nazi threat. The British surrealists met at the Downshire Street home of artist and collector Roland Penrose. Penrose had become an enthusiast for surrealism while living in France and in 1935 'found in Hampstead a climate which had some slight resemblance to that which [he] had left in Paris'.

Hampstead's international credentials were made visible with the construction of two iconic modernist buildings. In 1934 the Canadian architect Wells Coates designed a block of flats at Lawn Road, Hampstead, along archetypal white, geometric, 'international style' lines. The flats offered its residents a chic but progressive lifestyle with interiors fitted out with built-in plywood furniture made by the Isokon company, in which Coates was a partner. Further south, in Hampstead's Willow Road, the Hungarian architect Erno Goldfinger, another refugee, built a terrace of three uncompromisingly modernist houses. Goldfinger and his wife, the painter Ursula Blackwell, lived in one themselves and their home became a kind of salon for Hampstead's artists and intellectuals.

## THE RISE OF COMMERCIAL ART

Highbrow Hampstead discourses were just part of a broader spectrum of creative debate in London between the wars. The darkening social and economic climate around 1930 touched artists as keenly as other Londoners. 'The 1930 slump affected us all very considerably', recalled William Coldstream. 'Through making money much harder to come by it caused an immense change in our general outlook … Everyone began to be interested in economics and then in politics.' Coldstream explained that the Depression had turned him against avant-garde styles. 'It seemed to me important that the broken communication between the artist and the public should be built up again and this most probably implied a movement towards realism.' Similar views informed the foundation of the Artists International Association in 1933. Its founders saw their role as fighting Fascism, war and social injustice, a mission to which socialist realism seemed appropriate. Coldstream became a member of the AIA but also went on to found the Euston Road School, a private art school dedicated to the principles of 'objective representation' through meticulous observation.

The rise of the AIA artists also built bridges with commercial art. As London's creative industries expanded, so too did the number of commercial artists in the capital. Advertising needed illustrators, newspapers cartoonists and film companies art directors. Commercial artists were often looked down on by 'fine' artists' even though many had a foot in both camps: William Larkin, an outstanding printmaker, was also the art director for the agency J. Walter Thompson. The AIA's Cliff Rowe deplored the lower status accorded to commercial artists, not least because of the innovation their work often represented. 'There was a great deal of snobbery

within the profession … Then it was realized that the commercial artist was breaking through to a freedom of expression that the fine artists weren't achieving. Everybody began to respect the strip cartoonist and the silk screen people.' **MoL**

# SPORT & LEISURE

New facilities catered for a new age of mass leisure and healthy living in the interwar period. London acquired stadiums, dance halls, super-cinemas, lidos, sports grounds and golf courses.

*London Sports Grounds, 1938*

*West London was the healthy side of London, with space for many sports grounds.*

By the 1930s 'leisure' was a growing social concern. Many people were spending less time at work, thanks in part to stricter workplace legislation. Levels of disposable income were rising. The first comprehensive survey of Londoners' leisure habits was published in 1935 and it estimated that even ordinary working-class families only needed to spend sixty per cent of their income to cover the basic necessities of life.

The quotes included in the survey revealed that many Londoners did not feel like creatures of leisure. 'Recreation!' protested a railway worker in Willesden, 'Mother says there isn't any and I'm afraid she is not far wrong!' However, by the 1930s London's leisure industries were gearing up to a new scale of operation, tempting people out of their homes with the promise of spectacle, glamour and fun.

As with many aspects of London life, the sheer size of the city's population attracted entrepreneurs with large ambitions. Cinema was the most dramatic example of the way commercialized leisure flourished. By the 1930s, London had 258 registered cinemas, providing 344,000 seats. Many were part of Oscar Deutsch's Odeon chain, which spread through London's suburban high streets. The impresario Charles B. Cochran brought a range of spectacles to London, including circuses, prize-fight boxing at Olympia and musical revues. Londoners began to visit Billy Butlin's fun fairs and, from 1938, his holiday camp at Clacton.

## SPORT & 'AMUSEMENTS'

Sport also grew in scale and became more commercially-minded. The eleven professional football teams in London all expanded their grounds to meet spectator demand, some adopting the US model of the 'stadium'. Wembley was the super-stadium, a 100,000-spectator construction built in 1924 for the British Empire Exhibition. Ten years later, it was joined by the Empire Swimming Pool, built for the 1934 Empire Games. On its opening, the 70 x 18 metre (230 x 60 ft) pool was hailed as the largest indoor swimming pool in the world and a triumph of modern concrete construction. After Wembley, London's largest football stadium was Chelsea's at Stamford Bridge, which could accommodate 80,000 spectators. Arsenal built two new stands at their ground in Highbury during the 1930s, and six stadiums for greyhound racing were also added to the city's leisure facilities.

Greyhound racing was the boom spectator sport of the period. American in origin, it arrived in London in 1927 when a track was constructed at White City. London's second greyhound track appeared in the same year at Haringay, where a 50,000-seat stadium was built on a spoil tip left by the extension of the Piccadilly line to Finsbury Park. Haringay aimed to be a glamorous dog track and is said to have experimented with racing cheetahs. By 1933, London had seventeen greyhound tracks, attracting just over nine million Londoners a year, to the dismay of those who saw greyhound racing as just an excuse for betting. Concern about the connection between sport and gambling increased in 1929 when Haringay unveiled its latest mechanical wonder – the 'totalisator', a new, automated device for calculating bets placed and winning payments to be made.

The authors of the 1935 leisure survey drew a distinction between spectator sport, which they classed as 'amusements and entertainment', and participative sport, of which they approved. Opportunities for active sport increased enormously over the period as local councils and businesses embraced the idea that their responsibilities to their ratepayers and employees included the provision of sports grounds. By the end of the 1930s, the London County Council's parks department managed 366 cricket pitches, 436 football pitches, 29 hockey pitches, 726 hard and grass tennis courts, three 18-hole golf courses, 169 pitches for

LONDON SPORTS GROUNDS

Scale of Miles

REFERENCE

Bowling Clubs ● B.　　Golf Clubs ▶ G.
Cricket Clubs ■ C.　　Greyhound Tracks ○ G.T.
Football Clubs　　　　Tennis Clubs ● T.
— Association ● F.　　Polo Grounds ▲ P.
— Rugby ▲ R.　　　　Racecourses ○

*Sportswear for women*

Swimsuit by Straker Ltd, published in Needlework for All, 1933 (left); Golfing outfit, published in Ladies' Field and Fashion, 1925 (right).

Although sport was a universal enthusiasm, it remained divided on class and gender lines. Football was the game of the working man. By 1933 the eleven London professional football clubs were each attracting around 615,000 spectators annually – not all, of course, Londoners. 'Supporters travel all over England with their favourite team', explained the authors of the 1935 survey. 'The crowds, which are now composed mainly of men, follow the games with great interest and will stand watching in all sorts of weather. They enter into the spirit of the game and shout remarks of praise and disparagement at the players and the referees.'

Boxing was also a sport with 'a specially strong appeal to working men'. Although it was defined by the 1935 survey as a spectator sport, accounts record vigorous audience participation. 'If anyone imagines anti-Semitism to have died down', wrote the journalist Glyn Roberts in 1933, 'he should visit the Blackfriars Ring when Jewish boxers are appearing. So completely callous and open are the thugs and groundlings in their desire to see Hebrew blood spilt and Hebrew bodies prone that the Jewish Boxer really has more to contend with in the audience than in the ring.'

netball, 28 bowling greens, 63 putting greens, 9 athletics sports tracks and 17 lidos or open-air swimming pools.

Lidos became a particularly potent symbol of the contemporary cult of health, happiness and modernity. Designed to evoke the clean white lines and blue water of a fashionable Mediterranean bathing resort, they were, in the words of a London County Council booklet, 'brightly-coloured, architecturally-tasteful, spacious, airy and efficient swimming pools'. Lidos not only helped to promote physical fitness, they also helped 'to reconcile us in hot summer days to being still in London when everybody else is by the sea'. Between 1920 and 1933, the annual total number of bathers in London's municipal pools and lidos shot up from 3.9 million to 6.7 million.

Tennis and golf, by contrast, attracted a more middle-class following, particularly from women, for whom sporting activity was an indicator of new social freedoms. As with all aspects of life, old barriers were breaking down. 'The enthusiasm for walking is spreading through all classes', noted the 1935 survey approvingly. Walking had become looked upon in the poorer neighbourhoods of London as a sensible way of spending Sunday, instead of being the mark of a 'crank'. **CR**

## CLASS & GENDER

Turning land into sports grounds was largely a phenomenon of London's outer boroughs, which had spare space and clean air. West London, seen as the city's healthier side, was particularly affected and by 1940 had a heavy sprinkling of company playing fields. Among the largest were the two in Acton belonging to the London Passenger Transport Board and the London Gas and Coke company and J. Lyons & Co.'s large sports ground at Sudbury Hill. Sports grounds, with their associated networks of clubs and tournaments, played an important role in company morale and were seen as the sign of an enlightened employer.

*Travel poster 1933*

This poster was designed for the Rugby League cup final played at Wembley on 6 May 1933 between Huddersfield and Warrington.

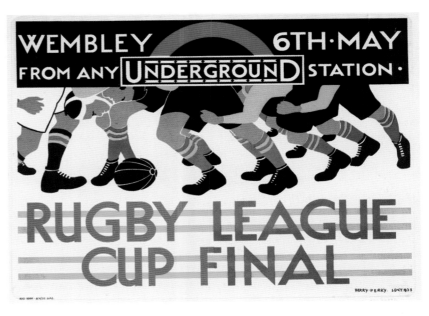

# LONDON'S NEW REFUGEE COMMUNITIES

New lines were drawn between different nationalities in London between the wars. Laws were tightened, but new groups of refugees arrived in London, fleeing Fascism in Europe.

**Italian children**

*These children in Saffron Hill, Clerkenwell, were photographed in 1935 by Margaret Monck, a photographer with an interest in London's poorer areas.*

World War I and its aftermath created 9.5 million European refugees, including two million Russians, displaced by the Russian Revolution. All European states began to control the movement of people; in Britain the new climate resulted in the much harsher Aliens Act of 1919 and the first appearance of the British 'blue passport', which, it was said, even the Foreign Secretary had to carry.

In London the new mood brought legal disadvantages to non-British Londoners, even those long-settled in the capital. World War I had decimated London's large pre-war German community. The handful who remained were now dubbed aliens and subject to the controls introduced by the 1919 Act. Certain jobs were now no longer available. Petty controls were introduced, including regulations for businesses wishing to anglicize their trading names.

As the 1920s progressed, fears about aliens were compounded by Britain's first experience of mass unemployment. In July 1920 the London County Council banned foreigners from all council jobs. By the middle of the decade the Musicians' Union was campaigning to ban the American jazz musicians, largely black, who populated the West End's bands and hotel orchestras.

Although London's German community disappeared from Fitzrovia, London's other national communities remained in their traditional haunts. The East End was a Jewish and Irish area. The Chinese had settled in Limehouse and Pennyfields; the Italians around Clerkenwell and Holborn (see above). During the 1920s and 1930s, London's Italian community began to drift towards Soho, traditionally a French district, but becoming more cosmopolitan with the arrival not just of the Italians but also Greek and then Turkish Cypriots. Soho also provided a home for Germans, Russians, Spanish, Belgians, Indians and Africans. 'It has barbers shops where English is spoken with every conceivable accent' said an admirer in 1933.

## THE COLOUR BAR

Citizens of the British Empire were not officially considered to be aliens, although anyone black-skinned was often caught up in the climate of suspicion. Lascar seamen were adversely affected by the 1919 Act, despite its stated intent of protecting their interests. Violence against 'foreign' seamen broke out in British ports during the summer of 1919. Further unrest accompanied the 1920 Aliens Order and the 1925 Special Restriction (Coloured Alien Seamen) Order. Many African, Indian and West Indian seamen with full British nationality were arbitrarily registered as aliens. In London, Lascar seamen tended to live in the very poorest parts of the East End (see opposite top).

Casual colour prejudice was a part of London life, and even the most respectable empire citizens could be subject to arbitrary 'colour bars' imposed by hotel or restaurant owners. The League of Coloured People was founded in London in 1931 by Dr Harold

**Mr Mix and family, 1938**
*These foreign residents of Hanbury Street, Poplar, were photographed by Cyril Arapoff for an unpublished* Picture Post *story about slum housing.*

Moody, with the aim of improving race relations and in particular addressing the personal injustices that many black Londoners experienced in their daily lives.

For many black-skinned Londoners, the main concerns of the period were political questions about the British Empire and the degree of identity it allowed to colonial nations within it. London became the focus for several pressure groups calling for political change. The India Freedom Association, for example, was formed in 1925 with the motto 'Freedom within the Empire if possible – outside if necessary'.

## THE SHADOW OF FASCISM

The rise of Fascism in Europe cast a shadow of suspicion over London's Italian and Spanish communities but rebounded more severely on Jewish Londoners. Anti-Semitism was often openly expressed in the 1920s and the formation of the British Union of Fascists in 1932 gave existing hostility a dangerous edge. Fascist marches through the Jewish East End led to their resounding defeat at the 'Battle of Cable Street' in 1936 (see page 265).

By this time Jewish families, like other Londoners, were moving to the suburbs: west to Ilford, or north to Edgware, Hendon and Finchley. The community, 150,000 strong by 1914, grew ever-stronger roots. Its institutions now included an enlarged London Jewish Hospital and the Jewish Museum in Woburn House, which opened in 1932. Jewish entrepreneurs opened factories and led London's film and cinema industries. Jewish musicians filled bandstands in the West End, where band leaders became household names, thanks to radio and the recording industry.

Elsewhere in Europe the outlook grew darker. The issue of immigration to Britain re-emerged in the 1930s as European Jews began to flee from systematic persecution in Nazi Germany. Despite the initial reluctance of the British government to accept migrants without pre-arranged jobs to go to, exceptions were made. A group of 3840 Basque children arrived in 1937 following the bombing of Basque towns by German aircraft during the Spanish Civil War. These children, with their teachers and priests, were settled in ninety-four 'colonies' across the United Kingdom. Those in London included homes in Barnes, Barnet, Clapton, Brixton and Hammersmith. Jewish children from Germany and the central European countries also arrived through the Kindertransport rescue scheme. Many Jewish adults also escaped to Britain with the help of organizations and individuals based in London, who provided the financial guarantees that the government continued to demand as a condition of entry. **MoL**

### THE KINDERTRANSPORTS

Following Germany's horrific Kristallnacht in November 1938, a delegation of British Jewish leaders approached the Prime Minister to discuss the mass evacuation of German Jewish children. The Kindertransport, as the operation became known, was organized at speed. The Refugee Children's Movement sent people to Germany and Austria to make arrangements: priority was given to those children most in danger. In Britain, a radio appeal for foster homes broadcast on the BBC Home Service generated some 500 offers.

The first Kindertransport train from Berlin left on 1 December 1938. Ten days later another left from Vienna. The trains crossed into the Netherlands and Belgium then continued to Britain by ship. Arriving at Harwich, the unaccompanied children travelled by train to Liverpool Street Station, where some were met by new foster parents. Trains from Prague were hastily arranged after the German army entered Czechoslovakia in March 1939. Transports of Polish Jewish children arrived in February and August 1939. Altogether 10,000 children were evacuated to Britain via the Kindertransport scheme. Many never saw their real parents again.

*Suzanne Schaefer, c.1937. A kindertransport refugee photographed in Berlin Zoo two years before her flight to England. Suzanne's mother escaped by other means and the two were eventually reunited in London.*

# WAR & POSTWAR LONDON

ondon's ordeal by bombing during World War II only strengthened its hold on the onal imagination. Photographs of St Paul's hedral standing proud during one of the worst hts of the Blitz created a powerful image of ish defiance and righteousness.

War left 100,000 Londoners homeless and a million buildings damaged or destroyed. population shrank from 8.6 million to 6.7 lion. Some had been evacuated; others had ted away as factories relocated elsewhere.

he idea of turning catastrophe to positive efit by rebuilding Britain as a utopia of al equality also became a London story. The don County Council put its muscle behind national crusade to banish bad housing and qualities in healthcare and education.

Itopia must have seemed far away in the late 0s. The aftermath of the war brought severe ters, food shortages, wage freezes and tighter oning as bread and potatoes became scarce. inequalities of class and wealth were ressed, so new sources of injustice emerged. onstruction brought a Caribbean workforce to don. Their experience of the supposedly fairer ety that Britain was building proved painful, was to shape London's future as much as new tower blocks and primary schools.

**A Brixton street, painted in 1948 by James Fitton**
James Fitton saw this derelict shop front 'blooming like a flower in such a drab setting'. A left-wing artist, he included a Vote Labour poster in the scene.

# THE BLITZ &
# THE V-WEAPONS

World War II brought the terrifying experience of heavy bombing and rocket attacks to London. During the 'Blitz' of 1940–1 firestorms raged throughout the city, and thousands died.

**Bomb damage, 10 May 1941**

*The aftermath of a bombing raid in the City, photographed by Arthur Cross and Fred Tibbs. Canvas fire hoses snake past the still-smoking ruins in Queen Strteet Place, looking south toward Southwark Bridge.*

London had first experienced aerial bombing during the 1914–18 war. When war was declared in 1939, it was expected that Germany would again mount raids on British cities. A programme for the evacuation of children, mainly from inner-city industrial areas, was quickly put into operation.

The Luftwaffe began a sustained bombing campaign – a *Blitzkrieg* or 'Blitz' – against London in September 1940. The first raid took place on 7 September 1940, the first of four days of saturation bombing. The target was the docks, but by 11 September much of the East End had been reduced to smouldering rubble. This first experience of bombing was terrifying, as Stan Harris, then a twenty-two-year-old, remembered:

The sky was black with the German bombers and fighters … we was frightened to go out in the garden in the shelter. And we all went under the stairs, so we never had a dog's chance if anything happened. And all the night through you could hear thud, thud, thud, thud and the whistles as the bombs were falling. And Canning Town, and Rathbone Street where the old shop was, that was alight from top to bottom, virtually eliminated.

Around 300 tonnes of bombs were dropped, leaving 430 Londoners dead and 1560 injured. People emerged from the shelters to find landmarks gone, homes destroyed and corpses in the streets. Thereafter, the raids came regularly, mostly at night.

The Blitz continued into the spring of 1941. German incendiaries, or fire bombs, were lethal in the older parts of the city, where fire spread quickly. The worst night occurred on 29 December 1940, when a high concentration of incendiaries was dropped on the City of London, creating a firestorm around St Paul's Cathedral. The German high command chose a night when the tide was low so that it would be difficult for the firefighters to get water from the Thames. The event became known as 'the Second Great Fire of London'.

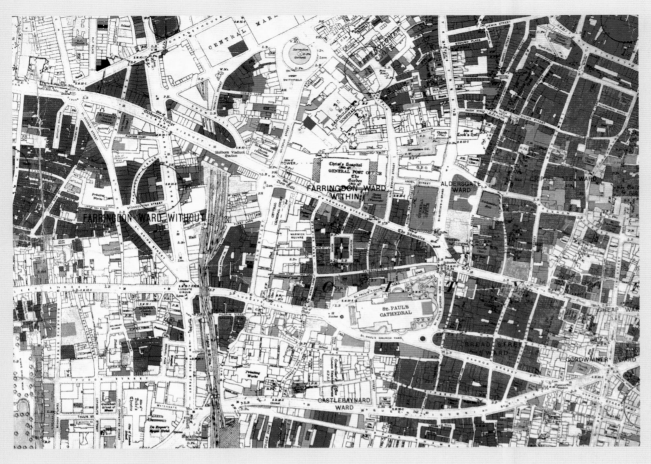

*War damage in the City by 1945*
A detail from a map produced by the LCC plotting the scale of bomb damage. Black shows areas of total destruction: purple, damage beyond repair; yellow, minor damage. The purple area to the top left was to be rebuilt as the Barbican complex, a symbol of the new City rising from the ruins.

Sheltering from the bombs became a daily concern for Londoners. The corrugated iron Anderson shelters provided by the government could only be used by those with gardens, and purpose-built brick street-shelters were few and far between. Many people in the poorer inner-city areas turned to the London underground for overnight shelter (see right). At first the government discouraged this, fearing a defeatist 'shelter mentality', but experience proved that in fact most people did emerge from the shelters each morning to carry on their normal business. Eventually parts of the underground became official shelters, with wardens, toilets and refreshment facilities.

The underground was not always safe, however. Sixty-eight people drowned when a bomb severed water pipes at Balham underground station and, in January 1941, a direct hit on Bank underground station killed 111 people.

## THE V-WEAPONS

The horrors of 29 December 1940 were repeated on 10 May 1941 when 1436 Londoners were killed by German bombs, the highest total for any single raid. The ferocity of the onslaught left fires raging across the capital and serious damage to major buildings, among them Westminster Abbey and the House of Commons (see left). But this ordeal marked the end of the most intense period of the Blitz. As the German war effort moved to the Eastern Front, air raids on London became less frequent.

After many raid-free months, a new wave of attacks began on 15 June 1944. The V1 pilotless flying bomb, or 'doodlebug' as it was nicknamed by the British public, brought a new level of fear to Londoners. Launched from France, the V1s were inaccurate and unpredictable, and their large payload caused high loss of life. The most serious V1 attack on London was at New Cross on 25 November 1944 when a V1 hit a crowded Woolworths, killing 160 Saturday-morning shoppers. Altogether the V1s killed over 6000 civilians and left 16,000 severely injured.

The V1s were followed in September 1944 by the even more terrifying V2 rockets, a highly destructive ballistic misile that might have crippled London had it been deployed earlier in the war. As it was, V2s killed nearly 3000 people and badly injured another 6000 before their launch pads were captured by the Allies in March 1945. There was no defence against these new missiles, and their super-sonic speed meant that their approach could not be heard before impact. Around 1000 V2s reached London, and if the attacks had continued the government might have instigated its emergency plan to evacuate the capital. Thankfully, Hitler's third vengeance weapon, the V3 guided missile, was never deployed. **MS**

*Underground shelter, 1940*
A photograph by Bill Brandt shows Londoners asleep in the Underground while sheltering from the Blitz.

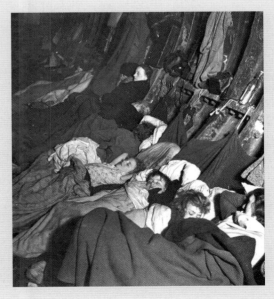

# EVERYDAY LIFE IN WARTIME

Government regulations flooded into Londoners' daily lives during the 'national emergency' of World War II. Ration books, clothing coupons and identity cards were all compulsory.

*Children with tin helmet, 1940*
*Photographed by George Rodger for the American magazine* Life.

'Business as usual' was the boast of wartime London, but daily life was very far from normal. Danger and death were ever-present. Everyday activities came under state control, as the government regulated what Londoners ate, wore and bought. People took on new jobs, devised new ways of entertaining themselves and learned to live in a new night-time London of darkness, shadowy figures and blacked-out street lights.

## EVACUATION

One of the certainties of modern warfare in the 1920s and 30s was that large cities would become targets for intensive air attack. The devastation of Guernica in the Spanish Civil War and of Warsaw and Rotterdam in the early months of World War II had brought home to the British government the dangers facing London well before the actual start of the Blitz. Even before war was declared on 3 September 1939, the evacuation of children from the capital had begun. The operation was organized by the London County Council (LCC), and within months about 600,000 children and expectant mothers had been moved to the relative safety of Kent, Sussex, Wales, Devon and Cornwall. Evacuation was not compulsory but parents accepted the government's view that London was now too dangerous for children, however distressing the separation. 'I watched the school teachers calling out their names and tying luggage labels in their coats, checking their parcels to see if there were warm and clean clothes,' noted Hilde Marchant, as she passed a school in Holborn on 1 September:

On the gates of the school were two fat policemen. They were letting the children through but gently asking the parents not to come further. They might disturb the children. So mothers and fathers were saying goodbye, straightening the girl's hair, getting the boys to blow their noses, and lightly and quickly kissing them.

## CHANGED ROLES

Adult roles and occupations also changed. Conscription into the armed forces became compulsory for all men between the ages of eighteen and forty-one, except those in essential industries. Women and older men moved into civil duties on the Home Front, becoming Air Raid Wardens or joining the huge army of clerks needed by the new government departments set up to manage the national emergency (see right). As had happened in World War I, women moved into jobs left vacant by men, and by 1943 all women aged eighteen to forty-five were required by law to register for work.

Many London women already had jobs in factories, but their working patterns were

### Baby's gas mask, 1940

*Gas masks were widely issued to civilians in the early war years, until it became clear that gas was to play little part in the war.*

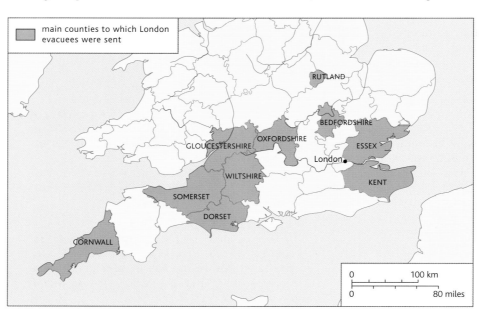

*main counties to which London evacuees were sent*

RUTLAND
BEDFORDSHIRE
OXFORDSHIRE
GLOUCESTERSHIRE
ESSEX
London
WILTSHIRE
KENT
SOMERSET
DORSET
CORNWALL

0  100 km
0  80 miles

### Evacuation destinations

London children mainly went to southern counties, but some went to Wales or further north.

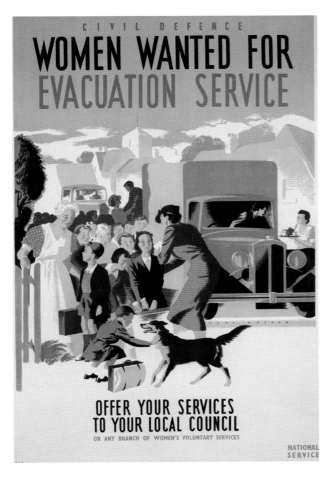

CIVIL DEFENCE

# WOMEN WANTED FOR EVACUATION SERVICE

OFFER YOUR SERVICES
TO YOUR LOCAL COUNCIL
OR ANY BRANCH OF WOMEN'S VOLUNTARY SERVICES

NATIONAL
SERVICE

*Evacuation Service poster, 1939*
*London's home-front relied heavily on voluntary work. Women and pensioners kept services running.*

also altered as production lines changed overnight. For example, Lebus of Tottenham, London's largest furniture factory, began to make hospital furniture, tent poles, aircraft fuselages and ammunition boxes. 'We also made this framework of a lorry in wood,' recalled Sissy Lewis:

… just the framework. It was then covered with canvas and I had to spray the windscreen, the radiator, the wheels and the number. It was then put on the road so the Germans would bomb that convoy of artificial lorries so the real lorries got through.

## FOOD & RATIONING

State control of the food supply was also immediate. In September 1939, the newly created Ministry of Food introduced ration books, a complicated but compulsory system that soon came to dominate the lives of everybody living in Britain. Rationing laid down strict controls for protein-rich essentials such as butter, bacon and cheese: each person was allocated a weekly amount. Bulk carbohydrate-rich foods such as bread and potatoes were not rationed. Other foods, including tinned meat, tapioca, sugar, pulses and breakfast cereals, were subject to a weekly points system, which allowed the consumer some choice over what to purchase.

Overall rations were not generous. 'You never starved, you just usually felt hungry,' remembered the Jamaican musician Coleridge

Goode. 'One ounce of butter a week. You had a choice whether you ate it all at one go or spread it thin over the whole week.'

Londoners found other ways of feeding themselves. Poster campaigns called on citizens to 'Dig for Victory' and 'Grow your own food' by cultivating their own vegetables. Many people already had an allotment and the old prohibition on keeping livestock on allotments was relaxed to allow the keeping of chickens, hens and pigs. Every available piece of land in London was turned over to agriculture. Hyde Park had its own piggery and Kensington Gardens replaced its flowers with rows of cabbages.

When bombing began to leave people homeless, the LCC provided cheap hot food for those who could not cook for themselves. Starting in the first days of the 1940 Blitz with a field kitchen on the Isle of Dogs, the Londoners' Meal Service was enormously successful. By 1943 the LCC was operating 242 feeding centres from school and hospital canteens, offering a good, basic meal for a cost of around one shilling. This was considerably cheaper than the five-shilling meal that government price controls required all restaurants to provide. Restaurants were allowed to continue in business during the war years, not least because eating out was seen as a morale booster.

## CLOTHING COUPONS

The supply and demand of other services and goods in London's shops also came under government control. Raw materials were diverted to the war effort, so firms manufacturing anything in wood, textiles or metal found their supplies limited and increasing controls on the sorts of products they could make. Customers experienced an ever-stricter regime of price controls and purchase taxes, until finally in June 1941 clothing and furniture both became subject to rationing by coupon. For clothing, every adult was given an annual quota of sixty-six coupons, and all garments were rated: a pair of shoes used up five coupons and a suit, eighteen coupons. The scheme created a flourishing trade in unused coupons. It also boosted the 'make do and mend' philosophy of repairing, altering or dyeing old clothes. 'Now it's patriotic to be darned and patched' declared one former teacher approvingly, to a Mass Observation recorder.

Wartime London was not all queues, blackouts, dowdiness and shortages, however. The cinema experienced a boom, with films from the United States providing at least a glimpse of glamour. *Gone with the Wind* opened in the West End in 1940 and played for several years. Radio brought a new generation of cheerful light entertainment programmes: *It's That Man Again* (ITMA), *Music While You Work* and *Desert Island Discs* all had their debut during the war years.

West End nightclubs and restaurants also kept going. 'Sure it was dangerous in the West End,' remembered the jazz drummer Tony Crombie:

I used to work in a first-floor club all through the bombs. No stopping for air raids, just kept straight on. People were fatalistic about it. But people were also tremendously happy. Everybody had that feeling that death was on the doorstep so they all had a good time. It's the happiest I've ever seen people in England.

**CR**

*War food, 1945*
*Dried milk and tinned food were staples of the wartime diet. Whale meat, shipped from Canada, was not popular.*

# RECONSTRUCTION: THE ABERCROMBIE PLAN

Patrick Abercrombie's Greater London Plan created a blueprint for London's future development. He envisaged a smaller, neater, more rational and more orderly capital city.

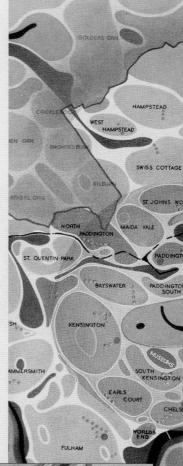

Planning for the reconstruction of London began before the end of the war. The London County Council published its County of London Plan in 1943, followed a year later by the Greater London Plan, a strategic plan commissioned by the Ministry of Town and Country Planning. Both were the work of Patrick Abercrombie, (1879–1957), professor of town planning at University College. They provided a bold blueprint for London's future development.

The 1943 Abercrombie Plan was presented to Londoners as a turning point for their city, an opportunity to build a better future. Leaflets and exhibitions publicized the proposals, which were received enthusiastically.

Abercrombie's thinking faced backwards as much as forwards. He aimed to preserve the best of the past while tackling the four 'major defects' of London, seen as traffic congestion, depressed housing, inadequacy and maldistribution of open spaces, and the 'indeterminate zoning' of houses and industry. 'Many people', he added, 'would add a fifth defect: the continued sprawl of London.' His vision harked back to the Arts and Crafts thinkers who saw the ideal city as small, clean and no threat to the English countryside.

At the heart of Abercrombie's proposals was his belief in 'decentralization'. He believed that London's sprawling growth should be contained by 'a rearrangement of population and industry … The numbers in the centre will decrease, those in the outer areas will grow.' He proposed ten new satellite towns. Harlow in Essex, with a population of 3000 in 1945, was to see an increase to 54,000. The growth of the suburbs would be curtailed by the strict enforcement of green-belt legislation.

Within London, he sought to surround each local centre with a mini-green belt, through which main roads would run. Different types of urban activity were to be clearly separated, and areas were to be 'zoned' by function. Industry was banished from the inner city, apart from the docks, which it was assumed would remain the engine of London's wealth.

Although Abercrombie wanted to preserve London's 'village' structure, he saw the need to rebuild some districts more or less completely. The plan contained many seductive illustrations of the future for

**Stepney**

*The plan's vision of future Stepney, with new housing blocks, green spaces and a new civic centre. The few survivals from the old Stepney include St. Dunstan's Church.*

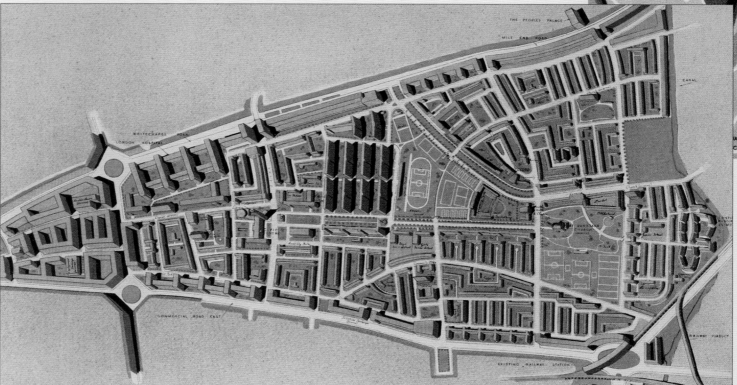

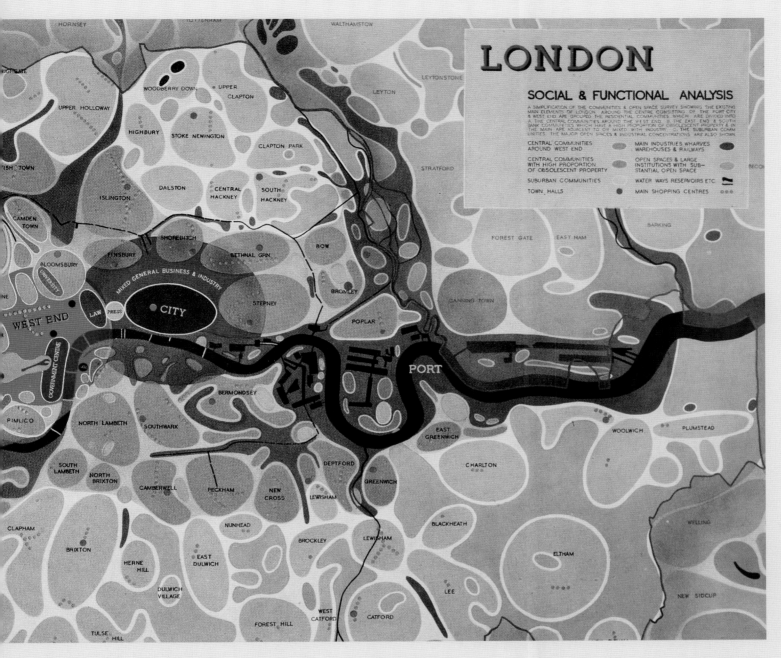

The map shows a "Social & Functional Analysis" of London with labels including:

**LONDON**

**SOCIAL & FUNCTIONAL ANALYSIS**

A SIMPLIFICATION OF THE COMMUNITIES & OPEN SPACE SURVEY SHOWING THE EXISTING MAIN ELEMENTS OF LONDON. AROUND THE CENTRE CONSISTING OF THE PORT, CITY & WEST END ARE GROUPED THE RESIDENTIAL COMMUNITIES WHICH ARE DIVIDED INTO A, THE CENTRAL COMMUNITIES AROUND THE WEST END. B, THE EAST END & SOUTH BANK COMMUNITIES WHICH HAVE A HIGH PROPORTION OF OBSOLESCENT PROPERTY & IN THE MAIN ARE ADJACENT TO OR MIXED WITH INDUSTRY. C. THE SUBURBAN COMMUNITIES. THE MAJOR OPEN SPACES & INDUSTRIAL CONCENTRATIONS ARE ALSO SHOWN.

CENTRAL COMMUNITIES AROUND WEST END — MAIN INDUSTRIES, WHARVES, WAREHOUSES & RAILWAYS
CENTRAL COMMUNITIES WITH HIGH PROPORTION OF OBSOLESCENT PROPERTY — OPEN SPACES & LARGE INSTITUTIONS WITH SUBSTANTIAL OPEN SPACE
SUBURBAN COMMUNITIES — WATER WAYS, RESERVOIRS ETC
TOWN HALLS — MAIN SHOPPING CENTRES

areas like Stepney (see left), notorious for their 'general drabness and dreariness'. The plan conjured up a vision of Stepney as a modernist utopia with tree-lined boulevards, high-rise housing blocks, community centres and schools, arranged around parks and green spaces. Roads were neatened.

## THE INFLUENCE OF ABERCROMBIE

Abercrombie's vision informed many reconstruction projects by local authorities in the 1950s, which embraced slum clearance and 'comprehensive redevelopment' in the name of modernization. But the vision had weaknesses as well as strengths. Above all, it was rooted in paternalistic assumptions and an instinctive dislike of the jumble and mess on which London had always thrived.

Street markets were one of the casualties. In the 1930s London had around ninety major street markets. Abercrombie recom-

mended relocating these into new pedestrianized shopping precincts. Many, such as Watney Street Market in Stepney, failed to thrive in their new surroundings. Green spaces, however, were one of the gains. Abercrombie proposed creating new parks along canals, particularly the Grand Union Canal in east London and the Surrey Canal in the south.

Abercrombie also proposed two new areas of regeneration in central London. He recommended developing the West End with 'inexpensive flats' to dilute the blocks of luxury apartments built before the war, and he earmarked the decaying, industrial South Bank for redevelopment as 'a great cultural centre, embracing amongst other features a modern theatre, a large concert hall and the headquarters of various organisations'. Six years later, the latter vision was realized through the Festival of Britain in 1951 and the creation of Shell's headquarters building.          **CR**

*Social & Functional Analysis map*
Abercrombie's analysis of London used four categories: an industrial zone (black); the centre of government and learning (red); inner-city communities with 'obsolescent property' (dark brown); and the suburbs (light brown).

# THE WELFARE STATE
# IN LONDON

The London County Council pushed forward the national mission to remove inequalities in welfare provision. The biggest transformation was in London's schools.

**Kidbrooke School, Greenwich, 1958**
*London's first comprehensive secondary school. With a colossal intake of 2000 girls, Kidbrooke was intended to replace five existing schools in south-east London.*

In July 1945 a nation exhausted by war voted in, by a landslide, a Labour party that had fought the election with the slogan 'Let Us Face the Future'. The new government, under Clement Attlee, was committed to social and economic revolution. In 1942 the Liberal Sir William Beveridge had been asked to examine the inadequate pre-war system of social insurance. In its place, he proposed a comprehensive system of social welfare. The *Beveridge Report* became a bestseller, with more than 600,000 copies sold. In 1945, with popular fears of a return to pre-war mass unemployment, the electorate was ready for change. In London Labour won forty-eight out of the sixty-two seats, nearly doubling the twenty-eight that they had achieved pre-war. Stepney even voted in a Communist. Having fought for freedom, Londoners now wanted equality.

London already had its own embryonic welfare state in the shape of the London County Council (LCC) which by the 1940s managed most of the capital's municipal housing and elementary schools. The LCC also ran the public assistance system, the ambulance service and the municipal hospitals, making it 'the greatest Local Health Authority in the Empire'.

The new national vision meant change for the LCC: the council kept its schools but lost its hospitals, which in 1948 were transferred to the new National Health Service. Overall, the new system, transformed the work of both local and national agencies in London by making welfare provision a universal right for all, rather than a stigmatised last resort for the ill and destitute.

## EDUCATION

London's education service had three pressing tasks in 1945: to repair or rebuild the 1150 schools destroyed or damaged by war-time bombs; to recruit more teachers; and to reorganize London's secondary education in order to enact the requirements of the 1944 Education Act, which had raised the school leaving age to fifteen, thereby making secondary education compulsory for longer. The LCC was to run an integrated system of secondary schools alongside its existing primary schools (as the former 'elementary schools' now became).

The London School Plan published in 1947 set out the council's bullish targets for more schools and more teachers. By 1957, sixteen new primary schools and twenty-five new secondary schools had opened, among them London's first comprehensive school, the colossal Kidbrooke in Greenwich (see left). Costing £560,000, Kidbrooke was designed for nearly 2000 girls and attracted huge publicity at the time. Facilites included 'housecraft rooms' for teaching office practice, catering and dressmaking.

The LCC favoured the comprehensive principle for its new secondary schools (instead of a tripartite system of separate grammar, technical and modern schools). It was felt that 'school life should promote a feeling of social unity among adolescents of all kinds and degrees of ability and that this could best be achieved in a comprehensive school'. However, in practice the pre-war patchwork of technical and central schools was maintained, along with assisted places to private schools so that 'boys who want to go to sea can follow a five-year course at the London Nautical School'. Ideological battles were yet to come.

All aspects of London education flourished. Between 1946 and 1953, the number of school pupils rose from 269,065 to 434,391 and the number of full-time LCC teachers increased from 14,273 to 17,938. Teacher-training courses expanded their intake, as did London's universities, as ex-service men and women took up govern-

ment grants aimed at those whose education had been disrupted by war service. Education was London's great success story.

## HEALTH CARE

The most fiercely debated area of reform was health care provision. Prior to the war, there had been great disparity between the health care available for those with different means, with services like dentistry a luxury that only a few could afford. The National Health Service Act was passed in 1946, and the National Health

establishment of a national service, not wishing to pass ownership of its hospitals to the state.

Perhaps the biggest innovation was the nationalization of hospitals. This had been pioneered during the war, when the two existing types – voluntary hospitals (ranging from tiny cottage hospitals to large teaching hospitals) and local authority hospitals – had been merged into the Emergency Hospital scheme. Fourteen regional hospital boards were created to manage the new system; after much debate and opposition from the London County Council, which wanted a central London region, London's hospital services were split between four regional boards.

The NHS suffered from financial problems from the outset: it had been hard to estimate costs, especially as medical science advanced and public expectations grew. The government's financial problems were exacerbated when defence expenditure increased sharply after the Korean War. Chancellor Hugh Gaitskill, in his 1951 budget, sought savings by imposing charges on NHS spectacles and dentures, which had initially been free. The Health Secretary Nye Bevan opposed any erosion of the principle of a free health service, and both he and Harold Wilson resigned in protest. Prescription charges of one shilling were introduced in 1952, as was a flat rate of £1 for ordinary dental treatment. The economic situation also made it difficult to build new hospitals: existing ones simply had to be adapted and patched up where possible.

The new welfare system aimed to look after its citizens 'from the cradle to the grave', as Winston Churchill had put it, and to foster solidarity by providing a common set of services for the whole population. This principle is clearly seen in the design of the Lansbury Estate in Poplar, east London, developed as part

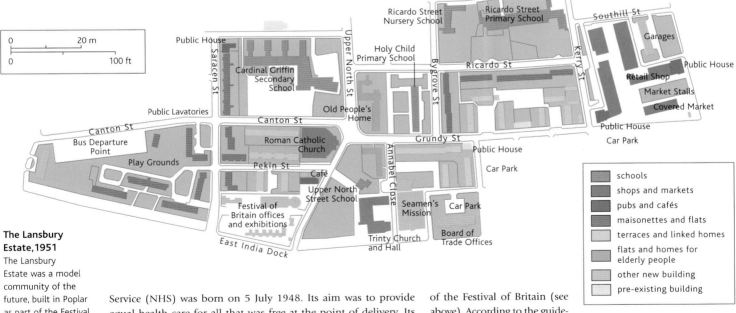

**The Lansbury Estate, 1951**

The Lansbury Estate was a model community of the future, built in Poplar as part of the Festival of Britain.

Service (NHS) was born on 5 July 1948. Its aim was to provide equal health care for all that was free at the point of delivery. Its establishment, however, was not without debate; opposition originally came from doctors and from the British Medical Association, fuelled by concerns that doctors might become salaried state employees and by ideological issues over state intervention in health care. The London County Council also resisted the

of the Festival of Britain (see above). According to the guide-book for this 'Live Architecture Exhibition', discussing the ways in which town planning could address perceived needs, 'the lives of a baby, a schoolchild, a teenager, a single worker, a married woman with a job, a mother and an elderly person are very different, but all have to live together as one community'. **MoL**

# THE FESTIVAL OF BRITAIN

London's South Bank was laid out with colourful pavilions, clean technology and a modern yet whimsical design style. Was this a vision of the future?

**Building the Dome of Discovery, 1951**
*The Dome was the largest aluminium structure ever built. It was 'not simply a gigantic mushroom', according to its designers. 'It was a considered a work of art as well as an achievement in engineering.'*

The Festival of Britain took place between May and September 1951. After the devastation of the war and years of austerity, it aimed to raise the nation's spirits while exploring ideas of Britishness and promoting the best in British art, design, science and industry. By the end of September, eighteen million people had taken part. The London centrepieces – the South Bank Exhibition (see right) and the Festival Pleasure Gardens in Battersea – were the Festival's most visible elements.

According to Herbert Morrison, in the official guidebook, the Festival was to be 'the autobiography of a nation … and millions of the British people will be the authors of it'. The Festival was about and for the British. It barely made reference to the rest of the world, for example representing the Commonwealth only in a small programme of exhibitions in South Kensington.

The South Bank Exhibition examined Britain in a series of large pavilions. The People of Britain Pavilion rooted the British firmly in pre-Norman history, while the Lion and the Unicorn Pavilion attempted to define their character. Overall, the Exhibition presented a selective and often romanticized past.

But the Festival also looked forward with optimism. It saw a 'New Britain' founded on communal values, where social progress would be achieved through collective action and provision. It also envisaged a future made more efficient and comfortable by scientific discovery. These advances were to benefit both men in the workplace and women in the home. The Country Pavilion on the South Bank, for example, showed the transformation of the farmer into a 'technician'. But alongside the display of tractors gently rising and falling on pistons was a somewhat uneasy assurance that mechanization did not mean the end of craftsmanship.

The Festival promoted the best in industrial design, recognizing its visitors as consumers. It celebrated new, well-designed, mass-produced, affordable goods, some 10,000 of which were displayed, while the Design Review offered a pictorial index of 20,000 more. To visitors tired of austerity, the promise was of a future that would be convenient, comfortable and notably materialistic.

The Festival's focus extended to the universe itself. The Dome of Discovery promoted astronomical exploration, with a telescope and a planetarium reached by an 'Escalator to Outer Space'.

The Festival was also meant to be fun. Marking the 100th anniversary of the Great Exhibition, it took inspiration from the Victorian period for many activities, notably the Festival Pleasure Gardens in Battersea. Modelled on London's 19th-century pleasure gardens, these were pure Victorian fantasy. Theatre, dance and music

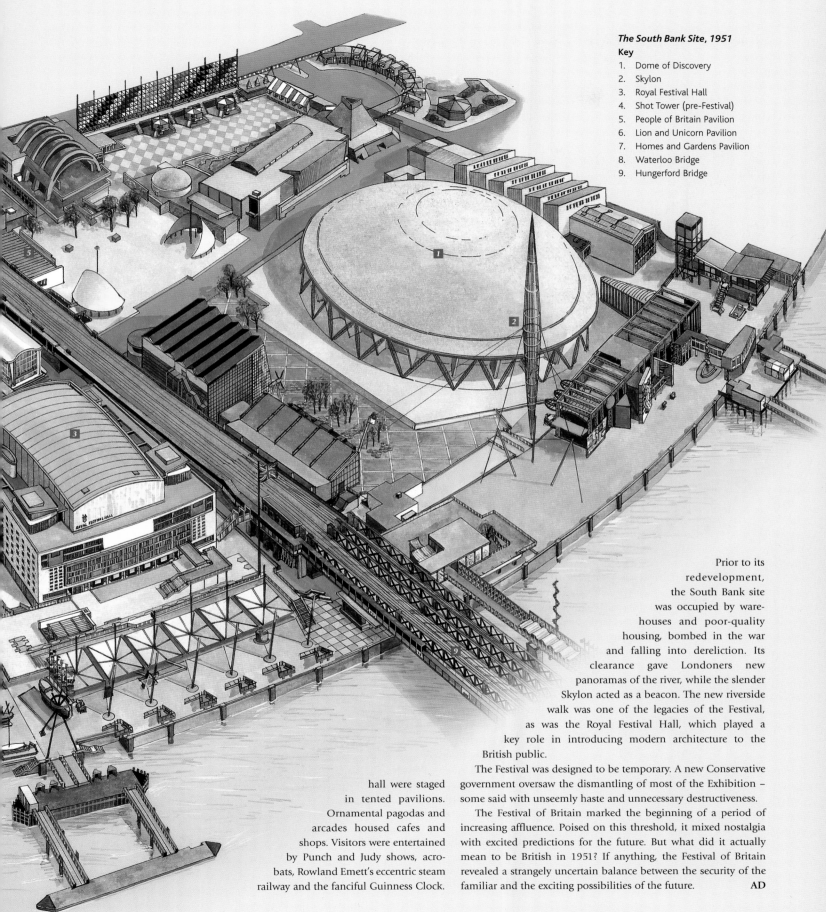

**The South Bank Site, 1951**
Key
1. Dome of Discovery
2. Skylon
3. Royal Festival Hall
4. Shot Tower (pre-Festival)
5. People of Britain Pavilion
6. Lion and Unicorn Pavilion
7. Homes and Gardens Pavilion
8. Waterloo Bridge
9. Hungerford Bridge

Prior to its redevelopment, the South Bank site was occupied by warehouses and poor-quality housing, bombed in the war and falling into dereliction. Its clearance gave Londoners new panoramas of the river, while the slender Skylon acted as a beacon. The new riverside walk was one of the legacies of the Festival, as was the Royal Festival Hall, which played a key role in introducing modern architecture to the British public.

The Festival was designed to be temporary. A new Conservative government oversaw the dismantling of most of the Exhibition – some said with unseemly haste and unnecessary destructiveness.

The Festival of Britain marked the beginning of a period of increasing affluence. Poised on this threshold, it mixed nostalgia with excited predictions for the future. But what did it actually mean to be British in 1951? If anything, the Festival of Britain revealed a strangely uncertain balance between the security of the familiar and the exciting possibilities of the future. **AD**

hall were staged in tented pavilions. Ornamental pagodas and arcades housed cafes and shops. Visitors were entertained by Punch and Judy shows, acrobats, Rowland Emett's eccentric steam railway and the fanciful Guinness Clock.

# BEATNIK LONDON

Soho was the place where outsiders felt at home. This cosmopolitan district attracted bohemians, drinkers, teenagers and sexual adventurers.

**The Soho Annual 1958**

*The Annual was produced by the Soho Association to drum up business for local restaurants during the Soho Fair.*

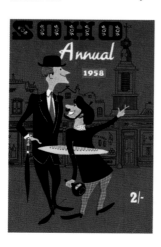

The 1950s brought a new mood to London's bohemia. There was a new soundtrack in the form of jazz; new – and sometimes bleak – intellectual ideas; a fresh political cause in nuclear disarmament; and a new experimentation in writing and art. Common to all of these was their appeal to the young and the alienated.

London's older bohemian areas, such as Chelsea and Hampstead, continued to cultivate an air of genteel intellectualism, but for the post-war generation, the place to be was Soho. This warren of narrow streets at the heart of the West End provided an oasis of existentialism within walking distance of the art schools. It encompassed European and African street life, restaurants, after-hours drinking clubs and jazz. By the 1950s it was also the capital's 'sexual gymnasium', for people of every persuasion. 'I felt that I had begun to discover – in the seeming chaos of the "smoke" – a secret village' said the jazz and blues singer and writer George Melly, remembering his early encounters with Soho in the years just after the war.

The area's village character came in part from its long-established cosmopolitanism. For centuries it had had a French and Italian population, but by the 1940s Soho also accommodated Cypriot, African, Maltese, Jewish and Chinese businesses and residents. The Chinese had begun to colonize south Soho around Gerrard Street during the 1930s, moving 'up West' from the East End. Soho's other main ethnic group was the Jewish community in north Soho, around Poland Street and Broadwick Street. The Jewish presence here was strongly associated with the rag trade, and as the clothing workshops and small factories started to move to larger premises in the streets above Oxford Street, so too did the residents, restaurants and synagogues. Jewish Soho also included the film industry, which by the 1940s had settled in Wardour Street – 'known to the cynical as the only street in the world where it is shady on both sides', according to writer Stanley Jackson.

*Soho Fair, 13 July 1958*

*Organized by the Soho Association as a promotion for local restaurants, the first Soho Fair was held in 1955. By 1958, the fair included a parade, a beauty contest, a waiters' race and a spaghetti-eating competition.*

## A SQUARE MILE OF VICE

Soho's reputation as a square mile of vice reached its peak in the 1950s. The streets behind Piccadilly Circus were notorious for male prostitutes; Kingly Street was the equivalent pick-up place for female prostitutes. Soho's 'girls' were a familiar sight on the district's streets until the 1959 Street Offences Act moved them inside. Sex was central to Soho's attraction for homosexual artists and writers. Soho's drinking clubs provided a second home for many of London's gay authors: Colin MacInnes (1914–76) lived in north Soho and his 1957 novel *City of Spades* was partly set there.

The most famous of Soho's drinking clubs was Muriel's, as the Colony Room was known to its members. It was founded by Muriel Belcher in 1947 in Dean Street. Autocratic and temperamental, Muriel created an ambience that suited the self-styled misfits and outsiders drawn there. Her club played a central part in the lives of a group of artists: 'Muriel's Boys' included Francis Bacon, Lucien Freud, Michael Andrews and Frank Auerbach.

Muriel's was one of many drinking clubs, ranging from barely legal 'bottle parties' to more established nightclubs like the Gargoyle in Meard Street, which provided dining and a four-piece 'orchestra' for dancing. A new sort of Soho club emerged in 1949 when a group of musicians led by the saxophonist Ronnie Scott decided to open their own club devoted to music, and in particular to the new, exhilarating form of jazz: bebop. Club 41 moved from Archer Street to Carnaby Street in 1950, where its short life was ended by a drugs raid. At Scott's trial, the magistrate famously asked 'What is bebop?' to which the Chief Inspector confidently replied, 'It's a queer form of modern dancing – a Negro jive.'

Music was in many ways the dominant Soho art form. The area had long provided support services to the West End's musical theatres and clubs. Archer Street was London's open-air job market for dance band musicians, who would gather hoping to be hired for casual work. The district was filled with music shops, rehearsal rooms and, increasingly throughout the 1950s, jazz clubs. In 1959 Ronnie Scott made a second attempt to run a club by musicians for musicians, this time in Gerrard Street, and on this occasion with more success.

By this time jazz was not the only music in town. Skiffle had exploded in 1956, as had Elvis-style rock and roll, and rhythm and blues was also beginning to surface. For a new, younger generation, Soho's attraction was not the jazz clubs and drinking dens, but the coffee bars. The first Soho coffee bar, the Moka, had opened in Frith Street in 1953, and its formula of espresso machine, arty decoration and jukebox set the pattern for others. Heaven and Hell had interiors reflecting its name; the Partisan offered a more intel-

**In the Cellar Club, c. 1960**
*Formerly the Skiffle Cellar, the Cellar Club in Greek Street was one of the centres of the Soho scene. The poster reads 'Skiffle, Jazz, Folksong, Spasm', which refers to the different forms of music that were featured at the club. 'Spasm' was an early name for skiffle.*

lectual ambience with chess boards and foreign newspapers. Many also provided live music. 'Soho had become a Mecca for hundreds of young musicians who drifted into London from Manchester, Liverpool, Birmingham, Glasgow, and Newcastle, their only possession a guitar, all hoping to get work in the many coffee bars,' recalled Bruce Welch, one such hopeful who arrived in London in 1958 and within a year was playing regularly at the 2-Is.

The 2-Is in Old Compton Street was Soho's most famous coffee bar. Opened in 1956, its tiny windowless basement became the hottest music venue in town. Hundreds of teenagers crammed into the sweaty space to see their idols perform. It was here that British rock 'n' roll came of age with such singers as Tommy Steele from Bermondsey, Adam Faith from Acton and Harry Webb from Cheshunt, who changed his name to Cliff Richard in 1958 on the release of his first hit record, 'Move It'.                    **CR**

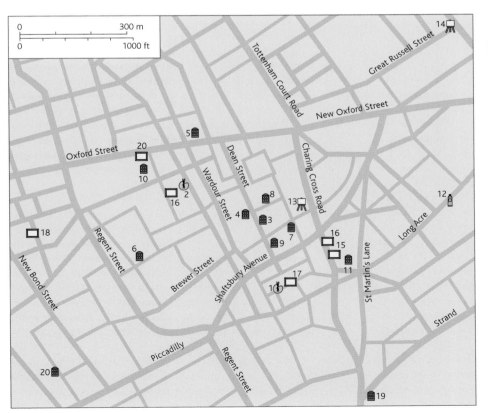

**Artists' Soho, 1950s**
Soho's cheap rents provided home and gallery space for artists, alongside clubs and pubs.

1. Gillian Ayres & Henry Mundy, 15 Lisle Street
2. Colin MacInnes (writer and art critic), 20 D'Arblay Street, 1956
3. The Colony Room Club, 41 Dean Street
4. The Gargoyle Club, 69 Dean Street
5. London Jazz Club, 100 Oxford Street
6. Barcelona restaurant, 17 Beak Street
7. Wheeler's restaurant, 19 Old Compton Street
8. The Dog and Duck pub, 18 Bateman Street
9. The French House pub, 49 Dean Street
10. Academy Cinema, 165 Oxford Street
11. Arts Theatre, 6/7 Great Newport Street
12. Brodie and Middleton, 79 Long Acre
13. St Martin's School of Art, 109 Charing Cross Road
14. Central School of Arts & Crafts, Southampton Row
15. Zwemmers, 26 Litchfield Street
16. Gallery One, 1 Litchfield Street, 1953–55, 20 D'Arblay Street, 1956–61
17. Artists International Association, 15 Lisle Street, 1947–71
18. Hanover Gallery, 32a St George Street
19. New Vision Group exhibitions Coffee House, Northumberland Avenue, 1953–58
20. Institute of Contemporary Arts, 165 Oxford Street, 1948, 17/18 Dover Street, 1950–68

**Map legend:**
- studios and homes
- art schools and academies
- meeting places
- exhibition space
- artists' supply shop

# THE LONELY LONDONERS

London's first body of postwar migrants came from the Caribbean. British citizens, they encountered a cold city, rather than a warm and welcoming motherland.

**Caribbean family in Trafalgar Square, c. 1959**

*This painting places Britain's Caribbean citizens at the capital's heart. The artist, Harold Dearden, had strong Christian beliefs but little else is known about him.*

The people who moved to London from the Caribbean between the late 1940s and 1961 changed the capital forever. As the first substantial community of black Londoners, they bore the brunt of the difficulty some British people found in adapting their attitudes to the change from empire to multiculturalism. Their presence tested the values that the British people professed to hold dear, pushing the issue of race relations to the centre of the national change in consciousness. Although the new arrivals were accused of being 'invaders', they were not by any legal definition 'aliens'. These were people with British passports and as much legal right to move to London as people from Yorkshire.

Immigration from the Caribbean began in earnest following the 1948 British Nationality Act. This act was in part a 'thank you' to British Commonwealth citizens for their war effort and in part a reflection of labour needs after the war. It bestowed citizenship on people from Commonwealth countries, creating a kind of global British labour market. In 1948 three ships arrived in Britain bringing 700 West Indian men seeking work in the country to which they now belonged. The first of these, *Empire Windrush*, was accompanied by a media frenzy. When the boat docked at Tilbury it was met by journalists and a camera crew who famously recorded the Trinidadian calypsonian, Lord Kitchener, performing a song he had composed to mark the occasion.

Migration from the West Indies grew throughout the 1950s. By 1961, around 177,000 Caribbeans had arrived in Britain, of whom around 100,000 had settled in London, the men mainly working in transport and construction and the women in hospitals and schools. Many organizations actively recruited Caribbean labour in the mid-1950s. In Barbados would-be emigrants were encouraged by government grants for those with the skills Britain needed as it rebuilt itself as a welfare state.

The new migrants tended to settle in the capital's poorer districts. The rundown terraces of Bayswater, North Kensington and Notting Dale became home to many as slum landlords exploited the fact that West Indians were turned away from rooms in more respectable areas. A second community, largely Jamaican, settled in Brixton, where the sympathetic Lambeth Council had welcomed the *Windrush* arrivals in 1948 and provided temporary accommodation in a former air-raid shelter at Clapham South. Brixton attracted many as it provided the nearest labour exchange and was relatively close to Waterloo Station, the terminus for boat trains from Southampton.

The new arrivals joined London's existing small community of West Indian intellectuals, teachers and doctors, many of whom had come to study. Their presence enabled the community to grow in cultural confidence. In 1945 the West Indian Students Union (WISU) was formed 'to help build up a Caribbean culture of our own'. WISU became a focus for intellectual life, as did the BBC radio programme *Caribbean Voices*, which from

1946 was broadcast from London and heard in the Caribbean every Sunday afternoon. *Caribbean Voices* became a forum for new writing from Caribbean writers in London. Its editor between 1954 and 1956 was the Trinidadian V. S. Naipaul, who had arrived in England to study in 1950. Naipaul later credited the programme with first encouraging him to write.

One of the writers in the *Caribbean Voices* circle was Sam Selvon, who arrived in London from Trinidad in 1950 when he was aged twenty-seven. Selvon's third novel, published in 1956, was a rich evocation of the lives of those who had arrived in the capital with little more than hope and curiosity. *The Lonely Londoners* describes the inner life of Moses, an old London hand, drifting through the capital as through a floating world, meeting new arrivals with their excitement and optimism, and reflecting on the grey city, the cold weather and the 'colour problem'.

> 'Sometimes I look back on all the years I spend in Bit'n', Moses say, 'and I surprise that so many years gone by. Looking at things in general life really hard for the boys in London. This is a lonely, miserable city.'

## THE NOTTING HILL RIOTS

Two years later, the Notting Hill riots showed London also to be a terrifying city. The area's Caribbean population had attracted the attention of British Fascists, stirring up the tensions that had grown as poor white families competed with poor black families for rooms and jobs. The slogan 'Keep Britain White' appeared everywhere . In August 1958 tension erupted into three days of rioting, during which white Teddy Boys came from as far away as White City, Tottenham and Acton to 'hunt niggers' and terrorize the Caribbean residents with petrol bombs and knives.

The police slowly regained order; they arrested 140 people, largely the white troublemakers, but also some black residents who had armed themselves in self-defence. The event shocked the nation and sparked lengthy debates about racial prejudice, community harmony and the scale of Commonwealth immigration. In a vicious postscript, a carpenter from Antigua, Kelso Cochrane, was stabbed to death in Kensal New Town by a gang of white men in May 1959. A much more positive event was the first West Indian carnival, held at the Porchester Hall in Bayswater in 1958.

**Man in Notting Hill,** *1961*
*Photographed by Henry Grant, this image shows one of the first generation of postwar immigrants from the Caribbean to London.*

By the end of the 1950s, 'the colour bar' was increasingly recognized as an obvious injustice that Britain would have to confront. Facing casual racial prejudice was part of daily life for many Caribbean Londoners, and it was not confined to working-class areas. In 1959 a Grenadian physician, David Pitt, stood for Parliament as the Labour candidate for Hampstead; his defeat was attributed by many to colour prejudice.          **CR**

**The Notting Hill Riots, August 1958**
Three days of fighting saw Notting Hill become a battleground as belligerent white gangs poured into the area from elsewhere.

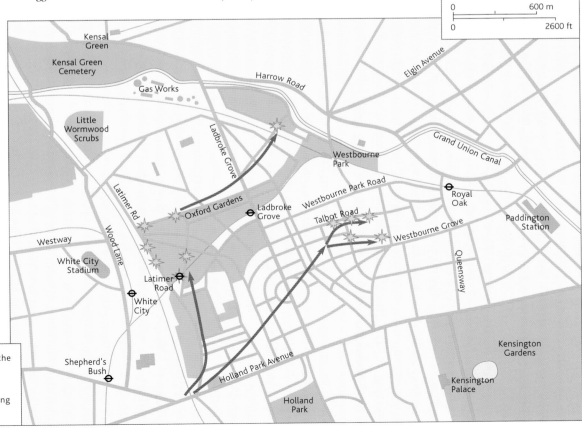

areas of slum clearance in the 1960s and 1970s

flashpoints of violence

routes of white gangs coming from Shepherd's Bush

# SURVIVALS
## EARLY 20TH CENTURY

**Finsbury Health Centre, 1938**
*A pioneering attempt to provide public health facilities for locals, the Finsbury Health Centre was designed by Lubetkin & Tecton.*
Underground: Angel

**Admiralty Arch, 1906–11**
*This monumental arch was completed in 1910 as part of the improvements to the Mall.*
Underground: Charing Cross

**The Port of London Authority Building, 1912–22**
*The PLA Building was designed by Sir Edwin Cooper as the headquarters for the newly established Port of London Authority.*
Underground: Tower Hill

**The Michelin Building, 1905–11**
*The Michelin building was built by the Michelin Tyre Company to a design by F. Espinasse as their London headquarters and a garage for fitting tyres.*
Underground: South Kensington

**The Daily Express Building, 1932**
*Designed by Ellis Clarke & Atkinson with Sir Owen Williams, the Daily Express Building was one of the great newspaper palaces of the interwar years.*
Underground: Temple or St Paul's

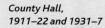

**County Hall,
1911–22 and 1931–7**
*County Hall was designed by
Ralph Knott for the London County
Council before World War I, but
not completed until after the war.*
Underground: Waterloo

**Liberty's department store:
the 'Tudor Building', 1924**
*Liberty's 'Tudor Building' expressed
the firm's pride in its Arts & Crafts,
English values. The architects were
E. T. & E. S. Hall.*
Underground: Oxford Circus

**The Carreras Building, 1926–8**
*Designed by M. E. & O. H. Collins
as a cigarette factory, the Carreras
Building's façade was supposedly
modelled on a temple to the
Egyptian cat goddess Bubastis,
a reference to the company's
cigarette brand 'Black Cat'.*
Underground:
Mornington Crescent

**The Hoover Building, 1932–5**
*This Art Deco icon was designed
by Wallis, Gilbert & Partners as
a state-of-the-art factory for
the US company Hoover.*
Underground: Perivale

**Selfridges, 1907–28**
*The large US department store in
Oxford Street was built in several
stages. The magnificent entrance
(above), with sculpture by Gilbert
Bayes, was completed in 1928.*
Underground: Bond Street

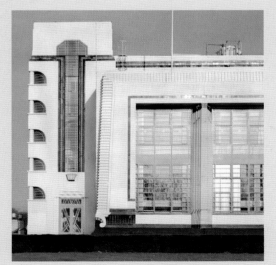

**Broadcasting
House, 1929**
*The headquarters
of the newly formed
British Broadcasting
Corporation,
Broadcasting House
was a cathedral of
modernity designed
by Val Myers.*
Underground: Oxford
Circus

# 1960s & 70s LONDON

The 1960s and 1970s were decades of mood swings. London shook off austerity to become the capital of a futuristic new Britain. Skyscrapers and flyovers, space-age fashions, optimism and pop made sixties London feel young.

But a darker London surfaced in the seventies as the economy took a downturn. The population fell to just under seven million and the jobs vanished along with the people. Was London an old city trapped in a cycle of dereliction and decay? As recession took hold so too did the terrible suspicion that London was dying.

Contrasts played out everywhere. The Greater London Council came to power in 1966 with a modernist mission to reinvent London from top down. Within ten years power had shifted to grass-roots action. Social divisions melted away in the sixties, as East End boys dated West End girls. But new lines were drawn. Words like 'ghetto' and 'underclass' re-emerged from London's 19th-century past. Carefree dolly birds gave way to sneering punks.

Beneath the mood swings, London was adjusting to profound changes. A youth revolution saw London's character, economy, values and image re-made by people under the age of thirty.

Unprecedented global mobility brought a multi-racial revolution, with equally far-reaching consequences. In 1960 London was still essentially a white city. By 1980 population statistics were telling another story, as were the mix of faces in London's primary schools.

Issues of migration, citizenship, race relations, rights and personal identity moved to the centre of London's political and cultural life during these years. By 1980 London faced the future as neither a modernist paradise, nor a dying Babylon, but a city of messy, exasperating but exuberant complexities.

**London from
Cromwell Tower, 1977**
London's new landscape of towers
and slab blocks, painted by Richard
Walker from a tower block on the
Barbican estate.

# THE RISE OF GREATER LONDON

London became officially larger in the 1960s, as the London County Council was replaced by the Greater London Council. Its initial strategic plan brought the first inner-city motorways.

**GLC strategic thinking, 1969**
*Dotted lines are roads needing enlargement; triangles are redevelopment areas; diamonds, road interchanges; 'T' indicates termini; purple, work zones; brown, 'settlement' zones; and circles, town centres.*

The creation of the welfare state made inevitable the reform of London's local government. Its new responsibilities required resources beyond the capabilities of the London County Council (LCC) and the metropolitan boroughs, bodies set up to reflect the needs and character of the 19th-century city. London entered the 1960s facing a revolutionary transformation of its government.

In October 1957 the Royal Commission on Local Government had proposed the abolition of the LCC and its replacement by a new council for Greater London, covering an enlarged area from Staines in the west to Hornchurch in the east. At the same time the lower level of government would be reorganized, replacing 117 metropolitan, county and district boroughs with 52 new London boroughs, each with a population of around 100,000.

The proposal was the natural development of changes that had been apparent since the end of the war. The Royal Commission's underlying aim was to create units of government that could operate strategically over a wide area and were 'large enough and strong enough to carry out the main range of local government functions'. The worry was that national government would take on running the capital if London's local government remained small in scale. The Royal Commission stated firmly its belief that London's future vitality would be best served through self-government.

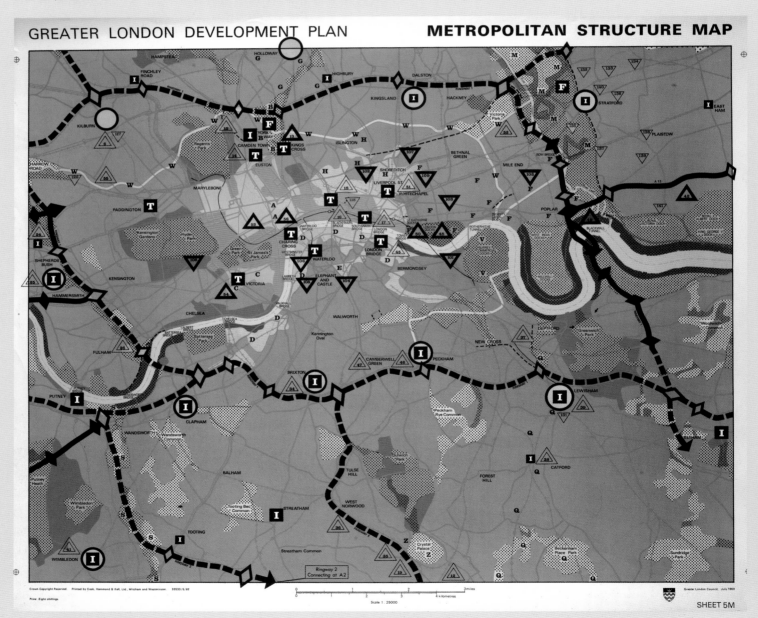

GREATER LONDON DEVELOPMENT PLAN     METROPOLITAN STRUCTURE MAP

SHEET 5M

The proposals for a two-tier system of local government were made on the assumption that the tiers would work harmoniously together. But even before the proposals were enacted, tensions emerged between the local and strategic levels. Boroughs in the south and west raised objections to being included in Greater London. The debates about reorganization were long and vociferous, raising passions about local identities, tradition and the grouping together of districts with little in common beyond geography. By the time the first elections for the new authorities took place in May 1964, the new London boroughs had been made larger and fewer, their numbers reduced from fifty-two to thirty-two.

The new London boroughs took over from April 1965. For Londoners the change was more than administrative. The new map of London government cut across many old local identities. Hendon had been absorbed into Barnet. Hayes and Harlington had been split: Southall passing to Ealing and Hayes to neighbouring Hillingdon. Old borough names disappeared, to be replaced by new entities, such as Tower Hamlets, made up of Poplar, Bethnal Green and Stepney. New street furniture was installed and new letterheads appeared on rates demands. Many of London's old turn-of-the-century town halls were abandoned in favour of new office blocks. There were inevitable cries that the whole process of change was a scandalous waste of ratepayers' money.

## A MOTORWAY BOX

While the new London boroughs were getting to grips with their responsibilities, the Greater London Council (GLC) began to flex its strategic muscle. Despite its augmented area, it was a less powerful body than its predecessor in terms of day-to-day service delivery. Many of the LCC's old responsibilities passed to the boroughs or to non-elected bodies. In the case of education in inner London, reorganization created a completely new body – the Inner London Education Authority (ILEA). The main focus of the GLC's work became roads, transport and strategic planning.

The first large-scale statement of intent from the GLC was the Greater London Development Plan, published in September 1969 (see left). This doorstopper of a document preached a message of order: 'London needs better organizing, not meaning more busy-bodying and interference with individual freedom, but basic planning.' It had a litany of virtuous words in its aims, which were to 'liberate' economic enterprise, to 'treasure' London's character, to 'conserve' its fabric of buildings, and to 'balance' home, work and transport. In practice, however, this meant more main roads.

The 1969 plan proposed three concentric 'ringways' that would encircle London and, together with the outward-facing 'radials', solve the city's traffic problem once and for all. It was an aggressively bullish vision that would cost £2,000 million and require the demolition of 30,000 homes. 'Everyone regrets,' said the plan, 'the disturbance of private property which this road planning involves,' and this was to prove true. In the 1970 GLC elections, eighty-five candidates stood as 'homes before roads' candidates. The public enquiry into the plan, the Layfield Panel, heard more than 28,000 objections before finally reporting in May 1972. Layfield's report criticized the ambitious scale of the GLC's plans and the vision of London as a 'motorway box' was amended when the plan was finally approved in July 1976. By this time, an economic downturn had made much of the vision unviable, although elements were to remain in the GLC's thinking for years to come. The outer ringway was finally completed in 1986 with the opening of the M25, while the inner-city ringway remained as the old North and South Circulars. The M11 extension in east London and the Westway in west London are also surviving fragments of the plan, as are Centrepoint tower (see below) and the regiment of high-rise office blocks along the Euston Road.

Other aspects of the plan also ran aground. The GLC's vision of a neatly ordered London with well-defined suburban centres alternating with office districts and factory zones was not endorsed by the boroughs where it cut across their own ambitions. In central London the GLC's central office district led to the planning battle-grounds of Piccadilly and Covent Garden, where the GLC found itself facing fierce opposition from a generation of articulate, belligerent and politically savvy residents. In the early 1970s, the new Covent Garden Community Association was successful in halting the GLC's plan to raze the historic fruit and flower market and replace it with office blocks. By the mid-1970s, the GLC's political make-up had changed and it adopted a less aggressive, more community-minded approach to strategic planning.     **CR**

***Centrepoint, 1974***
*The office block remained un-tenanted for many years, becoming notorious as a symbol of corporate greed. This protest urged that the homeless should be housed there.*

# SLUM CLEARANCE & HOME OWNERSHIP

London's postwar housing drive moved into a new phase. Slum clearance programmes moved thousands from terraced houses into high-rise flats.

***Cotton Gardens Estate under construction, 1968***
*A typical 1960s high-rise housing scheme in Lambeth. The massive twenty-two-storey blocks replaced old streets of terraced housing deemed to be slums.*

**New housing estates in Bethnal Green, 1960s**
Schemes such as the Cranbrook Estate cleared areas of terraced housing that had largely survived war-time bombs.

The creation in 1966 of the London boroughs and the Greater London Council (GLC) coincided with a new phase of anxiety about London's housing. In 1963, the terrorization of tenants by slum landlord Peter Rachman in Notting Hill had come to light as part of the Profumo scandal. In 1965 the Milner Holland report on London's housing concluded that the capital's housing stock was worryingly decrepit. Around 500,000 new homes were needed over the next ten years if London was to provide decent homes for its citizens. Immediately after the war the focus had been reconstruction; now it was slum clearance. Victorian terraces had to be swept away and Londoners rehoused in bright, clean, modern flats.

The new London boroughs embarked on the crusade against slums and slum landlords with enthusiasm. In 1961, 21 per cent of London's homes were local authority-owned. By 1981, the proportion had risen to 46 per cent, and 400 high-rise housing blocks had appeared, in all parts of London. Changing the landscape was a way of asserting civic identity, and several of the new boroughs built on a heroic scale (see right).

Southwark was one of the most ambitious, with a vision of the complete elimination of its housing shortage by 1980. Newham built 125 tower blocks, more than any other London borough, and completed twice as many new homes in the 1960s as the entire housing programme of Newcastle upon Tyne. Haringey embarked on the huge Broadwater Farm estate. Equally vast was Brent's Chalk Hill estate of 1900 houses and flats designed for families from overcrowded Willesden. By the end of the 1960s, London's highest tower block was the thirty-one-storey Trellick Tower in Notting Hill, built by the GLC. By the end of the 1970s, the height record had risen to forty-three storeys, with Shakespeare Tower on the Barbican estate qualifying as the highest housing block in Europe.

Most ambitious of all the 1960s schemes was Thamesmead, a space-age suburb of 60,000 dwellings built on the Woolwich and Erith marshes in east London. 'A desolate scene will be transformed for the well being of Londoners' promised the GLC. The construction problems of building on marshlands were immense and the initial idea was to build in the Dutch style, on concrete platforms held up by stilts. In the event, the land was drained and large quantities of concrete were poured into the foundations. The design incorporated all the latest architectural ideas about public housing. It mixed medium-rise tower blocks with low-rise slab blocks, and arranged them around a twisting 'spine' of long pedestrian walkways. Residents were taken from inner London borough waiting lists, and the first moved into their new homes in June 1968.

## A HIGH-RISE BACKLASH

By the end of the 1960s, faith in mass housing schemes had begun to falter. Construction faults were most dramatically illustrated by the collapse in 1967 of one corner of Ronan Point, a tower block in Newham, killing five and injuring seventeen. The backlash against tower blocks also raised questions about the assumptions on which slum clearance programmes were based.

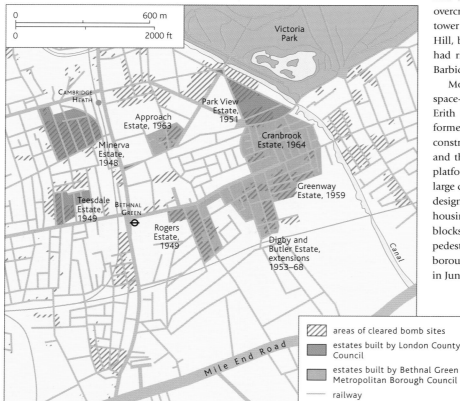

| 0 | 600 m |
| 0 | 2000 ft |

Victoria Park

CAMBRIDGE HEATH

Park View Estate, 1951

Approach Estate, 1963

Minerva Estate, 1948

Cranbrook Estate, 1964

Greenway Estate, 1959

Teesdale Estate, 1949

BETHNAL GREEN

Rogers Estate, 1949

Digby and Butler Estate, extensions 1953–68

Canal

Mile End Road

▨ areas of cleared bomb sites
■ estates built by London County Council
■ estates built by Bethnal Green Metropolitan Borough Council
— railway

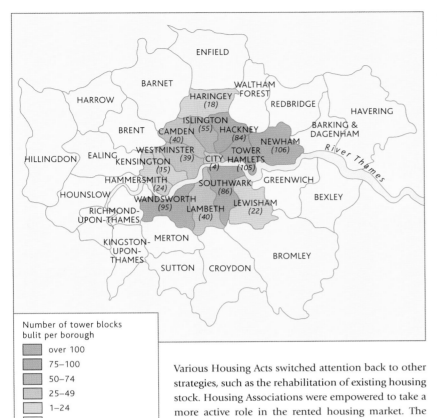

Number of tower blocks
built per borough

| | |
|---|---|
| ▨ | over 100 |
| ▨ | 75–100 |
| ▨ | 50–74 |
| ▨ | 25–49 |
| ▢ | 1–24 |
| ▢ | none |
| *(40)* | actual number of tower blocks built |

**London's Tower Blocks**

This map shows the numbers of multi-storey housing blocks (over ten storeys high) that were built in inner London boroughs between 1950 and 1970. Some were built by the LCC and GLC; others by the boroughs themselves.

***Tolmers Square, 1979***

*Residents fought a seventeen-year battle against demolition. The area, at the back of the Euston Road, was eventually redeveloped as offices.*

Various Housing Acts switched attention back to other strategies, such as the rehabilitation of existing housing stock. Housing Associations were empowered to take a more active role in the rented housing market. The community housing movement championed an approach to housing design that placed much more emphasis on the real needs of tenants.

## OWNER OCCUPATION

The new focus on improving existing stock reflected changes in London's housing market. While councils were moving their tenants into new estates, London's inner-city Georgian and Victorian terraced houses were attracting a new generation of owner-occupiers. In 1964, the word 'gentrification' was coined by sociologist Ruth Glass to describe the changes that occurred in an area when middle-class owners moved in. London's Georgian suburbs – Islington, Notting Hill, Camberwell and Kennington among them – were all affected by this phenomenon in the 1960s.

The arrival of a new breed of residents in such areas was quickly followed by an influx of property developers and the emergence of new tensions between landlords and tenants. Although the worst excesses of tenant harassment and evictions had been made illegal by a succession of post-Rachman rent Acts, many tenants in private rented accommodation found themselves displaced when landlords decided to seize the opportunity of realizing the newly inflated value of their crumbling properties. The 1970s saw a consequent mushrooming of tenant action groups to protect their interests (see right).

As the housing market became more complex, new worries began to emerge. Slums might have been cleared, but poorer Londoners remained trapped in a vicious circle of inner-city renting, which allowed them no opportunity to accumulate capital through home ownership in the rising housing market; their situation led at best to overcrowding, and at worst to homelessness. The potential for the very poor to sink through the system designed to help them was powerfully illustrated in 1967 by Ken Loach's television play *Cathy Come Home*, and out of the resulting furore emerged the charity Shelter.

Concern that home-ownership in London was being driven upmarket also began to be voiced. In Islington the value of a Georgian house bought for £6000 in the mid-1960s had risen more than twentyfold to £130,000 by the mid-1970s. Generally, London had always been a city where the majority of people rented their homes, but between 1960 and 1980 the statistics for owner-occupation began to rise.

By the end of the 1970s, despite the mammoth effort put into council house-building over the previous twenty years, London still had a severe shortage of housing, although the nature of the crisis had changed. The GLC's 222,000 homes made it the largest public landlord in the country but, against the background of a declining population, the GLC of the late 1970s decided to change its housing strategy.

Under the banner 'Inner London must live', the council moved away from provision to enablement: henceforth the council would aim 'to stimulate people into solving their own housing problems, making finance available for home-ownership, encouraging equity-sharing and co-operatives'. Mortgage lending was stepped up and in 1977 the GLC began to encourage long-standing council tenants to buy their homes from the authority. It was a strategy that would controversially be rolled out across the rest of the nation in the next decade under the Conservative government of Prime Minister Margaret Thatcher. **CR**

# FROM FACTORIES TO OFFICE BLOCKS

London's economy changed gear as manufacturing industry collapsed; the docks quit the inner city, leaving behind a landscape of dereliction. Elsewhere, office towers rose.

**Industry leaves inner London**
Manufacturing firms that survived the 1970s recession tended to move out of inner London. Some moved their operations abroad, others moved to new plants elsewhere in the United Kingdom.

During the 1950s, London's economy seemed well on the way to postwar recovery. Twenty years later, however, the city was in a state of shock. The economic stability on which London had rested over the previous 200 years had suddenly vanished, leaving behind the spectres of unemployment, factory closures and recession. Industry had collapsed – 38 per cent of London's manufacturing jobs disappeared between 1959 and 1974. The expected growth in office work, which had so obsessed the planners and politicians of the 1950s, had not materialized. Optimism about London's future gave way to pessimism.

The most traumatized sector of the economy in this period was the manufacturing industry. At the end of the 1950s, one in three of all London's workers was employed in factories, and in some sectors London's workforce made up a significant proportion of the national total: 20 per cent of British engineering jobs, for example, and 45 per cent of British ladies' tailoring were located in

the city. London's industrial heartlands lay in four places. In the inner city a perimeter of workshop quarters encircled the old City, from Clerkenwell for precision instruments to Aldgate for clothing. In west London a series of industrial zones stretched from the Park Royal Estate at Acton to the industrial quarters of Southall and Hayes – the former housing the large AEI vehicle works and the latter the mammoth electronics factory of Thorn EMI. To the east, the Lea valley had been colonized by furniture factories and engineering works. Finally, there was an industrial zone on both banks of the river, including the docks, which still employed 30,000 men in the early 1960s. Riverside industry included London's largest factories – Tate and Lyle's sugar refinery at Beckton, the cement works at Thurrock and the Ford motor works at Dagenham.

## A DE-INDUSTRIAL REVOLUTION

The factors that enabled industry to flourish in the 1950s were those that had brought industry to the capital in the first place: the sheer size of the metropolis, which allowed a self-sustaining network of contractors and subcontractors to flourish; easy access to global trade through the docks; and a workforce that could supply both high skills and low-paid labour in abundance. By the mid-1960s, all of these were rapidly being overtaken by circumstances. The loss of trading privileges to Commonwealth countries hit many London firms hard: Tate and Lyle's sugar exports halved during the 1960s, forcing the firm to close refineries at Plaistow, Fulham and Hammersmith. By the 1970s, there were other pressures too: the oil crisis sent fuel prices spiralling upwards, and as countries in the Far East underwent their own industrial revolutions, British firms found themselves struggling to compete. The west London glass firm Whitefriars closed in 1980, bringing to an end a manufacturing history that had begun just outside the City walls in the early eighteenth century.

The growth of factory closures and job losses during the 1960s and 1970s was unrelenting. Many firms shut down completely; others shed jobs or moved out of London. Pears closed its soap factory in Isleworth in 1962, Watney Mann's Albion Brewery in Whitechapel closed in 1979, Beckton gasworks closed in 1969 and Westland Helicopters closed its Fairey works at Hayes in favour of its base in Yeovil, Somerset. The closure of British Leyland's West London vehicle

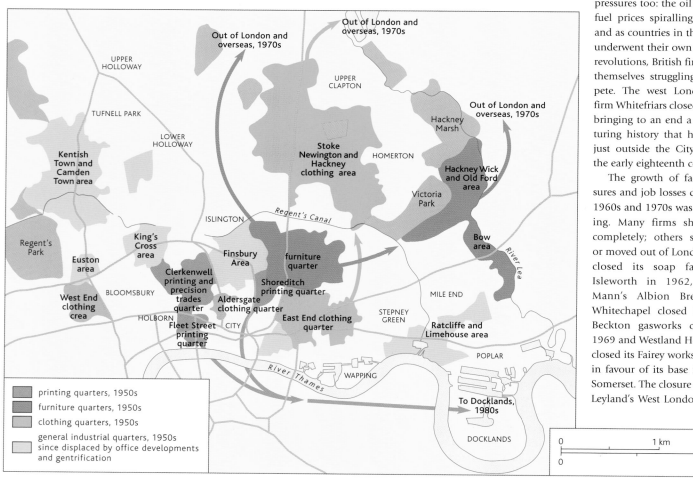

printing quarters, 1950s
furniture quarters, 1950s
clothing quarters, 1950s
general industrial quarters, 1950s since displaced by office developments and gentrification

Hyams built the 116-metre high (380-ft) Centrepoint, opened in 1967. Meanwhile, in the suburbs, Croydon turned its centre into a futuristic cityscape of concrete and glass. Over fifty office blocks were built between the mid-1950s and the mid-1970s, providing five million square feet of office space and jobs for 3000. New shopping centres, multi-storey car parks, ring roads and flyovers allowed Croydon to promote itself as 'the most consistently modern-looking area in the whole of England'.

In central London the area that was fast emerging as the most modern-looking was, in fact, also the most historic. In the City of London an eruption of towers and blocks accompanied the journey of the financial institutions into new territories of wealth creation. Dominating all was the giant 183-metre high (600-ft) Nat West Tower, built in the 1970s and London's only genuine skyscraper (see below). In 1958, London had been the first European capital to relax exchange controls, and had thus begun to attract European money markets to its Square Mile. Even before Britain's entry into the Common Market in 1973, the City had become the financial capital of Europe. As the City turned away from its domestic hinterland to face the global markets, it became an oddity, marked off from the rest of London by its unsettling combination of tradition and modernity. Its largely male workforce continued to wear Edwardian bowler hats and carry rolled umbrellas, but they worked in futuristic tower blocks and nobody quite understood what they did. The City's old wealth had been rooted in physical commodities; now its earnings were invisible.                                                          **CR**

**The Lesney factory, 1982**
*The firm made Matchbox toys and was one of Hackney's largest employers in the 1960s. Recession hit hard in the 1970s and the factory closed in 1982.*

plants meant that even the famous London buses would no longer be made in London. This de-industrial revolution left an aftermath of anger, distress and hardening industrial relations, but it also gave London a new landscape of dereliction. For many in the 1970s it seemed as if London was regressing to its post-Blitz incarnation as a city of corrugated iron, overgrown weeds, crumbling brickwork and ruins.

## CHANGING CITYSCAPES

The most visible example of London's decaying cityscape was the swathes of land that had once been the docks. The East India Docks were the first to close in 1965, and the last, at the end of the 1970s, were the giant dock complexes on the Isle of Dogs. Trade had moved downriver to Tilbury, where Britain's first container port opened in 1968. This left behind thousands of unemployed men and acres of empty warehouses in London. At St Katharine Dock, the fate of the warehouses came to illustrate two possible futures for redundant industrial buildings: adaptation for other uses or demolition. In April 1969, a group of artists led by Peter Sedgley took over the warehouses and turned them into a complex of 150 artists' studios. Three years later, the GLC decided that commercial development was a better option for the long-term regeneration of the site and the artists moved out, leaving property developers Taylor Woodrow to demolish the old warehouses and build the Tower Hotel in their place.

Tourism and office work were the twin hopes for future job growth. Planners and property tycoons joined forces in the effort to replace old buildings with new office blocks. In central London, Joe Levy made the Euston Road into a skyscraper canyon and Harry

**The City skyline, 1976**
*This view from St Paul's Cathedral shows the cluster of new towers, including the Nat West Tower and the Stock Exchange Tower.*

# SWINGING LONDON: FROM FAB TO PUNK

The young seized London for themselves in the 1960s and 70s. The city's image changed from stuffy to hip, bringing worldwide fame for Carnaby Street, King's Road and Camden.

**Swinging London bus, 1967**
*A Matchbox toy made by Lesney, the iconic Hackney toymakers.*

'This spring, as never before in modern times, London is switched on. Ancient elegance and new opulence are all tangled up in a dazzling blur of Op and Pop.' So declared *Time* magazine's cover story on 'Swinging London' in April 1966. The article identified London as the centre of 'fab' modernity, defined by a glamorous mix of youth, wealth and attitude. *Time*'s characterization of London stuck. Postcards and products spread the message that this was a swinging city where the young had taken over, with new ways of dressing, behaving and thinking. Old was out.

**Union Jack shirt, 1966**
*This shirt is from I was Lord Kitchener's Valet, a Carnaby Street boutique that had started life in Portobello Road selling old uniforms and Victoriana.*

Youth was the common factor for the movers and shakers in Swinging London. Art students such as Mary Quant, (twenty-five in 1961) had lived through the grey years of austerity and hungered for colour. London's young artists had been exploring Pop and Op styles since the 1950s. Working-class teenagers had money to spend, anti-establishment glamour and self-confidence. As the actor Terence Stamp (twenty-three in 1961) recalled, 'The working class was just dogsbodies up until then. Suddenly we were Jack the Lads. Everybody wanted to be like us.'

## THE NEW MAP OF LONDON

The youth revolution remade the cultural map of London, picking out districts to transform from dowdy to trendy. Carnaby Street, a backwater in Soho housing low-grade garment factories, became the most famous shopping street in Britain. The kingmaker of Carnaby Street was Scottish clothing entrepreneur John Stevens, whose menswear boutiques attracted a clientele who wanted to dress in colour and patterns, rather than grey suits (see left). Across town in Chelsea, boutiques like Mary Quant's Bazaar, opened in 1955, Top Gear and Hung on You re-invigorated the King's Road in similar fashion.

Chelsea and Soho were already bohemian areas, but the next generation of Londoners took anti-establishment preferences further by colonizing places that were definitely 'other'. Camden began to change from working-class suburb to youth-culture hotspot with the growth of Camden Market. The presence of the boutiques Biba and Bus Stop added new excitement to Kensington. Notting Hill, where the presence of the West Indian community gave the district a vibrancy and edge unmatched elsewhere, became a fashionably bohemian place to live.

While shops remade the daytime map, clubs changed the night-time flow around central London. Soho remained a mecca, its clubs evolving with the musical journey from rhythm and blues through pop and progressive rock to punk. The 100 Club on Oxford Street had begun life in 1942 as a jazz club; in 1976 it hosted a notorious two-day festival of Punk. Tottenham Court Road went hippy when the UFO club opened in an old 1920s dance hall. In 1967 the club moved its psychedelic happenings to a disused engine shed in Camden, the Round House. Camden's credentials as a centre of music and youth culture grew in 1973 with the opening of Dingwalls, a music venue housed in an old canal-side timber warehouse.

## ALTERNATIVE LONDON

**Swinging London, 1967**
*London's new image on an LP by Russ Sainty and the First Impressions, released on the budget-label Saga, based in Kensal Green.*

In the late 1960s the bright colours of Swinging London gave way to the darker tones of the counterculture. More overtly anti-conformist and political, this generation positively rejected the laws of 'straight' society. Across London, communes became a way of life. By the 1970s the 30,000 squatters in London included the citizens of the Free and Independent Republic of Frestonia, otherwise known as Freston Road, Notting Dale.

The counterculture left a legacy of do-your-own-thing, including publishing. The London listings magazine *Time Out* first appeared in 1968, run in true counterculture style as a workers'

## THE SCENE

**Map labels:**
Portobello Rd. (antique shops)
Victoria Sporting Club
Robert Fraser
Kasmin
BBC
Carnaby St. (mainly boys' boutiques)
L'Étoile
White Tower
Tiles
Sotheby's
Foale & Tuffin
Soho Sq.
SOHO
Oxford St.
Royal Opera House
Aldwych Theater
Trattoria Terrazza
MAYFAIR
New Bond St.
Palisades
Regent St.
Grosvenor Sq.
Berkeley Sq.
Leicester Sq.
Bayswater Rd.
Hyde Park
Strand
Embankment
Kensington Gardens
Serpentine
Park Lane
Annabel's
Clermont Club
Dolly's
I.C.A.
The Scotch
Trafalgar Sq.
Piccadilly Circus
Victoria
Thames
Tiberio's
Crockford's
Albert Memorial
Rotten Row
Hyde Park Corner
Mirabelle
Hilton
Piccadilly
Caprice
Christie's
St. James's Sq.
Whitehall
Royal Festival Hall
SOUTH BANK
Biba
Green Park
The Mall
National Theater (Old Vic)
Kensington Rd.
Knightsbridge
St. James's Park
Birdcage Walk
Parliament Sq.
High St.
Albert Hall
Hostess
Leslie Caron's home
Belgrade Sq.
Buckingham Palace
S. KENSINGTON
Brompton Rd.
Harrods
BELGRAVIA
Sloane St.
Cromwell Rd.
CHELSEA
Sloane Sq.
Blaise's Club
Guys and Dolls
Royal Court Theater
Hung On You
Bazaar
Hem and Fringe
PIMLICO
Le Reve
Casserole
Road
Top Gear
Countdown
King's
Fulham Rd.
Cheyne Walk
Chelsea Embankment
Thames
Granny Takes A Trip

**Legend:**
- Art gallery or auction house
- Theater or concert hall
- Casino
- Restaurant
- Discothèque
- Girls' boutique
- Boys' boutique

0   ¼   ½   1 mi.
TIME Map by R. M. Chapin, Jr.

'The Scene', 1966
This map from the American magazine *Time*, marked the establishment end of the swinging London scene, rather than its youth culture.

co-operative. Individualism was also part of the legacy. 'The purpose of this book,' explained Nicholas Saunders, writer of the counterculture handbook *Alternative London*, 'is not to push a way of life, but to give access to the ways in which you can express your individuality in a sincere way.'

## PUNK

In the late 1970s London's youth culture swung in a new direction. Punk was also anti-establishment, but more aggressively so. Its followers were the alienated 'blank generation'. Chelsea moved on

*London postcard*
Street scenes captured in a 1970 postcard.

*London Punks, 1981*
Photographed by Henry Grant.

FORTY CENTS                                      APRIL 15, 1966
LONDON: The Swinging City
TIME
THE WEEKLY NEWSMAGAZINE
VOL. 87 NO. 15

*Time magazine, 1966*
Liverpool-born cartoonist Geoffrey Dickinson's cover illustration captures London's old and new icons, such as a Rolls Royce and a Mini Cooper.

from Swinging London to become the epicentre of Punk culture, thanks in large part to the presence of one shop. Malcolm McLaren and Vivien Westwood opened a boutique in 1971 at the rundown end of the King's Road. Originally called Let it Rock, the shop evolved through various names to become the notorious SEX. McLaren was also the manager of the Sex Pistols, a living, spitting advertisement for McLaren and Westwood's outrageous clothes. By 1980 King's Road was famous for the crowds of punks who paraded up and down it each weekend.

London had always offered an arena for self-expression, but the youth revolution meant that individualism now came with a positive antipathy to all forms of traditional authority. The youth revolution ultimately changed not just the capital's global image, its clothes and record shops, but also the way the city allowed itself to be governed, its economy and values.                    **CR**

# THE RISE OF MULTICULTURAL LONDON

London wrestled with the twin issues of immigration and racial discrimination. New laws tried to shape a fair future for all British citizens but tensions rose.

***Supermarket shopping, c. 1978***
*A photograph by Henry Grant shows Asian women and children at a supermarket in Southall. This area of west London had become home to a large Asian community.*

The 1960s and 70s saw more immigration into the United Kingdom than ever before, altering the face of London forever. Debates about migration from abroad became entangled with questions of citizenship and racial discrimination at home. In 1968 the Home Secretary, James Callaghan, saw the new Race Relations Act, which tightened anti-discrimination laws, working hand in hand with the new Commonwealth Immigration Act, which tightened entry controls. Together they promised a way of '[creating] a society in which, although the government might control who came in, once they were in, they should be treated equally'.

Not everyone thought it was so simple. London was at the heart of an often angry debate, frequently spilling over into street violence. Londoners in the inner city were caught up in a vortex of clashing views as disaffection with the current state of British society was expressed from all sides. Nevertheless, these years saw London realize it was a multicultural city – a fact clearly visible in the faces of London schoolchildren (see right) or the dress of Londoners going about their daily business (see above).

## COMMONWEALTH IMMIGRATION

The Commonwealth Immigration Act of 1962 brought an end to the unrestricted immigration of the postwar years, and people from Africa, China, India, Pakistan and the rest of the Commonwealth flocked to Britain to avoid being locked out.

'Africanization' of countries in East Africa after independence saw the expulsion or mass migration of Asians on an unprecedented scale. Over 13,000 Kenyan Asians arrived in London in 1967, followed by 10,000 Ugandan Asians in 1971; by 1981, there were nearly 92,000 East African Asians in the city. Other groups included 12,000 Vietnamese war refugees, living largely in Hackney. Greek and Turkish Cypriots who arrived after the Turkish invasion of Cyprus in 1974 took up residence in Stoke Newington and Wood Green. The Chinese community in Soho doubled in the 1970s as an exodus from Hong Kong began, reaching a high of 20,000. In Lambeth, Hackney, Islington and Paddington nearly 30,000 West Africans had settled by 1971. This was a major change from the mainly West Indian migration of the previous decades.

In London, as elsewhere, newcomers were frequently treated as scapegoats for grievances, subjected to a range of prejudices, and viewed as competition for housing and jobs. Despite the introduction of the 1966 Race Relations Act, which made outright discrimination illegal, and the setting up of the Race Relations Board (1966) to encourage 'harmonious community relations', most immigrants found little support if they complained

The xenophobic mood was captured in 1968 by Conservative MP Enoch Powell's infamous 'Rivers of Blood' speech, in which he sought to whip up hysteria by implying that white Britons might become a minority. His calls for a halt to immigration were taken up by London's meat porters and dockers on 23 April 1968. With the slogan 'Back Britain, not Black Britain', thousands marched to Trafalgar Square in support of Powell. Far-right groups such as the National Front, which shared Powell's views, seized the opportunity to fan the flames of anti-immigrant sentiment.

But three years later, thousands of immigrant sympathisers, both black and white, marched in central London to protest against the tighter restrictions introduced by the 1971 Commonwealth Immigration Act. Denounced as a piece of legislation that discriminated against black Commonwealth citizens, this restricted entry to people with UK parentage. Exceptions continued to be made for refugees. London's Bangladeshi community grew in 1971 following the war of independence from Pakistan.

## LIVING IN LONDON

For security and familiarity, new immigrants to London followed the familiar pattern of settling close to their places of work, their community centres or places of worship. Immigrant communities were established in suburban boroughs like Brent, Croydon, Northwood and Woolwich, and transformed areas like Southall, where the first Sikh temple was built in 1959. Southall was one of the first areas in London to provide for a growing Asian consumer market; its High Street was transformed by Asian businesses, with BHS (British Home Stores), for example, replaced by the Asian-owned Bainwant Bros. Asians provided labour for the Woolf Rubber Factory and Jimnalls Bakery, and the area also saw Asian factories and businesses set up to meet a growing demand for Asian foods, saris and other imports.

The new communities began slowly to blend in. Their adoption of customs

**London's ethnic villages, mid-1970s**
Communities from the Caribbean islands and Ireland were well-established. Communities from India, Pakistan and Bangladesh were growing fast.

**Population in 1974**
- more than 8% born in the West Indies
- more than 8% born in South Asia
- more than 8% born in the Republic of Ireland
- more than 8% born in the West Indies and more than 8% born in the Republic of Ireland

ENFIELD
BARNET
HARROW
HILLINGDON
BRENT
HARINGEY
WALTHAM FOREST
REDBRIDGE
HAVERING
CAMDEN
ISLINGTON
HACKNEY
EALING
WESTMINSTER
CITY
TOWER HAMLETS
NEWHAM
BARKING & DAGENHAM
HAMMERSMITH
KENSINGTON
River Thames
HOUNSLOW
SOUTHWARK
GREENWICH
BEXLEY
RICHMOND -UPON-THAMES
WANDSWORTH
LAMBETH
LEWISHAM
KINGSTON -UPON-THAMES
MERTON
BROMLEY
SUTTON
CROYDON

**London school children, 1978**
Pupils at George Tomlinson middle school in Southall, photographed by Henry Grant.

considered British was gradual, but in many cases their acceptance in the wider London community came first through commercial initiatives: the new phenomenon of the 'open all hours' Asian corner shop. Later, thousands of curry houses, often owned by Bengalis from Sylhet, Chinese restaurants and Greek and Turkish cafes would spread to every area of the city.

In the inner city, Bangladeshis colonized Whitechapel and Spitalfields; housing shortages forced many to move the short distance to rundown areas in Shoreditch and Bethnal Green. Black and Asian households were sometimes placed in the poorest accommodation on council estates. These were hostile environments for newcomers, synonymous with inner-city deprivation. Some estates became no-go areas for Asians, where white prejudice

and anger seethed. The National Front turned Newham into a battleground for racist violence. 'Paki bashing' became a recognized activity, and many Pakistanis and Bengalis suffered daily abuse. The 1970s also saw racist murders in London. In 1978 the murder of Altab Ali, a Bengali clothing worker in Whitechapel, proved a tipping point in race relations. Around 7000 people accompanied his coffin in protest from Brick Lane to Downing Street.

National Front agitation surfaced again in Southall where on St George's Day 1979 several thousand Asians and Anti-Nazi League protesters demonstrated against the use of the town hall by the National Front. New Zealand-born Blair Peach, one of the protesters, was struck on the head and died of his injuries. Allegations were made against the police of indiscriminate batoning.

Tensions between black communities and the police remained close to breaking point throughout the 1960s and early 1970s. It was at the 1976 Notting Hill Carnival, and again a year later, that relations finally broke down in some of the worst rioting London had ever seen. Around 400 police and 200 civilians were injured. In the aftermath, long-standing grievances were left unresolved and tensions remained high into the troubled 1980s.          **SG**

# THE CHANGING FACE OF SPORT

London's major clubs turned professional, bringing in new money and a business outlook. But despite new stadiums, attendances at football matches fell.

**World Cup Willie, 1966**
*The first-ever mascot for a football world cup. Willie was used to brand a range of souvenirs, including keyrings.*

In the 1960s sport in London was irreversibly changed by the widening gap between amateurs and professionals. For London's old private sports clubs, the new decade brought a new commercial outlook. In 1968 the Wimbledon Lawn Tennis club, resolutely amateur since its foundation in 1877, opened up its tournament to professional players and embarked on a new era of sponsorship and prize money. Around the same time the Marylebone Cricket Club, another bastion of gentlemen amateurs, reorganized itself, making a clear distinction between amateur and professional cricket. The commercial aspirations of the London clubs that followed the professional road were marked by an outbreak of stadium building and property development. At Wimbledon, Lords Cricket Ground and Chelsea Football Club, new property investments underlined that sport was now a business.

Amateurs also had their new stadiums. While the private clubs went professional, amateur sport came within the remit of local government, in its new role as the deliverer of social benefits through the welfare state. London County Council led the way in dramatic style when it built the National Sports Centre at Crystal Palace, Britain's first purpose-built sports centre and hugely influential on all the smaller versions that followed. It housed Britain's first Olympic-standard swimming pool and top-class facilities for athletics. The building, designed by Sir Leslie

**Young fans, 1963**
*A photograph by Roger Mayne of fans at the cup-tie between Arsenal and Liverpool.*

Martin, opened in 1964, but the idea of a sports complex on this site (derelict since the Crystal Palace fire of 1936) had been in planners' minds for many years. The Abercrombie Plan had spoken of a 'long felt need for running tracks' in south London and had envisioned the Crystal Palace complex as one of a ring of new public sports centres around London. The metropolitan borough keenest to buy into the vision was Hampstead, which opened a glamorous new sports halls and swimming bath complex at Swiss Cottage in 1964.

## FOOTBALL & MONEY

Football proved to be the sport most changed by the new commercial environment. Before 1961, footballers in England were still governed by a maximum wage and a restrictive transfer system that favoured the clubs. In 1961, the maximum wage was £20 a week. Most footballers were paid a similar wage to other working men and were not unlike their supporters. Under threat of a players' strike, the maximum wage was abolished in 1961. Fulham chairman Tommy Trinder had previously publicly stated he would pay Johnny Haynes £100 a week if he could. He stayed true to his word and Haynes became the first player to earn this sum. In 1963 the restrictive transfer system was ruled a 'restraint of trade' when George Eastman sued Newcastle United for refusing to release him for transfer to Arsenal.

As wages increased for the elite, so too did commercial and promotional opportunities. The best players had long dabbled in such activities as sponsoring products and ghostwriting articles. However, the scale grew exponentially from the late 1950s. Johnny Haynes, for instance, was one of the first players with an agent and won a lucrative contract to advertise Brylcreem. In the 1960s, a new breed of footballer celebrities emerged and the 'swinging' capital became their playground, even for players like George Best who lived elsewhere. One club in particular became associated with the rich and glamorous – Chelsea. The club's ground, Stamford Bridge, was conveniently located near the fashionable King's Road and its board member Richard Attenborough regularly filled the director's box with famous faces to watch the young flamboyant team. In 1975 the opening of the new East Stand, designed by Darbourne and Darke, accentuated the club's image as stylish and modern.

As professional football became more corporate, money, power and the best players became concentrated in a small number of clubs, several in the capital. In 1961 Tottenham Hotspur were the first 20th-century team to achieve 'the double', winning the League Championship and the FA Cup in the same season, a feat repeated a decade later by their north London rivals, Arsenal. London clubs won the FA Cup eight times between 1960 and 1979, although only Spurs and Arsenal managed a First Division title win during this period. Spurs were also the first English team to win a major European trophy, taking the Cup Winners' Cup in 1963. London clubs and players were central to the most famous football event of the 1960s – England winning the World Cup at Wembley in 1966. West Ham's trio of captain Bobby Moore, hat-trick scorer Geoff Hurst and Martin Peters were instrumental in a victory that was watched on television by audiences around the world.

Televised football came of age in this period, transforming the game. Coverage focused on the top clubs and on national and international competitions. As armchair spectators became familiar with top-class football, their expectations grew, with consequences for the lower league teams. Television was a factor in declining match attendances: in London weekly gates for league clubs almost halved between the late 1960s and the mid-1980s.

*Football fans, 1976*
*A photograph by Jim Rice of fans on the way to Wembley for the Cup final between Manchester United and Southampton.*

## CROWD TROUBLE

Another factor was hooliganism. Crowd troubles were not unknown to football, but this period saw a darker mood take hold, as the game became a lightning conductor for other social tensions in the inner cities. In the early 1970s, groups of young 'skinheads' became increasingly, and sometimes violently, territorial about both clubs and sections of the terraces. By the mid-1970s, the skinhead image had disappeared, but the violence persisted. Organized gangs emerged; in London the Millwall Bushwhackers became notorious. Violence spilled out of the stadiums into the streets where heavy-handed policing contributed to a battleground atmosphere.

Violent hooliganism was often accompanied by racist politics. A small but growing group of black footballers had begun to emerge through the London clubs in the 1960s and 1970s. Players like Clyde Best at West Ham became role models for young black footballers, but also the targets for racist abuse, which ranged from insults and animal noises to bananas thrown onto the pitch. It was not until 1978 that a black footballer was picked for the England squad and by this time National Front sympathizers were leafleting outside some London grounds. The reaction came in the form of Anti-Nazi League groups, for example 'Spurs against the Nazis', but management still tended to turn a blind eye to the problem. Football's troubles were to get worse before they got better, scarring the game for the remainder of the century. **AD**

*Crystal Palace, 1964*
*London's showpiece sports stadium: intended for amateur use but designed to accommodate world class professional events.*

# GANGLAND & CRIME

The two most notorious gangs of the 1960s were run by the Kray twins and the Richardson brothers, from east and south London. Both crime empires spread to the West End.

The social and economic upheavals that created Swinging London reverberated in London's underworld. As new boundaries were drawn between what was legal and illegal, and new opportunities for profit-making business emerged, so too did new opportunities for crime. Gambling, vice, clubs, white-collar fraud, property development and Mafia-style money laundering were the key areas for London's modern-minded criminals in the 1960s. Drugs were added in the 1970s.

The most high profile of the 1960s-style criminals were the notorious sibling gangs – the Kray twins and the Richardson brothers. Organized crime had been part of London since at least the 1920s, but both these gangs added a postwar flavour to their activities. Although they were rooted in a home patch of working-class London – Bethnal Green and the East End for the Krays, Camberwell and South London for the Richardsons – both gangs exploited the new classless mood of the 1960s to move socially and geographically into the more lucrative activities associated with West End clubs and City investors.

Clubs, and particularly gambling clubs, were at the heart of gang crime in the 1960s. The Betting and Gaming Act of 1960 legalized gambling with the hope that this would sever the connection with crime. In fact the Act opened the door to a new wave of criminal activity, including Mafia-style takeovers and protection rackets. Esmerelda's Barn, a lucrative gambling club in Wilton Place, was taken over by the Krays in 1961 and was soon furnishing them with incomes of £40,000 a year. The roulette wheels were generally stacked in favour of the clubs and by 1969 there were 1200 licensed gambling clubs in London, far more than the authorities had originally envisaged. The Richardsons never made it to the West End, but at Mr Smith's gambling club in Catford, a notorious gun fight in 1966 turned out to have been a battle between Richardson's men and a rival gang over protection money.

'Clubs' also covered a host of small premises that had sprung up in the wake of the 1959 Street Offences Act, which effectively moved vice indoors. In Soho and Shepherds Market in Mayfair, strip clubs, massage parlours and drinking clubs burgeoned, many directly controlled by criminal syndicates like the vice empire run by Bernie Silver and Frank Mifsud. Porn shops were another innovation of the period. Like gambling clubs they needed a license and were subject to regulations, but police corruption ensured that the system did not always work as intended. By 1970, there were forty porn shops in Soho and the old bohemian, romantic sense that had characterized the district for so long had given way to a much harder atmosphere of money and exploitation.

## BUSINESSMEN-GANGSTERS

The bullish mood of 1960s business provided other opportunities for clever criminal gangs. The 'long firm' fraud saw false companies created to attract loans from investors and banks. Both the Krays and the Richardsons dabbled in overseas investments: South Africa, in the case of the Richardsons, while for Ronnie Kray there was an abortive attempt to build a completely new city in Nigeria. This semi-respectable activity gave the Krays a way in to high society, particularly via those who regarded the working classes as glamorous. Both MP Tom Driberg and Lord Boothby were drawn into the Krays' orbit. The latter successfully sued the *Daily Telegraph* in 1964 over allegations that he had had a homosexual affair with Ronnie Kray.

Beneath the veneer of modern-minded businessmen gangsters, the Krays and the Richardsons ran their empires with old-fashioned criminal values, using fear and physical violence. The trials of the Krays in 1966, following the murder of Jack 'the Hat' McVitie in the Blind Beggar pub in Whitechapel, were read with revulsion by middle England as they glimpsed into a nightmare world of brutality that underpinned the bright lights of modern Swinging London. The following year, the Richardson 'torture trial' brought even more ugly truths to the surface. Following Charlie Richardson's sentence, *The Times* tried to reassure its readers that the police were now hot on the trail of organized crime, 'But all [future gangs] will need to tread warily. For now they are up against a police organization so highly skilled and determined that no little back street despot will ever be able to cock a snook at law and order and hope to get away with it. They have Richardson and his bunch of bullies to thank for that.' Such confidence was severely knocked, however, by the

***Off Leicester Square, 1962***
*West End night-life, shown here, attracted a new breed of businessman gangster: the dividing line between licit and illicit businesses was blurred.*

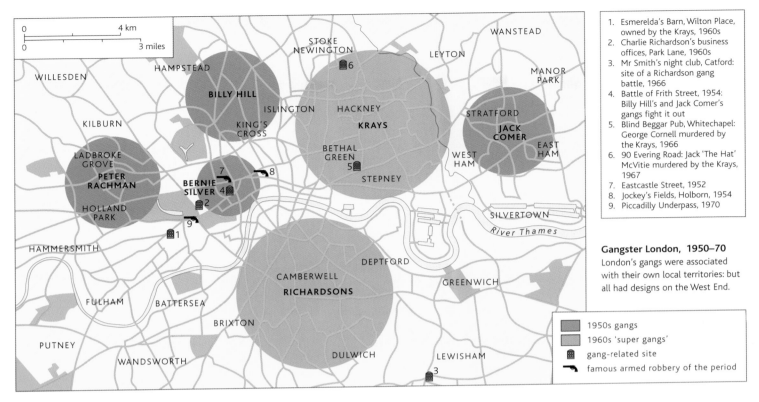

0 4 km
0 3 miles

1. Esmerelda's Barn, Wilton Place, owned by the Krays, 1960s
2. Charlie Richardson's business offices, Park Lane, 1960s
3. Mr Smith's night club, Catford: site of a Richardson gang battle, 1966
4. Battle of Frith Street, 1954: Billy Hill's and Jack Comer's gangs fight it out
5. Blind Beggar Pub, Whitechapel: George Cornell murdered by the Krays, 1966
6. 90 Evering Road: Jack 'The Hat' McVitie murdered by the Krays, 1967
7. Eastcastle Street, 1952
8. Jockey's Fields, Holborn, 1954
9. Piccadilly Underpass, 1970

**Gangster London, 1950–70**
London's gangs were associated with their own local territories: but all had designs on the West End.

| | |
|---|---|
| ▨ | 1950s gangs |
| ▨ | 1960s 'super gangs' |
| ▣ | gang-related site |
| ⚊ | famous armed robbery of the period |

police corruption trials of the 1970s, when it was revealed that almost one third of the Metropolitan Police's vice squad were taking backhanders from criminals.

Compared with the gangster entrepeneurism of the Krays and Richardsons, old-fashioned armed robbery for money seemed relatively innocent. The Great Train robbery of 1963, was a London-based crime that caught the headlines and was presented in the media almost as a daring escapade. This was also true of the Piccadilly Underpass Security van robbery in 1970, an ingeniously executed operation. One of the most sensational crimes in this period was also the most apparently innocent. In 1960, Goya's portrait of the Duke of Wellington was saved for the nation by the National Gallery and then promptly stolen while on display. The painting was recovered in 1965 when it emerged that the mastermind was not a gangland boss, but Kempton Bunton, an unemployed bus driver, who claimed he had stolen it to raise money to buy TV licences for pensioners.

By the 1970s, drugs were replacing clubs and vice as the new growth areas for London's criminal gangs. Cannabis and cocaine had been part of London's bohemian lifestyles since the 1920s, but neither drug was seen as a threat to the fabric of society. Heroin was not really known in London until the early 1960s, and it was not until the mid-1970s that its use began to spread to working-class areas of inner London and middle-class suburbs, leaving a trail of social and personal devastation in its wake. Drugs was one area of personal behaviour where the state tightened, rather than loosened, the boundaries of legality. In 1966 LSD was outlawed. In 1971 the Misuse of Drugs Act tightened the law considerably, introducing the offence of 'possession with intent to supply'. New laws proved impotent in the face of new surges of supply from heroin labs around the globe, including Vietnam following the end of its traumatic war in 1975.

Drugs heralded the rise of new criminal overlords with global networks and no need for local loyalties. The Kray era was already over when in 1969 the twins received life sentences. Both spent the 1970s in Parkhurst Gaol, where Ronnie joined the art class. In 1979 he was transferred to Broadmoor psychiatric hospital. **CR**

***Ronnie Kray's Crucifixion, 1972***
*The gangster's religious-themed artwork was painted in Parkhurst Gaol and given to his old associate Billy Webb, who regularly visited the twins in prison.*

# STRIKES, PROTESTS & DEMONSTRATIONS

Londoners in the 1960s and 70s took to the streets to demand rights, protest at wrongs and activate causes. Wars and freedoms jostled with identity and revolution in the city's politics.

**Anti-Nazi rally in Trafalgar Square, 1978**
*The rally was followed by a Rock against Racism concert in Victoria Park, East London.*

London in the late 1960s and 70s was a tense, troubled city. The combination of economic recession and an anti-establishment youth culture created a climate where grievances were not to be suffered in silence.

Direct action was traditionally associated with the labour movement's twin causes: the right to work and the right to strike. Now newer causes, global in scope, emerged to join them. The anti-Vietnam War and the anti-apartheid movements moved many to action. 'Identity politics' brought new campaigns into the open as women and gay Londoners marched to liberate themselves from social and legal constraints. Debates about race and citizenship were played out on London's streets, just as much as in Parliament.

## THE RIGHT TO STRIKE

The struggle for the 'right to work' was epitomized by London's dockers who, fearful of redundancy, challenged their employers and national government with a major dock strike in 1972.

Year on year the dockers had resisted dock modernization through wildcat strikes that brought the port to its knees. In 1972, the imprisonment of five London dockers for picketing the Midland Cold Store in Stratford triggered a national dock strike, and the ensuing campaign to free 'The Pentonville Five' was regarded by the *Observer* newspaper as the 'most significant challenge to the authority of any Government since the general strike of 1926'.

## PEACE NOT WAR

Throughout the 1960s, London's middle-class socialists and students took to the streets to protest against a range of issues including the Vietnam War, apartheid, nuclear arms and sexual inequality. From its formation in 1958, the Campaign for Nuclear Disarmament (CND) had organized an annual 'Ban the Bomb' march from Aldermaston to Trafalgar Square. From

*Philosopher Bertrand Russell at a CND protest march, Trafalgar Square, 1961*

1967 many CND supporters joined the Anti-Vietnam War and anti-apartheid demonstrations marching through central London alongside student activists, hippies, anarchists and socialists, including members of the Workers' Revolutionary Party (WRP) and the International Marxist Group (IMG). Although the protests were disruptive to London life, most were good-natured and peaceful. In March 1968, however, 100,000 Anti-Vietnam War protesters gathered in Trafalgar Square to hear Tariq Ali of the IMG and Vanessa Redgrave of the WRP deliver pro-revolutionary speeches. As the marchers progressed to the US Embassy in Grosvenor Square a massive police presence incited a violent confrontation lasting over two hours. Another conflict that bred bitter protests in London was the dispatch of British troops to Northern Ireland in 1969.

In 1976, workers from the Grunwick Photographic Film Processing laboratories in Willesden went on strike against poor pay and working conditions. Many of the 137 strikers were women from the East African Asian community and their struggle attracted the attention of socialist groups and union militants. Demonstrators, including trade union leader Arthur Scargill and his miners, were bussed into the area from all over the country to strengthen the picket line and transform the local dispute into a wider political struggle. Battles for control of the surrounding area sparked frequent clashes between the police and militant picketers until the eventual settlement of the dispute in 1977.

## BLACK IS BEAUTIFUL

Second-generation black Londoners saw street protests as the natural – perhaps only – way to be noticed politically. Inspiration came from the US civil rights movement, and its more radical offspring, Black Power. London's Black Panther Party helped to publicize real injustices, such as the beating meted out in 1972 by Brixton police to Jamaican-born Joshua Francis, a London Transport employee, while they were pursuing another man.

The street was also the place where the right-wing National Front (NF) tried to assert its power. In August 1977, the National Front turned its attention to the Afro-Caribbean community in south London, marching through New Cross, Deptford and Lewisham in a 'territorial bid' for the area. Against the NF were aligned marchers for 'peace', churchmen, anti-racist organizations and local groups including the All Lewisham Campaign against Racism and Fascism. The ensuing violent clashes between police and demonstrators resulted in injuries on both sides and the introduction of police riot shields in mainland Britain. The rioting exposed how easily outsiders could inflame a tense local situation and threaten public order in London's most volatile areas.

## PRIDE & LIBERATION

Two new causes surfaced. In 1971 London saw its first 'gay day' march, renamed a year later as Gay Pride. In 1970 angry feminists tried to disrupt the Miss World contest held at the Royal Albert

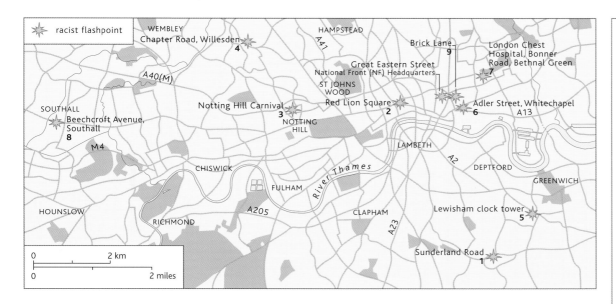

racist flashpoint

WEMBLEY
Chapter Road, Willesden
4

HAMPSTEAD

A41

Brick Lane
9

London Chest
Hospital, Bonner
Road, Bethnal Green
7

A40(M)

Great Eastern Street
National Front (NF) Headquarters

ST JOHNS
WOOD

SOUTHALL
Beechcroft Avenue,
Southall
8

Notting Hill Carnival
3

NOTTING
HILL

Red Lion Square
2

Adler Street, Whitechapel
A13
6

M4

LAMBETH

A2

DEPTFORD

CHISWICK

River Thames

FULHAM

GREENWICH

HOUNSLOW

A205

CLAPHAM

Lewisham clock tower
5

RICHMOND

A23

0    2 km

0    2 miles

Sunderland Road
1

1. 3 January 1971: firebombing of a party by a group of white boys and girls (22 people injured).
2. 15 June 1974: death of Kevin Gately when police and demonstrators clash at an anti-fascist rally.
3. 29–30 August 1976: clashes between police and local black community.
4. 1976: regular battleground between police and demonstrators during the Grunwick strike.
5. 13 August 1977: first use of riot shields by the police in mainland Britain, following an NF march through New Cross, Deptford and Lewisham.
6. 4 May 1978: scene of racist murder of Altab Ali.
7. 23 April 1979: attack on Asian workers leads to the media adopting the term 'Paki-bashing'.
8. 23 April 1979: clash between police and anti-fascist protesters leads to the death of anti-fascist activist Blair Peach.
9. 1970s: regular clashes between NF skinheads and local Asian youths.

**Violent London, 1960–80**
London's major flashpoints of violent protests and racist incidents in a troubled twenty years.

*A march in support of the Grunwick strikers, 1976*

*The Grunwick strike became notorious for the numbers of pickets who arrived from other parts of the country to support the striking workers.*

Hall. The Women's Liberation Movement held a series of marches through London in the early 1970s to demand equal pay for women and wages for housework.

In both these campaigns, street protests helped change public opinion and, in time, the law. Equal pay and sex discrimination laws were enacted. Gay activity was decriminalized in 1968, and gays began the slow progress towards full civil rights. The myriad new causes made London seem fragmented by identity politics, but big campaigns united all in the belief that the future could be changed: as one placard in a Trafalgar Square protest in 1978 declared, 'Queer Jew-Boy Socialist seeks a Better World' (see opposite top). **BC**

## THE LONDON SCHOOL OF ECONOMICS: A CENTRE OF STUDENT PROTEST

Student unrest in the 1960s was widespread in both the United States and Europe. In the UK, radicals studying at the London School of Economics (LSE) were at the forefront of student protests and demonstrations. The LSE movement was driven by the issue of the democratic right of students to influence the appointment of the school's Director. In 1967 students vigorously opposed the appointment of new director, Dr Walter Adams, an academic associated with the white-dominated racist regime in Rhodesia. Student action against Adams included the occupation of LSE buildings and a five-day hunger strike in protest against the suspension of student leaders, the South African David Adelstein and the American Marshall Bloom. Unrest continued after Adams took up his post. In 1969 students protested against the installation of steel security gates which, they claimed, made the college feel like a concentration camp. The subsequent destruction of the gates by radical students resulted in the arrest of twenty-five students and the closure of the LSE for three weeks.

*Student protesters outside the London School of Economics, 1969*

# MODERN LONDON

The tensions of the 1970s continued into the 80s. Hostility between the police and the black community in Brixton erupted into riots. Hostility from national government led to the abolition of the Greater London Council in 1986. And the IRA resumed its bombing campaign.

But the 1980s saw new reasons for optimism. After reaching its lowest point in 1983, London's population began to rise. Money began to surge through the City of London as the banking and financial service industries took over from the docks as the drivers of London's wealth.

The 1980s also saw the derelict docks transformed into Docklands, gleaming new office and residential districts lining the Thames.

In 2000, the creation of a new London strategic authority boosted the bullish mood. To the surprise of many, Ken Livingstone, the first city-wide mayor, championed growth. London was booming, with higher densities, taller buildings and lots more wealth-creating opportunities.

Debates raged over whether London should be run as a city of Welfare State interventions or free-market freedoms. But one thing was sure: London was irreversibly cosmopolitan, steeped in a distinctive urban mix of cultures, religions and ethnicities.

*History Painting, 1994*
*A striking image of the 1993 Poll Tax Riots, a historic outbreak of civil disorder in central London. The artist, John Bartlett, chose the subject for painterly, not political, reasons.*

# FROM DOCKS TO DOCKLANDS

Derelict land along the river was built over with extraordinary results. Docklands created a new London district and a new model for urban regeneration.

In 1968, the Isle of Dogs was completely dominated by its docks. Housing was limited and access was difficult. From the late 1960s trade began to move away from the old docks, and between 1975 and 1982 jobs on the island fell from 8000 to just 600. Dock closures left a great swathe of derelict land with little prospect of

island, between Wapping and the old Royal Docks. This was partly completed in 1987, but the vital Limehouse Link tunnel was not completed until 1993.

Although access to the island was somewhat improved, inadequate transport was unquestionably a deterrent to new businesses. The situation was made dramatically more favourable by the construction of the Docklands Light Railway (DLR), first proposed

**Docklands, 1998**
This map shows the new district, after seventeen years of LDDC-led redevelopment and £12,600 million investment.

**Burrell's Wharf**
*The same site at Millwall in 1937, as a paint works; and in 1997, with two apartment blocks.*

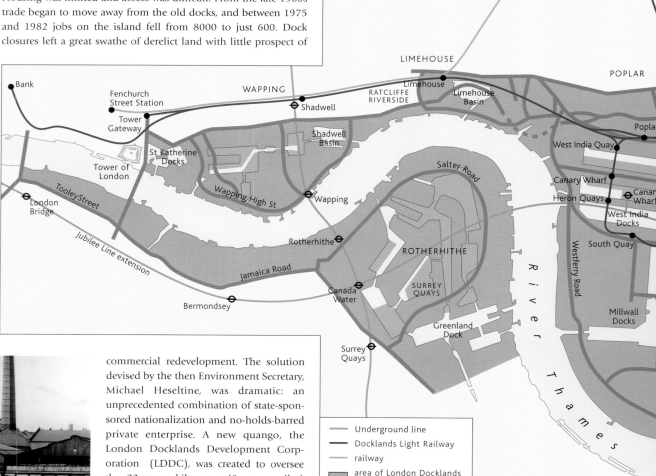

commercial redevelopment. The solution devised by the then Environment Secretary, Michael Heseltine, was dramatic: an unprecedented combination of state-sponsored nationalization and no-holds-barred private enterprise. A new quango, the London Docklands Development Corporation (LDDC), was created to oversee the 22 square kilometres (9 square miles) of former docks, including an 'Enterprise Zone' on the Isle of Dogs. The LDDC was granted unprecedented powers to encourage regeneration, including, most controversially, the right to circumvent the elected local authorities. From the outset, the LDDC recognized the need for better transport links. A new road was built into the heart of the development zone, but access to the island continued to be difficult. The Greater London Council had planned to end the wider problem of increased congestion in east London by building a new relief road just north of the

in 1982. Work on the DLR began in 1984, using the existing London & Blackwall Railway viaduct of 1840. The LDDC recognized that the new railway would have to link to the existing Underground network, so an extension to Bank station opened in 1991. Such was the success of the redevelopment that estimates of the DLR's passenger capacity had to be revised even before it began running, and longer station platforms had to be built. Approval was also given in 1989 for an extension of the London Underground Jubilee Line eastwards, with a station at Canary Wharf. This deep-level station was built in the drained eastern end of the West India Export Dock.

At first, development on the island was small-scale as the LDDC began to attract new industries and services. From 1986 onwards, however, banks and other companies began to move from the City, creating a demand for much larger, high-rise, accommodation. In 1987, the wharf area between the old West India Import and Export Docks was expanded as the foundation for the new Canary Wharf centre. This development of offices, shops and car parking

LDDC began to encourage private housing development. By 1988, the proportion of local authority housing on the island had fallen from 83 per cent to less than 40. Attempts were made to force developers to include low-cost starter homes in their schemes, but prices remained beyond the reach of many locals. House prices escalated as the office workers at Canary Wharf sought convenient homes and the area became accessible from the City and West End.

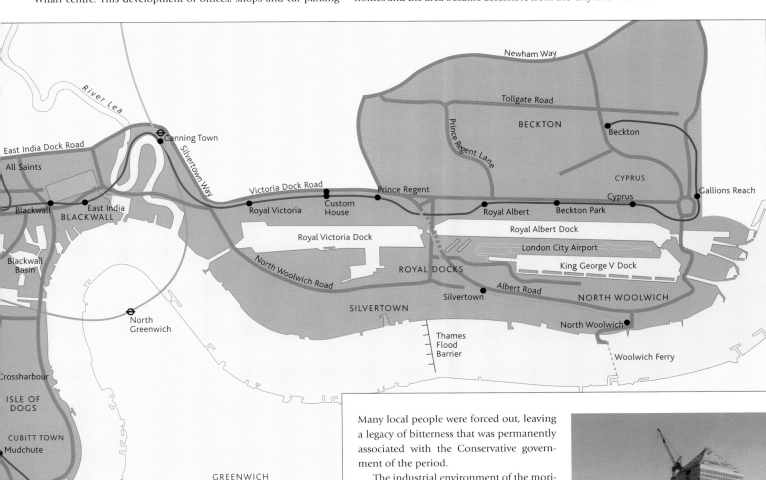

was for many years dominated by the lone Canada Tower, but with economic confidence growing from the late 1990s, it was joined by other tall buildings. Possibly the biggest controversy associated with redevelopment of the Docklands related to housing. Before the 1980s, the majority of residents lived on the Millwall side of the island and at Cubitt Town, in housing dating from the mid-19th century. In the 1930s several low-rise blocks of flats were built by the London County Council near Millwall Dock. The area was heavily bombed during World War II and some new social housing was built in the 1960s and 1970s. Most residents lived in local authority housing, and there was great hostility when the

Many local people were forced out, leaving a legacy of bitterness that was permanently associated with the Conservative government of the period.

The industrial environment of the moribund docks had been seen as a blight on the area in the late 1970s, but the riverside wharves and dock basins were presented in a positive light by both the LDDC and property developers. The area's maritime heritage, history and environment proved – and remains – highly marketable. The LDDC had spent £3900 million from the public sector and £8700 million of private money in building a new part of London. Docklands left a legacy across Britain as the enterprise-zone model of urban regeneration spread. In London it fed the appetite for the even more ambitious regeneration vision that emerged in the 1990s: the Thames Gateway. **TW**

***Canada Tower, Canary Wharf, 1991***
*The final construction stages of Europe's tallest building, painted by Carl Laubin.*

# INTERNATIONAL FINANCE IN THE CITY

London became a boom town for international finance in the 1980s. The 'Big Bang' in 1986 liberalized old trading practices and brought new wealth to the capital.

The City of London's financial markets were transformed in the 1980s. No longer an intricate old boys' network with restrictive trading practices – at least by reputation – the City became dynamic and international. London ranked alongside Tokyo and New York as an undisputed centre of global finance.

The new Conservative government kick-started change in 1979 with the abolition of exchange controls. The control, management and ownership of the London Stock Exchange (LSE) also came under scrutiny and it was evident that the LSE's rule book infringed restrictive practice legislation. As it became clear that a major reorganization was underway, there was a rush of new alliances between large banks, merchant banks and stockbrokers. Barclays Bank paired with Wedd, Durlacher and de Zoete; Rothschilds with Smith Brothers; Deutsche Bank with Morgan Grenfell.

On 27 October 1986, the 'Big Bang' (as it became known) threw out the old rule book and introduced new ways of working. The old division between stockbrokers and stockjobbers was scrapped, as was the old-fashioned face-to-face dealing on the trading floor. From now on trades were made on computer screens.

Most significant for London was the abolition of ownership restrictions on UK stockbrokers, which enabled international banks to move in. Almost all the City's major brokers and merchant banks came under foreign control. In 1985 the City's top firms were UK-owned, including long-standing names like Morgan Grenfell and Hambros. By 2005 there were no British firms in the City's top twenty, which was now made up of five American firms, four Swiss, four German, two French, two Dutch, two South African and one from Qatar.

## FUTURES, MARKETS & FOREIGN OWNERSHIP

Changes also were afoot elsewhere in the City. In 1982 a new type of stock exchange appeared, the London International Financial Futures and Options Exchange (LIFFE), which traded in complex financial products based on their future value.

At LIFFE 'open outcry' trading continued until 1988 and its floor traders became notorious for their brash, macho 'loads-of-money' lifestyle, which attracted a new generation of young working-class men into the city. 'A salary of £150,000 is by no means uncommon for traders like Gary and Tony,' reported the *Independent*, in August 1998. Also featured was a former carpet-fitter from Kent, now making £8 million a year.

Bowler hats and old boy networks gave way to international corporations. Although journalists deplored the idea of the City 'falling into foreign hands', nationality was irrelevant, according to the chief executive of the London Metals Exchange, Simon Heale, quoted in 2004. 'When I was a child

**The Lloyds Building**
*Designed by Richard Rogers, the building's startling appearance made it instantly famous, and much photographed: here by Tom Evans in 1989.*

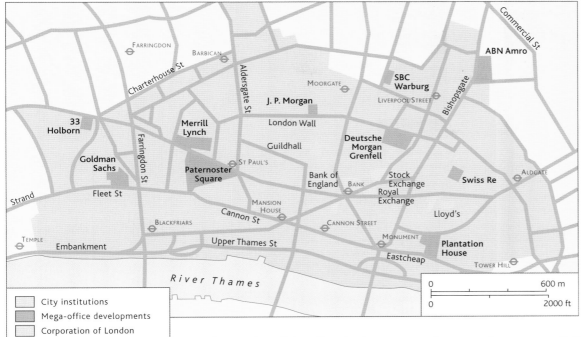

**Mega-office sites, 1997**
New or planned property developments provided over 27,850 square metres (300,000 sq ft) of office space in the City.

40,000 in Docklands. But the new financial centre in the east was catching up fast.

In 2001 Barclays announced its intentions to quit the City for new headquarters buildings in Canary Wharf, a move that sent shudders through City corridors. By contrast, three of the biggest international investment banks – Merril Lynch, Goldman Sachs and J. P. Morgan Chase, chose to remain. The City retained its aura as a 'sacred site', in author Peter Ackroyd's words, with its trinity of hallowed institutions – the Bank of England, the Mansion House and the London Stock Exchange. The latter re-committed to a City location in 2004 when it moved to new premises in Paternoster Square, next to St Paul's Cathedral.

During the 1990s London's financial sector gathered steam. A threat from Frankfurt for the title of financial capital of Europe was dismissed. By 2005 London was even rivalling New York, its freer markets attracting hedge funds and other new forms of moneymaking. 'Whilst New York remains the financial centre to beat, London has momentum' said *New York* magazine in 2007.

The City's internationalism was expressed in its buildings. The world's leading architects, among them Norman Foster, James Stirling and Santiago Calatrava, made the City into an architectural hotspot (see below). The workforce became international along with the markets. London's claim to be a world city was as much about its financial industries as its increasingly multicultural population. **MoL**

'I used to eat Corn Flakes. Thought they were as English as Marmite. But they're not – and it never fussed me … There's an emotion about ownership, but for businesses such as us, it's not an issue.' Despite its name and location, the London Metal Exchange, for example, was owned entirely by non-British firms whose businesses accounted for 90 per cent of all global trading in metals.

Twenty years on, the Big Bang's legacy was clear. Jobs in financial services had increased by over a third. The annual turnover of shares traded through London had rocketed from £101 billion to £2495 billion. The Big Bang also had also created a new plutocracy, with around 200 hedge-fund managers worth over £50 million. Opinions differed over whether this was good for London overall.

## THE NEW MEGA-OFFICES

The Big Bang had a visible effect on the look of the 'Square Mile' of the City of London. The opening of the Lloyd's Building (see opposite) in 1986 heralded a new generation of mega-offices, with vast floor-space and enormous ducting networks to accommodate the wiring needed for global communications. Between 1986 and 1989, 745,000 square metres (8 million sq ft) of the City's office space was expanded to nearly 2 million square metres (21.5 million sq ft) through rebuilding or major upgrades to existing office stock (see map above).

Despite the ingenuity of architects, these mammoth new blocks were not easily accommodated in the street plan of the medieval City. Some firms began to migrate east to the new cluster of skyscrapers on the Isle of Dogs. By 2001 the City's workforce stood at 250,000, compared to

**Billingsgate, 2000**
*Billingsgate fish market quit the City in 1982, leaving its arcaded riverbank building (centre) to be turned into office space.*

# TRANSPORT: M25, AIRPORTS & THE CHANNEL TUNNEL

A series of projects transformed London's transport networks – particularly international links. Within London, more cars brought more congestion and anti-road protest.

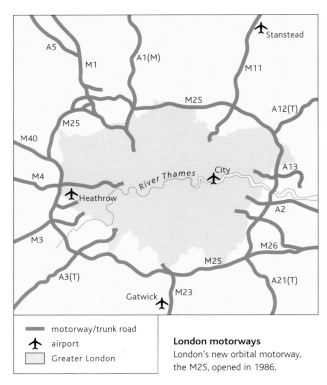

**London motorways**
London's new orbital motorway, the M25, opened in 1986.

Legend:
- motorway/trunk road
- ✈ airport
- Greater London

The last twenty years of the 20th century saw huge new investment in London's transport infrastructure. The pressure of a booming economy, a rising population and new models for financing grand projects created major changes in the way Londoners moved about their city and the way international travellers passed through it.

The list of projects was impressive. Between 1980 and 2000 London received two new motorways, the M25 (opened 1986) and the M11 (opened 1999); two new light rail or tram systems serving Docklands (which began operating in 1987 with extensions in 1991, 1994 and 1999) and Croydon (opened May 2000). The tube (Underground) network saw a £1.9 billion eastern extension of the Jubilee Line (1999) and the extension of the overground East London Line to run from Dalston in the north to Crystal Palace in the south. In 1988 Thameslink created a new north–south rail link across London. A new road bridge was built at Dartford in 1991, the first major infrastructure project in Britain to be financed entirely from private funds. Two new pedestrian bridges across the Thames were opened in central London in 2001, financed by the National Lottery's Millennium Fund.

In the redeveloped Docklands, where business travel was on the up, London got an entirely new airport. City Airport, which opened in 1987, was the capital's fifth international airport. The existing four also boomed, with a new fourth terminal opening at Heathrow in 1986 (see above), followed by new terminals at Gatwick in 1988, Stansted in 1991 and Luton in 1999. Heathrow, by now the world's busiest international airport with more than 51 million passengers annually, began to build a fifth terminal in 2006 which was finally opened in 2008. A new high-speed rail link was introduced between Paddington and Heathrow. Most significant of all was the start in 1994 of 'Eurostar' rail services between London, Paris and Brussels. Britain was no longer an island. It was now possible to work in London and commute from a home in northern France.

## CONTROVERSY & DELAY

Many of these projects were tied up with the regeneration of Docklands and the need to serve what was increasingly becoming one of London's great centres of employment. Typically, projects were financed through a mixture of private and public funding, a method that came with controversy and delays. The Jubilee line extension was held up for years amid wrangling over the financial contributions required from the different partners. The great un-built project of the period was CrossRail, which was bedevilled by disagreements between the public and private interests behind it. CrossRail had first been given the go-ahead in 1989, following a study of central London's overstretched commuter railways. This proposed three new projects: the east–west CrossRail, linking Ealing and Stratford through a new tunnel beneath central London; a new north–south Underground link between Hackney and Wimbledon, and the Jubilee Line extension. Progress stalled until 2004, when the Treasury gave the project a second, though still lukewarm, go-ahead. The successful Olympics bid of 2005 revived the project's prospects. 'CrossRail is even more important to London's long-term future than the Olympics,' said Mayor Ken Livingstone. 'It is also the transport system needed to underpin London's most rapid areas of economic growth, enabling the City and Canary Wharf to keep their global edge, supporting the renewal of the West End, and helping to lock in the benefits of 2012 to Stratford.'

## RESISTANCE TO NEW ROADS

Alongside the new investment in rail infrastructure, the period from about 1990 saw a cooling enthusiasm for road building. During the 1980s the number of cars in London had increased by 22 per cent and congestion grew worse in all parts of the capital, not just the centre. The M25 opened in 1986, the fulfillment of the postwar planners' dream to make London traffic flow smoothly. Two years later the new motorway achieved exactly the opposite result, creating the city's largest ever traffic jam, with 35 km (22 miles) of gridlocked vehicles.

***Approaching Heathrow, 2000***
*Heathrow added a fourth terminal in 1986 and a fifth in 2008. The impact on the local area began to cause serious concern.*

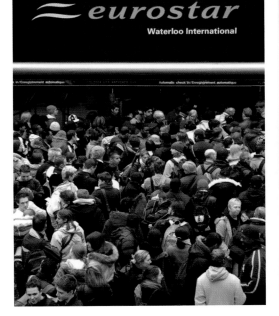

One of Britain's largest and longest anti-road-building protests took place in east London during the 1980s and 1990s, against the building of the M11 link road. The protest came to a climax in 1993 when the campaigners turned to direct action in the form of physical passive resistance to compulsory eviction from 400 houses in Leyton, Leytonstone and Wanstead. Residents transformed the Victorian terraces into a makeshift walled city, blocking up the entrances and creating new routes between the houses through the interiors and over the rooftops into the nearby trees. In January 1994, they declared the independence of the sovereign state of 'Wanstonia'. When Wanstonia fell to the bailiffs in February, the neighbouring state of 'Leytonstonia' declared independence. The last bastion of the protesters was Claremont Road, where the final evictions took place in December 1994 (see above right). By now the protest had become international news and the occasion was witnessed by the world's press and media. The M11 link road was finally opened in October 1999.

Meanwhile, in central London, traffic congestion had increased to intolerable levels. Average speeds had fallen to 9 mph and it was estimated that 50 per cent of car journey time was spent stationary.

Neither fierce increases in parking charges, nor the introduction of wheel clamping in 1983 for illegal parking, deterred car owners. In 2003, Mayor Ken Livingstone announced a radical strategy – a congestion charge for drivers entering central London – a first for a city of London's size. The results were generally seen to be a success, not just in reducing congestion but also in improving the air quality in central London and in raising money for public transport.

While the status of cars rose and fell, bicycles saw the opposite. The number of cyclist-commuters fell by 29 per cent in the 1980s to reach an all-time low in 1993, but then started to rise again. The steepest increase came after 2000, a reflection not just of the congestion charge but also of the terrorist attacks of July 2005, which cast a shadow over public transport. Cyclists also acquired a new sense of virtue as study after study showed that cycling was good for personal and social health: 'Good for London, good for you,' as the London Cycling Campaign slogan put it. **CR**

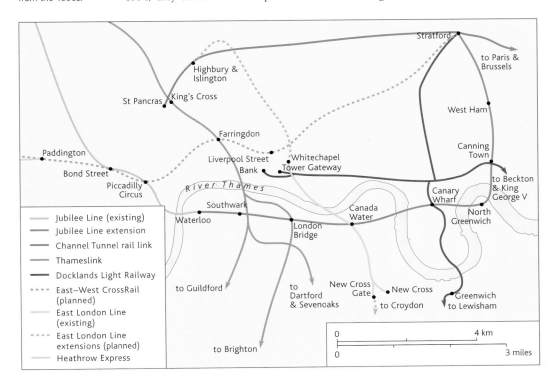

- Jubilee Line (existing)
- Jubilee Line extension
- Channel Tunnel rail link
- Thameslink
- Docklands Light Railway
- East–West CrossRail (planned)
- East London Line (existing)
- East London Line extensions (planned)
- Heathrow Express

# THE LONDON BRAND

London acquired a new image in the 1990s as the global capital of cool. In word city rankings, London scored high on cultural activity but low on quality of life.

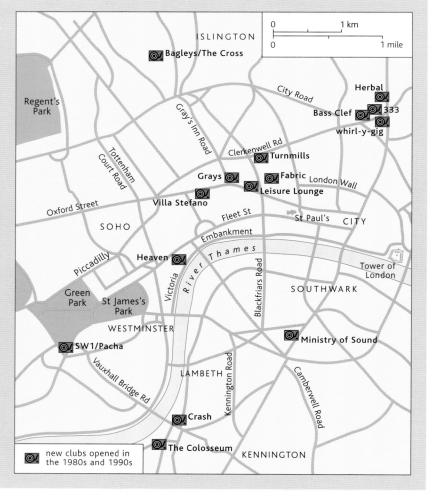

*The London Marque*
*Introduced in 1996 to represent London's vibrancy.*

In the 1990s Londoners were entranced to discover that their city was once again hip. 'It is incredibly cool and happening,' wrote Emma Soames in a 1996 *Daily Telegraph* magazine, 'with hip clubs and fab clothes and terrific art and great restaurants and unbelievably cool people who stay up all night … London is crackling with chic, jumping with ideas and is once again in the eye of the fashion storm.'

The magazine commissioned Sam Taylor Wood, 'one of London's rising young artists', to create an image of London life in the 1990s. Wood came up with a composite photograph showing five iconic Londoners of the age: 'the clubber, the artist, the party-goer, the shopper and the restaurateur'. The photograph was taken in a loft in Shoreditch, one of the iconic places of the age.

Soames, who remembered the 1960s, saw this London 'moment' as different from its predecessor by virtue of the serious wealth that was fuelling it: 'There is a huge influx of foreign money and an international chicarama buying into London, giving it a gloss it never had when it was all home-grown crushed velvet.'

Confirmation of London's new 'brand' came from abroad. In 1996, *Newsweek* magazine declared London 'the coolest city on the planet' (see opposite). In 2005 the award of the 2012 Olympic Games to London rather than Paris, underlined the city's international ranking. In 2007 *New York* magazine conceded that London no longer needed the description 'the Manhattan of Europe'. The British capital was now the world's most dynamic and cosmopolitan city, a universal magnet for entrepreneurial talent.

## THE CAPITAL OF COOL

London took comfortably to this new sense of itself. All Londoners could take pride in the fact that London fashion was a world leader and its creative industries were booming. Confidence and a sense of entitlement meant that anyone with the money could drink champagne in the fashionable Atlantic Bar and Grill, or go all-night clubbing at Turnmills. High Street chain stores brought designer fashion to everyone. Statistically, Londoners were getting wealthier. For the first time in the capital's history the number of home owners outstripped the number of tenants. Old distinctions between rich and poor districts blurred as fashionable clubs and restaurants popped up in previously dingy neighbourhoods such as Clerkenwell.

## CAPITAL OF CLUBBING

London's new brand was projected by new architecture above ground, and also by invisible places hidden beneath the ground. The young Europeans who flocked to Tate Modern by day also flocked by night to London's clubs and super-clubs.

The clubbing phenomenon of the 1980s and 1990s gave London a new night-time cultural map. Hitherto unremarkable districts became night-time destinations. The landmarks on this new map had little architectural presence, their entrances often just a modest doorway. Typical was the Ministry of Sound, which opened in an office backwater in Southwark. Another cluster of clubs was formed around Holborn, spreading to the area around Smithfield Market.

Clubbing was by nature a European, if not worldwide, phenomenon and in 1994 a happy synergy was created between the clubs and Eurostar trains. Travellers reported the regular sight of exhausted twenty-somethings packing the trains back to Paris on Sunday evening following forty-eight hours of non-stop hedonism in London.

*London's clubs, 1990s*
*Clubs were often located in non-residential office districts. Venues included office-block basements, underground storage space and warehouses, so their lives were often short.*

316

**Newsweek, 1996**
*The American magazine endorsed London's reputation as 'the coolest city on the planet'.*

**Viaduct, by Michael Johnson, 1998**
*Set on Holborn Viaduct in London, Johnson's allegory of modern Britain includes key capital-of-cool figures Peter Mandelson and Damien Hirst, along with mad cows and the disenfranchised poor.*

London's changing character affected the way it was promoted to visitors. The old tourism iconography of Beefeaters and Piccadilly Circus gave way to images of the Notting Hill Carnival and Camden Market. Tourism chiefs reinforced the branding of London as a young city, pulsating with multicultural rhythms and global foodstuffs. In January 1996, the Department of National Heritage, the British Tourist Board and the London Tourist Board created a new logo, 'the London Marque', to represent 'the true spirit and character of London' in their overseas marketing. The marque showed people joining hands (see opposite).

The changing symbol reflected changing visitor profiles. In 1996 nearly half of French visitors to London were aged sixteen to twenty-four. In 2003 a new consumer marque for London – 'Totally London' – projected a more street-wise and urban edge, underlining that the youth market was now a key sector in the London tourist trade.

London's cool image among the young owed much to the capital's street-style and its rising fashion stars. The designer Vivienne Westwood, a presiding genius of the punk scene, was the first to cross from subculture to haute couture. She was followed by a new generation of London fashion designers. Wallington boy John Galliano was awarded British Designer of the Year four times between 1987 and 1997. Alexander McQueen, the son of a cabbie who grew up in Stepney and cut his fashion teeth in the London clubbing scene, succeeded Galliano as head of Paris fashion house Givenchy in 1996.

The 'London Look', an eclectic mixture of street-style, eccentricity and individualism, went around the world with the models of the moment, Kate Moss from Croydon and Naomi Campbell from Streatham. Like the designers whose fashion-forward clothes they wore, they came to represent London's spirit of street-wise creativity.

## THE QUALITY OF LIFE

London's brand became important in the business world as 'liveability' issues became part of the competition between world cities for inward investment: international corporations could now set up their offices anywhere, so factors other than economic climate became important. Business consulting firms began to produce league tables, ranking world cities in terms of quality of life and cost of living. In 2004 Mercer's Index found London the second most expensive city in the world. In 2008 UBS made it the most expensive, because of the high cost of rented accommodation. In 2007 Mercer's quality of life index put London at a low 39th place.

These city rankings were much reported in the mainstream media and came as little surprise to Londoners. 'Revealed: dark side of the coolest city' said a headline in the *Evening Standard* in November 1996, reporting a new set of research statistics. The capital had England's highest rates of homelessness and reported crime. Some parts of London had a staggeringly high unemployment rate of 60 per cent. Rocketing house prices had put 'affordable housing' beyond the reach of the capital's key workers. Even without statistics, most Londoners could see for themselves that the city embraced poverty alongside wealth. Rough-sleepers, an attribute of the Victorian city, returned to the streets. Tuberculosis, a classic disease of poverty, re-emerged.

This more jaundiced view of the London Brand was expressed by the painter Michael Johnson in 1998 (see below). His state- of-the-nation allegory is set on Holborn Viaduct. Processing along the top are Arts Council officials, artist Damien Hirst, politican Peter Mandelson, businessmen, scientists and their mad-cow creations. Beneath lurk the poor, whose contributions to the National Lottery kept the capital of cool going.                    CR

# NEW LONDON LANDMARKS

A new generation of iconic London buildings changed the skyline from the late 20th century. Landmarks for Londoners, these buildings also expressed a new love of stylish architecture.

Some of the most impressive features of the invigorating stylistic jumble that is London's skyline have been added since the 1980s. These structures do more than simply provide a visual reference point. In a surprisingly short space of time, they have become as much a part of the international iconography of the city as Buckingham Palace, Big Ben, Tower Bridge or St Paul's Cathedral. They say 'London' to the world in the same way that the Empire State Building says 'New York' or the Eiffel Tower says 'Paris'.

### Tate Modern, 2000
*London's iconic early 21st-century art gallery was converted by Herzog and de Meuron from the former Bankside power station, and opened in May 2000. Here it is seen from the equally celebrated Millennium footbridge.*

The development of these new landmarks took place against a background of regeneration that transformed many cities across the United Kingdom. In 1980, the country was deep in recession. Over the following twenty years, as the economy began to recover, a brashly optimistic cultural trend began to emerge, which picked its way deftly through the stylistic back-catalogue, citing the Beatles and Donald McGill as much as Elgar and Pugin. The full flowering of this postmodern, neo-1960s 'Cool Britannia' mood coincided with a change of government, in 1997, and new injections of money from the public and private sectors. 'The capital of cool is in the throes of a building boom' read a 1997 headline, mapping thirty new projects giving London a complete facelift.

Many of the ambitious new-builds and redevelopments were made possible by the inauguration of the National Lottery in 1993, funds from which were disbursed via a number of bodies including the Heritage Lottery Fund. London did well out of lottery funding: by 2001 the capital had received a total of £1.3 billion for major projects costing over £10 million each. The largest grant was the £628 million toward the cost of the Millennium Dome in Greenwich (see above). Despite the building's distinctive profile, the Dome's perceived failure as a visitor attraction also blighted its potential as a symbol for London. By contrast, another millennium project, the non-lottery-funded London Eye (a giant Ferris wheel) on the South Bank, became a ubiquitous image on tourist souvenirs immediately on opening in 1999.

### The Dome, 2000
*The Dome was designed by Richard Rogers to house the ill-conceived Millennium Festival. It stood empty for several years after the festival, but in 2005 became a new entertainment venue known as The O2.*

Lottery funding also had a major impact on London's cultural infrastructure. The British Library relocated to St Pancras and a new home, designed by Colin St John Wilson, the largest public building to be constructed in 20th-century Britain. By contrast, the British Museum reclaimed an existing historic building, the old Reading Room of the British Library, which had sat in the middle of the museum unseen by the general public and, since the Library's departure, unused. In the process, the Museum created the largest covered public courtyard in Europe, protected from the weather by Norman Foster's extraordinary toroidal roof. Other projects included the £120 million rebuilding of Wembley Stadium and the £12 million reconstruction of Shakespeare's Globe Theatre on the Southwark riverbank, on a site very close to its 16th-century location.

*The Gherkin, 2003*
*Designed by Norman Foster, the Swiss Re tower in St Mary Axe added an arresting new shape to London's skyline. The building stood on the site of the Baltic Exchange, destroyed in 1992 by an IRA bomb.*

## ICONIC SKYSCRAPERS

London's new economic muscle also thrust up new skyscrapers. Among the earliest were Tower 42 and One Canada Square. Designed by Richard Seiffert and built for the National Westminster Bank (hence its popular name, the Nat West Tower) Tower 42 was under construction throughout the 1970s, but finally opened for business in 1980. At the time, it was the tallest skyscraper in Britain and it remains in 2008 the tallest within the City of London. For all its size, Tower 42 appeared sleek thanks to its polyhedral plan and its closely spaced steel mullions which run the height of the building.

In 1980, One Canada Square (better known as Canary Wharf) overtook Tower 42 to become, at 235 metres (770 ft), the tallest building in the United Kingdom. This huge, slab-sided skyscraper surmounted by a pyramid roof was often seen as a monument to 1980s capitalism, an embodiment of Thatcherism that echoed the big shoulder pads of the time. It certainly read like an assertion of power, impressing more for its sheer physical bulk than for the panache of its design.

If One Canada Square could be said to represent the Eighties, Norman Foster's 30 St Mary Axe (see right) was its equivalent for the Noughties. A near neighbour of Tower 42, it was judged by some observers the most striking and stylistically original building to be added to London's skyline since the 1960s. A glass and steel rocket, nicknamed the Gherkin, 30 St Mary Axe could be seen from almost everywhere east of Waterloo, its pointy head appearing unexpectedly at the end of numerous streets. Like Frank Gehry's Guggenheim Museum in Bilbao, it was a signature building that made a virtue out of seeming to have descended from Mars. Being circular in plan, it presented the same, instantly recognizable profile regardless of the viewpoint. With its unusual shape and the spiralling tracery of its diamond-shaped windows, it was the architectural equivalent of Brit Art or Brit Pop: at once robustly in-your-face and wittily elegant.

Nothing could be further from the lapel-grabbing design of the Gherkin than the aloof grandeur of Tate Modern (see opposite). Unlike other modern landmarks, this huge art gallery was not a new building, having existed in the form of Bankside power station since the late 1940s. Its transformation by architects Herzog and de Meuron came to be powerfully symbolic of 21st-century London, not because its architecture was quirky or provocative, but because of what it represented. Indeed, the exterior of the building remained largely unchanged, while the radical design changes were concentrated in the gallery's vast interior. Tate Modern embodied London's new identity as the epicentre of Brit Art, international creativity and contemporary visual culture. From its opening in May 2000, Londoners and visitors alike swarmed to Tate Modern, making it the city's top visitor attraction. **FM**

# LONDON'S MULTICULTURAL HEART

Multiculturalism moved to the mainstream of London's sense of civic identity. As old confrontations over rights faded, so new debates about values emerged.

**Buddhapadipa Temple, Wimbledon**
*The first Thai Buddhist temple of its type in the UK, the building was opened in 1982. The community it serves has been settled in London since the 1960s.*

The last twenty years of the 20th century saw postwar immigrant communities become an established part of the social and cultural landscape of the capital. London's cosmopolitanism was also expanded by the arrival of new migrant groups, ranging from refugees and asylum seekers to European professionals seeking the jobs and freedoms that London offered. London became a true world city, where everyone had the experience of living, shopping or working with someone from a different ethnic background.

The 1991 census was the first official count of ethnic minority Londoners, and throughout the 1990s a succession of studies and statistics underlined just how multicultural the city had become. In 1997 the London Research Centre produced the largest study to date, which included an 'ethnic map' of London's communities. *Cosmopolitan London: Past, Present and Future* rejoiced in the fact that London had numerous 'ethnic villages' but, in contrast to other world cities, no racial ghettos.

The visible signs of multiculturalism were indeed transforming many London localities. Greek and Turkish Cypriot shops, restaurants and businesses now lined Green Lanes in Haringey. There was a Japanese shopping centre in Finchley; Polish delicatessens in Hammersmith; Portuguese bakeries and Moroccan cafes around Ladbroke Grove in Notting Hill. Hackney was home for refugees from Kurdish parts of Turkey, Iran and Iraq, alongside the more established Afro-Caribbean community.

Southall had become a vibrant suburb, the largest Asian shopping centre in London, a 'chota Punjab' complete with its own Asian music station, Sunrise Radio, founded in 1989. A mostly Punjabi area with a 60–80 per cent Asian population, Southall's proximity to Heathrow Airport made it a natural staging post for new arrivals. Tooting in south London had become a multicultural home to Gujarati, Pakistani and Tamil communities. Green Street in Newham had been transformed by its Pakistani population into an area of specialist Asian fashion and jewellery shops. Wembley became home to Gujaratis from India and East Africa.

The exotic feel of these neighbourhoods turned many of them into visitor attractions in their own right. In 1986 Westminster Council began promoting Chinatown in Soho. A Chinese Pagoda and arch was erected in Gerrard Street, and the Chinese New Year procession was officially adopted as a key event for both tourists and the community. In 1997 Tower Hamlets Council adopted a similar strategy for Brick Lane, now rebranded as Bangla Town in recognition of its Bangladeshi community, the largest in Europe.

As these communities grew, new places of worship began to appear in London's landscape, in the outer suburbs as well as the inner city. The Shri Swaminarayan Mandir Temple in Neasden, built in 1995, provided a magnificent new centre for Hindus. The Sri Guru Granth Singh Sabha in Park Avenue, Southall, became the biggest Sikh temple outside India, built and paid for by the Punjabi community. In 1980 the Buddhpadipa Temple (see left) was built in Wimbledon for Buddhists of the local Thai and Chinese communities. Another important new arrival was the East London Mosque on Whitechapel Road, built in 1985 and extended in the 1990s as the congregation expanded.

The 2001 census figures showed Newham and Brent as the first boroughs with non-white majorities. The city remained predominantly white (74.4 per cent) but the largest ethnic minority group was the 350,000 (5.2 per cent) from the Indian subcontinent, encompassing a variety of peoples, religions and languages. Black Caribbeans were the next (4.4 per cent), followed by Black Africans (2.4 per cent). Of the 300 languages spoken in London, four of the top five were Asian: Bengali, Punjabi, Gujarati and Hindi.

## RACE, RACISM & VALUES

Despite the increasing value placed on London's multiculturalism by political and business leaders, race relations remained an issue for Londoners in general, and the Metropolitan Police in particular. The first half of the 1980s saw more clashes of the type that had become depressingly familiar in the 1970s. Relations between the police and the black and Asian communities boiled over in Brixton in April 1981. An incident of heavy-handed policing erupted into three nights of violence, an experience that was repeated on a smaller scale four years later. Southall also saw street fighting in 1981 when white skinheads caused disturbances on the night of a concert in a local pub. Somee 500 Asians and 200 skinheads were caught up in the fighting and 61 policemen were injured.

The defining event of the 1990s was the murder on 22 April 1993 of a young black teenager. Stephen Lawrence was stabbed to death on the corner of Well Hall Road and Dickenson Road in Eltham. The failure of investigating police to pursue those responsible led to a public enquiry, which proved to be a watershed in race relations. Uncovering an ugly truth about endemic 'institutional racism' in the Metropolitan Police, the Stephen Lawrence Inquiry prompted much soul-searching about exactly how honest Britain was being in its treatment of its non-white citizens. A legacy of Stephen Lawrence's death was the creation of the Race Relations (Amendment) Act and a more sober and self-critical approach to tackling the issues that race and cultural difference continue to throw up for the capital.

The value placed on London's cosmopolitan nature helped take the sting out of the debates about race and citizenship that had so bedevilled the 1960s and 1970s. However, new questions about migration emerged as new groups of people arrived in London: as refugees, asylum seekers, or economic migrants from the poorer countries of Europe. New tensions about multiculturalism also emerged as the focus of debate shifted from rights to values. In 1989 a group of Muslim men exercised their right to protest, gathering in Parliament Square to burn Salman Rushdie's book *The Satanic Verses* and demand the execution of its author for blasphemy. Newspapers reported the event with incredulity, as a kind of throwback to times long gone. The thought that the incident pointed to a possible future was dismissed as unlikely.    **SG**

**The world in one city**
Large numbers of non-white or non-British Londoners bring extraordinary cultural diversity to parts of the city. This map also identifies some of London's 'ethnic villages', as revealed in the 2001 census.

percentage of non-white or
non-British Londoners, 1990

more than 50%

40%–49%

25%–39%

less than 25%

• ethnic 'village'

# NEW DEALS FOR HOUSING ESTATES

Ambitious regeneration programmes harnessed public and private money from the late 1970s to repair and improve London's rundown housing-stock – but progress came with controversy.

**Cathall Road Estate, Leytonstone, 1999**
*Over twenty years after it was completed, the high-rise blocks of the 70s in the Cathall Road Estate were demolished and replaced by low-rise traditional housing.*

'The huge pressures on London mean that the GLC and the boroughs must continue to build and to build quickly,' said GLC architect Kenneth Campbell in 1976. Ten years later the focus had shifted completely. Now the mission was not building but regeneration. London's neglected council estates were to be repaired, revamped and reborn as sustainable communities. Regeneration was not just a matter of refurbishing rundown housing stock, but also of tackling the social problems that plagued the inner city.

Government money had started to flow into London's council estates during the 1970s through programmes such as the Urban Programme (1978) and Estates Action (1985). The pace quickened during the 1990s when regeneration initiatives came thick and fast. The Housing Action Trusts in 1991 were closely followed by the designation of City Challenge areas (1991) and the Estates Challenge Renewal Fund of 1993. In 1994, these programmes were rolled together into Single Regeneration Budgets, followed by the New Deal for Communities (1998). A host of smaller programmes ran alongside.

These funding programmes had a huge physical impact. The Cathall Road Estate in Walthamstow was built between 1966 and 1972 as a high-rise estate with two twenty-one-storey tower blocks. In 1991 it became London's first Housing Action Trust and embarked on major surgery. Old blocks were demolished and most of the estate rebuilt as low-rise terrace housing, in accordance with tenants' wishes (see above). In Brent, demolition was also the main tool for regenerating the Chalkhill Estate. This mammoth

estate of low-rise, concrete slab blocks had been built in haste in the 1960s to relieve overcrowding in Willesden. In the 1990s, few people mourned when the bulldozers went in. 'A lot of people had happy times raising their families in Chalkhill, but for most people this day will be a welcome relief,' said local councillor Ann John, at a ceremony to inaugurate the final phase of demolition in 2002.

Local authorities took to regeneration with enthusiasm. Hackney achieved the distinction of demolishing more tower blocks than any other council in Europe. Although critics saw such 'blow-downs' as unnecessary gestures that wasted recyclable housing stock and building materials. Southwark, the largest council landlord in London, ran the biggest Single Regeneration Budget project in the country, a £290-million scheme covering five council estates, including the giant Aylesbury Estate of 2700 dwellings housing 10,000 people. In 1997, the newly elected prime minister Tony Blair came to Aylesbury to launch his government's commitment to tackle inner-city deprivation and rescue the 'forgotten people'. In 1998 Aylesbury became a New Deal for Communities (NDC) scheme, the third largest in the country.

Throughout the 1990s, schedules for demolition and rebuilding rolled on, but progress was slow. In 2000, the murder of ten-year-old Damilola Taylor in the North Peckham Estate came to symbolize the difficulties of the task. Journalists visiting the estate reported on the failure of government money to transform what they saw as a 'concrete warren of despair'. But regeneration funding was hugely significant. Across London, small-scale but critical improvements gave estates a new lease of life. Physical surroundings were spruced up by adding hipped roofs to flat blocks, repainting balconies in bright colours and designing out areas of 'no man's land'. Funding also brought much-needed skills training and drug- and health-education programmes.

Many of London's estates emerged from the regeneration process with happier tenants. Broadwater Farm in north London was one of the success stories. Notorious for a horrific riot in 1985, twenty years later it was transformed by the residents themselves and a £33 million regeneration programme. As a journalist reported in 2005, 'police–community relations are now so good that after a drugs raid on a flat, officers were applauded by residents.'

## DEATH OF THE COUNCIL HOUSE?

Regeneration was not, however, without controversy. The late 1990s saw bitter debate about whether local councils should continue to build houses and act as landlords. The new model for financing and running social housing was partnership between councils, housing associations and private-sector house builders. The new vision for 'sustainable' housing estates was of mixed tenure – owner-occupiers side-by-side with tenants in mixed luxury and affordable housing. The difference between private and public housing had already been blurred by the 1980 Housing Act, which gave council tenants the right to buy their homes.

In 2000, the British government made regeneration funds conditional on the transfer by councils of their housing stock to housing associations. or 'Arm's length management associations' (ALMOs). Critics concluded that regeneration now meant 'privatization by the back door' and deplored the fact that some London

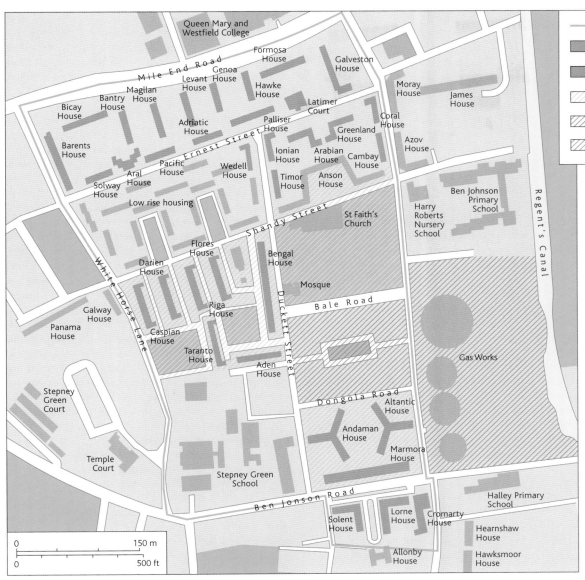

boundary of Ocean Estate

blocks built on original design 1940s

blocks built on amended design 1940s–60s

areas cleared and redeveloped from 2005

redeveloped as private affordable housing

rebuilt 1997–99 as social housing for a housing association

Queen Mary and Westfield College

Mile End Road

Formosa House

Galveston House

Genoa House

Levant House

Magllan House

Hawke House

Moray House

James House

Bicay House

Bantry House

Adriatic House

Latimer Court

Palliser House

Coral House

Azov House

Barents House

Ernest Street

Greenland House

Ionian House

Arabian House

Cambay House

Pacific House

Aral House

Wedell House

Timor House

Anson House

Ben Johnson Primary School

Solway House

Low rise housing

Shandy Street

St Faith's Church

Harry Roberts Nursery School

Regent's Canal

Flores House

Bengal House

Darien House

Mosque

Bale Road

White Horse Lane

Riga House

Duckett Street

Galway House

Panama House

Caspian House

Taranto House

Aden House

Gas Works

Stepney Green Court

Dongola Road

Altantic House

Andaman House

Temple Court

Marmora House

Stepney Green School

Ben Jonson Road

Halley Primary School

Solent House

Lorne House

Cromarty House

Hearnshaw House

Allonby House

Hawksmoor House

0 ——— 150 m

0 ——— 500 ft

## The Ocean Estate, Stepney, 1940–2000

The Ocean Estate saw an extensive and complex programme of redevelopment in the early 21st century.

than on the Ocean Estate in Stepney (see left). Built by the LCC in the late 1940s, the estate comprised forty blocks, named for faraway seas and ports. By the 1990s, residents were largely Bengali-speakers from the Bangladeshi community. Overcrowding and poor health had become serious problems because of the run-down, pest-infested buildings. Child mortality was shockingly high. In the late 80s, heroin addiction also began to affect the estate. Ocean's reputation as the cheapest place in London to buy heroin attracted more homeless addicts. In 2000, over 95 per cent of the 1100 council-rented homes were deemed to be substandard.

#### Children on the Ocean Estate, 2004

*Right-to-buy legislation changed tenure on all London's housing estates. Here, children pose with an estate agent's 'For Sale' placard.*

councils had already pulled out of housing altogether (in 1991, for example, Bromley Council had transferred its entire stock of 12,000 dwellings to a group of housing associations). The pace of change slowed further. In January 2004 Camden tenants voted not to transfer to an ALMO despite £283 million in promised regeneration funds.

Nowhere was the regeneration process more tortuous

In 1998 the Ocean Estate became a flagship of the New Deal for Communities scheme, under which it was promised £56 million in regeneration investment by 2011. Parts of the estate were demolished, but the scheme foundered amid allegations of large-scale misuse of public funds.

In 2003, a new £190 million scheme was devised: the estate was to be completely remodelled, with private house-builders erecting both luxury and affordable housing on the cleared sites and Sanctuary Housing Association assuming management of the council's refurbished or rebuilt properties. This scheme too began to founder when it emerged that much of the money earmarked for housing would have to be spent by the council buying back dilapidated property sold under right-to-buy legislation but now scheduled for demolition. A further setback came in 2006 when tenants voted to reject Sanctuary Housing, thus also rejecting the whole scheme. Ocean's slow progress exemplified the difficulties of trying to reconcile government policy, local authority finances, tenants' wishes and the knock-on effects of London's extraordinary housing market.

**CR**

# SHOPPING CENTRES

Shopping centres became more ambitious in scale, scope and aspirational appeal. They changed London's map and altered the way Londoners spent their weekends.

During the 1980s, London's purpose-built enclosed shopping centres became more than just places to shop. Increasingly designed as centres of community life, they began to assume greater significance in the city's social and transport maps. Incorporating multiplex cinemas, gyms, restaurants, entertainment and leisure centres, these buildings began to gather together under one roof a variety of activities previously carried out in separate premises. Shopping centre architects claimed to be 'reinventing communal experience' by designing out the 'rough edges' of urban living. Local councils saw shopping cetres as agents of regeneration. Londoners welcomed the convenience, but worried about the death of the traditional high street.

Londoners had first experienced modern shopping centres in the 1950s when town planners rejected traditional street layouts in favour of shopping precincts. Early shopping centres were essentially roofed-over precincts, and London's first opened in 1965 at Elephant & Castle, part of a dream to make the area the Piccadilly of south London. During the 1970s, many London councils followed suit in an effort to modernize their local town centres. Wandsworth's Arndale centre opened in 1971, a mixed retail and residential development. Other 1970s shopping centres included the Stratford Centre in east London (1973), the Lewisham Centre, south London (1975), Kings Mall, Hammersmith

**London's major shopping centres 1950–2000**

Some shopping malls were in regenerated existing town centres, others were built outside towns, creating new shopping destinations.

(1979) and Eden Walk in Kingston (1979). A second type of shopping centre arrived in 1976. Brent Cross in north London typified a new generation of US-style shopping malls, built on the fringes of town and designed for the car-owner. Brent Cross provided 74,322 square metres (800,000 sq ft) of retail space, and was seen at the time as a huge development.

## AN INCREASE IN SCALE

The 1980s and 1990s saw an outbreak of new local shopping centres, built on an even more ambitious scale. Hailed by local councils as catalysts of town centre regeneration, these local centres were as much about leisure spending as shopping, tapping into 'the money people don't even know they want to spend', as the managing director of the developers Chelsfield put it in 1999. Shopping City at Wood Green was opened in 1981 by the Queen. The Broadway Shopping Centre opened in Bexleyheath in 1983. Other developments were built at Ealing Broadway in 1985, the Treaty Centre, Hounslow (1987) and Dalston Cross in Hackney (1989). To some, these bright new urban spaces signalled 'the death of the high street', but to local councils intent on regeneration their popularity was a lifeline: it was the high streets without shopping centres that were dying.

The suburban shopping centre model was replicated in the West End, where many of the large department store buildings were broken up into mall-style collections of smaller 'boutique shops'. In Oxford Street the old department store Bourne and Hollingsworth closed in 1983 to reopen in 1986 as the Plaza Centre, with 10,000 square metres (107,639 sq ft) of retail space. In 1989 Whiteley's department store in Bayswater was transformed into an upmarket shopping mall with multiplex cinema attached. In 1982 the long established Kensington department store, Barkers, was turned into the Barkers Centre.

## MEGA-CENTRES

The 1990s also saw a new type of shopping centre, the out-of-town mega-centre serving regions rather than cities. Lakeside, at Thurrock, became London's largest shopping centre when it opened in 1990. Nine years later it was followed by Bluewater, just off the M25 in Kent. Bluewater was more than just regional in scale; it was 'Europe's largest and most innovative retail and leisure destination', according to its promotional material. It

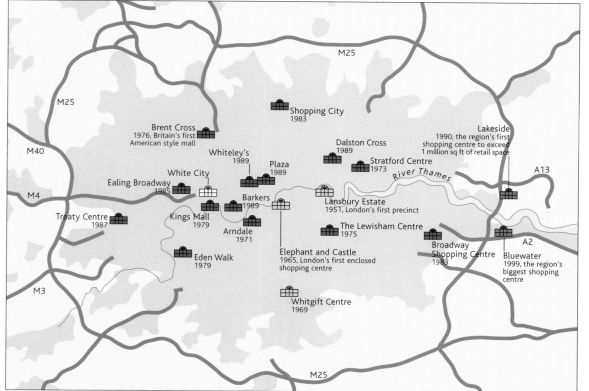

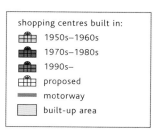

shopping centres built in:

- 1950s–1960s
- 1970s–1980s
- 1990s–
- proposed
- motorway
- built-up area

As the 20th century came to a close, shopping centres themselves came under threat. Questions of environmental sustainability came to the fore in the thinking of Londoners, and new questions began to be asked. Shopping centres were a 'must-have' for local centre regeneration, but they implied increased car use and new pressures on existing roads. Retail development brought private money and the promise of employment to often hard-up boroughs, but was the public interest really served by using London's scarce land for yet more facilities for shopping?

Debates about the role and meaning of London's shopping centres came to a head around 2000 with plans for a £500 million transformation of a site at White City. The developer promised a new, pedestrianized centre for west London incorporating over 150 retail units, an 18-screen cinema, and 40 restaurants and food shops, as well as social housing and bus and train stations. Supporters saw the opportunity for an architecturally striking new city quarter for London. Opponents deplored the inclusion of 4500 parking spaces and a projected 64,000 daily car journeys. 'The idea that in inner London you create a bloody great magnet for cars is totally opposed to everything we are trying to do in London', said Mayor Ken Livingstone in 2000. Following a change of developer, construction began. It remains to be seen whether retail projects of this scale will be sanctioned again in future without significantly more attention being paid to both environmental and social costs.          **CR**

*The Bluewater Centre, 2000*
Opened in 1999, as the largest shopping centre in Europe, Bluewater attracts 27 million visitors a year.

*Shops in Camden High Street*
Famous as a centre for alternative subcultures including goth, punk and emo, Camden provides a quite different retail experience from that of the purpose-built shopping centres. This view shows the original Dr Marten's shop.

offered 320 shops organized into three malls, themed to evoke a pastiche town: the 'Thames Walk', the 'Rose Garden' and the 'Guild Hall'. Bluewater had high aspirations. Its lavishly designed spaces were carefully thought out, not just to make shopping easy but also to emphasize the centre's values: safety, cleanliness, child-friendliness and 'respect' for a rather sanitized past.

In 1999 the Design Council decided to give Bluewater its 'millennium product' stamp of approval. Others saw Bluewater as a sinister caricature, creating an ersatz urban environment that allowed an Orwellian degree of control over visitors impossible in the high street. From design through to letting, Bluewater controlled the overall retail mix to appeal to its target customers, the car-owning and cash-rich comfortably-off.

## AN ALTERNATIVE EXPERIENCE

'The Bluewater philosophy is simple', stated the centre, 'to make shopping an enjoyable, stress-free experience, to treat its customers as Guests.' Paradoxically, one of London's most successful retail areas to emerge from the 1980s was at the other end of the spectrum. The anarchic Camden Market, with its second-hand goods and organic fast food, offered an altogether less sanitized experience. 'The crowds do not come [to Camden Market] to shop at Marks and Spencer', concluded Simon Jenkins, in 1999. 'They come for informality, atmosphere, and if they are honest, a touch of danger. At Camden Lock you risk being fleeced, cheated and pushed into the canal ... Tourists each weekend from France, Germany and Scandinavia love it.'

# BRAVO! LONDON: ARTS & CULTURE IN THE CAPITAL

Modern London's cultural life boomed. The dividing lines between high-brow art and low-brow leisure blurred as more Londoners began to see the arts as a necessary part of their urban lifestyle.

In 2000 it was estimated that on any one night there were 60,000 seats for live events in London. The city supported more than forty theatres, two opera houses and five symphony orchestras, plus an extravagant number of fringe theatre companies, dance groups, musicians, stand-up comedians and performance poets.

Arts activity in modern London benefited from two new funding streams. From 1982 until its abolition in 1986, the Greater London Council became a significant arts patron with a budget of £18 million a year, which largely went to small-scale, grass-roots activity. 'In the space of two years', reflected Mark Fisher, 'London changed from a city whose artistic life was dominated almost entirely by the great national institutions ... to one in which over 150 new community arts projects were competing for audiences.'

In the next decade the National Lottery took the opposite tack, channelling its grants, at least initially, to bricks and mortar, thus favouring established arts companies. Lottery money began to flow in 1994; after six years, the largest arts grants had gone to repair and refurbishment projects: £74 million to the Royal Opera House; £31.6million to the National Theatre; and £20.2 million to the Royal Albert Hall.

## TO SUBSIDIZE OR NOT TO SUBSIDIZE?

One legacy of the GLC era was a higher profile for artists from London's black and ethnic minority communities. GLC funding enabled companies like Tara Arts and venues like the Yaa Asantewaa Centre in Notting Hill to build firm foundations. In 1982 London's first Black Theatre season was held at the Arts Theatre. GLC funding also helped raise levels of debate about 'Black Artists – White Institutions', as the title of a 1985 conference at the Riverside Studios put it. A plan to turn the Round House in Camden into a black theatre centre fell by the wayside, but overall GLC funding was a significant factor in the renaissance of black arts (see left) in London during the 1980s.

London's largest single investment in the arts owed nothing to either the GLC or the National Lottery. The Barbican Centre (see opposite) opened in 1982, its £153 million cost shouldered entirely by the Corporation of London. The Barbican was Europe's largest arts centre; it reflected an earlier generation of thinking about 'palaces of the arts'. Like the Lincoln Centre in New York, on which it was partly modelled, the Barbican provided spaces both large and small: a 2000-seat concert hall, two theatres, three cinemas, two art galleries, a sculpture court and library as well as a conference centre and music school. It housed two established companies – the Royal Shakespeare Company and the London Symphony Orchestra – but the mix of spaces was intended to encourage flexibility in programming.

London's other modern concert hall, the Royal Festival Hall, also opened itself up to more flexible use. In the early 1980s, under GLC ownership, the RFH began an 'open foyer' initiative, with all-day opening and free events. After the abolition of the GLC, control passed to an independent board, which united the arts institutions on the Waterloo riverside under the new brand name 'South Bank Centre'. This created an even bigger arts complex, encompassing the National Theatre, the National Film Theatre cinemas, the Royal Festival Hall, the Hayward Gallery, a poetry library and, from 1989 to 1999, the Museum of the Moving Image.

The controversy surrounding the latter's abrupt closure fuelled debates about business culture infiltrating the arts. Despite lottery money, arts funding had become more competitive. Corporate and private sponsorship were now integral, as was generating new revenue. The V&A's 1988 advertising slogan 'An ace café with quite a nice museum attached' was notorious, but it expressed the new reality.

## ARTS & LIFESTYLE

Audiences for arts grew throughout the 1990s, but growth tended to be at the commercial, rather than the subsidised end of the market. Surveys showed that Londoners' favourite arts pursuit was going to the cinema. New clubs and venues testified to the healthy state of London's music scene. Popular interest in what was

**Time Out** *cover,*
**April 1981**
*The cover story in this issue of London's listings magazine dealt with black actors and classical theatre in the context of a National Theatre production of Measure for Measure with a black cast.*

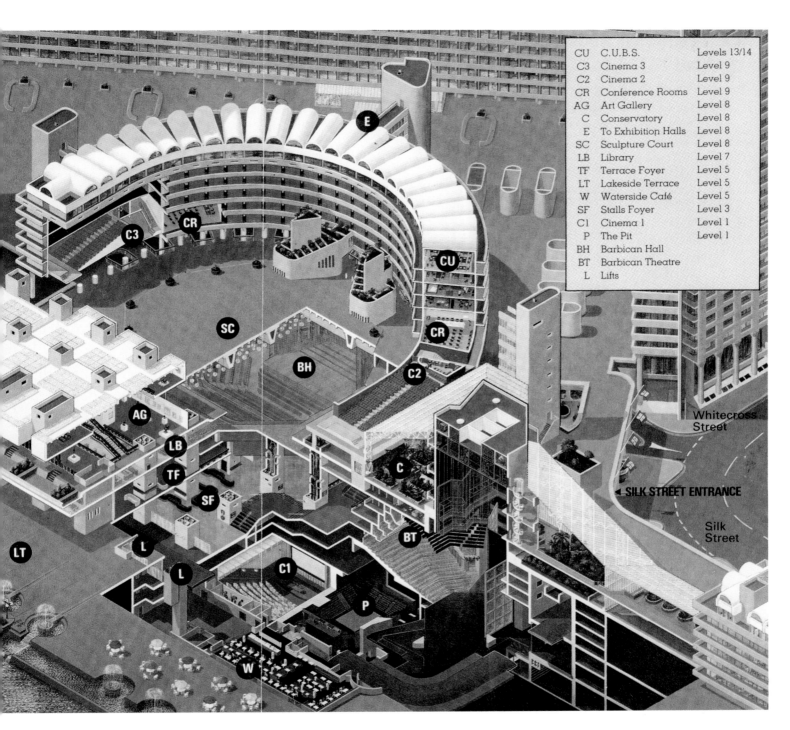

| | | |
|---|---|---|
| CU | C.U.B.S. | Levels 13/14 |
| C3 | Cinema 3 | Level 9 |
| C2 | Cinema 2 | Level 9 |
| CR | Conference Rooms | Level 9 |
| AG | Art Gallery | Level 8 |
| C | Conservatory | Level 8 |
| E | To Exhibition Halls | Level 8 |
| SC | Sculpture Court | Level 8 |
| LB | Library | Level 7 |
| TF | Terrace Foyer | Level 5 |
| LT | Lakeside Terrace | Level 5 |
| W | Waterside Café | Level 5 |
| SF | Stalls Foyer | Level 3 |
| C1 | Cinema 1 | Level 1 |
| P | The Pit | Level 1 |
| BH | Barbican Hall | |
| BT | Barbican Theatre | |
| L | Lifts | |

***The Barbican Centre***

*An isometric cutaway drawing of the Barbican Arts Centre on its opening in 1982, by John Roynane.*

increasingly called 'the creative industries', design and fashion among them, grew. London's new Design Museum, which opened in 1989, came out of the non-subsidized sector, being an independent charity funded by the Terence Conran Foundation

One activity that flourished between arts and leisure was stand-up comedy. It was a phenomenon of the 1980s, beginning in 1979 with amateur performances at one venue, The Comedy Store in Leicester Square, and growing within ten years to a professional cir-cuit with over 100 venues. In 1988 the London magazine *Time Out*, whose listings had helped the comedy scene expand, introduced the annual *Time Out* Comedy Awards. Fringe theatre, a 1970s phe-

nomenon that also owed a great deal to *Time Out*'s listings, contin-ued to flourish, with some fifty venues in and around London. Pioneer pub theatre The King's Head in Islington was typical in surviving on shoestring budgets and a fiercely loyal following.

*Time Out*'s pages showed how boundaries between the arts and urban lifestyle began to blur at the end of the 20th century. Going to a concert, shopping, eating out, visiting an art gallery, seeing a film were all part of London's rich mix of possibilities. As the GLA's first cultural strategy, published in 2004, pointed out, London's extraordinary choice in its cultural and creative resources 'is what many of us enjoy most about living and working here'. **CR**

# THE ART WORLD & LONDON

Contemporary art rose to be one of London's most powerful cultural activities. The 'Young British Artists' altered London's image while making their own fortunes.

**Art Sabotage, 1999**
*David Piddock's view of the Sensation exhibition at the Royal Academy, when a visitor vandalized Marcus Harvey's portrait of the child-murderer Myra Hindley. The title could refer to the YBAs' assault on the old art establishment.*

An unmade bed, a pickled shark, frozen blood: these eye-catching elements were all associated with a group of young artists living and working in London from the 1980s onwards. Their work came to dominate the British art scene and propelled London to the vanguard of the international art world. They also made art exciting for a wider and often youthful audience. Both factors helped transform London's cultural map and contributed to the capital's sense of itself as a place of cutting-edge creativity.

The buzz around the group began when sixteen enthusiastic art students from Goldsmiths' College, New Cross, first exhibited together in late summer 1988. This was to be an independent exhibition, showcasing their latest work. Second-year student Damien Hirst is credited with taking the lead in organizing the exhibition. Fellow exhibitors included Fiona Rae, Gary Hume, Ian Davenport and Sarah Lucas. The resulting show, 'Freeze', was staged in a disused Port of London Authority building in Surrey Docks. It was accompanied by a stylish catalogue, reflecting the sponsorship the group had won from the London Docklands Development Corporation and property developers Olympia and York. All this helped to make what was essentially a student show into a polished spectacle that attracted serious critical attention.

Freeze was visited by leading figures in the art world such as Nicholas Serota, director of the Tate, and Norman Rosenthal of the Royal Academy. If the initial attraction was in part Goldsmiths' reputation for innovative teaching, the media soon latched onto the art itself – self-confident, provocative and fresh. Perhaps the most significant visitor was the advertising tycoon Charles Saatchi, whose interest in art had led to the creation of his own gallery in St John's Wood in 1985. With the purchase of Matt Colishaw's *Bullet Hole*, Saatchi became patron to the new generation.

Freeze set the trend for warehouse-style exhibitions in post-industrial spaces. Hirst went on with other artists to organize two influential warehouse shows in 1990, 'Modern Medicine' and 'Gambler'. *A Thousand Years* was one of his installations at the time; it consisted of a rotting cow's head encased in a glass vitrine, complete with flies and maggots. The work was also acquired by Charles Saatchi.

In 1991 the 'Broken English' exhibition at the Serpentine Gallery marked a move to the heart of the art establishment for the Freeze group of Goldsmiths' graduates. Their work was shown alongside that of their contemporaries, including the sculptor Rachel Whiteread. Simultaneously, Davenport and Rae were nominated for the Turner Prize, the Tate's increasingly controversial award for artists under the age of fifty. In 1992, Saatchi staged the first exhibition of his collection, titling it 'Young British Artists' and giving a name to the group of emerging talents now taking the art scene by storm. Neat enough in itself, the name was quickly shortened to the even snappier acronym, 'YBAs'. Serious money began to flow, and media controversy about the merits and meaning of contemporary art reached new heights.

In 1997, the Royal Academy's blockbuster exhibition of Saatchi's collection, 'Sensation', ensured that many of the YBAs became household names through extensive media attention. Their use of unconventional materials and their regular focus on taboo subjects such as sex and death infuriated many, but inspired others. From Hirst's rotting cow to Emin's *Tent* to Marcus Harvey's *Myra*, the British art scene, with London at its centre, became talked about across the globe.

## COLONIZING POST-INDUSTRIAL SPACE

The use by artists of disused industrial buildings was not a new phenomenon for London. In the late 1960s and 1970s, groups of artists had begun to colonize the empty warehouses of Docklands and the condemned terraces of east London for studios and homes. By the 1980s, many London artists were finding short-lease property through two artist-run organizations, SPACE and Acme. SPACE, formed in the late 1960s when a group of artists occupied empty warehouses at St Katharine Dock, expanded its operations in the 1980s. By the end of the 20th century, the organization was running seventy studio complexes providing work spaces for hundreds of artists in disused factories, among them the old Yardley cosmetics factory in Carpenter's Road, Stratford. Acme operated as a housing association as well as a studio finder, seeking out homes for artists through low-cost short leases on terrace properties eventually destined for the bulldozer.

Acme properties famously included a whole street, Beck Road, Hackney, which at one point in the 1980s housed forty-two artists and their families. Beck Road attracted musicians as well as artists. It became, remembered former resident Philip Hoare, 'a post-punk colony … a kind of indie Coronation Street' whose inhabitants included the performance artist and Throbbing Gristle singer Genesis P. Orridge. 'Genesis had just instigated a new crypto-religious sect, the Temple Ov Psychick Youth, who, with their neo-Buddhist haircuts and army fatigues, would conduct candlelight processions on pagan feast days to the hospice for the dying at the top of the road.'

The artists, musicians, clubbers and fashion designers turned into a distinctive 'scene' in the 1990s, particularly in Shoreditch and Hoxton, with its studio parties and social networks. Artists were at the centre of this youthful commotion and their activities became the stuff of Cool Britannia legend. Sarah Lucas and Tracey Emin opened The Shop in 1993 at a vacant property on Bethnal Green Road, where they exhibited and sold their own work. A surge of independent galleries and exhibition spaces materialized in the area. Some were branches of established West End galleries, and the established London art market began its gradual shift to the east of the city.

In 2000 two events symbolized the enormous significance that contemporary art now had for London. The capital's leading dealer, Jay Jopling, opened his White Cube2 gallery in Hoxton Square, confirming that east London was now the centre of the wealthy international art market. The opening of Tate Modern in 2000, in the former Bankside power station, underlined how wildly popular contemporary art had now become. The legacy of the London art scene in the 1980s and 1990s was not just the hundreds of independent galleries and thousands of artists throughout the capital, but also the millions of visitors to Tate Modern, evidence that contemporary art had seized the public imagination. **AS**

**The East London Art World, 1980–2000**
London's vibrant 'Brit Art' scene from the 1980s onwards found its home in the post-industrial east of the city.

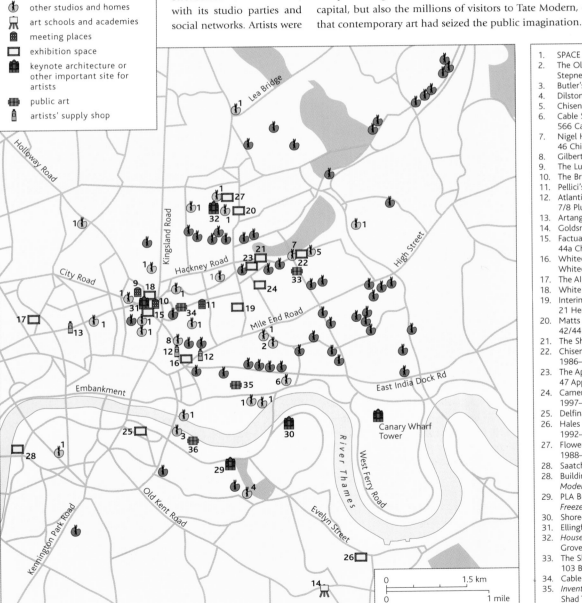

**Legend:**
- Acme houses & studios, 1972–
- other studios and homes
- art schools and academies
- meeting places
- exhibition space
- keynote architecture or other important site for artists
- public art
- artists' supply shop

1. SPACE studios, 1968–
2. The Old Jewish School studios, Stepney Green, 1971–
3. Butler's Wharf studios, 1973–81
4. Dilston Grove studios, 1969–
5. Chisenhale studios, 1980–
6. Cable Street studios, 566 Cable Street, 1984–
7. Nigel Henderson, 46 Chisenhale Road, 1984–
8. Gilbert and George, Fournier Street, 1967–
9. The Lux Centre, 2/4 Hoxton Square, 1997–
10. The Bricklayer's Arms, Charlotte Road
11. Pellici's Cafe, 103 Bethnal Green Road
12. Atlantis, 146 Brick Lane, 1993–9; 7/8 Plummer's Row, 1999–
13. Artangel, 36 St John's Lane, 1985–
14. Goldsmiths' College, New Cross
15. Factual Nonsense Gallery, 44a Charlotte Road, 1992–6
16. Whitechapel Art Gallery, Whitechapel High Street, 1901–
17. The AIR Gallery, Rosebery Avenue, 1978–88
18. White Cube, 48 Hoxton Square, 2000–
19. Interim Art, 21 Beck Road, 1984–99; 21 Herald Street, 1999–
20. Matts Gallery, Martello Street, 1979–92; 42/44 Copperfield Road, 1992–
21. The Showroom, 44 Bonner Road, 1988–
22. Chisenhale Gallery, 64 Chisenhale Road, 1986–
23. The Approach Gallery, 1st Floor, 47 Approach Road, 1997–
24. Camera Work Gallery, 121 Roman Road, 1997–2000
25. Delfina, 50 Bermondsey Street, 1996–
26. Hales Gallery, 70 Deptford High Street, 1992–
27. Flowers East, 199/205 Richmond Road, 1988–
28. Saatchi Gallery, County Hall, 2003–5
28. Building One, Drummond Road, *Modern Medicine* exhibition, 1990
29. PLA Building, Surrey Docks, *Freeze* exhibition, 1988
30. Shoreditch Town Hall
31. Ellingfort Road
32. *House* by Rachel Whiteread, Grove Road, 1993
33. The Shop by Tracey Emin & Sarah Lucas, 103 Bethnal Green Road, 1993
34. Cable Street mural by Ray Walker
35. *Invention* by Eduardo Paolozzi, Shad Thames, 1989

# TERRORISM & SECURITY

International terrorism threw a shadow over all Londoners' lives.
As the IRA bombing campaigns ended, so a new threat began,
this time from extreme Islamist groups.

**Missing persons, 2005**
*An improvised noticeboard was created at King's Cross station following the terrorist bomb attacks in London on 7 July 2005.*

On 7 July 2005, four bombs hit London, three within fifty seconds of each other at 8.50 a.m. on Underground trains, and a fourth on a bus travelling through Tavistock Square near King's Cross at 9.47 a.m. Fifty-two commuters died, along with the four bombers. These four young men are alleged to have been suicide bombers with links to the international Islamist terrorist network al-Qaeda. Mobile phone technology allowed images captured by commuters on the trains to be broadcast around the world almost instantaneously. In the rolling news coverage that followed, some key images emerged, most movingly the notices and photographs posted outside the Underground stations by relatives searching for their loved ones lost in the carnage and confusion (see above). But perhaps one image above all others came to define the attack: that of the destroyed red bus, symbol of London. This image underlined some of the characteristics that have made, and continue to make, London a target for terrorism: it is a capital, the home of the British monarchy, the heart of government, a global financial centre and a tourist destination par excellence.

It was another characteristic of the capital, however, that made it a target for a fortnight in 1999: London as a place of diversity and tolerance. Lone extremist David Copeland detonated three nail bombs between 17 and 30 April. The first exploded outside a busy supermarket in Brixton, targeting the local black community; the second detonated near to Brick Lane, heart and symbol of the Bangladeshi community; while the third killed two people in the packed Admiral Duncan pub in

**Destroyed bus, 7 July 2005**
*Wreckage of the bus destroyed on 7 July 2005 in Tavistock Square by a terrorist bomb. Thirteen people were killed and 110 injured in the explosion.*

Soho, long associated with the gay community. Copeland's campaign of hatred was halted when he was identified and arrested. His actions showed just how much damage one person could inflict.

## IRA CAMPAIGNS

For much of the last third of the 20th century, the main terrorist threat in London came from the Provisional Irish Republican Army (IRA). This was not without precedent: there were Fenian attacks in the late 19th century and IRA campaigns in 1939 and 1940 – but the 1970s attacks in the capital reached a new level. When the situation in Northern Ireland deteriorated after 1968, and particularly after the events of 'Bloody Sunday' on 30 January 1972, IRA attacks on London gained an impact that simply could not be achieved elsewhere, particularly in Northern Ireland. The IRA mainland campaigns of 1973–6 and 1978–82 took a significant toll on London, with 252 bombs or explosive packages and 19 shootings, resulting in 56 deaths and more than 800 people injured. The campaigns were organized by small self-contained

'cells' based in the city, such as the group that later became known as the 'Balcombe Street Gang' – a nickname gained with their capture after a siege in Balcombe Street, Marylebone, in 1976.

One of the best remembered attacks of the IRA came on 20 July 1982, when a bomb in Hyde Park killed four soldiers and seven horses of the Household Cavalry; two hours later, a second explosion killed seven bandsmen of the Royal Green Jackets in Regent's Park. Pictures of the slaughtered horses in Hyde Park came to define the attack in the international media. Another high-profile attack came the following year during the pre-Christmas shopping period in December 1993: an explosion at Harrod's department store killed six people and wounded nearly one hundred more. Throughout the campaigns of the 1970s and early 1980s, the targets included prominent individuals, members of government and service personnel, but, above all, civilian Londoners.

In the 1990s, the financial heart of the City became a target. On Friday 10 April 1992 a huge explosion in St Mary Axe killed three people and injured almost one hundred, causing extensive damage to the buildings in the area, notably to the Baltic Exchange, which later had to be demolished. Just over a year later, on Sunday 24 April 1993, a large truck bomb exploded in Bishopsgate, killing a young news photographer, injuring forty-four people, and causing damage worth millions of pounds to the modern City buildings and to the nearby medieval church of St Ethelburga. In 1996 another bomb hit the new financial centre of Canary Wharf.

Soon after the 1993 bomb, a security system dubbed the 'ring of steel' was erected around the City, consisting of roadblocks,

**Major terrorist incidents in London, 1970–1990**
The IRA was a major threat to London for almost thirty years. Fundamental Islamic terrorist groups took on that mantle less than a decade later.

checkpoints staffed by armed police officers (although this presence was curtailed after the IRA ceasefires), and an extensive network of CCTV (closed circuit television) cameras. This introduced an extraordinary new level of security surveillance and made the City of London the most watched place in the country. The 'ring of steel' was later widened, while the CCTV technology used became commonplace throughout the capital and beyond.

## LIVING WITH THREATS

From the 1970s onwards, hoax calls and evacuations of streets and stations, as well as terrorist attacks themselves, became a regular feature of life in the capital. Although such incidents caused caution and some fear, they did not appear to undermine morale among Londoners. The late 1990s was a period of relative calm as peace talks on Northern Ireland took place. But the beginning of the 21st century saw the arrival of a new threat – fundamentalist Islamist terrorism. After the al-Qaeda attack on the World Trade Center in New York and other targets on 11 September 2001, the subsequent wars in Afghanistan and Iraq, and an attack on the Madrid transport system in 2004, it was felt by many to be only a matter of time before London was hit. The predictions came to pass on 7 July 2005, and a further attack on the capital continues to be considered likely – perhaps inevitable. After 7/7 many media commentators applauded the calm and stoicism of Londoners and the speed with which they appeared, at least on the surface, to return to normal life.           **AD**

1. 31 October 1971: Post Office Tower
2. 8 March 1973: Old Bailey and Great Scotland Yard
3. 8, 10 and 12 September 1973: Victoria, King's Cross and Euston stations, Oxford Street (Selfridge's) and Sloane Square
4. 17 June 1974: Houses of Parliament
5. 17 July 1974: Tower of London
6. 22 October 1974: Brooks's Club, St James's Street
7. 7 November 1974: King's Arms pub, Woolwich
8. 22 December 1974: home of Edward Heath, Wilton Street
9. 5 September 1975: Hilton Hotel
10. 30 March 1979: Houses of Parliament (assassination of Airey Neave, Secretary of State for Northern Ireland)
11. 30 April 1980: siege at the Iranian embassy
12. 10 October 1981: Chelsea Barracks
13. 20 July 1982: Hyde Park and Regent's Park
14. 17 December 1983: Harrod's
15. 20 July 1990: London Stock Exchange, Threadneedle Street
16. 7 February 1991: three mortars fired at 10 Downing Street
17. 18 February and 28 February 1991: Victoria and London Bridge stations
18. 10 April 1992: St Mary Axe
19. 12 October 1992: Sussex Arms pub, Covent Garden
20. 16 November 1992: Canary Wharf (defused)
21. 24 April 1993: Bishopsgate
22. 26 July 1994: car bomb outside Israeli embassy
23. 10 February 1996: South Quay, near Canary Wharf
24. April 1999: Brixton, Brick Lane and Soho (Admiral Duncan pub)
25. 20 September 2000: rocket-propelled grenade attack on MI6 headquarters
26. 3 March 2001: BBC Television Centre
27. 7 July 2005: Underground trains near Liverpool Street, Edgware Road and Russell Square stations, and a bus in Tavistock Square

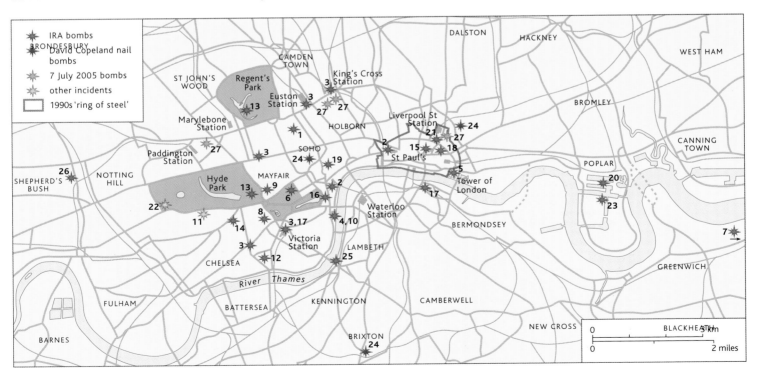

# INNER-CITY CHANGE

Parts of inner London have changed beyond recognition since the 1980s. A combination of gentrification, regeneration funds and fashionable buzz transformed run-down areas.

'Gentrification' is a buzzword of modern London. Clerkenwell has gone from dull to trendy; Hoxton from nasty to hip. Behind all outbreaks of gentrification lies the combination of regeneration money, property development and steeply rising land values.

The gentrification that attracted most comment saw middle-class owner-occupiers move into areas previously inhabited, if at all, by the renting working class. In the 1950s, young professionals had bought rundown Regency houses in Islington to 'do up'. In the 1970s, building-conservation militants squatted Georgian town houses in Spitalfields to save them from demolition. In both cases, the focus was on London's existing housing stock. In the 1980s, a new sort of gentrification emerged, in which post-industrial districts were colonized by young urban professionals.

The arrival of these 'yuppies' in local housing markets led to accusations of breaking up working-class communities. However, gentrification also brought benefits in raising the low spending power of districts and bringing people from different classes and cultural backgrounds together.

Nowhere in London did the forces of gentrification combine more powerfully than in Spitalfields. The district had developed in the late 17th century as an industrial suburb of the City, later acquiring a large brewery and wholesale fruit and vegetable market. Thereafter it deteriorated into a classic area of poverty, overcrowding, sweat shops and prostitution. By the end of the 1970s, it retained a Dickensian air despite the presence of one of London's newest and poorest immigrant communities, the Bangladeshis.

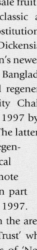

**Spitalfields old and new**
In Spitalfields, a number of different forces compete for change.

Tower Hamlets Council directed regeneration funds through a £7.2 million City Challenge programme from 1992, followed in 1997 by the £11.4 million Cityside programme. The latter aimed to 'pioneer a new model of regeneration', considering the needs of local businesses. One target was to promote the area as a cultural destination, in part by rebranding it as 'Bangla Town' in 1997.

Property developers were active in the area, not least the 'Spitalfields Building Trust' which had emerged from the 1970s groups of 'New Georgian' gentrifiers to buy up the houses and sell them to 'sympathetic' purchasers. A house bought in 1977 for hundreds of pounds changed hands in the early 1990s for just over £1 million.

The Corporation of London also had its eye on Spitalfields as a site for new office space. In 1986, as landlord of the fruit and vegetable market, the Corporation moved the market traders elsewhere and gave planning permission for a £500 million office scheme on the site. The scheme did not progress smoothly and the fifteen-year delay enabled the old market building to find a new use as a Camden Lock-style 'alternative' market, selling organic food, clothes and interesting junk. The market matched the zeitgeist perfectly, and by 2000 it had become an economic force to be reckoned with, attracting huge Sunday crowds.

In 2000, a new scheme was unveiled, this time incorporating three-fifths of the old market buildings and allowing the Sunday market to continue. It failed to placate objectors, who saw the development as an epic battle between global capitalism and the local community. In fact, however, parts of the Bangladeshi community welcomed the new trade that a large development would bring. The number of restaurants in Brick Lane had risen from eight in 1989 to forty-one in 2002, the largest cluster in Britain.

Another strand of gentrification in Spitalfields was the arrival of the creative and cultural industries, a new boom sector. The 4.5-hectare (11-acre) site of the empty Truman Brewery had been sold in 1995 and the new owners at first rented space to designers and artists. In 1998 the building was wired up and its clientele changed to small internet companies. By 2000, 300 such companies were based there, and the Brewery was dubbed 'Dot Com City'. The new young workforce created a trendy micro-climate of organic cafes, designer shops and night-time clubs and bars. On Sundays the synergy between the Brewery and the Old Spitalfields Market was overwhelming. As artist Tracey Emin, proud owner of one of the Georgian town houses, put it in 2005, 'come down here on a Sunday morning and I guarantee you will be in the trendiest spot in the world.'

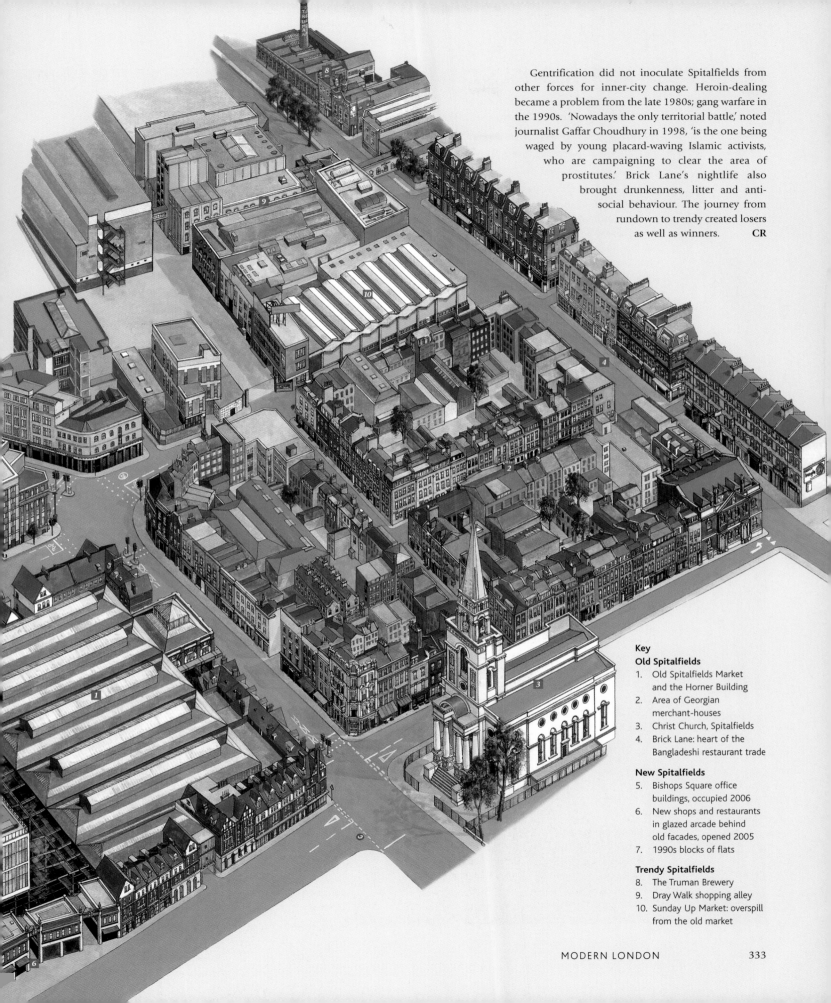

Gentrification did not inoculate Spitalfields from other forces for inner-city change. Heroin-dealing became a problem from the late 1980s; gang warfare in the 1990s. 'Nowadays the only territorial battle,' noted journalist Gaffar Choudhury in 1998, 'is the one being waged by young placard-waving Islamic activists, who are campaigning to clear the area of prostitutes.' Brick Lane's nightlife also brought drunkenness, litter and anti-social behaviour. The journey from rundown to trendy created losers as well as winners. **CR**

### Key

#### Old Spitalfields
1. Old Spitalfields Market and the Horner Building
2. Area of Georgian merchant-houses
3. Christ Church, Spitalfields
4. Brick Lane: heart of the Bangladeshi restaurant trade

#### New Spitalfields
5. Bishops Square office buildings, occupied 2006
6. New shops and restaurants in glazed arcade behind old facades, opened 2005
7. 1990s blocks of flats

#### Trendy Spitalfields
8. The Truman Brewery
9. Dray Walk shopping alley
10. Sunday Up Market: overspill from the old market

# LONDON MOVES EAST

The East Thames corridor was earmarked for regeneration in the early 21st century as London's 'gateway to Europe'. Preparations for the 2012 Olympics added impetus to the eastwards spread.

The regeneration of Docklands in the 1980s and 1990s shifted London's economic centre of gravity eastwards and began the process of turning London's East End, the capital's former industrial backyard, into an attractive and vibrant place to live and work. The lessons learnt in Docklands encouraged an even more ambitious regeneration project for east London, this time extending from Tower Bridge to the Thames estuary.

Planners had long deplored the tendency of industry and wealth to settle more comfortably in west London rather than east. In the 1990s, the prospect of the Channel Tunnel rail link entering the capital from the east offered an opportunity to redress the balance. Planners and politicians envisaged a new life for the eastern districts as Britain's gateway to Europe, the regeneration financed by the same type of public and private sector partnerships that had made such massive change possible in Docklands. In the early 1990s, national government set up an East Thames Task Force with the aim of coordinating a regeneration strategy and bidding for help from the European Union's assisted area funds. Although the territory stretched into Kent and Essex, the regeneration of the East Thames corridor came to be seen as critical to the capital's future, not least for offering a possible solution to London's growing problem of affordable housing.

**The Lower Lea Valley, 2000**

*This industrial area is earmarked for the 2012 Olympic Park. The Victorian match factory in the background closed in 1979 and became housing in 1988.*

**Olympic site fence**

*The entire site for the 2012 Olympics in the lower Lea valley was fenced off in 2007 by a continuous blue barrier that both intrigued and appalled Londoners.*

By 2000, the East Thames corridor project had become the Thames Gateway project and formed part of the Greater London Authority's first London Plan, which put the ongoing regeneration of east London as one of its main priorities. The Thames Gateway would see not just more houses, but also new jobs, bridges and transport infrastructure for the poorer communities on both sides of the river. Overall, the east offered London 'the greatest reservoir of large development opportunities which are also most accessible to London's greatest concentrations of deprivation'. The plan envisaged a minimum of 104,000 new homes built in the area by 2016.

The Thames Gateway label created an umbrella strategy beneath which local organizations and public/private regeneration projects operated. In March 2005, the Office of the Deputy Prime Minister announced a further £6 billion for projects. A typical example was the redevelopment of the historic Royal Arsenal at Woolwich, which ceased to be a military establishment in 1994. Here, the master plan saw the complete revitalization of the thirty-one-acre site, to create 3000 new dwellings alongside restaurants, retail, cinema and office developments. The giant project was a partnership between the borough of Greenwich and Berkley Homes, which had undertaken much of the new housing in the Gateway territory.

## STRATFORD: THE NEW WEST END

In the London area two factors added critical mass to the forces pulling the capital eastwards. The first was the decision to make Stratford a major transport hub for the new high-speed international trains coming through the Channel Tunnel. The development of Stratford International station brought in its wake a £45 billion private sector development: Stratford City. As its name suggested, this was a new mini-city creating 5 million square feet of new office space, 2000 new hotel rooms, 5000 new homes and a cluster of new tower blocks. Part of its aim was an ambitious plan to make Stratford 'the third most important retail centre in London after the West End and Knightsbridge'.

The second factor was the announcement in July 2005 that London was to be the host city for the 2012 Olympic Games. The main Olympic site was to be in the Lower Lea Valley, and London's arguments for the bid had made much of the regeneration benefits the Games would bring to east London as a whole. Although it would occupy only a small part of the Thames Gateway, the proposed Olympic Park was seen as focusing international as well as national attention on east London. It was claimed that the legacy of the Games would include permanent new jobs, new housing and the transformation of the post-games Olympic Park into an attractive 'Water City'.

## THE THAMES & CLIMATE CHANGE

Concern about climate change checked enthusiasm for the Thames Gateway. Sea levels were rising and so too was the risk of flooding in the Thames Estuary. In 2005 the London Assembly's environment committee pointed out that 'a major flood in the Gateway could cost between £12 and 16 billion, with about £4–5 billion coming from the new developments if precautions are not taken in the new developments'.

Existing flood defences relied on physical barriers. In the 1960s the LCC had built the new township of Thamesmead over the low-lying Erith Marshes. Buildings stood on concrete stilts and slabs; flood protection was provided by earth embankments. These were now deemed inadequate for a future of fiercer storm surges. The Thames Barrier, opened in 1986, was the heart of London's flood defence system. This massive edifice had protected London from tidal surges for twenty years, but climate change brought more frequent and alarming emergencies.

The Thames also dominated Thames Gateway discussions as an unavoidable barrier to north–south traffic flows. The Dartford Crossing, combining a road bridge and a tunnel (see right), had opened in 1991, but this left a long stretch of the river unbridged between the Dartford crossing and Tower Bridge. An 'East London River Crossing' had been talked of for years and a succession of schemes had failed to progress beyond the planning stage: in 1986, a soaring suspension bridge between Beckton and Thamesmead; in 1999, a £600-million package of a tunnel and two bridges; in 2004, a £450-million six-lane motorway toll bridge, criticized for being environmentally unsound.

Will the East London river crossing ever be built? Almost certainly yes, but any new bridge will have to take seriously the

environmental impact. For centuries, the Thames has shaped London's development. Despite being embanked, built across, over and under, the river remains a great determining force in the London story. Perhaps, in an era of climate change, the Thames is set to play an even greater role in the chapters and centuries yet to come. **MoL**

**Arrest at Nevada Bob's,** *by Julian Bell 1999*
*The backdrop to Julian Bell's painting is the Dartford suspension bridge, swooping across the Thames as it carries the M25 southbound.*

**Thames Gateway developments**
This map shows the developments planned for the Thames Gateway, around 2000.

- area of housing growth
- Greater London
- 2012 Olympic games site
- motorway
- Channel Tunnel rail link
- transfer of dock trade to Tilbury

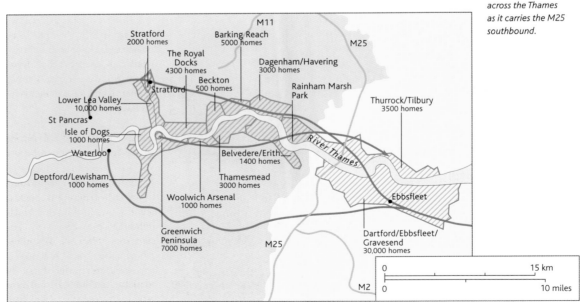

M11
M25
M2

Stratford
2000 homes

Barking Reach
5000 homes

The Royal Docks
4300 homes

Dagenham/Havering
3000 homes

Beckton
500 homes

Stratford

Rainham Marsh Park

Lower Lea Valley
10,000 homes

St Pancras

Thurrock/Tilbury
3500 homes

River Thames

Isle of Dogs
1000 homes

Waterloo

Belvedere/Erith
1400 homes

Deptford/Lewisham
1000 homes

Thamesmead
3000 homes

Woolwich Arsenal
1000 homes

Ebbsfleet

Greenwich Peninsula
7000 homes

Dartford/Ebbsfleet/ Gravesend
30,000 homes

0        15 km
0        10 miles

# FURTHER READING

## GENERAL HISTORIES

Several excellent overview histories of London have appeared in recent years, among them Roy Porter's *London: A Social History* (Hamish Hamilton, 1994); Francis Shepherd's *London, a History* (Oxford University Press, 1998); and Stephen Inwood's *A History of London* (Macmillan, 1998). A Museum of London publication, *The Archaeology of Greater London: An Assessment of Archaeological Evidence for Human Presence in the Area Now Covered by Greater London* (Museum of London 2000), surveys the archaeological evidence from the London area from prehistory to the recent past, with maps, gazetteers and an extensive bibliography. For the last two centuries, Jerry White's two volumes, *London in the Nineteenth Century: 'A Human Awful Wonder of God'* (Jonathan Cape, 2007); and *London in the 20th Century: A City and its People*, (Viking, 2001) provide an inspiring account of the capital at its most complex.

*The London Encyclopaedia* by Ben Weinreb & Christopher Hibbert (Macmillan, 1983, reprinted 2008) remains an indispensable reference work; as does, for London's buildings, the six revised London volumes of 'Pevsner', otherwise known as *The Buildings of England* series (Penguin and Yale, 1998–2003). A more concise buildings guide, with maps, is *A Guide to the Architecture of London* by Edward Jones and Christopher Woodward (Weidenfeld & Nicholson, 1983, reprinted 1992). *London Suburbs*, ed. Julian Homer, (Merrell and English Heritage, 1999) includes an illustrated gazetter by borough of suburban housing from the 17th to the 20th centuries.

Most of these books contain good further reading lists but the Bible of London bibliographers is the two volumes by Heather Creaton: *Bibliography of Printed Works on London History to 1939* (Library Association, 1994) and *Sources for the History of London 1939–45: A Guide and Bibliography* (British Records Association, 1998). Both are now searchable online at London's Past On-line (www.history.ac.uk/cmh/lpol/).

Thematic books about London's past include several published by the Museum to accompany exhibitions: *The Peopling of London*, ed. Nick Merriman (Museum of London, 1992), a short overview of pre-1945 migration to the capital; *London Bodies: The Changing Shape of Londoners from Prehistoric Times to the Present Day*, ed. Alex Werner (Museum of London, 1998,); *London Eats Out: 500 Years of Capital Dining*, by Edwina Ehrman and others (Philip Wilson, 1999); *Creative Quarters: The Art World in London from 1700 to 2000*, by Kit Wedd and others (Merrell, 2001); *The London Look: Fashion from Street to Catwalk*, by Christopher Breward and others (Yale, 2004); and *The Art of Satire: London in Caricature*, by Mark Bills (Philip Wilson, 2006).

Up-to-date information about research on London history can be found in a variety of journals and series publications, such as the *London Journal* and the *London Archaeologist*, which carries brief reports on recent archaeological discoveries. The London Topographical Society publishes reproductions of historic maps as well as more substantial books on the history, growth and topography of London. Since 1997, the Museum of London Archaeology Service (MoLAS) has published over thirty monographs on the results of its investigations in London, which comprise extensive documentary research on the history of the sites as well as the excavation reports. The monograph series continues, and is supplemented by an extensive series of smaller reports and popular booklets on individual sites and themes – see www.museumoflondonarchaeology.org.uk/English/Resources/Publications/.

## BRITISH HISTORIES

London of course features strongly in the three volumes of *The Cambridge Urban History of Britain*: vol. 1 *600–1540*, ed. David Palliser; vol. 2 *1540–1840*, ed. Peter Clark; vol. 3 *1840–1950*, ed. Martin J. Daunton (Cambridge University Press, 2000). *The Cambridge Social History of Britain 1750–1950*, ed. F. M. L. Thompson, (Cambridge University Press, 1990) covers its ground thematically but the three volumes include much London material, particularly volume 1, which has an overview chapter on the metropolis by P. L. Garside. The growing number of books about Britain's multicultural past also put London at the centre of the story – for example: *Staying Power: The History of Black People in Britain since 1504* by Peter Fryer (Pluto Press 1984) and *Asians in Britain: 400 Years of History* by Rozina Visram (Pluto Press, 2002).

## ON THE WEB

The explosion of digitization projects in recent years has opened up exciting new resources related to London's past. British History Online (www.british-history.ac.uk/) offers access to a huge number of original texts in transcript, from lists of medieval fairs to the volumes published by *The Survey of London*. The Old Bailey On Line website (www.oldbaileyonline.org) makes accessible the proceedings of London's Central Criminal court from 1674 to 1913, offering an extraordinary panorama of London at its most disorderly. Most of London's museums and archives have placed virtual exhibitions or online catalogues on the web – for example, Westminster Archive's Celebrating the Black Presence in Westminster, 1500–2000 (www.westminster.gov.uk). Collaborative web projects include Exploring 20th-Century London (www.20thcenturylondon.org.uk), which combines items from the collections of eleven museums across London to create a fascinating kaleidoscope of metropolitan stories; Untold London (www.untoldlondon.org.uk), which looks at material in London museums related to multicultural communities; and Ideal Homes (www.idealhomes.org.uk), which explores London's south-east suburbs. Photo London (photolondon.org.uk) is a gateway site, pointing to London's main collections of photographs. London's Screen Archives (www.filmlondon.org.uk/screenarchives/) does a similar job for London's moving image collections. Summaries of archaeological work on over 5000 sites in Greater London can be found on the London Archaeological Archive and Research Centre's online gazetteer (www.museumoflondon.org.uk/laarc/catalogue/).

In addition to the resources listed above, the following relate more specifically to the period chapters in this book.

## PREHISTORY

There are few books devoted to London's earliest past. Nick Merriman's *Prehistoric London* (HMSO, 1990) is still the most useful, though now somewhat dated. However, recent advances are helpfully summarized in a series of chronological chapters contained in *The Archaeology of Greater London: An Assessment of*

Archaeological Evidence for Human Presence in the Area Now Covered by Greater London (Museum of London 2000), and in London Under Ground: The Archaeology of a City, a volume of essays edited by Ian Haynes, Harvey Sheldon and Lesley Hannigan (Oxbow, 2000). Reports on recent archaeological work appear in the local county archaeological journal, the Transactions of the London & Middlesex Archaeological Society, and in a quarterly magazine, the London Archaeologist. The broader national picture is well covered in Chris Stringer's Homo Britannicus: The Incredible Story of Human Life in Britain (Allen Lane, 2006) and Richard Bradley's The Prehistory of Britain and Ireland (Cambridge University Press, 2007). Good websites now exist too: see, for example, that maintained by the National Ice Age Network at www.iceage.org.uk

## ROMAN LONDON

Roman Britain by Peter Salway (Oxford University Press 2003), part of the Oxford History of Britain series, provides a very full explanation and history of the whole of the Roman period in Britain. There have been so many archaeological excavations in Roman London over the last thirty years that no one publication can cover everything in detail. The most comprehensive publications, still essential reading, are by Ralph Merrifield, who published The Roman City of London (Benn, 1965) before the explosion of archaeological activity, and London: City of the Romans (Batsford, 1983) which incorporated some of the new exciting discoveries. More recent surveys, both entitled Roman London, by Dominic Perring (Seaby, 1991) and Gustav Milne (English Heritage, 1995), bring the story more up to date. For an authoritative assessment of London's archaeology of all periods see The Archaeology of Greater London (Museum of London, 2000). Important topics such as cemeteries, religion and the population and status of Roman London are all covered in Interpreting Roman London, ed. Joanna Bird, Mark Hassall and Harvey Sheldon (Oxbow, 1996), London Under Ground: The Archaeology of a City, ed. Ian Haynes, Harvey Sheldon and Lesley Hannigan (Oxbow, 2000) and Londinium and Beyond, ed. John Clark, Jonathan Cotton, Jenny Hall, Roz Sherris and Hedley Swain (Council for British Archaeology, 2008).

## EARLY MEDIEVAL LONDON

The whole of this period of London's history is covered by John Clark's Saxon and Norman London (HMSO, 1989), although this small book is now rather out of date. Little has been published recently on the early Saxon period in the London area, but Robert Cowie's chapter 'Saxon Settlement and Economy from the Dark Ages to Domesday' in The Archaeology of Greater London (Museum of London, 2000) summarizes the archaeological evidence. For the discovery of Saxon Lundenwic and the excavations in Covent Garden, see Alan Vince, Saxon London: An Archaeological Investigation (Seaby, 1990) and G. Malcolm and D. Bowsher with R. Cowie, Middle Saxon London: Excavations at the Royal Opera House 1989–99 (Museum of London Archaeology Service Monograph 15, 2003). Although these archaeological works have superseded Christopher Brooke's London 800–1216: The Shaping of a City (Secker & Warburg, 1975), the latter remains a sound study of the historical evidence, particularly for the Norman period. See also the early chapters of Christopher Thomas, The Archaeology of Medieval London (Sutton, 2003), Gustav Milne The Port of Medieval London (Tempus, 2003) and John Schofield The Building of London from the Conquest to the Great Fire (Sutton, 1999).

## LATER MEDIEVAL LONDON

Caroline Barron's London in the Later Middle Ages: Government and People 1200–1500 (Oxford University Press, 2004) is the most up-to-date work on London in this period. For a survey of the archaeological evidence, see Christopher Thomas, The Archaeology of Medieval London (Sutton, 2003). Mary D. Lobel (ed.), The British Atlas of Historic Towns Vol III: The City of London from Prehistoric Times to c.1520 (Oxford University Press, 1989) provides the most detailed reconstructed maps of the medieval city. Bruce Watson, Trevor Brigham and Tony Dyson detail the history of one of medieval London's most important structures in London Bridge: 2000 Years of a River Crossing (Museum of London Archaeology Service Monograph 8, 2001). John Schofield, in The Building of London from the Conquest to the Great Fire (Sutton, 1999), describes the development of the buildings of London – houses, churches, public buildings, palaces and fortifications – from its Roman and Saxon origins until the destruction of 1666, while his Medieval London Houses (Yale University Press, 1995; reprinted 2003) is a very detailed study of the evidence, from documents, surviving buildings and archaeology, for the plans, structure and appearance of houses of all types in London.

## TUDOR & EARLY STUART LONDON

The Oxford Illustrated History of Tudor and Stuart Britain (Oxford University Press, 1996), edited by John Morrill, offers one of the best general surveys of the period, and the comprehensive bibliography is helpfully divided into specific topics and themes. Readers wishing to find out more about Tudor London could do no better than to pick up a copy of John Stow's A Survey of London, first published in 1598 and now available in a paperback reprint with an introduction by Antonia Fraser (Sutton, 1994). Just as for the earlier periods, John Schofield's The Building of London from the Conquest to the Great Fire (Sutton, 1999) provides valuable insights into London's structural history. Simon Thurley, in The Royal Palaces of Tudor England: Architecture and Court Life 1460–1547 (Yale University Press, 1993), describes the development of Henry VIII's palaces in the London area, while Julian Bowsher's The Rose Theatre: An Archaeological Discovery (Museum of London, 1998) gives the most up-to-date account of the Elizabethan London playhouses. The best account of London's book trade is provided by Peter Blayney in The Bookshops in Paul's Cross Churchyard, London (The Bibliographical Society Occasional Paper 5, 1990). On the subject of food and drink see Edwina Ehrman and others, London Eats Out: 500 Years of Capital Dining (Museum of London/Philip Wilson 1996).

## LATER STUART LONDON

London and the Civil War, edited by Stephen Porter (Macmillan, 1996), provides an accessible account of London's involvement in the turmoil of the early 17th century. Walter Bell explores the story of the Great Plague of 1665 in The Great Plague in London in 1665 (revised edition, Bodley Head, 1951). The Great Fire and its aftermath are considered by Gustav Milne in The Great Fire of London (Historical Publications, 1986), Stephen Porter in The Great Fire of London (Sutton, 1996), and T. F. Reddaway The Rebuilding of London after the Great Fire (Jonathan Cape, 1940). The diaries of Samuel Pepys, which cover the years 1660 to 1669, throw a great deal of light on the events and the character of this period; the best edition is that in eleven volumes edited by Robert Latham and William

Matthews, *The Diary of Samuel Pepys* (G. Bell and Sons 1970–1983, reprinted by HarperCollins, 1995–2000). A. R. Hall, *The Revolution in Science 1500–1700* (Longman, 1983) describes the impact of science at this time, while the development of the navy is explored in Paul M. Kennedy's *The Rise and Fall of British Naval Mastery* (Macmillan, 1983).

## GEORGIAN LONDON

London events and characters feature strongly in Roy Porter's *English Society in the 18th Century* (Penguin, 1982). First published 80 years ago but still invaluable for the richness of its detail is Dorothy George's *London Life in the 18th Century* (1925, reprinted Penguin 1966). Sheila O'Connell's *London 1753* (British Museum, 2003) uses the British Museum's print collection to focus on five areas of central London. Peter Guillery's *The Small House in Eighteenth-Century London* (Yale, 2004) provides stimulating new insights into London's more modest Georgian buildings. The standard work on its architecture remains John Summerson's *Georgian London* (Pimlico, 1988; new edition Yale, 2003). In recent years, understanding of 18th-century London has been transformed by new sources relating to the lives of the poor and marginalized. Rictor Norton's *Mother Clap's Molly House: The Gay Subculture in England 1700–1830* (London, 1992) is one of several recent studies of gay activity. Tim Hitchcock's *Down and Out in Eighteenth-Century London* (London, 2004); L. D. Schwarz's *London in the Age of Industrialisation: Entrepreneurs, Labour Force and Living Conditions, 1700–1850* (Cambridge, 1992); and Robert Shoemaker's *The London Mob: Violence and Disorder in Eighteenth-Century England* (London, 2004) all offer new insights into an age once characterized as elegant. There are, of course, splendid contemporary accounts of life in the 18th century capital. James Boswell's *London Journal, 1762–3* (new edition Edinburgh University Press, 2004) remains a classic. Less well known is Daniel Defoe's *Colonel Jack* (1722, new edition Pickering & Chatto, 2008) a vivid tale of an orphan's adventures, beginning on the streets of London.

## REGENCY LONDON

*London World City, 1800–1840* (Yale, 1992), edited by Celina Fox, gives an all-embracing illustrative general account of the capital in this period of transition. *George Scharf's London: Sketches and Watercolours of a Changing City, 1820–1850* (John Murray, 1987), ed. Peter Jackson, depicts the urban topography in astonishing detail. James Hamilton's *London Lights* (John Murray, 2007) explores the men and women who contributed to the financial, entrepreneurial and intellectual life of the city. For insights into the political and working life of the capital *The Autobiography of France Place 1771–1854* (Cambridge University Press, 1972) should be read alongside Iorweth J. Prothero's *Artisans and Politics in Early Nineteenth-Century London* (Dawson, 1979), Ian McCalman's *Radical London* (Cambridge University Press, 1987) and David Green's *From Artisans to Paupers: Economic Change and Poverty in London 1790–1870* (Scolar Press, 1995). John Pudney's *London Docks* (Thames and Hudson, 1975) remains the best general introduction to London's port at this period, and for the river, Bill Luckin's *Pollution and Control: A Social History of the Thames in the Nineteenth Century* (Hilger, 1986) should be consulted. The life of the financial city is well documented in David Kynaston's *The City of London: A World of its Own, 1815–1890* (Chatto & Windus, 1994). For London's entertainments, Richard Altick's *The Shows of*

London (Belknap Press, 1978) provides the most comprehensive survey.

## EARLY VICTORIAN LONDON

Francis Shepherd's *London, 1808–1870: The Infernal Wen* (Secker & Warburg, 1971) gives a good general survey of many aspects of the early Victorian metropolis, as does Jerry White's *London in the Nineteenth Century* (Penguin, 2007). Charles Dickens's novels of London life can be read alongside Peter Ackroyd's excellent biography *Dickens* (Sinclair Stevenson, 1990). Henry Mayhew's writings are essential reading, and a good selection can be found in *London Labour and the London Poor* (Penguin, 2005). James Winter's *London's Teeming Streets 1830–1914* (Routledge, 1993) examines the capital's congested thoroughfares and the improvements undertaken during the course of the century. The best case study of a 19th-century London suburb is H. J. Dyos's *Victorian Suburb: A Study in the Growth of Camberwell* (Leicester University Press, 1961 and 1973). A good popular introduction to London's transport network, covering the omnibus, underground and trams, is *The Moving Metropolis: A History of London's Transport since 1800* (Laurence King, 2001), ed. Sheila Taylor and Oliver Green. The appearance of the capital is charted for the first time in photography in Gavin Stamp's *The Changing Metropolis: Earliest Photographs of London, 1839–79* (Viking, 1984).

## LATE VICTORIAN LONDON

The evolution of London's government is treated in Ken Young and Patricia L. Garside's *Metropolitan London: Politics and Urban Change, 1837–1981* (Edward Arnold, 1982). Gavin Weightman and Steve Humphries's *The Making of Modern London 1815–1914* (Sidgwick & Jackson, 1983) is a well illustrated work that uses oral history. Poverty and the poor are central to an understanding of late 19th century London, and good studies on the subject include Anthony S. Wohl's *The Eternal Slum: Housing and Social Policy* (Edward Arnold, 1977), E. Ross's *Love and Toil: Motherhood in Outcast London, 1870–1914* (Clarendon Press, 1993), Anna Davin's *Growing up Poor: Home, School and Street in London 1870–1914* (Paul and Company, 1997) and G. Stedman Jones's *Outcast London: A Study of the Relationship between Classes in Victorian Society* (Clarendon Press, 1971). The East End is examined in W. J. Fishman's *East End 1888: A Year in a London Borough among the Labouring Poor* (Duckworth, 1888) and *Jack the Ripper and the East End* (Chatto & Windus, 2008), ed. Alex Werner. Lynda Nead's *Victorian Babylon: People, Streets and Images in Nineteenth-century London* (Yale, 2000) focuses on the modernity of metropolitan life, especially from the women's perspective. Stephen Inwood's *City of Cities: The Birth of Modern London* (Macmillan, 2005) chronicles the major changes in the capital from the 1870s to World War I.

## EDWARDIAN LONDON

London's imperial character at the start of the 20th century is explored in *London 1900: The Imperial Metropolis* by Jonathan Schneer (Yale, 1999). Its architectural character is discussed in Michael Port's magisterial *Imperial London: Civil Government Building in London 1850–1915* (Yale, 1995). For popular culture, see Andrew Horrall's *Popular Culture in London, c. 1890–1918: The Transformation of Entertainment* (Manchester University Press, 2001); and Gavin Weightman's well-illustrated *Bright Lights, Big City: London Entertained, 1830–1950* (Collins & Brown, 1992).

A good introduction fo the suffragette campaign is *The Suffragettes in Pictures* by Diane Atkinson (Sutton, 1996) which draws on the suffragette photograph collection held at the Museum. Two engaging accounts of life at different points on the Edwardian social scale are: Maud Pember Reeve's survey *Round about a Pound a Week* (1913, republished Virago, 1990) which surveys working-class life in Lambeth, and C. H. Rolph's *London Particulars: Memories of an Edwardian Boyhood* (Oxford University Press, 1962) which describes growing up in a policeman's family.

## INTERWAR LONDON

*Twenties London: A City in the Jazz Age*, by Cathy Ross (Philip Wilson and Museum of London, 2004) surveys the city in one of its most exuberant decades. For the national background, see *The Long Weekend: A Social History of Great Britain, 1918 –39*, by Robert Graves and Alan Hodge (1941, new paperback edition Abacus, 1995) and Ross McKibbon's *Classes and Cultures: England 1918–1951* (Oxford University Press, 1998), an insightful account of changing experiences in a newly democratic age. The capital's spread is discussed by Alan A. Jackson in *Semi-Detached London: Suburban Development, Life and Transport, 1900–1939* (Allen & Unwin, 1973). More rakish aspects of interwar London are covered in Matt Houlbrook's *Queer London: Perils and Pleasures in the Sexual Metropolis, 1918–1957* (Chicago University Press, 2005) and D. J. Taylor's *Bright Young People: The Rise and Fall of a Generation 1918–1940* (Chatto and Windus, 2007). The latter takes its cue from Evelyn Waugh's classic novel of doomed and gilded youth, *Vile Bodies* (1930, reprinted by Penguin, 2000). Contemporary writing includes Hubert Llewelyn-Smith's seven volumes of *The New Survey of London Life and Labour* (P. S. King & Son, 1930–5), and some terrific essays and journalism: Thomas Burke's *London in My Time* (Rich & Cowan, 1934), H. V. Morton's *London* by H. V. Morton (Methuen, 1941) and C. L. R. James's *Letters from London* (1935, reprinted by Hurst, 2003). Louis Heren's marvellous *Growing Up Poor in London* (Hamish Hamilton, 1973) recalls a childhood in interwar Poplar.

## WAR AND POSTWAR LONDON

Gavin Weightman and Steve Humphries' *The Making Of Modern London: a People's History of the Capital from 1815 to the Present Day* (1983–6, reprinted Ebury Press, 2007) is particularly good on the war and its aftermath, using Londoners' own voices to tell the story. 'History from below' also informs *London at War, 1939–1945* by Phillip Ziegler (Pimlico, 2002); Maureen Waller's *London 1945* (John Murray, 2004); and *Living through the Blitz* by Tom Harrison (Penguin, 1976) which draws on the Mass Observation archive. The 1950s has recently been the subject of two authoritative books: Peter Hennessy's *Having It So Good: Britain in the Fifties* (Penguin, 2007) and David Kynaston's *Austerity Britain: A World to Build* (Bloomsbury, 2008). For the Festival of Britain, see the essays in *Twentieth Century Architecture No. 5, Festival of Britain* edited by Elain Harwood and Alan Powers (Twentieth Century Society, 2001). *Family and Kinship in East London*, by Michael Young and Peter Willmott (1957, reprinted Penguin, 1969) is a classic account of working-class life in postwar Bethnal Green. *The New Look: A Social History of the Forties and Fifties* by Harry Hopkins (Secker & Warburg, 1963) muses on 'some of the extraordinary experiences that have befallen us in these crowded years "since the war"'.

## 1960s AND 70s LONDON

The story of London's postwar high-rise housing is comprehensively chronicled in *Tower Block: Modern Public Housing in England, Scotland, Wales and Northern Ireland* by Stefan Muthesisus and Miles Glendinning (Yale, 1994), which also includes a useful gazeteer by borough of all London's tower blocks. The planning issues of the sixties are set out in Peter Hall's *London 2000* (Faber & Faber, 1963). The political problems of the seventies fill *London: The Heartless City* by David Wilcox with David Richardson (Thames Television, 1977). *Swinging Sixties: Fashion in London and Beyond 1955–1970*, ed. Christopher Breward, David Gilbert and Jenny Lister, (V&A, 2006) provides an excellent overview of the capital's youthquake and has some great illustrations. Jonathan Green's *All Dressed Up: The Sixties and the Counterculture* (Jonathan Cape, 1998) remembers the counter-cultural revolution. *Notting Hill in the Sixties* by Mike Phillips with photographs by Charlie Phillips (Lawrence & Wishart, 1991), and *Roots to Reckoning* by Charlie Phillips, Armet Francis and Neil Kenlock (Seed Publications, 2005) are both eloquent photographic records of London's Afro Caribbean community during a time of struggle.

## MODERN LONDON

*London from Punk to Blair*, ed. Joe Kerr and Andrew Gibson (Reaktion Books, 2003) offers an eclectic collection of essays and photographs about London's more recent past. Michael Hebbert's *London: More by Fortune than Design* (John Wiley & Sons, 1998) looks at the city's story from a planner's perspective, but is particularly insightful about post-GLC London and its *grand projets*. The new architecture of Docklands is described in Alan Cox's *Docklands in the Making: The Redevelopment of the Isle of Dogs, 1981–1995* (Athlone, 1995); its social transformation in Janet Foster's *Docklands: Cultures in Conflict, Worlds in Collision* (University College London Publications, 1999). London's multicultural character is explored, semi-autobiographically, in *London Crossings: A Biography of Black Britain* by Mike Phillips ( Continuum, 2001); and more sociologically in *The New East End* by Geoff Dench, Kate Gavron and Michael Young (Profile Books, 2006). Gentrification is the subject of *London Calling: The Middle Classes and the Remaking of Inner London* by Tim Butler and Garry Robson (Berg, 2003). Change in Spitalfields is recounted in Charlie Forman's *Spitalfields: A Battle for Land* (Hilary Shipman Ltd, 1989).

# INDEX

Italics indicate a map or illustration. Alternative names (Queenhithe) are in parentheses; additional information [friary] is in brackets.

# MAP & IMAGE CREDITS

The authors would like to acknowledge the followng sources used for maps in this book: **pages 14–15 maps 1–4 and 6** P Gibbard, *History of the Northwest European Rivers during the last Three Million Years*; **map 5** R. L. Jones and D. H. Keen *Pleistocene Environments in the British Isles* (1993); **44** W. Rodwell (ed.) *Temples, Churches and Religion: Recet Research in Roman Britain*; **48 top** B. Jones and D. Mattingly *An Atlas of Roman Britain* (1980); **94** P. Blayney *The Bookshops in St Paul's Cross Churchyard* (1990); **103** M. Carlin *Medieval Southwark* (1996).

Almost all the images and items reproduced in this book come from the Museum of London's collections. Further information about most can be found in the Collections section of the Museum's website: www.museumoflondon.org,uk.
  The following list provides details of the artists, photographers or other sources for the paintings, prints and photographs we have used, where these are known. Copyright details and other acknowledgements are given where copyright is not owned by the Museum. Images provided by the Museum of London Archaeology Service (MoLAS) are also listed.
  Penguin Books and the Museum of London are grateful to all lenders and copyright holders who have allowed their works to be reproduced here. Every effort has been made to trace copyright holders; the publishers apologize for any errors or omissions in the list below and would welcome these being brought to their attention.

**Half-title page** London, woodcut from William Caxton's *The Chronicles of England* (1497 edition); **Title page** *Canary Wharf* (detail), oil painting by Carl Laubin, 1991 © the artist; **Page 9** *London from Southwark* (detail), oil painting, anonymous (Dutch School), c. 1630

**PRELUDE**
**10 top** Map of 'Londinium Augusta', engraving in William Stukeley, *Itinerarium Curiosum*, 1724; **10 bottom** Roman house and bath house, engraving from *Illustrated London News*, 1848; **11 bottom** Bucklersbury Roman mosaic, chromolithograph from J. E. Price, *A Description of the Roman Tessellated Pavement Found in Bucklersbury*, 1870

**CHAPTER 1**
**12–13** *Central London in the Second Millennium BC*, reconstruction by Frank Gardiner; **19** *Uxbridge Camps*, reconstruction by Frank Gardiner; **20** *Yeoveney Lodge Causewayed Enclosure*, reconstruction by Alan Sorrell; **21** Bronze Dagger from Teddington, engraving, from *Surrey Archaeological Collections*, 1858; **23** *Ploughing Scene*, illustration by Derek Lucas

**CHAPTER 2**
**26–7** *Londinium c. AD 120* (detail), reconstruction by Peter Froste; **29 top** *Londinium c. AD 60*, reconstruction by Peter Froste; **29 bottom** Roman

bronze arm, photograph by Andy Chopping/MoLAS; **31 top** *Londinium c. AD 120*, reconstruction by Peter Froste; **38 top** *Roman Couple*, illustration by Derek Lucas; **39 bottom left** Reconstruction of a Roman woman's head, commissioned for the BBC television programme 'Meet the Ancestors'; **46–7** *Roman Newgate*, reconstruction by Alan Sorrell; **49 top** *Londinium in the 4th century*, reconstruction by Peter Froste

**CHAPTER 3**
**50–1** Westminster Abbey, detail from a Victorian copy of the Bayeux Tapestry © Reading Museum Service; **52** Glass vessels from Prittlewell, photograph by Andy Chopping/MoLAS; **55 bottom** Gold pendant, photograph by Andy Chopping/MoLAS; **58 top** *Westminster from the River*, engraving by Wenceslaus Hollar, 1647; **58 bottom** Impression of City of London Common Seal, City of London Records Office; **60** St Bartholomew the Great, photograph by Mike Seaborne; **63 bottom left** Excavation of Jewish mikveh, photograph by Andy Chopping/MoLAS; **63 bottom right** Jewish tombstone, redrawn after an engraving in *Gentleman's Magazine*, 1753; **64** London Bridge, detail from panorama by Anthonis van den Wyngaerde, c. 1544, © Ashmolean Museum; **65** Tower on London Wall, photograph by Mike Seaborne

**CHAPTER 4**
**66–7** *London in about 1400*, reconstruction by Amédée Forestier, 1912; **69 top** Charter of King John, City of London Records Office; **70** Goldsmiths' Row, detail from an engraving after a painting of the coronation procession of Edward VI, © Society of Antiquaries; **71** *Guildhall in the late 15th century*, reconstruction by Terry Ball (private collection), © the artist; **73 top** Holy Trinity Priory in about 1500, digital reconstruction by Richard Lea; **73 bottom** Choir of St Paul's Cathedral, engraving by Wenceslaus Hollar from William Dugdale *The History of St Paul's Cathedral in London*, 1658; **74 top** St Mary Spital, reconstruction by Faith Vardy/MoLAS; **76** The Steelyard, detail from an engraved panorama by Wenceslaus Hollar, 1647; **78** Excavated revetment at Billingsgate, 1982–3, photograph by Jon Bailey/MoLAS; **79** London Bridge, engraving by John Norden, about 1600

**CHAPTER 5**
**84–5** Copperplate map, detail of the south-western plate, drawn by Tracy Wellman, after the original in the Anhaltische Gemäldegalerie Dessau, Germany; **88** Richmond Palace, drawing by Anthonis Van Den Wyngaerde, 1562; **89** Nonsuch Palace, detail from John Norden's map of Surrey, in John Speed *Theatrum Imperii Magnae Brittaniae*, 1616; **93** St Paul's School, engraving in William Maitland *The History and Survey of London*, 1756; **94** *Old St Paul's* (*Sermon at St Paul's Cross*) by John Gipkyn, 1616, © Society of Antiquaries; **96** Plan of property in Giltspur Street by Ralph Treswell, before 1611, by kind permission of Christ's Hospital; **96–7** *House in Pancras Lane*, illustration by Roger Hutchins, 2008 © Penguin Books Ltd.; **98** *The Rose Theatre, 1587–92*, reconstruction by C. Walter Hodges, © Estate of C. Walter Hodges; **99** *London from Southwark* (detail), oil painting, anonymous (Dutch School), c. 1630; **100** *The Royal Exchange*, engraving by Wenceslaus Hollar, c. 1660; **101 top** *A table of the Chiefest Citties and Townes in England*, c. 1600 © Society of Antiquaries; **101 bottom** Map of London attributed to Ralph Agas (details), c. 1561, © Guildhall Library, City of London; **102 bottom** *The Old Tabard Inn*, watercolour by Louise Rayner, 1870; **103 bottom** *'Hot Bak'd*

*Wardens'*, etching by Marcellus Lauron from *The Cryes of the City of London*, c. 1688

**104–5** Survivals: Medieval & Tudor, all photographs by Mike Seaborne (except Lambeth Palace gateway)

### CHAPTER 6

**106–7** *The Great Fire of London*, oil painting, Dutch School, 17th century; **109 bottom** Charles II's cavalcade through the City of London, 22 April 1661, oil painting by Dirck Stoop, 1662; **112** *A plan of the City and Liberties of London after the dreadful conflagration in the year 1666*, engraving after Wenceslaus Hollar; **114** John Evelyn's plan for the rebuilding of the City of London after the Great Fire in 1666, engraving by Benjamin Cole © Guildhall Library, City of London; **115** Christopher Wren's plan for the rebuilding of the City of London after the Great Fire in 1666, engraving by Henry Hulsbergh © Guildhall Library, City of London; **116 top** *The Royal Exchange of London*, engraving by R. White and T. Cartwright, 1671; **116 bottom** *Fresh Wharf, London Bridge*, oil painting by William Marlow, 1762; **118** Covent Garden, detail from an engraving by Sutton Nicholls, c. 1731; **119 top** *A New Plan of the City of London, Westminster and Southwark*, from John Strype's edition of John Stow *A Survey of the Cities of London and Westminster*, 1720; **119 bottom** Bloomsbury Square, detail from John Rocque's *Plan of London, Westminster and Southwark*, 1746; **120** *The Hospitall at Greenwich*, engraving from *John Stow A Survey of the Cities of London and Westminster*, 6th edition, 1755; **120–1** *Prospect of London and the Thames from above Greenwich*, oil painting, Flemish School, 1620–30; **121** *Samuel Pepys*, oil painting by John Hayls, 1666, National Portrait Gallery, London; **122** Portrait believed to represent Robert Hooke, oil painting, anonymous, © Natural History Museum

### CHAPTER 7

**124–5** *Blackfriars Bridge*, watercolour by Nathaniel Black and Thomas Rowlandson, 1798; **126** *Devonshire Place and Wimpole Street from the New Road, St Mary le Bone*, engraved by G. Barrett, from a drawing by C. H. Riley, 1799; **127 top** *The Middleton Family*, oil painting, British School c. 1796–7; **127 bottom** *London going out of town, or The March of Bricks and Mortar 1*, etching by George Cruikshank, 1829; **128** Exchange Alley, surveyed by Thomas Jeffries, 1748; **129** *The Inside of the Royal Exchange*, engraved by F. Bartolozzi from a drawing by Philllipe J. de Loutherbourg, 1788; **131** *London in Miniature*, published by Edward Mogg, 1809; **133 top** The Lord Mayor's Coach, designed by Sir Robert Taylor, 1757, on loan to the Museum of London from the Corporation of London; **134** *May Morning*, oil painting by John Collett, 1761–70; **135** *Omai, a native of Ulaietea*, engraved from a portrait by Nathanial Dance, c.1774; **136** King Ancheigo, inscribed 'King Ancheigo Reigo Gabon River', watercolour, anonymous, date unknown; **137** *The Rev.d Mr. Kicherer, Mary, John and Martha*, engraving by T. Williams, 1804; **138** *The imports of Great Britain from France*, engraving by Louis-Phillippe Boitard, 1757; **139** Detail from *An Exact Survey ... Cities of London & Westminster*, John Rocque, 1746; **140–1** *Covent Garden Piazza and Market*, oil painting by John Collett, 1771–80; **142** *A General Prospect of Vaux Hall Gardens shewing at one View the disposition of the whole Gardens*, Samuel Wale, I. S.Muller, Bowles and Carver, Robert Wilkinson, 1745–51; **143 top** *An Inside View of the Rotunda in Ranelagh Gardens*, engraved by N. Parr from a view by Canaletto, 1742–50; **143 bottom** *The Ascent of Lunardi's Balloon from St George's Fields*, oil painting by J. C. Ibbetson, 1788–90; **144** *An Englishman's Delight or News of All Sorts*, published by W. Richardson, 1780; **145 top** *The Distressed Poet*, engraving by William Hogarth, 1741 (1822 edition); **146** *A peep behind the scenes: Covent Garden Theatre*, watercolour by John Nixon, 1802; **146–7** The Theatre Royal, Drury Lane, illustration by Roger Hutchins, 2008 © Penguin Books Ltd. This illustration is based on the research of Richard Leacroft, published in *The Development of the English Playhouse* (1973); **148** *The Exhibition of the Royal Academy*, 1787, engraving by Henry Ramberg, Pietro Antonio Martini and A. C. de Poggi; **151 top** *Interior of Duke's Place Synagogue, 1809*, aquatint by Rudolph Ackermann, Thomas Rowlandson and A. C. Pugin, from *The Microcosm of London*; **151 bottom** *The Gravel Pit Meeting House, Hackney, erected 1810*, watercolour by Edmund Atkin; **152** *An Execution outside Newgate Prison*, drawing by Thomas Rowlandson, 1805–10; **153** *Jack Sheppard seated in his cell, Newgate*, drawing by James Thornhill, 1724; **154** *Ganymede & Jack Catch*, etching by M. Darly and John Wilkes, 1769–71; **155** *'How d'ye like Me?'* mezzotint by Carrington Bowles, c. 1772; **156 top** *'Light your Honour?'*, mezzotint by James Wilson, published by W. Humphrey, 1772; **156 bottom** *A Harlot's Progress*, engraving by William Hogarth, 1732 (1822 edition); **157 top** *The Female Bruisers*, oil painting by John Collett, 1768; **157 bottom** *The Beauties of Bagnigge Wells*, published by Sayer and Bennett, 1778; **158 top** *Workhouse in St James' Parish*, aquatint by Rudolph Ackermann, Thomas Rowlandson and A. C. Pugin, from

*The Microcosm of London*, 1809; **158 bottom** *Gin Lane*, engraving by William Hogarth, 1750–1 (1822 edition); **161 top** *A Ward in the Middlesex Hospital*, aquatint by Rudolph Ackermann, Thomas Rowlandson and A. C. Pugin, from *The Microcosm of London*, 1809; **161 bottom** *St George's Hospital*, engraving, anonymous, after 1733; **162–3** *'The devastation occasioned by the rioters of London firing the new goal of Newgate'*, engraving published by Alexander Hogg, June 1780

### CHAPTER 8

**164–5** *The Rhinebeck Panorama*, watercolour probably by Robert Havell Jr, c. 1806; **166** *The Quadrant, Regent Street*, aquatint by Rudolph Ackermann after Thomas Hosmer Shepherd and J. Bluck, 1822; **167** *Hyde Park Corner and Constitution Arch*, oil painting by James Holland, c.1833; **168** *His Royal Highness the Prince Regent and Duke of Wellington etc First Visit to Waterloo Bridge on the 18th June 1817*, aquatint by Rudolph Ackermann; **169** *The Vauxhall Cast Iron Bridge*, engraving, anonymous, 1818; **170** *Calvert's Brewery*, watercolour by Robert B Schnebbelie, 1820; **170–1** *Messrs. Potts' Vinegar Manufactory, Bankside*, watercolour, anonymous, 1840–9; **172–3** *The Bank of England c. 1830*, illustration by Roger Hutchins, 2008 © Penguin Books Ltd.; **174** *Burlington Arcade*, engraving by Thomas Hosmer Shepherd and W. Tombleson, 1828; **174–5** *Messrs Harding Howell & Co, 89 Pall Mall*, aquatint from Rudolph Ackermann's *Repository of Arts*, 1809; **175 top** *Mr. Blade's Upper Showroom*, aquatint by J. Gendall from Rudolph Ackermann's *Repository of Arts*, 1823; **175 bottom** *The Haberdasher Dandy*, etching by C. Williams, published by Thomas Tegg, 1818; **176** *The Opening of St Katharine's Docks*, painting by William John Huggins, 1828, © PLA Collection/Museum of London; **178** *The Annual Fete of the Licensed Victuallers' School*, oil painting by E. F. Lambert, 1831; **179 top** *Tom, Jerry and Logic ... at 'All Max' in the East*, aquatint by George and Robert Cruikshank, published in Peirce Egan's *Life in London*, 1820–1; **179 bottom** *A shilling well laid out: Tom and Jerry at the Exhibition of Pictures at the Royal Academy*, aquatint by George and Robert Cruikshank, published in Peirce Egan's *Life in London*, 1820–1; **180 top** *Sir Robert Peel*, mezzotint after Sir Thomas Lawrence, 1828; **180 bottom** *A Watchman Making his Rounds*, watercolour by Thomas Rowlandson, 1795–1800; **181 top** *Dashall Objects to the Restraints of the Charleys*, etching by William Heath and William Sams, 1822; **182–3** *Representation of the Election of Members of Parliament for Westminster in 1818* (detail), aquatint by Robert Havell after George Scharf, published by Colnaghi and Co.; **183** *An Eclipse as seen over London in 1832*, lithograph by John Doyle, 1832

**184–5** Survivals: Georgian and Regency, all photographs by Mike Seaborne, 2007–8

### CHAPTER 9

**186–7** *Trafalgar Square by Moonlight*, oil painting by Henry Pether, 1861–7; **188** *The Houses of Parliament from Millbank*, oil painting by David Roberts, 1861; **189** *T. Duncombe Esq presenting the Petition in the House of Commons*, detail from an anonymous engraving, 1842; **190–1** *The Crystal Palace, 1851*, illustration by Roger Hutchins, 2008 © Penguin Books Ltd.; **190** *All the World going to see the Great Exhibition of 1851*, etching by George Cruickshank; **191** *The Great Exhibition*, chromolithograph by Joseph Nash, 1851; **192** *The 'Silent Highway'-man: your money or your life*, by John Tenniel from *Punch*, 10 July 1858; **194** *The Thames Embankment Works between Waterloo and Blackfriars Bridges*, watercolour by E. Hull, 1865; **194–5** *New Oxford Street*, watercolour, anonymous, 1875–80; **195 top** *Peabody Square, Westminster*, wood engraving, anonymous, 1869; **195 centre** *The Great Fire in Tooley Street from Nicholson's Wharf*, lithograph by J. Bell, 1861; **196 top** *The Crossing Sweeper*, oil painting by William Powell Frith, 1858; **196 bottom** *Covent Garden Market* (detail), oil painting by Phoebus Levin, 1864; **198** *Shillibeer's Omnibus*, lithograph by S. Gans, 1829–35; **198–9** *A Street Scene with Two Omnibuses*, oil painting by James Pollard, 1845; **199** *View of the Pool of London*, watercolour by W. Fenoulet, 1840; **200** *View of the London and Croydon Railway*, Edward Duncan, 1838; **201 top** *Railway Bridge over Westminster Road*, watercolour, anonymous, c.1850; **201 bottom** *Building the Stationary Engine House, Camden Town, 28 April 1837*, John Cooke Bourne, 1839; **202–3** *The General Post Office: One Minute to Six*, oil painting by G. E. Hicks, 1860

### CHAPTER 10

**204–5** *From Pentonville Road looking West: Evening*, oil painting by John O'Connor, 1884; **206 top** *Queen Victoria's Golden Jubilee*, watercolour by W. Hardy, 1887; **206 bottom** Whitehall, photograph, anonymous, c. 1880; **208–9** *Bedford Park*, chromolithograph by S. M. Trowtschild, 1882; **209 centre** Totterdown Fields Estate, an advertisement in *Workmen's Trains and Trams* timetable booklet, 1914; **209 bottom** *A Tennis Party at Burroughs Lodge, Hendon*, watercolour by Howard Gull Stormont, 1887; **210** *Over London by Rail*, wood engraving by Gustave Doré, from Blanchard Jerrold and Gustave

Doré, *London, a Pilgrimage*, 1872; **211** Little Collingwood Street, Bethnal Green, photograph by John Galt, 1900–7; **213 top** *Charing Cross Station*, lithograph, anonymous, 1864; **213 bottom** Constructing the Underground Railways, photograph by Henry Flather, c. 1869; **214 top** *The Sweater's Furnace; or the real 'curse' of Labour*, by Edward Linley Sambourne, from *Punch*, 17 March 1888; **216** Albert Chevalier, photograph, anonymous, c. 1910; **217** *Behind the Bar*, watercolour by John Henry Henshall, 1882; **218 top** *Inside The Athenaeum*, drawn by J. Walter Wilson for the *Illustrated London News*, 11 March 1893; **218 bottom** *Portrait of Oscar Wilde*, printed cartoon by Carlo Pellegrini ('Ape'), from *Vanity Fair*, 24 May 1884; **220** *The Bayswater Omnibus*, oil painting by George William Joy, 1895; **221** *Portrait of Frederic Leighton*, watercolour by Jacques Joseph Tissot, reproduced in *Vanity Fair*, 29 June 1872; **223 top left** The Fiszers, photograph, anonymous, c. 1907; **223 top right** A Jewish couple celebrating the Jewish New Year, photograph, anonymous., c.1900; **223 bottom** The Pavilion Theatre, lantern slide from the Whitechapel Mission donation, c. 1900; **225 top** *A London School Board Capture*, from the *Illustrated London News*, 9 September 1871; **226** *A Poor House*, oil painting by Gustave Doré, 1869; **227** Outside a Newsagent's window, photograph, anonymous, c. 1910; **229 top** Night meeting at the Blackfriars Shelter, photograph, anonymous, from the Salvation Army donation, c. 1910

**230–1** Survivals: Victorian, all photographs by Mike Seaborne, 2007–8

### CHAPTER 11
**232–3** *Popularity: the Stars of the Edwardian Music Hall*, oil painting by Walter H. Lambert, 1901–3; **234** *Coronation Street Scene, June 1902*, watercolour by C. E. Flower; **235** Aldwych, photograph, anonymous, c. 1915; **236 right** Bourne Estate, Clerkenwell, photograph by Mike Seaborne, 2005; **237** Map of LCC housing, taken from an insert in *London Housing*, London County Council (1937); **238** *Regent Street Quadrant by Night*, watercolour by William T. Wood, 1914; **240 top** *London News Boy*, poster designed by Elijah Cox, c.1919; **240 bottom** Fleet Street, photograph by George Reid, 1920s; **243** Lyons Corner House, photograph, anonymous, c. 1915; **244 top** *Gallery Box at the New Bedford Music Hall*, oil painting by Walter Sickert, c. 1906–7 © DACS; **244 bottom** *Mornington Crescent*, oil painting by Spencer Gore, 1911; **246** Suffragettes battle with police, photograph by 'Barrett', 1910; **247 top** Women's Sunday, 21 June 1908, photograph, anonymous; **247 bottom** Vera Wentworth and Elsie Howey, photograph by World's Graphic Press Ltd, 1908; **248 top** *Gun Week in Trafalgar Square*, watercolour by G. Bron, 1918; **248 bottom** *Zeppelin*, drawing by Edwin Bale, 1915

### CHAPTER 12
**250–1** *Amongst the Nerves of the World*, oil painting by C. R. W. Nevinson, 1929 © Bridgeman Art Library; **251** *London, Winter*, oil painting by C. R. W. Nevinson, 1928, © Bridgeman Art Library; **252–3** British Empire Exhibition poster designed by C. R. W. Nevinson, 1924 © Bridgeman Art Library; **254** *Laggard Leaves*, oil painting by Harry Bush, 1925 © the artist; **255 bottom** Housing Bonds poster, produced by Greenwich Borough Council, 1922; **257** *To the Theatres* poster, produced for LCC Tramways by Leigh Breton Studios, 1927; **260** Charing Cross Road, photograph by Wolf Suschitzky, 1935 © the photographer; **261 bottom** Croydon Aerodrome, photograph, anonymous, 1930s; **262–3** Map of the Port of London,1966, © PLA Collection/Museum of London; **263 left** Opening of the King George V Docks, photograph, anonymous, © PLA Collection/Museum of London; **263 right** Canary Wharf, photograph, anonymous, 1938 © PLA Collection/Museum of London; **264** Election Poster, produced by the Municipal Reform Party, 1925; **267 top** *Hampstead Heath Roundabout*, watercolour by Arthur Watts, 1933 © the artist; **267 bottom** *London in the 17th century*, oil painting by Humphrey Jennings, 1936 © the artist's estate; **268** Map of London's Sportsgrounds (detail), reproduced from Bacon's *Large Scale Atlas of London and Suburbs*, 1930s; **269 top** Women's sportswear, photographs by the Bassano studio, 1925 and 1933, © NPG/Museum of London; **269 bottom** Rugby League Cup Final poster, designed by Herry Perry for London Transport, 1933 © London Transport Museum; **270** Italian children, photograph by Margaret Monck, 1935 © the photographer's estate; **271 top** Mr Mix, photograph by Cyril Arapoff, 1938 © the photographer; **271 bottom** Suzanne Schaefer, photograph, anonymous, c. 1937

### CHAPTER 13
**272–3** *London Landscape*, oil painting by James Fitton, 1948 © the artist's estate; **274** Bomb damage in Queen Street Place, 11 May 1941, photograph by Arthur Cross & Fred Tibbs, reproduced by kind permission of the Commissioner of the City of London Police; **275 top** War damage, detail from *The London County Council Bomb Damage Maps 1939–45*, published by the London Topographical Society and London Metropolitan Archives, 2004

© London Metropolitan Archive; **275 bottom** Underground Shelter in South East London, 11 November 1940, photograph by Bill Brandt, © Imperial War Museum; **276 top** A Young East-Ender, photograph by George Rodger, 1939–40 © Magnum; **278** Stepney Reconstruction Area, drawn by Eileen Sherwell, published in the *County of London Plan*, by J. H. Forshaw and P. Abercrombie, 1943; **279** Social and Functional Analysis, drawn by Arthur Ling and D. K. Johnson, published in the *County of London Plan*, by J. H. Forshaw and P. Abercrombie, 1943; **280** Kidbrooke School, photograph by Henry Grant, 1958; **281** The LCC Ambulance Service, photograph by Henry Grant, 1951; **282** Building the Dome of Discovery, photographs by Henry Grant, 1951; **282–3** *The South Bank Site, 1951*, illustration by Roger Hutchins, 2008 © Penguin Books Ltd; **284 top** The Soho Fair, photograph by Roger Mayne, 1958, © the photographer; **285** In the Cellar Club, photograph by Bob Collins, c. 1960 © the photographer's estate; **286** *Caribbean Family in Trafalgar Square*, oil painting by Harold Dearden, c. 1959 © the artist; **287** Man in Notting Hill, photograph by Henry Grant, 1961

**288–9** Survivals: Early 20th Century, all photographs by Mike Seaborne, 2007–8

### CHAPTER 14
**290–1** *London from Cromwell Tower*, oil painting by Richard B. Walker, 1978 © the artist; **292** Metropolitan Structure Map, reproduced from the *Greater London Development Plan*, 1969; **293 bottom** Protest at Centrepoint, photograph by Henry Grant, 1974; **294** Cotton Garden estate, photograph by Henry Grant, 1968; **295** Tolmers Square, photograph by Henry Grant, 1979; **297 top** The Lesney Factory, Hackney, photograph by Barry Gray, 1982; **297 bottom** The City, photograph by Henry Grant, 1976; **299 top** 'The Scene', from *Time*, 15 April 1966 © *Time*, Inc./Time-Life Pictures/Getty Images; **299 centre** Cover of *Time*, 15 April 1966 © *Time*, Inc./Time-Life Pictures/Getty Images; **299 bottom** Punks in Hyde Park, photograph by Henry Grant, 1981; **300** Supermarket in Southall, photograph by Henry Grant, 1978; **300–1** Class at a Southall school, photograph by Henry Grant, 1978; **302** Football spectators, photograph by Roger Mayne, 1963 © the photographer; **303 top** Football fans, photograph by Jim Rice, 1976 © the photographer; **303 bottom** Crystal Palace Athletics Stadium, photograph by Henry Grant, 1964; **304** In the West End, photograph by Bob Collins, 1962 © the photographer's estate; **305** *Untitled*, oil painting by Ronnie Kray, 1972 © the artist's estate; **306 top** Anti Nazi League Rally, photograph by Henry Grant, 1978; **306 bottom** Bertrand Russell at a CND protest, photograph by Henry Grant, 1961; **307 centre** Supporters of the Grunwick strike, photograph by Henry Grant, 1976; **307 bottom** London School of Economics student protest, photograph by Henry Grant, 1969

### CHAPTER 15
**308–9** *History Painting*, oil painting by John Bartlett , 1994 © the artist; **310 centre** Burrell's Wharf, photograph, anonymous, 1937, © PLA Collection/ Museum of London; **310 bottom** Burrell's Wharf, photograph, 1997 © London's Found Riverscape Partnership; **311** *Canary Wharf*, oil painting by Carl Laubin, 1991 © the artist; **312** Lloyd's Building, Leadenhall St, photograph by Tom Evans, 1989 © the photographer; **313** Billingsgate, photograph by Mike Seaborne, 2000; **314** House near Heathrow, photograph by John Chase, 2000 © the photographer; **315 left** Eurostar, photograph by Anna Wright, c. 2000 © the photographer; **315 right** Claremont Road, Leytonstone, photograph by John Chase, 1994; **317 top** Cover of *Newsweek*, 4 November 1996 © *Newsweek*, Inc.; **317 bottom** *Viaduct*, oil painting by Michael Johnson, 1998 © the artist; **318 centre** The Millennium Dome, photograph by Mike Seaborne, 2003 © the photographer; **318 bottom** Tate Modern, 2008, photograph by John Chase, 2008 © the photographer; **319** The 'Gherkin', photograph by Mike Seaborne, 2003 © the photographer; **320** Buddhapadipa Temple Wimbledon, photograph by Mike Seaborne, 2007 © the photographer; **322** The Cathall Rd Estate, photograph by Mike Seaborne, 1999; **323** On the Ocean Estate, photograph by Mike Seaborne, 2004; **325 top** Bluewater shopping centre, photograph by Mike Seaborne, 2000; **325 bottom** Shops in Camden High Street © Hemis/Corbis; **326** Cover of *Time Out*, April 1981 © *Time Out*; **327** *Barbican Centre*, drawing by John Ronayne for a visitor leaflet, 1982, © the artist/City of London; **328** *Art Sabotage*, oil painting by David Piddock, 1999 © the artist; **330 top** Missing persons posters at King's Cross, photograph by Mike Seaborne, 2005; **330 bottom** Destroyed bus, 7 July 2005, © Dylan Martinez/AFP/Getty Images; **332–3** *Spitalfields old and new*, illustration by Roger Hutchins, 2008 © Penguin Books Ltd; **334 top** Olympic site fence, © Rex Features Ltd; **334 bottom** The Lower Lea Valley, photograph by Mike Seaborne, 2000; **335** *Arrest at Nevada Bob's*, oil painting by Julian Bell, 1999 © the artist